Passing Rhythms

Passing Rhythms

Liverpool FC and the Transformation of Football

Edited by
**John Williams, Stephen Hopkins and
Cathy Long**

BERG

Oxford • New York

First published in 2001 by
Berg
Editorial offices:
150 Cowley Road, Oxford, OX4 1JJ, UK
838 Broadway, Third Floor, New York, NY 10003-4812, USA

Berg is an imprint of Oxford International Publishers Ltd.

Library of Congress Cataloging-in-Publication Data
A catalogue record for this book is available from the Library of Congress.

British Library Cataloguing-in-Publication Data
A catalogue record for this book is available from the British Library.

ISBN 1 85973 397 2 (Cloth)
1 85973 303 4 (Paper)

Typeset by JS Typesetting, Wellingborough, Northants.
Printed in the United Kingdom by Biddles Ltd, Guildford and King's Lynn.

For our families and all Liverpool supporters in the
Flat Iron pub, Liverpool 4.

Contents

Contents

Notes on Contributors

Dr Raymond Boyle is Head of the Film and Media Studies Department and a member of the Stirling Media Research Institute based at the University of Stirling. He has published on sport and the media and is co author (with Richard Haynes) of *Power Play: Sport, the Media and Popular Culture* (2000). He sits on the editorial board of *Media, Culture and Society*.

Liz Crolley teaches in the Department of Languages at Manchester Metropolitan University and she has written widely on football. She is a review editor for *Soccer and Society* and is the co-author, with Vic Duke, of *Football, Nationality and the State* (1996) She is also the co-author of *Imagined Identities? Football in the European Press* (2001).

Dave Hill is a writer and researcher who has a special interest in issues of 'race' and masculinity. There are plans to publish a new version of *Out of His Skin*, Dave's seminal book on John Barnes and racism in football, which was first published in 1989. He is also the author of *England's Glory* (1996), a book about the 1966 World Cup Finals, and he has published widely on sport, and on relationships and the family, especially in the *Guardian* and the *Evening Standard*. His latest project is a book on masculinity and sex.

Stephen Hopkins teaches in the Politics Department at the University of Leicester and is an associate member of the Sir Norman Chester Centre for Football Research. He is a Liverpool season ticket holder and his main research interest is in the politics of Northern Ireland

Cathy Long works for the FA Premier League and the Football League on supporter panels research. She also co-ordinated and reported on activities at the Fans' Embassies for the Football Supporters' Association during Euro 2000 in Belgium and Holland. She is currently working on a project on football families and is an active researcher on the music scene in Liverpool. She is a Kop season ticket holder.

Colin Moneypenny is a Liverpool supporter, FSA member, and was the Liverpool City Council Committee Clerk to the Hillsborough Working Party.

Rick Parry is an accountant by trade, but as the first Chief Executive of the FA Premier League he is also one of the architects of the 'new' football in England. A life-long Liverpool supporter, and with a goalkeeping son coming through the junior ranks at the club, Parry took over as Chief Executive at Liverpool in 1996 and he now has the task of piloting the club into the new commercial sporting future.

Andrew Ward is a freelance writer who has written a number of books on the history of football. He is the co-author (with Rogan Taylor) of *Kicking and Screaming: an Oral History of Football in England* (1995). He is currently the Royal Literary Fund Writing Fellow at the University of Aberystwyth.

John Williams is the Director of the Sir Norman Chester Centre for Football Research at the University of Leicester, and he has published widely on football fan cultures and the structure and future of the game, including *Is it All Over: Can Football Survive the Premier League?* (1999). He is currently writing *Into the Red*, a book based on Liverpool FC and the 2000/2001 League season in England.

Introduction

John Williams, Stephen Hopkins and *Cathy Long*

Writing about football

This book is about football in the city of Liverpool, but it is mainly about the history and place of one football club in that city, Liverpool FC. The other major football club in Liverpool, Everton FC, has a key role to play in the very beginning of our account of the origins of professional football on Merseyside, but it soon fades from obvious view. In fact, of course, Everton, though not often mentioned explicitly in what follows, never fully disappears from our vista at all. 'The Blues' are forever helping, dialectically, to shape their Liverpool football counterpart in their vital co-struggles for Merseyside – and latterly national – footballing hegemony. The nature and meaning of this domestic struggle between near neighbours, born of the same seed, also changes as the respective identities of these clubs shift over time.

Today, for example, in an era of football 'brands' and global marketing, when 'What is increasingly being produced are not material objects but signs' (Lash and Urry, 1994: 14), footballing antagonisms and rivalries in the city are as likely to revolve around *symbolic* – as well as commercial and spatial notions of Liverpool FC as a 'national' or 'global' club, with Everton as a more 'local' or 'regional' concern – as they are around more historic and domestically-rooted religious, kinship or territorial distinctions around Merseyside football (Williams, 2000). The meanings and values specifically attached to Everton Football Club deserve their own extended investigations, of course, not least because of the club's extraordinary history, but also because of more recent struggles around the ownership and control of this famous North West football club. But this is the subject of another book: it is not our task here.

Local histories, fan remembrances, life biographies and statistical accounts are pretty much all available now on most top football clubs in England. They are part of the astounding growth of recent interest in football as a cultural product: football is certainly one of the key media sports 'texts' which are at the leading edge of the recent 'culturalization' of economics (Rowe, 1999: 70). The market for books and other media texts about football and its fans seems to be an ever-expanding one. Indeed, as this book was being written, a number of popular other books about Liverpool FC and the recent managers and players of the club, emerged

(Keith, 1999; Kelly, 1999; Souness, 1999; Barnes, 1999; Molby, 1999; Hansen, 1999). This is a signal, of course, both of the century's end and the enduring national popularity of Liverpool FC, but also of the extent to which the really great days of the Liverpool club are now increasingly seen as a matter of historical fact, to be celebrated and reviewed as new anniversaries come and go. Most recently at a home match in December 1999, the club and its fans celebrated the 40th anniversary of the arrival in Liverpool of the architect of the modern Anfield approach, the still-idolized and iconic Scottish manager of the club in the 1960s and early 1970s, Bill Shankly.

Recent contributions from football supporters and writers who, using person-alized accounts, have excavated the recent history of their own clubs, all tell us something about the character and traditions of those clubs and of their fans. Nick Hornby (1992), famously, has trawled through Arsenal's recent past and has offered hope for all young male suburban football fans who are wracked with questions about place, identity and especially, perhaps, concerns about the role of *gender* in shaping their football allegiances. Colin Schindler's (1998) account of Manchester City's (and Lancashire County Cricket Club's) place in the North West sporting landscape mainly in the 1950s and 1960s tells us much more about ethnicities and family/sport relationships drawn from a very different era, even if such accounts are tinged with more than a little distorting nostalgia. Nick Varley's (1999) review of the post-Hillsborough English football landscape is quite different, set as it is against memories of his active support among sometimes truculent Leeds United fans in the 'hooligan' era of the 1970s and 1980s. This is also a very different north of England from that 'lived experience' of 'northernness' and football support on Merseyside during the same period. Jim White's (1994) recent treatise on 'following' Manchester United in the mid-1990s is shaped, substantially, by the suffocating dominance of United by Liverpool in the 1970s and 1980s, hence the book's rhetorical title: *Are You Watching Liverpool?* Finally – although there are many more books we could mention in the same vein – Alan Edge's (1999) funny and heartfelt description of the 'pseudo-religious' aspects of supporting Liverpool Football Club, mainly in the 1950s and 1960s, is definitely one for those fans who are weaned on the familial traditions of generations of local club support in 'two-club' football-obsessed northern cities. Edge, at times, like Schindler, talks fondly and sadly here of a world which now seems almost completely lost.

The scope of the work reported on above is entertaining and impressive, and we can learn something about the 'meaning' and the particular culture of football clubs and their supporters from nearly all of these popular sources. But these are also partial and deeply personal accounts. None of these popular books does what we try to do here, namely to consider the deeper significance of the relationship between professional football and other local cultural practices in a major footballing city in England. We would also argue that few, if any, *academic* accounts of football supporters or football culture do the same thing as we are trying here, either. Indeed, a common approach to football fans and 'spectator cultures' in Britain and elsewhere in recent years has been to look only at its *contemporary*, rather than its *processual* manifestations over time, and to *equate* such cultures either simply with 'hooligans' or else with those largely male 'activist' supporters who are involved in fanzine culture or supporter organizations (see Giulianotti, 1999, Ch. 3 for an example). The vast bulk of 'ordinary' fans effectively disappear from these accounts (see also King, 1998). We favour a rather wider approach here, and we try to examine fan traditions and cultures from a number of perspectives which, when taken collectively together, we would argue, rather more successfully locate football, both historically and culturally, in the life of one of the great trading cities of the North West of England.

Our main propositions are these: first, that football has become a central part of the taken-for-granted 'social practices' that characterize the social formation in the city of Liverpool and help – along with highly distinctive patterns of politics, work and consumption, relations of religion, gender and ethnicity and socio-economic and spatial distributions – to provide the city with a specific 'structure of feeling', to use the 'frustratingly underdeveloped' (Taylor et al., 1996) notion originated by Raymond Williams (1965). Williams's concerns with the 'ordinary', 'lived' cultures of specific social formations and the intangible 'elements of impulse, restraint and tone', as well as the 'specifically affective elements of consciousness and relationships', which shape such formations at the local and regional level (Williams, 1977: 132; Taylor et al., 1996: 5), fits well with our own preferred approach to the analysis of the contemporary 'place' of football in the city of Liverpool at the turn of the twenty-first century.

Secondly, we contend that Liverpool FC's relative fall from national football dominance in the 1980s, and its more recent struggles to revive the club's fortunes, can tell us much which is significant in furthering our understanding of the *wider* transformations of English football in the 1990s. Here, we are interested in the new occupational practices in the sport, the rise of a new doctrine of 'profession-alism' in English football, the links between footballing and general well-being and post-Fordist prosperity in host areas, the tensions involved in opening up the game to continental influences, and the new commercial and cultural imperatives involved in the TV-dominated global version of the game's recent development.

The way top football in England has been transformed culturally, but perhaps especially *economically*, over the past decade is a theme which runs though many of the contributions to this book. Top football clubs in England, such as Liverpool, these days are no simple sporting concerns: they are also now sites for multi-various forms of consumption and they have important global symbolic, as well as economic, resonances. Television is at the heart of these changes. In the 1970s and 1980s, when Liverpool was *the* dominant force in the British game, club income was made up very substantially of revenues taken directly through the turnstiles. In 1998/99 matchday income made up only 37 per cent of cash inflows into FA Premier League clubs, with TV revenues now accounting for some 30 per cent of total income. This TV figure will rise again following a new television deal established between the FA Premier League and various media partners from 2001 which will more than double income from these sources for top clubs (Deloitte and Touche, 2000: 44). Liverpool FC also recently announced that its own new media partner, the Granada leisure group, will seek to exploit the club's 'brand' value around the world by selling initially delayed coverage of the club's activities and matches over the internet.

But almost matching these new revenue streams have been ever increasing demands from top players and their agents. Although Liverpool FC was reported to be in the top ten richest clubs in the world in 1998 (Deloitte and Touche, 1999), and had net assets of £46.1 million in 1998/99 (the fifth highest in England and compared to Manchester United's £107.9 million), *wages* at Liverpool FC in 1998/99 took up an astonishing 80 per cent of club turnover. Football analysts, Deloitte and Touche (2000: 20), eschewing just for a moment their generally positive support for 'free market' developments in the sport, warned sternly that wages of over two-thirds of football club turnovers were unlikely to be sustainable in the long run.

Already it must be clear that this is no simple *homage*, of course, to Liverpool FC or to the people of the city; far from it. The history – especially the recent history – of football at Anfield is, it must be said, run through with extraordinary and unmatched playing success in England: it includes eighteen League titles and four European Cups. It seems barely plausible, even through the long lens of history, to argue, as the *Independent* (16 December, 1999) did recently, that *Arsenal* (eleven League titles; no European Cups), not Liverpool, was the most successful English football club of the twentieth century. But, notwithstanding this extraordinary record on the pitch, the recent history of football in Liverpool is also intertwined with real tragedy, as well as with established local patterns of both inclusion and exclusion.

The City and the Club: some History

In many ways, the city of Liverpool is a vibrant, creative and highly inventive urban base. In its music and in its sport, especially, the people of the city reveal and celebrate themselves and their heroes in ways that belie the negative images often peddled elsewhere about the 'failings' of its culture and of its people. Liverpool has historical claims on the basis of its role as a dynamic and cosmo-politan seaport, and to evoke in its people both a 'natural' tendency towards democratization and also a fierce independence (Lane, 1997: 7; 59–98). The people of the city are especially prominent today, nationally, in popular cultural and performance domains – sport, music, comedy, drama – although this strong sense of a wider public perception of 'Liverpool-ness', as read mainly through sport and popular culture, especially, is probably a relatively recent tradition, dating back only to the late 1950s.

Many of the people in the city also jealously defend its openly 'emotional', Celtic 'separateness' and 'opposition' to conventional English formations (Walter, 1991), and they also guard its reputation from what sometimes seems to the people who live in Liverpool like sustained public attack from outside – about 'militant' politics, about crime, family life, poverty and conflictual industrial relations. It is in this sense that some people who live and work in Liverpool hold the view – perhaps mistakenly and obsessively so – that: 'Liverpool is the only city in Britain (apart from London) upon which other Britons have definitive opinions', and who believe Liverpool 'is seen as a city of problems where the people themselves are reckoned to be part of the problem' (Lane, 1997: xiii).

Liverpool certainly does have deep-seated – perhaps intractable – post-industrial problems of insecurity and underemployment, of crime, deprivation and racism, and a political culture which many of the people in the city still find macho, opaque or unwelcoming (Parkinson, 1985). In such circumstances, to talk glibly here about top football clubs on Merseyside simply 'reflecting' or somehow 'representing' the aspirations of their local 'communities' in the year 2000 is both to simplify the long history of local social and economic problems in Liverpool and the structure of local identities which this troubled history has helped to solidify. In addition, it fails to recognize the new ways in which top football clubs, such as Liverpool FC, now must locate themselves *internationally* in the new 'global' age of the sport (Williams, 1999) in terms of their responses to new, more affluent, supporter markets that stretch way beyond both regional and national boundaries. It also understates the *independent* creativity and resourcefulness of Liverpool FC supporters themselves, as the club they passionately support tries to recapture the footballing successes which were writ large for an earlier generation of followers of the club.

The city of Liverpool has been in long-term economic decline probably since the period immediately before the First World War. The central dependence for local employment on the unskilled and uncertain occupations of the docks and its ancillary industries has meant that the commercial fortunes of Liverpool have ebbed and flowed with those of its international sea trade. In 1914, the Port of Liverpool accounted for 31 per cent of the UK's visible imports and exports. By 1938 the Liverpool share had already fallen to 21 per cent (Lane, 1997: 14). Only from the global depression of the 1930s did the relative lack of a local industrial base in the city and its overdependence on the port become of critical concern to local politicians. Even in the late 1940s, unemployment in Liverpool rose to two-and-a-half times the national average and it has been some way above the national average ever since, catastrophically so in the 1980s (Parkinson, 1985: 11).

Until the mid-1960s, Liverpool's share of national sea trade remained reasonably constant, but the movement, from this period onwards, of manufacturing industry, population – Liverpool suffered particularly here – and the growth of cheaper, overseas competitors accelerated Liverpool's fall from a position of world significance to one in which the city's new service industries of heritage and tourism are the only real reminder today of the city's once dominant sea-trading traditions. Between 1966 and 1994 Liverpool's share of all ship arrivals in the UK was halved and east coast UK ports had effectively eclipsed those on the west (*ibid.*: 23). In the wake of wider economic depression under the neo-liberal political onslaught of Thatcherism in the 1980s, unemployment – especially youth and long-term unemployment – reached quite staggering proportions in some parts of Liverpool (see Williams, 1986).

In specifically footballing terms, the decline of Liverpool FC from a position of world strength has been more recent and rather less emphatic, though the connections of this football failing to the wider economic decline of the city should not be underplayed. However, the successes of the major local football clubs on Merseyside in the 1980s were at least a minor bulwark for local people when set against the realities of startling economic meltdown. Back in 1901 and 1906, when the port of Liverpool was still a world trading power, Liverpool FC won its first League Championships. More League titles followed in 1922 and 1923, and one more immediately after the Second World War, in 1947. In 1954, the club was relegated to the obscurity of the Second Division, before being revived by the arrival of Bill Shankly in December 1959. Shankly's teams won League Championships in 1964, 1966 and 1973 and two FA Cups, in 1965 and 1974. Then, under Bob Paisley, Joe Fagan and Kenny Dalglish, from 1976 to 1990 Liverpool won an astonishing ten League titles in fifteen seasons, finishing second in all other seasons except 1980/81 (when they were fifth). During this period, too, the club were also FA Cup winners twice (1986 and 1989) and European Club Champions four times (1977, 1978, 1981, 1984), as well as dominating the domestic League Cup competition.

In the 1990s, by way of contrast, Liverpool won but two trophies – the FA Cup in 1992 and the more lowly Coca-Cola Cup in 1995. We chart in this book the decline of Liverpool FC from its real dominance of the 1970s and 1980s to the relative struggles of the 1990s. In this context we are mindful of King's (1998: 207) important contention that the reversal of fortunes between Liverpool FC and the now dominant and publicly owned Manchester United also correlates symbolically with the contrasting economic developments of the two cities. Although there are clearly other forces at work here, there seems little doubt that, 'in an image-saturated age, where brand-sign value is paramount' (Rowe, 1999: 72) the fame and success of Manchester United *has,* indeed, contributed to the wider resurgence of the city of Manchester in the post-Fordist world economy. We look here at the beginnings of recent attempts in Liverpool to harness the commercial and symbolic power of the two main Merseyside football clubs in attempts to get them to contribute more strategically to the wider economic restructuring of the city.

New Directions

We also map in this book recent indications of a relative resurgence of the fortunes of the Liverpool club both on and off the field. In this last respect, according to club 'insiders', a home defeat against modest Leicester City in April 1999 proved to be a watershed of sorts ('Loss to Leicester opened the door to Granada', *Sunday Telegraph*, 18 July 1999). After the game, the club's directors were reported to have gathered to consider the future of the club. The questions raised here were definitive: did Liverpool FC want to end up on a par with middle-sized, mid-table domestic football rivals? Or did the club want to compete effectively, once more, with the 'new' giants of the world game, such as Real Madrid, SS Lazio and Manchester United? A new future for the club had already been set in motion by the appointment months earlier of City analysts Schroeders to look at the prospects for a commercial buy-in at Liverpool FC, a club still effectively owned and controlled by the local Moores family, owners of the Liverpool-based conglomerate, Littlewoods.

The eventual result of these deliberations was the purchase by the North West-based Granada group in 1999 of a 9.9 per cent share in the Liverpool club, worth £22 million. The club was reported to be especially interested in using Granada's merchandising expertise in order to promote the Liverpool FC 'brand', via Granada's network of hotel (Trusthouse Forte) and restaurant (Little Chefs) interests *(Guardian,* 14 July 1999). In return, Granada would run a future Liverpool FC TV station and be given lucrative internet rights in order to market more effectively the club's considerable global appeal. Liverpool FC, a relatively benign local 'family' fiefdom pretty much since its earliest days as a professional club, and one which had made a virtue of its very *lack* of 'distracting' external commercial partners, even in an age of public flotations and diverse forms of club ownership, was now, itself, beginning to look to a very different – a rather more corporate and 'global' – future. Part of this new future may involve a new 70,000 capacity stadium, built on nearby Stanley Park, to replace the hemmed-in and commercially limited space currently occupied by the club's historic Anfield Road base. Liverpool FC had, in fact, spent £7.3 million redeveloping Anfield in 1998/99 alone (Deloitte and Touche, 2000: 80). According to Liverpool fanzines at least, at the start of the

2000/2001 season the club was in grave danger of overstretching its ambitions on proposed ground redevelopment when the important matter of *team* rebuilding was still far from complete.

Even in a city ravaged by economic depression and the restructuring of the global economy, two locally controlled businesses with a combined turnover of not much over £70 million (1998/99 season, Deloitte and Touche, 2000) may not sound like an important major focus for regional economic regeneration. But, in an era of 'cultural citizens' (Rowe, 1999: 69) sports texts also have very high 'sign value' in the new global economies of 'signs and space' (Lash and Urry, 1994: 14–15). In the mid-1990s there were small signals that the city might, ham-fistedly, be trying to put this fact to work: Robbie Fowler and Ian Rush appeared on Merseyside Development Corporation ads to 'remind' potential employers that the Merseyside area had 'other' kinds of strikers too. Global sports businesses these days also mean selling 'signs' globally, while trying to produce some jobs *locally*. In July 1999 a survey of the economic benefits of football in the city of Liverpool carried out by the Football Research Unit at the University of Liverpool (Johnstone et al., 1999) estimated that in the region of 3,000 full-time jobs in the wider Merseyside economy are dependent on the football industry. The report also argued that 1,400 part-time jobs are produced by the clubs on matchdays and that for every 100 jobs in the retail sector around the two football grounds, five are dependent on matchdays. For every £1 spent by the two clubs combined, 31p remains within the local Liverpool economy. Around 78 per cent of interviewees in service sectors (pubs, bars, sports shops, restaurants) noted a 'significant increase' in takings when Liverpool FC play at home and estimate the increase in takings to be 10–25 per cent. A smaller proportion of businesses (37 per cent) noted the same increase for Everton home games, again reflecting the national and inter-national draw of Liverpool FC *versus* the more local appeal of Everton. Although it is unclear how exactly the figure is arrived at, the report estimates that 750,000 visitors come to the city of Liverpool for what the authors call 'football-related' reasons (*ibid.*: 26).

Echoing our own observations about the lack of 'embeddedness' of the two football clubs in Liverpool in local political and cultural networks and in the local economy – in part a consequence of these successful clubs being controlled by strong political and economic Conservatives in a city dogged in the 1960s and 1970s by lack of political leadership and a failing economy, and in the early 1980s by economic ruin and a radical form of 'centralised municipalism' (Parkinson, 1985: 18–20) – the report argues for more collaboration between 'stakeholders' in the city. Stakeholders here are taken to include the clubs, supporters, the City Council, the Mersey Partnership and local businesses. Some local *accountability* was on the agenda here, promised, too, in a limited way *nationally* in 2000 by the establishment of an Independent Football Commission to check on relations between top English clubs and their fans, via new *Customer Charters* (see FA Premier League, 2000: 39–41). A possible starting point for a new relationship on Merseyside is outlined by the Liverpool study. (Johnston et al., 1999: 27):

- A collaborative network of shareholders is needed to ensure that the local football industry adds to the competitive advantage of the entire locality and is used to avoid a competitive cycle of decline within the whole economy
- The two Premiership clubs need to be (and be seen to be) an embedded and highly valued part of the local Merseyside economy
- There is a need to develop a collaborative approach to enticing more football-related tourism into the city centre, i.e. to develop an integrated tourism and football industry strategy (Johnston et al, 1999: 27)

These suggestions may seem both obvious and important but also highly *relevant* recommendations for the City of Liverpool and its people, though how they might play in the new 'global' economies of top football, where television income and returns from the internet from a *global* market seem likely to be the major new income generators at clubs such as Liverpool FC, is unclear. The report concludes, unsurprisingly:

> There is no blueprint to the future of the football industry on Merseyside. There is no co-ordination, or plan, about how this sector might be developed for the benefit of the two clubs, the local economy and the Merseyside community. There needs to be a first step in realising the potential of the football industry on Merseyside. (Johnston et al., 1999: 27)

An important part of this general shift of emphasis at Liverpool FC in the late 1990s, and a signal for wider shifts in the English game towards the end of the century, was its appointment for the first time in 1998 of a *foreign* football manager, the French technocrat, Gérard Houllier. Houllier's arrival in Liverpool, and that of other foreign football coaches in England, is a sign not only of the sorts of accelerated 'global flows' – of capital, players, spectators and coaches – predicted by post-Fordist global economic developments in sport (King, 1998: 206), but it also signals the relative shedding by English football of its historic and icy isolationism, which has been such an established feature of the game's relations with foreign rivals, at least since the establishment – without the reluctant English – of the world governing body FIFA in 1904 (Wagg, 1984; Tomlinson, 1991). In the 1990s, the flood of foreign players into the English game has provided more ammunition for the historic tensions which have always existed here between the needs and aspirations of top clubs and the fortune of the England national team (Williams, 1999). These concerns reached something of a climax in 2000 when

England failed to qualify for the knock-out stage of the European Championships – a competition won by a French side containing a core of FA Premier League-based stars. Surprisingly for some, one of the *England*'s keenest and least critical supporters in Holland and Belgium was Anglophile Liverpool manager, the Frenchman Houllier.

Notwithstanding these first signs of a new, more commercialized and more internationalized direction for the structure of the club, and one shaped in part by financial partners drawn from *outside* the city of Liverpool, there are still important ways, of course, in which Liverpool Football Club still 'stands' for, still symbolizes, the hopes for 'something better' among the 'Red' half of the city. This remains the case, too, even if some local followers of the club are now excluded from attending football by price, or by the new climate around the sport which seems, to many, increasingly to prioritize commerce and order over the playing side of the game, and over the local passions which have traditionally – and sometimes dangerously – been roused in support of *both* of the established Liverpool football clubs. We return to some of these important issues later in the chapters which follow.

Finally, we also want to look seriously in this book at something which is little covered in discursive academic books about football. Indeed it is not much covered either, in any analytical way, in popular football books or by more than a small number of broadsheet football journalists. That is, we want not just to look seriously at the cultural effects of the game and at its economic and social importance – though these *are* central issues we want to cover – but also to say something here about the way the sport is both managed and *played* in England, and especially in Liverpool. Talking here of both organization and aesthetics, and also about the specific management strategies and capabilities – and limitations – at Liverpool FC over time, we hope this exploration may stimulate further social science work in this much neglected area, which is otherwise likely to be left to the much narrower focus provided, for example, by physical educationalists and the sometimes crude positivism of sports scientists.

Introducing the Chapters

We begin at the beginning. Chapter One examines the historical origins of Liverpool Football Club, its intimate early relationship with Everton, and the unusual development of non-sectarian football clubs in a city that remained marked by religious and sectarian undertones, even into the post-Second World War period. **John Williams** explores the evolution of football in the city of Liverpool from the 1890s through until the late 1950s, within the wider context of Liverpool's economic and social profile in these years. He tries to account for how and why football became such a central feature of the cultural landscape of the city in an era before the maximum wage and national celebrity cultures. Clearly, the basis is laid here for the bedrock of the distinctive supporter cultures at Liverpool FC which emerged more clearly and much more publicly in the 1960s and 1970s.

In Chapter Two, **Raymond Boyle** investigates aspects of the complex inter-relationship between football and religion as experienced in two 'Celtic' British cities, Liverpool and Glasgow. Understanding the connections, as well as the contrasts, that clearly exist between the two cities, Boyle uses material from interviews with supporters to gain genuine insight into the 'religiosity' of many aspects of social life in the increasingly secular, multicultural city societies of contemporary Liverpool and Glasgow.

Andrew Ward (with **John Williams**), in Chapter Three provides a rich and unusual reading of the character of *Bill Shankly*, Liverpool manager from 1959–1974 and the founding father of the 'modern' Liverpool club. John Williams, first, provides some important general context here, making it clear exactly how Shankly both adhered to aspects of 'scientific' management first established in English football back in the 1930s, but also differed markedly in his approach to player preparation and motivation at Liverpool in the 'modern' era of the post-maximum wage 1960s. Using largely original sources, Andrew Ward's warm and evocative analysis of the combination of factors that helped Shankly to his unique place in the affections of Liverpudlians, then demonstrates the way in which Shankly matched, and to some degree manufactured, the Liverpudlian spirit of the time.

Stephen Hopkins addresses in Chapter Four the *playing* styles adopted by Liverpool teams under the managerial dynasty set in place by Shankly, and maintained by Bob Paisley, Joe Fagan and Kenny Dalglish until the end of the 1980s. Playing techniques or styles, and their aesthetic appreciation, have not figured very highly in the recent huge growth of football literature, but this chapter seeks to explore the fundamental character and social and cultural roots of 'the Liverpool way', with its emphasis upon passing and movement. The importance of the collective ethos of teamwork, the nature of Liverpool's experiences in European competition, and the lessons learned from contact with other footballing cultures exploring similar principles form part of this unique analysis of an era of yet-unmatched dominance by Liverpool FC.

In Chapter Five, **John Williams** concentrates upon the question of *supporter traditions* and styles at Liverpool, and the changing nature of this support since the early 1960s. By focusing attention upon the nexus of football, music and youth culture, but also looking at more *generalized* supporter traditions at the club, Williams highlights continuities and discontinuities in fans' perceptions, and external judgements with regard to the 'character' or 'identity' of Liverpool's supporters. An engaged – yet critical – analysis, this chapter discusses in detail responses in the city and outside to the aftermath of Heysel and Hillsborough. A final section uncovers the contemporary fan and fanzine cultures associated with

Liverpool, and places them in the wider context of ongoing, rapid change in the national and international game.

Dave Hill, in Chapter Six, revisits and extends some of the territory covered in his 1989 book *Out of his Skin*, which analysed John Barnes' reception in Liverpool as the first black player to be signed by the club, in 1987. The impact of Barnes's arrival on the 'submerged' racial issues on Merseyside and in English football at large is taken further here as this chapter explores the nature of the contrast between the situation then and the rather different situation now. Hill recognizes that important elements of the issue of race and racism have been exposed to critical enquiry during the last decade, and that black players have written themselves into Liverpool's history in a way that looked a long way off as little as fifteen years ago. He nevertheless argues strongly that the 'bigger story' of Liverpool the city, Liverpool the club and their relationships with people who don't fit the description 'white' still requires careful and considered scrutiny.

In Chapter Seven, **John Williams** analyses the development of the Liverpool club in terms of management and administration in the crucial period between the mid-1980s and 1998. Williams shows how the club both accumulated and then lost strategic advantages on its competitors during this period and argues, paradoxically, that the unparalleled success of Liverpool in the two decades when the club was the dominant force in English football actually hindered some of the necessary processes of adjustment to the rapidly changing new football world, and the global realities of the football industry at the turn of a new century. The ambivalences of discourses associated with 'tradition' or 'modernization' are interrogated fully, with the departure of Roy Evans in 1998 (after more than 30 years with the club) and the arrival of Gerard Houllier viewed as seminal, yet complex, events in the ongoing negotiation of this transitional era.

In Chapter Eight, **Stephen Hopkins** and **John Williams** address the new 'Europeanization' of Liverpool FC – and of the English game – following the arrival of new manager Gérard Houllier. The authors guide the reader through the debates about the quality and future of English football in an era when foreign managers and players begin to dominate key aspects of the English game. The editors' extensive interview with Liverpool manager Gérard Houllier provides a fascinating account of his long-standing attachment to Liverpool as a city (Houllier spent a year teaching and writing a Masters' thesis on poverty in Liverpool in 1969) and his depth of understanding and feeling for the people (as fans and as citizens), something that is unusual for a top club manager in England. Still, this is no misty-eyed account, for Houllier is also critical of aspects of the club's recent administration. He reveals his philosophy and plans for Liverpool FC, both in terms of the short-term team-rebuilding, and also the necessary longer-term restructuring of the club. As well as the enthusiasm of Houllier for the game in general, what shines through this interview is his deep-seated admiration for what was achieved by Liverpool FC, and the style in which their football has, traditionally, been played.

In Chapter Nine, **Liz Crolley** and **Cathy Long** examine the issue of *gender* and football in Liverpool, paying special attention to the role of female players, as spectators and as general football enthusiasts in the city. The authors do this, in part, by talking to past and present female Liverpool fans. They also try, critically, to 'unpack' the notion that the game in England has been 'feminized' recently, and they offer challenging contentions about the 'masculine' standing terraces of Liverpool's Spion Kop experienced by female fans as a generally safe and inviting space, rather than the dangerous terrain identified in official reports. Finally, the authors explore the extent to which recent changes in football in Liverpool and elsewhere in England are actually supported or welcomed by most female fans.

Rick Parry has now seen the development of 'new' football in England both from his pivotal position as Chief Executive of the fledgling FA Premier League, and later as the Chief Executive of Liverpool FC, as the club faces an uncertain and changing future. In Chapter Ten, Parry provides excellent insights into the sorts of choices which faced the FA Premier League in the early 1990s, and he also offers the League's rationale for striking lucrative but controversial partnerships with satellite broadcasters in the early 1990s. He then surveys the powerful European football arena and locates the Liverpool club in terms of policy issues and debates about the likely future direction for the sport and its clubs in Europe and the world in the twenty-first century.

Finally, **Colin Moneypenny** is a Liverpool supporter, prominent member of the Football Supporters Association (FSA) in Liverpool, and Hillsborough survivor who offers a moving comment on the continuing struggle for 'Justice' for the Hillsborough bereaved. He is strongly critical of administrators and officials in their handling of both Hillsborough and Heysel, but he also notes how the awful events at Sheffield presaged a rather less intense, less aggressive, period for rivalries between opposing supporter groups in England. His assessment properly leaves our final thoughts with the families of the 96 who lost their lives on 15 April 1989 and those of the 39, mainly Italian, fans who perished in another tragedy involving Liverpool, at the Heysel Stadium on May 29 1985.

References

Barnes, J. (1999) *John Barnes: the Autobiography*, London: Headline.

Deloitte and Touche (1999) Annual Review of Football Finance, Manchester: Deloitte and Touche Sport.

Deloitte and Touche (2000) Annual Review of Football Finance, Manchester: Deloitte and Touche Sport.

Edge, A. (1999) *Faith of our Fathers: Football as a Religion*, Edinburgh: Mainstream.

FA Premier League (2000) FA Premier League Handbook, Season 2000/2001.

Giulianotti, R. (1999) *Football: a Sociology of the Global Game*, Cambridge: Polity.

Hansen, A. (1999) *A Matter of Opinion*, London: Partridge.

Hornby, N. (1992) *Fever Pitch*, London: Victor Gollancz.

Johnstone, S., Southern, A., and Taylor, R. (1999) *The Economic Benefits of Football in the City of Liverpool*, Football Research Unit, University of Liverpool.

Keith, J. (1999) *Bob Paisley: Manager of the Millennium*, London; Robson.

Kelly, S. (1999) *The Boot Room Boys*, London: Collins Willow.

King, A. (1998) *The End of the Terraces*, London: Leicester University Press.

Lane, T. (1997) *Liverpool: City of the Sea*, Liverpool: Liverpool University Press.

Lash, S. and Urry, J. (1994) *Economies of Signs and Space*, London: Routledge.

Molby, J. (1999) *Jan the Man: From Anfield to Vetch Field*, London: Victor Gollancz.

Parkinson, M. (1985) *Liverpool on the Brink*, Hermitage, Berks: Policy Journals.

Rowe, D. (1999) *Sport, Culture and the Media*, Milton Keynes: Open University Press.

Schindler, C. (1998) *Manchester United Ruined My Life*, London: Headline

Souness, G. (1999) *Souness: the Management Years*, André Deutsch.

Taylor, I., Evans, K. and Fraser, P. (1996) *A Tale of Two Cities: Global Change, Local Feeling and Everyday Life in the North of England*, London: Routledge.

Tomlinson, A. (1991) 'North and south: the rivalry of the Football League and the Football Association', in J. Williams and S. Wagg (eds) *British Football and Social Change*, Leicester: Leicester University Press.

Varley, N. (1999) *Parklife*, London: Viking.

Wagg, S. (1984) *The Football World*, Brighton: Harvester.

Walter, T. (1991) 'The mourning after Hillsborough', *Sociological Review*, **39**(3): 599–626.

White, J. (1994) *Are You Watching Liverpool?* London: Heinemann.

Williams, J. (1986) *Football and Football Hooliganism in Liverpool*, Leicester: Sir Norman Chester Centre for Football Research, University of Leicester.

—— (1999) *Is It All Over: Can Football Survive the Premier League?*, Reading: South Street Press.

—— (2000) 'Pool's apart', *When Saturday Comes*, September, No. 16.

Williams, R. (1965) *The Long Revolution*, Harmondsworth: Penguin.

—— (1977) *Marxism and Literature*, Harmondsworth: Penguin.

Out of the Blue and into the Red: The Early Liverpool Years

John Williams

The Origins of the Liverpool Clubs and Tales of Early Fandom

Students of the two main Liverpool football clubs know full well that Liverpool FC's origins actually lie inside Everton Football Club. When the Sunday school of St Domingo's was sited on Breckfield Road North in May 1870 and the adjacent Methodist chapel was formally consecrated in July 1871 it was to be the beginning of not one but two great north-west professional football clubs. In fact, despite its later centrality, football came rather late to Liverpool, with the Liverpool and District Football Association itself not appearing until 1882 and with the earlier Lancashire League being dominated by clubs from the eastern Lancashire cotton towns. Historian Tony Mason has speculated that the unique industrial structure of Merseyside, centring on sea trade rather than on manufacturing and producing a large semi-skilled and non-unionized casual workforce, may have played a part in inhibiting football's early growth in the city. He also points out, however, that the large number of clerks who made their living out of administering the trading industries in the city was probably central to the eventual rapid growth of the sport on Merseyside (Mason, 1985: 1). The late arrival of the Saturday half-day holiday for Liverpool's casual workers especially inhibited the growth of football playing on Merseyside. The local press in Birmingham recorded 811 football matches in the 'second city' in 1879/80. In Liverpool the local press noted only two (Russell, 1997: 13.)

The nineteenth-century muscular Christians who proselytized sport for moral health and Godliness in the working-class areas of Liverpool began their work on the urban poor, perhaps not surprisingly, with the gentleman colonizers' sport of cricket and with the popular American-imported baseball (still played in Liverpool). But working-class and lower-middle-class young men in the Anfield area soon demanded more physically robust team games for the winter months. Despite the early local popularity of the handling game, rugby, it was initially cricket and then street football which was favoured here and, under the auspices of the church's patrician Reverend Chambers, a football club, St Domingo's, was established in

1878 growing out of the summer's cricketing activities around the church. One year later, and with football clubs sprouting up elsewhere in the city – numbers grew from 2 in 1878 to 151 by 1886 – St Domingo's became Everton Football Club, locating their headquarters in a pub in Everton village, the Queen's Head. Everton played its first game – which it won – against nearby St. Peter's on 23 December 1879.

By 1880 Everton were already playing in the Lancashire League, using public land for home matches on Stanley Park. However, as 'football fever' took hold in working-class areas throughout England in the 1880s, and as football crowds grew in the North West, a league ruling in 1882 required that the new club find an enclosed ground for its home fixtures. At a club meeting hosted in his own Sandon Hotel in Anfield by John Houlding, an Irishman, a football follower and errand-boy-made-good as a self-made brewer and notable local Conservative politician, it was decided to rent a roped-off pitch off Priory Road, Anfield, for this purpose. But soon, following complaints about noise from the site, the club was once again without a home. With a brewer friend of Houlding's, John Orrell, called in to help, another venue was provided by Orrell for rent, at Anfield Road, where Everton first played on 28 September 1884, beating Earlstown, 5–0.

In the years which followed, the new club prospered and, like other successful football clubs of the day, terraces and small stands were erected at the new ground at Anfield Road to accommodate paying crowds which were now sometimes numbered in their thousands and were supporting professional players from 1885. However, the uncertain nature of club fixtures which resulted in many post-ponements and blank match days – and, thus some disappointed customers – eventually encouraged the small businessmen who ran twelve larger football clubs in Lancashire and the Midlands to ape the match arrangements of the established English County Cricket Championship. On 17 April 1888, at the Royal Hotel in Manchester, they agreed to establish a regular fixture list under the auspices of the new, national, Football League. One Alex Nisbet represented Everton at the inaugural League meeting, though more established neighbours Bootle FC were riled at being overlooked by the new organization, claiming, with some reason, to have a better ground and larger crowds than Everton (Inglis, 1988: 9–10).

With a regular list of fixtures and with dockworkers winning the right to half-day Saturdays in 1890, crowds continued to grow at Anfield Road. The national status of the Anfield ground was also rising, as evidenced by its hosting of an England v Ireland international match in 1889. The longevity of the place links of professional English football clubs is that even by 1991, some two years after the Hillsborough disaster, some 58 Football League clubs were still at the stadium sites they first occupied between 1889 and 1910 (Inglis, 1991: 10). In contrast to the often strong local opposition among planners and residents to the siting of new stadia today, so powerful and popular was the new professional football industry, and so prestigious to a local municipality was the siting of a new football ground, that clubs were able to monopolize some of the prime open land which might otherwise have remained or become private property. As Simon Inglis points out:

> A football ground was in many ways as much part of a burgeoning corporation as a public library, town hall and law courts, and was certainly used by more people. Furthermore, a football ground was often the only place in a town outsiders would visit. (Inglis, 1991: 12)

The civic pride invested in early professional English football clubs and their stadia was cemented, in the main, by highly localized forms of funding and control and by local sponsorship. This was certainly true in Liverpool. But a rift was also growing between the powerful Houlding and his colleagues at Everton. Houlding not only owned part of the land at Anfield Road but he also acted as the agent for the landlord for the rest. As the Everton club's profitability grew, Houlding decided to increase the Anfield Road rent, from £100 to £250. By 1891 Houlding had also formed a new limited company with a view to buying the Anfield ground and nearby land also owned by John Orrell, allegedly at a considerable potential profit to himself. Everton members were disgruntled. On 15 September 1891 the *Liverpool Football Echo* reported that an Everton member had told a shareholders meeting that: 'it seemed to him that they could expect nothing but the policy of Shylock from Mr. Houlding. He was determined to have his pound of flesh, or intimidate the club into acceptance of his scheme'.

When the Everton club's 279 members rejected the new rent proposals, in October 1891 Houlding served notice for his own club to leave land he now partly owned. In February 1892, Everton were set to quit Anfield, as four club shareholders agreed to contribute £1,000 each towards the £8,000 cost of a new ground at nearby Goodison Park, on the north side of Stanley Park. On 12 March 1892 a meeting of Everton members overwhelmingly voted Houlding out of office, and the move across the park was cemented. After Everton had departed Anfield, Houlding claimed that it was the 'teetotal fanaticism' of Everton's Methodist members which had forced him into his actions and which had produced the rancorous split. The *Liverpool Review* (19 March 1892) emphasized that the schism at Everton was 'purely a business one'. Greed and ambition certainly played their part, but to his credit Houlding also resisted the temptation to then sell his Anfield Road site for housing development and, instead, he set about 're-inventing' Everton FC – once more, at Anfield.

The New Liverpool FC

Houlding wanted to keep the name Everton for his 'new' football club, but the FA ruled in 1892 that the name should stay with the majority group. Although a rugby union club called Liverpool Football Club already existed in the city, on 15 March 1892 Houlding responded to the FA ruling by forming his own football club, rather grandly called the Liverpool Football Club and Athletic Grounds Company Limited, to play in the now empty Anfield Road venue. He charged the new club just £100 in rent and immediately donated £500 to its coffers. The club's application in the same year to join the Football League was rejected, however, on the grounds that 'they did not comply to regulations'. Everton's opposition to their upstart neighbour's bid for League membership was presumed to be the crucial factor in Liverpool's rejection (Inglis, 1988: 25).

Forced to join the Lancashire League instead of the more prestigious Football League, Liverpool's first fixture – a friendly against Rotherham Town at Anfield on 1 September 1892 – suffered badly from the fact that Everton also played its first Goodison fixture on the same day. The already established club hosted over 10,000 fans, while newly formed Liverpool could muster only a handful of spectators and could not even cover the Yorkshire club's financial guarantee. Early Liverpool matches in the Lancashire League – like the first, a local 'derby', at home to Higher Walton – attracted only 200 fans. But enthusiasm for the club soon spread; when, on 10 September 1892, Liverpool defeated Stockton to go top of the local league, Anfield crowds were already reported to have swelled to over 3,000 (Kelly, 1991: 7). Liverpool won the Lancashire League title and the Liverpool District Cup in 1892/93: both trophies were stolen, costing the club £130 in replacements (Rippon, 1980: 5).

Crowds of this size, however, were still 'lost' in Anfield. The Anfield Road ground in the 1890s could already accommodate up to 20,000 spectators, 4,000 of them on an exposed bank of wooden terraces at the Anfield Road end of the ground. At the Oakfield Road end a smaller stand stood in front of open fields, an area which would eventually house the new standing Kop. Fans who watched from here remember this part of the ground with the sorts of fears which were tragically realized much later in the English game. The original south end at Anfield was recalled by one early fan as 'A very old wooden stand with newspapers on the floor. I often used to wonder how it didn't catch fire, with people throwing their cigarettes down' (Liversedge, 1997: 22). On the west (Main Stand) side of the ground stood a modest pavilion and paddock, while the narrow Kemlyn Road stand was squeezed between the near touchline and the tight, terraced housing of the Kemlyn Road itself, behind (Inglis, 1996: 218).

By this time, an Irish rugby devotee who had been converted to football by his Everton involvement, 'Honest John' McKenna, a man who had controversially taken Houlding's part during the Anfield Road dispute, was becoming a key figure in the new Liverpool club. McKenna, from County Monaghan, was a grocer's boy who became a vaccinations officer in the West Derby district of the city. He lived modestly all his life in a terraced house near the Anfield ground. McKenna became famous in Liverpool football circles for his legendary player scouting trips to Scotland which resulted in the famous 'Seven Macs' Liverpool team of the 1890s – including one English 'Mac', goalkeeper McOwen. McKenna had recognized the tactical advantages of the co-operative cross-field passing popular in Scotland against the individual dribbling techniques still favoured in England. It was a lesson which would stand Liverpool in good stead throughout most of the following century.

Protestant or Catholic?

McKenna and Houlding, partners in the shaping of the new Liverpool club, were also both prominent local Freemasons and Conservatives and Houlding was also a well-known Orangeman with strong links to the Protestant-inclined Conservative Working Men's Associations. This fact, the existence of a large Irish Catholic community in Liverpool, and the strong – but not exclusive – early recruitment of Scottish Protestant players by Liverpool probably accounts, at least in part, for the popular mythologies which still persist today, about Everton's supposed Catholic heritage and Liverpool's alleged Protestant base. However, there seems no strong evidence for Everton's Catholic leanings nor for them recruiting fans strongly from 'Catholic' parts of the city. Also, both clubs had a tradition of contributing quite evenly to Catholic and Protestant 'good causes' in the city, and there is no pattern of player recruitment by the clubs which indicates any obvious sectarian divisions between them. As early as 1927 the teams from the city emerged on the field together for derby matches and, unlike the situation in Glasgow, for example, there are plenty of historical accounts from Liverpool of divided family loyalties and city-wide support for whichever of the local clubs was left playing in important cup ties or Cup Finals. There is evidence, in short, of a strong Liverpool footballing tradition around the clubs of both separation and togetherness, a tradition which does little to support notions of a divisive sectarianism between the clubs and their supporters (see Boyle, in Chapter Two). By the mid-1930s a social survey of Merseyside commented that: 'The intense religious antagonism which undoubtedly exists – and which from time to time breaks out into more than verbal strife – is also peculiar to Liverpool, but it should be added that this has declined in recent years' (Jones, 1934: 322).

Nevertheless, popular sentiments about the alleged religious leanings of the two clubs lingered well into the post-Second World War period, sentiments which remained important for some of the clubs' supporters in a city where education, for example, continued for many to be delivered along 'religious' lines. Indeed, strong 'religious' areal divisions in housing persisted in Liverpool until the city slum clearance programmes of the 1950s and 1960s, and employment practices on the docks and elsewhere in the city in the 1930s and 1940s could be shaped by religious background (Lane, 1997: 84–6). Longstanding football fans remember the two Liverpool football clubs still 'unofficially' recruiting youngsters from the Liverpool Boys' teams of the time largely along the lines of religious denomination well into the 1950s. This may have suited the clubs, of course, avoiding as it did unnecessary competition for local talent. The Protestant Irish roots of Liverpool FC are probably seen to strongest effect today in Belfast itself. The staunchly Protestant Shankill Road area in particular has been 'insularized' from the global push of 'Catholic' Manchester United, as well as from Everton; instead, Liverpool remains supreme as FA Premier League club of choice here. Everton, meanwhile, invested for a short spell in the 1990s in Home Farm, a Dublin football club, in an effort to revive the stream of Ireland player imports into Goodison Park, which was still strong in the 1950s.

However, the later example of Kenny Dalglish – a Rangers' supporting Protestant who went on to become a hero at both 'Catholic' Celtic and 'Protestant' Liverpool – is a good marker on the real mix of sentiments involved in football allegiances in the city of Liverpool today, perhaps especially as Liverpool FC has latterly become more of a 'national' and 'international' club in terms of its support. It has been argued that Liverpool FC's recent strong connections with Glasgow Celtic, in fact, go back to 1966 when supporters of the two clubs were reported to have joined forces for Liverpool's UEFA Cup Winner's Cup final against Borussia Dortmund in Glasgow in that year. This new alliance followed violent scenes involving Celtic fans at Anfield earlier in the tournament (Scraton, 1999: 21). These links, if they already existed, were certainly cemented, first by Liverpool playing at Celtic for Jock Stein's testimonial in 1986, and then by the support offered to Liverpool by the Celtic club and its fans following Hillsborough – including a match in Glasgow to raise funds for the Hillsborough victims.

Joining the Football League

In 1893, and unknown to other Liverpool FC officials who were quite happy to see the club find its feet slowly in the local leagues, it was John McKenna who applied on the club's behalf to join the newly expanded Second Division of the Football League. Under pressure from the emerging Liverpool FC, ambitious neighbours Bootle FC had fallen on hard times, and out of the Football League, allowing scope for Liverpool's opportunist application. When the club was duly elected, still reluctant club directors agreed that McKenna himself should travel to London to arrange the new fixture list. He did so along with representatives from Arsenal, Middlesbrough Ironopolis, Newcastle United and Rotherham United, all clubs elected into the League in the same year. By 1902 the gregarious and popular McKenna, a man of reputed even temperament who was known to speak with the humble and the elite on equal terms, was elected to the League

Management Committee, and in 1910 he became the third President of the Football League itself, a position he held until his death in 1936 when he was 81 years old. He stayed on the Liverpool board until 1922, only then fully devoting himself to his work with the Football League.

On 9 September 1893 Liverpool FC played its first home Football League fixture at Anfield, against Lincoln City, in front of a reported 5,000 fans. A 4–0 win signalled an amazingly successful first season drive for promotion – 26 wins out of 28 matches – via the end-of-season 'Test Match' system against the bottom three clubs in the First Division. With the club in the First Division in 1894/95, Anfield gates rose quickly, showing the obvious hunger among mainly working people for football in a city which was now already supporting two of the top sixteen football clubs in England. Frequently averaging over 10,000 spectators, Everton's were, comfortably, the highest attendances in English football until the late 1890s. Liverpool's attendances more than doubled between 1895/6 and 1896/7, from an average of just under 5,800 to just over 12,000. By the early 1900s Liverpool had pretty much already caught up their local rivals on this score, at the same time marking out the city of Liverpool as an authentic footballing 'hot bed' at the turn of the century, comparable to any site for the sport in England, even in the football-mad North. As Mason points out (1996: 46), 'Professional football . . . was a Northern innovation at which Northerners were top dogs. Not only did they play it better than Southerners, they also watched it with more knowledge and intensity.'

On 13 October 1894 the city rivals met for the first time, at Goodison Park, in front of 44,000 fans, as well as the Lord Mayor and other local dignitaries. As early as the early 1880s, in fact, politicians had been keen to be present at football matches in the north, courting electoral interest from players and fans alike (Tischler, 1981: 138). Both teams, already embracing the new, 'modern' approach to match preparation, were using hotel retreats to prepare for major fixtures such as these. Everton's superior strength and experience produced a 3–0 home victory. Nearly 30,000 spectators also watched the return match at Anfield, a 2–2 draw, and early rivalry was predictably fierce. 'Local rivalry keeps the game alive', one contemporary remarked, 'It is never so much alive as when Liverpool and Everton meet. Then, the wonder is that instead of everybody being alive, everybody is not killed dead, as an Irishman would say' (Leatherdale, 1997: 132).

The step up to the top level had tested the Anfield club's resources and support, however. As relegation looked increasingly inevitable for Liverpool, one observer of the time reported that even under the astute stewardship of Secretary-Manager Tom Watson – recruited by McKenna from Sunderland in 1896, and reputedly 'the most popular man in all football' – at some Liverpool home matches, 'there were not enough spectators to go around the field' (Hodgson, 1978: 13). The Liverpool police might certainly have preferred larger football crowds in the city, having early on identified the sport as an important guard against disorder and drunkenness. The Chief Constable told the Royal Commission on the Liquor Licensing Laws in 1898 that before football Liverpool working men would simply move from pub to pub after work. Things had changed, as football seemed to have had a 'civilizing' and sobering effect on local men according to this senior officer (quoted in Mason, 1980: 176):

> I think that now when there is a match on the Everton or Liverpool grounds, a great number of working men, the instant they get paid, rush off home as quickly as they can, get a wash and a change, leave their wages with their wives, and are off to see the football, and I think that has led to a great decrease in drunkenness.

The First Championships and the New, 'People's' Kop

Despite these early relegation setbacks, with McKenna's backing and the recruitment of more quality players, these early 'yo-yo' years at Liverpool soon gave way, albeit briefly, to real success. In 1901 the club won its first Football League title, with a team built round the staunch, blond Scottish defender, Alec Raisbeck, and the English centre forward, Sam Raybould, dramatically clinching the Championship in the last match of the season at West Bromwich. On returning to Central Station in Liverpool at midnight on that mild Monday evening of 29 April 1901 the players were met by thousands of Liverpool fans and even a drum and fife band. The celebrations went on long into the night, and it mattered little to the supporters of the club that players in the victorious team were not raised in Liverpool; it was the territory of the *crowd*, not that of the players, which mattered. Players with no organic ties to the place of their clubs were given the task of bringing glory and social cohesion, shape and meaning to the lives of working men in the harsh industrial heartlands of northern England (Holt, 1989: 171). Not that the city of Liverpool was unfamiliar with transient populations. The Port of Liverpool, then close to the height of its powers, imported cotton for Manchester to spin and weave. Its core workforce was unskilled and casual and was substantially employed on the basis of the seasons, weather and tide. The city had a 'continuously transient population of seafarers to give it colour, variety and cosmopolitanism' (Lane, 1997: xvii). Socially and culturally the city was humming – and not only with its new-found footballing success. But new problems for what was now the leading football club in the city, Liverpool FC, were also just around the corner.

Liverpool FC, in a very short time, had become a relatively well supported and 'commercialized' and wealthy club for the period, and it little favoured the maximum players' wage of £4 introduced in April 1901 by a Football Association which was still troubled by what it saw as the pernicious effects of professionalism.

Key members of the first League Championship team at Anfield, for example, were reputed to be earning as much as £10 per man, as Liverpool FC recorded a profit for every season between 1900 and the curtailing of football by the First World War, in 1915. McKenna complained bitterly about those FA 'amateurs' being involved in the business decisions of professionals, a theme which would emerge many times later, of course, in disputes between the northern League clubs and the patrician and 'unworldly' southern-based FA (Tomlinson, 1991).

By 1904, when the FA eventually handed over to the Football League and its members complete control of professional clubs' financial affairs, objections to the maximum wage among the clubs had rather died. McKenna, himself, had changed his views in the light of the 'exorbitant demands of players' which made it difficult to see 'how free trade can be allowed' (*Athletic News*, 2 January 1910). Poorer clubs actually *liked* the imposed wage ceiling, of course; it offered welcome opportunities to keep down costs, provided strict regulation and control of players, and offered opportunities for the least well off to compete more equally with the northern city giants. Liverpool FC and other richer clubs were also hardly inconvenienced. They had simply got around the ruling by inventing additional 'jobs' for top players or simply by paying them 'under the counter'. Self-interest, and the militancy of the Player's Union, rather than any ideological opposition to laissez-faire policies, were what determined McKenna's attitude – and that of others like him (Tischler, 1981: 65). Everyone – except the Union and the players who were not paid illegally – was happy, and this also helped release funds for limited work on grounds. Around the same time, and once again with Liverpool back in the Second Division, a roof was built at the Anfield Road end of the Liverpool ground, perhaps in fond expectation that more goals might be scored at home games at this lower level (Kelly, 1991: 12).

Mason (1985: 5–6) has illustrated the extraordinary stability of the Liverpool FC Board from the early years of the new century right up until the Second World War, made up as it was for most of this period by brewery managers, local merchants, solicitors and, for a time, an undertaker and even a schoolteacher. These were by no means the wealthiest or most influential people in the town; they were, above all, comfortable and respectable local citizens who knew how to tend to local business and to 'community' interests. The early directors were also carefully selected by John Houlding in order to ensure a large measure of personal control over the club – especially given his problems at Everton (Tischler, 1981: 74). Brewers were especially prominent in hosting northern clubs, charging rent for ground use and selling their products at matches. Despite early talk in the city of making the club more popular and of, 'putting football in the hands of the people', it was clear that this did not include even ordinary shareholders – mainly clerks, managers and bookkeepers – never mind the modest sixpenny spectator. The members of the Liverpool board clearly meant, in this respect, themselves (Mason,

1985: 6). As Russell (1997: 71) has argued, in the early years of professional football, 'While the working-classes might have imposed themselves on the game, they exercised little real control over it.' Nothing much was to change in this respect over the next hundred years.

In 1905/06 Liverpool won the League Championship again, just one year after another promotion, and Everton won the FA Cup. Liverpool was the national centre of football excellence with an aggregate average attendance of 34,400 fans, higher than for any English city outside London. Tom (T.V.) Williams, later Liverpool chairman and the club's first life president, first heard singing in the Liverpool crowd during the promotion campaign of 1905 (Keith, 1999: 53). Many more people in Liverpool than actually attended matches also had an investment, emotional or otherwise, in the outcome of matches there; a survey in 1907 revealed that nearly 80,000 football pools coupons were collected in a single week in the city (Holt, 1989: 183). Some connection to football was, clearly, widespread in the Merseyside area. Some Liverpool fans also already travelled to away matches; around 1,000 Liverpudlians were reported to have made the trip for a vital match at Bolton in 1906. In the same year, the club's directors, encouraged by the gate returns from the second League Championship season, and perhaps anticipating more new support and better prospects for increasing gate receipts, entered into the second phase of major ground development at Anfield. For this, the celebrated Scottish Engineer, Archibald Leich, was called in. According to the proud *Liverpool Echo* (25 August 1906): 'The entire scheme is modelled on a new departure from what football grounds are generally supposed to be. The stands . . . are as safe as skill and good workmanship can make them.' The Anfield pitch was raised five feet and the ground was, for the first time, totally enclosed, reportedly by 'fancy brick walls' and with turnstiles on all four sides (Inglis, 1996: 218). At this time, too, Leich designed and built the barrel-roofed Main Stand, with its famous curved mock-Tudor gable, which survived until 1970. There were now 3,000 covered fans housed here on seats, with an enclosed standing paddock area below.

But even the new Main Stand was dwarfed by the huge cinder and wood-support banking which was rising out of the fields behind the old open terrace at the (Oakfield) Walton Breck Road end of the ground. Known originally, if rather inaccurately, as the Oakfield Road bank, the new standing area was not the first major bank of terracing at an English football ground, but with 132 treads from top to bottom it was quite probably the tallest. From the back of the open Kop supporters had a 'spectacular' view of Liverpool, 'all the way across Anfield and Stanley Park and down to Goodison' (Kelly, 1993: 15). According to Simon Inglis (1996: 219), Arsenal had already used the term 'Kop' to describe football terracing in north London. Perhaps local journalist, Ernest Edwards, of the *Liverpool Daily Post and Echo* had heard the term being used in London? In any case, Edwards is accredited with 'christening' Liverpool's great, dark bank 'Spion Kop', after a hill in Natal District upon which many young infantrymen from local regiments had perished in a losing battle in January 1900 in the still-strong-in-the-memory Boer War.

The imposing new standing Kop, with a capacity for some 28,000 fans, was clearly no staunchly home preserve at this time; in 1907 Blackburn Rovers supporters on the Kop were reported to have 'waved their colours to a set motion and sent forth a weird, unearthly cry', when the teams appeared for a League match; contrast this with the views of a local weekly paper, *Porcupine*, which argued in 1905 that 'We in Liverpool are more reserved or less enthusiastic than our brethren up country . . . Liverpudlians rarely wear their colours conspicuously, even when they travel abroad' (Mason, 1985: 16). Goal celebrations on the Kop at this time comprised mainly of ranks of male fans, in their flat caps and mufflers, joyously throwing their hats in the air and chancing on getting their own headgear returned. Local betting syndicates were also rife among Kopites, as they were at most other major football grounds of the time. Even opposing fans on the Kop were invited to be involved in informal home fans' 'sweeps' on the first scorer (Kelly, 1993:19). Betting coups might replace lost wages: attendance at football frequently drew workers from their jobs, much to the consternation of local employers. While an FA official in Liverpool noted that dock workers in the city in the winter months 'Rush home from work and hand over their wages before going to the match' (*Liverpool Football Echo*, 28 February 1909), one northern mill owner complained that working men in the north had adopted the motto: 'if your work interferes with football, give it up' (Quoted in Tischler, 1981: 127). Fans' support, however, was far from unconditional, and directors at top clubs at the beginning of the century already knew they had to strive, by fair means or sometimes foul, to produce a winning team in order to attract larger crowds.

Women fans were clearly something of a feature of the landscape at Anfield at this time, but some men saw little in the new Kop to further attract members of the fairer sex. In the *Liverpool Echo*, a local male fan complained, soon after its opening, about the narrowness of the Kop turnstiles, which meant that if the club directors thought that, 'any gentleman would ask a lady to squeeze through such an aperture, to the destruction of her dress, they are mistaken' (Inglis, 1996: 219). It is hard to imagine too many females in valued dresses braving the driving wind and rain and the various other trials on the new banking, though the Kop did harbour very young children, including young girls, even in its earliest days (see Liversedge, 1997: 22). The *playing* was tough, too, emphasizing the sort of 'entertainment' both male and female fans now expected. In April 1914, for example, a survey of the top 1,701 players in England and Scotland found that only 61 had survived the season without missing a match through injury. Poor medical and training facilities extended the amount of playing time footballers lost through 'accident or illness' (Tischler, 1981: 97).

In 1913/14 Liverpool reached the FA Cup Final, played at Crystal Palace, for the first time. It was an all-Northern affair, against Lancashire rivals Burnley, and the first to be played in the presence of the King. It was an occasion on which to parade, ritualistically, the distinctiveness of Northern cultures to the 'soft' South. But the Cup Final was also a growing *national* event, rich in the symbolism of community and country: 'What it sought to assert, in the face of division, was a civic and national unity of seamless communities' (Hill, 1996: 107). Northern fans were determined, however, to resist the sophistication – and exploitation – of London, a common feature of complaints about Wembley FA Cup Final trips later. Spectators for the 1914 Final, for example, had to pay a shilling (5p) admission to the pleasure grounds before gaining access, for an *additional* payment, to the football stadium. This was naturally frowned upon by the thrifty Lancastrians who had 'gone down' for the Cup (Hill, 1996: 104). Liverpool lost the Final. It would take another fifty years of hard work to secure a Cup Final victory.

The Inter-war Years

The formidable Tom Watson, Liverpool's first identifiable 'manager', died in 1915 and he was briefly followed into the manager's chair at Liverpool in 1920 by David Ashworth, an ex-referee, and then by Matt McQueen, an ex-Liverpool player who had first arrived at the club in 1892. Forced to retire by ill health, McQueen himself was eventually replaced by the club secretary, George Patterson, in 1928. As Stephen Wagg (1984) has shown, the role of early football managers was not to select or coach the team, but to deflect local accountability from directors in the face of increasing demands for success from club supporters. Managers only slowly developed any sort of public profile until, in the 1930s, they began to make the transition from glorified clerks to tacticians and horsetraders (Wagg, 1984: 57). Formal coaching was resisted by professional players in England right up to the 1960s, and early football 'managers' spent most of their time in suits and in the office, identifying upwards, with the club proprietors, rather than downwards with the players on the shop floor (Wagg, 1984: 48). Most managers – with the exception of early technocrats such as Herbert Chapman at Huddersfield Town and Tom Buckley at Wolves – would certainly not have signed players themselves or tried to instruct professionals on how to play. Manager Tom Watson, for example, famously remained in his office during the second half of Liverpool v Newcastle United at Anfield in 1909, thus missing a comeback by his side from 2–5 down to a remarkable 6–5 victory.

By 1921 the Kemlyn Road enclosures at Anfield were covered, but it was not until 1928 that local architect Joseph Watson Cabre was asked to place a roof on the Kop, with Anfield then claiming covering on all four sides, a capacity of 68,000 fans, and scope for 45,000 'reds' as shilling spectators under cover. The acoustics produced by the new roof offered encouragement to working-class standing supporters who wanted to generate more of a 'participatory' supporter culture at Anfield, and to get more 'involved' with their heroes on the pitch. It was also the beginning of spectator rituals that still survived at the club more than 70 years later. Though singing of club songs and popular tunes seems already to have been established at some other football clubs by the late 1920s (Russell, 1997: 100), it seems it was still largely absent at Liverpool. Harry Wilson, a Kopite from the late 1920s onwards, recalled the informal but clear 'class' divisions inside Anfield in this early period, and also the effect on the Liverpool crowd of the arrival of the new Kop roof (Kelly, 1993: 16):

> There was no singing in those days, I can tell you that. But there was lots of chanting. We used to chant the names of the players. When Harry Chambers, our centre forward, scored we'd all chant, 'Cham-bers, Cham-bers'. He was one of our favourites. And then there was Elisha Scott, the greatest goalkeeper of them all. We called him 'Lisha' He was idolised by the Kop. They would shout, 'Lisha, Lisha'. When the players came out on to the pitch they would run down to the Kop end, just as they do now, and Lisha would wave to us. He also used to give us a wave when he left the pitch. He was a great favourite . . . The opposition fans would be there as well [on the Kop] but there were never any problems . . . It was a very working-class crowd on the Kop, mainly dockers and the like. The 'toffs' were in the Paddock and the stands. We called them 'the mob' or the 'toffs'.

In the 1920s and for the whole of the inter-war period it was possible to walk all the way around inside Anfield, and some fans used to 'follow' their clubs at half time by changing ends, bringing plenty of visitors onto the Kop to join the locals (Taylor and Ward, 1993: 28). Links established with visiting supporters at home could even be used to set-up future away trips. The football camaraderie is very clear in accounts of football support at this time, but working men could also fall out at football. Football culture enshrined older forms of toughness and rudeness, a working-class code of 'masculinity' rather than a middle-class 'manliness', and one which strongly resisted the 'civilising process' of fair play and sportsmanship (Holt, 1989: 173). Life on the football terraces was not always sweetness and light, though the police were seldom called in to sort out disputes in the crowd. 'Fights didn't last that long', according to Kopite, Harold Atkinson. 'In fact, some of the Kopites used to sort it out themselves' (quoted in Taylor and Ward, 1993: 29).

In 1933 Liverpool signed the Rangers centre forward, Sam English. When the feisty English tangled soon afterwards with a rival defender in front of the Kop, a member of the home crowd enthusiastically came to his rescue. The incident is recalled by a Liverpool supporter, Billy O'Donnell (Taylor and Ward, 1993: 31):

I'm standing on the Kop one day with a little friend of mine who also idolised Gordon Hodgson. Well, this English got in a little bit of trouble with a full-back, who was a bit rough, a bit of a character, and they were wrestling with one another, and Gordon Hodgson got in between them. Well, my mate jumped up, 'I won't be long, Billy', he says. He jumps over the barrier and he gets mixed up in it. This [police] Inspector grabs him, and he lets fly at the Inspector. I never saw him for six months after that. 'I won't be long', he says. He got six months.

As can be seen from the example above, the working-class members of crowds at matches in this period were far from paragons of virtue. Nor were images of football crowds at the time overly idealized. In fact: 'The impressions of contemporary observers were all that football belonged to the working-class, whether this was described as the "rougher element", "working men" or even a "howling, booing mob"' (Fishwick, 1989: 56). Football spectators of the time were mainly working-class men of working age who were generally young enough to endure what was often a long walk to the ground and two hours standing in often poor conditions at the match for what was frequently a cold, wet and sometimes depressingly dull fortnightly ritual (*ibid.*: 64).

The size of crowds at Goodison Park and at Anfield, however, was reasonably stable throughout the inter-war period, though usually these were well below respective stadium capacities. In 1914/1915, as the First World War took hold, average crowds at Everton had fallen from 25,250 in 1913/14 to 18,530, and at Liverpool from 24,315 to 16,805. In the 'War season' of 1914/15, scandal briefly enveloped Anfield: four Liverpool and four Manchester United players were suspended by the FA *sine die* after allegations about match fixing following the Good Friday fixture between the two relegation-threatened clubs at Old Trafford. This impropriety seemed to have little effect on fan enthusiasm. Both Liverpool and Everton averaged almost 30,000 fans at home games in the season immediately after the War, in 1919/20, enjoying, as did other football clubs, the working-class hunger for leisure and sport in Britain after the carnage of battle, with minimum admission charges now raised from 9*d* to one shilling.

In both 1922 and 1923 the Elisha Scott-inspired Liverpool were League Champions again, with Anfield crowds for these seasons averaging 36,105 and just under 33,500, respectively. The defensive strength of the Liverpool team was widely admired. Although working-class fans enjoyed seeing skilful forwards outwit thumping full backs, it was more the capacity to work hard, to take punishment and to play the required role in a team performance which were the qualities northern football crowds looked for (Holt, 1989: 163). Merseyside fans keenly *played* football, too, in the inter-war period, on the city's parks and open fields. A survey of Liverpool in 1934 found that 15,000–20,000 adults played the game 'fairly regularly' in the city alone (Jones, 1934: 291).

Trams and bicycles were favoured forms of transport to Liverpool matches at the time; tram drivers often used to park their vehicles near kick-off time and watch the games, and those riding bikes contributed to the local informal economy around Anfield by paying for them to be minded in nearby gardens and yards (Kelly, 1993: 19–20). But droves of fans would also, maybe, grab a bag of chips and walk home after games, even to the South End of the city (Taylor and Ward, 1993: 28). Kids would be deposited by Kopites in the 'boys pen', which took up a section of the terraced area of the Kemlyn Road side of the ground in the 1930s, to be collected again after the match. For the rest of the decade, average crowds at Anfield stayed in the high 20,000s/low 30,000s, as the club struggled for consistency on the field. Average attendances in the First Division as a whole increased from just over 23,100 in 1913/14 to 30,700 in 1938/39.

Football attendances generally fell in the North, including Liverpool, in the recession years from the mid-1920s, but by the late-1930s crowds in the city were actually quite similar in size to those which had watched football in the city more than a decade before. Neither of the Liverpool clubs, however, averaged home gates of 40,000 or more in any season during this period – a figure consistently exceeded by the dominant Arsenal club in the Herbert Chapman years in the 1930s, for example. But, in 1920/21, aggregate crowds in the city of Liverpool averaged a period high of just over 72,600, and for the whole inter-war period, and despite crippling economic depression, aggregate football crowds in the city only once dipped below 50,000 fans, in 1932/33. The First Division average in this season was the lowest reported for the inter-war depression years, at 23,225. As a source of specifically *northern* comparison, crowds at Newcastle United dropped to an average of just 19,483 in 1935/36; aggregate combined crowds in Sheffield only ever exceeded 50,000 right at the end of the inter-war years; and aggregate average crowds in Manchester, combining 'gates' at City and United, fell to as low as 37,200 in the hard times of 1931/32.

Though faced with recession, as well as with the rising number of entertainment competitors in the 1930s – nationally, the number of cinemas grew from 3,300 in 1929 to almost 5,000 in 1938 (Fishwick, 1989: 51) – the city of Liverpool remained a football stronghold in the 1930s. Liverpool FC could not match the draw of some of the more glamorous London clubs of the time, especially the all-conquering Arsenal, which were in any case much better sheltered from the effects of national recession and also identified by the fans in the North as a symbol of southern economic advantage (Russell, 1999: 20). Nevertheless, the city of Liverpool was, arguably, *the* centre for northern football support in England in the inter-war period.

Football players of the time also remained culturally and economically *connected* to the people who supported them. Contrasts elsewhere were striking. In 1930 the American baseball star Babe Ruth visited Liverpool and met Everton's

Dixie Dean. Both men had recently scored a record 60 goals (Dean) /home runs (Ruth) in their respective sports. Dean was earning £8 per week and was astonished to learn that Ruth earned £300. Average weekly manufacturing earnings in Britain were £3 a week at the time. Despite these disparities and the growing size of football crowds, the effects of the national economic depression in England and the weak bargaining position of players kept most footballers 'contented'. A £9 maximum wage was agreed for players after 1945, with a bonus for a win (£2) and a draw (£1). By 1952 the maximum football wage had been raised to £15 and £12 in the off season. The *average* professional player, however, earned only around £8 compared to the £10 average industrial wage, a fact which encouraged player unrest and corruption and which led to many clubs making 'under the counter' payments (Szymanski and Kuypers, 1999: 93).

Cost clearly limited football attendances in the city in the 1930s, as it did elsewhere especially in the north and even when entry prices were relatively cheap. From the earliest days of the Championship sides at Anfield, for example, people who couldn't afford to attend matches would simply stand outside the ground and, on hearing a roar inside, would collectively ask 'Who scored?', to be quickly answered from within (Liversedge, 1997: 22). The perimeter gates at matches in the city would be opened at three-quarter time to allow for early departures and opportunities for those outside to watch the last 20 minutes of games. That the general enthusiasm for football in the city in the entire period up till the Second World War remained high cannot be doubted. When the Pilgrim Trust reported on unemployment in Liverpool in 1938 it noted that unemployed men who could not afford the shilling entrance fee still used to turn up on Saturday afternoon just to watch the crowds going to the match (Mason, 1985: 20).

The 'Golden Age'?

After the Second World War, football attendances in England soared to record levels. In 1946 Entertainment Duty, first levied in 1916, was reduced for theatre and sports, and the Chancellor specifically requested football clubs to reduce the minimum admission price from 1*s*. 6*d*. to 1*s*. 3*d*. Football was not alone in flourishing in Britain: in the post-war glow, 45 million fans watched greyhounds in 1947, three million went to cricket and 300,000 a week to speedway. Cinema attendances topped one billion (Szymanski and Kuypers, 1999: 43–4).

In 1946/47 Liverpool's fifth League Championship season drew average crowds of 45,732, bettered only by the 49,379 average at Newcastle United. Liverpool had signed star centre forward Albert Stubbins from Newcastle for a record fee of £12,500 just after the War. Stubbins, Jack Balmer, and a young Billy Liddell, tore up defences in 1946/47 under then Liverpool manager, George Kay. Kay, an Irishman and an ex-player, notably in the first Wembley Cup Final for West Ham

United in 1923, and renowned for his 'deep thinking' about the sport, had been appointed in 1936. He had shrewdly taken his team to the USA to build up on their frugal post-war diet for the successful campaign. He was also praised later by Stubbins and Bob Paisley for his willingness to offer organization on the field, but to allow good players the freedom to 'go out and play', something which was to become an established trait at the club under both Shankly and Paisley (Keith, 1999: 32). But a collective slump in Liverpool form, predictably, soon followed. Despite the fact – or maybe because of it – that the city of Liverpool in the early 1950s remained badly scarred and dishevelled from war damage and that the city itself was 'poverty stricken, having had nothing like its share of the post-war boom' (Channon, 1976: 21), up till Liverpool FC's eventual relegation in 1953/54, attendances at Anfield nevertheless remained consistently high. But they were generally rather lower than those enjoyed in North London, at Tottenham and Arsenal, where average gates now regularly topped 50,000, and also at rejuvenated Newcastle United, even minus their prized goalscorer, Stubbins.

Aggregate average football crowds in Liverpool came close to 90,000 for the first time, in 1948/49, when attendances in England also reached an all-time peak of 41.27 million admissions. In September 1948 the record football crowd for the city of Liverpool – 78,299 – was shoe-horned into Goodison Park to watch the 1–1 draw in the local 'derby' match. In the same year, the record Football League attendance of 83,260 watched bomb-damaged Manchester United entertain Arsenal at Maine Road. By February 1952, when Liverpool had its own record home gate of 61,905 for an FA Cup tie against Wolves at Anfield, minimum League admission prices had already been raised to 1s. 9d. They were raised again, in 1960, to 2s. 6d. Nationally, and perhaps unsurprisingly, English football attendances dropped in that one season, at the start of the 1960s, by 3.9 million. The post-war football 'boom' was deemed to be over, though many football clubs, Liverpool among them, were actually destined to enjoy their own best average attendance figures in the 1970s, rather than in the national 'peak' years for attendances of the 1940s and early 1950s.

In the 1940s and early 1950s football remained the ruling passion of working men without television and cars, whose world still revolved around the communal passions of the works, the pub and the match (Holt, 1989: 297). Rising living standards, growing levels of car and television ownership, and an increasingly 'privatized' and domestic focus for personal consumption are generally blamed for declining football attendances in England in the 1950s and 1960s (see, Dunning et al., 1988). TV sets especially, a rarity in 1950, could be found in 75 per cent of all households by 1961 (Russell, 1997: 135). The relative growing power of women to demand different from their men in weekend leisure time was almost certainly another feature of the changing place of attending football in the lives of more affluent working men (Walvin, 1994: 166). The working week also was gradually shortened to five days, so the early industrial link with football diminished. 'Football started to become the province of the die-hard fan rather than the recreation of the working man' (Szymanski and Kuypers, 1999: 46). These changes, plus the growing contrast between the privations of facilities at football grounds such as Anfield which had changed little since the 1930s under club directors who could see no reason to change what was offered, added to shifting leisure priorities.

The growing attractions of staying home on Saturdays, for DIY, gardening and other home entertainments – including more and more Saturday afternoon TV sport – began the long decline of mass active working-class support for local football clubs as a central and 'organic' feature of the way skilled working men, in particular, 'connected' to their towns and cities and defined themselves socially, culturally and geographically. Later, the impact of hooliganism would make more fast this initial social division in post-Second World War football crowds (Dunning et al., 1988). From 1953 to 1977 football attendances nationally fell by an average of 1.4 per cent per season, but admission prices rose 4.2 per cent per season, revealing a relative 'price inelasticity' of football. At the same time the wealth of the population increased and consumer expenditure grew by 2.4 per cent per year. Thus, increased consumer income enabled clubs to charge higher prices but it also created competition from alternative pastimes (Szymanski and Kuypers, 1999: 45).

On the Kop, and in the rest of Anfield, life was also slowly changing for spectators. The old 'boys pen', later quite brilliantly captured in all its terrifying glory by Alan Edge (1997: 64–66) had been moved some years before from the Kemlyn Road into the Kop and it was the first sign of the later, more informal, segregation by age which was to become such a defining feature of terrace life on the football 'ends' in Britain from the early 1960s. For 'big' matches in the early 1950s it was not unusual even for adults to climb into the boys pen on the Kop to escape the crush on the main terrace (Paul, 1998: 122).

Of course, lacking 'penning' arrangements or any reasonably sophisticated system of *counting* fans onto the Kop, and also with adults passing children over the turnstiles for free entry, it was impossible to gauge with any real accuracy, when and whether the terrace was actually 'full' at any time. The spectator tragedy which occurred at Burndon Park on 6 March 1946, in which 33 people died and 500 were injured when an exit gate was left open by a man leaving the ground, thus allowing thousands more spectators inside, was less likely to happen at Liverpool simply because of the sheer scale of the Kop terrace. But Anfield, in general terms, was no 'safer' than any other football ground of the time, and injuries caused by a swaying and excited crowd were a common feature of life on the Liverpool terraces in the post-war period. This became more of a problem from the early 1960s onwards, however, especially as core goal-end terrace support became exclusively younger, and ever more vociferous.

Floodlit football finally came to Anfield in 1957, a move which also stayed the mass absenteeism on the docks and in other local industries when midweek games had been staged in the city in daylight (Kelly, 1993: 25–6). The very rhythms of the sport in England were now beginning to change, especially as English clubs began to take their first, tentative, steps into Europe. On the administrative side of affairs, even following promotion to the top level in 1961/62, the Liverpool club remained pretty much in the Dark Ages, sometimes to literally tragic effect, though they were certainly not alone in this at the time. Jimmy McInnes, a club administrator, hanged himself in the turnstile area at the Kop end of the ground, soon after Shankly's arrival, allegedly because of pressures produced by lack of resources or the necessary staff or technology to deal with the new demands from spectators (Paul, 1998: 120–1).

Most fans at this time simply queued and paid their money at the gate; neither segregation of rival fans, nor fan safety seems a major concern of the time. But, singing among the crowd seems finally to have arrived at Anfield in the early 1950s in interesting circumstances, which also display aspects of the sharp humour of the people of the city, and their abject refusal to be co-opted by 'official' sources. Albert Stubbins, who played for Liverpool from just after the Second World War, remembers hearing 'witty' remarks from Kopites while playing in the early 1950s, and also, 'some singing, but it was usually drowned out by the vast noise' (Kelly, 1993: 22). A visit to Anfield by Wembley's own Arthur Kagan around the same period probably set the Kop off for some of the major singing 'performances' which still lay some time ahead.

Kagan was the man who was made famous in this period for his conducting of the community singing before Wembley FA Cup Finals, and he toured Football League grounds in the 1950s. At Anfield, before a match against Matthews' Blackpool, Kagan arrived, complete with a brass band, in order to 'conduct' the home end Liverpool club's supporters in what was still for these times some unusual pre-match singing. Things did not go as planned. As Kagan and his band went hard at one popular tune, the Kop, to its own collective amusement, and probably surprise, piped up with quite another song, wilfully refusing to follow the frustrated Kagan's lead (Kelly, 1993: 26–7). Others who have since tried, 'officially', to guide the Kop's singing, especially from the pitch, suffered similar fates. Nor were Liverpool supporters easily convinced later by new ways of presenting the sport – music, video screens, or electronic scoreboards, for example – in the 'entertainment-driven' era of the 1990s. If sport in the United States was a 'highly orchestrated production' (Schaff, 1995: 45), and some English football clubs had followed this lead, it found no welcoming space at Anfield among fans, administrators or staff. These events involving Kagan, however, were the early post-war signs of the exuberant, creative and irreverent singing cultures on the Kop, which were only to get fully into gear about a decade later.

The career end for the great 1950s hero of the Kop and of other Liverpool fans, Billy Liddell, a flying Scottish winger but a modest man and a devout Christian, probably symbolized the end of an era at Anfield – and in English football. Liddell played in every part of the team, except in goal, and every new Liverpool signing in the 1940s and 1950s was ritually photographed on arrival shaking the great man's hand for the benefit of the local press and fans. Liddell, like many other highly localized top football players of the 1950s, was retained firmly within the cultural confines of the everyday working-class world from which players of the time were mainly recruited.

From this, traditional/located base, players drew their style: of playing, bearing and appearance (Critcher, 1991: 74–5). The status of northern sporting hero of the sort inspired by Liddell's career and routine presentation of self would soon be replaced by the more extrinsic status of sporting celebrity, an attribution based on personality, not character (Holt, 1996; Giulianotti, 1999: 118). Constructions of sporting 'northernness' in Liverpool also had quite different cultural meanings and inflections, of course, from those attributed for example to the great industrial/ rural cotton towns of Lancashire, whose once dominant football clubs were about to fall into sharp decline. For one thing, to move east out of Liverpool, into Warrington, Wigan and St Helens, was to move almost immediately into deep rugby league country and into quite a different set of local sporting practices and traditions evoked by these tightly knit industrial villages.

Billy Liddell, and other top footballers of his day, neither suffered nor would have enjoyed the sort of massive public exposure which awaited most top sportsmen in the approaching television age for sport. He seldom appeared on TV and his image was only really available to local kids in Liverpool on cigarette cards and, to men, in articles in football magazines such as *Football Monthly*. Liddell was not, and could not be, a 'celebrity' in the sense in which we understand the term today, but he was still celebrated by youngsters and their parents in Liverpool, even if, as a young Alan Edge recalls, few youngsters of the time would actually have *recognized* Liddell if they had met him face-to-face (1999: 42).

All of this would soon change. As images of players became more recognizable, players would also become more socially and economically distant from many fans. Soon, few players would travel on the tram or bus anymore, or live among even affluent working-class supporters, as had been common in the 1950s and before. Instead, here we are on the brink of the emergence of lifestyles and identities for top footballers in England, after the end of the maximum wage in 1961, which would increasingly stress image management, commerce and consumption as central, defining features for the sport's new stars (Wagg, 1984: Walvin, 1986: 33–4).

Liddell, like Preston North End's Tom Finney, had also *worked* while he had been a professional player. Liddell was an accountant, Finney a part-time plumber.

Also, as Tom Finney's testimonial did at Preston North End in the same year, 1960, Liddell's retirement from Liverpool after 22 years at the club and a then record 536 appearances, signalled the emergence of a quite new set of social and economic relationships in English football, as well as the effective end of a long-established set of quite specific *supporter* traditions in the sport. Above all, it signalled the beginnings of the redefinition of football, in Stephen Wagg's words, 'as a television show' (Wagg, 1984: 133). Here, too, the technocratic vocabulary of 'the professional' and 'the job' would increasingly replace the traditional language of northern football of toughness and virility, thus producing a new code in the sport whose moral categories were altogether less distinct (ibid.: 151).

As Dave Russell (1997: 154–5) points out, the whole style of Tom Finney's testimonial event, with its speeches and traditional songs, belonged to a mode of civic culture and spectator behaviour at football that had emerged in the nineteenth century and was now coming to an end. In just a few years, both Liddell and Finney, loyal club servants and essentially gentle and 'ordinary' sons of their clubs and its followers, but men blessed with quite extraordinary gifts, would seem increasingly anachronistic figures as the effects of the lifting of the maximum wage and the new 'commercialism' in 1960s football kicked in. Football crowds were about to change, too, in the youth-dominated swinging 1960s – as we shall see later, dramatically so.

References

Channon, H. (1976) *Portrait of Liverpool*, London: Robert Hale.

Critcher, C. (1991) 'Putting on the style: aspects of recent English football', in J. Williams and S. Wagg (eds) *British Football and Social Change*, Leicester: University of Leicester Press.

Dunning, E., Murphy, P. and Williams, J. (1988) *The Roots of Football Hooliganism*, London: Routledge.

Edge, A. (1999) *Faith of our Fathers: Football as a Religion*, Edinburgh: Mainstream.

Fishwick, N. (1989) *English Football and Society, 1910–1950*, Manchester: Manchester University Press.

Giulianotti, R. (1999) *Football: a Sociology of the Global Game*, Cambridge: Polity.

Hill, J. (1996) 'Rite of spring: Cup Finals and community in the North of England', in J. Hill and J. Williams (eds) *Sport and Identity in the North of England*, Keele: University of Keele Press.

Hodgson, D. (1978) *The Liverpool Story*, London: Arthur Barker,

Holt, R. (1989) *Sport and the British*, Oxford: Oxford University Press.

—— (1996) 'Heroes of the North: sport and the shaping of regional identity', in J. Hill and J. Williams (eds) *Sport and Identity in the North of England*, Keele: Keele University Press.

Inglis, S. (1988) *League Football and the Men Who Made It*, London: Willow Books.

—— (1991) *The Football Grounds of Great Britain*, London: Collins Willow.

—— (1996) *Football Grounds of Britain*, London: Collins Willow.

Jones, D. C. (1934) *The Social Survey of Merseyside*, London: Liverpool University Press.

Keith, J. (1999) Bob Paisley: *Manager of the Millennium*, London: Robson.

Kelly, S. (1991) *You'll Never Walk Alone: the Official Illustrated History of Liverpool FC*, London: Queen Anne Press.

—— (1993) *The Kop: the End of an Era*, London: Mandarin.

Lane, T. (1997) *Liverpool: City of the Sea*, Liverpool: Liverpool University Press.

Leatherdale, C. (ed.) (1997) *The Book of Football*, Westcliff-on-Sea: Desert Island Books.

Liversedge, S. (1997) *Liverpool, We Love You!*, Stroud: Soccer Books.

Mason, T. (1980) *Association Football and English Society, 1863–1915*, Brighton: Harvester Press.

—— (1985) 'The Blues and the Reds: A history of the Liverpool and Everton Football Clubs', *History Society of Lancashire and Cheshire*, University of Liverpool, mimeo.

—— (1996) 'Football, sport of the North?', in J. Hill and J. Williams (eds) *Sport and Identity in the North of England*, Keele: University of Keele Press.

Paul, D. (1998) *Anfield Voices*, Stroud: Tempus.

Rippon, A. (1980) *The Story of Liverpool FC*, Ashbourne: Moorland Publishing.

Russell, D. (1997) *Football and the English*, Preston: Carnegie.

—— (1999) 'Associating with England: social identity in England', in G. Armstrong and R. Giulianotti (eds) *Football Cultures and Identities*, London: Macmillan.

Schaff, P. (1995) *Sports Marketing: Not Just a Game Anymore*, New York: Prometheus Books.

Scraton, P. (1999) *Hillsborough: the Truth*, Edinburgh and London: Mainstream.

Szymanski, S. and Kuypers, T. (1999) *Winners and Losers: the Business Strategy of Football*, London: Viking.

Taylor, R. and Ward, A., with Williams, J. (1993) *Three Sides of the Mersey: an Oral History of Everton, Liverpool and Tranmere Rovers*, London: Robson.

Tischler, S. (1981) *Football and Businessmen*, New York and London, Holmes and Meier.

Tomlinson, A. (1991) 'North and South: the rivalry of the Football League and the Football Association', in J. Williams and S. Wagg (eds) *British Football and Social Change*, Leicester: University of Leicester Press.

Wagg, S. (1984) *The Football World*, Brighton: Harvester.

Walvin, J. (1986) *Football and the Decline of Britain*, London: Allen Lane

—— (1994) *The People's Game: the History of Football Revisited*, Edinburgh and London: Mainstream

Williams, J. (1994) 'English football stadia after Hillsborough' in J. Bale and O. Moen (eds) *The Stadium and the City*, Keele: Keele University Press.

—— (1999) *Is It All Over: Can Football Survive the FA Premier League?* Reading: South Street Press.

Football and Religion: Merseyside and Glasgow

Raymond Boyle

Indeed, to state that sport is a modern, secular form of religion is something of a cliché. (Bale, 1994: 134).

Like Liverpudlians, Glaswegians pride themselves on their corporate sense of humour, their love of an eccentric, their ability to laugh loudly in the darkness. (Moir, 1995).

The Scouse lads on Hertford Road think England will beat Scotland, but apart from that, feel a closer affinity to Glasgow than London. 'You know in Glasgow, they are pretty much like us, like', yells one. 'There's only two things that matter, football and getting bevvied' (Lappin, 1996).

Introduction

Football fandom has often been described as displaying many of the symbolic and ritualistic aspects of religious belief. Liverpool fan Alan Edge (1999) went as far as to subtitle his book about his love affair with the club simply *Football as a Religion*. For other supporters, following a football club can also be part of a wider social network which may involve specific religious affiliations, such as those Celtic fans who might view their Catholic identity as being integral with their support of that club.

Football, almost inevitably, dramatizes the religious conflicts and inequalities that exist around the world where the game is played (Giulianotti, 1999: 17). Religious or ethnic tensions can sometimes 'settle' on the sport or else, more usually, football clubs are historically and culturally tied to religious or sectional affiliations.

This is especially the case in the British context, of course, in the city of Glasgow, although even here there is considerable debate today about the extent to which sectarianism fundamentally underpins the affiliation to, and rivalry between, the two major Glasgow clubs. Liverpool is often compared to Glasgow, partly because of the working-class occupational and religious traditions in the two cities, partly because of the strong Irish influence in the history and cultures of the two locales, but also because of the particular passion for football in both Liverpool and Glasgow. So in this chapter, and although it is fashionable in some circles to describe modern-day football as a new 'religion', my aim is *not* to examine in any depth the ways in which the game *itself* might be compared in its rituals and traditions to the religious devotions of other faiths. I have much more limited ambitions here. Instead, I want first to try to say something about the differences in this respect between the character of football support in these two great northern British cities, Liverpool and Glasgow. Secondly, I want to spend a little time looking at the 'religious' connotations of the Hillsborough disaster as it was experienced by fans in the city of Liverpool, and also the specific role of 'Celtic expressiveness' in both the style and the depth of the mourning which followed in the city. Finally, I want to return to a modern-day comparison of football and religion in the two places, and to say a little about the importance of new 'cross-religious' links, as it were, which have been established recently between Liverpool FC and Celtic FC and between the supporters of these two football clubs.

This chapter draws, then, on interviews with supporters and examines the role that religious identities have had in shaping the fan culture which surrounds football in Liverpool and Glasgow. By contrasting the two cities – both ostensibly very similar in character – we can see the way that even in an increasingly secular society aspects of religiosity have helped mould the character of both the cities and the footballing culture which each helps to sustain.[1]

And if You Know Your History . . .

Both Liverpool and Glasgow are cities unique in Britain, long associated in popular consciousness with football, a strident working-class culture, urban deprivation and particularly in the case of the latter city sectarian violence. In addition they have strong connections with Ireland, both being subject to a massive wave of Irish immigrants in the nineteenth century. All immigrants help to shape the character of the cities in which they settle; the mainly Catholic Irish in Britain were no different, bringing aspects of their cultural and religious beliefs to a largely hostile indigenous population.

The development and origins of football and football clubs throughout England and Scotland are closely associated with various Church organizations. Initially the Christian Churches viewed football as a way of channelling the energy of the new urban working-class. Sport was accepted as a healthy pursuit which could

---

1. This chapter draws upon work and interviews with supporters (whose names have been changed) in both cities undertaken as part of research for R. Boyle, (1996) *Football and Cultural Identity in Glasgow and Liverpool*, unpublished PhD, University of Stirling: Stirling.

install both moral and spiritual values into this potentially volatile section of the population and keep them away from other less respectable forms of popular culture. However, such was the popularity of the sport of football, and the financial rewards available within the professional game, that by the 1870/80s it had become an organized and institutionalized mass spectator sport on both sides of the border.

Although coming to the game later than other cities, by the end of the nineteenth century Liverpool was widely regarded as the footballing centre of England. The origins of Liverpool and Everton can be traced to the formation in 1878 of St Domingo's. The club changed its name in order to attract a wider cross-section of players and called itself Everton after the local district of the city. The driving force behind the club was a one-time Lord Mayor of the city, local businessman and Tory politician, John Houlding, as discussed in Chapter One (see pp. 17–20).

In 1892 after falling out with his fellow club members on the Everton Board, who promptly relocated with the team to Goodison Park, Houlding now had a ground at Anfield, but no football team. He recruited individual players from Scotland (nicknamed the Scottish Professors), put together a team drawn from players many of whom were in fact Irish Glaswegians, and formed Liverpool Football Club. Ironically then it was an Orangeman who effectively founded the two biggest clubs in the city of Liverpool, and the steady flow of Scottish footballing talent (which would include Shankly, St John and Dalglish among others) to Anfield had been established.

There is little doubt that the origins of the clubs in the city are important in understanding how neither club became closely identified with a specific religious community in the city. While the question of how extensively these two clubs became associated with particular ethnic or religious groupings can be contentious, it appears that it was only in Glasgow that football took on sectarian overtones. In Liverpool there are some suggestions that popular folk memory recalls the 1920/30s as a time when Everton was seen by some as the Catholic club on Merseyside but there is little evidence to back this up.

What was crucial however was that neither club imposed a religious ban on who could or could not play for them, and as a result, the Merseyside rivalry was unlike that which existed in Glasgow between Celtic and Rangers, with the latter operating at various times in their history a Protestant-only signing policy, clearly marking the club as anti-Catholic. Indeed the recent autobiography by former Rangers player and Manchester United manager Sir Alex Ferguson (1999) makes clear that this anti-Catholic signing policy was still evident in the late 1970s.

In Liverpool there was a period during the 1950s when Everton (partly due to the large number of Irishmen they had playing for them at the time) did in the eyes of some fans become identified as the team supported by Catholics. However, neither Everton nor Liverpool operated sectarian player signing policies and with the origins of the clubs being such, any religious identification was at best transient (see Chapter One, pp. 19–20).

Football and Sectarianism

While there are great footballing rivalries throughout the world, most are based on regional/national differences (Barcelona/Real Madrid) or particular intra-city rivalry (Inter Milan/Milan). In Glasgow it is the identification with specific religious and ethnic groups that makes the derby games between Rangers and Celtic different.

Bradley (1994: 432) has argued that: 'Many Catholics in Scotland have an identity in relation to both Ireland and Scotland which varies in intensity and emphasis depending on circumstance and environment.' He suggests that the close interplay between a religious identity (Catholic) and a cultural identity (Irish) mark out this group as being a distinct ethnic community in Scotland. It could be argued that this ethnicity finds one arena of public expression in its support of Celtic F.C. In this sense the linkage between football support, religion and identity differs from the situation in Liverpool. Here there is no clear religious or ethnic identity attached to any specific club in that city despite the existence of a strong city-wide identity heavily influenced by nineteenth-century Irish immigration.

Support for a football club, with its emphasis on collective symbolic displays of loyalty and ritual, lends itself to being a very public marker of identity among groups. Bale (1991) has argued that many football supporters view their football stadium as a 'sacred space', which carries with it quasi-religious connotations of communal experience, a point which is developed below.

That sectarianism has shaped the culture of Scottish society is not disputed by social commentators (although there is a marked dearth of material on the subject). However there is disagreement as to the extent of this influence, and its presence in contemporary Scottish society. The sectarian culture which predominated in nineteenth-century Liverpool and which remained well into the twentieth century from the 1970s onward ceased to be a major force in the city. However in Scotland, and in particular in the west of the country, the debates about the continued influence of sectarianism in contemporary society retain a public profile which simply does not exist anywhere else in the UK outside of Northern Ireland.[2]

---

2. Witness the public furore surrounding the speech entitled 'Scotland's Shame', given by the composer James MacMillan at the 1999 Edinburgh festival in which he argued that anti-Catholic prejudice was still rife in Scottish society. He was attacked by a number of commentators as having overstated a problem, which they suggested did not exist, while others commended him for speaking out.

This clear religious affiliation with Catholicism among Celtic supporters is in marked contrast to the situation in Liverpool, a point noted by supporters of Liverpool:

Dave: I mean you do have Everton or Liverpool families, but it's also common to find supporters of both clubs under one roof, you don't expect to find that in Glasgow.

Helen: I was never aware that there were separate Catholic schools like there are in Glasgow.

Pete: I think there was a big sectarian divide in Liverpool from the generation before, my parents told me about it, similar to Glasgow. But it seemed to fade away in the 1960s, you had separate Catholic schools in the city, but it was never a big thing. There is still a Protestant/Catholic divide in the city, but not like Glasgow, and it's never, as far as I am able to see, affected the football. So you can't say one was a Catholic team or one was a Protestant team.

Mike: I get young people in my taxi cab and they don't know who the Catholic team was. Some of the older people do, but a lot of the younger ones don't. A lot of it's to do with success, and following success and wanting to be associated with success, you've had success at Liverpool for almost 25 years.

Helen: Everton, who were supposed to be Catholic, had a lot of support from North Wales, which doesn't tie in because that part of the country isn't Catholic.

Among contemporary supporters in Liverpool sectarianism was not viewed as being an issue, whereas race and racism were deemed important in modern Liverpool (see Chapter Six).

Pete: Yeah it's strange really, I think that race is the bigger problem than religion in Liverpool. Because let's face it the founder member of both clubs was an Orangeman. Among younger fans there was a broad consensus that attaching a religious dimension to football support was in fact a problem, or a potential problem.

Liverpool, Religion and Football

The focus of this section is on the aftermath of the Hillsborough disaster of 1989. What is of particular interest is the extent to which religion, religious ritual and football all played a key role in shaping the manner in which Liverpool mourned the supporters who died at the FA Cup semi-final match. Moreover, it offers a striking insight into the central position that ritual occupies in the life and culture of the city of Liverpool.

This sense of ritual is directly informed by the city's past (the influx of Irish immigrants in the nineteenth century) and its more recent economic and political isolation within contemporary Britain. It also presents a contrasting view of the position of religion and religious ritual in public life to that which exists in Glasgow. As we see below, far from viewing the link between religion and football as a problem, as is sometimes the case in Glasgow, in post-Hillsborough Liverpool it became a positive force. In part it allowed a sense of collective identity to find expression in the form of public rituals. This enabled the city to engage in a process of collective mourning. In many ways how the city of Liverpool coped with this tragedy offers an insight into the extent to which religiosity and football are intertwined in that city.

Walter (1991) has argued that the mourning which took place in Liverpool after Hillsborough offers a rebuttal to the conventional wisdom that people in late twentieth-century Britain were unable to deal as publicly with death and bereavement as they had in times past. He argues:

> Though there are major class, ethnic, gender and regional variations, British people have in the twentieth century become less expressive about their grief in public; lengthy periods of mourning that were expected in Victorian days collapsed in the 1914–18 war, and by mid-century people expected to get back to normal as soon as possible (Walter, 1991: 606).

The outpouring of public grief in the city of Liverpool in the days and weeks that followed Hillsborough were, it could be argued, unique to that city and are explained in part by the influence of the traditions and rituals of its Irish-Catholic-descendant working-class, and both the centrality that football occupies in the city's sense of identity and the marginal position of the city in the political and cultural life of English society.

One of the dominant characteristics of the mourning which took place in the city was that it was public, much of it spontaneously organized and centred around both traditional places of mourning (the Catholic and Anglican Cathedrals) and Anfield, the home of Liverpool F.C. It was here on the morning after the disaster that fans gathered to pay their respects to those who had died and to seek solace among supporters going through similar pain.

> *Jane*: I woke up on Sunday the 16th, didn't really sleep. And I just had to go down to Anfield. I really thought that there would maybe be a few people there, but that was all. I'm not really religious but it seemed right to go to the Shankly Gates at Anfield. When I got there there was hundreds of people, all with the same idea. The club opened the gates and we walked around the ground and laid flowers at the Kop end of the ground, and cried openly in public among friends.

The football ground became what Taylor (1989) called part of 'a mass popular religious rite'. The ground became a shrine, with the Kop end of the ground bedecked with flowers, scarves and other football memorabilia. Over a million people would file past the Kop over the next two weeks (many queuing for up to six hours just to get in). Bale notes: 'Mourners filed slowly past as they would at a cemetery. The stadium, not a church, was selected for this rite, making it a sure site for topophilic sentiments' (Bale, 1991: 132).

While there are quasi-religious overtones to much football supporting, the ritual of regular attendance at games, collective chanting and singing and a particular devotion to a club and its ground, it was never more pronounced than in Liverpool in the days and weeks after Hillsborough. Ian Taylor notes:

> The reconstruction of the ground as a shrine is a natural extension of existing relationships of the club to the fan: football grounds across the country have always had an almost religious hold on football fans and, indeed, on the families and kin on whom these, mainly male, fans have imposed their weekend and midweek-evening obsessions (Taylor, 1991: 5).

In addition, the spontaneous nature of the public collective outpouring of grief was commented upon not only by those directly involved. For example, a photographer, Steve Shakeshaft, sent by his newspaper to cover the story, arrived at Anfield only to find:

> I felt I was imposing. I had to take photographs, and yet I didn't want to. I felt as if I was exploiting the situation [. . .] A Salvation Army band followed us into the ground, and they grouped around in a circle inside the penalty area and then began playing 'Abide With Me'. It was so spontaneous. We were all in tears. Suddenly, I had a different perspective on the Kop and all those who stand on it. It had become a shrine, their shrine (Kelly, 1993: 182).

In general the coverage of the Hillsborough disaster in the national media, and the press in particular, generated a great deal of resentment among many people in the city. The portrayal of Liverpool fans as drunken louts, who looted the dead and abused the police as they attempted to offer assistance, was not only carried in the many national newspapers, but reproduced in papers throughout Europe. The *Sun* in particular suffered a drop in its Merseyside circulation of up to 150,000 as a result of its untrue stories, although it was not the only paper to upset people in the city. The *Daily Mirror* was the first to be criticized for its use of explicit colour photographs of fans being crushed to death against the fences at the Hillsborough stadium.

Tony Walter offers this explanation of much of the hostile reaction among other parts of England to the public communal outpouring of grief after Hillsborough. It is worth quoting at length because it raises a number of central themes in this chapter:

> In white UK culture, there are (apart from class differences) two cultures: an English reserve and a Celtic expressiveness. These are seen dramatically in the different feel of Manchester versus Liverpool, or even Edinburgh versus Glasgow. Celtic expressiveness offends English reserve (though it may be enjoyed by the English on holiday in Southern Ireland). To the English, Celts are dangerously unpredictable, and a crowd of Celts even more so – hence the stereotype of Liverpudlian football supporters as always liable to get into trouble, despite their generally good humour and unusually good police relations. Hence perhaps also the stereotype of the Liverpool worker as likely to take unofficial strike action at the drop of a hat (Walter, 1991: 607/8).

He argues that the expressive nature of the public mourning was in part a reflection of this Celtic cultural influence on the city of Liverpool, in turn fuelled by the sense of 'non-Englishness' felt by many in the city.

The contrast, however, with Manchester (itself a city with a large community of Catholic/Irish descent) seems misplaced. Differences between these two cities (both economic rivals in the north-west of England) are best understood by their differing patterns of economic development, decline and regeneration, rather than being purely cultural (although there is at times a link between the two).

There is no doubt, however, that the enormous influx of Irish into Liverpool has left a residual stamp on the character of the city, and its own self-identity. Samuel notes:

> The Irish brought with them into the country a complex of popular devotional practices, whose warmth and externality were often contrasted with the more reserved tradition of worship which prevailed among the English (Samuel, 1989: 101).

However accurate Walter's analysis, and its generalizations leave it open to criticism, there is no doubt that this view reflects the self-image held by many in the city as to its relationship with the rest of England. This perception of difference is reinforced by the position and character of the city in various aspects of popular culture, of which the tradition of supporting football is one of the most high-profile.

It should be noted that not all reaction was hostile to the city. Many football fans shared in the grief felt by the city. Over a million people passed through Anfield to pay their respects, well over double the population of the entire city. Significantly, the first match to be played by the club was at the invitation of Celtic F.C. and took place in Glasgow before an emotional crowd of over 60,000, with all proceeds going to the Hillsborough Disaster Fund.

The ties between the clubs for many supporters revolved around Kenny Dalglish, the former Celtic player and then Liverpool manager. But the ties between the clubs pre-date this and clearly have much to do with the mutual respect and friendship that developed in the 1960s between the two managers who laid the foundations of the modern clubs, Bill Shankly and Jock Stein. During a match in 1973 Celtic made a presentation to Shankly at Celtic Park. Shankly noted that:

> It was a magnificent gesture by Celtic to even consider making a presentation to me and as for the Celtic fans, their reception gave me an even greater thrill if that was possible. Any nervousness about being introduced onto the pitch disappeared as he 'heard the crowd and felt so much at home, it was like standing in the middle of the Kop at Anfield' (*The Celtic View*, 8 August 1973).

The adoption by Celtic fans of the Liverpool anthem 'You'll Never Walk Alone' also stems from this period and the communal singing of this at the post-Hillsborough match was commented upon by Ken Gaunt of the *Liverpool Echo*.

> Liverpool players came out in ones and twos to a great reception in the warm-up, but that was nothing compared to the thunderous roar of applause as the teams came out to the haunting strains of 'You'll Never Walk Alone'. Thousands of green Celtic scarves suddenly took the salute in one of the most remarkable messages of friendship I can ever remember at a football ground (*Liverpool Echo*, 1 May 1989).

There is little doubt that the relationship between both clubs and sets of fans became significantly closer after this particular match.

The role of official religion

In addition to the spontaneous organization of communal mourning there were also the formal religious rituals. The Catholic Cathedral in the city attracted twice its capacity to a Requiem Mass on the Sunday after Hillsborough. Memorial services were held in many local churches and in the Anglican Cathedral on the 29th of the month. However, something else occurred in Liverpool that emphasized the blurring of the religious lines of division that were once evident in the city and that still inform much of the public life of Glasgow. This involved the coming together of the Anglican and Catholic Churches in the city. Their leaders, Bishop David Sheppard and Archbishop Derek Worlock, spoke out together, defending the city against attack and ridicule from outside. In addition, they also argued for solutions to its economic and social problems, while all the time projecting a more positive image of the city to the outside world.

Walter (1991: 621) notes that perhaps more so than any other city in the UK 'Durkheimian religion – in which religious or neo-religious totems represent the entire community – operates in Liverpool.' He argues that this situation has become more acute with the collapse of traditional local politics which began to occur in the 1980s. While it has to be asked to what extent the large black community in the city feel represented by either the predominantly white Catholic or Anglican clergy, it is true to say that this coming together of the Churches, speaking on behalf of the city, does not occur in Glasgow.

While in that city in particular the Catholic Church frequently speaks out on a range of social and political issues relating to the Scottish situation (Cardinal Winning in particular), it makes no pretence that it is doing anything other than defending the interests of the Catholic community and certainly not speaking for the city as a whole.

The overwhelming post-Hillsborough sense in Liverpool was of a city pulling together to grieve for its own: Protestants and Catholics attending services together, with the unique sight of professional football players and fans helping and supporting each other at services and funerals. It represented a unique moment in the history of the city, and, it could be argued, produced a city-wide solidarity the like of which is rarely seen in contemporary urban Britain.

> *Nancy*: It was a truly weird time to live in the city. They say that Liverpool is small and that everyone knows everyone's business. But at that time it felt like a small village. Actually at times it was suffocating, and I know a lot of people needed to get away for a while.

> *Pete*: Yeah I mean you don't want to get sentimental about it, but there was a sense of togetherness, I don't know if it's the Irish thing or what, but I can't see that public grief being displayed elsewhere in England.

> *Dave*: It sounds clichéd but everyone did feel a sense of loss and grief. It engulfed the city. I couldn't have coped without the public rituals. I mean there was the private grief as well, but the thought that you could see people and they were feeling the way you were was very important. I'm not religious, but that sense that you are not alone is very important. It was like an extended family in the city, it sounds daft to say it, but that was how it felt. I mean football means more than it should to this city and for that to happen at a match, well . . .

Walter sums up the aftermath of Hillsborough as:

> A city retaining an unusual blend of Celtic and working-class mourning patterns, which it enacted in highly dramatic form due to the unique circumstances surrounding Hillsborough, was on view to the whole nation. Middle-class people throughout the country saw on Merseyside a model for the handling of grief to which they aspired, yet lacked the communal identity to achieve (Walter, 1991: 623).

The most recent comparison which saw public mourning on this scale was that which followed the death of Diana Princess of Wales and which was centred in

London. However, rather than being generated by a sense of traditional community, this appeared in part to represent a specific media-connected community. It is also significant that by the second anniversary of her death the public displays of remembrance predicted by the media had failed to materialize.

It could also be argued that in part the survival of that communal model (or aspects of it) in Liverpool is in part a result of the economic and political isolation felt by the city, particularly in the 1980s and into the 1990s. This isolation involved a turning inward for community strength and an outward articulation of that identity through its high-profile and, until recently, highly successful football teams. What, then, does this tell us about the relationship between football and religion in the cities of Liverpool and Glasgow?

Religion and Football: a Sense of Belonging

What clearly emerges from this chapter is the fact that religion and displays of religiosity occupy different social roles in both cities. In Glasgow, religious labelling (and this usually is limited to being either Catholic or Protestant despite the multitude of faiths evident in contemporary Glasgow) is still an important boundary-marker of difference between social groups in certain circumstances. In other words, in specific situations, affiliation to either Celtic or Rangers football club or whether the name of the school you attended began with a Saint's name marks you as either Catholic or Protestant (and of course this can often be innaccurate).

Being earmarked as a Catholic also carries with it connotations of Irishness and support for things Irish and this in turn can be held by some as an indication of that person's lack of loyalty to all things supposedly Scottish. To a few the fact that a person is Catholic means that they can never be truly Scottish.

Of course much of this operates at the level of generalization. All Rangers fans for example do not hold bigoted attitudes towards Catholics, and all Celtic supporters do not necessarily feel that they are Irish. However, to play down the role of religious labelling in the west of Scotland is to be guilty not only of denying its influence (both historical and contemporary) but also of presenting Scottish culture as some sort of homogeneous entity not subject to the internal contradictions and tensions that all national cultures experience. More importantly, it denies the importance of confronting issues of division and, in this instance, specifically the issue of sectarianism. As Scotland embarks on a new political era, with its own Parliament, recognizing that a problem exists remains an important first step towards finding a solution.

This point was made by novelist Andrew O'Hagan in a polemical article entitled 'Scotland's Fine Mess'. He commented on his experience of an Orange Walk in the town of Alloa during the summer of 1994:

The first of 130 buses roared into West End Park [. . .] The Bannockburn True Blues adjusted their gear. They began to flute and drum and march out of the park [. . .] There was wildness in every direction: you felt anything could go off. I felt very Catholic, very open to assault. [. . .] England, for all that's said, is not really a target of everyday Scottish venom. We save most of that up for ourselves; we spend it recklessly on each other (*Guardian Weekend*, 23 June 1994).

Interestingly, the issue of a Catholic/Protestant divide does not exist to any great extent in modern Liverpool. If religious discrimination is viewed as a problem in Glasgow then it is not seen as such in Liverpool.[3] Historically, sectarianism had an important influence on the political and economic development of the city, yet with the city's economic and political decline, internal city divisions have, to a large extent, been replaced by a more common citywide identity. Perhaps the major internal issue to threaten this cosy city image is that of race and racism. The invisibility of the city's black community from dominant images of the city is as striking as it is worrying.

Again, it is worth emphasizing that while much of the discussion in this chapter has been on the issue of religion, it is true to say that the population of both cities is overwhelmingly secular in nature. However, this does not negate the importance of religious labelling or aspects of religiosity in the culture and identity of both cities. Glasgow is not the warring sectarian battleplace of some media representations, yet vestiges of sectarianism do exist and are not confined to the working-class population of the city. Witness the resignation in 1999 of Rangers Vice-Chairman Donald Findlay QC, following his capture on video singing sectarian songs as Rangers players celebrated winning the domestic treble. Some commentators suggest that the 'Old Firm' rivalry simply continues 'because the fans enjoy it so much. They are not about to give up their ancient traditions just because they no longer believe in God' (Kuper, 1994: 218). To what extent this rivalry could be sustained without it having any connection with the contemporary social and economic reality of life in Glasgow is hard to believe. However complex this connection may have become over the years, for many this rivalry is fuelled by more than mere rhetoric.

In Glasgow, the position of a separate state-funded Catholic system of education is vital in sustaining a specific identity among the Catholic population of the west of Scotland. In addition, the Catholic Church takes an active part in the public issues of the day affecting its laity in this part of Scotland (Boyle and Lynch, 1998). By contrast, the situation in Liverpool sees both the Anglican and the

3. The signature tune from the 1960s television series *Z Cars* was played by Everton before matches. It was apparently played once before a match at Celtic Park during this period. One fan recalls the Celtic supporters 'went bananas and started shouting for it to stop. The reason? They thought it was an Orange tune and, when you think about it, I suppose there is a similarity' (Quinn, 1994: 179).

Catholic Churches occupying central positions as representatives and spokespeople for the city in a way that neither the Catholic Church nor the Church of Scotland does in Glasgow. Ironically, in terms of profile, the situation in Liverpool is more akin to the position of Church spokespeople in Northern Ireland, where media time is often given to Church leaders calling for consensus between the separate communities which they claim to represent.

In Liverpool, as the reaction to Hillsborough demonstrated, quasi-religious links between football and organized religion take on a heightened cultural significance in this particular city, partly due to its historical character and its contemporary position within English culture.

There are links between football and aspects of religiosity in Glasgow and Liverpool. The continued interest and popularity of football in these cities, while a testimony in part to the resilience of working-class culture in the cities, is also an indicator of the importance of ritual and spectacle in urban life. What you find in both cities is an interweaving of public and private culture, of religion and sport, the configuration of which is informed by the specific characteristics of the cities. In common they play a central role in the identity of many people in both these cities, yet in many ways, as shown above, they manifest themselves differently and tell us how, for all their similarities, Glasgow and Liverpool are very different cities.

Yet this is not to downplay the more secular links which help bind clubs such as Liverpool and Celtic together. Post-Hillsborough, alliances between supporters of the clubs have been strengthened, both by the epic UEFA Cup matches of 1997 and more recently by the arrival at Celtic in 1999 of the two Liverpool legends, Kenny Dalglish as Head of Football Operations and John Barnes as Head Coach. Ironically this is at a time when the former Rangers manager Walter Smith is in charge at Everton. In many ways, the 'traditional religious' allegiances between the cities is being superseded by new more secular patterns of loyalty and interest.

While Glasgow and Liverpool have both been shaped by the influx of nineteenth-century Irish immigrants, it is clear that this process has been different in each city. Differing political and economic environments have conspired to give each city a distinctive character. One characteristic shared by both is the important position that football occupies in their cultural lives. It seems reasonable to assume that, despite any impact that political and economic change may have on both cities, football will remain symbolically important in Glasgow and Liverpool, both reflecting and giving shape to a range of identities.

Acknowledgements

I would like to thank all the fans who spoke with me, and the editors for their helpful comments on an earlier draft.

References

Bale, J. (1991) 'Playing at Home: British football and a sense of place', in J. Williams and S. Wagg (eds) *British Football and Social Change: getting into Europe*, Leicester: Leicester University Press.

—— (1994) *Landscapes of Modern Sport*, Leicester: Leicester University Press.

Boyle, R. and Lynch, P. (eds) (1998) *Out of the Ghetto? The Catholic Community in Modern Scotland*, Edinburgh: John Donald.

Bradley, J. (1994) 'Ethnicity: the Irish in Scotland – football, politics and identity', *Innovation*, 7(4).

Edge, A. (1999) *Faith of Our Fathers: Football as a Religion*, Edinburgh and London: Mainstream.

Ferguson, A. (with Hugh McIlvanney) (1999) *Managing My Life: My Auto-biography*, London: Hodder & Stoughton.

Giulianotti, R. (1999) *Football: a Sociology of the Global Game*, Cambridge: Polity.

Kelly, S. (1993) *The Kop: the End of an Era*, London: Mandarin.

Kuper, S. (1994) *Football Against the Enemy*, London: Orion.

Lappin, T. (1996) 'Engerlaaand Engerland', *Scotsman*, 15 June.

Moir, J. (1995) 'A man of two halves', *Observer Life Magazine*, 17 September.

O'Hagan, A. (1994) 'Scotland's Fine Mess', *Guardian Weekend*, 23 June.

Quinn, J. (1994) *Jungle Tales: Celtic Memories of an Epic Stand*, Edinburgh: Mainstream.

Samuel, R. (1989) 'An Irish religion', in R. Samuel (ed.) *Patriotism: The Making and Unmaking of British National Identity*, London: Routledge.

Taylor, I. (1989) 'Hillsborough, 15 April 1989: Some Personal Contemplations', *New Left Review*, No. 177.

—— (1991) 'English football in the 1990s: taking Hillsborough seriously', in J. Williams and S. Wagg (eds) *British Football and Social Change*, London: Routledge.

Taylor, R., Ward, A. with Williams, J. (1993) *Three Sides of the Mersey: An Oral History of Everton, Liverpool and Tranmere Rovers*, London: Robson.

Walter, T. (1991) 'The mourning after Hillsborough', *Sociological Review*, **39**(3): 599–626.

Bill Shankly and Liverpool

Andrew Ward with *John Williams*

Introduction

What we want to try to do in the first part of this chapter is to look at the circumstances of Bill Shankly's arrival in Liverpool in 1959 and to try to locate him and the Liverpool coaching staff of the time within the context of wider shifts in the post-war English game and debates about the domestic 'governance' of the sport, at least with respect to the issues of football management and coaching. John Williams tries to set the scene in this respect, by arguing that the Shankly era at Liverpool both recalls earlier developments in coaching and football club administration in Britain and also stands some way at odds with aspects of emerging new orthodoxies in England in the 1960s and 1970s about how football should be both played and coached.

Then, Andrew Ward in the second, longer, part of this chapter tries to evoke something of the particular *flavour* of the man, and of the Shankly years on Merseyside, and also of his relationship with supporters and players in Liverpool. How does Shankly both engage with and contribute to the particular 'structures of feeling' in the club and the city in the 1960s? Ward displays this in a highly original way by presenting a number of *vignettes* which highlight important aspects of Shankly's character and his approach to relationships in the sport. Much of this material is from original, unpublished, sources and is used in this inventive and unusual way especially to try to highlight the special features of Shankly's relationship to football, to Liverpool Football Club and to the city of Liverpool itself. Let us begin, then, by briefly trying to locate Shankly and his influence more broadly within the British game.

The Shankly Era Begins

Promotion for Liverpool FC from the Second Division under the young Bill Shankly in 1961/62 ushered in the beginning of a new era for the football club, a time when Liverpool FC would pursue European football adventures for the first time and the club would remain, for very different reasons, resolutely centre stage in public debates about football and its possible futures. In the early 1960s, Liverpool FC was becoming an international focus because of the synergy between music and football in the city and the cultural inventiveness of its fans; in the 1970s the spotlight fell on Liverpool because of the excellence and dominance of the club's extraordinary football team and management; in the 1980s it was more footballing excellence, but also an altogether harsher glare on the character of the city following the fatal hooliganism at Heysel and the crowd disaster at Hillsborough; by the 1990s the focus was on the prospects for reviving the club's football status in a new, global era, but also on the new economics of the sport as the club struggled to adapt to the new era of the game's development, eventually investing in a new business structure, a talented foreign coach and a roster of imported foreign players (see Chapters Eight and Ten).

The so-called 'December earthquake' when Bill Shankly arrived at the club in the winter of 1959 (Hodgson, 1978) almost blew itself out before the footballing transformation at the club could even begin. Shankly had explosive early confrontations with the club's conservative directors, who were accused by the ambitious and abrasive Scot of complacency and of being, 'scared, like gamblers on a losing streak who were afraid to bet any more' (Hodgson, 1978: 78). Shankly persuaded the Liverpool board to 'modernize' the poorly developed Melwood training ground in 1960, and he aimed at transferring out twenty-four players in just over a year after his arrival in December 1959, bringing in key young replacements, especially from his native Scotland. Even as a young manager of a Second Division club in the late 1950s it was clear that Shankly's ideas were from a very different era from that represented by the departing Phil Taylor, who had served the club as player, coach and manager since 1936. The *Liverpool Echo* reported on 14 December 1959 that:

> Shankly is a disciple of the game as played by the Continentals. The man out of possession, he believes, is just as important as the man with the ball at his feet. Continental football is not the lazy man's way of playing soccer. Shankly will aim at incisive forward moves by which Continentals streak through a defence when it is 'closed up' by British standards. He will make his players learn to kill a ball and move it all in the same action . . . he will make them practice complete mastery of the ball.

Shankly was determined to introduce 'modern' methods of training and preparation with his new club; as early as February 1960, for example, Liverpool players flew to Plymouth for a League meeting with Argyle, something which was highly unusual for the time, especially for a club in the Second Division of the League. Shankly also described the crumbling and disjointed Anfield ground of the time as an 'eyesore'. He was right. There had been no serious structural work on the stadium since 1928, and in 1963 a new 'daringly modern' (Inglis, 1996: 220) cantilevered stand for 6,700 fans was built to replace the shambolic barrel-roofed Kemlyn Road stand. As if to salute this expensive and impressive new structure, following promotion from the Second Division Shankly's young team carried off the League title in 1964 and, for the first time in the club's history, the FA Cup in 1965. With the Cup Final profits the Anfield Road end of the ground was also re-roofed, as Anfield was slowly transformed to meet the new demands of a European football age.

On the coaching side at Anfield, Shankly had inherited what were to become a number of key figures in the successful period which followed. They included later manager, the low-key but knowledgeable Joe Fagan, and chief coach Reuben Bennett, a severe physical education disciplinarian who used to wail at the 'softness' of players and tell his injured men to rub the offending area with a wire brush or even a kipper (Kelly, 1999: 59). Ex-Liverpool players Ronnie Moran and Roy Evans would join the back room later, but the most important of all the coaching staff was Bob Paisley, a long-serving Liverpool player himself, who had been offered the job of reserve team trainer by club director and later chairman and president T.V. Williams in 1954. Paisley took over at Liverpool from Albert Shelley, the archetypal white-coated British football club trainer, who by this time was limited to sweeping out the changing rooms and swapping banter with the hardened professionals. Paisley, a north-easterner from a mining background, already had a 'native' interest in fitness and the body which he attributed to his father's prodigious strength in the mines and a northern working man's industrial/rural deep interest in the performance of pigeons and his beloved racehorses. Paisley often compared players to racehorses, noting their common 'edginess', and also the ways in which both football players and thoroughbreds responded to *different* sorts of training, dependent upon their temperament. Even when he became club manager Paisley was probably most at home in the local bookmaker's studying form (Keith, 1999: 12; see also Chapter Four). He shared many of the pragmatic, 'communitarian' values and football enthusiasms of Shankly's own Scottish industrial heritage, which produced a crop of great British football managers from Shankly, Matt Busby and Jock Stein through to Alex Ferguson (Giulianotti, 1999: 128; McIlvanney, 1995).

Paisley had taken a correspondence course in physiotherapy, but Williams had also secured an open letter from local friend John Moores, founder of the Littlewoods group, requesting that Paisley be allowed in local hospitals to study medical methods and operations. For years the training staff and players at the club trusted to Paisley's intuitive insights into injury, but he was also aware of the paucity of specialist knowledge in the sport about treatment of injuries. He was one of the few trainers in the Football League in the 1950s to have any formal medical qualification (Kelly, 1999: 33). Paisley was also tactically astute, more so than Shankly. Their combination of strong, inspiring leader and shrewd 'medical' and tactical second-in-command dominated the English game for the following 25 years. Incredibly, in a total of 784 matches in charge at Liverpool, each missed only one match on the bench – Paisley due to illness, Shankly to scout elsewhere.

Shankly's predecessor at Liverpool, Phil Taylor, had resigned in 1959 after failing to take the club out of the Second Division and had also suffered humiliating defeat at the hands of non-league Worcester City in the FA Cup. Taylor had retired from playing at the same time as had Paisley and became club coach to Don Welsh in 1954. Welsh was sacked two years later, the first Liverpool manager to suffer this fate and followed since only by Graeme Souness. Tellingly, however, Bill Shankly had been interviewed for the job when Welsh had been appointed and was told, ominously, that the directors reserved the right to change the team (Wagg, 1984: 157). This time Shankly insisted he take charge at Liverpool with complete control over team matters, signalling the arrival of the 'modern' manager at Anfield, more than 30 years after the emergence in the 1920s of the first modern football technocrat, Herbert Chapman, at Huddersfield Town, and later the dominant force at 1930s Arsenal.

Chapman, like Shankly, believed in the unchallengable centrality of the manager's expertise – the board could deal with tickets and economics – and in 'organized' systems of play, which focused on the *team* not the individual. He was also concerned, again like Shankly, not just with the *playing* skills of his professionals, but with their general attitudes and lifestyles: 'How does he behave? What sort of life does he lead? Unless the answers are satisfactory, I do not pursue the matter further' (quoted in Wagg, 1984: 49). He understood the importance of delegation to a trusted staff and also the crucial matter of player fitness. He appointed Tom Whittaker as trainer and in the latter's resort to modern science in the treatment room threatened to revolutionize the whole approach in the game to physical fitness (Young, 1968: 175). At Anfield, Paisley and Bennett kept meticulous records on the fitness and preparation of players and strived for improved medical expertise.

Unlike his starch, be-suited contemporaries, Chapman, like Shankly, was also a players' manager who argued that one must get close to players, share their difficulties, understand their problems: though, if truth be told, at Liverpool Bob Paisley was more a players' *pal* than was Shankly. Finally, Chapman, again like Shankly, was an innovator who had a genius for psychological ploys and public relations and club promotion. Chapman experimented with a white football and numbering on players shirts, and introduced a 45-minute clock at Highbury. He had the press in thrall. Shankly sought more a special relationship with *fans,* but he was also a marvellously untutored proselytizer for the club on TV and with the press. Managers at Liverpool who followed him had quite a different approach to such matters as the press became more voracious – and vicious – and television much more intrusive and demanding in the TV age of football.

Shankly and his staff at Liverpool shared much, then, with the early revolutionary Chapman approach, but like most coaches and managers in England they were also much more reluctant to embrace aspects of the newly emerging post-war coaching orthodoxies. Wagg (1984: 74–100) describes well the struggle in the English game between the traditional 'muddy boots' approach of the English ex-professionals-turned-managers and the 'chalky fingers' philosophies of the new generation of qualified football technocrats, sponsored by the Football Association and led by the first England manager, an ex-school-master, Walter Winterbottom. Later, Charles Hughes, the Technical Director at the Football Association championed so-called 'scientific' approaches to coaching and playing which stripped the sport down to the conclusions of data analysis which purported to show that 90 per cent of goals scored came from moves of five passes or fewer. This peculiar form of 'industrial deskilling' (Giulianotti, 1999: 133), which effectively championed the long ball game in England, was followed more recently, in the 1990s, by new calls for a more 'scientific' approach to football coaching here. One dimension of this, recalling aspects of the obsessive scientific Taylorism of Charles Hughes, is the endless match analysis, conducted for the FA, designed to try to quantify the key features of some optimum international playing style. As this sort of rank positivism continues, the England team at the outset of the twenty-first century continues to fail, miserably, in the face of much more flexible opponents. Key deficits here seem to be in the processes of preparation, mental agility and strength, and in the crucial areas of creative decision-making and technically proficient and imaginative play.

Hostility among football professionals and managers back in the 1950s and 1960s to the new 'football theorists' – the 'outsiders', the blazered 'amateurs' at the FA who had never played the game, so what could they know? – was rooted both in a strongly defensive professional ideology and in an assertion that by invoking a more 'scientific' approach to coaching, especially, the theorists were in danger of making a 'simple' game unnecessarily complicated. In the 1960s, the old League player's ethos of native skill and masculine toughness had to be reconciled with a new orthodoxy based on formal knowledge and detail to strategy (Wagg, 1984: 100). At Liverpool, following Shankly's arrival, the struggle was soon on. Early in his reign, Shankly, Paisley, Fagan, Reuben Bennett and Ronnie Moran attended an FA coaching course at Lilleshall, reporting to their hosts on Saturday evening. Paisley was unimpressed and Shankly hated the formal 'theorizing' and wanted to leave immediately. He lasted until Tuesday, and never returned. Moran and Fagan, however, enjoyed meeting other coaches and went back for five or six years. According to rotund Liverpool 'keeper, Tommy Lawrence, Shankly 'didn't like Lilleshall, he didn't like boards with diagrams on them or somebody talking posh about football, that wasn't Bill' (quoted in Kelly, 1999: 77; see also Chapter Four). Until the arrival at the club more than 30 years later of Gérard Houllier, formal approaches to 'scientific' coaching were largely decried at Liverpool in favour of tried and trusted schemes of preparation honed under Shankly and Paisley and passed on via custom and practice to those who followed.

Why was all this 'book learning' necessary, it was argued at Anfield, when regularly playing in *Europe* also meant that coaches at the club were open to, and could adapt, innovations from abroad? After an unusual and comprehensive defeat, home and away, by Red Star Belgrade in 1973, for example, the Liverpool coaching staff concluded that the old 'stopper' English centre backs were now outmoded and they successfully converted more mobile midfielders – Hughes, Thompson – to these defensive positions (Keith, 1999: 119). Experience and flexibility, rather than theory and what were deemed to be fixed practices, were extolled as the central virtues at Anfield.

This surprise European defeat by Red Star occurred, in fact, during what was to prove to be Shankly's last season at Liverpool. Despite a crushing FA Cup Final win against Newcastle United and with a team crammed with new young talent including Ray Clemence, Phil Thompson, and the player who was to become the standard bearer for the new football commercialism, Kevin Keegan (Wagg, 1984: 144), Shankly resigned. Although he routinely told his staff he was 'packing in' the game, this was a stunning moment. Perhaps he sensed another, more consumer-driven period of the game's development lay ahead, where *players* would hold more of the whip-hand, and where television would increasingly dominate? Football had certainly changed enormously since his early days as a manager. Perhaps he fretted at his lack of serious European success? Perhaps, as some have argued, his decision was a spasm, quickly regretted? Whatever the reason, here was the end of the beginning of a period of club dominance in the English game which would surpass even Chapman's remarkable record at Huddersfield and Arsenal back in the 1920s and 1930s. Bill Shankly, often at odds with the new coaching gurus at the FA, had been a central figure in establishing the modern 'Liverpool way'.

Nine points of Shankly

In this section Andrew Ward selects nine features that helped to mould Bill Shankly into the unique managerial talent that oversaw Liverpool Football Club from his arrival in December 1959 to July 1974 when he suddenly retired. Some of these features are common to many football-club managers. It is the combination that produced the legendary influence which has been the subject of a stream of recent books about Shankly the man and his Liverpool legacy (Thompson 1993; Bowler 1996; Kelly, 1996; Bale, 1996; Darby, 1998; Keith 1998).

Bill Shankly moved to Liverpool in December 1959 after a decade of managing at Carlisle United, Grimsby Town, Workington Town and Huddersfield Town. He joined a club that was consistently missing promotion to the old First Division by one or two places. Helped by an injection of money for the signings of two fellow Scots, Ian St John and Ron Yeats, Shankly turned the club around inside three years. The Second Division Championship (1961/62) was followed by three League Championships (1963/64, 1965/66 and 1972/73), two FA Cup Final victories (1965 and 1974) and the club's first European trophy, the UEFA Cup (1973).

Through Shankly, and the mythologies which were generated by his presence, we can understand what *kind* of organization Liverpool Football Club became in the 1960s and early 1970s. Also, through these key features, we can sense how Shankly matched, and to some degree manufactured, the Liverpudlian spirit of the time. The relationship between Shankly and the bulk of Liverpool fans was largely compatible. Both sides were tough and cocky with plenty of swagger. Together they were a bit lippy and a little crazy, and they made each other laugh. As Kelly (1996) explains in the introduction to his recent Shankly biography, the people of Liverpool and Shankly *shared* the same fighting spirit, humour and obsession with football.

The Obsession

One cold April night, in the early 1950s, a party of football-club managers travelled by train together from London to Aldershot. They had met in London to help prepare the Football League AGM agenda, and now they were on their way to play a charity football match – Bob Jackson's All Star XI against Aldershot, then of Division Three (South). Snow was falling, toes were freezing, and there seemed little chance of the game being played. As the train approached Aldershot a third of the ground was visible, shrouded in snow, and the majority view was confirmed. The game would be postponed.

The group walked from Aldershot railway station and entered the ground. Johnny Carey, then manager of Blackburn Rovers, was the first to see that the referee was conducting a pitch inspection. The referee was skating around and falling over, and the pitch was obviously unfit. Carey relayed the news to the others.

The young Workington Town manager, Bill Shankly, was down the terraces and over the perimeter wall in a trice. A few well-balanced strides on the icy surface and he was coercing the referee: 'It's fit tah play, Sah, it's fit tah play.' And so they played.[1]

1. Told to Andrew Ward by his father, Tim Ward, who also played for Bob Jackson's All Star team of managers.

All managers love football and live football but Bill Shankly's obsession for the game went further than most of his peer group. Similarly, most managers construct football analogies from everyday situations but Shankly was a master at it. If a player said 'Good morning, Boss', he would reply 'Aye, a good morning for football'. He would start training with a simple homily – 'It's great to be alive, boys, all you need is a round ball and the green grass' – and take it from there.[2] A rainy day was 'a good day for skidding the ball'.[3]

His obsession sometimes bordered on craziness or rudeness because he didn't waste time on preamble like 'How's the family?' or 'How are you?' It was straight to the football (Taylor and Ward, 1993: 95/6). Denis Law, who played under Shankly at Huddersfield Town in the late 1950s, has described Shankly as a football fanatic who never talked about anything else but football. Law accepted 'football talk' at a match, but after the game Shankly drove Law crazy.[4]

Neville Smith, author of *The Golden Vision*, a play set around Everton football fanaticism in the 1960s, tells of how he once met Bill Shankly on a Liverpool–London train in the late 1960s. It was over the Christmas holiday period and the League fixtures were being staggered for the first time. Liverpool had no game that day but there were a couple of matches in London so Shankly was going to watch one of them. It wasn't because he was watching a player. 'It's a game,' was Shankly's explanation. While everybody else was at home with families, Shankly was going to one of the few games available.[5] The obsession legend bubbled over when Shankly claimed to have celebrated his wife's birthday by taking her to a reserve-team match.

Shankly's obsession had always been there, but it must have been aggravated by frustrated ambition. As a Preston North End player he won three medals – FA Cup runners-up (1937), FA Cup winners (1938) and Wartime Cup winners (1941) – but defeat to Arsenal in 1938 had cost his club the Cup and League double and the Second World War had stopped him from adding to his five Scotland caps. Shankly later said that his best playing years were from age 28 to 33, and that those years had coincided with the war (1941 to 1946) (Keith, 1998: 75).

---

2. Interview with Brian Hall for *One Hundred Years of Merseyside Football*, a 32-part radio series broadcast by Radio City (Sound of Merseyside). The majority of interviews were conducted by Rogan Taylor and the scripts written by Andrew Ward. Footnotes here refer to material not used in the radio series or the subsequent book (Taylor and Ward 1993).

3. Interview with Tommy Smith for a six-part BBC-2 television series called *Kicking and Screaming*. The series was produced by Jean-Claude Bragard and the consultant was Rogan Taylor. Footnotes here refer to material not used in the series or the subsequent book (Taylor and Ward 1995).

4. Interview with Denis Law for *One Hundred Years of Merseyside Football*.

5. Interview with Neville Smith for *One Hundred Years of Merseyside Football*.

As a professional player and a manager, Shankly went from 1941 to 1962 without winning a trophy. That's a long time in football. Similarly, Liverpool Football Club went from 1947 to 1962 without winning anything of note. The frustration of their fans matched Shankly's.

Also, when Bill Shankly reached fifty, he wasn't even the most successful manager in his own family. That honour belonged to his brother Bob, who took Dundee to the Scottish League Championship in 1962 and to a European Cup semi-final a year later. It is often said that younger brothers, striving to catch up, are more likely to have football ambitions, and Shankly was the youngest of five brothers.

Similarly, again, Liverpool fans could be bridled, in a familial way, by Everton fans. The most persistent taunt was that Liverpool had never won the FA Cup. When Shankly's team finally did win the Cup, in 1965, it led to amazing scenes of 'red' celebrations. A few days after the Final, Liverpool entertained Inter Milan in a European Cup semi-final. Some fans set off to Anfield at nine in the morning to make sure of seeing the 7.30 pm game. At eleven o'clock in the morning Anfield was surrounded. The gates were opened soon afterwards and thousands were in that ground from noon to nearly half past ten at night (Taylor and Ward, 1993: 120). Thousands wanted to see the Cup. Thousands were as obsessive as Shankly. Without realizing it, Bill Shankly and Liverpool fans had been moving in parallel since the Second World War.

Scottish Socialism

There were no charter flights from Speke Airport, Liverpool, to Reykjavik, Iceland in 1964. When Liverpool made their European Cup debut, after winning the League under Shankly in 1963–64, it meant a coach ride from Liverpool to Scotland and a flight from Prestwick in Ayrshire. Having played West Ham in the Charity Shield on the Saturday, the team left on the Sunday. As the coach neared its destination, Shankly had an idea:

> *'We've got a couple of hours to spare,' he said. 'Let's go to Butlin's at Ayr.'*
> *The coach-driver pulled in at the gates of Butlin's Holiday Camp.*
> *'Who are you?' asked the man on the gate.*
> *'Bill Shankly, Liverpool Football Club, we're going to Reykjavik in Iceland.'*
> *'I think you've taken the wrang road.'[6]*

The idea of taking a European Cup team to a Butlin's Holiday Camp might seem ludicrous nowadays, but it says a lot for Shankly's roots that this seemed a

---

6. This story is taken from a number of sources, notably Keith (1998: 140), Kelly (1996: 161) and Taylor and Ward (1993: 134).

wonderful idea at the time. He was brought up in Glenbuck, a coal-mining village 30 miles inland from Ayr, and he had learned his basic values from the coal-mining community – you work hard and you work for each other. Every day was a day to be appreciated but if you wanted something special you went to Ayr.

Part of Liverpool's success in the 1960s and 1970s was built around the socialist ethic of collective effort with equal wages and no prima donnas. Liverpool supporters warmed to this all-red 'political correctness'. There was no room for anyone thinking he was above anyone else.

Bowler (1996: 8–9) links Shankly's lifelong socialism to his Glenbuck upbringing, in particular his work in the mines and the formative influence of the General Strike (when Shankly was twelve): 'His political ideas grew from that time, leaving him a lifelong socialist who played like a socialist and managed like a socialist. Everything about Shankly was geared to fostering a community, a powerful team spirit that acknowledged the fact that no individual component was more important than the greater good.'

The work ethic also showed in training. A succession of players signed from other First Division clubs – Geoff Strong (Arsenal), Phil Chisnall (Manchester United) and Tony Hateley (Chelsea) – expressed surprise at how much harder the training was at Liverpool (Keith, 1998: 41). Shankly drew a distinction between exercise (less than needed in a match) and training (more than needed in a match). The epitome of this was the 'sweat-box' or 'shooting-box'. Players worked in pairs in a square box surrounded by four shooting boards. One player would shoot and the other player would have to hit the rebound in his stride. It was like a four-way squash game and was very hard work (Bowler, 1996: 160).

Shankly never lost his sense of how hard life could be. When he moved to Liverpool he lived in the same three-bedroom semi-detached house from 1960 to his death in 1981. The link between his origins and his socialism is best shown when Shankly hosted a Radio City chat show with Prime Minister Harold Wilson in November 1975. A transcription of the occasion shows their informed discussion of the Ayrshire coalfield and the values instilled from such communities (Keith, 1998: 184–210).

And, of course, Glenbuck was a football community. A village of fewer than a thousand people, it had produced top-class professional players such as Sandy Brown and John Crosbie at the turn of the century, and Shankly's two uncles on his mother's side – Bob and Billy Blyth. Glenbuck's footballers never lost their quintessential *Scottishness*. As Shankly told Welshman John Toshack after signing him from Cardiff City in 1970, 'Never lose your accent' (Keith, 1998: 175). This attitude suited Liverpool fans. They had always welcomed Scottish players, right from the 1890s when the club fielded predominantly Scottish teams (see Chapter One). In the 1950s the only playing star was the much-loved and devout Christian, Billy Liddell. He had hailed from a Scottish coal-mining community. Just like Bill Shankly.

Simple Strategy

Throw-in to Liverpool in the mid-1960s. In their own half. On the right-hand side. Quickly taken. Waist high to Chris Lawler, the full-back, about six yards away. Lawler stoops and heads the ball back to the thrower. Liverpool in possession. In their own half. Coming forward.

This rehearsed throw-in, repeated hundreds of times without losing possession, was about as complex as Bill Shankly's tactical innovation ever became. His basic philosophy, derived from his Socialist origins, was very simple: You pass the ball to another red shirt and then take up another available position.

> Pass, move, receive the ball.
> Pass, move, receive the ball.

You keep moving into good positions and give your team-mate alternatives. You play to each other's strengths and your team keeps possession of the ball. And if you're losing you don't change the system. You keep going till the end.

Bill Shankly was not a man for ostentatious display or fancy talk. He was certainly not a man for jargonized team-talks. He despised expressions such as 'penetrative through-ball' and 'overlapping full-back' (Taylor and Ward, 1993: 97). He would have agreed with Joe Mercer that the way to learn how to play football was by practising with a ball and playing against better and better players (James, 1993: 16). His approach contrasted strongly with that of the Don Revie/ Syd Owen player dossiers in use at Leeds United in the late 1960s and early 1970s.

Shankly and Bob Paisley were probably more inventive in training than on the playing pitch. For instance, they introduced shaped blocks of wood which changed the direction of shots when placed in front of goal; they gave specialist practice to the goalkeepers; and they paid close attention to other defensive tactics.[7] Shankly moved midfielder, Tommy Smith, alongside Ron Yeats as a central defender, telling Smith that he would be 'Yeatsy's' right leg. Less successful was the signing of the tall but technically weak Tony Hateley which caused a switch in attacking tactics. Because Hateley was a brilliant header of the ball but poor in build-up play, Liverpool briefly switched unsuccessfully to a high-ball game. Hateley was replaced by John Toshack, who not only was excellent with his head but had a better touch with his feet.

Tommy Smith recalls the 1966 Charity Shield match, when Shankly decided that Liverpool would try something different. 'Let's try a free-kick', Shankly said. 'Let's try somebody running over the ball and then maybe passing it sideways.

---

7. Interview with Tommy Smith for *Kicking and Screaming*.

Sort it out among yourselves.' When Liverpool got a free-kick at Manchester United's Stretford End, Tommy Smith jumped over the ball, Gordon Milne jumped over it and Willie Stevenson did likewise, leaving the ball on its own. 'Ah, forget it', said Shankly later.[8]

It sums up Shankly's whole approach to tactics. What mattered most was getting the *right players*.

Tough, Skilful Northern Players who had Served Apprenticeships

Playing against Tottenham in the Cup in the early 1970s, Tommy Smith injured a thigh muscle in his left leg. He knew that if he was seen to be injured Shankly would leave him out of the side. He was also aware, as was everybody at Liverpool, that Shankly did not like his players to strap their legs or put plasters on cuts because that was showing weakness to the opposition. In the treatment-room that week, Smith talked to trainer Joe Fagan.

'Maybe I can get away with this, Joe', said Smith. 'If you shave the top of me leg, I'll put a tight, sticky bandage on and we'll organize a pair of long shorts. I think I can get away with it.'
'Well, it's down to you', said Fagan. 'But let's not do it while Shanks is here.'
Smith got on the table, shaved the top of his leg, and was having his leg strapped when Shankly walked into the treatment-room.
'Oh Jesus', said Fagan.
Smith, lying flat, guessed who must have come in.
'What are you doing?' asked Shankly.
'Tommy's just putting a strap on the leg', said Fagan.
'You told me you were fit', Shankly said to Smith.
'I am, it's just a little safeguard.'
'Oh no, son. No strapping.'
'Well, I'm putting it on.'
'No, you're not.'
'I am.'
'No, you're not.'
'You can sod off, it's my leg.'
'Oh no, son, it's not your leg, it's Liverpool Football Club's leg, son.'
Shankly walked out.
Joe Fagan burst out laughing[9]

Shankly's players had to be tough. He didn't sign players who missed matches with injury. (Frank Worthington and Freddie Hill were only two of those turned

---

8. Interview with Tommy Smith for *Kicking and Screaming*.
9. Interview with Tommy Smith for *Kicking and Screaming*.

down on medical grounds.) There are legendary tales of Shankly reacting to injured players by ignoring them or making an amazing suggestion. One time while he was the manager at Carlisle United, during a five-a-side game, the unconscious Geoff Hill was carried from the field and laid on the dressing-room table, unattended, while the others finished the game (Bowler, 1996: 101). When Carlisle United goalkeeper Jim MacLaren injured a leg in the early 1950s, Shankly told him to walk *slowly*, so the opposition didn't notice that he was limping (Kelly, 1996: 54).

Shankly once told Neville Smith, 'I don't talk to players when they're injured. Good players don't get injured.'[10] The benchmark was set by Gerry Byrne, when he played through almost all the 120 minutes of the 1965 FA Cup Final with a broken collarbone. The Liverpool players of the 1960s and 1970s did their utmost not to miss matches. When Liverpool won the Second Division title in 1961/62 they used only seventeen players and three of those played only five games between them. The 1965–66 Championship team consisted of twelve players with two others sharing four games at the tail-end of the season. In 1972/73 the Championship was won by only fourteen players (plus Lane and Storton).

As a player at Carlisle United and Preston North End, Bill Shankly was enthusiastic, energetic, hard and fair. He was a small, wiry wing-half who always gave one hundred per cent and had a bit of skill. He covered an enormous amount of ground and seemed to tackle players from ten yards away. He urged on his colleagues with cries of 'Come on, yee, get in there!', even when they were trailing hopelessly with only a few minutes to play. He had no concept of an end-of-season match and all matches went to the final whistle.

As a manager, Shankly served an apprenticeship in the north of England. He spent over ten years in total at Carlisle United, Grimsby Town, Workington Town and Huddersfield Town, and this apprenticeship factor featured strongly in his quest for players. It is difficult to think of a Shankly equivalent in the modern game; someone who managed a series of lower-division 'outpost' clubs before being appointed to an unfamiliar club with great potential at the age of forty-six. It would have been a little like Asa Hartford or Joe Jordan being appointed manager of, say, Wolverhampton Wanderers in 1996 or 1997.

Shankly expected players to serve similar apprenticeships as himself and he identified most strongly with players from the working-class communities of Scotland, northern England and south Wales. He would never take a Londoner away from London, for example. When he did sign players from London clubs he knew that they had been raised elsewhere: in the north-east, like Geoff Strong (Arsenal) or the Midlands, as with Tony Hateley (Chelsea). Shankly looked for

---

10. Interview with Neville Smith for *One Hundred Years of Merseyside Football*.

players with 'good character' who had proved themselves in lower-level football. He told chief scout Geoff Twentyman to concentrate his efforts on the Third and Fourth Divisions (Kelly, 1996: 212). When he signed players such as Larry Lloyd (Bristol Rovers), Ray Clemence (Scunthorpe United), Peter Wall (Wrexham) and Alec Lindsay (Bury) he subjected them to additional apprenticeship spells in Liverpool Reserves.

Not all Shankly's lower-division signings became first-team regulars – there was also Stuart Mason (Wrexham), Frank Lane and Trevor Storton (Tranmere Rovers) and Alan Waddle (Halifax Town) – but the failures were not that expensive. And Kevin Keegan, signed from Scunthorpe United for a meagre £33,000, more than compensated for any losses. Shankly felt a special closeness to Keegan because Keegan's father was a coal miner. Similarly, Shankly took to Ian St John, who was still working in the steelworks when signed from Motherwell. Even the Liverpool club Secretary, Peter Robinson, appointed in 1965, had served his own football-administration apprenticeship in places such as Crewe and Scunthorpe.

Although Shankly, and contemporary First Division managers such as Harry Catterick (Everton) and Jimmy Hagan (West Brom), had served managerial apprenticeships, they differed significantly from managers such as Matt Busby (Manchester United) and Bill Nicholson (Tottenham Hotspur), who had hardly been out of the First Division as players or managers. Busby's signings came from clubs such as Arsenal (David Herd and Ian Ure), Celtic (Pat Crerand), Chelsea (Alex Stepney), West Ham (Noel Cantwell) and even Torino (Denis Law). Although Shankly spent large sums wisely on Ray Kennedy, Strong, Emlyn Hughes (Blackpool) and Peter Cormack (Nottingham Forest), such other big-money signings, as Phil Chisnall, Hateley, Jack Whitham (Sheffield Wednesday) and Alun Evans (Wolves), were not as successful as his lower-division coups.

As we have seen from his response to injured players, Shankly could also be abrasive, unsympathetic and aggressive. He was a boxing fan who loved gangster films. His favourite film-stars were the likes of Jimmy Cagney and Jack Pallance who excelled in tough-guy roles. Shankly would come into the players' dressing-room and throw photographs of people such as Bugsy Moran, Legs Diamond and Eliot Ness on the big, square dressing-room table: 'You think you've got a hard time coming up this afternoon? See about them. When these lads did anything wrong they'd get shot. You think you're a hard man, son? This is a hard man. He used a Magnum and he shot 55 people . . .'[11]

But Shankly's definition of courage extended far beyond the physical components.

---

11. A number of sources, including Taylor and Ward (1993: 99–100) and interview with Tommy Smith for *Kicking and Screaming*.

Courage is also the ability to get up when things are getting you down . . . to get up and fight back. Never to know defeat, let alone accept it. To have principles – be they of fitness or morality – and stick by them. To do what you feel you must do, not because it's the most popular thing to do but because it's the right thing to do.

Courage is skill, plus dedication, plus fitness, plus honesty, plus fearlessness. It is a big word, but it is one which should hang above your bed if you really want to be a footballer – and to be one that is a credit to the game and yourself (quoted in Bale, 1996: 128).

Shankly was keen to sign players of character and commitment, and he wanted his chief scout, Geoff Twentyman, to investigate every aspect of a player's life (Kelly, 1996: 211). Shankly wanted players who were dedicated to the game and passionate about it, not those who were likely to go out drinking excessively or those who might crack under pressure. But such players had to be skilful too. They had to be able to control the ball and pass it in the Liverpool way. Shankly once walked out of a game before kick-off because he saw in the warm-up that the fancied player couldn't control the ball and pass it.[12] He walked out of another game because he didn't like the way the player rolled over and feigned injury (Kelly, 1996: 211–12).

Shankly laid the foundations at Liverpool by choosing players who showed the personal responsibility of playing for the club (Keith, 1998: 175). The Liverpool way was to sign skilful, resilient players who could fit into the passing and movement game, players who would respond to tough training principles and serve an apprenticeship in playing the Liverpool way, players who could take responsibility for themselves and make decisions on the pitch for the good of the team.

A Way with Words

One day the great England centre-forward Tommy Lawton visited Anfield to see his contemporary Bill Shankly. Shankly called in the teenage groundstaff players and introduced them to Lawton, who scored 22 goals in 23 internationals and would probably have been England's all-time record goalscorer had the war not intervened.

'This is the greatest centre-forward who ever lived', said Shankly. 'He could head a ball harder than most of us could kick it. The only way to stop him was to stop the ball getting to him.' Shankly spent ten minutes extolling Lawton's strengths. 'Right, Tommy,' he said eventually. 'Now tell them who was the best wing-half you ever saw and why I was.'[13]

12. Interview with Larry Lloyd for *Kicking and Screaming*.

13. This is a story told by a number of people in football. Andrew Ward first heard it from his father.

Shankly had a way with words and a means of attracting an audience. As one of Shankly's close colleagues once said, 'He couldn't open his mouth without saying something.' Sometimes Shankly was serious and it came out funny. Sometimes it was carefully calculated:

> *If it had been a boxing match it would have been stopped at half-time.*
> *We beat them five-nil and they were lucky to get nil.*
> *The best team drew.*
> *He must be a good goalkeeper, he saved one of my shots last week.*
> *There are two teams in Liverpool – Liverpool and Liverpool Reserves.*
> *Aye, Tony Currie's probably a better player than Tommy Finney, but Tommy Finney's fifty-odd now.*

When Ron Yeats signed from Dundee United, Shankly was typically proud of his big centre-half and called him a Colossus. Liverpool beat Sunderland comfortably in the first home game and Yeats had been dominant. Yeats was just coming out of the bath when Shankly invited all the journalists into the changing-room. 'There's the big man there,' said Shankly. 'Go and walk round him' (Taylor and Ward, 1993: 96).

When Alan Ball was signed by Everton from Blackpool, Shankly phoned up the new signing to welcome him to the city. 'Congratulations, son,' said Shankly. 'You'll be playing near a great side' (Keith, 1998: 127–28). Sometimes it was difficult to tell whether the jokes originated with Shankly or not. In 1969–70, Everton won the League convincingly with their fabulous midfield trio of Kendall, Ball and Harvey. The story was that Shankly went to his barber for his fortnightly haircut. 'Anything off the top, Mr Shankly?' 'Aye, Everton.'

And when Neil Armstrong took his first step on the moon in 1969, news of his famous first words spread quickly around Anfield: 'It's just like Goodison Park – there's no atmosphere.' It was immaterial whether the jokes were started by Shankly or an anonymous fan. A symbiosis had formed between Shanks and Liverpool supporters.

Our Players are Better than Their Players

> *One Saturday in the early 1970s, Liverpool manager Bill Shankly took his usual position in the Anfield corridor where he could watch the Ipswich Town players arrive. After seeing what he needed to see, Shankly burst into the Liverpool dressing-room and delivered a typical oration that belittled the opposition:*

> *'You'll have no problem today. I've just seen a centre-half whose glasses are like milkbottles. They're that thick, he's blind. I've just seen a little boy that plays midfield, his legs are like that, he won't be able to run . . .'*

The Liverpool players had heard this sort of thing many times before, but they were still fired up by it. By ten to three – ten minutes to kick-off – they were ready to go out and beat Ipswich.

'Take your shirts off', said Shankly.
'What, Boss?'
'Take your shirts off.'
They pulled off their shirts.
'Throw em on the floor', said Shankly.
They threw them on the floor.
This was a new approach. The players hadn't heard this team-talk.
'Now go and have a bath', said Shankly.
'Wait a minute, Boss,' said one of the players. 'What's going on?'
'Well, you lot go and have a bath, I'll throw these shirts out on the field and the shirts will beat Ipswich by themselves.'

Shankly was famous for raising his own players' determination through comic, crazy team-talks like the one above (Taylor and Ward, 1995: 282–3). Players hung on Shankly's words and he rarely failed them. At the same time Shankly had a way of reducing the power of opponents: one had a heart as big as a caraway seed; another couldn't trap a bag of concrete; and a third, on a cold winter's day, would only want to play if he could wear a numbered overcoat.

Denis Law chuckles when he recalls the time when Huddersfield Town played Liverpool in the Second Division in 1959/60. Shankly was manager of Huddersfield at the time and his team-talk reduced Liverpool to the most awful team in the world. A few weeks later, when Shankly joined Liverpool, Law was told by Shankly that Liverpool were the greatest team in the Second Division and would soon be the greatest team in the world.[14]

Ian Callaghan remembers an occasion when Shankly prepared the team for a match against West Ham. Shankly played down the skills of Martin Peters and Geoff Hurst and described the great Bobby Moore as a robot. After the game he told Callaghan that they'd just beaten a great team, and Bobby Moore was one of the greatest players in the world.[15]

In *Crazy Horse*, Emlyn Hughes tells the story of his first ride in Shankly's car and how the Liverpool manager was stopped by the police. 'Do you realize who I've got in the car?' said Shankly. 'The future captain of England.' Hughes was nineteen at the time (Hughes, 1980).

Ron Yeats remembers how Shankly used to come and sit beside people and talk to them: 'Hey, you're playing against what-do-you-call-him today. You'll not

14. Interview with Denis Law for *One Hundred Years of Merseyside Football*.
15. Interview with Ian Callaghan for *One Hundred Years of Merseyside Football*.

give him a kick. Ask him, "Why are you on the same pitch as me?"' (Taylor and Ward, 1993: 100). In Friday team-talks, Shankly would demonstrate one or two things on a magnetic board and then use the setting to relax the players. It was common for him to sweep magnetic opponents off the board with the words 'They can't play anyway.' Similarly, when using Subbuteo players to symbolize the opposition, he would sometimes hold one back in his hand and then throw it flamboyantly across the room with a dismissive comment.

Shankly later attributed his memorable team-talks to what he learned during his early coal-mining days, when he saw how humour could help fellow workers relax before the task in hand. He recalled how one man in the pits told a story of how he single-handedly pushed a truck full of coal for a mile in the pit before realizing that it had come off the rails (quoted by Bale, 1996: 26 and Keith, 1998: 15).

This basic message – our players are great, their team are terrible – was perfect for Liverpool fans because it appealed to the natural Scouse cockiness and there were ready-made rivals in Everton (Keith, 1998: 124 and 149–50). But Shankly did not pursue this tactic relentlessly. Everton player Terry Darracott recalls how Shankly stopped him in the street a couple of days before his League debut and told him 'You'll do great, son.' Shankly could even raise the spirits of an Everton player.[16]

The Network of Friends (off the pitch)

Shankly told a story about his RAF boxing days during the Second World War. One evening in Manchester he was fighting an Army man in the finals of the Northern Command. In the dressing-room before the fight, Shankly took out some precious rubbing-oils that he had been given by Preston North End.

'How did you get them?' asked the man next to him.
'I can get them,' said Shankly. 'Do you want to use some of them?'
'Oh, yeah.'
'What are you in?' asked Shankly, watching the other boxer rub the oils in his body.
'The Army.'
'Who are you boxing?'
'A fellow called Shankly.'
'Have you got a towel I can borrow?'
'Yeah, use this one.'
Shankly took the towel and rubbed the oil off the other boxer.
'Hey, I'm fighting you, I'm not letting you have my oil.'[17]

16. Interview with Terry Darracott for *One Hundred Years of Merseyside Football*.
17. Told to Andrew Ward by his father, who encouraged Shankly to tell it on a number of return journeys from All Star charity matches in the 1950s.

Bill Shankly was everybody's friend until he got you into that arena. He was a great networker who was forever telephoning people in the game and making fair and supportive comments to them. He was very good at contacting people to congratulate them or commiserate with them. His network began with his family. His brother Bob managed Falkirk, Dundee, Hibernian and Stirling Albion and his other brothers had met a lot of footballers when playing for clubs as far afield as Barrow, Portsmouth, Blackpool and Southend. When Bill Shankly signed ex-Hibernian player Peter Cormack for £110,000 from Nottingham Forest before the 1972/73 season, he had heard all about Cormack from brother Bob.

Having managed clubs outside the First Division Shankly had a bigger natural network than the Busbys and Nicholsons of his era. Surprisingly, none of his biographers discuss the partnership with Fred Ford, who was trainer-coach at Carlisle United when Shankly was manager. Ford, who stayed in the game until his death in 1981, had as much intensity as Shankly (see Swann and Ward, 1996: 102–4); and he was in charge of Bristol Rovers when Larry Lloyd was transferred to Liverpool.

Shankly was probably not the first to joke that football was more important than life and death but he was probably the first to suggest it at a time when mass communication was able to run with it. Like the boxer Muhammad Ali, who learned his verbal bravado from wrestler Gorgeous George, Shankly had undoubtedly learned things mixing among Third Division (North) managers such as Fred Westgarth of Hartlepool United (see Alister and Ward, 1997: 53–6). Later, in August 1967, Shankly recruited Geoff Twentyman as Liverpool chief scout. Twentyman had played under Shankly at Carlisle United.

The most brilliant part of Shankly's network was his boot-room team, the loyalty of which helped sustain Liverpool through the 1980s. Kelly (1996: 118–25) discusses the origins of their dedication in deserved detail. Shankly inherited Bob Paisley, Joe Fagan and Reuben Bennett, but of course there were connections. Shankly had once wanted Fagan to sign for Grimsby Town, and Scotsman Bennett, a former Dundee trainer, was known through brother Bob.

If Shankly was the motivator, Bob Paisley was the real tactician. Paisley could sum up players quickly and assess their strengths and weaknesses. Paisley and Fagan could organize canny psychological tricks, such as ensuring that Tommy Smith was given the wrong pre-match meal at the Holiday Inn so that he was in a suitably bad mood for the match.[18]

Ron Moran, club captain when Shankly arrived at Liverpool, later joined the backroom staff as a coach. Shankly won over Moran when he sent him a letter with advanced notification of what he intended to do when he arrived at Liverpool.

18. Interview with Tommy Smith for *Kicking and Screaming*.

One of Shankly's virtues was his consideration. He never got above his station. He was never quite sure whether the dustbinman might have a better opinion. If you were passionate about football, then he would talk to you about the game. Bernard Bale recalls his first meeting with Shankly as a *Soccer Star* journalist. 'My time is football laddie', said Shankly. 'I'm busy with football, and you're busy with football – so let's talk about football and let the time worry about itself' (Bale, 1996: 127). Shankly's attitude to football was the same with everyone. Paul (1998: 94–104) and Darby (1998: 145–68) include stories from fans which show that it was easy to form a relationship with the man if you were a football fan.

Reaching the People

The Liverpool players were touring the city again in an open-top bus. Thousands of people lined the streets.

They were nearing the library when manager Bill Shankly suddenly turned to Brian Hall and said, 'Hey, son, who's that Chinaman with the sayings, you know, what's that man?'
Hall looked at Shankly as if his manager was mad.
'Chairman Mao?' asked Hall.
'That's him, son, that's him. That's the man. Aye.'
He's definitely cracking up, this fellow, thought Hall.
Then they reached St George's Hall and Shankly stood up in front of 300,000 people. Cheering burst out. Shankly held his arms aloft and the cheering stopped.
'Chairman Mao has never seen such a show of red strength as this', said Shankly. The cheering recommenced.
Perfect, thought Hall. Brilliant. The man's a genius.[19]

This was one of many times when Shankly talked to Liverpool fans and the people responded. Shankly orchestrated them. His arms could silence the largest of crowds. Then he addressed them in simple language with two clear messages – we have the greatest team in the world and you are the greatest fans. As Bowler (1996: 211) says, Shankly spoke without a safety-net. Simple expressions like 'you are the people' became sententious through their spontaneous delivery and sincerity. And Shankly was not beyond rescuing a fan's scarf and tying it round his own neck (Bowler, 1996: 151; Kelly, 1996: 23).

Shankly's effect on the people is best demonstrated by the supporters' reaction after the 5–1 European defeat to an outstanding Ajax team in Holland. Shankly

19. A number of sources, including Keith (1998: 133 and 146) and Taylor and Ward (1993: 101).

managed to convince 54,000 people that Liverpool could beat Ajax by six in the second leg. The ground was full for a game that was lost from the first minute (although Shankly still argued that had Peter Thompson's sixth-minute shot gone in rather than hitting the bar then they would have won the tie). As Bill Nicholson once remarked, Shankly never lost, not even in defeat (Keith, 1998: 154).

Shankly's messages appealed to the Liverpudlian confidence of the time. The Beatles were the most famous music group in the world, and in their slipstream came Gerry and the Pacemakers, Rory Storm and the Hurricanes, Billy J Kramer and the Dakotas, The Four Most, the Searchers and the Swinging Bluejeans. Cilla Black was a big pop star and local poets such as Roger McGeogh, Adrian Henri and Brian Patton were creating a national stir. Comedians Ken Dodd and Jimmy Tarbuck were household names, and the city produced a string of boxing champions from Alan Rudkin to John Conteh. Liverpool and Everton were winning trophies regularly and Roger Hunt, Ian Callaghan and Ray Wilson had played for England in the successful 1966 World Cup Finals. And, for several years in the late 1960s and mid-1970s, Harold Wilson ran Britain from the nearby Huyton constituency. All in all, the city had optimism, employment and good humour.

At Anfield the crowd had their say. They worshipped the team (*We're the Greatest in Europe and Shankly is Our King*), they commentated on the game (*Eee-aye-addyo, Rowdy's won the toss*) and they coached from the side-lines (*attack, attack, attack, attack, attack*). They introduced other aspects of Liverpool music culture: they adopted an old Cabaret song, 'You'll Never Walk Alone', which had been revived by Gerry and the Pacemakers; and they mass-sang the latest Beatles number, either for hours before the match or sometimes spontaneously during it.

In one incident in 1963 a player was concussed during a match. The trainer came on and helped the player to his feet, and then the player slumped forward across the trainer, who held his weight. The Liverpool fans burst into song: *He loves you, yeah, yeah, yeah.*[20]

Always a Player

> When Liverpool players trained at Melwood, the gates were left open and fans gathered three or four deep around the touch-line.
> One day in the early 1970s, a bigger crowd than usual watched a five-a-side match between the staff team and the young lads. Schoolchildren on holiday, sailors in port, workers on strike, they swelled the attendance to the level of an acceptable Fourth Division crowd.

20. Told to Andrew Ward by his father after the team he was managing, Derby County, had lost 5–0 at Anfield in January 1964.

> *Shankly, then nearly sixty, was on form that day, knocking his passes around, running the show.*

> *'Eee, just think,' he said to a colleague, looking at the crowd. 'They're watching this for free.'*[21]

Almost all managers bemoan the passing of their playing careers but few hang on to them as tenaciously as Bill Shankly did. In fact, Shankly never really let go of his playing days. In his 1960s, after retirement, he was still enjoying impromptu Sunday afternoon games with children. They would play for a couple of hours and then Shankly would go off and say, 'We had a great game, we won 19–17' (Taylor and Ward, 1993: 102–3).

Shankly's life had a theme of informal small-sided games. In his Scottish youth there were five-a-side competitions (Bowler, 1996: 36–7). During his managerial days he was five-a-side obsessed, with players at Grimsby recalling Scotland v England or Single v Married (Kelly, 1996: 75). When manager of Huddersfield Town he played on a local recreation ground (Kelly, 1996: 87–8) and then at Liverpool came intensive three-a-side games (Bale, 1996: 119) and the legendary five-a-sides at Melwood or in the Anfield car-park.

The car-park matches sometimes involved local dustbinmen on the days their round took them to the club. Shankly liked to arrange confidence-boosting games for his youngsters against the binmen, the latter considerably handicapped by their big boots and sacks tied round their heavy clothing. One day Shankly turned up just after the players had started a game. He was told that he couldn't play because the sides were equal. Shankly went away and came back five minutes later riding on a milk-float. The milkman complained that he'd never played football in his life. 'That's alright,' Shankly said, 'You can go in goal for them.'[22]

The Staff team was unbeaten for years, but only because the staff all had whistles. They took turns to blow for fouls and would add time on if they were losing. Joining in with the youngsters every day helped pass on the club's values. The staff watched players' reactions and studied their character. Shankly taught them good habits, which included little details such as practising one-twos when fetching the ball from behind the goal, just to get to know your players a little better.

Whereas Everton's Harry Catterick was a directors' manager who generally wore a suit to work, Bill Shankly kept his office near the changing-rooms, wore a tracksuit and was always looking for a game. He wanted to be close to the players and wanted to know all that was going on in their lives. 'Are you sleeping well?'

21. Told by Tom Saunders at a coaching course in 1972.

22. Told to Andrew Ward by his father after an evening with Bob Paisley. The story may have been adapted in the telling but people in football accepted it because it showed Shankly's playing obsession and his canny way of getting on the best side.

he would ask them. He also knew who was having trouble with their drains, whose roof needed repair and whose garage doors had fallen off. He was constantly checking whether jobs had been done for the players. And he was also checking whether the groundstaff had done their jobs properly (Taylor and Ward, 1993: 97–8).

After retirement, it was the day-to-day involvement with the players that Shankly missed the most (Taylor and Ward, 1993: 104).

References

Alister, I. and Ward, A. (1997) *Barnsley: A Study in Football, 1953–59*, 2nd edn, Oxford: Crowberry.

Bale, B. (1996) *The Shankly Legacy*, Derby: Breedon Books.

Bowler, D. (1996) *Shanks: The Authorised Biography of Bill Shankly*, London: Orion.

Darby, T. (1998) *Talking Shankly: The Man, the Genius, the Legend*, Edinburgh, Mainstream.

Giulianotti, R. (1999) *Football: a Sociology of the Global Game*, Cambridge: Polity.

Hodgson, D. (1978) *The Liverpool Story*, London: Arthur Barker.

Hughes, E. (1980) *Crazy Horse*, Manchester: Arthur Barker.

Inglis, S. (1996) *Football Grounds of Britain*, London: Collins Willow.

James, G. (1993) *Football with a Smile: The Authorised Biography of Joe Mercer*, Leicester: ACL Colour Print and Polar Publishing.

Keith, J. (1998) *Shanks for the Memory*, London: Robson.

—— (1999) *Bob Paisley: Manager of the Millennium*, London: Robson.

Kelly, S. (1996) *Bill Shankly: It's Much More Important Than That*, London: Virgin.

—— (1999) *The Boot Room Boys*, London: Collins Willow.

McIlvanney, H. (1995) 'No power, no glory', *Sunday Times*, 5 November.

Paul, D. (1998) *Anfield Voices*, Stroud: Tempus.

Shankly, B. (1976) *Shankly*, Manchester: Arthur Barker.

Swann, G. and Ward, A. (1996) *The Boys from up the Hill: An Oral History of Oxford United*, Oxford: Crowberry.

Taylor, R. and Ward, A. with Williams, J. (1993) *Three Sides of the Mersey: An Oral History of Everton, Liverpool and Tranmere Rovers*, London: Robson.

Taylor, R. and Ward, A. (1995) *Kicking and Screaming: An Oral History of Football in England*, London: Robson.

Thompson, P. (1993) *Shankly*, Liverpool: The Bluecoat Press.

Wagg, S. (1984) *The Football World*, Brighton: Harvester.

Young, P. (1968) *A History of British Football*, London: Stanley Paul.

−4−

Passing Rhythms: The Modern Origins and Development of the Liverpool Way

Stephen Hopkins

A recent major work on the social and cultural aspects of football's development as the global sport, makes the telling point that 'playing techniques, styles and their aesthetic appreciation have been notably absent' from the rapidly increasing literature devoted to the game (Giulianotti, 1999: 129). While the recent growth in academic, as well as popular and journalistic, writing about football has largely concentrated upon elements of fan support, behaviour and culture, there has been a much smaller growth in interest in the way in which the game is played, and the ways in which this interacts with other aspects of any particular club's historical and cultural identity.

This chapter seeks to examine 'the Liverpool way' of playing, with an exploration of the early years and development of the 'modern' Liverpool (under the managers, Bill Shankly, Bob Paisley and Joe Fagan). The intention is not simply to reduce discussion of this rich, complex area to a question merely of tactical formation, significant though tactical variations are. What is of particular interest here is how the 'style of play' is understood by fans (and players and staff at the club, at least to an extent) as a central element of their self-identification; popular myths have developed concerning the 'right' way for a Liverpool team to play, and these are strongly held, transmitted to new generations of supporters and players, creating an unbroken link with the past, and consolidating a complex process of identity construction. In a period of transition in the management of the club, with the arrival in 1998 of Gérard Houllier signifying for some an overdue 'revolution' in the club's management philosophy, and relative lack of success on the pitch, this popular historical memory does not fade away: indeed, if anything, the symbolism attached to Liverpool's playing traditions is perhaps stronger in the contemporary period, as supporters seek a means to negotiate the rapidly changing circumstances of the club, and the game more generally. Although there is not space here to discuss the recent developments, in the much less successful 1990s (see Chapter Seven for aspects of the 1990s management of the club), this chapter should provide some pointers for an appraisal of the elements of continuity and change that have been part of the transmission of the 'Liverpool Way' to the contemporary era.

Equally, there is not space either to trace the early origins of the club's playing style, although some elements of Liverpool's early development are included in Chapter One, and in Kelly (1996). However, as Giulianotti (1999: 137) points out, 'the exact origins of most cultural paradigms or genres are very difficult to establish', and we must avoid the error of attributing linear historical 'lines' to what is, in fact, a complex dialectical process, involving teamwork and individual creativity, continuity and change, in terms of tactical appreciation and style of play. Giulianotti (1999: 137) further argues that 'football people at any one time are brought up to value one or two "traditional" playing styles. A "revolution" occurs in this footballing community when the dominant tradition loses power to a new model'. It seems to me that changing playing styles are rarely as 'revolutionary' as this argument suggests, and that transitions generally occur within a pre-existing historical framework. 'New' styles have to be 'fitted in', both practically and symbolically, to the prevailing pattern of play familiar to the players/ supporters, and they have to be made consistent with long-held, collective beliefs regarding the club's playing identity.

Of course, identities do change over time, and occasionally this can be properly described as revolutionary. The transformative effect wrought by Bill Shankly's arrival as manager at Liverpool in December 1959, followed by fifteen years of building a style, on and off the pitch, that became known as 'the Liverpool way', is an example that might well serve to support Giulianotti's argument. We turn to a brief and incomplete look at the way in which the Liverpool way came to prominence, and the evolution of the 'boot room' philosophy during the 1960s and 1970s.

Shankly, Paisley, and the Liverpool Way: The Struggle for Simplicity

Just go out there and express yourself in your own way, but be part of the machine that keeps moving the round thing'. (Phil Neal in Taylor and Ward, 1993: 163).

Many people came here to watch training sessions in those years thinking there was some particular kind of magic, and they'd come down to Melwood [Liverpool's training ground] and we'd allow them to watch and, after the training session, they would feel as though they'd been cheated. They would say, 'Well, you mustn't be showing us it all. You must be hiding something from us.' The whole method was simple. It was based on a rapport with management, good management, good players and the freedom to express themselves. (Tom Saunders in Taylor and Ward, 1995: 286–7).

The stories and anecdotes relating to the genius and charisma of Bill Shankly are legion, and there have been countless attempts to distil the essential characteristics of his approach: in Chapter Three, Andrew Ward has provided a full explanation of Shankly's relationship with Liverpool, the club, the city and its people, as well as a survey of some of the large volume of publications celebrating this authentic hero. Here, it is particularly the approach to playing the game that is of interest.

The watchword of Liverpool's approach under Shankly, and subsequently under Paisley and Fagan, was simplicity. Shankly, in common with many of his contemporaries in the British game in the 1960s, was disdainful of the pseudo-scientific tactical approach to the game, preferring to concentrate on the players and encouraging them to do the simple things correctly. Steve Wagg (1984: 73–100) discusses in detail the painfully slow 'coming of technocracy' to the British professional game in the post-war era. He recalls the frosty reception for the successful touring side, Moscow Dynamo, who played a series of games at the invitation of the Football Association in the autumn of 1945 (see also Downing, 1999). The basis of the 'public condemnation by football people of Dynamo' was that 'masculinity, as well as individuality . . . were felt to have been sullied' through their emphasis upon 'pretty-pretty' passing, tactics and teamwork. Immersed in a British football culture that continued to treat coaching with suspicion well into the 1950s, or even later, the Liverpool staff undoubtedly took time to digest the lessons of football's rapid development elsewhere. The elements of the game that Shankly and the back room staff (which he mainly inherited, the likes of Reuben Bennett or Bob Paisley, who became first-team trainer in August 1959, or promoted from within, like Ronnie Moran, full-back and club captain in 1959, who eventually retired from Anfield in 1998) thought were central revolved around 'good players, playing with freedom within a sensible framework' (Bowler, 1996: 217).

A certain degree of myth-making has built up around the preparations employed at Liverpool; a mystical quality has been attributed, for example, to the regular five-a-sides that dominated training during the season. Undoubtedly, although Shankly was dismissive of tactical devices, particularly those designed to stop the opposition playing, he was nevertheless very keen on a structured and methodical training regime. Intuition, psychology, man-management, all were facets of the Shankly character that were channelled obsessively towards playing the game. However, if the rhetoric of 'scientific' tactics was derided by Liverpool under Shankly, it would be equally wrong to view their approach as unstructured, based only upon some kind of impressionistic 'feel' or simple enthusiasm for the game.

A *collective* approach, based on the understanding that the team is all, and the individual nothing without the team, helped to produce a team ethos founded on self-respect, discipline, trust and dedication to the overall cause. Some have likened the spirit generated as similar to a harmonious family, while more politically minded observers (following Shankly's famous interview in 1975 with then Prime Minister Harold Wilson; see Keith, 1998: 184–210) saw Liverpool's approach as a 'form of socialism'. Here, I agree with Giulianotti's caution concerning the functional position that 'views football culture as a straightforward reproduction of wider social relations' (1999: 128). It is, of course, no accident that men like Shankly, Paisley, Jock Stein, Matt Busby and later Kenny Dalglish and Alex Ferguson were imbued with a strong collectivist mentality, being socialized when and where they were, in mining communities in the West of Scotland or Durham, and yet the teams produced by Liverpool and Manchester Utd over the last forty years, and the styles of play promoted as integral to the respective clubs' identities, have emphasized different, perhaps even contradictory, values. The 'Liverpool way' has privileged pass-and-move, a 'shape' or pattern of play that was efficient and, above all, controlled (mechanistic, according to its critics). Simply, and reductively, where Liverpool's football was primarily based on two touches (control first, and then pass), Manchester Utd can be characterized as one-touch, moving forward quickly, with flick-ons and a greater emphasis upon individual trickery. The point here is that these footballers' and managers' similar objective social circumstances could be shaped and expressed in football, according to different aesthetic appreciations of the 'right' way to play.

To return to the Liverpool way, there were tried and tested methods of preparation, some of which were innovative for the time. Ian Callaghan (1975: 28; see also Ian St John in Taylor and Ward, 1995: 284) recalls the 'sweat box': 'a wooden box formed of boards. A player goes in on his own with four men . . . in each corner throwing balls at him from all angles which he has to control and hit'. The numbered shooting boards were another example of this planning on the training pitch. Roger Hunt also remembers the 'training boards where we had to receive a ball, trap it, shield it, control it, shoot on the turn, all the things that you have to do within a game, match situations, playing under pressure . . . In that sense, it was tactical as well as technical work . . . It was all sharp, quick exercises, pressure things in short bursts' (Bowler, 1996: 216). The significance of these routines was that the players were asked to practice in training, repeatedly, elements of the game that they would be required to reproduce in match situations; later on, during the unsuccessful 1990s, new manager Houllier would argue that Liverpool had lost some of their urgency in training. At least some of the players had come to regard training as little more than 'filling in time' between matches.

To illustrate the continuity that existed in Liverpool's preparation from the 1960s through until the early 1990s at least, it can be seen, from a variety of later players' accounts, that a similar set of exercises and priorities were to be found at Melwood: Alan Hansen recalls (Taylor and Ward, 1995: 286) that 'You used to have a stupid thing – well, I thought it was stupid (at first) – where if you passed it and didn't move two or three yards you were penalized, and that soon taught you that you had to move'. Interestingly, Phil Neal (1986: 81–6), when he arrived at Anfield from Northampton Town in 1974, was 'exhilarated' by Liverpool's insistence on working primarily on ball skills, rather than simply doing stamina work, as he had been used to. Nonetheless, Neal was struck by the fact that training 'never varies, week-in week-out the routine is exactly the same'. While recognizing that this 'repetitive diet' had remained largely unquestioned because it had brought success to the club, Neal couldn't help 'wondering what the atmosphere would have been like had they not been so successful'. He went on to say that he would have preferred more variety in training exercises, but 'as long as the side keeps winning all the powerful voices in the "boot-room" will be able to claim without fear of contradiction that the results on the field fully justify the system. I'd go even further and suggest that something as simple as superstition could be at the heart of the matter . . . It's a very old-fashioned club in many respects'.

Arriving at Liverpool soon after Neal's departure, John Barnes (1999: 90–2) also expected 'some kind of initiation into the mystique of Liverpool playing. Liverpool's secret training methods were part of football's folklore; no one knew what they were but everyone was convinced they existed. Me too . . .'. For Barnes, the five-a-sides that followed 'a very light warm up' came as a relaxation after the regimented Watford style, but he was surprised to learn that they involved 'no tactical work, none whatsoever. All the strategic stuff was done within the small-sided games. Liverpool believed that everything we faced in five-a-sides would be encountered again on match day . . . Liverpool's training characterised Liverpool's play – uncomplicated but devastatingly effective'. Barnes underlines the competitive nature of training ('Cup Finals on a small pitch'), and argues that 'if there was any secret to Liverpool's success it lay in the fact that the fixation with five-a-sides gave us an extra edge on match days. Bigger pitches and goals made us feel we had more room'. Moreover, Barnes touches on another critical aspect of the club's self-perception: despite some redevelopment work, Melwood 'remains pretty basic. It doesn't bear comparison with some of the sumptuous Italian training grounds like Inter Milan's Appiano Gentile . . . It surprised me how rudimentary it was. That was typical Liverpool; all they were worried about was the football. Coming from Watford, which was so organized with a really close community relationship with the fans, it all seemed so different. Anfield's code was essentially: "Run on the pitch and win"'.

In a partially contrasting account, Jan Molby (1999: 61–5), who had spent two seasons at Ajax in the early 1980s before Joe Fagan signed him for Liverpool, was surprised at the relatively relaxed training regime, and the lack of emphasis on tactical variation: 'Compared with what I'd been used to at Ajax it was very low-key. There were no flying tackles, nobody was working very hard. Basically, it didn't amount to all that much . . . All the staff [Joe Fagan, Ronnie Moran and Roy Evans] were joining in, and I found it difficult to take in at first.' One explanation for this apparent difference is that Molby joined Liverpool during the pre-season build-up to the Charity Shield, and they were renowned for starting pre-season slowly. Another, more interesting, explanation stems from the cultural differences between English and Dutch football, and the strength in depth of the respective leagues:

> [At Ajax] you had to play for your life and train for your life. You could be in a team which won 5–0 on a Saturday but, if you didn't perform in training during the week, you wouldn't keep your place. It put everyone under pressure and led to a quick turnover of players . . . Every morning we played possession football, 8-a-side in a very confined space (a small square), one-touch, two-touch, with some shocking tackles going in. It was very high-powered stuff. Some of the training sessions were much tougher than some of the games, which we cruised through (Molby, 1999: 38–9).

In England, not only were there considerably more games to play, there were very few where the players could play within themselves, as Molby had been used to at Ajax: 'We [Liverpool] could go away and be two or three nil up but the other teams just wouldn't give in. They'd keep going because their fans would demand it.'

This also points to another important aspect of the Liverpool way, one that Shankly was especially focused on: continuity of personnel (see Chapter Three and Yeats, 1966: 47). A settled side, playing according to each other's strengths, was the goal, and Shankly was famously unimpressed by players who were injury-prone. Bob Paisley (1983: 31; see also Bowler, 1996: 303), acting as physiotherapist, recalled that Chris Lawler was 'in the middle of his run of over three hundred consecutive appearances. Chris hurt his foot on the Saturday, and in training I told him to take it easy. Bill saw me talking to him and asked: "What does that malingerer want now?"' Later on, Phil Neal played with a broken toe, wearing an enlarged boot, in order to maintain his place. Selecting the right sort of character, as well as the right kind of player, was a crucial part of the Liverpool way; often Shankly would be drawn to those players who viewed their profession as a craft, and took real pride in their work.

There is an unresolved debate regarding the extent of Shankly's tactical awareness, as against the consensus that exists concerning his extraordinary motivational powers. Ronnie Moran (Bowler, 1996: 223) argues that 'tactically Bill was far advanced . . . He would combine a lad who was quick in the head but not so fast with one who could run'. On the other hand, Roy Evans (who joined Liverpool in 1964, but whose playing career was cut short by injury) considers that Shankly was 'idealistic. He wanted perfection. He wasn't a coach, he wasn't a tactician, he was an enthusiast and a teacher. He preached simplicity' (Bowler, 1996: 246). Tommy Smith recalls (Bowler, 1996: 223–4, 231–2; Hey, 1997: 42) that while Reuben Bennett would watch Liverpool's forthcoming opponents, Shankly didn't want extensive dossiers on the opposition, in case 'we frightened our bloody selves to death'; rather, 'if we came up against the best players, someone who could run the show, we wouldn't man-mark him like other teams. We just kept in communication . . . We played to a system. It depended on togetherness and we worked on it in five-a-sides. We never moved up, we kept it dead flat so if anyone ran beyond the back four they'd put themselves offside. We never ran out to catch them'. Here, we also see the origins of the goalkeeper's role as occasional sweeper behind this flat back four, a function performed most effectively by Ray Clemence.

Smith also argues, more controversially, that Shankly was 'the first to go for a 4–4–2 . . . which a lot of people think England [managed by Alf Ramsey] started, but I can honestly say that it was Liverpool that were one of the first teams to play that way. I came across it playing for the England youth team in Switzerland – they used to call it the "Swiss bolt". The boss brought it in for us, and we perfected it'.

However, alongside this emphasis upon continuity, there was also a ruthless approach to players who could no longer maintain the required standard on a regular basis. Ron Yeats, one of Shankly's favourites, acknowledges, 'he knew exactly when to replace you, and I don't think anyone had any qualms about it . . .' (Taylor and Ward, 1993: 145). In came Larry Lloyd, Ray Clemence, Brian Hall, Steve Heighway and Kevin Keegan, in Shankly's 'second' team of the early 1970s. Typically, this ruthlessness was combined with a sympathetic attachment to 'his' players, those that had served the club loyally, and would now have to hang up their boots. As Shankly knew only too well from his own experience, when a player has to stop, there is an irreplaceable void. The most important aspect of this inevitable process of generational turnover is that fundamental principles were not disturbed for any newcomer; they had to fit in to the prevailing pattern without upsetting the equilibrium. Jan Molby (1999: 65–6) shows how this attitude lived on in the 1980s; while nervously awaiting his debut, he pressed Joe Fagan about what his role should be: '"Play", he said "Play. Don't do anything silly, just play within the system" . . .'. For Phil Neal (1981: 145), 'when Liverpool bought me and other players, we were told to play our natural game. Playing with the lads and training with them week after week made modifications to their game and to ours. The newcomers and the old hands learn to work together by combining their skills, not by playing to a set, mechanical pattern'.

The final word on the question of Shankly's attitude to tactical issues can be left to the man himself. Although he went on several occasions, along with other members of staff, to Lilleshall (the FA's coaching centre), Shankly quipped, 'It was an education because everything they did, I did the opposite . . . God Almighty! I could have written a comic cuts book about it! They were trying to tell me that you could make football players! They had a set plan all the time, but when it broke down, there was nowhere to go. Talk in a language the players understand, simplify and clarify . . . We're not too fond of coaching, coaxing is a better word' (Bowler, 1996: 245–6).

If there is disagreement over Shankly's tactical acumen or interest, then Bob Paisley is regarded uniformly by his players as a deep thinker about the game, an excellent (and at times uncanny) judge of a player's physical condition, but generally a poor communicator. There is, however, some argument concerning the extent to which Paisley's image was carefully honed, to perhaps lull opponents into a false sense of security. Stories abound of his uncomplicated tastes, whether in clothes, food or football. His captain, Graeme Souness (1985: 49–53, and 1999: 188–91), recalls Paisley's flat cap and carpet slippers, worn whenever possible because of an injured ankle. In Paris, after the European Cup final victory against Real Madrid, Paisley looked incongruous in the palatial splendour of the team's hotel, and Souness recalls him 'sitting back with a cigar, a glass of whisky and wearing those old-fashioned slippers . . . Completely relaxed and apparently not at all excited'. Before training every morning, Paisley would stop in at a local garage for a cup of tea, while he picked out his horses from the paper, and Souness used to meet him there for a chat. He simply felt comfortable in this kind of uncomplicated daily routine, familiar to millions of other working-class men of his generation. I tend to agree with Stan Hey's assessment that 'it would do Paisley a disservice to try to define him as the last true football man, with its connotations of centre-partings, boot-room camaraderie and home-spun values, because although he embraced all of these, he was also one of the great thinkers and modernisers of the English game' (1997: 183).

After Paisley's death, in an unusual tribute, an editorial in the *Independent* (15 February 1996) made the point that Paisley was:

> A working-class man who made good, but whom extraordinary success failed to corrupt or sour . . . What is truly remarkable about this is the fact that Paisley was never feted in the way that other, far less successful, soccer managers have been . . . He did not have a way with the press, was not actively considered to become an international manager . . . Bob Paisley stands for all those hundreds of thousands of his generation whose intelligence and loyalty achieved much, but whose attributes went largely unrecorded and underestimated. And who did not mind.

Souness (1985: 53) agrees that he was a 'football "intellectual"'. Had he been more articulate he would have been hailed as one of the greatest thinkers and managers on the game'. Stan Liversedge (1995: 48), Liverpool's programme editor for many seasons, and ghost-writer of successive managers' notes, agrees that 'anyone who took Bob Paisley for a fool would have spent his money badly . . . He was a canny fellow, all right — and don't let that woolly-cardigan image fool you'.

A couple of striking examples of this forward-thinking approach, rarely associated with Paisley, come from his autobiography: 'Soon, I think we shall see a European League, and then, with supersonic travel, and the emergence on to the football scene of hitherto non-soccer-playing nations, there could even be a World League by the end of the century' (Paisley, 1983: 95). It is worth noting the date of publication, and the fact that very few of his contemporaries were contemplating these sorts of seismic shifts in the global game. Or, again, as far as the induction of younger players into the game is concerned, Paisley (1983: 102–3) makes a strong case for root-and-branch reform, involving 'the setting up of special schools at which the development of their football talent would run parallel to their general, academic education. It would not be at the expense of normal education but as an addition to it. The lads would have the benefit of their natural talent being nurtured and developed by expert coaches, and not by ambitious and inexperienced schoolmasters . . . The current rules often mean that when a youngster is old enough to link up with a professional club, he has already formed too many bad habits which are difficult to eradicate ; . .' It is easy to imagine the pride Paisley would take in the £12 million Academy opened by Liverpool in Kirkby in 1998.

Paisley's image as a 'kindly, avuncular . . . favourite uncle type' (Hey, 1997: 184) should not therefore deter us from his ambitions for Liverpool, and his willingness to gently, but firmly, remind commentators of his prowess. When Liverpool won the European Cup in 1977, and became the first British side to retain it the following year, Paisley (1983: 28) acknowledged that Shankly 'had to take a lot of the credit for what happened . . . But on the other score, there is a bit of credit due to me and the staff, because we changed the whole team over'. Only four of the players involved in 1978 against Bruges had played under Shankly in the first team (Clemence, Heighway, Hughes and Thompson). In 1978, before the defence of the European Cup, Hey (1997: 189) interviewed Paisley, who pointed out as a matter of fact, not immodestly, that 'in their history, Liverpool have now won, or been runners-up in the league, FA Cup and European Cups 36 times. And I've been involved on 26 of those occasions, as player, assistant manager, or manager.' It is not hard to see how this record inspired the players, and despite his apparent uncertainty with the media, he commanded real respect. Souness (1985: 49) argues that although 'he may have been regarded as a fatherly figure by the supporters . . ., let me tell you, he ruled at Anfield with a rod of iron . . . He was a commanding man and there were few who dared mess around with him. If we looked as though we were becoming a little complacent . . . Bob would say, "If you have all had enough of winning, come and see me and I will sell the lot of you and buy 11 new players"'.

In terms of playing style, the Liverpool way was firmly entrenched, and while Paisley was busy integrating players such as Phil Neal (right-back), Joey Jones (left-back), Terry McDermott and Jimmy Case (midfield) into the team during his first two seasons in charge, fundamentally the passing game remained central. Neal (1981: 148–9) underlines two simple foundations of Paisley's approach: "'If the ball's controlled, keep it controlled." By this he means that, if you receive a controlled pass along the ground, give a controlled pass along the ground . . . Another saying of the Boss is that the longer you keep the ball the less time the next man to receive it has. This has become known as the "early ball" game.' A crucial aspect of Paisley's approach was the search for players who could display flexibility out on the pitch, who were intelligent enough to make decisions and communicate with each other during the maelstrom of fiercely competitive matches, and who did not 'hide', but actively sought out responsibility. As Tom Saunders, long-serving Youth development coach, observed, 'I can't recall a time here where players have been looking towards the bench for advice for what should happen next . . . It's a decision-making game, and you want men who can assume responsibility and make decisions on the pitch while the game's going on' (Taylor and Ward, 1993: 174). Neal (1981: 144) makes the point that 'the management put absolute trust in the players. They never clock us in and out but trust us to be a credit to ourselves and the club'.

Ray Kennedy, whom Paisley famously 'converted' from his previous role as a striker with the Arsenal double-winning side of 1971, into a graceful, yet strong midfield passer, was viewed by Paisley (1983: 14–17; see also Lees and Kennedy, 1994) as 'one of Liverpool's greatest players and probably the most under-rated . . . his contribution to Liverpool's achievements was enormous and his consistency remarkable'. The qualities he admired in Kennedy, apart from his origins in the north-east, were his 'ability to open up a game and give you the width of the park . . . He had so much control and was such a good shielder of a ball that an opponent virtually had to knock him over to take the ball off him. He had a great footballing brain, and his striker's instinct in the box never left him'. This stress upon intelligence, and its flexible application on the pitch, were hallmarks of Paisley's favourite players; Alan Hansen confirms that 'Bob Paisley used to say the first two yards of professional football was in the head. When he first said that, I thought, "What a load of rubbish", but the more I played the game, the more I realised he was spot on' (Taylor and Ward, 1995: 287).

In Graeme Souness (bought in January 1978 from Middlesbrough), Alan Hansen (who came from Partick Thistle in April 1977) and Kenny Dalglish (bought from Celtic at the start of 1977/78, to replace Kevin Keegan), Paisley created the spine of a team that had intelligence and drive, and that went on, in 1978/79, to win the League in perhaps the most complete fashion ever. As Phil Neal argued, Paisley had 'developed a team that, at one stage, I felt could possibly run itself. He had so many leaders within the team, particularly the '79 season, when we scored 85 goals and conceded only 16 goals in the league' (Taylor and Ward, 1993:167). This average of two goals per game or above was matched by the Liverpool Championship-winning teams of 1982/83, 1985/86, 1987/88 and 1989/90, and it gives the lie to an oft-repeated claim that this particular Liverpool side put the accent too heavily on defensive qualities, and were too ready to grind out efficient 1–0 victories (of which there were six in the League). In short, the accusation has been that this side was dour, mechanical, and lacking flair. What is at issue here is precisely the question of the club culture and playing style of a team.

Though Liverpool in the late 1970s and early 1980s are seen by many football fans (and even by some Kopites) as an efficient 'machine for winning', while the late 1980s team (of John Barnes, Peter Beardsley and John Aldridge) are contrasted as 'the great entertainers', the truth is much more complex. What is satisfying and aesthetically pleasing to Liverpool supporters may well incorporate elements from both of these stereotypes, but my argument is that 'the Liverpool Way' emphasizes the hard work involved in winning, and then repeatedly winning over and over, season after season. As soon as the Championship or Cup is safely tucked away, the celebrations barely over, Bob or Joe would be moving on, the slate wiped clean, reminding the players that it would be more difficult next year. Dalglish (1996: 143) illustrates Ronnie Moran's deliberately low-key reaction to a hard-won victory, '"I've got a job for another week."' Souness (1985: 52) notes that Paisley 'would moan and grumble . . . and generally bring us down to earth. The only time he would relent and hand round a bit of praise and a few laurel wreaths was when we had actually won a trophy. Next morning it would be back to basics and start all over again'.

Necessarily, if this slightly puritanical ethos is one of the primary aspects of the club's self-image or character, then playing with an ostentatious or devil-may-care flamboyance (*extravagance* is a better term here, conveying a derogatory and condescending impression) is rightly to be mistrusted. It is ludicrous, of course, to suggest that Liverpool in these years did not play with style; it was simply that Liverpool's aesthetic was not the same as, say, Manchester United's emphasis upon glamour (some Kopites refer disparagingly to Manchester United as 'the Glams', among other epithets). When Manchester United finally won the Championship (for the first time since the 1960s) in 1992/3 and then again in 1993/4, it was generally portrayed as a triumph for this glamorous self-image, as a vindication of their club's identity, although in neither season did they average two goals per game.

Paisley, himself, saw the 1978/79 team as 'the best of the Liverpool Championship sides I have been associated with in one capacity or another' (Paisley, 1983: 22). Again, continuity was vital. In winning the Championship in 1965/66, Liverpool had used only fourteen players, the lowest total in the history of the League, with five ever-presents (Lawrence, Byrne, Yeats, Smith and Callaghan). In 1978/79, the total was fifteen, with Clemence, Neal, Ray Kennedy and Dalglish ever-present, Souness missing only one game, and Thompson, Case, Alan Kennedy, Hansen and McDermott all featuring in thirty-four matches or more. For Paisley, this record, while partly a question of luck, has to do with the 'factor of competition, which makes players unwilling to drop out because they're worried about getting back in, particularly when the team is winning' (Paisley, 1983: 118).

Significantly, however, the avoidance of injury cannot be reduced to fortune or the willpower of players, it is also a matter of the correct physical and mental preparation, and here not only was Paisley, as we have mentioned above, a very accurate diagnostician, but he also firmly believed in a training regime that combined established principles (the programme was designed to integrate skill, strength, stamina, speed and flexibility), with the need for flexible responses. Attention to detail was critical, and the desk diaries that accumulated season by season in the manager's office, with entries almost every day, dealing with all types of apparently inconsequential material, 'ranging from weather conditions for a match in September to the fact that a certain player was late for training on a day in March' (1983: 13), provided a mine of information regarding the raw materials available to the staff. This intelligence-gathering was unobtrusive, and not 'scientific' in any dogmatic way, but Paisley enjoyed studying players and their physical and mental responses, and it was no accident that his 'relaxation' was often spent in the company of horse-racing trainers (such as Frank Carr). Souness (1985: 52) provides a good example of Paisley's love of racing and gambling, a passion he shared with many other working men in the city, and several of his players: 'He was certainly keen on the horses and I have even known him come in at half-time – when things were going well – and tell the boys which horse won the 3.30 at Catterick.'

Unlike Shankly, Paisley's obsession with the game was tempered by his methodical approach, and at least one of the players who served under both managers, Chris Lawler, 'found Bob much easier to deal with than Shanks, because he listened to your problems. Shanks would just ignore you' (Hey, 1997: 186; see also Bowler, 1996: 276). With a core of five of the 1978/79 team still available (Neal, Thompson, Hansen, Dalglish, Souness) and the addition of players who became regulars in the early 1980s (Bruce Grobbelaar in goal, Mark Lawrenson at centre-half, Sammy Lee, Craig Johnston and Ronnie Whelan in midfield, and Ian Rush up front), in 1982/83, in Paisley's final season, Liverpool continued to adhere to the same basic philosophy of how the game should be played, and very similar methods for transferring those principles from training ground to match conditions.

Allez les Rouges: Liverpool's Playing Style and European Football

We don't go around with our eyes shut (Bob Paisley in Hey, 1997: 188).

We learned in Europe that you can't score a goal every time you get the ball (Geoff Twentyman in Bowler, 1996: 267).

Liverpool's emphasis upon passing the ball, maintaining options for the player in possession through unceasing movement of, and off, the ball, and defending collectively when the ball was lost, was not necessarily European in its inspiration. However, it is true that Liverpool's style did develop through the assimilation of new ideas and tactical ploys, as they qualified annually for European competition from 1964 until 1985, when, after Heysel, the club was banned from Europe until 1991. It is not the intention here to provide a record of Liverpool's participation in the Fairs'/Uefa Cup, the Cup Winners' Cup or the European Cup (see Hale and Ponting, 1992 and Kelly, 1992), but to offer some thoughts on the more general impact that playing in Europe had upon the playing styles adopted.

Even as early as 1964, Liverpool's first season in the European Cup, the League Champions were exposed to influences that would help shape their approach to the game well into the future. Although a good deal of controversy still reigns over the semi-final elimination at the hands of Internazionale in the San Siro (Bowler, 1996: 228–234; Hale and Ponting, 1992: 18–21), the home leg was judged by many to be one of the finest games of the era. The Inter side, famed for its *catenaccio* defence, and coached by Helenio Herrera, had proved their credentials by defeating Real Madrid in the previous year's final. After the first leg, Herrera was full of praise for Liverpool's tactical nous, but the second leg proved a bitter reverse, with complaints by Liverpool about their preparation being affected by Milanese supporters, and accusations of match-fixing after two of the goals were fiercely contested by Shankly.

Liverpool took at least two significant lessons from this experience; in the future, when playing abroad, there was a strong sense of suspicion regarding the conditions that awaited the visitors, on and off the pitch. Undoubtedly, travel and facilities in the 1960s and 1970s were not comparable with the standards enjoyed by subsequent teams, but there are a number of anecdotes relating to these exaggerated concerns and fears, including Liverpool's decision to take their own food and bottled water, to arrive only the afternoon before the match, and to try to isolate the team from any problems that might arise (Taylor and Ward, 1993: 185–93; Paisley, 1983: 50–70; Souness, 1985: 94–106; Dalglish, 1996: 103–19). These precautions maybe served a dual purpose, in building team spirit in perceived conditions of adversity, and in concentrating the players' minds; eventually, Liverpool were capable of absorbing hostility and intimidation, settling themselves, and imposing their own game.

Second, Liverpool learned the virtues of patience and possession. Arguably, it was through the experience of playing over two legs in European competition that Liverpool refined their playing style, adopting elements of the continental game which were complementary to the acknowledged strengths of the English game. This produced a 'measured aggression' (Bowler, 1996: 232) that emphasized control of the tempo of the match, self-discipline and a ruthless streak. On the pitch, away from home, Liverpool teams attempted to maintain possession in a systematic fashion, often moving the ball around the back four (including the goalkeeper), frustrating the opposition and quietening the crowd. Attempting to 'draw the opposition onto them', Liverpool hoped to exploit counter-attacking opportunities, as they arose, but they wouldn't be unduly concerned if the match was played at a slow tempo. If, by chance, they fell behind, Liverpool learned through bitter experience that they risked more misery by 'chasing the game', throwing caution and discipline to the wind. A 1–0 defeat was not disastrous, and could often be repaid with interest at Anfield. The Ajax defeat in December 1966 (7–3 on aggregate, after a 5–1 reverse in the first leg in Amsterdam) was put down by Shankly, at least in part, to loss of discipline after conceding two goals in the opening quarter of an hour of the away leg, although in hindsight the quality of the Ajax team ought not to be dismissed (Bowler, 1996: 250–1; Paisley, 1983: 54; Callaghan, 1975: 41; Barend and Van Dorp, 1999).

Later on, after a damaging defeat by Red Star Belgrade (4–2 on aggregate, with 2–1 defeats in both legs of the second round tie) in the 1973 European Cup, Bob Paisley attempted to derive the lessons that could be drawn:

> Our approach was a bit frantic. We treated every match like a war. The strength of British football lay in our challenge for the ball, but the continentals took that away from us by learning how to intercept. We discovered it was no use winning the ball if you finished up on your backside. The top Europeans showed us how to break out of defence effectively. The pace of their movement was dictated by the first pass. We had to learn how to be patient like that, and think about the next two or three moves ahead when we had the ball. (David Lacey, *Guardian*, 15 February 1996)

According to Paisley (1983: 59), Dalglish (1996: 107–9) and Souness (1985: 97), the team of the late 1970s and early 1980s, even with two European Cups under their belts (Borussia Moenchengladbach in 1977, in Rome; Bruges in 1978, at Wembley), still managed to commit a similar costly error against Nottingham Forest in the away leg of the first round in 1978/79: 'When we were a goal down we were looking for an equaliser instead of accepting that as a reasonable result in the first leg of a European Cup tie . . .', said Paisley, while Dalglish considered that 'this naive reaction probably stemmed from the fact that we were playing familiar League opponents'. Souness described it 'as one of the biggest lessons I have ever received in European football'.

However, the value of an away goal was also learned after experiencing elimination by Vitoria Setubal in 1969/70 (losing 1–0 in Portugal, before winning the return 3–2) and by Ferencvaros in 1974/75, when a 1–1 home draw was followed by a frustrating 0–0 in Hungary (Ferencvaros are distinguished as the first continental team to win at Anfield in January 1968, 1–0 on the night and 2–0 on aggregate, and also as the only side to beat Liverpool twice over two legs). Dalglish recognized early in the 1980s, when Liverpool defeated Athletic Bilbao 1–0 away after a goalless draw at Anfield, on the way to winning the European Cup for the fourth time, that 'the important thing is that the opposition haven't scored; many good teams have fallen out on the away goals rule'. One of Liverpool's best-ever results in Europe proved the same point, when in the European Cup semi-final in 1981, a 0–0 home draw with Bayern Munich was followed by a thrilling 1–1 result away, with Ray Kennedy scoring with fewer than 10 minutes left, and Karl Heinz Rummenigge's equalizer not enough to stop Liverpool's qualification on the away goals rule. Sammy Lee had famously man-marked Bayern's most dangerous creative force, Paul Breitner, out of the game, illustrating that Liverpool were now also prepared to adjust their tactics to take account of opposition strengths. Souness (1985: 50) recalls that Paisley 'loved that game', and many Liverpool supporters would also have it very close to the top of any list of favourite matches. These lessons from playing in Europe had to be relearned, sometimes painfully, for a new era and by new players, when Liverpool were readmitted to European competition in 1991. For instance, defeat by the single goal at Anfield, in the second leg of a second round UEFA Cup tie, against the moderate Danish side Brondby in 1995/96, had followed what many considered a 'tie-winning' scoreless draw in Copenhagen.

On occasion, of course, Liverpool learned by simply coming up against talented and committed opponents, who outplayed them and deserved their victories. Although comprehensive defeat was rare enough, and the respect given to a team such as Ajax may have appeared grudging, the Liverpool staff were quick to recognize and appreciate quality football. One example of such a defeat was provided by the 1979/80 first-round European Cup exit against the Soviet Union's finest side, Dynamo Tbilisi. The Georgians lost 2–1 at Anfield in the opening leg, but several observers judged that 'only abysmal finishing prevented them inflicting a home defeat on the English Champions' (Hale and Ponting, 1992: 136–7; Paisley, 1983: 60–1; Kelly, 1992: 104–5; Dalglish, 1996: 109–10; Souness, 1985: 98–100).

Although Liverpool had played teams from East Germany (Dynamo Berlin, Dynamo Dresden three times), Poland (Wroclaw), Hungary (Ferencvaros, Honved), Romania (Dinamo Bucharest, Petrolul Ploiesti) and Yugoslavia (Red Star Belgrade), this was the first meeting with a team from the Soviet Union. It was clear that the playing style of the Soviets was not dissimilar to Liverpool's, based as it was upon accurate, economical passing and good movement, controlled build-up play and an ability to interchange positions. Players of the calibre of Chivadze (who scored Dynamo's goal), Shengeliya, Kipiani and Gutsaev also had skills to match the best in Europe. Significantly, this side seemed unruffled by the intimidating reception they received, and they were temperamentally strong, not a feature then associated with East European or Soviet sides. Drawing in Tbilisi

0–0 at half-time, Liverpool still had hopes of scraping through, but a goal by Gutsaev meant Liverpool were forced to attack, and conceded two more late goals on the counter. Bob Paisley alluded to the difficult travelling arrangements and the players being woken by fan demonstrations in the early hours of the morning of the game, but still knew Tbilisi were 'a very confident and skilful side'. Typically, Paisley 'had a long chat over a drink' with Tbilisi coach Akhalkatsi, partly no doubt in an effort to glean potentially useful information, but also because here was a man who clearly shared similar ideas about the way to play football. Dalglish reckoned 'We deserved to fail . . . Liverpool were simply beaten by the better side'; for Souness, despite some gamesmanship, Tbilisi 'were undoubtedly the better side and good value for their eventual . . . victory'. Dynamo lost in the second round to Hamburg, but this excellent team gained some reward in 1981, winning the Cup Winners' Cup against Carl Zeiss Jena.

Since Liverpool's return to European competition, the record has not been particularly impressive. An excellent opportunity to complete the full set of European club trophies, by adding the Cup Winners' Cup in 1996/97, was squandered with a disastrous performance in the away leg in the semi-final at Paris Saint-Germain. Still, it was seen in the late 1990s that with qualification for the Champions' League being a top priority for Gérard Houllier's new team, Liverpool would need to adapt their playing style to such a different format if they were again to take on and succeed against the Continent's most accomplished sides.

Some People Think It's Fun to Entertain: The Liverpool Way in a Changing Football World

> Life at Liverpool was simple. No wild predictions, no arrogance, no petulance (Dalglish, 1996: 143).

> The largest part of our game is still ball control, accurate passing and good movement. And it's also about patience, which demands intense concentration . . . The perfect player hasn't been born, so you have to ensure that you can cover people's weaknesses within the framework of the team (Paisley in Hey, 1997: 190).

In the domestic sphere, Liverpool continued to dominate English football, first under Joe Fagan, who like Bob Paisley had risen through the boot room ranks, and was by no means sure that the manager's job was his destiny but took it on because he was asked to by the club, and then Kenny Dalglish, who became player-manager in 1985 (Kelly, 1995; Dalglish, 1996; McIlvanney, 1995: 56–9). The style of preparation and play didn't change radically, and the football and administrative sides of the club remained under the guidance of most of the same individuals.

Of course, there were new faces on the playing staff from time to time (with John Wark, Jan Molby, Gary Gillespie, Kevin MacDonald, Michael Robinson and Paul Walsh all playing quite substantial roles under Fagan), but in general Liverpool supporters became adept at comparing (rather than contrasting) individuals who performed similar functions within the overall continuity of the team pattern. Defensively, the core of the team under Fagan's managership remained Alan Kennedy, Neal, Hansen and Lawrenson, with Grobbelaar in goal. Remarkably, in 1983/84, four of these five were ever-present in the league, and Neal missed only one game. Part of the explanation for this was undoubtedly the intelligence and experience of these players; as Paisley pointed out, 'If you can win the ball by interception [rather than tackling] it not only cuts down on injuries . . . it also means you can use the ball better because you've got it cleanly, you're not at full stretch, and you're in space.' (Hey, 1997: 190–1). In midfield, Liverpool relied upon the complementary virtues of good passing, strong running, physical and mental toughness, characterized by Souness, Lee, and Johnston, with Steve Nicol, Ronnie Whelan, Molby and Wark all breaking through. Up front, Dalglish and Rush continued to work as a genuine partnership (42 league goals combined in 1982/83, 39 in 1983/84, 20 in 1984/85). Never did a player bear out Bob Paisley's maxim, about the pace of a footballer comprising mental as well as physical quickness, so completely as Dalglish did. His manager stressed that:

> The judgement in Kenny's passing bears the hallmark of great golf shots. And he can read ground conditions the way cricketers can. He has the uncanny knack of knowing a ball will bounce, carry or skid on a particular surface . . . Kenny can make a team spark collectively with his gifted ability to read situations, and offer other players so many options with his wide-ranging distribution and vision. Of all the players I have played alongside, managed and coached in more than forty years at Anfield, he is the most talented. When Kenny shines, the whole team is illuminated (Paisley, 1983: 87–8).

When Joe Fagan, a Liverpudlian by birth (as opposed to the honorary status conferred upon Shankly and Paisley), became manager, he was endorsed by the latter for the telling reason that 'above all, he was not the sort of man who was going to come in with different ideas that could have ruined the club' (Paisley, 1990: 33). It was certainly never held against him that, when offered the chance to sign for Liverpool by George Kay in 1938, Fagan opted to join Manchester City, and then had to wait nine years for his debut! Like Paisley, Fagan was 'reliable rather than flashy' as a player, and was equally dependable as one of the backroom staff. Brought to the club from Rochdale by Phil Taylor in 1958, he was already known to Shankly, who had tried in vain to sign him when manager at Grimsby, and was kept on as reserve-team coach. An undemonstrative and self-deprecating man, Fagan's players generally recall a sense of their manager as one of a number of influential members of the staff (alongside Ronnie Moran and Roy Evans), lacking ego, but determined to overcome 'the fear of disappointing the supporters' (Paisley, 1990: 34).

If this description sounds slightly dismissive, that the Liverpool 'system' was merely kept ticking over under Fagan's leadership, then it should be recalled that in his first year, Liverpool completed a historic treble (winning the Championship from Southampton, the League Cup for the fourth time in a row against Everton, and a fourth European Cup against Roma, in Rome). This 'fine-tuning' also produced another appearance in the European Cup final in 1984/85, and a semi-final exit in the FA Cup, although in the end it was a barren year, Liverpool's first season without a trophy of any shape or size for nine years. Fagan had to make do without Souness, who had decamped to Sampdoria, but exemplified the Liverpool way with his pragmatic insistence: 'Souness has gone; forget about him, we've got a job to do without him' (Ponting, 1996: 198). So, while it is fair to say that the circumstances of Fagan's leave-taking (after the chaos of Heysel) overshadowed to some extent his team's achievements, nonetheless, his role over twenty-seven years at Liverpool ought to be remembered more often than it is.

It is not possible here to detail the beginning or acceleration of the apparent decay of the 'Liverpool Way' in the 1990s, but it is clear that under managers Dalglish (1986–91), Souness (1991–94) and Evans (1994–98), although all three were steeped in the traditions that had brought the club unparalleled success, the football world was rapidly changing, and Liverpool could not remain immune from these developments. The debate regarding the responsibility for Liverpool's relatively turbulent attempts to adjust has recently been joined with a vengeance, with revealing (though, of course, partisan) accounts by ex-managers Dalglish (1996) and Souness (1999; see also Kelly, 1994), as well as by players who each spent a decade or more at Anfield (Barnes, 1999: 237–56; Molby, 1999: 161–99; Hansen, 1999). The significant point here is that all of these accounts stress the deep impression created by the individual experience of the 'Liverpool Way'. For Barnes (1999: 109–17), when he joined Liverpool in 1987, they had 'an instantly recognisable shape that was unique to them . . . Anfield's emphasis was on passing the ball and keeping moves simple. Players fitted into the Liverpool way while giving it an added dimension'. This structure or pattern, what Barnes refers to as a team's 'DNA', was based upon retaining control of the ball, although 'as a footballing breed, the English never treat possession with the reverence it deserves. Possession is almost a dirty word. Liverpool are the best in England at keeping possession, but send them into Europe, against a team like Celta Vigo [who eliminated Liverpool from the UEFA Cup in 1998/99, 4–1 on aggregate], and Liverpool look ordinary'.

All of these ex-players have continued to involve themselves fully in the game away from Liverpool, whether as managers or coaches (Barnes at Celtic, Molby at Swansea and Kidderminster, Dalglish at Blackburn and Newcastle, and Souness at Galatasaray, Southampton, Torino, Benfica and Blackburn, not to mention other former Liverpool players currently or recently in management such as Kevin Keegan, Phil Neal, John Toshack, Ronnie Whelan, Nigel Spackman, Steve McMahon, David Hodgson, John Aldridge, Nigel Clough), or alternatively as media pundits and commentators. (As well as Hansen and Lawrenson, who has also had a spell in management, on *Match of the Day*, other ex-Liverpool players are continually to be found on radio or TV broadcasts: Barry Venison, David Fairclough, Jim Beglin, Ian St John, Michael Robinson, in Spain, to name only a few.) Their contributions are of a variable standard, but they are undeniably informed by their playing experiences, and their opinions on the game often reflect a sense of attachment to Liverpool's playing style. Of course, despite the 'revolutionary' appointment of Houllier, and his fellow French coach, Patrice Berguès, it also remains the case that Liverpool have a large number of their former players still closely involved in the running of the club (Phil Thompson as Houllier's assistant manager, Sammy Lee as coach, Steve Heighway in charge of the Youth Academy, Ron Yeats as chief scout).

There clearly remains something significant with regard to the footballing education received by these men at Liverpool and, despite undoubted differences that exist in terms of the level at which these former players are contributing to the game, it is nonetheless hard to imagine any of them actively renouncing their identification with the 'Liverpool way'. Even those who spent only a relatively short time on the playing staff, or played in the more recent, less successful, era, appear still to have found the experience crucial to their ideas about how they want football to be played.

There is certainly some truth in the suggestion that in the 1990s, as Giulianotti has posited (1999: 142), the increasing 'inter-penetration of sporting aesthetics, techniques and tactics . . . [means] hybridity can only expand as we enter the post-modern milieu of increased labour [player] migration, television coverage and international competition'. However, this apparent convergence in playing styles is mediated by the particular cultural traditions and identities of individual clubs. For Liverpool, the death of Bob Paisley in February 1996 was, of course, felt with great emotion, perhaps the more so because supporters recognized that here, genuinely, was definitive proof that an era in football had passed. Several of the obituaries, including those in the Liverpool fanzine, *Through the Wind and Rain* (no. 30, Spring 1996), drew attention to the enormous changes that had occurred in the football world since Paisley had stepped down as manager. In December 1999, to mark the fortieth anniversary of Bill Shankly's arrival at Anfield, prior to the home match against Coventry many of the players from the 1960s and 1970s paraded in front of the Kop, and there were fulsome, moving tributes paid, with nostalgic reminiscing for older players and supporters alike. However, there was also some ambivalence, not with regard to the great man's legacy, but because such an occasion would inevitably overshadow the first tentative steps that Houllier's young team were taking on the road to re-establishing Liverpool as a footballing force in the land. The club and its supporters are in the process of wrestling with this inescapable dialectic; all associated with Liverpool are proud of a past that deserves to be celebrated, particularly in these days where football's 'history' appears to have begun with the Premiership in 1992, but building for a successful future requires a recognition that the game has changed radically. This has occurred on the pitch, in the styles of play adopted, though perhaps this aspect of modernization has not been as dramatic as the upheavals in the 'social world' in which football exists.

If, when, Liverpool do win the League Championship once more, it will be understood (and felt) by the many thousands who celebrate it, including Gérard Houllier himself, as a continuation of the footballing tradition represented by men such as Bill Shankly, Bob Paisley and Joe Fagan. More importantly, it will also be seen by a large proportion of those who celebrate as a vindication of the wider moral, social and political values enshrined by these men. After all, in order to stay the same, things must change.

References

Barend, F. and van Dorp, H. (1999) *Ajax, Barcelona, Cruyff: The ABC of an Obstinate Maestro*, London: Bloomsbury.

Barnes, J. (1999) *John Barnes: The Autobiography*, London: Headline.

Bowler, D. (1996) *Shanks: The Authorised Biography of Bill Shankly*, London: Orion.

Callaghan, I. and Keith, J. (1975) *The Ian Callaghan Story*, London: Quartet Books.

Dalglish, K. with Winter, H. (1996) *Dalglish: My Autobiography*, London: Hodder & Stoughton.

Downing, D. (1999) *Passovotchka: Moscow Dynamo in Britain, 1945*, London: Bloomsbury.

Giulianotti, R. (1999) *Football: A Sociology of the Global Game*, Cambridge: Polity.

Hale, S. and Ponting, I. (1992) *Liverpool in Europe*, Enfield: Guinness.

Hansen, A. (1999) *A Matter of Opinion*, London: Partridge.

Hey, S. (1997) *A Golden Sky: The Liverpool Dream Team*, Edinburgh: Mainstream.

Keith, J. (1998) *Shanks for the Memory*, London: Robson.

Kelly, S. (1992) *Liverpool in Europe: The Complete Record from 1964*, London: Collins Willow.

—— (1994) *Graeme Souness: A Soccer Revolutionary*, London: Headline.

—— (1995) *Dalglish*, London: Headline.

—— (1996) *The Illustrated History of Liverpool, 1892–1996*, London: Hamlyn.

Lees, A. and Kennedy, R. (1994) *Ray of Hope: The Ray Kennedy Story*, London: Penguin.

Liversedge, S. (1995) *Liverpool from the Inside*, Edinburgh: Mainstream.

McIlvanney, H. (1995) *McIlvanney on Football*, Edinburgh: Mainstream.

Molby, J. (1999) *Jan the Man: From Anfield to Vetch Field*, London: Victor Gollancz.

Neal, P. (1981) *Attack from the Back*, London: Arthur Barker.

—— (1986) *Life at the Kop*, London: Queen Anne Press.

Paisley, B. (1983) *Bob Paisley: A Lifetime in Football*, London: Arthur Barker.

—— (1990) *My Fifty Golden Reds*, Warrington: Front Page Books.

Ponting, I. (1996) *Liverpool Player by Player*, London: Hamlyn.

Rush, I. (1986) *Rush: Ian Rush's Autobiography*, London: Grafton Books.

Souness, G. with Harris, B. (1985) *No Half Measures*, London: CollinsWillow.

Souness, G. with Ellis, M. (1999) *Souness: The Management Years*, London: André Deutsch.

Taylor, R. and Ward, A. with Williams, J. (1993) *Three Sides of the Mersey: An Oral History of Everton, Liverpool and Tranmere Rovers*, London: Robson.

Taylor, R. and Ward, A. (1995) *Kicking and Screaming: An Oral History of Football in England*, London: Robson.

Wagg, S. (1984) *The Football World*, Brighton: Harvester.

Yeats, R. (1966) *Soccer with a Mersey Beat*, London: Pelham Books.

–5–

Kopites, 'Scallies' and Liverpool Fan Cultures: Tales of Triumph and Disasters
John Williams

Introduction

I want to look in this chapter at the changes in support and supporter styles around Liverpool FC from the early 1960s to the present day. I'll talk here mainly about younger (though not always 'youth') male supporter traditions – there is a focus on female supporters of the club in Chapter Nine – though I do draw on the perspectives of older fans, too. I want to stress, strongly, that the overall character of Liverpool fans owes much to the contribution of its often neglected older fans and perhaps especially to its female followers and their welcome and resolute refusal to be excluded from these cultural 'male preserves' in the city (see Chapter Nine, and also Williams and Woodhouse, 1999).

I also want to try to say something here about the connections between local oral traditions, music cultures and football fandom in Liverpool, especially in the formative years of the Kop as a 'singing end' in the 1960s. In doing this I am trying to respond to calls for more work on football fans which concentrates on the specific, local traditions of club support and the 'cultural power' that supporters exert in relation to the sport and to their own clubs (see Clarke, 1991).

In the early 1960s, of course, Liverpool FC was becoming an international focus because of the synergy between music and football in the city and the cultural inventiveness of its fans; in the 1970s the spotlight fell on Liverpool because of the excellence and dominance of the club's extraordinary football team and management; in the 1980s it was more footballing excellence, but also an altogether harsher glare on the character of the city following the fatal hooliganism at Heysel and the crowd disaster at Hillsborough; by the 1990s the focus was on the prospects for reviving the club's football status in a new, global era, but also on the new economics of the sport as the club struggled to adapt to the new era of the game's development, eventually investing in a new business structure, a talented foreign coach and a roster of imported foreign players (see Chapter Ten). I want to try to cover all these issues here. I'll begin with some opening comments on the Liverpool Kop.

The early Kop

Following the arrival of the more media-conscious Bill Shankly and the *footballing* success he brought to the club in the early 1960s, at the slowly modernizing Anfield base the main Liverpool home terrace, the cavernous Spion Kop itself, was about to become something of a focus for national, and even international, celebrity. When the Kop played out its final hours as a standing terrace in 1994, press and TV crews from all over the globe came to record the event. Arthur Hopcraft's early insightful and essentially sympathetic profile of the Liverpool Kop, and of other English football terraced ends of the 1960s – 'the privileged places of working-class communion' (1971: 161) remains one of the classic pieces of pre-Hillsborough football writing about standing football crowds in England. Interestingly, what Hopcraft seemed to find alluring and impressive about terrace life in the 1960s was, by the early 1990s, being quoted at length in official reports as being exactly the reasons why the football terraces had to be left to the past (Taylor, 1990). For these reasons at least, it is worth quoting his description at some length here. For Hopcraft (1971: 162), these great terraces were:

> . . . [H]ideously uncomfortable. The steps are as greasy as a school playground lavatory in the rain. The air is rancid with beer and onions and belching and worse. The language is a gross purple of obscenity. When the crowd surges at a shot or a collision near a corner flag a man or a boy, and sometimes a girl, can be lifted off the ground in the crush, as if by some massive, soft-sided crane and dangled about for minutes on end, perhaps never getting back to within four or five steps of the spot from which the monster made its bite. In this incomparable entanglement of bodies and emotions lies the heart of the fan's commitment to football. The senses of triumph and dejection experienced here are never quite matched in any seated section of a football ground. It is the physical interaction which makes the monster the figure of unavoidable dreams it becomes. To kill off this animal, this monstrous, odorous national pet would be a cruel act of denial to us.

In the early 1960s in Liverpool, and with the Kop in its early pomp, many Liverpool football supporters, mainly working-class men, spent some of their greatest communal moments grasped and flung around in its lurching, soft-sided grip. But the Kop's effects were not always so benign; it could also bite. In December 1966 the usual tens of fans who were treated for injuries, as the giant beast rippled back and forth, were multiplied tenfold as at least 200 supporters were carried out injured from a steaming, packed terrace as Liverpool tried, unsuccessfully, to rescue a first-leg disaster in a European Cup tie against the rising Dutch Champions, Ajax. Inglis (1996: 219), perhaps unfairly, describes the Kop as being 'a fairly unmanageable terrace throughout its 88 year history'. In fact, the Kop was often described by many Liverpool supporters, male and female, as being the 'safest' place in the ground, especially in the 1970s and 1980s (see Chapter Nine). But it could also play with, frighten and damage even its staunchest allies.

Finally, these still great civic spaces in the city, the football terraces at both Liverpool and Everton, acted – as they did in parts of North London and elsewhere in de-industrializing Britain (see Robins and Cohen, 1978) – as a stable point of reference, identification and *belonging* in the early 1960s, in a city which had been torn about by the modernizing planners charged with clearing the Liverpool city centre of its poverty-infested but communal bullrings and back-to-back houses (see Channon, 1976: Ch. 1). With working-class families now decanted from the centre to high-rise blocks along the Everton Valley and to new, isolated and unemployment-blackspot housing estates in Huyton, Netherley and Kirkby on the periphery and outside the city boundaries, the two football clubs acted as collective points of city communion, continuity and neighbourhood solidarity, especially for working-class men. In 1969, the Liverpool city council called a belated halt to its high-rise relocation policy, but by now its slogan of 'City of Change and Challenge' resonated barely at all with those who had seen the Liverpool city centre, and its tough local communities, effectively gutted. Observed one commentator of the time, 'Not only in the major operation of its heart has Liverpool come near losing its soul – drastic surgery *outside* the central area had grave psychological consequences' (Channon, 1976: 31).

Football, Youth Culture and Music in Liverpool in the 1960s

Things other than urban disruption and football were also already stirring, loudly, in Liverpool at this time. This was a heady period, especially for male youth in the city. The so-called 'Mersey Sound', led by the international pop music success of the Beatles, had thrust Liverpool into the world spotlight. The city's football clubs were also enjoying success together – Everton's 'school of science' had won the League title in 1963 – in a way seldom experienced even in the long history of the professional game in Liverpool. Even the new 'modern' Labour Government of 1964 was led by a Prime Minister, Harold Wilson, who represented a Liverpool constituency, Huyton. Wilson also cleverly used his local connections to emphasize the supposed youthful 'energy' of his new administration, especially in his carefully prepared publicity shoots with the ubiquitous Beatles. This was also a period in which British drama, theatre, and popular culture, more generally, celebrated specifically northern working-class traditions, probably for the first time, for example, in the new British 'kitchen-sink' realist TV dramas – including the Liverpool-based successful police series, Z Cars – and in the popular 'realist' wave of British films and novels of the time. Culturally, at least, it was a relatively good time to be young, working-class, a football fan and from Liverpool in the early 1960s.

At the same time, as new traditions for travelling and watching football began to emerge in England in the 1960s, with younger supporters at the forefront, brash young supporters of Everton and Liverpool were already developing an early reputation for football 'trouble'. Early themes here focused on the 'instrumental' nature of Merseyside football delinquency; on theft, for example. A police sergeant in Liverpool told the author James McClure that in the late 1950s and early 1960s, even before 'football special' trains arrived, unwary football visitors arriving in Liverpool by train would be directed by locals into Gerard Gardens or other city housing estates to be stripped by waiting predators: 'We used to have them trooping into St. Anne's Street [police station] without their coats, their boots, and their shoes: their money had been taken off them and everything' (McClure, 1980: 269). A popular club comedian joke in the early 1960s was also that Liverpool FC supporters could be spotted by the 'railway carriage door' they were supposed to wear in their jacket lapel (having wrenched it from its moorings on a football trip).

By November 1964 the national press was reporting that 'shopkeepers lock up when Everton are in town', and local police forces were already promising 'get tough' measures when Liverpool fans were visiting (Dunning et al., 1988). In fact, of course, when Celtic fans came to Anfield for a UEFA Cup Winners Cup tie in 1966, and fought before and after the game, littering the pitch with bottles during it, this was easily the most serious crowd trouble yet seen in the Anfield part of the city. Some of this early English focus on Merseysiders as hooligans was clearly media hype and some was a consequence of the sheer numbers of younger Merseyside fans who were now travelling away with their successful football clubs, unchaperoned, almost for the first time. But some was also the result of the convenient 'export' of aspects of real cultural traditions in the city. Such traditions had been forged out of and around the trading industries and cultures of Liverpool – especially those in the docks – and also the perceived 'necessary' resort by young men, sometimes, to theft and to barter in a city where unskilled labour, high levels of unemployment, routine street-smartness, and merciless masculine status hierarchies were long-established as key recurring features.

At the same time as this more 'subterranean' reputation of Liverpool fans was spreading among some rival fans, the mainstream public 'reading' of the Kop – and therefore of Liverpool supporters at large – was very different. The regular televising of football highlights on the BBC began in Britain in August 1964, at Anfield. The choice of venue was highly appropriate. Liverpool were League Champions, and the club was guaranteed a large and vociferous following, especially as the British pop industry, a growing cultural and economic force in the early 1960s, was then dominated by Brian Epstein, the Beatles, and other Liverpool artistes. One emerging local band, Gerry and the Pacemakers, musicians and also fans of the club, reached the top of the singles charts late in 1963 with a reworking of a grandiose old musicals' standard, 'You'll never walk alone'. The themes of the song – struggle, pride, community, 'hope in your heart' – seemed ideal for the trials and emotions of football fans, and its 'walk on' chorus, slowly, began to be sung on parts of the Kop. (The later, impressive, Kop anthem, the self-penned 'Scouser Tommy', adds images of stirring Liverpool heroism in foreign wars to this seductive mix.) The Liverpool club, with Bill Shankly's enthusiastic support, eventually responded to growing informal pressure by agreeing to play the Pacemakers' version of the song on the p.a. before matches as a means of getting the home fans 'involved' and of intimidating visiting teams. It was, as we now know, enthusiastically embraced by the Anfield crowd.

Other songs followed, especially local pop hits with 'sing-along' choruses, which could be used, simultaneously, to celebrate the city's global, cultural success, as well as being easily adapted for specific local football use. More prosaically, older, familiar tunes were incorporated into local repertoires: 'Ee aye addio', followed by any appropriate 'football' ending and sung to the tune of the playground song 'The farmer's in his den', was a simple, staple part of the Kop's early song book. It is also likely that the long tradition of performing Liverpool comedians, the strong poetry and oral history cultures in the city, as well as the deep-rooted folk song and music hall and public house strands of popular musical performance, based especially around the cultural exchanges made possible by sea trade, all fed the Kop's new reflexive and creative appetites as a performer at the match: as part of the active text of a game. These performance and oral traits – plus the occupational and informal trading and exchange cultures in the city – are deeply embedded parts of the 'local structures of feeling' on Merseyside (I. Taylor et al., 1996). This extension by Ian Taylor and his colleagues of Raymond Williams' original concept is useful in the way that it draws on and combines historical discourses and myths, as well as on local patterns of consumption and employment, gender and 'race' relations and spatial environments, in order to reveal markers of local social formations and identity, and also expressions of local character.

Once the Kop had fully developed its public reputation for innovation and wit – and for its urban vim and vinegar, too – it was soon clear that the production of some of the newer, more inventive, vocal material required more than simple spontaneity and informality. According to Hopcraft (1971: 166), in the 1960s 'The Liverpool crowds have been imitated but never adequately, no other fans being able to match their invention, to say nothing of the sustained indecency'. Much of the singing in the crowd was spontaneous, an immediate response to incidents on the field. But the Kop also soon acquired its own local 'writers' in order to keep the great crowd fed with new songs, as 1960s Kopite Phil Aspinall told Stephen Kelly (1993: 67–8):

We used to make the songs up in a pub. In our case it was always The Albert, next door to the Kop. But there are a number of pubs dotted round Liverpool where the same kind of thing goes on. If the songs were long, we'd have to organize it. We usually do that before the game, while we're having a few drinks. If the words were easy and the tune was catchy, you might be able to start it in that afternoon. Sometimes it would take a few games before it really got going. They're easy tunes in the main, and people soon catch on once they've got the tune. On the Kop it would snowball and everyone would be singing it in three or four minutes . . . I've been drinking in The Albert since the 1960s. We'll be singing most of the night – you know, old Beatles and Elvis numbers – until we get thrown out.

European nights at Anfield soon became established as 'special' occasions when the Kop and its various informal bards were expected to turn out in force – and with new songs. This was in tune with Shankly's own thinking, of course, that foreign teams could be intimidated by the physical prowess and commitment of his players and by the howling reception they received from the 25,000 souls who now gathered under the roof of the home end at Anfield (see Chapter Three). The European night-game crowds in the 1960s also assembled inside Anfield from 5.30 p.m. onwards for these pay-at-the-gate events, so the atmosphere inside the stadium by kick-off time was simply intense. Innovation and the sense of 'border-crossing' and experimentation was more generally in the air at European matches. Liverpool's famous all-red kit was first introduced, in fact, as a 'European' strip in a tie at Anfield, against Anderlecht, in November 1964. Shankly tried the strip on Ron Yeats, the club's towering centre back, just before the match. Convinced the new gear made his players look more fearsome, the manager simply asserted that this should be the club's new strip (Kelly, 1993: 139–40). Anderlecht, a top European club side of the time, were crushed, 3–0.

The Kop also busily collected chants and songs on their own European journeys, of course. The titanic struggles with France's St Etienne in 1977 produced 'Allez les rouges', for example, a song eventually 'revived' for the 'new' Liverpool under French manager, Gérard Houllier. An estimated 25,000 Liverpool fans also famously travelled by bus, plane and train to Rome in 1977 for the club's first European Cup Final victory, with a new song 'Roma', sung to the tune of 'Arrivederci Roma', and penned by Phil Aspinall and his mates on their way to an away game at Newcastle (Kelly, 1993: 68). According to the club's players, themselves still low after an FA Cup Final defeat just days before, it was the sight of the huge bank of Liverpool red in the Olympic Stadium, as the players inspected the pitch, which stirred the side to victory.

The central place for football in the lives of working-class men in Liverpool in the 1960s, and in other working-class cities like it, is easily romanticized now, especially as today's leisure options proliferate (for those who can afford them) and ties of family and place have been so weakened by post-Fordist shifts in patterns of work, by changes in social and geographical mobility and by shifts in gender relations (see King, 1998). Football clubs today are now also more 'available' for support by those who inhabit a space outside the 'traditional' ties of family and neighbourhood. 'Going to the match' then was both a respite from work and from home and also an exploration of friendship, communal worth, and, essentially, of local working-class masculine solidarities both at work and at play (Holt, 1989). But it was also focused strongly on an *aesthetic* – the grace, the style and the pace of professional players – and on spectator *performance* – the physicality, the creativity and harmony of the crowd – in a way which called up qualities and sensitivities in working men which had few other appropriate or satisfying outlets.

Although the Liverpool Kop, in its deep partisanship and darker mode, had 'all the menace of an hysteric's nightmare' (Hopcraft 1971: 164–6), in the 1960s it was also a place where tough Liverpool dockers, factory workers and tradesmen could collectively warm, for example, to the sensuous skills of the slight Hungarian inside forward Varga as he guided Ferencvaros to a rare Fairs Cup win at Anfield during the 1967/68 season: 'More than any other English city', Hopcraft wrote in 1971, 'Liverpool experiences its hope and its shame through its football.'

For Liverpool supporters in the 1960s, such as Alan Edge (1999: 138), it was the case that before marriage and the kids set in with new responsibilities and constraints, watching football at Anfield with close male mates offered three or four years of an 'exclusive arrangement' which tied working men, perfectly, to each other, to their favourite football pub, and, thrillingly, to their own 'spec' on the Kop. But it was not so for *all* Liverpudlians, of course; in a deeply segregated and racist city, there was little space for black people from Liverpool to assert their own allegiance to either of the major Merseyside football clubs (see Williams, 1988; Hill, 1989; and Chapter 6).

Saturday's Kids

At the same time as singing was being established at Anfield, penetrations of the football world by aspects of what was, even by 1964, a rapidly expanding teenage leisure industry also had the effects of exacerbating divisions by age inside football grounds. At Liverpool, as elsewhere, younger fans began, noisily, to colonize the areas behind the goals in the early 1960s. The Kop, however, because of its sheer scale, and also its lack of lateral fencing, managed to incorporate, initially at least, both the new more vocal and more disruptive fandoms of youth, and the more established, older, and more traditional fan styles which gathered around the younger core area. At other venues this was much more difficult to achieve, especially as hooliganism accelerated and as older, 'respectable' fans gradually evacuated these smaller terraced spaces, effectively giving them up to the sorts of masculinist, 'neo-tribal' struggles which were to become such a defining feature of football culture in England for the next twenty-five years (see Dunning et al., 1988). In short, we were about to move into quite new, and sometimes disturbing, football times in England.

The emerging new forms of terrace *patois* were, of course, largely the preserve of the young. The influence of popular musical forms and a more general concern with consumption, style and the exploration of existing local cultural traditions have been a central feature of football's youth cultures on Merseyside at least since the early 1960s. As the maximum wage was lifted in 1961, so the players themselves were also slowly moving into an era of new and more conspicuous lifestyles and, increasingly, onto the stage of impression management and public celebrity (Wagg, 1984).

The generally favourable TV and press coverage provided of Liverpool fans especially the all-singing, all-dancing Kop – throughout the 1960s and into the 1970s also served to mask, however, some important local developments. By the late 1970s, for example, more and more young Liverpool hard cases had left the by then 'safe and boring' Kop for the 'Anny Road End' at the other end of the Liverpool ground. These 'deserters' were among the most belligerent, but also the most vociferous and most inventive young Kopites, who railed, especially, against the bland media construction of the great Liverpool terrace as a partisan but essentially good-humoured enclosure (including an early 'anthropological' feature on the BBC's *Panorama*). Instead, they sought more immediate football action, set-up as they now were against the visitors' enclosure at the far end of the ground. Exchanges between the Kop and its recalcitrant offshoot at the other end of the stadium became more fractious as the 1980s wore on. If, for the new Anny Roaders, the Main Stand fans were older 'moaners', and the Kemlyn regulars the dull, scarf brigade, 'family' Kopites were, increasingly, just 'gobshites' (Edge, 1999: 142). Some Liverpool fans identify *this* early splintering – rather than the falling 1980s crowds or the later reduction in Kop capacity, post-Hillsborough – as the real beginning of the long-term decline of the Kop as a raucous, impassioned and sometimes dangerously unpredictable home end (Kelly, 1993: 43–4).

The national media image of generally 'peaceful' local derby games in Liverpool – families and friends split only by their football support – helped to continue the national popular profile of Liverpudlians as roguish but essentially collectively *non-violent* football fans. Meanwhile, other terrace 'contests', this time around consumption and style, were hotting up. Regular European football travel for most Liverpool fans from the mid-1960s onwards meant adventure, some lasting friendships, broadened cultural horizons, and many extraordinary footballing successes and memories (Goodwin and Straughan, 1996). For some younger male fans from the city, however, it was also an extravagant dip into the exotic and exposed style pots of Europe.

Going abroad for football at first meant the intoxication of foreign football travel, and bringing back a rival hat or scarf for its rarity value and to show others you had made the trip. Soon, for younger fans, it also offered opportunities for scanning, buying – and sometimes stealing – designer leisure gear not yet available in the UK. Young scousers in Paris for the European Cup Final of 1981, for example, eschewed the usual tourist sites giving priority instead to an ultimately fruitless search for a mythical Adidas [trainers] Centre in the city (Goodwin and Straughan, 1996: 39). As economic depression intensified in Liverpool during the Thatcher years, so too did the determination of those on the margins of the legitimate enterprise culture to continue to strut their stuff; especially as football supporters from the South began to work on well-established North/South footballing divisions by taunting rivals from north of Watford with hefty money wads or even by the 'flashing' of designer underpants! (see Williams, 1991). On Liverpool match trips abroad, while the majority got on with routine football travel, other forces were stirring. Apart from the usual hunt for free food and drink, attractive options for 'work' at matches abroad now narrowed down to two main targets: the travelling 'professionals' took on the jewellery stores; the committed 'casuals' could run easily through a continental sports shop or a men's outfitters. Billy Wilson, a young Kopite at the time, followed style trends in the city like many young men did – probably a little *too* closely (Kelly, 1993: 46–8):

> The late 1970s and the early 1980s were the period of the 'style wars' . . . Sports gear was the essential ingredient, preferably exotic, continental brands. It has been said that most of it was 'lifted' from unsuspecting shops on the continent at away European ties. So, they'd be kitted out in continental anoraks/training tops/cycling tops/sports coats. Then the trainers had to be the correct type to be cool . . . [In] the late 1970s/early 1980s I recall wedge haircuts being very essential to any cool Liverpool fan. After the Italian games in 1984 and 1985 a lot of Italian banners, tops and hats were sported on the Kop . . . I would say that the Kop drops something when they see that other clubs' supporters have copied their ideas, whether it be clothes, banners or whatever . . . Liverpool supporters feel they created this whole 'new-mod' scene, and laughed off counter-claims from London and Manchester.

This interest in stealing at football abroad seems to be an *English*, rather than simply a Liverpool theme (Williams et al., 1989). But the focus by what was always a small minority of Liverpool fans on stealing and 'grifting' around football and elsewhere, is also probably quite a common feature of life in those declining post-industrial seaports which house a large and vibrant unskilled urban underclass. The combination of regional separateness, an intense focus on football as an expression of local aspiration and identity, the centrality of sea trade in local economies, coupled with industrial decline and innovative street cultures draws strong connections, for example, between the dominant 'structures of feeling' of the city of Liverpool and those in 'independent' southern European cities such as Marseilles and Naples (see Bromberger, 1993).

Responses of other Liverpool fans to this kind of behaviour were ambivalent. On the one hand, there was fury at the easy crude stereotypes, increasingly peddled on TV and elsewhere, about the alleged dishonesty of *all* people from Liverpool. These sorts of affront were also opposed later, as we shall see, by Liverpool football fanzines. Such media stereotypes continue unabated in the early twenty-first century along with tired and routine abuse from rival fans that Liverpudlians all 'sign on', live in 'slums', and are, predictably, 'cheating scousers'. On the other hand, although stealing on football trips was never sanctioned by the majority of Liverpool supporters, it probably became grudgingly accepted by many; after all, it was reckoned, this sort of *instrumental* hooliganism was 'better' than fans *fighting*, and at least it never disrupted the game. Targets for theft were also, usually, larger anonymous businesses *outside* Merseyside, and, if abroad, well, the continentals looked as if they could at least *afford* it. Hard times, it was reasoned, produce unavoidable costs.

Orchestrating the so-called 'style wars' back in Liverpool from the early 1980s was *The End* fanzine, inspirational and pseudish offspring of musician/fan Pete Hooton and colleagues, and arbiter of all things stylish in football, music and club cultures in the city (see also Redhead, 1991; 1997). Gradually, the very strong music base of the early issues of *The End* faded, to be overtaken by endless accounts of the designer labels which were 'in', those which were now *passé*, and exhaustive theses on trainers, haircuts and exactly how to wear jeans. Over? On *top* of trainers? Split, flared or straight? Here, too, was contained the identikit profile of the new, true Liverpool 'scally': love of the right (usually Indie) music, and clothes; adeptness at robbing; keen on having a draw (smoking dope), rather than sinking gallons of ale; being scandalized by ignorant 'woollybacks' (from nearby St Helens, Warrington, and especially from 'agricultural' Leeds); and showing open resistance to any media-stimulated form of music or football cultural shift – no Merseyside football fan would ever describe *himself* as a 'casual', less still join some named football 'firm'. Topping all of this was an explicit and appalled rejection of the real hooligan 'gobshites' elsewhere who were still trashing football grounds and attacking 'anoraks' or 'woollybacks' (ordinary fans).

In fact, throughout the 1970s and 1980s hooligan groups at Liverpool, all still tied, unconventionally, to particular parts of the city, were best known elsewhere and in Liverpool itself less for their organization or their general fighting prowess than they were for their alleged dangerousness when faced in Liverpool, for their commitment to 'robbin', for their outrageous expertise in 'bunking in' at away matches and, on some occasions especially later when in Europe, for their full-on project crime (Williams, 1988: 16). In general, Liverpool hooligans were not typically well known at all for the sort of nihilistic and sometimes racist violence and vandalism which, increasingly, characterized some English football hooligan crews – at Manchester United, at Leeds United, and at Chelsea in the 1970s, for example. Away travel, and especially some matches at home, might bring unavoidable and pleasurable contact with 'their lads', of course; but hooligan traditions on Merseyside had never easily sanctioned simply expressive forms of violence around football, especially if they threatened to bleed, uncontrollably, into the staging of the match itself (see, Cotton, 1996; Edge, 1999: 142–4). In the early 1980s, in fact, the Liverpool police, strategically, denied knowledge of any *named* Liverpool football gangs at all, though the fighting which sometimes went on in Utting Avenue outside the away end at Anfield made it clear that some locals were still 'well up' for any serious challenges from outside the city (Williams, 1988: 21).

These notions, and the still dominant public profile of younger Liverpool football supporters as sometimes 'fly' *football* fans, rather than fighting hooligans, are among the reasons why the tragic incidents at the Heysel Stadium in 1985 hit the city so hard, of course, and why they also brought instant – and understandable, if probably ill-judged – assertions from Merseyside that those involved simply 'could not be from Liverpool' (Williams, 1986). In short, this locally valued image of authentic Liverpool 'scals' – promoted in fanzines such as *The End* and among young men in the city, as essentially sharp urban rogues who could 'look after themselves' when they needed to, who could organize their own, illicit enterprise and consumption cultures, and who loved their football – was about to come under some very close scrutiny. Europe was about to go badly wrong for Liverpool.

More generally, this determined *separation* of football – or, at least, *the match* – from 'trouble' at Liverpool, both confirmed and reinforced the notion, still strongly held in the city, that the fans of the club *valued* and protected the sport rather more than was the case in cities such as London, Manchester and Leeds, where hooliganism had been allowed to take a much more central and disruptive hold, especially in the 1970s. This tied in with ideas about the more 'sophisticated' football allegedly played by the Liverpool club in the 1970s and 1980s, which combined the physical attributes of the English game with the patience and technique more usually associated with football on the continent (see Chapter Four). Liverpool FC's place as a fixture in European football competition from the mid-1960s onwards also imbued local football cultures with a sense that the club's fans were both more knowledgeable and, increasingly, more sporting than those elsewhere in England, especially as they welcomed to the city fans and clubs from some of the continent's less familiar outposts. This general sense of the club and its supporters as passionate *and* insightful and gracious about the game was something which was also sustained, of course, by the relatively benign national media image of footballing Liverpudlians, at least in the 1960s and 1970s, as seen through the prism of the Kop.

There is, clearly, a lot of local chauvinism solidly at work here, but all these mythologized traits – these football stories that people told and retold about themselves in the city – also contributed to real local traditions which are still guarded and celebrated at Liverpool, and which are difficult to track in quite the same form elsewhere. This generosity of footballing spirit lives on at Anfield. Visiting goalkeepers continue, almost always, to be applauded into the Kop goal, and sections of the home crowd, almost always, show their respect for 'good football' played by the opposition. Booing home players, or jeering at ex-Liverpool players who return to Anfield with other clubs is also generally condemned among the club's fans and is asserted to be 'not the Liverpool way'. Few Liverpool players, in any case, have left the club in acrimonious circumstances in order, provocatively, to 'better themselves' elsewhere, unless, of course, they went abroad.

An example of this local feature came after another damaging Liverpool home defeat in 1999, this time by the then newly-promoted Watford. It produced the 'usual' Kop response of warm applause for the visitors. The reception drew approving comment from Watford manager, Graham Taylor, but it also resulted in a public appreciation of the grace shown by Liverpool fans in defeat, written by Peter Drury for the *Independent* (20 August 1999):

> It remains a rare pleasure to visit a match at Liverpool FC. The Kop makes it so . . . Nobody booed when the Watford team-sheet was read out; everybody clapped when the Watford goalkeeper ran towards them for the start of the second half. Then at the end – and here was the highlight for anyone who clings, anachronistically, onto ideals of mutual respect, sportsmanship or simple decency – they stayed behind to applaud their victorious visitors . . .
>
> On the Kop they love Liverpool but they understand that, without an opponent, there isn't a game. Without Watford and Swansea, and even Everton and Manchester United, Liverpool is a pretty pointless entity. Pointless is precisely what Saturday became for Liverpool. Happily, the Kop offered that pointlessness some meaning.

Drury exaggerates, of course, the 'sporting' ethos of the Kop: his comments seem much more in tune, in fact, with the more middle-class notions of fair play associated with sports such as cricket and rugby union, rather than with the desperate desire to win, at almost all costs, vividly expressed on almost all football terraces in the North virtually since the game was professionalized in the late nineteenth century (see Holt, 1989). Nevertheless, his account is properly appreciative of values which are still cherished by many Kopites: namely, a willingness to concede to a deservedly better or fighting performance by the opposition, perhaps especially if it is from a skilled foreign foe or from a battling and courageous domestic underdog. This sporting cosmopolitanism, especially in relation to foreign clubs and players, coexisted, however, with powerful forms of 'domestic' racist exclusion in the home crowd: as visiting *foreign* black players might, on occasions, be lauded by Liverpool fans for their skill and vision, so *local* black people – black *Liverpudlians* – saw, and occasionally experienced, the Kop as an exclusive and hostile space (see Chapter Six). In the mid-1980s, racism and xenophobia were about to loom large in the Liverpool story abroad.

Heysel: the end of Europe

Getting a handle on the seriousness of hooligan cultures in terms of their effects on 'ordinary' Liverpool fans in the 1970s and 1980s is not always easy. Up until 1980, crowds at Anfield continued to top an average of over 40,000, reaching club record levels of 47,221 as late as 1976/77, and during an extraordinary and unprecedented period of individual English football club success. In nineteen seasons from 1972/3 Liverpool won an astonishing eleven League titles, finishing out of the top two clubs only once. In 1980/81, as the club 'slumped' to fifth place in the League while still winning the European Cup for a third time, Anfield crowds fell to an average of 37,547, and stayed broadly around the same mark (below 40,000) throughout the 1980s, even as League Championships and European and domestic Cups were delivered to Liverpool 4, as if by order.

Was this drop in attendances a sign of a 'hooligan effect'? Possibly, though after the deep shock of Heysel in 1985, and even though some long-time fans probably stopped attending matches, Anfield attendances actually went up in the 1985/86 'double' season, against the background of what was initially an open-ended ban on all English clubs from European competition, and a national slump in English match-attendance figures. The 1980s fall in Liverpool home attendances was probably associated more with the troubled image of the sport and the effects of economic depression in the city, even as numbers of fans at Anfield drawn from *outside* Liverpool were probably already rising (Williams, 1997). Everton's average home crowd, rather more locally drawn than Liverpool's, collapsed in 1983/84 to below 20,000, the lowest figure at Goodison since before the First World War, though it soon recovered again as Everton then produced a Champion-ship team in 1985.

Watching matches only at home can, of course, insulate one from the worst effects of hooliganism. The 'fun' was definitely in travelling away. There may be some generational effects also at play here. For Alan Edge, for example, the dreaded 'hooligans' at football were simply 'bastards' who had quite maliciously spoiled the traditions and experience of supporting football for older fans who had also loyally followed the club, home and away, in the 'peaceful' eras of the 1950s and 1960s, before match transport or even motorways were at hand (Edge, 1999: 141–5). For some younger male fans, of course, the prospects for some argy-bargy with the police and rival fans was increasingly just part of a 'lively' afternoon at the match. For all those in between, the aggressive tribalism which now characterized fan conflict at the sport was simply something to observe and to be both avoided and endured.

Accounts presented since that time of Liverpool hooliganism in the 1970s and 1980s read like a nostalgia call for thin adventure yarns in which fights just 'happen' and young girls are even casually 'gang-banged' in the back of football coaches (Cotton, 1996). How serious was it all? Writers such as Scraton, for example, actually seem totally confused by the hooliganism question, at one point bemoaning the racism, sexism and homophobia of the terraces (but not the violence?) in the 1980s (1999: 10), and the next, offering what others (Lea and Young, 1984) might describe as a 'left idealist' argument about media-orchestrated moral panics and national statistical trends on football hooligan arrests in the 1980s which are taken to confirm that the State and its agents had simply 'exaggerated' the hooligan problem all along (Scraton, 1999: 30).

In a sense, the tragedy at Heysel in 1985 temporarily stilled the views of those who merely dismissed hooliganism as a media 'fabrication', or else as just the universal and timeless, harmless rituals of working-class 'lads' (though such accounts were not slow to return later. See for example Armstrong, 1998). There was pious bile after Heysel from the hated (in Liverpool, certainly) bucolic, little-Englander Thatcher Government, of course, which clearly could see no role for itself in creating the public climate which was so ripe in England for the existence and promotion of the sort of casual xenophobia and machismo which underpinned events there and which had led indirectly to the deaths of 39 mainly Italian fans. (Racism, of course, was hardly unknown in Liverpool.) Instead, talk among Mrs Thatcher's Ministers was soon of bringing more (middle-class?) families into football, of identity cards for all fans, and of new police campaigns aimed at finally bringing the hooligan to heel (see Giulianotti, 1994; King, 1998).

In Liverpool, itself, sentiments after Heysel were mixed, ranging from deep shock and real shame that some people from the city were directly involved in such an appalling football tragedy, to open anger at the predictably spiteful and vicious press coverage that football, and especially the city, attracted as a result of the disaster. The city's strong self-identity, its semi-Celtic local culture, its long-term industrial decline and depopulation, and its social, cultural and geographical relative isolation from the mainstream of Englishness, all allied to a formal and deep popular opposition to the politics of national government in Britain in the 1980s, turned Liverpool in on itself for mutual support after Heysel, as would also happen again later following the disaster at Hillsborough (Walter, 1991).

Initially convincing claims that London-based racists might have had a hand in events in Brussels surfaced soon, but they were never proven, and knowledgeable Liverpool fans 'on the ground' were also unconvinced by this explanation of events. There was understandable local anger, at the quite abject performance of UEFA officials in siting the Final match at such a poorly appointed stadium in Brussels,

and at their ill-advised arrangements for ticket sales and distribution for w.
after all, the blue riband match in European club football. Peter Robinsc
Liverpool club's Chief Executive, had warned UEFA beforehand that the stac
and its ticketing arrangements were unsatisfactory, possibly dangerous, by English
standards. No heed was taken of his remarks.

Suggestions in the press and on TV from fans returning to Merseyside, however,
that Italian fans simply should not have been in adjacent pens to Liverpool
supporters and that *this*, and flimsy lateral stadium fencing, was the major reason
for the tragedy, came uncomfortably close to victim-blaming. Were we, perversely,
demanding at Heysel the sorts of spectator pens or unclimbable fences which
actually contributed to killing fans, later, at Hillsborough? Violence aimed by AS
Roma fans at Liverpool supporters after the previous Final in Rome in 1984 was
also, plausibly, raised as a possible contributory cause. This may well have played
a part. But citing this was also as if proposing that violent retribution might have
been *reasonably* sought by Liverpudlians on *any* available Italian in 1985, even
those drawn from Juventus in the *North* of Italy.

Difficult to accept, too, were chauvinist claims by some returning Liverpool
fans that the inept Belgian police were *really* to blame because they were simply
too *cowardly* to intervene against earlier Juventus hooliganism, or in the exchanges
between rival fans which took place before the fatal charge (see Williams, 1986).
In short, Heysel clearly had plenty of the ingredients of what now passed pretty
much for *accepted* young male supporter rituals at English football, if not elsewhere
in Europe. Taken abroad, and placed suddenly out of context in a crumbling stadium
and with a hesitant police force, and disaster was in the offing. Pete Hooton, himself,
saw it all unfold (Taylor and Ward, 1993: 243–4):

> It was the type of skirmish that you'd seen 100, 200 times before, on grounds all round
> the country, over a fifteen year period and you thought to yourself, 'Well, that's a skirmish
> and within a couple of minutes there'll be a police-line there and they'll force both sets
> of fans back and there'll be a no-man's land of 50 metres.' That didn't happen. That's
> when people started to think, 'What's going to happen here?' . . . There was no one
> taking control . . . People realised the police were actually scared. It was a sense of,
> 'There'll be a bit of trouble.' I don't think anyone thought of walls collapsing anyway,
> but you've got to apportion blame to Liverpool fans because they charged over . . . It
> was a sense of *fait accompli* in a way: 'This is our end, get out.' It wasn't getting
> controlled and people panicked.

Comments such as these offered the context for setting Heysel against the backcloth
of more than fifteen years of routine football violence by English football fans at
home and abroad (see Williams et al., 1989). As Hooton suggests, however, it was
difficult to take the moral high ground on Merseyside by arguing that scousers
had 'only' really ever been abroad on football and 'robbin' escapades, and that

the *real* English hooligans actually resided in small 'woollyback' English towns and in London. This was especially difficult, too, when published Liverpool fans' despatches emerged later, reporting on both their 'shopping' abroad *and* their own minor football tussles on foreign soil (see Cotton, 1996).

In the main, however, it was certainly *true* that the Liverpool club and its fans had had a 'good' record at football abroad, especially when compared to the violent and sometimes racist trashings dished out by other English crews over many years (Williams et al., 1989). Many Liverpool fans were also completely estranged from the England national side in the 1980s – Ireland was favoured by many, and the England team was, in any case, southern-based, and was profoundly *her* (Thatcher's) team – and so Liverpudlians had relatively little to do with the extreme England hooliganism on the continent in the 1970s and 1980s (Williams, 1986). But Heysel? Well, no matter what the real intentions in Brussels, this was now something on quite a different scale.

One positive outcome of Heysel was the setting up in Liverpool, in 1985, of a new, non-club-based, national supporters group, the Football Supporters Association (FSA), by long-standing club supporters Peter Garrett and Rogan Taylor. The FSA was also the springboard for a new national supporter fanzine movement, which later sprinkled some of its authors among the established football writers and in sports television (Haynes, 1995). The FSA was also central to the public debate about the second major football disaster involving Liverpool supporters in the 1980s: this time the club's followers were clearly involved as *victims* rather than as alleged perpetrators.

Heysel, on the face of it at least, had done little to disrupt the established *football* pattern at home. Although all English clubs – including new Champions, Everton – were banned from Europe, in 1985/86 Liverpool won the domestic 'double' for the first time, and under new player-manager Dalglish began to build another impressive team for the late 1980s. Only a surprise FA Cup Final loss to lowly Wimbledon prevented another Liverpool 'double' in 1987/88. But the club was soon faced by another spectator tragedy of such proportions that not even the trauma of Heysel could offer adequate preparation.

Hillsborough: new nightmares

For those who have followed the Hillsborough case – and in Liverpool, even now, it is seldom ever really off the public agenda for football followers at Anfield, and for others – certain key phrases about the Inquiry hearings covering the afternoon of 15 April 1989 have now taken on an almost totemic resonance: 'the 3.15 p.m. cut off point'; 'accidental death'; 'defective camera 5'; 'disgraceful lies'; 'missing video tapes'; 'the truth'; and so on. TV coverage has also put some of these phrases into the national domain. Nevertheless, it is still incredible just how many people seemed to know so little of the important detail of the incidents in Sheffield, at least until the Jimmy McGovern ITV drama about the tragedy was screened in 1996. Hillsborough also remains sensitively high in the public consciousness of the city because of the highly moralistic way it has been linked by the national press and TV with wider social issues in Liverpool, including the alleged excessive 'sentimentality' of people in the city, but especially perhaps the social context of the later Jamie Bulger killing – poverty, parenting, family dysfunction, etc. – and with Liverpool's alleged endemic problem of crime.

I do not want to rehearse again here in detail the events of 15 April 1989, or to look at length at what happened to the families of the bereaved later. That can easily be followed elsewhere (Scraton, 1999; Scraton et al., 1995; Taylor et al., 1995). It is relevant, however, to try to say something more about the wider context of Hillsborough, outside of football.

More specifically, the promises of broadly collectivist social policies for wealth-creation and of 'one nation' welfarist social policies in Britain had already grown distant and hazy by the late 1960s, and by the 1980s the earlier consensuses around notions of local and regional 'civic pride' and around a sense of collective 'social cohesion' seemed to have been substantially dislodged, as policy aims, by national government strategies which lay a much more profound stress on the importance of ownership and choice in the private sphere and on individual striving for personal success of the kind most closely associated with 'Thatcherite' social and economic policies.

If, under the twin pressures of commodification and privatization in 1980s Britain, public spaces were neglected and 'a narrower range of "strangers" are met in public space, and, increasingly, experiences of public life are with a more homogeneous group of others' (Brill, 1989: 30), then these developments suggest an important theoretical and socio-political connection between disasters of that period in public places in England of a kind little made in the press coverage of Hillsborough, or in the report of the official Inquiry into the disaster, chaired by Lord Justice Taylor (1990). In this sense, according to Ian Taylor (1991: 12), for example, such disasters – on public ferries; on the railways; in the London Underground; at football matches, etc. – were all

[C]learly an expression of a kind of careless inefficiency and neglect for the public interest which characterises the British service industry in general. The Hillsborough disaster was the product of a quite consistent and ongoing lack of interest on the part of the owners and directors of English league clubs in the comfort, well-being and safety of their paying spectators: this particular failure within football that I am condemning is a generalised problem in English culture – the lack of regard by authority (and thereby what we now call 'service providers') for the provision of well-being and security of others.

If the wider context for the tragedy is, properly, a debate about public policy and public provision in Britain, in *footballing* terms Hillsborough was much more about the direction and management of the sport and of its spectators. The disaster was not of course *caused* by hooliganism, but it was certainly fundamentally *about* what had become routine collective responses to problems which were now regularly produced by some fans at English football. How else could the necessary balance between safety and security be so badly wrong at a major football match in Britain as it was in the late 1980s (see Ian Taylor, 1991)?

Once police hesitancy and mismanagement of Liverpool supporters outside Hillsborough had led to the ushering in of the fateful unsupervised group of fans who were simply seeking a decent vantage point for the game but who now added to the overcrowding in unescapable pens, the very design of the Sheffield stadium offered little scope for remedial action at that late stage. Given the awful, but hardly unimaginable, catalogue of police mistakes on the day, Hillsborough was simply like many other English football grounds of the time – a potential death trap. The general chaos, horror and lack of preparedness for something on this scale at football, and early police presumptions that what they were seeing must be *hooliganism*, not unfolding disaster, meant that the seriously injured (who might now be saved in similar circumstances) then had little chance of survival (see Scraton, 1999).

If the disaster itself was avoidable and tragic, the treatment later by the police of the families of the dead and injured was little short of inhumane and repellent (see Taylor et al., 1995). Personal and professional damage limitation – the attempted rationalization, or 'cover up' – soon swung brutally into action. What was truly shameful here, to many observers, were the police attempts to continue to fly the drunken fans/broken gate stories about alleged Liverpool 'hooligans' – later aided by the *Sun* – and seemingly to treat the bereaved like little more than contemptible rubbish. After all, these were just football supporter families (many people on Merseyside would add 'from Liverpool' here), people with no obvious power to organize or to question the police case, or even their own desperate treatment at the hands of the South Yorkshire force. 'They *can* be rubbished', must have been the thinking from some of these public 'servants'. How little these senior police officers knew (see Moneypenny's Afterword at the end of this book for more on the fans' struggle).

Ironically, of course, many of those supporters who died in Sheffield would have been among the very first in the ground, arriving early to get a good 'spec' behind the goal. They would, in fact, have been among the very *last* supporters to have been 'on the ale' on the day. Many Liverpool and Forest fans at Hillsborough *had* been drinking, of course. This was English FA Cup semi-final day, after all, traditionally a major day for a football 'bevvy', as most young (and older) male fans still know. Insistent police questioning on this aspect implied that simply having a drink somehow made quite innocent fans culpable for their own deaths.

But Jimmy McGovern's Hillsborough TV drama documentary also takes obvious, but important, liberties on this and on other points, presumably for dramatic and possibly 'political' effect. According to the TV drama-doc, apparently, *no* fan goes ticketless to Sheffield, or even for a single pint before the match, as the police later pummel away grotesquely with questions to bemused and broken parents and relatives about football and drink. Drinking, in fact, is strategically *expunged* by McGovern from the culture on this day. Nor do we get any sense from the TV version – though we do get it from the real ordinary police constable statements which emerged much later – of quite how *damaged* relations had generally become between some young male supporters and the police at football at this time. This, sadly, was just one of the reasons why police responses were so completely inappropriate on the day.

In fact, until quite disastrous policing decisions intervene, McGovern's TV depiction of an ultimately tragic football day, arguably and oddly, in fact looks much more like the spruced up 'new' football experience of the late 1990s than it does an account of the then sometimes deeply troubled sport and the macho posturings 'across the barricades' more characteristic of policing and fan cultures at English football in the 1980s. One learns nothing here, for example, about how or why these ugly, sunken football pens – real death traps – had come almost to be accepted by many fans then, and in one of our most 'modern' football grounds.

Some other context, which reveals much more about troubling aspects of the general character of the sport and of prevailing footballing masculinities at that time and before, is probably also important here in order to understand exactly how the police – but also we ourselves, as fans – could get it quite so badly wrong at football in 1989. This sort of necessary broader contextualization, with its realist account of then existing English male terrace culture, is present in some academic accounts of Hillsborough (see for example Taylor, 1991), but it is arguably, still missing from some of the later, established descriptions and explanations of events on 15 April 1989 which are still more strongly favoured on Merseyside (see for example Scraton, 1999; Scraton et al., 1995).

Fans at Liverpool today

Today, of course, following the public inquiry into the disaster in Sheffield, most of the brutal perimeter fences have gone from major football grounds and so, at the big clubs, sadly, have the terraces. The Liverpool Kop finally succumbed to seats on 30 April 1994, its emotional last stand made against ungracious visitors, Norwich City; another 0–1 defeat. When Minister for Sport, Tony Banks, commented in October 1997 that he might look again at the question of bringing back 'safe' terraces, he was taken immediately to task by the Hillsborough Family Support Group in Liverpool, who spoke of the important progress on safety and on hooliganism at football since 1989. The *symbolic* shift to seats is probably also important here; a sign of the sport finally moving on from a generally troubled period in the 1980s. This was, perhaps, more strongly felt in Liverpool than elsewhere.

By the end of its standing days, in fact, the Kop was but a pale ghost of earlier manifestations, licensed as it was after Hillsborough to hold only 16,480 standing spectators, way below its early 28,000 capacity. The 12,000 fans who are now allowed to *sit* on the new Kop were soon accused, locally, of assuming the general demeanour of an *audience*, waiting to be engaged by events on the pitch, rather than a passionate and committed *crowd*, urging the team on and straining to be involved as the day's drama unfolds. The Kop's bards still work hard at their new songs and chants – a whole raft of new material emerged to greet new, foreign players in 1999 – but it *is* much more difficult in the seats to rouse fellow supporters into song. Noticeably, too, very few local, unaccompanied teenage fans of the sort who made up an important part of the Kop's original standing and singing core now attend at Anfield. Can they afford to? Would they want to sit?

Most longstanding fans at Liverpool probably share the deep ambivalence about 'new' football expressed in Kevin Sampson's excellent seasonal diary for 1997/98: they are glad that away games are not quite the bear pit they could sometimes be in the 1980s, but they are also saddened that the culture has lost some of its passion and edge from that time (Sampson, 1998: 46). Certainly, Simon Inglis's (1996: 224) assessment of the new Kop as, 'exceptionally well designed and logically arranged . . . providing clear circulation routes throughout', was hardly likely to set supporters' pulses racing in this new era.

Generally, football supporters in England are also dealt with by the authorities rather differently now. Like it or not, they are a little more *cared* about these days. Fans probably think about their own safety a little more now, too, though the rolling, standing Kop in its pomp, offered for many a sense of collective security and belonging which is quite lacking from the highly individualized experience of watching from seats (see, Chapter Nine). But the seated Kop is no middle-class enclave, far from it. Nor does it lack for wit or for seeking out inspiration for laughter in the course of a match, something noticed by the new manager, Houllier. Although memories of the old standing terrace are themselves highly mythologized, the Kop *is* less collective and less spontaneous today; it misses its ribald and fluid young core, from where most of the early songs sprouted. These days, attempts at songs often roll forlornly around small banks of seats all over the Kop, most of them not taken up by the whole. The Kop, perhaps inevitably like most football 'ends' – and public culture itself – is also cruder – and more cruel – today than it was in its prime.

But new sorts of abuses of *spectators* also emerged in the 1990s. If there was a Thatcherite contempt for the public and for public services and spaces a decade before, now, in times of relative plenty for the sport, there came a new contempt, this time for the much trumpeted football *customer*. Clubs followed the letter, but hardly the spirit, of Lord Justice Taylor's post-Hillsborough recommendations on seats and new facilities at football. He envisaged access for all fans and at reasonable prices, something which is certainly possible today (Taylor, 1990). The reality, in the 1990s, was very different, as ticket prices soared and 'excluded' fans, including many in Liverpool, turned to TV coverage in order to try to remain 'connected' with their local clubs (Williams, 1999; Williams and Perkins, 1999). Despite these effects, towards the end of that decade, most Liverpool home games sold out in advance, and the club began to discuss moving to a new 70,000 seat stadium nearby (see Chapter Ten).

'Post-fan' Liverpool Culture

In Liverpool today, at least in the 'post-fan' (Giulianotti, 1999) reflexive realm of local supporter fanzines, four 'supporter' issues, apart from spiralling ticket prices, were major talking points in the 1990s in the main fanzines, *Through the Wind and Rain* (TTWAR) and *Red All Over the Land* (RAOTL). One, inevitably, is Hillsborough and its aftermath, which was covered, extensively. A second is a near-obsessive concern in the fanzines – especially in the local TTWAR – with the *media image* of the city of Liverpool and, as part of this, with relations with Manchester United, the new, and much nastier, 'Everton' for the late-modern period. A third is a more general theme concerning the alleged changing character and geographical spread of Liverpool supporters – and their need to be better schooled into more 'appropriate' forms of fandom. A fourth is the question of how the club could best respond to the new economic realities of football in the 'global' age. I have said quite a bit about Hillsborough already. Let me now end by saying, briefly, something on each of these other key themes.

The sourness of the Liverpool/Manchester United relationship is widely traced, in Liverpool at least, to an alleged lack of media respect for the great Liverpool teams of the 1970s and 1980s, and the corresponding supposed fawning by the media over much less successful United teams of the same era and since. Relative recent economic and social decline in Liverpool is also liable to play a part here, especially as Manchester has profited in recent years. It is clear, however, that this media effect was something also deeply felt by players at Liverpool during this period, and it was used by coaches at the club to motivate the team, especially in matches against United (Souness, 1999: 84). In the 1990s, media treatment of United became 'caught up' somewhat by the real success of the Manchester club under Alex Ferguson, though this did not really diminish some Liverpool fans' focus on United as a convenient local hate-figure to supersede even Everton.

In the mid-1980s, negative sentiments between United and Liverpool followers reached something of an extreme point, with fans and even on one occasion *players* suffering attacks at the fixture. By the early 1990s, events at Hillsborough had quelled the use by Liverpool fans of the inflammatory, so-called, 'Munich song', which referred to United fans and staff killed in the 1958 air tragedy (see, TTWAR, No. 11, 1991). This improved relations between Liverpool and United fans for a time. But in 1995 another watershed was probably reached when the Kenny Dalglish-managed Blackburn Rovers arrived at Anfield needing a win on the final day of the League season to win the Championship and thus deprive Manchester United of the title. Some Liverpool fans openly wore Blackburn shirts at the match and cheered Alan Shearer's opening goal for the visitors. Scuffles broke out among home fans on the Kop as small pockets of Liverpool supporters, enthusiastically, supported the opposition. A late winning goal for Liverpool was greeted with only stifled cheers in the crowd, and apparent gloom on the pitch – until it was learned that United had failed to win, thus giving the title to Blackburn after all; but more importantly not to United.

These incidents reveal something of the real complexities of football club support and enmities, of course, and they also point to some of the ambiguities of the Liverpool fans' approach to United. For example, most Liverpool supporters refuse to take up the more generalized distaste for United – by sharing an identity with rival supporters in singing anti-United songs – on the grounds that this both condemns Liverpool to a common, 'other' status, and reveals publicly an unhealthy and obsessive concern with their regional rivals. Some fans born in Liverpool also insist on continuing to hold up *Everton* as the 'proper' focus for fan enmity, thus stressing the continuing importance of *localism* for authentic club support. At the same time, however, Liverpool football fanzines have been full of pages of snippets of press coverage of United and Manchester (TTWAR's *Mancwatch and Satanic Curses*; *Neighbourhood Watch* in RAOTL, etc.) which are used to 'confirm' the alleged media obsession with United, for example, at the Manchester based North West edition of the *Mirror*, known locally in Liverpool football circles such as these, as the *Daily Manc* (see, TTWAR, *passim*).

This kind of fanzine coverage, which also defends the city more generally from alleged media bias, is of course one way of trying to 'shore up' support for the club against the affections of those who come to support the club from *outside* Liverpool. It is also, in part, a response to anti-Liverpool invective from the much more vicious United fanzine, *Red Issue*. But it also reflects something deeper about the city's character and conscious 'separateness' during recent hard times, when it has been such a focal point for the effects of damaging shifts in economic and industrial trends and policies – which have been much less powerfully felt in

Manchester – and for the harsh, and often unfair, glare of the media on a range of incidents connected to the city, spanning the Toxteth riots, and the Heysel and Hillsborough football disasters through to the Jamie Bulger case.

The alleged changing *character and geographical spread* of Liverpool supporters in the 'new' football era has also been something of a focus for Liverpool fanzine insights. This is especially interesting because the two main Liverpool FC fanzines are made up of one edited locally, in Bootle (*Through the Wind and Rain*) and one edited outside the city, in Loughborough (the appropriately named *Red All Over the Land*). Fans come from all over Britain and beyond to watch Liverpool home matches these days, of course. In 1997, around one in six (16 per cent) Liverpool season ticket holders lived more than 50 miles from Anfield; the figure for Everton was just 6 per cent. Of Liverpool season ticket holders, 73 per cent were born within 20 miles of the club, compared to 87 per cent of Everton fans who were born close to Goodison. Only one-quarter of those season ticket fans who travelled 50 miles or more to Liverpool home matches were actually locally born (Williams, 1997). Everton *seemed* a more local club than Liverpool. Clearly, some fans travelling to home matches at Anfield were returning to the city; but many more were signalling the status of Liverpool as a national, and international, club second only in this respect in England to Manchester United.

Routinely, on match days now, Liverpool fans from Scandinavia and on occasions from Germany, especially, are identifiable in local pubs or on the Kop. Small groups of British *Asian* Liverpool fans, mainly drawn from outside the city, are also a new feature on the seated Kop. The Liverpool club also has an International Supporters Club, numbering some 60,000 members, and chat on Liverpool fan web sites is frequently sprinkled with contributions from Liverpool followers around Europe and in South East Asia and the Americas.

There are a number of issues at stake here: one is the social and geographical origins of fans; another is maintaining the quality and supposed 'uniqueness' of Liverpool support; a third is the emergence of a new kind of consumer/fan at Anfield. Symptomatic of these sorts of concern is a letter to TTWAR (No. 33, 1997: 30). Here, the 'sit back and entertain us' section of the new Kop is taken to task for its general lack of support and its booing and moaning at home players. These are, the writer concludes, 'probably the same people who are emblazened with every piece of merchandise going'. In TTWAR No. 37 (Winter, 1997) a regular contributor's tirade against 'out of town supporters' provoked a 'Tebbit-test' response in No. 38 (1998: 51) from a London-based Liverpool supporter of 25 years' standing, who admits that he 'never once realised that because I had the audacity to be born outside the city I should be excluded from Anfield – presumably unless I pass some test of knowledge or loyalty'. In No. 41 (Winter, 1998: 51) an *Asian* Liverpool supporter – the fanzines are one of the few cultural spaces in the city where 'race' is featured even slightly as an issue in relation to the club –

welcomes the new diversity in the club's support and new attitudes towards racism, before concluding that:

> Seeing some of the passionless, uninformed, camera-clicking, burger-eating Liverworld bag wavers calling themselves 'supporters' now, I sometimes wish it was like the old days! Anfield is not a theme park, but some people are treating it like such. No wonder the atmosphere is crap.

In TTWAR No. 36 (Autumn, 1997: 25) a contributor summed up a number of related supporter/style issues when he asked:

> Where has the 'knowledgable' supporter got to? You know, the ones we used to be praised to the skies for? Well, it looks as if they've buggered off someplace. Priced out of the game, or simply disenchanted – and he's been replaced by MISTER LIVER-WORLD . . . Their lack of knowledge and lack of patience is doing my head in . . . I've worked out a foolproof plan for identifying these idiots, should you have the misfortune to be sat next to one at the match. They're sneaky, and they always wait until the game starts. A replica shirt is a clue, McManaman or Redknapp on the back makes it clearer, and the Liverworld bag between the feet is a complete giveaway. If they're wearing those trainers that look like mini-spaceships, act fast and ask a steward if you can move, there and then.

RAOTL, predictably perhaps, has a slightly different take on the issue of the club's support. For one thing it has a regular feature aimed at reporting on and promoting singing at Anfield, usually listing in a table the 'performance' of Liverpool fans home and away. It also regularly carries the lyrics to famous songs at the club. All of this is likely to be regarded as education too far for TTWAR, which assumes a much more knowing, a more local, and more 'organic' readership than does the non-local RAOTL. The latter's approach to the traditions of the club are also much more *formally* conceived, and could probably only come from *outside* Liverpool. RAOTL agonizes over the sensitive issue of loyal 'out-of-town' supporters (good) and new travelling 'day trippers' (bad). It *is* concerned about recent developments at Anfield, and it feels some hearts and minds instruction in Liverpool traditions is required for new recruits. In an article called 'Sing your own songs', in RAOTL No. 30, (1998: 37), 'Johnny Red' has his sights on members of the club's official International Supporters Club (ISC) as likely instigators of embarrassingly 'bad' singing at Anfield. He recommends, without apparent irony, a Liverpool fan induction process:

> Due to the numbers involved in starting this crap singing, their accents and the way they were dressed, I would hazard a guess that they were an ISC branch on a day out . . . I had the idea that some sort of Liverpool fans code of practice could be drawn up by

the ISC which outlines the history of the club, the fans, the Kop, etc., and various dos and don'ts. I feel that the club has an obligation to maintain our traditions or we will slide even further towards blandness . . . This could be done in the form of an 'education pack', or slide show. This may sound desperate, but something has to be done . . . We have always had the most knowledgeable and sporting fans; we are in danger of losing that reputation and something needs to be done now.

This regular emphasis in Liverpool fanzines on the real cultural *knowledge* of true fans which is set against the empty and wanton *consumerism* of new arrivals links well with the final 'supporters' issue I want to mention briefly here, namely, the alleged craven commercialism of the Liverpool club, and the recent ownership and economic policies at Liverpool. These matters have received some recent fanzine coverage on a number of fronts. There has been fury, for example, about the 'McDonaldization' of the Kop; a branch of the burger chain was controversially included in the Kop rebuild, and the famous giant yellow 'M' now adorns the great stand and even promotes a family area in the new Kop seats. In TTWAR (33, Winter, 1997: 34) an appalled correspondent suggested that:

Stewards should patrol the Kop with a big net pulling out anyone under 12 with a painted face or with a Liverworld bag, and eject them immediately. You have to be cruel to be kind. I won't harp on about commercialism, and Robinson doesn't give a fuck anyway, but the arse who permitted the 'M' on the side of the Kop should be dragged through the streets by dogs.

In similar commercial vein, a statue of the great Kop hero, Bill Shankly, which is outside the club shop, carries a crass reminder of the club sponsors' support for its construction. At Anfield, these days, one assuredly enters the branded territory of brewing giants Carlsberg and club kit sponsors Reebok. Concern over recent club kits has also focused on the overbearing role of sponsors in introducing non-traditional Liverpool colours – green, black, even blues – into club products (see, TTWAR, 15, Winter, 1992: 6).

The symbolic and topophilic importance of the stadium and the sanctity of the totems of the club are deeply important to football supporters, of course (Bale, 1994: Ch. 6). This is certainly true at Liverpool. Steven Kelly, committed editor of TTWAR, responding to readers' requests in 1997, perhaps tellingly, for more *humour* in the fanzine replied instead with a stern reminder that

The corporate infestation of Liverpool is not a laughing matter, and to trivialise everything in a, 'Oh well, what can we do, let's have a laff', sort of way is the '90s equivalent of fiddling while Rome burns. This club MEANS something to me, and to you, too, hopefully. Laugh away while they screw every last penny out of you, while they demean everything of significance to a great football club and its marvellous supporters. I'm sure Reebok, McDonalds, Carlsberg, Sky, Moores, Robinson and Parry will say, 'Keep laughing suckers' . . . Recognize the reality of football in the late 20th century, and come to the conclusion that something must be done soon. (TTWAR 35, Summer 1997: 8).

Actually, TTWAR is, darkly, very funny indeed; but it is also, importantly, *deeply* serious. These sorts of crucial issue, along with possible structural changes in the sport, continue to be debated passionately in both TTWAR and, less convincingly, in RAOTL. Ideas for a European Super League, the spread of Rupert Murdoch's TV/football business interests, the alleged 'takeover' of the sport by 'accountants' (including Liverpool's Rick Parry) and the new investment in Liverpool FC by the Granada group in 1999, are all regarded, in these *culturally* knowledgeable football circles, with deep suspicion. At Liverpool, however, perhaps more than at any other British football club, the new and corrosive corporate era for football can be comfortingly set against a recent and 'better' past, when action *on the pitch* is fondly remembered as all by which the measure of a football club was properly made. As *Prometheus* told readers of TTWAR (No. 40, Autumn, 1998: 41):

The sad, but inescapable, truth is that the game has already changed out of recognition in a very short space of time. We are still nostalgic for the Shankly and Paisley eras, when what you achieved on the pitch determined whether you were considered a contender for the greatest club in the world. The hard work, creativity and industry of the players and back room staff were enough to put us in a super league all of our own. These days, performances on the pitch seem to matter less than share dividends and corporate marketing strategies. You, there! Just pay up and shut up . . .

Nostalgia burns brightly here, of course, as the writer is happy to point out. TTWAR, especially, is an articulate, informed and an unapologetically *political* forum where the Liverpool club's past is constantly set against a less satisfying present. It proffers a profoundly local and *masculinist* cultural space – there is barely a female contributor, though little *explicit* sexism either – and it is one which also, predictably, privileges certain types of fan in the debate about authenticity: the subtext, almost always, here is that the *real* fans of the club are male, young, probably working-class and ideally local (see Chapter Nine). But this is also a voice which is an important and very *necessary* counter to the commercial output of the football club to which it is so utterly devoted. However, for all their insight and passion, for all the extraordinary knowledge and respect the fans at Liverpool have for the traditions of the club and for its great managers and players, it is not always easy to detect in these debates among fans about the 'beautiful game', a clear and workable vision of a preferred *future*. Mapping a reasonable future for *all* fans is something which is extremely difficult to prefigure, of course, in these days of the global economics of sport. The recent past? Now, *that* still beams on this Red side of Merseyside – like a veritable beacon.

References

Armstrong, G. (1998) *Football Hooligans: Knowing the Score*, Oxford: Berg.

Bale, J. (1994) *Landscapes of Modern Sport*, Leicester: Leicester University Press.

Brill, A. (1989) 'An ontology for exploring urban public life today', in *Places*, Fall: 25–30.

Bromberger, C. (1993) 'Allez L'OM, forza Juve': the passion for football in Turin and Marseilles', in S. Redhead (ed.) *The Passion and the Fashion*, Aldershot: Avebury.

Channon, H. (1976) *Portrait of Liverpool*, London: Robert Hale.

Clarke, A. (1991) 'Figuring a brighter future', in E. Dunning and C. Rojek (eds) *Sport and Leisure in the Civilising Process*, London: MacMillan.

Cotton, E. (1996) *The Voice of Anfield*, Chorley: Sport in Wood.

Dunning, E., Murphy, P. and Williams, J. (1988) *The Roots of Football Hooliganism*, London: Routledge.

Edge, A. (1999) *Faith of our Fathers: Football as a Religion*, London: Mainstream.

Giulianotti, R. (1994) 'Social identity and public order: political and academic discourses on football violence', in R. Giulianotti, et al. (eds) *Football, Violence and Social Identity*, London: Routledge.

—— (1999) *Football: a Sociology of the Global Game*, Cambridge: Polity.

Goodwin, J. and Straughan, L. (1996) *Reykjavik to Rome: Everton and Liverpool Fans in Europe*, Birkenhead: Picton.

Haynes, R. (1995) *The Football Imagination: the Rise of Football Fanzine Culture*, Aldershot: Arena.

Hill, D. (1989) *Out of his Skin: The John Barnes Phenomenen*, London: Faber & Faber

Hodgson, D. (1978) *The Liverpool Story*, London: Arthur Barker.

Holt, R. (1989) *Sport and the British*, Oxford: Oxford University Press.

Hopcraft, A. (1971) *The Football Man*, Harmondsworth: Penguin.

Inglis, S. (1996) *Football Grounds of Britain*, London: Collins Willow.

Kelly, S. (1991) *You'll Never Walk Alone: the Official Illustrated History of Liverpool FC*, London: Queen Anne Press.

—— (1993) *The Kop: the End of an Era*, London: Mandarin.

King, A. (1998) *The End of the Terraces*, London: Leicester University Press.

Lea, J. and Young, J. (1984) *What's to be done About Law and Order?* Harmondsworth: Penguin.

McClure, J. (1980) *Spike Island: Portrait of a Police Division*, London: Arrow.

Paul, D. (1998) *Anfield Voices*, Stroud: Tempus.

Redhead, S. (1991) *Football with Attitude*, Manchester: Wordsmith.

—— (1997) *Subculture to Clubcultures*, Oxford: Blackwell.

Robins, D. and Cohen, P. (1978) *Knuckle Sandwich*, Harmondsworth: Penguin.

Russell, D. (1997) *Football and the English*, Preston: Carnegie.

St John, I. (1967) *Boom at the Kop*, London: Sportsmans Book Club.

Sampson, K. (1998) *Extra Time*, London: Yellow Jersey Press.

Scraton, P. (1999) *Hillsborough: the Truth*, Edinburgh and London: Mainstream.

Scraton, P., Jemphry, A. and Coleman, S. (1995) *No Last Rights*, Liverpool: Liverpool City Council/Alden Press.

Souness, G. (1999) *Souness: The Management Years*, London: André Deutsch.

Taylor, I. (1991) 'English football in the 1990s; taking Hillsborough seriously', in J. Williams and S. Wagg (eds) *British Football and Social Change*, Leicester: Leicester University Press.

Taylor, I., Evans, K. and Fraser, P. (1996) *A Tale of Two cities: Global Change, Local feeling and Everyday Life in the North of England*, London: Routledge.

Taylor, J. (1998) *Body Horror*, Manchester: Manchester University Press.

Taylor, P. (1990) *The Hillsborough Stadium Disaster 15 April 1989: Final Report*, London: HMSO.

Taylor, R. and Ward, A., with Williams, J. (1993) *Three Sides of the Mersey An Oral History of Everton, Liverpool and Tranmere Rovers*, London: Robson.

Taylor, R., Ward, A. and Newburn, T. (1995) *The Day of the Hillsborough Disaster*, Liverpool: Liverpool University Press.

Wagg, S. (1984) *The Football World*, Brighton: Harvester.

Walter, T. (1991) 'The mourning after Hillsborough', *Sociological Review*, **39**(3) : 599–626.

Williams, J. (1986) 'White riots: the English football fan abroad', in A. Tomlinson and G. Whannel (eds) *On the Ball*, London: Pluto.

—— (1988) *Football and football hooliganism in Liverpool*, Leicester: Sir Norman Chester Centre for Football Research, University of Leicester.

—— (1991) 'Having an away day', in J. Williams and S. Wagg (eds) *British Football and Social Change*, Leicester: Leicester University Press.

—— (1997) *FA Premier League National Fan Survey, 1996/97*, Leicester: Sir Norman Chester Centre for Football Research, University of Leicester.

—— (1999) *Is It All Over: Can Football Survive the Premier League?*, Reading: South Street Press.

—— (1999) 'Safety and excitement at football: post-Hillsborough football spectator culture', in *Fire, Safety and Service Recovery in Sports Stadia*, Preston: University of Central Lancashire.

Williams, J., Dunning E. and Murphy, P. (1989) *Hooligans Abroad*, London: Routledge.

Williams, J. and Perkins, S. (1999) 'Ticket pricing, merchandising and the new football business', London: Report for the National Football Taskforce.

Williams, J. and Woodhouse, D. (1999) *Offside? the Position of Women and Football in Britain*, Reading: South Street Press.

$-6-$

From Barnes to Camara: Football, Identity and Racism in Liverpool
Dave Hill

Out of His Skin

It was a wet, windy autumn night in east London, but a bleaker one in Liverpool. I was in my car listening to the live BBC radio broadcast of the season's first Merseyside derby, giddy with rage and frustration over what I was hearing. Alan Green's commentary was not the problem. The cause of my consternation was the sound from the crowd, the unbearable eruptions of abuse from massed Evertonians every time a particular Liverpool player got anywhere near the ball.

That player was John Barnes, playing against the men from the other side of Stanley Park for the first time in the red shirt. When this match took place – October, 1987 – Barnes was already an exceptional figure in the English national game thanks both to the shining talents he'd already displayed for Watford and England, and to his unusual background as the son of a senior figure in the Jamaican military. Now, as the Evertonians' baiting rose to successions of crescendos, Barnes was also turning into the powerful symbol of a disorder within football culture, something which those inside the game seemed unable to even recognize, let alone begin to cure – racism, in many forms.

In a small way, I helped make Barnes into that symbol. First, following a second derby a week later which was similarly disfigured (there were four that season altogether), I wrote an article in the *Independent* newspaper arguing that the reactions Barnes had triggered since joining Liverpool brought sharply into focus the unchallenged prevalence of racism within English football at large and also its peculiar manifestations on Merseyside. How strange, I observed, that the city of Liverpool was the home of one of the longest-established black communities in Britain, yet its two great football teams had somehow remained almost totally white during a twenty-year period in which black players had become conspicuous at just about every other professional club in England. And this was in spite of a clear passion for the game among ordinary black Liverpudlians who played for amateur teams and followed the professional game on TV and in the press, but were almost never seen on the celebrated terraces or in the stands of Anfield or Goodison Park.

There seemed much more to find out, and plenty to be said about it. Yet, although Barnes's treatment had inspired debate in the Merseyside media, the only strong voice heard nationally was Green's who, to his great credit, condemned the 'racial stuff' on air during that first derby. Other broadcasters and virtually all the press ignored it: apparently, such crowd behaviour was to go on being accepted as 'part and parcel of the game', even when so extreme that it dominated it.

The more others failed to tackle the matter, the more intent I became on doing the job myself. I wrote a proposal for a book and my literary agent duly set about trying to sell it. Initially, she sent the idea to a number of conventional sports publishers. There were no takers. Yes, they said, they'd love to do a book about Barnes, who, to the intense of annoyance of terrace taunters up and down the land, had been the star of a series of brilliant displays by an all-conquering new-look Liverpool team assembled by manager Kenny Dalglish. But the publishers wanted an authorized biography, almost certainly a standard 'ghost job', and that wasn't what I had in mind at all.

It's worth remembering that this was in football writing's BFP period – Before *Fever Pitch* – when football books with pretentions to proper journalism were few and far between: Eamon Dunphy's *Only A Game?* (1976) Hunter Davies's *The Glory Game* (1972), Arthur Hopcraft's collection of essays and profiles *The Football Man* (1971) . . . that was about it. Furthermore, the book I wanted to write was never going to be one that John Barnes himself would wish to associate himself with, and for entirely understandable reasons. Even if any contribution he might have wished to make to it had been emollient and diplomatic to a fault, the book as a whole was certain to reflect badly on the club he had just joined, its famous local rival, many fans of both, and on the city of Liverpool itself whose cosy 1960s image as a city of good-natured scallywags was already badly damaged. First, there was the stigma of mass unemployment. In its wake the Toxteth riots – and the inquiry chaired by Lord Gifford which followed – put Liverpool's race relations under the national spotlight for the first time. And then, of course, there was the grim disaster at the Heysel stadium in Brussels, where violence by followers of Liverpool before the European Cup Final led to the deaths of thirty-nine mainly Juventus fans.

Given all this, had John Barnes assisted me in my enterprise it could only have brought a heap of trouble on his head. This would have been particularly unfortunate given that the project had been inspired by my sympathy and admiration for this remarkable player. I made a half-hearted approach to his then agent, just to be polite. I was pleasantly relieved when, as expected, I was rebuffed. I had gone through the necessary motions. Now I was free to write the book that really needed writing while leaving John Barnes equally free to say completely truthfully that he'd had nothing to do with it after it came out.

This, in fact, is exactly what happened when *Out Of His Skin: The John Barnes Phenomenon* was published in September 1989. It had finally been commissioned by that most literary of publishing houses Faber & Faber and for the decidedly modest (though very welcome) advance of £4,000. Of this, the usual ten per cent went to my agent and most of the rest was eaten up by the cost of tickets, train fares and overnight accommodation in some of Liverpool's less glamorous hotels. It was, in other words, never going to be a money-spinner for me. It did, though, sell nearly 15,000 copies – quite a respectable performance – and, best of all, it created a small but rather satisfying stink.

The book told the story of John Barnes against the social background that made his move to Liverpool so significant and his experiences there so revealing. To me, Barnes's impact at Anfield had the effect of exposing and dramatizing submerged racial issues on Merseyside and in English football at large. My thesis was that while there was never any formal anti-black policy at Anfield with regard either to players or supporters, the customs and traditions of the club had made it extremely difficult for anyone with a dark-coloured skin to thrive or feel comfortable there. There was, in other words, a sinister hidden underside to the compelling mythology around Liverpool Football Club which had evolved in the era of Bill Shankly and which contributed to and reflected the wider rough-diamond romance of Beatle City.

This mythology surrounding Liverpool FC was a powerful and, in many ways, a wonderful thing. It had had me under its spell since about the age of eight when, despite being from a modestly middle-class home in a small town in Somerset, I was captivated by the football ethos of a proletarian northern city personified by the 'hard-but-fair' reputations of Ron Yeats and Tommy Smith, the exuberance of Emlyn Hughes, the eccentricity of Tommy Lawrence, the flair of my first hero Peter Thompson on the wing, the wry, rugged populism of Shankly himself and, of course, the Kop.

Much of my infatuation with the Liverpool football team was down to the seductiveness of that certain Liverpool style conveyed through the media to me as a child just as vividly by figures as diverse as John Lennon and Jimmy Tarbuck and even by The Liver Birds. But one of the wonders of my pursuit of the John Barnes story was that I was confirmed in my belief that this was a style rooted in substance. Close to twenty years on from the day in 1970 when I sat at the bottom of the stairs in my parents house and wept over Liverpool's shock exit from the FA Cup at the hands of lowly Watford, I found myself talking to ordinary Liverpool people who were just as witty, warm and irreverent as was advertised by the Liverpool legend. My boyhood idealization of Liverpool FC still had some justification because so many of the good things I'd always believed about the city were still true. The trouble was, there was another, less attractive truth as well. This was what the John Barnes phenomenon laid bare.

Dave Hill

A New Liverpool?

So, what is the purpose of this rather lengthy recap? A small part of it is to establish that, despite being far from Liverpudlian or, these days, even a supporter of Liverpool FC (more a fascinated sympathizer, really) I have at least some credentials for the task of making sense of issues around 'race' and racism as they arise in the often unique context of Merseyside football. (I'm not black, either, since you ask, although the most gratifying compliments I've received from black people, including one or two professional footballers, was that they wouldn't have known that from reading my book.) But the main reason for starting this chapter by looking back to the events of the 1987/88 season is to evoke a sense of contrast between the situation then and the rather different situation now.

It is only thirteen years since John Barnes was, unforgettably, photographed back-heeling bananas off the pitch at Goodison Park, and he has only just hung up his boots to become chief coach at Celtic. Yet the events and passions triggered by his first appearances in a Liverpool shirt might easily be mistaken for ancient history. That is certainly the first impression created by considering the long list of black players who have subsequently turned out for the Reds.

Under Graeme Souness, Dalglish's eventual successor as Liverpool manager (following Ronnie Moran's brief spell in charge), Barnes was followed by two of the most unlikely black guys to wear a Liverpool shirt: Michael Thomas, whose last-gasp goal for Arsenal had deprived the Anfield club of the 'double' at the end of the 1988/89 season; and David James who, being a goalkeeper, played in one of the positions black footballers have always been least likely to occupy (despite the first black pro in England being a goalkeeper, Arthur Wharton). As well as these, the Souness regime also brought Mark Walters down from Glasgow where (also under Souness) he had been the first black player to turn out for Rangers. Then, when Souness gave way to the leadership period of Roy Evans and his subsequent co-manager Gerard Houllier, Evans brought another black goalkeeper into the squad. Tony Warner never got further than the subs' bench at Anfield and eventually became first choice at Millwall following a spell in Scotland. But it is important to mention him, not least because he was locally born. The first of other black additions arrived thanks to the cheque book: Irish international defender Phil Babb, Cameroonian international defender Rigobert Song, striker Stan Collymore and Paul Ince, the first black player to captain England.

Most recently Houllier has provided Liverpool fans with a new favourite by importing the Guinean-Frenchman Aboubacar 'Titi' Camara from Marseille. Although – at least as I write – Camara has not secured a regular place in the starting line-up, he has endeared himself to the Liverpool crowd with his strength, his skill on the ball and, significantly, his on-field personality. He may be very different from them, but he has something important in common with Liverpool figures of legend in that he seems slightly larger than life. In a symbolic way, Camara has also shown himself to be larger than death. Not only did he run out to play from the kick-off against West Ham in October 1999 despite learning of the death of his father earlier in the day, he scored the only goal of the game.

The sight of Camara turning with outspread arms to celebrate his strike seems to me a rather beautiful image in the context of a Liverpool fan culture marked more deeply than most by mortality and the need to come to terms with it. The Spion Kop, of course, takes its name from a hill in South Africa where many troops from the Liverpool area perished during the Boer War, and the song 'Scouser Tommy' has its catastrophic images of soldiers from the city under fire in foreign fields. The contrasting legacies of Heysel and Hillsborough speak pretty much for themselves. Similarly, Bill Shankly's tongue-in-cheek remark on the relationship between football, life and death is too famous to need repeating here.

Liverpool fans won't need reminding that not every black player joining the club has been a big success. The erratic James became a notorious liability at times – 'Calamity James' to some. Walters and Thomas had their moments, but Collymore's intermittent golden ones were dulled by the pall of disturbance and disappointment he seems to cast wherever he goes. Babb went in and out of favour before being cast into the reserves, and not everyone is convinced about Song, who was transferred to West Ham United late in the year 2000. As for Ince, he arrived at Anfield handicapped by past exploits with Manchester United. Intent on being 'the Governor', he appears to have lived up to the nickname more off the pitch than on it, where his leadership ambitions were actually required.

But these chequered exploits are in no sense evidence that blacks and Liverpool Football Club don't mix. The fortunes of these players were no more nor less uneven during the difficult late 1980s and 1990s than those of the white players, be they white English, Scottish, Irish, Scandinavian, North American, Eastern or Western European. And on the upside, the best years of John Barnes will be remembered just as long as will the teenage feats of Michael Owen, while Camara has already achieved a small yet special place in Anfield folklore. The overall picture is perfectly clear: since the tempestuous months which followed Barnes's first appearance in 1987, black players have written themselves into Liverpool's history and will continue doing so, a transformation which looked a very long way off as little as fifteen years ago.

Meanwhile, a similar metamorphosis has occurred at Everton, despite those many Goodison fans who took such dismal delight in celebrating their white 'purity' by comparison with Barnes's supposed contamination of their Anfield counterparts' racial profile. Again, each story is different. Everton's first black signing, the Nigerian World Cup star Daniel Amokachi, was well liked, even though he struggled. (Was this simply because he added a little novelty interest to a prosaic and fitful side? Or was there also something slightly self-conscious – even a little penitent – about Evertonians' embrace of this big-hearted failure, especially following their ill-treatment of Barnes?) Joe Royle's managership saw the arrival of defender Terry Phelan and also Earl Barrett from Royle's previous club Oldham Athletic. Royle also blooded Bradford-born Danny Cadamarteri who was embraced for energy, commitment and his ability to come up with something unexpected, though his star faded under Walter Smith. Smith experimented unsuccessfully with Ibrahima Bakayoko and began the 1999/2000 season hoping for better from Abel Xavier, a versatile Mozambican defender signed from PSV Eindhoven who quickly entered the Pantheon of Preposterous Haircuts. Smith also provided the club's first bona fide black hero in ex-Arsenal striker Kevin Campbell, whose goals rescued the Blues from relegation in the FA Premier League basement dogfight of 1999.

These developments among the playing staffs of the two big Merseyside clubs are impossible not to notice. It is, perhaps, especially remarkable that Campbell returned to English football from Trabzonspor after being the object of racist observations made in public by the Turkish club's chairman. Once upon a time Everton would have been one of the last clubs he'd have turned to following such an episode. But what do they signify about the bigger story of Liverpool the city, Liverpool the club and their relationships with people who don't fit the description 'white'? When John Barnes ghosted down the wing leaving defenders tackling shadows and received the adulation of the Liverpool crowd, did it mean he had made racism disappear just as dramatically as his arrival had exposed its full virulence? Did his irresistible form and the easy affability of his contacts with ordinary Liverpool people mean that every Liverpool supporter who'd ever shouted the word 'nigger' would think long and hard before doing it again? Had Anfield, for so long regarded as hostile territory by black Liverpudlians, suddenly been remade as a place of welcome, a place where they could at last become part of that Liverpool identity which the Kop had done so much to define and which I was so beguiled by as a child? Was local black talent more likely now to be recognized and nurtured by the club's scout network and youth development programmes?

Some certainly hoped that all these things were so. But was that much too wishful thinking? Was it more pertinent to ask whether Anfield's acceptance of John Barnes actually gave apologists for racism a most convenient argument for redoubling their insistence that the best way to deal with it was to ignore it? (After all, they might point out, that's what Barnes himself was doing, wasn't it?) And could it be that the subsequent importation of a few talented black individuals into a couple of famous football teams simply created an illusion of 'colour-blindness' that helps conceal the same dynamics of suspicion and exclusion festering underneath?

In the bright, sometimes blinding, light of what might be called 'New Football' all these questions deserve careful consideration – including the ones which more sophisticated observers of racism's workings may consider so naive as not to be worth asking. While the idea that one brilliant footballer can somehow wipe away the ingrained antipathies of an entire football fan culture with a few dazzling dribbles and a clutch of classic goals is perfectly absurd, no one should underestimate the implications of either what Barnes achieved or what he was obliged to endure.

Football's Anti-racism

As recently as the mid-1980s, racism was the subject that no one in positions of influence or authority in football could be bothered to talk about. Today, it is talked about constantly in the sporting media, whether because Leeds fans think it's 'a laugh' to sing songs about gas chambers to Spurs fans, or because white Englishman Neil Ruddock makes a wisecrack about garlic on the breath of black Frenchman Patrick Vieira. Racism, and how to combat it, has become part of the debate about the extraordinary renewal of the national game, along with the virtues of all-seater stadia, the dominance of Sky TV, the spiralling of wages and the influx of foreign stars. Racism is now at the centre of football debate, and this amazing transformation can largely be traced back directly to the trials and the triumphs of John Barnes on Merseyside.

The first and clearest evidence of this came with Lord Justice Taylor's report on the Hillsborough disaster. Its principle purpose, of course, was to investigate the nightmare at the Leppings Lane end and make recommendations about supporter safety in the future. But in the process of furthering the rehabilitation of football supporters – a process begun by the disaster itself – after decades of blanket demonization, the Taylor report drew attention to those unattractive aspects of football crowd culture that had previously been ignored. Consequently, racist chanting became a criminal offence. Would the subject have been addressed quite so urgently if the club whose fans had perished at Hillsborough was not also the club whose most exciting player had been very publicly subjected to some of the most extreme racial abuse ever see in England? Probably not.

That was just the beginning. Before long, in 1993, the 'Let's Kick Racism Out Of Football' campaign was jointly launched by the Professional Footballers' Association and the Commission For Racial Equality with the backing of most professional clubs, the main supporters' organizations and the then newly formed FA Premier League. This was the first phase of what evolved into the Kick It Out campaign which sought to address other manifestations of racism in football as well, such as racial abuse by players and discriminatory employment practices at clubs. Racism, in all its forms, also became the subject of an ambitious report by the government's Football Task Force, published in March 1998, which recommended a stiffening of the law and more vigorous forms of action at all levels of the game from junior and park football right up to the giddy heights of the FA Premier League.

But how did the situation evolve in the particular circumstances of Merseyside? There are several angles on this. Where black professionals are concerned, it is plain that Barnes's success at Liverpool smoothed the way for the flow of black players into the Anfield dressing room and, indirectly, into Goodison Park's as well. This would certainly have happened anyway, but the fact that Barnes had proved such an impressive ambassador for 'blackness' – whatever that was taken to mean by those who felt threatened by it – must have made it easier for others who followed.

This can only be a good thing, and not just for the top rank of black professionals who can nowadays think of Liverpool (and Everton) as possible employers rather than clubs whose supporters were among the most vocally racist in the country. Sceptics may be right to claim that a preponderance of black players in a team may be evidence of nothing more substantial than the kind of racial tolerance that can only be described as skin deep. Even so, the breach of the glass barrier which so heavily impeded black participation prior to Barnes has a symbolic importance which should not quickly be dismissed. It matters that Liverpool look different these days. It matters because of the wall-to-wall whiteness of its great teams in the past, and it particularly matters because those teams, even the ones with hardly a single scouser in them, were seen to personify other qualities seen as constituent of an authentic Liverpudlian working-class identity: tough, canny and spartan rather than fragile, guileless and flash – the very failings the football culture so often presumed to be synonymous with blackness.

Of course, there is a general sense in which the conspicuous addition of black players to the Liverpool team profile simply contributes to another racial stereotype perpetuated by sport, the one which deems that blacks are inherently more athletically gifted and therefore less intellectually able, and which contributes so insidiously to the underachievement of black boys at school. On the other hand, the sheer variety of black players who've performed on the big Merseyside stages has helped challenge the received wisdoms held by so many whites of earlier generations. Every black player who made his name in the 1970s seems to have put up with the assumption of white managers, coaches or fellow players that they might have flair when the sun was shining, but didn't have the blood or the bottle to scrap for an away point in mid-February. Only a total dope would make such assumptions now. Michael Thomas and Paul Ince might not have been everything Liverpool wanted them to be, but no-one could accuse them of being too soft for a ruck in the mud.

But so much for the symbolism of black bodies in red shirts. While that symbolism carries a force for good, which ought to be acknowledged, it cannot be held to represent the end of racism as an issue for Liverpool FC. My most poignant feelings when watching John Barnes at the start of his Liverpool career came from the realization that, even in his pomp, his place in the affections of too many Liverpool fans was very fragile indeed. It could all have been so different. Rumours, since denied, that he'd rather have joined a London club accompanied his arrival. The first few home games at Anfield had to be rescheduled thanks to a problem with the sewers. This was just as well for Barnes: who knows what sort of shit he might have had thrown at him by the more committed bigots among his new home 'fans'? Instead, he turned in three marvellous away performances, so by the time he made his Anfield debut the bulk of the home faithful were falling at his feet.

At the time Barnes himself was in no position to make these kinds of point. But he makes it very bluntly in his recent book (*Barnes: The Autobiography*, 1999: 95–6):

> For me the solution was simple – deliver on the pitch to make the fans love me. The Kop would have slaughtered me with racial abuse if I had faltered on the field. I knew that . . . What a target I would have been. The Kop treated out-of-form white players cruelly, so they would have crucified a struggling black. A bad aura already clung to me because Liverpool fans believed I only came because Arsenal did not step in. Had I played badly, it would have been hell for me. Pure hell.

Barnes also knew as well as anyone that a racist fan is quite willing to tolerate a 'black bastard' as long as he's doing a good job for his team. You don't have to know too much about either football or double standards to be sickened by the fact that many of the same fans who valorize a black star in their own team have no hesitation in hurling racial abuse at the black stars of opponents, especially if their own black star isn't playing. Liverpool fans did exactly that during John Barnes's first season when the Reds travelled to Norwich City for a League match in April 1988. On arriving at Carrow Road I learned that Barnes was out through injury, and felt immediate sympathy for Norwich's black winger Ruel Fox. I knew that Barnes's absence would be taken by a vocal element of Liverpool's travelling supporters as a licence to racially abuse Fox. When this duly occurred, it was no less repellent for its utter predictability.

Other incidents during the same season revealed an awareness among Liverpool supporters of precisely that type of double standard within their own ranks. A fairly bleak example arose during an away match at Luton Town. Travelling Reds supporters had been forced to slip in among the locals due to Luton's notorious ban on away fans. Black players were long-established at Luton – Ricky Hill,

Brian Stein, Mitchell Thomas – and were represented in the team that day. Meanwhile, Barnes was in the Liverpool side. When he got the ball a number of Town fans started up the regulation gorilla grunting, and a nearby Scouser felt moved to respond: 'Ah shurrup, will yer?: youse have got niggers of yer own.'

Then there was the game away to Watford, where Barnes received a friendly welcome from the fans of the little club he'd previously served so well. Thanks mainly to Peter Beardsley, who played beautifully that day, the game was won for Liverpool well before the end and Barnes was substituted. One Liverpool fan showing, I'd like to think, an ironic appreciation that Reds' fans were really no better than Everton's underneath the surface, responded by appropriating one of the racist chants Evertonians had used in the Merseyside derby games: 'Liverpool are white!' he cried, as Barnes left the field. 'Liverpool are white!'

As for Barnes, himself, he already knew that his adoration by the racist patrons at Anfield was highly conditional. It was also, quite literally, impersonal: 'I was fairly circumspect about all the adulation, about all the cries of "we love you, we love you". Liverpool's fans did not love John Barnes, the person. They worshipped John Barnes, the no. 10 who plays for Liverpool' (1999: 96). This realism was borne out in the later years of Barnes's time with Liverpool. After serious injuries had robbed him of his pace he re-emerged as a different kind of player under the Roy Evans regime. During the 1995/96 season he performed well in a central midfield 'holding role', a key component in a system he was widely credited with helping to devise, built around striker Robbie Fowler and Steve McManaman in a 'free' role. This team almost did great things. But not quite. And later, when its form slumped, Barnes bore the brunt of the more critical fans. While some had longer memories and admired Barnes for fighting back to fitness, others reached for insults unpleasantly adjacent to the standard clichés about black players: he was lazy, he was soft, he wasn't trying hard enough. Old habits die hard.

Liverpool 4 versus Liverpool 8

Those who at the time indignantly insisted that even if terrace racism used to be a feature of the Anfield atmosphere it wasn't any more, because Reds' fans all loved Barnes, would do well to reflect upon these sentiments, and on the player's own feelings on the matter, even at the time of his greatest triumphs. But the truest and most damning measure of how far Liverpool FC had to travel as an institution, if it was to be truly accessible to every Liverpudlian, was the reaction to Barnes mania among the city's black football lovers. Whether watching their amateur league games from the touchline, or chatting with them in the pub or in their homes, the story from these black scousers was always the same: they don't want us there – not as players, not as supporters, not at all.

Presented with this perception, a number of white Reds' fans (and one former player) were quick to belittle it back in the 1980s with the standard disclaimers: 'They've got a "chip on the shoulder" or "They won't mix".' But the black scousers' stories were all the more persuasive because they seemed to illustrate a theme of social exclusion which ran not just through football. Like anyone with half an eye for a city's racial landscape, I noticed very quickly the almost total absence of black people from Liverpool's streets and shops as well as from almost all its residential areas – rich and poor alike – outside the 'south end' postcode of Liverpool 8 and its fringes. Nor was this just my personal impression: reports and surveys into employment and housing swiftly confirmed that in most parts of Liverpool black Liverpudlians were nowhere to be seen.

Liverpool's two great soccer stadiums seemed to exemplify this informal apartheid, and with it the city's most distressing paradox: on the one hand it had acquired so much of its personality from being one of Britain's most vibrant and cosmopolitan seaports; on the other, the deep-rooted black element of this historic cultural mix seemed to have been erased from the city's otherwise attractive collective identity.

The black scousers I met felt this exclusion keenly. These included several members of an impressive multi-cultural park team called Almithak, who told stories of uncomfortable experiences with the intimidating citadel that was Anfield in the past. Some recounted going to the ground as fans – Liverpool fans – and becoming marginalized and terrorized – if not by direct threats and insults from other Liverpool fans around them, then by the waves of abuse aimed at visiting black players such as Cyrille Regis or Garth Crooks. Others talked of being spotted as talented schoolboys and invited to train with other promising lads under the aegis of the Liverpool youth system. At first they were pleased to be noticed, but later found their noticeability invited less gratifying attention: coaches insisting they played on the wing even though their position was midfield or centre-back; white players cheerfully calling them 'Sam' – short for 'Sambo'.

Incidents like these may not have been motivated by malice. But in some ways it might have been easier if they had. At least with an out-and-out racist a black person knows the score. But being assailed by unthinking, even benignly-meant, white racist assumptions about inherent aptitudes (sporting or otherwise) and acceptable nicknames, can be trickier to deal with, especially if you are far from your own patch and in a minority of one. Different individuals responded in different ways. Some took issue with their treatment, and were rewarded by being tagged 'chippy'. Others just drifted away. In either case the sentiments were much the same as those of alienated would-be black Liverpool fans. Or Everton fans, for that matter. Emotionally, culturally, even geographically, they were always made to feel completely out of place.

I found this was especially true among black Liverpudlians from the environs of Liverpool 8 – a 'bad area' as white taxi drivers often called it when driving me there – and this deep legacy of suspicion had been firmly cemented by memories of the few black players who had turned out for either Merseyside club before the arrival of Barnes. There had been two for Everton. One was a local player called Cliff Marshall who made a handful of appearances but never established himself. The other was striker Mike Trebilcock. To me at least his story is a bit of a mystery. Although he was dark, he was not very dark – possibly of mixed race – and was never described to me by anyone, black Scousers included, as an example of a 'black player'. However, he was certainly thought of one by racist Liverpool fans. Kopite John Mackin, writing in the Liverpool fanzine *Through The Wind And The Rain* (Issue 13, Autumn 1993) recalls 'a peculiarly graphic song about [Trebilcock] which beggars belief now'.

Trebilcock was signed for a small fee from Plymouth Argyle and never became a regular first-choice player, but he appeared in the 1966 FA Cup Final against Sheffield Wednesday because England international Fred Pickering was unfit. The game provided the nation with one of it's more dramatic Wembley showcases, won 3–2 by Everton thanks to a late goal by winger Derek Temple, following a desperate Wednesday defensive mistake. The drama of those closing moments clearly accounts for much of the reason why that final is remembered for Temple's winner. Yet it still seems very odd that the scorer of both Everton's other goals has been all but forgotten. It was Trebilcock, of course. And given this contribution on that famous day, it seems odder still that he moved from Goodison soon after and, if my information is correct, went to live abroad.

I have not properly researched the stories of Marshall and Trebilcock and must therefore resist leaping to conclusions. But I can speak with more conviction about the experiences of the only black player ever to have represented Liverpool prior to John Barnes, and the bitter legacy they left among the city's black people. Howard Gayle was not just a black guy; he was a black guy from the 'wrong' part of Liverpool. As a player, he was quick, skilful and brave. As a person, he was young and raw and had resolved, long before he joined Liverpool Football Club, that if anyone ever called him a 'sambo', a 'nigger' or a 'coon' he wouldn't take it lying down. To Gayle, that wasn't being 'chippy' – that was following the basic rules of self-defence and self-respect.

At first, Gayle progressed well. Bill Shankly predicted he would become the first black player to represent the full England team. But his career at Anfield never developed in the way Shankly envisaged. Gayle eventually made his first team debut under Shankly's successor, Bob Paisley as a substitute in a home game against Manchester City in October 1980. After that he returned to the reserves until, in April 1981, found himself thrown, completely unexpectedly, into a European Cup semi-final second leg, away to Bayern Munich. In the first leg at Anfield the German team had secured a goalless draw, and Liverpool's position for the return had been made all the more precarious by a long injury list. As a result the inexperienced Gayle found himself on the substitute's bench – but not for very long. Only a few minutes into the match Kenny Dalglish limped off and Gayle was sent on to replace him.

For most fans the significance of that match lies solely in the result: with a display of typical endurance and escapology, the Reds snatched a one-all draw and so went through to the Final in which they won the European Cup for the third time. But for Howard Gayle, and those many black Liverpudlians who knew him and his family or simply wished him well, the night has a bitter legacy. It wasn't because Gayle didn't perform. On the contrary, he was tremendous, playing almost alone up front and running the Germans ragged. Everyone who saw him thinks so, including his team mates. Yet shortly before the end of the ninety minutes Paisley took him off – the substitute was substituted.

Why did Liverpool's manager take this unusual step? The conventional view is that he did it because Gayle was exhausted and looked in danger of getting sent off. Paisley himself says as much, writing later about these events. Gayle's performance had been all the more impressive for being produced in the face of relentless provocation from the German defenders and the racial abuse of the crowd, yet as the final whistle neared it was clear that Gayle's temper was becoming frayed. Even very fair-minded fans believe that Paisley's decision was wise. But Gayle and his supporters back in black Liverpool read something else into the decision. A substitute substituted despite playing a blinder? A black player withdrawn because his temperament was judged too brittle? Would Paisley have done the same thing, they mused, if Howard Gayle had been white?

Maybe he would, maybe not. Maybe he was wrong, maybe he was right. But Gayle's suspicion that he'd been slighted was intensified by the club's subsequent refusal to offer him the contract he desired or the opportunities he felt that he had earned. He felt he deserved better. As well as impressing in the cauldron of the Olympic Stadium, he'd also shone in League matches towards the end of the season and scored in a one-all draw away to Tottenham. The *Guardian*'s Robert Armstrong sang his praises and those of another newcomer, a striker from Chester by the name of Ian Rush: 'Both have shown they possess the nerve and flair required for the big occasion.' Yet Gayle soon became convinced he had no place in Paisley's plans. True, there were other pretenders to first-team places, Rush included. True, Paisley seemed to have already decided that wingers weren't to be part of his plan. But Gayle felt there was more to it than that. He was eventually transferred and, during a spell with Birmingham City, fulfilled at least part of Shankly's prediction of national honours by representing England three times at under-21 level in 1984. But his career never fulfilled its early promise.

Some insist that racial judgements played no part in this story: Gayle, they say, was probably just not good enough and, furthermore, he was a 'difficult' character; sardonic, touchy and too fond of dubious company. But for some white

Liverpudlians any black guy from the 'wrong' part of town is, by definition, dubious. And for some within the club Gayle's disinclination to put up with racial comments or find certain racial 'jokes' funny marked him out as 'difficult' and 'touchy', whereas Gayle himself had learned to live his life by different standards. And, to much of black Liverpool, the treatment of Howard Gayle was damning evidence that even when a black player had proved that he was good enough to play for Liverpool at the highest levels, somehow a way would still be found to squeeze him out. It is not a fanciful theory. After my book had gone to the printer I was introduced to a Danish football reporter who had once asked Paisley during an interview why Liverpool was almost alone at that time in having no black players in its first-team squad. According to the reporter, Paisley's reply was direct and also revealing about the limits of his own North East and Liverpool 'football' upbringing: 'We don't trust them', he was alleged to have replied.

Liverpool FC Now

All of this took place around twenty years ago, and Liverpool Football Club looks a great deal different today. Howard Gayle's disaffection has not been forgotten by those who felt it by association, but his name may well mean nothing to new generations of black Britons, whether from Liverpool or elsewhere. Barnes has left his mark, and even though (thanks to injury) he lost his spark – and the support of some of the Anfield crowd – towards the end of his Liverpool years, his contribution to one of the finest Liverpool teams ever will not be easily wiped away. Now, under the Houllier revolution, the Liverpool team is more cosmopolitan than ever while, in keeping with national trends, its supporters now travel to fill expensive Anfield seats from further and further afield. Thanks to these upmarket demographics of 'new' football, the ground has been opened up to some ethnic minority groups. Even in the mid-1980s a small number of affluent Chinese Liverpudlians were regular attenders, and they've now been joined by a small but noticeable influx of 'middle-class' young British Asians, mostly from outside Liverpool.

Yet none of these developments seems to have lessened the separation between the club and a sharply marginalized section of the city's population. Liverpool might claim that the 1.4 per cent 'non-white' supporters they attract (according to the *1997 FA Premier League Fan Survey*) is a tiny bit bigger than for most other FA Premier League clubs and not much further behind Arsenal – league leaders in this respect with 4.1 per cent – than anybody else. But it is still a tiny figure in a city with such a long and variegated multi-cultural history. And even if it gets a little bigger in years to come, it probably won't be due to attracting the custom of many local black fans. FA Premier League ticket prices are now beyond the range of even quite affluent citizens. Even if a fear of racism fails to deter the people of black Liverpool from turning up at Anfield, given that so many are economically disadvantaged they are likely to be priced out of the market anyway.

Meanwhile, on the playing side, appearances still suggest that local black football talent is more likely to be recognized outside Liverpool than within it. It is, perhaps, ironic that Everton have made the greater efforts to reach out to Merseyside's black citizens. They've recently appointed a young education and community officer, Alan Johnson, who is from Liverpool and is black. It is doubly ironic that Johnson has found through his work that black kids living in and around Liverpool 8 are mostly Reds' fans, partly because Liverpool are seen as the more successful club, and partly because of the legacy of Barnes.

At the same time, Liverpool FC continues to have next to no effective 'grass roots' community mechanisms which really reach into the black parts of the city. And all reports suggest that the racial constitution of youngsters recruited to Liverpool's football youth schemes is almost as uniformly white as ever. There may be black players on the park, and that may be more important than some sceptics are inclined to think. Beyond that, though, the subtle, often unconscious, dynamics of exclusion seem very little altered.

All this helps to put the John Barnes legacy into a clearer perspective. In sharp contrast to Howard Gayle, he was fortunately placed to break through the barriers against black participation. His outstanding talent was, of course, vital. But so, too, was the fact that, in Kenny Dalglish, Liverpool now had a manager – still a player-manager, in fact – who was drawn from a different generation and who knew from his own playing experience that black players were no more nor less deserving of Liverpool's 'trust' than white ones. And Barnes was well equipped to handle his situation on a personal level too. The product of an impeccably middle-class Jamaican background and, it seems, all the confidence that went with it, Barnes looked down on racist fans and players alike as ignorant and pathetic – and therefore found it easier to rise above the fray. Life for Howard Gayle had never been that way.

Whatever their respective merits as players, the differing fortunes of Gayle and Barnes help crystalize the bigger picture of Liverpool FC and issues around 'race'. The discomforts and uncertainties of Gayle in the dressing room reflect those of other black Liverpudlians about the entire institution that is Anfield. Barnes, on the other hand, showed both how racist behaviour might be suspended, even challenged, yet also how conditional the acceptance of a black player by his home crowd can be.

In a way, the two men represent the themes of continuity and change also identified by supporters and academics alike. In the Liverpool fanzine *Through the Wind and Rain* in 1998 (Issue 41: 51), for example, an Asian Reds fan from Birmingham commented on the 'casually racist hard core' of Liverpool support pre-Barnes, which made it 'more intimidating going to Anfield than away games'. He goes on:

The hypocrisy that grew around the time of John Barnes's signing and the condemnation of Evertonians' behaviour was irritating and encouraging. Irritating because a lot of Reds opposed his move, and I knew they'd have been the same if he'd signed for Everton. Encouraging, because people were waking up to the fact that racism was unacceptable. I hoped this would be a turning point and that black people would be encouraged to attend games. It didn't really happen in any significant numbers, and problems persisted.

Les Back, Tim Crabbe and John Solomos in their recent article on 'Racism in football' (in Adam Brown (ed.), 1998 *Fanatics!*) make a similar point. 'It is clear', the authors observe, in talking about racist abuse by Evertonians at those first Merseyside derbies in the 1980s that spurred me to write my book, 'that while John Barnes was the referent in each of the key chants . . . their targets were the predominantly white Liverpool supporters'. They continue:

> Everton fans were making a statement about the perceived normative identity and racial preferences of Merseyside which could only work if those preferences were shared by the Liverpool supporters . . . The intention was to 'wind up' the Liverpool supporters on the premise of a shared antipathy towards 'niggers' which is located within a common understanding of the racial characteristics associated with the Scouse identity. (Back et al., 1998: 78)

The general climate at Anfield on matchdays has certainly changed a lot, too, since the 1980s. The overt baiting of visiting black players is no longer an obvious feature – though opposing *foreign* players, black and white, can still get their share from individuals when local passions are roused. But no matter how many black players appear in a red shirt, and no matter that more and more of Anfield's seats are now occupied by the backsides of affluent folk from Liverpool and from out of town, some of those who make the atmosphere inside the ground – who make the ground *their* ground – almost certainly still regard being white as a prerequisite for being Red. Until that is challenged effectively – and changed – New Football at Anfield will go on looking too much like Old Football did to those it disdained to embrace.

References

Back, L., Solomos, J. and Crabbe, T. (1998) 'Racism in football: patterns of continuity and change', in A. Brown (ed.) *Fanatics! Power, Race, Nationality and Fandom in European Football*, London: Routledge.

Barnes, J. (1999) *John Barnes: the Autobiography*, London: Headline.

Davies, H. (1972) *The Glory Game*, London: Weidenfeld and Nicolson.

Dunphy, E. (1976) *Only a Game?*, London: Kestrel.

Hill, D. (1989) *Out of his Skin: the John Barnes Phenomenon*, London: Faber & Faber.

Hopcraft, A. (1971) *The Football Man*, Harmondsworth: Penguin.

Hornby, N. (1992) *Fever Pitch*, London: Victor Gollancz.

Williams, J. (1997) *FA Premier League National Fan Survey, 1996/97*, Leicester: Sir Norman Chester Centre for Football Research, University of Leicester.

−7−

The Fall of Liverpool FC and the English Football 'Revolution':
John Williams

The End of Football History?

For an unprecedented twenty-five years, from the mid-1960s to 1990, under the football management of Bill Shankly, Bob Paisley, Joe Fagan and Kenny Dalglish, Liverpool FC were *the* dominant force in English football and, for seven years from 1977 to 1984, unquestionably the strongest club side in Europe. Leeds United in the late 1960s and early 1970s and, briefly, Everton in the mid-1980s posed challenges to this domestic ascendancy, but it was only as Arsenal, and later Manchester United, began to emerge as major footballing powers in England in the post-Hillsborough period from 1989 did Liverpool's stranglehold on the game in England really begin to loosen.

At the same time, football in England in the early 1990s had begun to hum to the new rhythms of global capitalism and to an increasingly internationalized market for both players and coaches. As this new era rapidly took hold, demanding new responses, Liverpool Football Club was still mired in the aftermath of the single biggest post-war football tragedy in Western Europe. The club turned, instead, once again to those familiar verities focused around the traditions of single-minded, but by now rather anachronistic forms of club administration on the one hand, and, on the playing side, to the still powerful aura of the club's famed 'boot room' coaching dynasty.

In this chapter, then, we want to examine some of the specifics of the recent decline in the fortunes of Liverpool FC against the background of wider shifts in the English game. We want to stress here the *relative* nature of this decline, of course; Liverpool's worst finish in the FA Premier League since 1992 has, after all, been a respectable eighth. We, nevertheless, *do* want to argue that a combination of the recent transformation of European professional football and the relatively static response by Liverpool FC to such shifts are important matters in understanding recent changes in the game and also the Liverpool club's drift from national and European club dominance. We want, then, to focus here, especially, on the *management* changes and continuities at the Liverpool club in the 1980s and 1990s, but we also want to try to locate these changes in terms of wider shifts in the business and management of football clubs during this extraordinary period of the game's development in England. Our argument is that Liverpool was, in some important senses, both temporarily numbed to, and 'overtaken' by, wider developments in the sport, changes which prefaced a much more intimate and necessary connection between the football and 'business' sides of the routine activities of top football clubs. In the new, more globalized era of the sport's development, Liverpool FC is now trying to reposition itself once again, not just nationally as a football club but also in terms of its function as a global 'brand' or 'sign' in the important international market place for transcultural sporting identities. This is crucial, as media sports signs – symbols, logos, texts – are increasingly at the leading edge of the recent 'culturization' of global economics because of their value to media systems, their capacity for flexibility and inter-connectedness, and the ease with which they flow through global networks (Rowe, 1999: 70–1).

We Think we'll Manage

There has actually been very little *academic* work on football club administration, coaching and football *management* in England. Stephen Wagg's (1984) marvellous and underused account of the development of English football into the TV age does most to reveal and explain important changes in the functions and role of the football manager in the post-war English game. Most recent academic work on football, however, has concentrated either on supporter cultures (e.g. Brown, 1998) or on the new economics of the sport (e.g. Morrow, 1999). Giulianotti's (1999) recent sociological work on football at least has a chapter on *playing* the game and on the diffusion of coaching styles, but it has little to say on football management per se. King's (1998) impressive work on the social transformation of the English game has virtually nothing useful to say about management and coaching. Recent accounts on football management drawn from psychology are aimed at a 'popular' audience and lack depth and a strong analytical frame (see Sik, 1996). They read rather like the (better) work of journalists on this issue (Lambert, 1995). Sarah Gilmore's (2000) interesting recent work on football managers, nevertheless, approaches the issue from the straitjacket of discourses drawn from management studies. Recent *anthropological* accounts of the world game have little useful to say about football management and football coaching at all (Armstrong and Giulianotti, 1999).

Despite this general lack of academic focus on management, coaching and playing the game some commentators, such as the French anthropologist Christian Bromberger (1993: 120) do, interestingly, argue that club styles of play reflect local milieus. Bromberger argues that, aesthetically, for example, 'the styles of

Olympique Marseilles and Juventus are strongly opposed, each reflecting a particular vision of the world of mankind and the city'. He discusses the value system of Juve – the so-called 'three Ss' of simplicity, seriousness and sobriety – and argues that this is rooted in the industrial rigour and discipline of the Agnelli family who own the club and the Fiat automobile empire (see Giulianotti, 1999: 140).

This is a similar point to the one we have been trying to argue for at various moments in this book. That is, that the character and style of a club such as Liverpool FC owes something to local 'structures of feeling' in the city of Liverpool itself. The approach, positioning and role in the city of the football club has been shaped both by the close but 'friendly' rivalry with Everton, the ethnic and occupational make-up of Merseyside and the cultural practices and values of the city itself, and *also* by the particular 'communitarian' values brought to the club, especially by the coaching and management dynasty established under Bill Shankly from 1959. In this instance, then, we would argue that the 'sense' of the football club comes more from the approach to managing, coaching and *playing* the game and from the relationships established between club staff and supporters and the specific *playing* traditions at Liverpool FC, especially since the early 1960s, than it does from any particular philosophy of club *ownership*.

This sort of claim, of course, fails to answer a crucial question, namely, what accounts for success at a top football club? In general football texts and coaching manuals, in England at least, the answer to this question tends to be reduced either to the mundane citing of 'hard work' and discipline, or to mythologized references to the specific 'chemistry' of teams, or to the undefinable attributes of individual players or managers, rather than to any specific *organizational* features or to established *processes* which might, for example, link fans, players and clubs. Although we would reject aspects of their overly narrow comparisons between football clubs and 'other' kinds of business, a slightly more sophisticated approach to this issue is offered by the economist Stefan Szymanski and business consultant Tim Kuypers, who have recently tried to identify what provides top football clubs with what they call 'competitive advantage' (Szymanski and Kuypers, 1999: Ch. 6). Only twenty-three clubs have won English League titles since 1888. Four clubs alone have won more than half of all League titles (Liverpool, Manchester United, Arsenal and Everton). Liverpool have won an unrivalled eighteen championships, including eleven between 1973 and 1990, the last time the Merseyside club won the championship. What marks out *these* clubs in particular, apart from their size and fan base (which is in fact a relatively weak indicator, in any case, of club success)?

Szymanski and Kuypers argue that these 'winning' football clubs have, or have had, *distinct capabilities* which, by their nature, are exceptional attributes which cannot be easily reproduced elsewhere. They identify *four* such capabilities (1999: 194–245), as follows.

First, *strategic assets,* in a business sense, refers to a scarce resource which provides an advantage in competition which, once possessed by one firm (club), cannot be possessed by others. This constitutes a monopoly over a necessary input in the production process: e.g. raw materials obtainable only from a particular location, or else some specialized equipment. Examples in a sporting context might be an outstanding player or more likely an inspirational and astute football manager. We have argued that Bill Shankly and his coaching staff at Liverpool provided such an asset, though Szymanski and Kuypers also warn that the advantages accrued here are unlikely to extend long beyond the end of any manager's tenure. At Liverpool, of course, a set of practices with regard to preparation of players had been laid down, had been institutionalized at the club and, also, a coaching *team* had been groomed to succeed Shankly. Moreover, senior players at the club were also charged with responsibility and leadership in a way which was probably uncommon elsewhere (Rush, 1996; Souness, 1999). Finally, the approaches established at Anfield also marked out the club's coaching staff as reliable early *identifiers* of necessary strategic assets (players) which could then be purchased cheaply from other firms (clubs). Shankly bought both Ray Clemence and Kevin Keegan from lowly Scunthorpe United for small fees. Each went on to become world-class players for Liverpool in the 1970s. Alan Hansen, Liverpool's kingpin defender for the whole of the 1980s, was plucked, at 20, by Bob Paisley from Partick Thistle for just £100,000.

The second strategic advantage identified by Szymanski and Kuypers is *innovation.* This they define as the ability to generate incremental improvements to existing products. Successful football clubs are likely to have a greater capacity to innovate than their rivals, and at a lower cost. We have seen, already, Liverpool's early capacity to buy players cheaply and to *improve* its purchases. Such innovations are likely to be quickly imitated in business, however, and so they are limited in the advantages they are likely to offer. But, in an era when involvement in *European* football competition was limited to a small number of clubs from each country, Liverpool's routine involvement in European competition from 1965 right up to the Heysel ban of 1985 also provided extensive opportunities for cross-fertilization of systems and ideas which came much less frequently to other English clubs. We have described in chapter four the ways in which routine local chauvinisms and anxieties about foreign travel at the club were mixed with a real openness on the part of the coaching staff at Liverpool specifically to *European* football experiences. These led to admittedly ad hoc innovation and adaptation on the playing and coaching side at the club throughout the 1970s and 1980s, something which contributed to Liverpool's combination of English and 'continental' playing styles.

The third strategic asset highlighted by Szymanski and Kuypers is that of *reputation.* This the authors define as a distinctive capability which comes from the established position of a product in the marketplace. A good reputation makes a product more attractive to consumers: they know what they are buying. Reputation is a hard capability to replicate or imitate. The authors point to the history and glamour of Manchester United in this respect, arguing that reputation is something which can only be acquired, if it can be acquired at all, in specific conditions and over a long period of time. But in the 1970s and 1980s the popular image of Manchester United among many top British *players*, at least, was that it was indeed a high-profile 'national' club, but one which was essentially underachieving. Professional ideologies strongly pointed at that time to top player transfers to *Liverpool* in order to win trophies, but to *United* perhaps for wages, publicity and profile. Significantly, for example, the sacking of United manager Dave Sexton in 1981 was widely attributed *by* the media *to* the media and to his failure to develop an attractive 'public image' (Wagg, 1984: 193).

All of this meant that in the pre-global football era at least, the routine playing success of Liverpool offered the club pretty much an open hand in the choice of the top British players they wanted; simply in *professional* terms, few players could afford to be seen to turn down a move to Liverpool. Perhaps only players at Manchester United and at local rivals Everton were effectively 'off limits' to the Reds at that time. This strong professional ideology, linking Liverpool FC with footballing success, also probably accounts for the larger number of rather more *cerebral* football players – Dalglish, Hansen, Souness, Lawrenson, Barnes – who, importantly, were the core of the dominant Liverpool teams of the 1980s. Coaches at Liverpool were also happy to let good *players* decide on basic strategies, and so were relatively unthreatened by the arrival at the club of players with ideas or strong *football* personalities. Following the establishment of freedom of movement of players in England in 1978, the advantages in this respect of more affluent, and *successful*, clubs such as Liverpool increased further. This reinforced the seldom believed claims at the time from Anfield that there was no complex, technocratic secret to the club's success: it was simply about signing the best players and letting them play (see Hansen, 1999; and Chapter Four).

The fourth strategic asset offering competitive advantage to clubs or firms is *architecture*. This, according to Szymanski and Kuypers, is a unique *organizational* structure, sometimes associated at football clubs perhaps with the manager and coaches, the players, or sometimes with the relationship between the team and supporters, or with the institutions of a club. Taken *together* these organizational advantages amount to a 'powerful source of competitive advantage, distinctly associated with Liverpool and never emulated elsewhere' (Szymanski and Kuypers, 1999: 204). The authors go on to argue that the coach's mythologized 'boot room' at Anfield was a unique and key source of *institutional* architectural advantage at Liverpool in the 1970s and 1980s.

We will return to discuss the 'boot room' and its fate at some length later in this chapter. What I want to do here is to look briefly at how Liverpool FC has responded *as an organization* to the challenges posed by the rapidly changing dynamics of professional football over the last fifteen years of the twentieth century – that is, I want to concentrate in the years following the Heysel disaster in 1985. It was from around that time that some of the strategic advantages discussed above finally began to unwind at Liverpool, even as the club continued in its domestic footballing dominance, for a few years at least, under new manager Kenny Dalglish.

After Heysel

On the *administrative* side of club affairs at Liverpool, local businessman and Conservative Party and Sports Council figurehead John Smith was confirmed as the Liverpool FC Chairman from 1976. Smith's powerful business expertise, and his network of contacts in political and sporting circles in Britain and beyond, were aimed to be the new stimuli for a more strategic and 'corporate' approach to club policy-making. In December 1976, for example, Smith announced that Liverpool FC were about to launch a unique export drive designed to sell the club overseas and to market its goods all around the world. It all *sounded* impressive, but the available technology and the resources allocated here were very modest. Liverpool FC, like most other top English clubs of the time, was barely 'selling' itself *domestically* with any degree of rigour or sophistication, never mind tapping into available *international* markets. Moreover, the low base from which the club had begun its supposed commercial reconfiguration was also made clear in Smith's very prescient comments on what was going to become football's new 'commercial age':

> Clubs cannot manage on their takings through the turnstiles. Every other means of expanding revenue has to be used for clubs to exist. Sponsorship is one of the biggest. We are the only club in the UK and, I believe, the only one in Europe not to have perimeter advertising around the ground. So we can offer what no other club can offer – exclusivity (quoted in Keith, 1999: 146–7).

At the same launch the long-serving club secretary Peter Robinson, who had largely guided Liverpool quite brilliantly at home and abroad up to the devastation and the six-year footballing exclusion from Europe brought by the Heysel Stadium disaster in 1985, was also offered a new seven-year contract at Liverpool and a new, rather strange, title of general secretary. Post-Heysel, and following the even deeper trauma of the Hillsborough tragedy in 1989, Robinson and his staff seemed determined to try to continue the core aspects of the previously successful recipe of what then passed for normal club/fan relations at Anfield. This involved, centrally of course, the continued delivery to Liverpool fans of a winning football team. But it also included a willingness to try, initially at least, to maintain reasonable ticket-pricing policies at Anfield in order to cater for a local audience badly hit throughout the 1980s by Thatcherite policies and by economic depression (Parkinson, 1985; Williams, 1986). Even in the new national thrall for football in the 1990s, Robinson was initially very nervous about increasing match ticket prices in a city where wages were generally low and *local* passion for football was very high.

It meant, too, the perpetuation of what seems to have become the 'modern' Liverpool FC tradition of a general quite low regard for those addressing the club's public face; stories, among fans, of the poor treatment of supporters, visitors and journalists approaching the club in this period are legion. It was not unusual, for example, for foreign visitors to the club to be left, untended and ignored, outside Anfield. Press talk about the lack of basic hospitality at Anfield was also rife. Insider accounts written about the successful Liverpool teams of the 1970s and 1980s also stressed how the club's coaches had warned *players* about courting publicity by talking too much to the press, an apprenticeship which would later dog players who went on to become managers, as they faced a much more demanding 'media age' of the game's development (Souness, 1999: 221).

Added to all this was the internal resistances and structural inertia to the processes of simple administrative modernization – in ticketing, in merchandising, in routine customer services and in public relations, for example – which were increasingly becoming commonplace at top football clubs both in England and in Europe. Liverpool's successes in the 1970s and 1980s extended over such a lengthy period, and depended so completely on events on the field and the club's strategic ability to attract top players – something which seemed quite secure at that time – that it was easy for Liverpool's staff and directors to assume that the model which had worked so successfully for so long would simply continue to deliver. But the world of football, on both the playing and the administrative sides, was actually already changing rapidly.

After 1984, it would be fifteen years before another English club, Manchester United – and by this time one owned by a PLC and with a team packed with *foreign* players – would triumph again in the European Cup (now the rather more taxing and definitely more lucrative Champions League). Laudably, in many respects, the tenacious but essentially paternalistic hold on the ownership of the Liverpool club by the Moores family, owners of the locally based Littlewoods empire, meant that the raw free market ideologies which would sweep more boldly through the sport in the early 1990s were unlikely to take a strong early hold at Liverpool (see King, 1998). Indeed, the extraordinary work with bereaved families by the Liverpool club and its staff around the aftermath of Hillsborough in 1989 was a clear reminder of the very caring, *human* bonds which still tied the club to its supporters, perhaps especially to those actually residing in the city of Liverpool (Williams 1999a; Walter, 1991). Nevertheless, it was also clear that on both the administrative and football sides of the club little cognisance was yet being taken of wider shifts which were already occurring in some of the central practices involved in running a very large European football club.

This general, strenuous emphasis inside Anfield on very 'traditional' work, largely on the football side and inspired by Shankly's legacy and ideas, at the expense of even quite modest developments on the coaching and preparation side and elsewhere, was understandably championed by some Liverpool fans as both a healthy sign of continuity and a proper focus on established *footballing* priorities. This strategy was seen as a welcome bulwark against creeping 'impression management' in football and the growing emphasis on the language of commerce, and on the role of new business elites in the sport (see King, 1998; Wagg, 1984). Manchester United's later struggles against the predatory Rupert Murdoch, for example, were watched with something approaching ghoulish glee on Merseyside. But it also actually meant a crucial falling-behind in the day-to-day necessities, both on the field and off it, of a late modern football club of Liverpool's size, traditions and ambitions. As John Smith's 1976 comments suggest, Liverpool FC had actually led on some early basic commercial issues, and not always to the liking of the club's supporters. Liverpool was the first club in England, for example, to strike a deal for shirt sponsorship, with Japanese high-tech company Hitachi, in 1978. But there was little sign of a wider strategy here designed both to modernize the club and build on its key distinct capabilities which had been built up throughout the 1970s and 1980s. Thus, by the mid-1990s, and as a simple measure of what was by now the club's relative infrastructural and commercial 'Luddism' in this respect, there still existed no reliable computerized – or otherwise systematized database of Liverpool FC's 25,000 season ticket holders, the club's core supporters and investors. Names and addresses of the club's major sponsors, the fans, were kept on dog-eared cards in a series of boxes.

The Liverpool club's general approach to administration, then, supreme in the club's halcyon days when 'business' in the European football context essentially meant bums on seats, guarding the sanctity of competition, working routinely with TV outlets, and dealing with the travel and the staging of matches, seemed increasingly out of step, in fact, with some of the significant new developments running through the European game in the 1990s. This was especially so regarding matters of club structures, the growing complexities involved in television deals, the necessity of effective national and global marketing, the spreading international market for football players, new approaches to player conditioning and coaching, and the growing importance of extra-UEFA international club relationships (see Williams, 1999b and Chapter Ten).

Added to this, if – as King (1998: 207) argues – in the new 'global' era football *cities* were to be the new driving force in the world game, with top clubs helping to denote which cities are politically and economically important and thus worthy of investment by international capital, then the city of Liverpool in the 1980s was some way from being the sort of nascent regional powerhouse likely to be favoured by top football clubs. Liverpool's poverty and militant municipalism, for example, and its docks-centred casual employment and substantially employer-absent branch economy, were stacked against effective local or regional entrepreneurial development (see, Parkinson, 1985: Ch. 1) There was little prospect on Merseyside, then, for the sort of small firms and cultural-industry development in centres such as Manchester, or for the sort of neo-Thatcherite football-related commercial development which was to feature so strongly later under entrepreneurs such as John Hall in Newcastle (Williams, 1996). Poorly managed and rapidly depopulating, and with a large, unskilled workforce which was overly dependent on the failing docks, and with few new private-sector white-collar service jobs attracted to the city, Liverpool in the 1980s was an unattractive commercial proposition for both foreign and domestic capital (Parkinson, 1985).

Administratively, Liverpool FC, by now a multi-million-pound business and with fans spread worldwide, retained a simple, hierarchical structure with little in the way, for example, of devolved responsibility to effective departmental heads. By the end of the millennium, astonishingly, the club remained the only one in the FA Premier League – probably the only major football club in Europe – still to have no official internet website of its own. It eventually 'piggybacked' on an existing fans' site and later, with Rick Parry now to the fore, moved into business with the Granada media and leisure group to better exploit the club's lucrative internet rights. In short, both in 'business' and in playing terms, the game was very quickly moving on in the early 1990s as Liverpool FC, still stunned by Hillsborough and its traumatic aftermath, and still rooted in some of the tried and successful methods of the past, clung on to a general system of operation that had fixed them at the top of the European football tree, but in quite a different phase of the sport's development.

Eventually, as relations between top clubs in the FA Premier League themselves threatened to fragment in the face of new opportunities for developing TV football markets, Rick Parry, the then FA Premier League Chief Executive and one of the architects of the new league – and also a longstanding Liverpool *fan* – was recruited by the club in 1996 in an attempt to try to pilot it successfully into the new global era. In the same year, and reflecting the obvious tensions in the collective hierarchy of the FA Premier League clubs, a Harris poll of UK TV football viewers was predicting, admittedly implausibly, that already-dominant Premiership champions Manchester United might earn up to £380 million a year from go-it-alone pay-per-view football coverage (Giulianotti, 1999: 93).

Peter Robinson, still an important figure at Anfield, remained at Liverpool as an influential director as Parry initially struggled to get to grips with his new challenge and with Robinson's own powerful legacy. Robinson finally retired from

Liverpool in the summer of 2000. Parry found himself saddled with an administrative set-up at Liverpool which was still geared for a period already twenty years in the past but one which was, in fact, even more extravagantly out of its time because of the failure of the club to grasp properly the *real* pace of change, for example, in the expanding use of new technologies.

Liverpool FC, then, despite the early promises from John Smith back in the 1970s, had also underestimated the growing importance of new football markets and the necessity for new forms for relationships with supporters for those top football clubs still bent, in the late 1990s, on stable European footballing success. The club still lacked effective liaison structures and was slow in terms of developing a forward-looking vision of how links with fans and other partners at home and abroad might best evolve in the age of 'new' football. Both an enthusiastic modernizer, and a man with a strong feel for the club's very special traditions and local relationships, Parry had joined a ship which seemed uneasily stranded between the compasses which had helped plot a marvellously successful course in the club's recent, but nevertheless now 'distant' past, and the need for very new charts and equipment for the tricky navigation that, unquestionably, lay ahead. Parry, above all else, is according to a city analyst 'Someone who knows the value of football to television companies.' (*Guardian*, 12 July 1999). Following a later tie-up between the Granada media and leisure group and the club, engineered by Parry, a spokesman for Granada commented, ominously, 'The worlds of football and television are in some senses symbiotic' (Gibson, 1999; see also Chapter Ten).

King Kenny

While *administratively* Liverpool FC was moving slowly and cautiously in the 1980s, specifically on the *footballing* side of club affairs, continuity was – unsurprisingly – also strongly stressed. It was a celebrated and brilliant Liverpool player, Kenny Dalglish, who had picked up the club's football managerial reins in the immediate aftermath of the Heysel disaster and Joe Fagan's retirement on the morning of the fateful European Cup Final against Juventus in 1985. Dalglish was steeped in the recently established Liverpool traditions under Shankly and Paisley of ebullient team spirit, signing 'good' players, a rejection of the 'star treatment' even for key performers, and an 'uncomplicated' approach to match preparation and tactics and strategies of play (see Dalglish, 1996: 51–61; see also Chapter Four). But he was also drawn from a very different footballing generation than that of his predecessors. He was already comfortably well-off as a top player and he extolled more the newer, politically conservative and 'privatized' virtues *outside* the game of providing for his immediate family, of 'executive' leisure – in this case, predictably, golf – and a willingness to explore commercial opportunities, than he did the older more communitarian values of, say, a Shankly, Paisley or

Fagan. If this was also, as Stephen Wagg (1984) has argued, the age of the football manager in the full glare of publicity, Dalglish, a very private man if one with a cruel and biting sense of humour out of the public eye, was clearly ill-equipped for the increasingly pressing requirements of the national sporting stage (see also Hansen, 1999, Ch. 9).

There were obvious strengths inside the institution Dalglish took over in 1985, but there were also growing signs of the traditional 'Liverpool way' now beginning to look a little dated, at least when judged against some of the new developments coming on-stream in the sport. Even for cerebral players at Liverpool, for example, such as key defender Alan Hansen, 'team spirit' was still a vital part of the club's success (Hansen, 1999). Ian Rush's later accounts of the intense team bonding at Liverpool and the drinking cliques inside the club in the mid-1980s, was also a marker on the *general* nature of the occupational culture inside many top British football clubs at the time (Rush, 1986; 1996).

The 'best' Liverpool social sessions of the 1980s were held once the *serious* football action was deemed to be over, but they still could be impressive affairs. On 18 May 1982, for example, Liverpool travelled on the day to relegated Middlesbrough for a final Tuesday night fixture, the League title already having been secured once again. By the middle of the afternoon Rush and his senior colleagues were in a Teesside pub, downing lager. 'It was the first of quite a few pints I sank in the next couple of hours. And the rest of the lads were enjoying themselves too.' The squad stumbled back to their hotel rooms for coach Ronnie Moran's 4 p.m. room-check. The match ended in a disjointed 0–0 draw. 'Apparently the Middlesbrough players had got wind of our afternoon session', reported Rush. 'They were half embarrassed at playing us.' (Rush 1986: 99). After the last match of the next season 1982/83, Liverpool left on a short tour of Israel. In Tel Aviv, the night *before* the first tour game, a group of the younger Liverpool players got badly drunk. Rush fell over in a bar and a 'free fight' broke out *between* the players over who had 'pushed' him. The next morning, equipped with shiners and facial gashes, a group of Liverpool players, including the tyro Rush, were up before a stern Bob Paisley, but no further action was taken.

Drinking by players on this scale was no novelty in English football, something confined to Liverpool; far from it. Tony Adams's recent 'confessions' show it was certainly still central to the occupational culture of top English football clubs even a decade later (Adams, 1998). Moreover, Liverpool were still, arguably, the top football club in Europe in the early 1980s, when Hansen and Rush were also fast approaching their prime. But, traditional British team spirit and strength, and this kind of chaotic and abusive treatment of the body, were unlikely to triumph for too long in the new football era. Indeed, when England lost to host nation Sweden in the 1992 European Championships, England manager Graham Taylor complained that the Swedes and other football nations were no longer intimidated by the collective physical power and 'togetherness' of the English. They were now, simply, technically superior and athletically better prepared. They now played the 'English style' *better* than the English (see Williams, 1999b).

Perhaps another small but important symbolic indicator of Liverpool's general approach even to major matches in the 1980s was that, distressingly for the new young Liverpool boss, Dalglish was forced to conduct his first formal managerial press conference immediately after the Heysel disaster in a club *tracksuit*. This was because the Liverpool players had travelled to and from Brussels for the European Cup Final in tracksuits and had returned to Merseyside immediately afterwards (ibid.: 133–4). The press conference called at Anfield to announce Dalglish's appointment, even as the dead were being assembled in Belgium for identification, was described later by one writer as 'Possibly the crassest piece of public relations in football history' (Kelly, 1999: 173).

Even for lengthy trips for crucial European club matches at this time, to distant parts of the old Soviet Bloc, for example, Liverpool persisted in training at Melwood on Tuesday morning, making the gruelling trip in the afternoon/evening, playing the match often the following afternoon, and returning to England immediately after the match. This seemed to work, it was argued: why change it? On the related and important *medical* side of club affairs, up to now taken care of by the recently retired Bob Paisley, Ian Rush also agreed (apparently approvingly) in the mid-1980s that Liverpool FC broke all the accepted rules (Rush, 1986: 145):

> Liverpool operate just about exactly the opposite to the way most people believe a football club should be run. Take the medical side of the club, for example. We have all the latest equipment at Anfield, costing thousands of pounds and we don't have anyone qualified to use it! Ronnie Moran and Roy Evans, our two coaches . . . just read the instructions on the various pieces of equipment and operate it from there. It's hard to imagine, I know. Millions of pounds worth of footballers being treated with less fuss and less knowledge than your pet dog would expect at the vet!

It was soon clear to new manager Dalglish that much of what was available, in terms of guidance or training, on exactly *how* to manage at a club such as Liverpool in the late-1980s remained very much at the *intuitive* level. Dalglish, for example, would have to make the potentially difficult move from player to club manager simply with the support of the club's extraordinary backroom staff. His instant promotion from player to player-manager would be impossible in, say, Italy or Germany, where football coaches are required to be formally qualified for their jobs. As a push towards more professional status and better preparation for football managers in England, but also as a response to some of the glaring *technical* deficiencies in the English game, the technical director of the FA, Howard Wilkinson, wanted to introduce similar sorts of FA-controlled accreditation here (see, Lambert, 1995: 55). Dalglish's 'qualifications' for the managership at Liverpool in 1985 were that he was arguably the most talented British player of his generation, he had a shrewd knowledge of the game and, crucially, he *knew* Liverpool Football Club. On his first day in his new job back at Anfield, however, he was also, tellingly, mystified by what it was the manager of Liverpool FC actually *did* at the club, especially in the closed season. Sitting in his office with 'wee uncle', the legendary Bob Paisley, the following exchange took place (ibid.: 134):

> 'What am I doing sitting in here', I asked Bob. 'There's nothing happening. The phone's not ringing. There's nobody training. All the players are still on holiday'.
> Bob said: 'That's part of the job at this time of year'.
> 'Oh', I said.
> It didn't sound too good to me. I just sat there and talked to Bob about football, which in itself was an experience.

Dalglish, later described the Liverpool manager's job as, 'never complicated . . . one of the most straightforward jobs in English football' (Dalglish, 1996: 180). This was because Peter Robinson and John Smith still dealt with major financial, and most other football administrative, matters at Liverpool. The job of the Liverpool manager was to pick the team and to *let them* win football matches. Technical preparation was minimal: not even set pieces – corners or free kicks – were practised in the club's training. Dalglish even picked as his team captain the nervously introverted and largely silent Hansen, simply because he felt the Scot was 'lucky' (Hansen, 1999: 40). Perhaps because of this deceptive simplicity, Dalglish soon seemed to get to grips with football management, Anfield-style. Astonishingly, he not only guided his squad to the club's first, and only, domestic 'double' – League Championship and FA Cup wins – in his first season in charge in 1985/86, but he also later successfully, if briefly, rebuilt the Liverpool side around a new generation of exciting attacking players between 1988 and 1990, including, especially, the talented Jamaican-born winger, John Barnes (see Hill, 1989 and Chapter Six).

The Boot Room Implodes

The famous Anfield 'boot room', was, in physical terms at least, little more than a cubbyhole at the Anfield ground, containing four kit hampers and a couple of cupboards, and wall slats where the players' boots were stored on hooks. This was profoundly a *man's* space, a shop floor environment, in what was a supportive but harsh culture; current assistant manager Phil Thompson remembers, for example, the beer and topless calendars in the boot room, renewed each November, and a source of considerable attraction to the club's young apprentices (quoted in Kelly, 1999: 60).

The mythology of the boot room began under Shankly when coach Joe Fagan helped out with coaching and support at local Runcorn-based non-League club Guinness Exports. By way of thanks, the Runcorn club sent crates of beer and Guinness across to Joe at Anfield, thus providing the early fuel for animated in-house discussions about club training, players and systems but also providing the opportunity for the club's coaching staff to entertain visiting managers and coaches after home matches. Shankly himself not a drinker save occasionally to quell his nerves about flying, was not a boot room regular. This was a place, instead, where his lieutenants and sergeant majors could pore through injuries and illnesses, discuss the morning's training, and run the rule through the new recruits while looking for developing weaknesses in the long-servers.

The boot room was the professional touchstone of the Liverpool club's playing success for some twenty-five years; a place where the club coaching staff would also meet on Sundays to discuss players, coaching and tactics, and, after matches, to suck in knowledge from other clubs about coaching techniques and 'likely' players in lower divisions (Dalglish, 1996: 143). In the early days of the original boot room, before the advent of the players' lounge and the requirement that players join wives and sponsors after the match, senior players also popped their head in for a natter and a beer with the coaching staff before setting off home. Other 'outsiders' were also allowed access. Tom Saunders, staff coach with the FA and head teacher at Liverpool West Derby Comprehensive, a man steeped in schools football in England, joined the Liverpool club full time in 1970, primarily to organize the recruitment and development of young players. Opera-loving Saunders also watched future match opponents for Shankly and Paisley and, lacking some of the rough edges of the shop floor, he was also a crucial link between the youth and coaching side at Liverpool – including the boot room – the manager, and the club directors.

The boot room itself was eventually demolished, after Dalglish had left Liverpool, as part of the Anfield stadium rebuilding programme, and under pressure from UEFA, ironically, for the provision of a larger *media* interview area at the club. If the boot room was essentially about sharing and soaking up football information, the Liverpool club, since Bill Shankly at least, had never placed great store by doing any more than simply humouring the national press. Dalglish, himself a single-minded and sometimes wilfully obtuse character, especially in his dealings with the media, but also a man who suffered from a severe lack of self-confidence, was accused by some critics of having destroyed the 'threatening' *institution* of the boot room during his spell as manager – a charge he later strenuously denied (Bowler, 1996: 276). Dalglish had actually installed a bar in his own office at Anfield, thus crucially re-directing some of the important post-match drink and gossip among coaches and managers *away* from the boot room base of Liverpool coaches Ronnie Moran and Roy Evans. Whatever the motivation for this development, it was probably the first concrete sign of a real shift in the successful Anfield coaching dynasty which had been inspired from the late 1950s by Bill Shankly.

As the exciting late-1980s Liverpool team quickly began to wane, with key players – Nicol, Rush, Hansen – beginning to age, and Dalglish's new signings – Speedie, Rosenthal, Carter – failing to match up to stringent Anfield standards, self-doubt and gloom began to envelop a clearly strained Dalglish. In 1989 the Hillsborough tragedy and its aftermath in Liverpool hit the manager and his family hard (see Chapter Five). He reported later that he had contemplated resigning his job early in 1990 following a 'creepy' return with Liverpool to Sheffield in front of an empty Leppings Lane terrace, where Liverpool fans had perished only months earlier (Dalglish, 1996: 179). Instead, he hung on until March 1991, before leaving, suddenly, after a coruscating FA Cup replay with Everton, pleading accumulated stress rooted in coping with the terrible aftermath of the 1989 disaster. The manager and his family, essentially very private people, had been key, and almost ever-present, figures in the public mourning which had engulfed the city in the months following the tragedy. After a cursory and largely uninformative press conference at Anfield, Dalglish and his family left immediately for a holiday the United States, leaving long-serving coach Ronnie Moran to step briefly into the Liverpool managerial breach.

Soon, another ex-Liverpool player and Dalglish colleague, Graeme Souness, an excitable and aggressive, but successful, player-manager at Glasgow Rangers, would take over at Anfield. He joined a club which was, arguably, still struggling as an organization to deal fully with the effects of the events of 1989, as well as with the pace of change in 'new' football as an industry, with six years' exclusion from European football competition, and with the very special pressures brought by a quarter of a century of near-constant footballing success at the highest level (see Chapter Four).

Dalglish himself summed up the philosophy of the Liverpool boot room as: 'Give the opposition very little and get as much as you can out of them' (Dalglish, 1996: 143). Szymanski and Kuypers (1999: 240) describe the boot room at Anfield as a: 'distinctive capability . . . [an] 'architecture', a source of competitive advantage derived from the network of relationships inside an organization, which not only benefits the individuals involved but also enhances the organization itself'. Souness remarked on the importance of the boot room, not only for club talk, but for 'documentary' records, of a kind which were probably innovative in the early years of Bill Shankly's tenure. Paisley, Moran and Fagan kept detailed written records of events at Melwood, the club's training ground. According to England inter-national Phil Neal, a policy of custom and practice reflected in comments such as 'Have a look, see what we did last year' was a common response among the club staff to try to right a slump in form or an outbreak of injuries (quoted in Kelly,

1999: 116). For Souness, the boot room was important for its 'continuity . . . that stems from a set of volumes stored at the ground and kept up to date without fail every day. It is the football bible as far as the Anfield staff is concerned, and contains the answer to almost every problem, and every situation which could arise in the day-to-day running of a successful club' (*Management Week*, 14 December 1990). The boot room was also important for its *symbolism*: it stood for a set of values which evoked notions of occupational solidarity and *democratization* – coaches and other staff 'chipping in' – as well as the idea, in an increasingly commercialized and commodified realm, of the club as a closely knit 'family', characterized by traditions of generational inheritance.

On the basis of accounts such as these, Szymanski and Kuypers, in their review of strategic advantages in English football clubs (1999: 239–40), concluded that:

> The boot room, then, appears to have been some kind of database for the club, not merely of facts and figures, but a record of the club's 'spirit', its attitudes and its philosophy . . . The boot room might be thought of as the equivalent of 'reputation' in the context of an organization, an established set of traditions which oblige newcomers to adapt themselves, to fit in, largely because the very success of the organization makes rebellion or radical departures lack credibility.

The Souness years

Graeme Souness's accession to the manager's job at Liverpool in early 1991 chimed well with what were then wider prevailing free market ideologies of management which were the product of the then dominant Thatcherite political philosophy in Britain – Souness was himself a publicly keen admirer of Thatcher and her neo-liberal policies. Known for his opulent style, Souness, no typical British footballer he, married a divorced heiress, sought exclusive private education for his children (at Millfield school) and, unusually, openly left Liverpool FC in 1984 for the less successful Italian club, Sampdoria, simply because of the better money on offer in Italy. Known inside football as 'Champagne Charlie', his general approach to life fitted, glaringly, less well with aspects at the time of the wider culture and politics of the city of Liverpool or, indeed, and more importantly, with what had become some of the accepted approaches to management and coaching at Liverpool Football Club.

Souness was a respected, rather than a loved, ex-player at Liverpool, and he was a man with a formidable reputation for toughness both in sport and in business. Indeed, Souness's approach to playing the game – his calculated violence and intimidation, mixed with cunning and great skill – was indicative of the extent to which the uncertain ethics of business and gamesmanship had increasingly intruded into football and become assimilated into the conventional wisdom of the game and sanctioned in its ideology (Wagg, 1984: 148–9). He had been welcomed back to the club by most Liverpool fans precisely because of his uncompromising competitiveness and supposed winning mentality, expressed in his turbulent recent successes as manager of Glasgow Rangers. Above all, he was welcomed to Anfield because of his *Liverpool FC* heritage. He was unlikely, nevertheless, simply to 'fit in' with the established management traditions at Anfield.

It was soon clear that Souness felt the club he had rejoined was still immersed in the nostalgia of past playing achievements, and he strove for change on the playing and coaching side. He was critical, later, of the lack of real commitment from the senior professionals at the club who, he felt, were either already past their best playing days (the injured, overweight and reluctant Barnes) or were allegedly too concerned about testimonials or a last football pay day (Nicol, Whelan, Rush) (Souness, 1999: 85–9). The new manager obviously felt he had inherited a team which had little backbone for a fight on the field, and which was already going alarmingly backwards so soon after its early 1980s European football dominance in which he himself had been a key figure as a player.

Originally recruited and publicized as a 'boot room' disciple, but one who had also a modernizer's steely glint to the club, Souness quickly moved unwanted players on and also brought in new players to the club on what were, by this stage, rocketing salaries. This was the moment when the new FA Premier League commercial boom in English football was getting under way and new TV income from BSkyB was already boosting the bargaining power of players and their advisers (Williams, 1999b). With established players on agreed contracts and new arrivals pocketing higher wages, this buying and selling strategy produced further disharmony in an already unhappy Liverpool dressing room. Also, the earlier internal 'boot room' discussions about what *exactly* the club needed and precisely *which* players the club might sign – something which had already begun to recede under Dalglish – now virtually disappeared in a much more hierarchical managerial set-up under Souness. Finally, almost for the first time since Bill Shankly had taken over at Liverpool, first-team players were allowed to leave the club – Staunton and Beardsley, for example – to go on to comparable playing success elsewhere. Their replacements – Dicks and Clough – little matched up to the loss of these established internationals. Talented youngsters coming through the Liverpool production line – McManaman, Fowler, Marsh, and the Dalglish signing, Jamie Redknapp – tempered the effects of these sorts of negative player 'exchange' sufficiently for Liverpool to win the FA Cup under Souness in 1992. The competition in this cup campaign had been weak, however; this was but a temporary glow.

Souness, a man who had of course played at the highest level abroad, also began tending seriously to Liverpool players' diets for the first time, and he moved all the club's training activities and its day-to-day focus away from Anfield to the

Melwood training ground. This sort of detailed attention to the preparation of players was naturally to become much more common in England, especially following the arrival of foreign coaches in the late 1990s. This necessary modernization of day-to-day routines at Liverpool also meant, however, that the daily visits by players to Anfield and the collective coach ride to Melwood for training, during which the elusive and vital Liverpool 'team spirit' was mainly sparked, also disappeared. Players now arrived for training alone in cars. 'Boot room' meetings, partly as a consequence, also became less central to the coaching and playing culture of the club. Finally, Souness had also taken over at the club at a time when it lacked real stability and enough top quality on the playing side, and when it was also missing effective boardroom leadership and real vision and dynamism in the area of club administration. In short, the club as an *institution* was clearly ailing, and it had been for some time. David Fairclough, a player with the club in the late 1970s who had, unusually, like Souness played abroad, had seen signs of Liverpool's demise a decade earlier (in Kelly, 1999: 241):

> I felt that the boot room had run its course. It might sound controversial, but having seen and done things abroad in Switzerland and in Belgium, and seen how the game was changing, I thought when I was in Switzerland that Liverpool, even though they were still European champions, were falling behind. I could see the game changing. I thought, ultimately, Liverpool would have caught up by the time I got back, by broadening their vision a little bit. I don't think Liverpool or English clubs were aware of what was going on on the continent . . . It is a European game now, and Liverpool have this attitude that 'We are Liverpool, we are the best, why should we change things, we've won trophies.' . . . We should have been more aware . . . I think Liverpool were a bit blinkered.

In 1993, under Souness, there also occurred a crucial *symbolic* moment for the club and a sign of the power of new money in the game. Wracked by defensive lapses, Souness moved to sign Tim Flowers, an emerging and talented young goalkeeper at Southampton. Ten, even five, or perhaps even *three* years before, Liverpool would comfortably have secured their man, drawing on their distinct capabilities of *reputation* and *innovation* to pull the young player on board. Now Flowers *rejected* a move to Liverpool in favour of Dalglish's offer of high wages and ambition at the Jack Walker-funded provincial Blackburn Rovers, where the goalkeeper went on to win a Premiership title in 1995 and England recognition under Kenny Dalglish. Symbolically and materially, this was a crushing reverse, and along with poor playing results added to the growing sense that the Liverpool club was in decline as others were quickly emerging, and also that the Liverpool manager, in the parlance of the boardroom and the press, had 'lost the confidence' of some of his senior players and also some key members of the Liverpool board.

Souness was eventually accused by fans, Liverpool coaches and the press of traducing the legacy left by Shankly and those who had followed him, and of riding roughshod over the by now mythologized Anfield 'boot room' footballing philosophies. Although the club *was* changing, change was clearly necessary. The truth about Souness, however, is that he had arrived at the club as its distinct capabilities were already being allowed to drain away. But Souness was also simply a poor man manager and, unlike many of his predecessors, at best an inconsistent judge of top players. He had also *played* at Liverpool with some of the squad he now had returned to the club to manage and, unlike Dalglish, he found this difficult personally. He had made actually quite modest – though prescient – changes to player preparation at Liverpool, even if a much more intensive training regime at the club was blamed by fans for a dramatic increase in player injuries.

As Liverpool's results worsened in the early 1990s, and as Souness's own health and his stock with club supporters and local commentators declined further following more ill-judged signings, the writing was soon on the wall. The public exposure of his commercial links with the *Sun* newspaper in 1992 – which was still fiercely boycotted across Merseyside following its insensitive and distorting Hillsborough coverage – added rancour to the inevitable parting. After the sort of dithering which was to become characteristic of the Liverpool board's hesitant management style in the early 1990s, Souness's resignation was eventually accepted by his close friend and now club Chairman David Moores following a shattering home FA Cup tie loss against Bristol City in January 1994.

Definitely Maybe: the Time of Roy Evans, 1994–1998

Damaged by the Hillsborough-related mistakes of an acerbic and apparently insensitive manager, and also by the 'modernizing' discourses and techniques and the ill-judged transfer and man-management practices of Souness, the Liverpool club turned, once again, in 1994 to what seemed the greater certainty and stability offered by a recognized boot room disciple. Bootle-born Roy Evans, twenty years on the Liverpool club coaching staff, stepped up, perhaps reluctantly, to take charge, ostensibly to try to re-engage once more with earlier, more successful Liverpool traditions (Hopkins and Williams, 1999). Briefly, it seemed it might prove an unlikely master-stroke.

Increasingly, in these so-called 'new times', when the predominant vocabulary inside the game is one of markets and 'brands', the very notion of a working relationship with a football club which spans, as it did for Evans, more than thirty years in all, and the sense of historical continuity, loyalty and integrity, and even duty, which that can evoke can appear outmoded and anachronistic. Evans was the sort of servant who personified the historical commitment and the collective spirit of a British football club – as well as, admittedly, sometimes the ingrained paternalism of some football club Chairmen.

Any serious audit of the Roy Evans years at Liverpool needs to acknowledge at least two important things. First, the scale of the problems he faced in rebuilding the club after its post-Hillsborough demise under a drained Kenny Dalglish, and the chaotic revolution 'led' by Graeme Souness between 1991 and 1994. Secondly, the very real quality of the team that Evans, Doug Livermore and long-time coach Ronnie Moran constructed on the basis of the 3–5–2 (or wing-back) system, particularly in 1995/96 when, but for a dark November when too many points were dropped against poor opposition, even the vaunted 'double' of League and FA Cup might, once again, have been within Liverpool's reach.

Under Evans, but with John Barnes closely in support on and off the field, Liverpool re-established their national credentials as *the* passing team in England in the mid-1990s. They kept possession of the ball better than any other side, they passed the ball relentlessly, they committed fewest fouls, and they played the purest football, in keeping with the club's long-established collective ethos of simplicity and teamwork. In his careful support and development of emerging young 'scousers' such as Steve McManaman and Robbie Fowler, especially, Evans also reinvigorated local traditions for nurturing young players at the very heart of the club's ambitions. The intelligent and talented McManaman, especially, had lost his way under Souness; under Evans he became the creative hub of an exciting new team. For all this, the club's League Cup Final triumph of 1995 against First Division Bolton Wanderers represented merely the barest of rewards.

Evans, a traditional English club *coach*, rather than a football manager, was essentially a nice man who lacked the cunning and disciplinary ruthlessness of some of his Anfield teachers. His approach to the football press, for example, suggested a dangerous openness and naiveté. 'If you get too close to one newspaper you can give yourself problems', he reasoned. 'If you stay reasonably honest with the media, they will be reasonably honest with you' (quoted in Lambert, 1995: 126). Evans *liked* his footballers, and he wanted to be their friends. In Bill Shankly's day, by way of contrast, if you were a player and merely injured you effectively ceased to exist, because you were of no use to the club (see Chapter Three).

Maybe Evans had always hated the necessary cruelty of this kind of approach to football club management. He was publicly criticized by the media for being 'too close' to the players, though after the destructive and abrasive management style of Souness, a renowned half-time teacup thrower, a new direction in this respect was also probably necessary (Lacey, 1998). The Liverpool approach under boot room product Evans was also a mystery to some new foreign players at the club. Abroad, if a player was dropped from the team the coaches talked to him, explained his deficiencies and worked on his weaknesses to try to get him back in favour. The psychology of man-managing intelligent, and sometimes sensitive, athletes was a central component of running a successful football club on the continent. At Liverpool, players left out of the first team were not typically faced with explanations or shows of real support. They effectively disappeared from view until they had magically 'found' their form once again.

Evans was certainly dogged during his time in charge at Anfield by recurring accusations about other aspects of the 'laxness' of his regime; his younger stars were dubbed the 'Spice Boys' by the media for their alleged penchant for celebrity culture and the high life. They were, damagingly, compared in this regard to the allegedly more 'focused' young players who were then emerging under the fierce and puritan management of Alex Ferguson at Manchester United. Some of Evans's more senior players, especially the expensive and perplexing Stan Collymore – a man 'lost in the mist of his own mind' according to one of his previous managers, Alan Smith (quoted in Sik, 1996: 115) – also seemed completely unwilling to come to heel, at one point flatly refusing to play for the club's reserve team. For many commentators, Evans seemed a weak character who had problems facing up to difficult decisions.

In point of fact, although lacking the disciplinary steel of some of his predecessors, Evans was in many ways simply following the tenets of the regime established under the Liverpool boot room dynasty when, as we have already seen, players were never route-marched, but were treated as 'adults', and senior professionals would be expected to keep in check their own socializing and the potentially dangerous excesses of younger members of the squad (Souness, 1999: 88). Published accounts of life at Anfield by later 'drinkers' recruited by Souness – the laddish Neil Ruddock, for example – showed that aspects of the occupational culture identified by Ian Rush during the 'good times' at Liverpool in the 1980s were still in place during the hard times later. But, under an increasingly puritanical and watchful media eye, as new methods of player preparation were emerging, and at a time when the sport was massaging it's own new glossy image as a 'family' product, Evans seemed to be struggling for good sense and judgement among some of his talented, and monied, younger players, but also for reliable *senior* dressing room leaders in this last important respect.

This was a very different era, of course, from the one in which Evans himself had been guided as a young coach. In the 1960s or early 1970s, few players at Liverpool ever spoke to Bill Shankly or Bob Paisley about *financial* rewards; players were recruited, simply, because they *wanted* to play for the club. Money could be dealt with later. Few players refused the offer of a contract at Liverpool. Even in the late 1980s, the club's own players were still very limited in their options for career movements – where could they go after Liverpool? Also, players' salaries were still firmly managed, they were as yet relatively unaffected by agents, TV income, or the very high wages already offered by some clubs abroad. By the mid-1990s, however, the celebrity status of top footballers, the more open international market for players, and the contracts and wages now offered even to moderate performers in the new TV age, meant a whole new set of concerns for football managers and club officials (see Williams, 1999b; Morrow, 1999). In this new post-Fordist occupational culture for players, where flexibility and mobility were the watchwords, players moved more frequently, and showed little loyalty to their clubs, or supporters, and expected little in return. The Bosman transfer ruling later offered players even more scope for reflexivity and shaping their own careers, irrespective of club and supporter claims on their loyalties (see, Williams, 1999b; and interview with Houllier; and also Chapter Ten). Significantly, Steve McManaman, perhaps the key Liverpool player under Evans and a local boy who had spent his entire career at the club, 'waited' on a Bosman transfer in 1998/99, eventually leaving for record wages at Real Madrid, with no transfer fee payable to Liverpool.

All of this growth in the power of players, their alleged lack of club loyalty, the penchant of Liverpool stars for the high life, and the laxness of Evans's regime, was used as the damning background to the abject defeat of Liverpool in a poor 1996 FA Cup Final against arch-rivals Manchester United. The Liverpool players had turned up for the match, in full media glare, sporting ostentatious cream 'designer' suits and 'Tarantino' sunglasses. This publicly languid approach and the Liverpool capitulation in what was arguably the club's most important match of the 1990s, simply provoked more media and supporter hostility aimed at Evans's alleged indolent and fabulously wealthy footballing underachievers.

In the following season, 1996/97, the experienced John Barnes, still a key ally of Evans's inside Anfield, was sent by the Liverpool club to observe the famous Ajax youth system. Barnes was apparently destined to continue aspects of the boot room ethos at Anfield, even in these very changed, and for Evans, troubled times. A new £12 million Academy for youth development was established at the club soon afterwards, under ex-player Steve Heighway. But, further alleged player indulgences, and inevitable defensive frailty and failures on the field, finally provoked the frustrated Evans, seemingly, to dispense with his entire playing strategy which he had built up so carefully since 1994. The key symbolic moment marking out this shift probably came with the signing, in 1997, of an experienced midfield ball winner, a 'hard man', but a technically limited and ageing player with a discipline problem: exit a slowing but still astute John Barnes, to be replaced at Liverpool by an already failing, self-styled 'Guv'nor', England international midfielder Paul Ince.

What followed in this belated new Evans approach was a decline from the seriously flawed excellence of the Liverpool squads of the mid-1990s to a much more anonymous and less fluent team later. The emergence of the mercurial Michael Owen, in 1997, served only to mask real weaknesses elsewhere, especially in defence (see, Cornwall, 1999, on Owen). At the beginning of the 1998/99 League season, and under pressure for more managerial change, but *without* sacking the loyal and liked Evans, the Liverpool club announced a surprising new direction. Evans and Gérard Houllier, ex-French national team manager and ex-Technical Director of Coaching in France, were unveiled to a disbelieving press as the new *joint* managers of Liverpool FC. The beginnings of a new 'continental' era to the coaching and development of players at Liverpool was about to take hold.

The New Future

Following the eventual uncertainties and traumas under the troubled Dalglish, and the harsher failures under Graeme Souness, by the end of the Roy Evans era at Liverpool, and despite his own difficulties in securing any of the major trophies for the club, many of the core strengths of the Liverpool club were still clear and intact. Evans, in fact, had produced a team which at certain moments was very close to title success. Attendances at Liverpool were still strong, the club's fan base more than loyal and secure. The stadium at Anfield was being modernized, though it was also clear that its size and facilities could yet restrict the club's preferred future as a top European club for the next century. Developments on the 'business' side of the club were also accelerating, with new deals in place with media partners which would later release large capital sums for new player investment. The club was, finally, planning for a future in what was likely to be a new European elite of top football clubs.

Liverpool FC's capacity among English football clubs in the late 1990s to be able to draw on a *national* and even an active *international* following was surpassed only by the corporate giant which was nearby Manchester United. The club's new Youth Academy was also nationally acclaimed and was continuing to produce able first-team candidates. However, between 1997 and 1998 wages and salary costs at Liverpool had climbed, with no proportionate noticeable improvement in playing performance. By 1998/99 Liverpool was paying 80 per cent of turnover in salaries and wages, reflecting both the residual 'narrowness' of the club's commercial activities and the wage inflation both inside the club and in the game more generally (Deloitte and Touche, 2000). In fact, the club's turnover in 1998 was by now comfortably less than *half* that of Manchester United. Liverpool FC had, critically, yet to play in the new extended version of the European Cup, the new international stage for top European football talent, and a TV-driven competition now securing vital extra revenue for its competing clubs. In an age of increasing reflexivity and mobility for footballers, top foreign players – and many domestic ones, too – were increasingly choosing their English clubs on the basis of *current* European credentials and lifestyle choices, and not in terms of past footballing glories. In the 1990s, neither post-industrial Merseyside, nor Liverpool FC, seemed especially attractive options to Europe's football crème. In short, many of the distinct capabilities referred to by Szymanski and Kuypers, and which the Liverpool club had nurtured, perhaps not always consciously, in the 1970s and 1980s, were simply no longer quite as relevant in this new 'globalized', more capital-intensive and more technically proficient and 'scientific' period of the sport's development. Liverpool FC then took a new direction to try to reassert the club's position in this new era. We pick up the story of Gérard Houllier's introduction at Liverpool, and what it also said about wider developments in the British game, in the next chapter.

References

Adams, T. (1998) *Addicted*, London: Collins Willow.

Armstrong, G. and Giulianotti, R. (1999) *Football Cultures and Identities*, London: MacMillan.

Bowler, D. (1996) *Shanks: The Authorised Biography of Bill Shankly*, London: Orion.

Bromberger, C. (1993) 'Allez L'OM, Forza Juve; the passion for football in Marseilles and Turin', in S. Redhead (ed.) *The Passion and the Fashion*, Aldershot: Avebury.

Brown, A. (ed.) (1998) *Fanatics! Race, Power, Nationality and Fandom in European Football*, London: Routledge

Cornwall, P. (1999) 'The making of Saint Michael', in M. Perryman (ed.) *The Ingerland Factor*, London: Mainstream.

Dalglish, K. (1996) *Dalglish: My Autobiography*, London: Hodder & Stoughton.

Deloitte and Touche (2000) *Annual Review of Football Finance*, Manchester: Deloitte and Touche.

Gibson, J. (1999) 'Stakes rise in battle of the box', *Guardian*, 14 July.

Gilmore, S. (2000) 'Out of the frying pan: new theories of Football Management', unpublished PhD, University of Portsmouth.

Giulianotti, R. (1999) *Football: a Sociology of the Global Game*, Cambridge: Polity.

Hansen, A (1999) *A Matter of Opinion*, London: Partridge.

Hill, D. (1989) *Out of His Skin: The John Barnes Phenomenon*, London: Faber & Faber.

Hopkins, S. and Williams, J. (1999) 'The departure of Roy Evans from Liverpool', *When Saturday Comes*, No. 143, January.

Keith, J. (1999) *Bob Paisley: Manager of the Millennium*, London: Robson.

Kelly, S. (1999) *The Boot Room Boys*, London: Collins Willow.

King, A. (1998) *The End of the Terraces*, London: Leicester University Press.

Lacey, D. (1998) 'French technocrat left to nail the door shut on Liverpool's bootroom', *Guardian*, 12 November.

Lambert, C. (1995) *The Boss*, London: Vista.

Morrow, S. (1999) *The New Business of Football*, Basingstoke: MacMillan.

Parkinson, M. (1985) *Liverpool on the Brink*, Hermitage, Berks: Policy Journals.

Rowe, D. (1999) *Sport, Culture and the Media*, Milton Keynes: Open University Press.

Rush, I. (1986) *Rush*, London: Grafton.

—— (1989) *Ian Rush: My Italian Diary*, London: Arthur Barker.

—— (1996) *Ian Rush; an Autobiography*, London: Ebury.

Sik, G. (1996) *I think I'll Manage*, London: Headline.

Souness, G. (1999) *Souness: The Management Years*, London: André Deutsch

Szymanski, S. and Kuypers, T. (1999) *Winners and Losers: the Business Strategy of Football*, London: Viking.

Walter, T. (1991) 'The mourning after Hillsborough', *Sociological Review*, **39**(3): 599–626.

Wagg, S. (1984) *The Football World*, Brighton: Harvester

Williams, J. (1986) 'White riots: the English football fan abroad', in A. Tomlinson and G. Whannel (eds) *Off the Ball*, London: Pluto.

—— (1996) 'Sir John Hall and the New Geordie Nation', in S. Gerhmann (ed.), *Football and Regional Identity*, Munich: LIT.

—— (1999a) 'Hillsborough: ten short years', *When Saturday Comes*, No. 147, May.

—— (1999b) *Is it all Over: Can Football Survive the Premier League?*, Reading: South Street Press.

—— (2000) 'Ian Rush', in P. Stead and H. Richards (eds) *For Club and Country: Welsh Football Greats*, Cardiff: University of Wales Press.

Young, P. (1968) *A History of British Football*, London: Stanley Paul.

−8−

Gérard Houllier and the New Liverpool 'Imaginary'

Stephen Hopkins and *John Williams*

Introduction

In the nearly five years Roy Evans spent as manager of Liverpool (1994–98), much of the traditional football culture and the economics of the English game were in the process of being radically transformed (King, 1998). This was occurring at the level of business and finance (Deloitte and Touche, 1999; Morrow, 1999) but on the playing side in terms of managing and coaching, football was also globalizing and facing new demands in terms of professionalism (Williams, 1999). A new generation of imported foreign coaches, players and managers were in the vanguard of these shifts. Often treated with undisguised media disdain initially, the success generated by Arsène Wenger (at Arsenal) and Gianluca Vialli (at Chelsea) had the effect of convincing many English fans that their clubs were not only in safe 'foreign' keeping, but that this technocratic innovation brought by foreign coaches was by now long overdue.

These sentiments have been powerfully reinforced, of course, by the poor performances of the England national side in the 1998 World Cup and, especially, at Euro 2000. Wenger and Vialli had also been especially successful in recruiting talented foreign stars to their increasingly wealthy and powerful clubs − if not always managing to hold on to them in the new post-Bosman era. In this era, it is the larger football clubs and leagues which are in the ascendant − which can mean problems for national teams (King, 1998; Williams, 1999). According to Wenger: 'Foreign players are a threat in rich countries like Italy and England because young [home grown] players have no real chance to play. But in France, for example, it is good because the exodus gives young people a chance' (quoted in Fynn and Guest, 1998: 91).

This chapter seeks to illustrate where Liverpool FC might fit into this 'transitional' phase in the development of English football, by examining the principles and early practice of Gérard Houllier as manager of the club. We centre this analysis around a lengthy interview which we conducted (see pp. 184–193). However, while much of what Houllier says could be read as a 'manifesto for change', it also quickly becomes clear that things are rather more complex than this.

Houllier's passion for elements of the traditional English game in general and for Liverpool FC in particular, not to mention his more generalized Anglophilia, stand out. English football reporters covering Euro 2000, which Houllier watched as a technical expert on behalf of UEFA, were amused to hear this Frenchman not only defending some of the qualities of the English game (while commentators in England were ready to condemn it in *all* its aspects), but also identifying himself as an England *supporter*, experiencing the real pain of the defeats against Portugal and Romania, and the short-lived high after a poor German team were beaten in Charleroi.

This is no convenient cover for Houllier's real feelings. In the interview that follows, Houllier openly confesses himself to being bored when he had to sit through highly skilled but cagey, slow-moving Italian league matches as the French national coach. The high pace of the English game excites him. It is also clear that, right from the beginning of his association with Liverpool as a city, in 1969, here is a man and a football manager who is no mere technocrat. Houllier certainly does not view the sport (or the Liverpool club) as in any way divorced from its social and economic surroundings. Quite the opposite. In fact, he sees no contradiction between a highly disciplined, carefully planned, and well-organized administration of the club – something easily associated with technocratic foreign coaches – and a passionate, empathetic desire to connect with the 'spirit' or 'heart' at the core of the club's identity.

There are several key themes that Houllier concentrates upon in the interview, and they resonate loudly in some of the recent debates concerning the direction being followed more generally by the footballing elite in England. For instance, he addresses the question of increasing player mobility, and the large numbers of foreign players now working in England; he also raises the interrelated issues of traditional English styles of play, and the general culture associated with the game in this country. At a more parochial level, he also demonstrates he has an understanding of what we have called, taking from Raymond Williams, the 'structure of feeling' in Liverpool about the sport. He knows something, for example, about why the Liverpool club has, and has had, such a critical place in the life of the city, and the special role the particular approach to playing the game in Liverpool holds in what he calls the 'imaginary' of the Liverpool people.

Preparing for Liverpool

Let us say something, briefly, about Houllier's links with Liverpool, and how he ended up as the club's first overseas manager and a potentially key figure in the wider English game. Houllier was a long-time admirer of the club, who had decided to come to the city in 1969 (aged 22) in order to work on his Masters dissertation – on poverty in the city. He lived briefly in Liverpool, teaching at Alsop school in the north of the city, playing local league football, and supporting Liverpool as a visiting 'Kopite'. His first game at Anfield, in the company of current first-team coach Patrice Berguès, saw Liverpool beat Dundalk 10–0 in the European Inter Cities Fairs' (now UEFA) Cup. He struck up a friendship with Liverpool Secretary Peter Robinson, which cemented Houllier's admiration for the club and the values it espoused on and off the field. A sporadic visitor to Anfield in subsequent years, in 1986 Houllier (by now the coach of Paris Saint-Germain) brought along another friend and football coach, Arsène Wenger, to share his appreciation of the English game (George, 2000).

Houllier's own ambitions to be a professional player had been dashed early on by his father's insistence that he should learn to teach. However, his father was the director of a small amateur club, and passed on his passion for the game to Gérard. Houllier made his way in the sport in France as a young, innovative coach with a reputation for meticulous attention to detail and a determination to apply a more 'scientific' approach to player preparation and strategies for play. After beginning as player-coach at Le Touquet in 1973, aged only 26, the young Houllier spent a couple of years as youth coach at Arras, before he took over at modest Noeux-Les-Mines. Between 1976 and 1982, Houllier guided this obscure team from the fifth to the second division of the French League. Recruited by another club from the old coal-mining region of the Nord-Pas de Calais, Houllier then took Lens into the French first division and to a UEFA Cup place, before leading Paris Saint-Germain to their first French League title in 1986.

Overtures from England, in the shape at least of Peter Robinson's recommendation to Spurs' then chairman Irving Scholar, came to nothing. Later on, after Kenny Dalglish stood down as Liverpool manager in 1991, Houllier was apparently considered for the vacant post, and the FA also thought about him as their inaugural technical director. However serious these possibilities were, the appointment of a foreign coach/manager in English football during the late 1980s/early 1990s would have been an imaginative, though not entirely unprecedented step, but also one that would undoubtedly have been greeted with hostility in many quarters. Indeed, it may be true to speculate that particularly *at Liverpool*, where the principle of 'boot room' succession still dominated, such a move would have been looked at askance by many of the club's devotees.

By 1988, Houllier had been appointed assistant to French national team coach Michel Platini, eventually taking over the top job in 1992. His 16-month spell as coach of France ended when the national team failed to qualify for World Cup 1994 after a last-minute home defeat to Bulgaria. As national technical director, Houllier then concentrated on youth development in France, contributing via this route to the emergence of the 1998 World Cup and Euro 2000 winning

French squads. Houllier was by now widely respected in UEFA and FIFA circles because of his central role in the dramatic transformation of the moribund French game.

Houllier came to the wider attention of the footballing elite in England when he captivated an FA national coaching conference in Birmingham in May 1997, with his use of video clips and coaching drills to illustrate the power of forward passing on counter-attack – 'the rattlesnake effect', as he described it to a rapt audience of English coaches (Ridley, 1997). The importance of the initial pass forward was a theme he would return to many times later at Anfield. At the same coaching conference, the FA pledged to follow for the English game the lead on youth development Houllier had established so successfully in France. Howard Wilkinson's 1998 *Charter for Quality*, which later established youth academies at all the major professional clubs in England, owes much to the transformations in France which were engineered under Houllier's astute direction.

A second theme that Houllier develops in our interview is the need for football technique and skills to be closely integrated with the evolution of players' all-round education and culture. This 'holistic' view of sportsmen is really quite alien to English football, where the culture is expected to produce young players who require direction, discipline and supervision almost all of the time. Thus, English footballers are little prepared to be good decision-makers on the field. In strictly playing terms, Houllier stresses the need for players who can demonstrate *flexibility* during matches, who have the intelligence to see the broad contours of a game, and to adapt according to different challenges that will be posed by tactically astute opponents. Supporting this argument, Houllier points to the fact that *substitutes* won the Euro 2000 final for France and the 1999 European Cup for Manchester United, and therefore, 'In the modern game now, you need a strong bench with flexibility, players who can create new problems for the opposition' (Ridley, 2000; George, 2000).

The English Failing: Players and Player Culture

During his two close seasons at Liverpool, Houllier has signed eleven new players, transforming the side within eighteen months. The rapid movement of players through top clubs has become more generally a new feature of the sport's late-modern development (Giulianotti, 1999; Williams, 1999). Clearly, Houllier also believed that the squad he inherited at Liverpool lacked sufficient depth to compete with the best in England and Europe, but he has also admitted that he was surprised by the scale of the rebuilding that he judged to be necessary (Ridley, 2000). He has preached the virtues of constructing a solid defensive foundation, around a 'square base' composed of central defenders and two central midfielders. Liverpool fans who had become used to inconsistency and costly individual and collective lapses in concentration during the 1990s, were pleasantly surprised to find Houllier's team with the tightest defence in the FA Premier League in 1999/2000, conceding only thirty goals.

On the flanks, he has sought out capable defenders, but of greater significance here is the premium Houllier places upon the attacking abilities of wide players, even when, nominally, they occupy primarily defensive roles. The expectation that seasoned German internationals Marcus Babbel and Christian Ziege (significantly, in place of *local* youth-team products) will provide this kind of flexibility remains to be definitively tested. Nonetheless, what is clear is that they represent a close approximation to Houllier's vision of responsible, mature, intelligent, and astute footballers who can also cope with the physical demands of the English game. Houllier has stressed, repeatedly, the sheer athletic endeavour required from footballers in this era, and it remains the case that the high tempo of English league football (in comparison with that of the Italian, French or Spanish leagues) means that this requirement necessitates a much more professional approach to the physical and mental preparation of players.

Thus, Houllier recognized the need for a root-and-branch revision of the prevailing player culture. This was partly a question of player discipline and professionalism during a specific period at Liverpool, which had reached a low ebb during the previous decade (see Chapter Seven), but it also had wider ramifications for ingrained aspects of English football's 'code of masculinity'. This pitted well-worn stereotypes of 'laddish' English behaviour and mentalities that had been the professional footballer's stock in trade over several generations (Wagg, 1984; Williams and Taylor, 1994), against a new emphasis upon the all-round education and personality of the modern elite player.

The *Guardian* journalist Richard Williams, writing after Euro 2000 and another close season when English footballers had rarely been out of the limelight, argued that young footballers' cultural experience was narrowly confined to 'What they see or hear or read in the over-heated and hyper-sexualised mass media, in the tabloid exposes and prying docu-soaps . . .' (R. Williams, 2000). In the same article, John Cartwright, director of Crystal Palace's academy for young players, and one-time technical director at the FA's coaching school at Lilleshall, is quite brutal in his assessment of the problematic, heavily masculinst values of many young English footballers:

> If you even try to speak properly, people think you must be a fool. We've developed a thug culture. Football follows the culture of the country, and sometimes vice versa. We've played thug football and we've produced a thug relationship between the player and the spectator . . . There have been gradual improvements. Coaches and players have come in from abroad and they've shown a different attitude to preparation. But we still go out there with a gung-ho attitude. If you can't think it out, fight it out.

Even well before the frantic inquest into England's national malaise during the summer of 2000, Henry Winter, one of the most thoughtful of current English football journalists, was bemoaning Kevin Keegan's insistence that 'We need to revert to more traditional qualities, like getting into them . . . I want intensity and aggression to become trademarks of my England side'. As Winter noted, 'Some of Keegan's players need to control their aggression, not unleash it.' The national team manager insisted that the 'tempo' and the 'intensity' of the English game could still bring success in international football, something that Houllier might agree with – but only up to a point. However, as Winter puts it, other necessities of the modern international game must also feature, namely, 'composure', 'shape' and 'possession'. For Winter – and almost certainly for Houllier too – 'Keegan's idea of tempo involves sustained velocity when the best teams . . . race through the gears, keeping the ball well and then counter-attacking on espying a defensive chink' (Winter, 1999).

Houllier argues forcefully that respect for teammates and opponents, communication and inter-personal skills (crucial in an era of media saturation coverage of sport), and commitment to embrace a 'learning culture' where change is not necessarily viewed as threatening – these are the sort of values and skills that will mark out successful football clubs in the future. Again, these points have a wider relevance. In terms of communication, for example, it has been pointed out that 'At Euro 2000 many of Keegan's players were sullen and uncommunicative. With a couple of honourable exceptions, what thoughts they may have had about what was unfolding in Holland and Belgium remained locked inside minds that have been closed to the joys of thinking and talking publicly about the subtle complexities of the game.' (Hayward, 2000).

If a certain suspicion of the voracious British media – especially the tabloids – is to be expected from English players, there is no doubt that this refusal or inability to reflect and theorize about the game is also a potent indicator of the paucity of the cultural resources that the bulk of English footballers can currently draw upon. This deep 'anti-intellectual strain' in English football (present, too, among many administrators, managers, coaches and supporters) clearly reflects a more generalized cultural problem, but after Euro 2000, there were some signs that insularity and chauvinism could be challenged more forcefully now than perhaps at any previous time in the recent development of the game in England. Speculation even extended to either appointing a foreign coach to manage England, or, given Keegan's evident deficiencies, asking Houllier or Wenger to 'help out' with the preparation of the English team (Powell, 2000). Interestingly, the advocates of this idea were not immediately laughed out of court, but Houllier himself, perhaps mindful of one failed 'joint experiment' at club level, immediately quashed the idea.

It is by no means clear that this struggle over the professional ethos and identity of footballers in this country will be easily resolved, for there are powerful currents that stand out against this perceived dilution of 'traditional' strengths of the English game. Houllier seems to understand the complexity of this issue and, critically, argues that this type of cultural transformation need not stifle spontaneity or belittle the spirit of collectivity and teamwork that, for example, the drinking culture in English football was supposed to embody. Indeed, he often uses aspects of the vocabulary and imagery of this old culture ('When each of my players wears the Liverpool shirt, I expect him to die for it'), but sees no contradiction in marrying this attitude with meticulous professionalism, and a much more rigorous and serious approach to planning for success.

When Houllier took charge at Liverpool he, predictably, took firm steps to tackle drinking: 'There used to be a time when, as soon as the young go through to the first team, they have to start drinking to show they are men . . . That's finished; if they do that, they last two years.' He also made the specific comparison with Arsenal's new regime: 'Arsene Wenger started by changing the attitude of players as regards their training, their diet and their behaviour off the pitch. We've done that here, with a good response. I don't think we have a booze problem. Previously, perhaps, but not now' (George, 2000).

Managing at Liverpool and the 'new' English game

On his arrival at Liverpool, as we have seen, as well as being internationally acclaimed Houllier also had the added attractions to the Anfield hierarchy of being a knowledgeable respecter of the club's traditions and, following the alleged excesses of the Evans regime, a reputed disciplinarian. He had turned down other British clubs, effectively to job-share at Anfield. Lacking the heavy egotistical baggage of some of his English equivalents, he also even seemed genuinely moved by his new appointment, and he appeared convinced that joint decision-making was perfectly possible at a top English football club, even one which was now frantically rebuilding in full media glare. 'Gérard must be in heaven', commented Alain Tirloy, a friend of Houllier who had also played under him at Lens in the early 1980s. 'He's always been completely mad about Liverpool' (Brodkin and Henley, 1998).

Predictably, however, the new managerial partnership did not last long. Press mutterings about the lack of a single 'decision-maker' at the football helm at Anfield added to the pressures on the new pairing; but it was poor performances and results which claimed Evans in the end. The Liverpool team which lost at home to Spurs in a League Cup tie in November 1998, a result which finally led to Evans's resignation, capitulated feebly. It was, like many of Evans's talented teams of the time, simply overpowered. This experience confirmed Houllier's insistence that physical strength and athletic ability were now absolutely vital as prerequisites for a successful team. Equally, passing for the sake of passing, and maintaining possession (often in their own half) with no clear attacking purpose, had become problems in the Evans' years, and Houllier made no apology for his conviction that Liverpool needed to revert to 'passing and movement', particularly movement *forwards*.

Houllier recognizes that this can easily be construed as a call for the introduction of 'long-ball' football and, particularly at Liverpool, this would not only be met with resistance from many players, but also from many of the supporters. He argues that he is not suggesting that Liverpool should take lessons from Wimbledon (the arch-exponents of 'route one' play), but that the Liverpool emphasis upon passing had become something of a fetish in recent years, producing an exaggerated 'purity'. As a result, home matches against lesser opponents ended up all too often in draws rather than victories. He also brought in new players who could improve Liverpool's *physical* presence (the central defenders Stéphane Henchoz and Sami Hyypia and the midfielder Dietmar Hamann are good examples). There were also to be important attempts to change Liverpool's off-pitch preparation.

At his valedictory press conference Roy Evans, tellingly, remarked that the players at the club had been 'his best friends'. Typically, too, when approached by the press for a comment about the 'new way' ahead for the Liverpool club, Gérard Houllier commented that 'Out of decency', and because he had 'so much respect for Roy Evans and what he was for this club', journalists should ring him again after an appropriate period of 'mourning' (Ridley, 1998). A *Guardian* editorial at the time (13 November 1998), significantly, and probably correctly, 'read' the departure of Evans from Liverpool and his replacement by Houllier in rather broader terms. This was not just a seminal moment in the recent history of Liverpool FC; it was also an important social marker for aspects of the wider transformation of 'new' football in England:

> The fate of Roy Evans at Liverpool is a sad one. He has been a loyal servant of a great club, and his going puts paid to its proud Shankly tradition of longevity in the dug-out; the 'double header' with Gerard Houllier has been personally humiliating. The Liverpool board has given the impression it believes foreign managers make magic. Ruud Gullit's far-from-immediate impact at St. James Park, let alone Liverpool's structural problems, ought to dispel that. But in the longer run the arrival of these French coaches must be deemed good news. They bring with them – witness Arsene Wenger – standards of education and culture hitherto unknown in club management, and above all they import sports professionalism antithetical to the drunken amateurism still evident in certain quarters . . . French managers, like Italian, Dutch and German are trained, examined and middle class. And that, like it or not, is football's future.

Following Evans' departure, Liverpool's immediate and long term future now depended substantially on whether Houllier – certainly an urbane, cultured and educated Frenchman of the sort described above, a man with a highly professional approach to his job, but one who actually also liked the 'difficult' areas of the city and the young players they produced – could successfully *manage*, as well as coach, in the English FA Premier League. It would also depend upon whether the Liverpool club, under Houllier and Chief Executive Rick Parry, *together*, could properly negotiate its move into the football age which was likely to be dominated by the so-called 'G14' grouping of European super clubs. Here, the balancing of the playing side of the club's activities, with the necessary *commercial* and *structural* development needed in order to keep pace into the new millennium with the sprawling economics of the Manchester Uniteds, Barcelonas and Milans – and perhaps the River Plates and Flamencos, too – would be crucial.

Houllier's first full season in charge of the club in 1999/2000 was dogged by injuries, suspensions and not a little ill luck. Club form was inconsistent, but improvements had clearly been made in key areas, especially in defence. His determination to recruit younger players, and to do so heavily from abroad, startled some Liverpool supporters, and the media made much of this arriving 'foreign legion'. His reasoning for this *continental* spending spree was that the technical quality of available players in Britain was simply too low, and their price too high for the money he had available to spend. There was also the rampant inflation of the English transfer market to take into account (Morrow, 1999). Other clubs were also investing heavily abroad, with the number of foreign players (who were full internationals) in the Premiership reaching 130 by 1999/2000 (*Rothmans Football Yearbook*, 2000). Nevertheless, the central core of the Liverpool team which began the 1999/2000 season was not only very young and inexperienced; it was also resolutely English, and it actually hailed from Merseyside. In some matches at the start of the new campaign, as many as six or seven players in the Liverpool line-up were actually young 'scousers'; not even the Shankly era could produce figures to match these. When Liverpool thrashed Southampton 7–1 at Anfield in January 1999, all of the scorers were local graduates from the club's youth team.

Houllier's transfer coffers were boosted by a large part of a controversial £22 million cash injection into the club from the Granada media and leisure group in 1999. This new financing was also a sign, of course, of the new commercial diversification of the administrative approach of the club under the direction of the increasingly influential Rick Parry. By the summer of 2000, reports suggested that the club was analysing the possibility of building an entirely new ground, only a matter of several hundred yards away from Anfield, on Stanley Park, with a projected capacity of 70,000 (Parry, 2000). Parry claims that Manchester United make £1 million more than Liverpool for every home match staged. He also knows that stadium capacity, income and the size of one's international fan base will be crucial factors in the event of the establishment of some future European League, which may well be organized by the top clubs themselves (see, King, 1998).

Houllier's maxim is that in the 'global' age, fans of the club will care little about the nationality of the players in the side if they can soon begin a new period of sustained success. This was an approach, of course, which had also stood the club in good stead back in the 1890s when 'honest' John McKenna was ransacking Scotland for players for the first great Liverpool side of the early 1900s. It was there again in the 1970s and 1980s when the team was successfully stocked with Scots and Irish players. Was the famous first 'team of the Macs' at Anfield really any less startling a century ago than was the recruitment of Smicer, Camara, Hyypia and the rest in the newly 'globalized' sport of 1999?

The FA Premier League now offers highly attractive salaries and an international stage for some of the world's top players, even if the hype about the quality of football played in England was still rather forced and overblown. The new 'scientism' of this continental drift extolled the virtues of greater club 'professionalism'; a more holistic view of player development and education; the need for rigorous control of player diets; a place in the game for top-class medical back up; and careful psychological, as well as physical, player preparation for matches (Williams, 1999). This new direction seemed, finally, to herald the beginning of the end of the 'muddy boots/chalky fingers' more informal traditions of the English approach to football coaching, which had been exemplified, in many ways, by the cosy mystique and information gathering of the Anfield boot room (Wagg, 1984). It also ruled out of court the associated ideas that player bonding in the club bar, and a strong dose of British 'team spirit', were still sufficient to overcome most of the tactical and playing challenges now posed in the British game and in Europe.

Early signs

Houllier's strong insistence on 'professionalism' in his staff was, then, very clear; senior players who were deemed to be 'negative' influences at Anfield were soon on their way out of the club. Ironically, the explosive and departing ex-England captain Paul Ince cited 'lack of respect' from Houllier towards senior players as a central weakness in the new Anfield regime. As the 1999/2000 season progressed, with a 25-match run in the League where Liverpool lost only twice, it appeared as though this very young team (often Hamann, at 26, was the oldest player in the side) was definitely responding well to the new regime. But for a terrible run of results in April and May, when Liverpool failed to score in their last five League games, a place in the European Champions' League would certainly have been secured. Chief Executive Rick Parry argued that 'If you leave aside the way it finished and judge the season as a whole, it was ahead of schedule' (Parry, 2000). Other close observers in the city were not quite so charitable.

Houllier is clearly both a technocrat and a humanist; a man who has an organic vision for the club and one which is designed to span the next decade, rather than a few months. He has signed young, ambitious players who are willing to make a personal investment in the new Liverpool project. In the interview he talks of the importance of the players' collective involvement in a football 'adventure'. He is also fully aware of how far, and why, the Liverpool club has now fallen behind the 'new' football innovators – and how long it might yet take the club to catch them up. Houllier also shows, in what follows, an engaging vulnerability, a realism about the immediate future, something which is not always matched by the club's keenest followers. As he points out, the wider difficulties of managing players on and off the field today bear little relation to the sorts of work performed so magnificently by Shankly, Paisley and Fagan in the club's recent past.

Houllier has warned that it may take five years for Liverpool FC to even begin to close in on its previous heights. By May 2000, Liverpool had clawed their way from the lower levels of the League table into a top four position and a European qualification spot – the minimum now demanded by most of the club's fans. Whether Houllier is actually allowed the time needed to see through his putative 'revolution' for the Anfield club – especially in an era when the demand for football success, urged on as it is by a rapacious English popular press, is measured in weeks, not years – remains, as they say, to be seen.

Can he carry the Liverpool fans with him, this modest, 'owlish' Frenchman? Will he have a wider role to play in the transformation of the English game? Will he also carry, especially, those supporters who have seen such great things from the Liverpool club in their living memory, and who still value the strongly local links of Liverpool FC? Can the club, in the wider sense, restructure itself in a way which matches up to the new futures for football in Europe, where, according to Houllier in our interview, a new European (or World?) League looms on the near horizon? Despite the club's preparations in case of a European breakaway, Rick Parry argued recently that he had never been a supporter of the proposition. Still, 'it's actually a huge dilemma that we may be faced with one day . . . If, for example, we were offered a place and all the big guys are going, do we take it or do we stay true to our principles?' (Parry, 2000). Most supporters – and Parry, himself – already knew the answer to this question.

One early hint of what might be in store for Houllier from club supporters came from a Liverpool visit to Leeds United in August 1999. Among a lively away contingent at Elland Road, a group of 'scouse' fans unfurled a new banner for the season. It read: *'Cosmopolitisme Vaincra'* ('Cosmopolitanism will triumph'). A year on, an uncertain start to season 2000/2001 had some Liverpool supporters calling for his head. It was already clear that, both on and off the field, Houllier's reign at Anfield, and his time in England, would be at the very least an interesting ride.

The Gérard Houllier Interview

The interview which follows was conducted by John Williams and Cathy Long and it took place over two days: on 21 September 1999 before a Liverpool home League Cup tie v Hull City, and on 24 November after a Liverpool training session. John Williams transcribed and re-assembled the written account. The meetings took place in Houllier's compact office at the Liverpool training ground, Melwood.

Can you recall when you were first aware of Liverpool – of the city and of the club?
When I was a student in France. There were two clubs here, Everton and Liverpool. If you play football, if you're a football fan, and if you are involved in foreign languages you know the clubs in England, I think. That was one of the reasons I came here the first time, because when I picked on Liverpool – to come and teach here – I knew it was a football town. I was already 'Liverpool-minded', not Everton.

Why?
I don't know; I always liked Liverpool. You are just brought up with it. Everton were the better team then. But even before coming here to the city I knew it was Liverpool for me. I remember, as [one of] the teaching staff, one of the first questions the boys would ask you is not where you are coming from, it's: 'Are you Liverpool or Everton?' – and you better have made your mind up first!

What kind of image did people in France have of the city of Liverpool when you were growing up
You mean thirty years ago? Well, a big port, you know, a big harbour, and not much more than that. I would say the image now is darker. They will think that Liverpool is a dull city and it is difficult to live here, because of the tradition of strikes and everything that happened here in the past 20 years maybe. In my university years when I decided to come and teach here for one year [1969–1970], I had to write a thesis for a final degree. I wrote a thesis about growing up in a deprived area of the city for the MA at Lille. It was an English MA, but I chose to write on social issues. So I worked here and I was linked to a youth club, and all sorts of things went on there. I won't tell you what sort of situations I got involved in! So the Liverpool 8 district I know well!

I picked Liverpool because of the football and because of Liverpool, the city. At that time I was Liverpool-orientated, but I knew there were two clubs so I said, well, maybe when I cannot go to [watch at] one club, then I'll go to the other. But, as soon as you arrive here you know that's finished. Because if you are committed to one club you're not committed to the other one . . . What struck me here is that you can have within the same family people supporting Everton and also Liverpool. I couldn't believe that! That's impossible on the continent. It's odd but interesting – funny.

Tell us about your time as a fan.
I went to see games – it was in the Kop. I went every time I could go. But sometimes I was playing myself so I couldn't go. But it was quite nice, I enjoyed it. I played for the Old Boys of the school I was working at [Alsop]. I enjoyed local football. It was a good atmosphere. The Kop was very unusual. You wouldn't find that in France or anywhere else 30 years ago – maybe in Marseilles, maybe. The noise, the singing, the moving. It was swaying all the time; you could hardly see half of the game! It was quite an atmosphere. When I came back and saw games like St Etienne, for instance [European Cup, 1977]. Or even when I saw cup finals where Liverpool were involved. Then you could feel there was a very strong link between the fans and the club. And, of course, that became even more acute to me with some of the games we played at Anfield this year. A couple of games we were down two–nil and we won three–two or four–two and it was a great atmosphere.

Was it something about the English game, the way football is played here, which was attractive to you, especially?
At that time the English game had a reputation to be direct football. Some guys would say it was 'kick and rush'. But Liverpool had a tradition of better football at that time; playing the ball round the floor, and so on. They were supposed to be successful because they were more continental in their approach to the game and had more skills. You know, the mid-1980s is the beginnings of television starting to show football in Europe and I would say so, Liverpool did have more of a continental style. It's true that I always think at some stage the football you play must some way, somehow, please and entertain your fans. And, if it entertains them it must appeal to their emotional, or to their subconscious, things. I think there are some values here [in Liverpool] which are very important.

First, the effort. Here, you can miss a pass, I mean if you miss a pass but you run 20 yards and do a tackle they [the crowd] applaud you. That means something. Provided the players show effort, they show a resilience and tenacity in their effort, that's very important. I don't know about football in London, but if you miss a pass in Chelsea maybe it's different than if you miss a pass here. I think even in my first professional club in France, Lens, which is a bit like Liverpool – it's a mining area, it went through difficult periods because of the mines collapsing, and so on – they like that effort, too, first and foremost, no matter the talent, they like that.

The second thing is that you know the Liverpool club has a tradition of passing football. Whether it is linked to the fact that the passing is a language between people – it's a bond between people, it's a link between people when you play football. Everybody involved in the passing, everybody working for the same aim, and so on. Has this got something to do with it? It must, probably, appeal to the 'imaginary' of the people [in Liverpool], that's what I think. All I know is that having been a technical director I notice that the football you play in some towns, even in France, is not the same and it couldn't be the same. And it has got something to do with the way of living, the culture, the history; it's funny.

Is there something about the working-class industrial traditions of towns like Liverpool and Lens which attracts you?

I've always liked the town, Liverpool. I know the town has not a good reputation abroad. I know that some people would come through various districts of the city and would say, 'Well, this is absolutely ugly', or 'This is dirty', and it's funny because I surprise myself because I say, 'Well, I like it!'. Don't ask me why, but I like it. I like the people and their sense of humour, this is important, this is a part of it. This is part of the game here. I think the people here like to have a good time. They like to have a laugh. Have you noticed, when there is something funny in a game, they always laugh? There was a game – I think against Watford – and there was a lot of tension and we were playing poorly and they, Watford, were one–nil [up]. And something happened. And they [the fans in the Kop] were all laughing!

What do the people here want from the team?

I know, for sure, that the people here like to take pride in what's on the field. They take pride in the people, the players, who've got the shirt. Talking in the city and everywhere, it's the first thing the fans want. When you talk about the link, the bond between the fans and the club, first of all they like to be really, really proud of the club and the team. And then there is no matter of national identity. They don't matter if it is Song or Riedle, or whether it's Fowler. It is totally out of order if you think they prefer the local lads. The fans want the team to be successful, to play well.

But, here, you cannot reach places or win trophies without a certain way of doing it. Because of the tradition, because of the culture of the football that was on the field here for years and years, with the good teams, with Keegan and Dalglish and all those players, it was different from the other football of other clubs. Here, you have got to play a certain type of football. I knew that when I came as a supporter, but even more as a manager in France and as a technical director I would watch Liverpool and the way they would play. I don't think you could play the Wimbledon type of football here. Suppose I would come here and say: 'Well, this is the quickest way to get from box to box, let's do that'. Well, it wouldn't work. And that's not just because of the players. Football is more than just eleven players; it's an environment, it's a context and they [the fans] have had so much of the good football practice in the successful years that you could not break away from that.

Even now I am trying to break away from the passing: well, not from the passing, because I like the passing. But I want to pass forwards, God, yeah. They [the players] like to pass the ball. Two years ago Liverpool made more passes than any other team, they were the best passing team in the Premiership. But to me that doesn't mean anything. You can be the best passing team and win nothing. You have to verticalize, and to go deeper with passes. The passing, like a bond, was more, 'Let's keep our hands like that' [a sideways clasp], but I think we have to be more provocative than that, and go forward.

These fans have been to matches for 20 or 35 years. They have been to many games. They know the type of football that was developed here. They've kept that in mind. They know more when the team is playing well. You cannot win without a bit of 'the manner' here. You can't win without entertaining here. It's my philosophy, but I think it's even more here [among the fans]. They like winning, but they like winning in the way they want to win. It's got to be a good, entertaining and fascinating way of playing it. That's important. We can win one–nil and play crap and they would not like that.

Is the English game too focused on action, not enough on thinking?
The English game is changing now. I mean you cannot say that Manchester United is playing a 'typical' English game. The football in Italy and France is very, very skilful, sometimes the level of skill is very high. It's very tactical, but the pace is not as high as here. Here, you never have a free half-a-second. The physical demand of the game here is much higher than anywhere else. When you go to Italian football it's a different sport. I was the French national

coach so I had to go and see my players playing everywhere, including Italy. Sometimes I got absolutely bored, because there was nothing! Suddenly, five minutes of good football and then a slump again. But here, in England, if you go and see Stockport playing Tranmere you get a lot of excitement, and this is a good thing about it. An English Champions League team, they can have problems against Watford, or Wimbledon, because it's difficult to play games of that intensity all the time.

Here, football is different. But, personally, I think the English football is also changing. Tactically it is getting richer. You have different systems, different approaches, more discipline now. The skill level is not bad at all. Don't be misled; it is because the pace of the game is so high here that players make mistakes. I mean, Michael Owen, if he played in a French team he will probably never miss a control of the ball.

How do you get this sort of change?

There are experienced players at the club. I say, 'Why don't you just sit there and pass the ball when you are ahead? Just pass the ball, and move, and pass, and move. What's going to happen is that you are going to tire them out.' But my players wanted to keep the pace of the game at the same level!

I think there is a crowd influence in this. The crowd plays a part because they want that. They like that, and they always want 100 per cent effort. They don't understand that, sometimes, you just need to keep the ball. They think we are taking risks when we do that. In Italy you would not see this crowd impatience. This is a habit of always playing 'pacy' football. To me, the best football means that you master the rhythm.

Is it a special problem of teaching English players to change?

They think, if they are not giving 100 per cent, maybe they are feeling guilty of not doing their job. Abroad, the youth development of players implies a professional youth development. A sociologist is a professional job, you have to go to university, to be trained. The same thing to be a professional player at the age of 20; you need five years of hard work as a professional, youth trainee. And if you don't do that now you can't be a professional at a club like this. Those days of coming to the club at 20 to be a professional footballer, that's finished now. The Academy system means that now, you have to be aware that to be a professional player and to respond to between 50 and 70 games a season, between 15 and 20 years old you must learn your trade. And you learn your trade through physical strengthening, the technical, the tactical and the mental processes. I hope the Academy system will bring here what it brought in France and in other countries: that you can feed good habits of professionalism into players at 15 and 16 years of age. That's what Lippi [Juventus coach until 1998] told me. He said the good thing about buying a French player is that he has a good education, good attitude, very professional, very focused and tactically fully aware. He knows all the systems; he can play in that, play in this. In about ten years, of course, that will be the same here. Provided the youth coaches change as well.

Is it difficult to make these sorts of changes in Liverpool?

It is always difficult to change in a city which has a long history and a tradition behind it. You will always have people who say, 'Well, in the past we had 12 players, we played 70 games, and it went alright.' 'In the past we had no physio, and we didn't need a physio.' Those same people now use a mobile phone at the moment, so they have changed! It's always more difficult when there is a great tradition of success. The past weighs heavy here.

I think the club is very strong, very powerful. One of its main roots is the fans, the supporters, because they feed that strength at the club. The players on the park will feel that strength from the back. They know how important it is; when we travel we see a full stand of Reds. But the loyalty to the club in the Bosman era is to me extremely limited. One of the appeals of the club is its tradition and its name. The other one is the fact we have a young team at the moment – which is interesting. I would say that all the players except one we have taken into the side this season are young players, between the ages of 23 and 26. So you can think about passion and everything. I prefer to think we have a good bunch of players here, whatever the nationality. They just bloody want to win something together. And its got to be for them and for the fans, but it's got to be for them [the players], first. To me the passion comes from the inner competitiveness of the players. Do they have the drive, do they have this thing? Some local lads are top class; Carragher is a model of commitment, passion, everything on and off the pitch and in training.

How did you 'sell' the club to new players in this period?

We have been extremely fair to all of them. We've said, 'This is where we are and this is what we want to do.' This is our target, to get back into the top three. It will take time because our team is relatively young and inexperienced. We've got the quality, we just need to build that success on the way together. But we'll be a professional club. You forget about the booze, forget about parties. You're part of the deal; you don't want to do it, if you don't feel for it, then get away.

You see, there are definite routes. You can have the Chelsea route. We were offered Deschamps [French captain]. He is over 31 and is experienced, and is a very good player, could have been a top-class player for a couple of years. But we preferred Hamann [German international], who is 26 and who needs to build up his trophies with us. Deschamps has already won European Cups, the World Cup. It's a different route. We have taken the route of faith and belief in what we do. Everyone is talking about the city resurging, about Liverpool coming back. I think our team is about the same. The players we've signed are young, they want to succeed, they are committed to the club, they enjoy being here: let's go.

Managing a club in England must be very different from being a technical director in France.

I was talking to Arsène [Wenger] about this. When I was a manager and then I became national team manager and then national technical director, as a technical director, even given the huge amount of work I had to do, I could still keep in touch with reading *Le Monde* every day, reading papers, books, and so on. But when you are a club manager it is very focused. All that goes. Not being involved in a club I missed what we in France call 'the powder', the gun and fire. I needed to go out into the trench again! It was a very strange move I did. Liverpool was important in that, but they pinched me in a way. I would have gone to another club anyway. When you have just passed your 50 and you say, 'Oo-la-la, listen: you're the top position in France, good salary, good respect from everybody in UEFA and FIFA, life could not be better'. I said, if I don't go into the fire now I will never go back.

Did anything surprise *you when you came to Liverpool?*

The approach to the professional side of the job was totally different from what I expected it to be, in terms of preparation, application and concentration. I don't think some players felt the relationship between the training and the game was important. They didn't understand the connection. Players thought training was something to pass the time between matches. For instance, the game requires a maximum concentration, but that means they must focus during training. The players enjoyed the good side of the job. This job is not just about being focused for an hour and a half. Keegan said, the way you train, you carry it over into games. That is changed here now. It is not perfect, but it has changed.

Do you ever think fans care too much for a club like this one?

I prefer that they care too much than that they don't care! It's important to have a heart and a passion. The Heysel disaster and the tragedy at Sheffield probably links in even more the fans and the players. I think the players at that time were very affected. And there is the memorial and a service each year for Hillsborough. When you suffer together, you are drawn together. Even if you wanted to forget you can't, and that helps to make the club. No player has ever told me that he has not been moved at the [Hillsborough] service held in April.

What is it about football, itself, which makes it so appealing to you?

My father was a player, then a team manager, and then a team director. I was immersed in football. I think people like football because of the dramatic intensity of the game. I mean, you are never sure to be winning or losing. It's not like basketball or handball, where there are many goals. In volleyball you can see right at the start who is going to win. In football here you can never say who is going to win. I think the people like football because your breath is being taken all the time. There's always a drama somewhere. The new stadiums now mean that people are sitting very close. There's like a communion with the players. In France it is not like that. In France the players are 'on the stage'. Here they're not on a stage; the players are here and the fans are there with them. Like life, you have good times and bad times in matches. The rhythm of a game could be like the rhythm of your life.

Why have Liverpool fallen behind other clubs do you think?

The physical demands of the modern game, especially in Europe, that has gone so high. They are athletes of football now, that's what they are. That makes the entertaining side of the game. The combination of skills and the physical thing makes the game entertaining. The pace, the challenge, the movement. In that case it has gone very high in some leagues in Europe. Here, it's physical, it's tough, but sometimes it's not the same. One difference here is the European gap of five years. Until 1985, Liverpool were top. When you play with someone and they beat you, you have to respond. It's not complacency here [in Liverpool]. It was just, 'We were winning and it worked. We were just doing five-a-side and it worked'. Like in life, if you don't question and try to update your methods, you will be left behind. The passion of this game is that it is traditional, it is orthodox, but at the same time you have to be adventurous; you do this, but sometime you have to do something which is more forward thinking. That's how you progress. Here, it was: 'This is the way we play, this is the way we train, this is the way we travel'.

At the moment we haven't changed everything. There are a couple of sectors I still want to work on. Some of my worries are about the youth and the way we deal with them. You have to do better all the time. We missed that European experience because between 1985 and 1990 Europe has changed, I can tell you. And the second thing is that here [in England] the clubs have changed. Arsenal, Tottenham, Leeds, Chelsea, Manchester, they have all changed. Would you know that other clubs have cameras everywhere analysing the play? Here, there was no change at all like that.

Was it difficult to change the coaching at the club?

The tradition of the boot room meant nothing had changed here. Changing the coaching was easy. We still do a lot of work with the ball. The only players who did not want to change, we got rid of. We knew that, because they preferred not to do anything. The good thing about working here is that there is a lot, a lot, of tremendous assets to the English players. The frame of mind, the attitude, the enthusiasm. They like the game. They've got a big heart, they put everything into it. I would say that I prefer to be a coach for the English players than working with young players in France. It's easier maybe on some aspects of the game with the French, but from the human point of view it is much more exciting here. Because I knew the type of environment the young players used to live in, and what it would mean for them to be there in the team, nobody wants to help them more than I do. It might be easier to work with other players from a technical point of view. But I enjoy the human things about working with the players here, especially, in some ways, with the players who come from the city itself.

Do you think the way clubs in England play makes it harder for English players to play in international football?

That's a very good point and I had a discussion on that one day with [Michel] Platini and he thought the English play too quickly and make technical errors. When they play at international level and they have to master a different rhythm, a different pace to the game, they can't do it: because they are used to playing flat out all the time. I believe in skill. The game will go with skill, I believe that. In ten years time you won't be able to tell if a player is right- or left-footed. In ten years time you will have to be able to do that to succeed. Skilful players solve problems on the field.

How has management in football changed over the past 20 years?

When a player knows he has two years on his contract, now with Bosman, he can just sit. The manager, ten years ago, was extremely powerful. Now you have counter-forces from everywhere. Because the profile of the player has changed, the profile of the manager has changed, too. The power of the players means a new way of managing. Twenty years ago a manager could tell players to do this, and do that. Now that's finished. Now you manage different nationalities, different players. They're more aware of their interests and their careers, through their agents. They're multi-millionaire, multi-national. At the same time, passion, commitment, teamwork, this is still what you need from them. This is something which gives players something to work for. There is some kind of pride to belong to Liverpool, there's no doubt about that. Here, it is different from other clubs because of the great traditions of Liverpool. But the job of the manager is still to create an environment in which players can produce their best. The job is more human now than it used to be twenty years ago, because it was easy twenty years ago. You *told* players what to do then. Now it's finished; today you have to explain. The most important word with top players now is 'Why?' 'Why do we do this, why do we do that?' This is a very important move in the mind of the players.

Players are human. They need confidence. They need a positive feedback; they need targets; and they need a strong sense of belonging. The manager must create a kind of 'human adventure'. There must be an atmosphere of work at the club, but it must also be relaxed. You need jokes, sometimes. You have to put the players in the best condition to find the motivation to play. Players like to be treated the same way. But you must have a slightly different approach to each of them. Players expect from their manager three qualities: you must be an expert in football – a top man in that. But you must also be able to communicate the message. You must also have a strong personality. If they get on top of you, you have had it. The third thing is that you must have a plan, a logic or a strategy. You must know where you are going and how to get there. A group reduces the amount of the initiative of the individual. You need to try to keep that. You must keep enterprise and initiative as well as having a strong spirit and a strong team.

What do you think will be the future direction of the game?
I think we are bound to have a European League. It is inevitable. They have resisted with the new version of the Champions League, but in five years we will have a new league. The power of players also means a new way of managing. All players say they love their club, and to be fair, most of them do. But we can also admit that the attraction to English football has something to do with the attraction to the English pound. They have a short career and they have to make the most of it. I am angry at the media at the moment because they lack respect for managers. The players have the attention of the media, they have the money; they can be very powerful if the manager has not a strong personality.

Players here can sign the biggest contract in the world, but as soon as they pass the gate [into Melwood] everybody is worth the same rate, they have no privileges and they do the work. Some players, though, they sign the contract, they take the money, they wave to the crowd, and they give ten minutes of football at the end of the game to show that they are 'committed'. The rest of the time they are invisible. They may fool some of the fans, but not me.

References

Brodkin, J. and Henley, J. (1998), 'Houllier'll never walk alone', *Guardian*, 14 August.

Deloitte and Touche (1999) *Annual Review of Football Finance*, Manchester: Deloitte and Touche.

Fynn, A. and Guest, L. (1998) *For Love or Money: The Business of Winning*, London: Boxtree.

George, R. (2000), 'What makes this man tick?', Liverpool Season 2000/01: Official Matchday Magazine, *The Big Kick-off*.

Giulianotti, R. (1999) *Football: A Sociology of the Global Game*, Cambridge: Polity.

Hayward, P. (2000), 'Islanders marooned as adventurers disappear over the horizon', *Daily Telegraph*, 4 July.

King, A. (1998) *The End of the Terraces*, London: Leicester University Press.

Morrow, S. (1999) *The New Business of Football*, Basingstoke: Macmillan.

Parry, R. (2000), 'The Road Ahead', Liverpool Season 2000/01: Official Matchday Magazine, *The Big Kick-off*.

Powell, J. (2000), 'Just say non to the foreigners', *Daily Mail*, 28 June.

Ridley, I. (1997) 'Houllier hails the revolution', *Independent on Sunday*, 18 May.

—— (1998) 'Houllier must do it the hard way', *Observer*, 15 November.

—— (2000), 'Houllier first among equals', *Observer*, 13 August.

Rothmans Football Yearbook, 2000–2001 (2000).

Wagg, S. (1984), *The Football World*, Brighton: Harvester.

Williams, J. (1999), *Is it all over? Can football survive the Premier League?* Reading: South Street Press.

Williams, J. and Taylor, R. (1994) 'Boys keep swinging: masculinity and football culture in England', in T. Newburn and B Stanko (eds) *Just boys doing Business?*, London: Routledge.

Williams, R. (2000), 'Wild things', *Guardian*, 12 August.

Winter, H. (1999), 'England cannot force themselves on Europe', *Daily Telegraph*, 12 October.

Sitting Pretty? Women and Football in Liverpool

Liz Crolley and *Cathy Long*

Introduction

> Shankly was a great motivator but Paisley was the brains behind the team. You have to be tactically aware as well as being able to inspire. Evans was great at getting the team to pass the ball, but now Houllier's getting the shape of the team right as well.

The above is an excerpt from a conversation overheard between two Liverpool football fans. It is the kind of exchange that goes on in public spaces all over the city. The fact that those involved were two middle-aged women in a hairdressing salon in Liverpool should surprise only those who don't know the city well. In some areas of the UK it is perhaps still seen as unusual for women to be 'involved' in football. In Liverpool, however, and although attending matches is still strongly dominated by men, football is a major part of living in the city – for almost everyone.

Men and women of all ages participate in the game in some way, whether as players, avid supporters or casual fans. Children are inculcated into supporter traditions at an early age, especially because it is easy to 'lose' potential recruits to the opposing side of the sport's blue and red divide on Merseyside (Edge, 1999). Those who take little or no interest in the game are in a distinct minority and are likely to suffer the sort of cultural exclusion which is catastrophic for male identities and sometimes damaging for those of local females.

Our aim here is to outline some 'typical' experiences of female football fans in Liverpool, to open a wider debate about the role of women in football and to discuss the contention that football is now more 'female-friendly' or has become more 'feminized' in England and in Liverpool (Coddington, 1997). This is done by using interviews with female Liverpool football fans as well as by drawing on personal experiences and other sources. Like any investigation into football culture in Liverpool, a backdrop of essentially working-class values and traditions in the city, including very traditionally defined gender roles, needs to be borne strongly in mind. Our evidence, however, casts doubts over the adequacy of these narrowly-defined roles within the football context.

Since the mid-1980s, a wealth of literature has been written which focuses on women's role in sport. Interest in this subject matter has often been triggered by an interest, especially perhaps, among 'feminist' academics based in the USA. While it is not our specific aim to contribute to the feminist debates over the wider role of sport in society, it is important that we bear in mind some of the conclusions of this recent body of research. This will also help better to contextualize the evidence of our own oral testimonies. Some of the key themes of recent sports theorists which are relevant to our study include:

- the role of sport in creating and defining a sense of masculinity. 'From the ancient Olympiad to the present, sport has been a primary site for defining, cultivating and displaying Western ideals of masculinity' (Sabo and Curry Johnson, 1998: 202). Traditionally-considered masculine characteristics of physical prowess, strength and courage are still positively associated with football, both by players and by fans and by both by females and males.
- the role of sport in reinforcing male hegemony. 'Sport in the twentieth century has given men an arena to create and reinforce an ideology of male superiority' (Duncan and Messner, 1998: 170). By making characteristics which involve the expression of physical prowess or strength more or less synonymous with masculinity, male superiority becomes self-fulfilling.
- the marginalization and alienation of women via sport. 'By excluding women from this arena . . . sport provides opportunities for men to assert their dominance at a time when male hegemony is continually challenged and opposed in everyday life' (ibid.). We will also see evidence that, despite the recent changes in football culture and the process of 'feminization' that will be discussed later, women can still be marginalized and alienated at times, sometimes deliberately, but more frequently inadvertently.
- the trivialization of women's role in sport (especially via the popular media) and the formulae of exclusion. In our data some women complain that they are not considered to be as committed as fans as were their male counterparts. Women's football is not taken seriously by most commentators, certainly not in England, and there still persists strong elements of the masculinist legacy of the notion that football is still 'a man's game'. Media coverage of women's role in sport is often reduced to 'the humorous sexualisation of women' (ibid.: 182) in which women's participation in sport is either ridiculed or patronized.
- questions raised over sexuality and gender. 'Sport experiences masculinise girls and women' (Kane and Jefferson Lenskyi, 1998: 188). Females involved in sport, as fans, but especially as players, may well have their sexuality questioned. In our own sample, several females felt that following Liverpool FC required them, somehow, to become 'honorary males'. But again, we realize that football culture is evolving in such way that, nowadays, many females can – and do –

go to football in 'feminine' garb – a skirt, make-up, or even carrying a handbag – and that this can be socially acceptable in the football context. Equally, we see evidence of infinitely complex notions of masculinity; the 'out-of town' fan (from outside the city) in particular casting new nuances onto formerly accepted concepts.

All the above issues, which routinely arise in theorizing on women and sport, are relevant to our own small study and they provide a useful starting point from which to examine the current situation and developments which appear to be taking place in changes in the 'new' gender order of English football.

Playing and Watching

Women's general role in football in England is slowly being redefined as they are increasingly visible both on and off the field (Lopez, 1997). After a slow start on Merseyside, there is now, for example, a Liverpool FC 'Ladies' team, and the women's game in England, though some way behind its equivalents in Scandinavia, Germany, the USA and China, is slowly beginning to make an impact on the footballing world (Williams and Woodhouse, 1999). However, marginalization of women's football continues in England as the game still struggles to attract sponsorship and TV coverage and it receives only modest funding support from the Football Association. As Hargeaves (1994) points out, female sport remains very much a subsidiary of (male) sport, and its role is trivialized.

Liverpool Ladies, despite their recent progress, still play their home matches in the Premier Division of the National Women's League at the local police playing field and there is little or no marketing or promotion of their games; even finding out the kick-off times of fixtures of top women's matches can be an ordeal. It is in schools that there has been a recent boom in female participation. More young girls now play football at school, an important development not just for the growth of football but for the fitness, personal development and identity of girls. Traditionally, of course, when boys leave school, many of them continue to have a kick-about with their friends at a local park or nearby field. Local junior clubs also cater extensively for boys' football. Girls, on the other hand, are still encouraged to associate physical team sport with a challenge to conventional femininity, thereby raising 'difficult' questions about sexuality and gender identities. Girls are also more likely to have been inculcated into netball and hockey as team sports; these sports involve considerably more organization, and more specialized kinds of facilities and equipment. So, relatively few girls continue to play team sports after their education, especially as peer-group pressure, too, presses for young girls to be conventionally competitive in seeking out the company of boys. Increasing numbers of girls also now opt for aerobics classes or gym sessions as a way of socializing and keeping fit, though these options are likely to be more limited – and regarded as less appropriate – in a strongly working-class city such as Liverpool. In contrast, of course, football can be played almost anywhere.

Perhaps unsurprisingly, in the age of 'new' football in England, it is in the media that women have begun to play a more obviously conspicuous role in football. Although many of the women now employed to front football programmes on television, such as Sky Sports's Clare Tomlinson and ITV's Gabi Yorath, may be conventionally attractive, but they also 'know' their football (Williams and Woodhouse, 1999). Yorath's father was an ex-player; Tomlinson was a committed season ticket holder at Spurs. Women have also now become established as part of the sports teams on radio and in some sections of the sporting press (e.g. Eleanor Oldroyd at BBC Radio Five Live, Amy Lawrence at the *Observer*; Alyson Rudd at the *Times*), though few women actually write or comment on the women's game. Women's football remains largely excluded from mainstream media (again marginalizing this arm of the sport). But it is also in the administration of the men's professional game that perhaps progress made by women has been less significant. Marginalizing female players seems somehow more explicable – if still depressing – than the exclusion of females from key administrative positions, where strength and technique are no longer factors. No female holds a senior role at Liverpool Football Club, for example. None has ever held such a position. It is hard to avoid the conclusion that this is a product of institutionalized exclusion, rather than accident or coincidence.

Even a visit to Liverpool FC's official club shop today can be something of an alienating experience for female supporters of the club. This is ironic, of course, given that 'shopping' is supposed to be a strong female identifier. In an age when football club superstores sell pretty much everything from wallpaper to school shirts, and when females make up around one in eight of all fans – and many more of those who actually shop in the club store – there are still few women's items on sale. As for female involvement as football fans, rather than just as consumers of football products, it is our aim here to provide some insight and reflection.

Football Feminization?

Despite these strides made in recent times, football in the UK is still perceived as being a sport played by men, and male dominance in the sport remains pretty much unquestioned. However, in recent years there has been much talk of the alleged 'feminization' of football (Coddington, 1997). This, usually, refers to a perceived change in the climate and atmosphere within football grounds rather than to any real modification in the power structures within football clubs or in the game in general. It implies some sort of change in football culture for the supporters. 'Feminization' is taken to suggest either an increase in the number of female fans in football grounds or that the presence of females is increasingly significant in softening the behaviour of football crowds, or both. Giulianotti (1999: xi) claims in his eloquent sociological study of football as a global sport that: 'Though football reflects the wider distribution of gender-related power in most societies, the game is also undergoing varying degrees of feminization among players, spectators and officials.' We are interested in this notion of 'feminization': we also need to know more about how to 'read' female perceptions of various aspects of this 'new' football culture today.

First, it is useful to refer to the often reported rise in the number of female football fans (Williams, 1997). While some research suggests small rises in the number of female fans at top clubs, lack of data prior to the 1980s means that there is simply no conclusive evidence to prove that significantly more females attend football today than did so in the past (Waddington, et al., 1996). Oral records and historical accounts suggest that, contrary to much speculation, it was not uncommon for females, actively, to follow their favourite football teams in the 1940s and 1950s. During the course of our own research we have come across innumerable cases in Liverpool of women, now over the age of 50, who went to football in their youth, gave it up when they had a young family and were forced to let other commitments take priority, but have recently gone back to attending matches at Liverpool FC. **Margaret**, now in her sixties, is one of these fans:

> I used to go to the match with my sister, Milly, when I was a teenager. We had a great time and were looked after by all the men as if we were their daughters. Then we both had to stop going when we got married and couldn't afford to go any more. It was only when I went back to work, when the children were a bit older, that we both started going to football again.

Notwithstanding the fact that some women have, clearly, always been attracted to football as fans (Mason, 1980; Fishwick, 1989), and that many women were present at matches prior to the recent so-called 'revolutionary' changes in the game, it would not be surprising to find recent increased female participation in football support. After all, female involvement in almost all public leisure activities has probably increased over the last two decades. But a number of more specific questions about the game also come to mind here. Has football really become as 'female friendly' as we are led to believe? Has football really been 'feminized' – and what exactly does this mean? Or, has football resisted changes which are perhaps taking place at a faster pace in other spheres of society? What is it that makes football unattractive to some females and yet so compulsively attractive to others? Has football ever been really 'unfriendly' towards females?

The oral testimonies of older female fans suggest that the 'feel' of the standing Liverpool Kop in the early 1990s, for example, was actually little different from that of being present on the Kop and other football terraces in the 1950s, although a few of our interviewees did suggest that the Kop of old 'respected women more' or that the men were 'more polite towards women' than it later became. Shifts in expectations between generations are important here, of course. Older women probably expect, and expected, men to behave differently – to be more 'chivalrous' towards women – than do the younger female products of the so-called post-feminism era. Most younger female supporters today probably aspire to equal, rather than special, treatment by men at football, as in all things.

There is some evidence that the promotion in the 1980s of the ideologies of the 'family' for football was a deliberate attempt by the then Thatcher government to 'soften' the rough image of football's support during the latter half of that decade by promoting more female support for the sport when hooliganism had hit something of a peak (Giulianotti, 1994). Government Ministers might have hoped that attracting a higher proportion of women to football crowds might have a potentially 'civilizing' effect on rowdy male spectators, thus curbing their sometimes violent and aggressive behaviour. This policy, which saw the introduction and expansion of special areas, often designated as 'family stands', enjoyed some success, arguably, in encouraging more women and children to enter football grounds. Family areas were advertised as 'safe' spaces. Any 'feminization' effect here, however, would surely be limited to these designated areas; it would have relatively little impact on the goal-end terraces, where hooligan problems were actually perceived to exist (Dunning et al., 1988).

It is questionable whether more female fans actually took their place *alongside* those male fans who, it was hoped, were going to be 'feminized' or 'cleansed' of the more traditional, overtly masculine and violent image of football fans at that time. More effective, here, was probably the discourse of 'the family' which was widely used in Liverpool and elsewhere in the early 1990s to discuss the aftermath of the Hillsborough tragedy in 1989 (Brunt, 1989; see also Chapter Five). Here, football fans were reported as victims, not as violent perpetrators, and the stories which unfolded about Hillsborough victims, male and female, located them within conventional codas about family life. Probably for the first time in more than two decades, English football fans were widely discussed in the media outside the conventional masculinist and hooligan frame – instead, 'ordinary' supporters turned out to be 'like us': they were fathers, sons, daughters and aunts. Thus, the role of female fans in the sport was acknowledged, albeit in the most tragic of circumstances. What followed Hillsborough was certainly a less 'closed' and less masculinist popular view of the culture. But is it really the case that it was specifically more women attending football which diluted the 'masculinist' atmosphere of matches? Or, were more women simply attracted to football at a time when other factors – new stadia, seats, marketing, decline of hooliganism, etc – were already reshaping aspects of the culture in this general direction? It is worth examining, in this context, the reasons why women begin to follow football clubs in the first place.

Why Do Women Like Football?

Sport socialization research (that is, research into how social forces shape involvement in sport) has most frequently been explored via social-learning theorists. In most studies into sport socialization research, the family, peer-groups members, teachers and role models are identified as the primary agents of sports socialization (Higginson, 1985). During early childhood, results of research show that the family and peer group are clearly more influential than the school in shaping the behaviour of both girls and boys under the age of twelve. Then, the balance of influences shifts. Among the girls, the family declines in importance, the peer group increases in importance, and sometimes teachers do too. Unsurprisingly, those girls who receive positive reinforcement for interest in a sport are more likely to remain involved than those who receive negative messages (Greendorfer, 1987).

Our research concurs with much of this sport socialization theory. Females who became hooked on football in early childhood quoted parents, then peer group, as significant influences, whereas those who developed an interest in football during adolescence more often quote peers alone as the prime influence. Few mentioned school, however, as being a major agency in developing their interest in football or in a club such as Liverpool. But those who liked football enjoyed playing sports at school. Girls who received positive reinforcement for their interest in football were usually those who either socialised with male peers a lot, or who had brothers who were interested in sport. Hence, it is easy to see how the link between girls liking football and girls being 'tomboys' can be made.

Research suggests that most female interest in football clubs is sparked in much the same ways as is male interest (Williams, 1997). The experiences of the two authors, for example, in terms of football background and the 'football family', differ significantly, but in neither case was gender a central issue. For many children growing up in Merseyside in the 1970s, it was largely understood that you supported your *local* team, and so it was rare for anyone in Liverpool to support a team other than Liverpool or Everton. We all knew exactly who supported Liverpool and who followed Everton in much the same way that children in the city who don't go to church still 'know' whether they are Catholic or Protestant.

Quality of football was not a determining factor here. At the age of five (or whatever) there was no such thing as 'quality' to take account of, though performances were judged on results. To play badly and win was a confusing contradiction. Even by the time we grasped a fuller understanding of the workings of the Football League table, we were already hooked – as a blue or a red. Media hype for football then was nothing like on the scale we enjoy/suffer today. BBC's

Match of the Day, the sole exponent of football on the television in the early 1970s, was on so late at night that by the time many children were old enough to be allowed to watch it, football allegiances had already probably been established. TV was not a factor. Parental influence usually encourages an interest initially, but other factors – school, friends – play their part. **Julie** claims that 'I got hooked because I actually went to matches from a young age. Here, the spirit of terrace culture played its part. I just loved the atmosphere.' **Pam** believes that although the gender issues seemed irrelevant at the time, being a female football fan actually made you that bit extra-special. It provided for a distinct and attractive additional status:

> As a young fan, being a girl was irrelevant to my interest in football. It seemed so natural for me to love football, until it became obvious that everyone else found it odd. Then I became something of an oddity – a girl who knew her football – something special, something to be talked about. I was different – even more reason for me to stick with football! I wasn't afraid of terrace culture. On the contrary, it could be very female friendly.

Parents could be highly influential, of course, in a child's choice of football team. That isn't to say that Evertonian parents inevitably spawned Evertonian children, or vice versa. Children either followed their parents' lead, or else wilfully rejected their pressures. Children might also, artfully, oppose the football choice of an older sibling or, in a 'divided' football family in Liverpool, follow either a mother or a father's lead. Parents – especially male parents – also worked harder on *boys* as potential active recruits to the match. Many fewer girls were regarded as youngsters who may eventually be taken to football by a male parent. Nevertheless, the influence of parents was rarely irrelevant, in this context: unless, of course, these were parents who, perversely, lived in the city but were not interested in football at all!

In the 1970s and 1980s, most girls in Liverpool rarely played football in school. Except for occasional rumblings of discontent, we largely accepted the fact that football was a 'boys' sport' and that we were destined to play netball and hockey. Putting fifteen or sixteen girls onto a hockey pitch for the first time could have been chaotic, of course. No one had seen or played the sport before. But, somehow, we all knew where to stand: we just took up the familiar positions of our *football* heroes.

Although female fans did have football heroes at that time, they were never strictly role models. We always knew we would never follow in our favourite player's footsteps and we never dreamed of lifting the FA Cup at Wembley, as many of the boys did. Today, this sort of role-modelling is a little more appropriate for young girls; the women's FA Cup Final is even televised, today, as long as you can grope towards the right satellite TV station and search out the timing in the press. One is more likely to lift the WFA Cup at Millwall or Oxford, however, than at Wembley Stadium. It is not quite the same. Although opportunities for girls to play football are increasing (Liverpool Football Club now runs coaching sessions for girls as well as for boys), those females who take playing football seriously are still in a distinct minority. Young girls in the city are well aware that girls' football is still tolerated rather than supported locally, and they also know well it does not lead to high-profile, professional football; there is no career option here for female players. In three years' time the new professional league for women in England may offer other options (Williams and Woodhouse, 1999). There is some evidence to suggest that the stigma of playing contact sport seriously is also still strong for females, despite recent changes. Most younger female fans we interviewed are not, or were never, interested in playing football themselves. Perhaps kids at school now see things differently?

Actually going to a football match for young girls is a very special experience. They are both immune to some of the demands made of football 'lads', and often cosseted by male sections of the crowd. **Jane** comments:

> The match atmosphere attracted us in the same way as it would attract lads, but we were different. There were never any pressures on us to be 'macho', to 'act like men', to grow up before we wanted to, or to join in the fighting in Stanley Park and along Utting Avenue after the game. We could even go along to watch with immunity. Female fans enjoyed a freedom to appreciate football culture and on top of it all the men made us feel special, looked after us, protected us from swaying crowds and generally spoiled us. We became part of a big family, our football family.

This notion of the 'football family' has probably always existed at Liverpool and elsewhere. Perhaps in the past there weren't quite as many females in the 'family' as there are today, but the idea of football being a 'family' experience, in this wider sense – not in the sense used by marketing men at football clubs – is not a new one. Most people at Anfield enjoy the company of the 'football family', a series of connections in a complex but largely informal network of relationships. Links here are made and acknowledged unobtrusively but with certainty; a nod at 'away' matches, a simple 'Hiya' or 'Alright' at home. To be included on the Kop, in this way, or as a loyal traveller, is to belong, to have a place.

For a number of years, **Cathy** went to the match with two other girls. The introduction of seating on the Kop coincided with her two friends moving away. Maybe it's because she's not with 'the girls' anymore; maybe it's because the terrace has gone: but her football experience is different now: 'I still miss the closeness we had and the other people we stood with on the Kop. Some people said seating would encourage more women to the game, but we liked the atmosphere on the terraces just as much as the men did.'

Liz's experience of the Kop has been very different from **Cathy**'s. Her football 'family' has always seen males and females mixed together. The ratio has varied over the years, but women have always been in the minority. Far from feeling alienated or excluded from the terrace culture, the overwhelming experience, for her, like that of so many girls and women we interviewed, has been one of welcome inclusion; although women can be treated differently at times, even by the 'family'.

The feelings conjured up by girls and women describing their experiences on the Kop so often contradict the rather negative images frequently portrayed by the media and the sports critics of the macho, aggressive and violent football crowd. Yet, should it really surprise us that most male fans can actually be so accepting – and even protective – of female fans? Are there characteristics of the football fan that the media and fans alike choose to ignore? There is this particular side to football culture – which often involves looking more closely at the terrace work of older male fans, especially – that makes Skinner and Baddiel's laddish portrayal of the generic football fan in TV's *Fantasy Football* (see Carrington, 1999; Crolley, 1999), or the Brimson brothers' nostalgic portrayal of 'lads' football (Brimson and Brimson, 1997) appear highly over-simplistic and even insultingly unidimensional.

There have always been elements of football culture that appear decidedly 'unmasculine'. Fans of both sexes vent their emotions at the match. They talk openly, male and female, of 'loving' their team and certain players: 'We love you Liverpool', 'She Loves You', 'I can't help falling in love with you', and so many more songs and chants at the match are really, well, quite . . . feminine. Giulianotti (1999: 156) hints at a more complex notion of masculinity in the sport when he argues that 'football cultures have always embraced diverse expressions of masculinity – and appreciated its expression in different forms'. Although in this context he refers more specifically to the style of *play*, his comment can easily be transposed to refer to terrace culture, too. Far from reflecting a narrow drama, made up of overtly macho elements, the bonding experience in football is far more complex. Indeed, some of the most touching, the most emotional and moving moments we both experience take place in the football context. Where else, one might ask, do even grizzled men get to hug each other – and sometimes us – unabashed?

King Kenny

An illustration of how male football fans can reveal characteristics which hint at a more complex expression of footballing masculinity than that to which we are accustomed emerges, for example, in the relationship between fans and the team or manager, which can be astoundingly intense. It can go beyond mere admiration or even adoration and is more complex than simple hero-worshipping. The fact that it is the same men who so often claim not to be able to verbalize their emotions that make public proclamations for the men who shape their football teams should not be trivialized!

Bill Shankly became a father-figure to many Liverpool supporters drawn from an earlier generation. His hero status is assured and his departure from the club in 1974 shocked the city (Taylor and Ward, 1993; see also Chapter Three). More recently, it was for a short time Kenny Dalglish's *status* at Liverpool FC that epitomizes how fans, male and female alike, can have feelings for a club servant that go way beyond that of the conventional fan/player (or fan/manager) relationship. When Dalglish suddenly left Liverpool Football Club in 1991, it was, for many Liverpool fans, as though he had walked out on them after years of a seemingly happy relationship or 'marriage'. Some felt betrayed. Others went into a temporary state of shock. Committed fans of the time can probably remember where they were when the news broke. Dalglish had been such an important part of the lives of Liverpool fans in a critical and successful phase of the club's history, but also in one deeply scarred by tragedy. He had 'stuck by us' and helped us through the hard times post-Heysel and Hillsborough. Maybe female fans, especially, felt this more deeply than men. And then he was gone. We could try to explain this by telling ourselves he was troubled and that there was nothing we could have done to keep him: that he just couldn't handle this sort of intense relationship anymore.

Then, Kenny joined Blackburn Rovers, and so soon after leaving Liverpool. As one distraught fan put it, 'It was like finding out he'd run off with your sister.' Many fans, female and male, still have mixed feelings about Kenny's success at Blackburn Rovers and his troubles at Celtic. It's too painful for many. There is still an incredible pride among Liverpool supporters with respect to Dalglish – witness their mischievous chanting of his name at Newcastle United after he had been sacked by that club. Some Liverpool fans probably harbour secret desires that, one day, he will come back; others find the pain of the break-up has made them, surprisingly, bitter. Some are more forgiving than others. In short, the emotions felt here are deeply felt and in some cases remarkably similar in nature and range to those experienced by many individuals who go through personal or domestic trials. Is all this simply 'displaced' emotion? Are these apparently 'sensitive' male fans – dockers, factory workers, office staff alike – the same macho hooligans we were told needed a 'feminizing' influence in the mid-1980s?

Perhaps terrace culture has never really been quite as 'masculinized' as we have been led to believe. It is certainly not homogeneous. Or perhaps there exists a 'covert', hidden masculinity at football, which involves a more emotional side to the character of men that is kept 'contained' within the private sanctuary of the football ground. After all, in the crowd one is not really 'accountable' for what one does and how one acts. It is these collective feelings and expressions of intimacy, as much as being able to let off steam together at the match, which form a central feature of the bonding process which takes place within the football ground. We talk often about the violence, little about these male emotions expressed at football.

Our own experiences suggest that the concept of masculinity within the football context is rather more complex than is usually recognized. It is not appropriate to adopt, uncritically, a social-scientific role theory. Role theory simplifies the complexities of gender (Stacey and Thorne, 1985) by relying on the notions of a single 'male sex role' and a single 'female sex role'. This consequently perpetuates mythical conceptions, almost stereotypes, of masculinity and femininity and does not allow for the development of relational processes through which notions of masculinity (and femininity) can be constructed, contested and redefined. Our view is that a binary vision of masculinity and femininity is inadequate. Many theorists tend to divide fans into 'male' and 'female' and treat (cultural) gender synonymously with (biological) sex, in binary terms which might no longer be appropriate in today's society. We suggest that we can no longer segregate fans into 'masculine' or 'feminine' categories. We should recognize, instead, the evolving complexities of gender identities.

Sexism in 'The Family'

Before the introduction of seats at football, the collective feeling of shared identity, among both males and females on the Kop, was strong. The Kop could be a forbidding place for those with the 'wrong' accent or lacking the necessary intuitive insights into the sport; it was never a true melting-pot of the social classes and diverse social groups. Black Liverpudlians, especially, felt the culture much less welcoming (see Hill, 1989) and fans from outside the city; 'posh' supporters or 'day trippers' may have found the Kop more suspicious, less inclusive.

Nevertheless, 'football families' across the Kop consist of groups of people from highly diverse social backgrounds. Maybe now, as the standing Kop as we knew it has gone, we view the past in a more favourable, nostalgic, light. For its last few years we had been talking about how the standing Kop just 'wasn't the same as it used to be', that the atmosphere had faded, that it had lost its strong sense of passion and identity. Yet compared to the 'new' seated Kop, it still had a strong feeling of togetherness, of mutual suffering yet support, something like being part of a 'class' or work struggle. The shared experiences of the 'red side' of the community could be found there. Seen in this context it is perhaps no surprise that women want to be part of this community, perhaps especially as their exclusion from such experiences in other aspects of the city life – in work, and in formal politics – has often seemed so acute in Liverpool (Parkinson, 1985).

We need to beware of the danger of warmed-up nostalgia, as it is clear that for some girls and women experiences of football culture have involved unpleasant encounters, albeit sporadically. Many of the female fans we interviewed recounted tales of how they had been singled out on the terraces and treated in a disagreeable manner. Most also claimed that there had been moments in their football-following careers when they had been made to feel uncomfortable because of their sex. It was generally agreed, too, that since the Kop became seated these moments had become less frequent. In a seated environment there are fewer opportunities for men physically to intimidate women; the standing Kop offered an anonymity for abuses. The seats better identify and expose male culprits.

Helen, however, says she has the misfortune currently to sit on the Kop in front of what she calls a genuine misogynist; a man who actually still thinks it's cool to be aggressively sexist. Hence, she has been subjected to his taunts and snide comments such as 'Get back to your kitchen where you belong!', 'You slag!', 'You bitch!', 'Women shouldn't be allowed out except to go shopping!' and so on. Men around her seem to think this fan is an irritating idiot and several times his status as 'a moaner' about the *team* has almost got him into serious trouble with other supporters. But none say a word when he launches into his specifically sexist abuse. The truth is, no one really takes this part of his match-day persona seriously. He's just being 'a lad'. Sexism is not stigmatized in the same way that, say, racism is at football these days. Anti-racist campaigns in football have raised the profile and awareness of the issue to such an extent that, although far from eradicating the problem altogether, today the bigots are stigmatized and quietened. No one bats an eyelid, however, at sexism. 'If women can't take it, they shouldn't be here', seems to be the response. There is also an assumption that to address overt sexism at football would effectively sanitize the culture; that somehow only 'middle-class' (and therefore unwanted) women fans could possibly object to being abused in this way.

The repercussions can be more sinister. At Arsenal away a couple of seasons ago, an incident took place on the steps at the end of the game. A 'scouse' lad in his late twenties was 'groping' a very young girl; when she protested, he began calling her a 'slag' for even being at a football match. Several hundred men were around at the time, and dozens were in the close vicinity. Yet no one stepped in to defend the young girl. No one else got involved. The notion that football is always a 'safe' space for females is, clearly, by no means watertight. In this specific context, sex divides and empowers/subjugates, even as common football club support ostensibly unites.

Almost any female who goes to football as a younger fan probably has experiences of this kind to recall. Sexism can range from an inappropriate glance to a vicious verbal attack or even a physical assault. Sexism at its most extreme can be aggressive, threatening and intimidating. Most female fans probably consider it a price you inevitably pay for entering this 'male' world. Such incidents are infrequent and, generally, football-going for women is still a positive experience. Arguably, female fans suffer this sort of prejudice because our sex makes us more immediately visible and different, in much the same way as some fans deride obvious 'out-of-town' followers at Anfield. Male attempts to undermine opposing players using sexist innuendo – the attacks on the Beckhams, David and Victoria, for example – are similarly inappropriate and are unlikely to be taken up by female fans interested in gender issues.

However, evidence drawn from interviews of young female fans at Liverpool suggests that relatively few fans have recent experiences of overtly aggressive sexism to recount. There are fewer reports of collective sexist chants or wolf-whistles around football grounds today than there were a decade ago. On the whole, female fans' tales of football are upbeat and the 'gender issue' is rarely perceived as a significant problem. Yet anecdotes of more subtle examples of sexism are still commonplace. Female supporters feel resented by some men. Female fans sometimes complain that they are seen as fickle, as not true fans, people who are ignorant of footballing matters, or who only go to football because they 'fancy' the players.

The more subtle illustrations of sexism that take place today involve instances when (male) fans belittle women's views or refuse to accept that we have valid opinions (trivializing female support). When **Cathy** started a new job in Manchester in a male-dominated office in the early 1990s, she was the only member of staff who went to matches, but was effectively excluded from office conversations about football. In similar vein, even in Liverpool as she began another new job in the mid-1990s, her new boss accused the men in the office of being 'unfriendly' to the 'new girl' by talking endlessly about the game.

Some male fans seem to find it troubling or confusing that many females go to football for the same reasons as males. Maybe they misunderstand the nature of the footballing experience? There is much talk of it being a fundamental experience of 'male bonding'. Perhaps it is better described as an experience, simply, of 'bonding'. It happens that for most men they are bonding with other men; but even where this is not the case the presence of women does not always change the male experience. It is often said to **Liz**, for example, by the men in her own football 'community', that the experience of attending for them now – with **Liz** involved – is actually much the same as it had been previously in all-male groups.

Recent Transformations

Recent transformations in football culture have probably made the game more attractive – or at least less unattractive – to some women. Improved facilities in football grounds are usually mentioned as being an attraction to women – yet no *real* fan, male or female, could be put off following their team because of a dirty toilet or a cold, stale pie. Nevertheless, fortunately, the days are long gone – if not forgotten – when women 'away' fans needed a police escort right across the pitch to the home end at some grounds if a half-time toilet visit was required. Invariably, the public return to the 'away' end would be accompanied by 'We know where you've been' ringing around the ground.

The changed image of football is likely to appeal to certain females, just as it is likely to appeal to certain males: the game is no longer perceived as being a hotbed of hooliganism and violence, for example. Most fans of both sexes are glad of that. The role of women in society has changed too: we are no longer excluded from social life or from work outside the home and we increasingly participate in leisure activities. Women who were already interested in football now feel more able to attend matches, and are not afraid to admit to an interest in the game. The new perception of football as a more 'cross-class' and 'cross-gender' leisure option has also meant that women generally don't feel as alienated from the game: it is now more acceptable for women to talk about football and to actively support in a way that was seen, narrowly, as 'unfeminine' only a few years ago.

Perhaps some 'traditional' male fans have resented the encouragement of football support among females? Perhaps they feel threatened? Their territory is being 'invaded' and the last bastion of maleness/masculinity is being eroded, when other male roles are also under attack (see Brimson and Brimson, 1997, for an example). Sport, and football in particular, is no longer quite as active in perpetuating male superiority as it has done throughout most of the nineteenth and twentieth centuries. Perhaps, as football culture has evolved over the last decade, the more 'traditional' fans – males and females *together* – are trying to resist some of these changes. They have, at the top level at least, witnessed subtle changes in the type of people who attend football, an increase in prices, an unwanted 'feminization'/'de-masculinization' of the sport, and they resist by deriding all those they see as representing this shift under one label: 'newcomers'.

At Liverpool FC, it is often the 'out-of-town' fan, rather than the female fan, who is at the receiving end of most of the derision from traditional ('scouse') fans. Nevertheless, the gender card is relevant here, too, as 'out-of-towners' are often indirectly derided for not expressing their 'masculinity' in the same way as 'scousers' do. Their dress code is totally different; many of them wear colours, scarves, for example. They might even carry a merchandise bag. They dare to stray from the classic mega-short hair 'style' which is regarded as compulsory for 'proper' 'scouse' lads these days. They arrive at the ground too early before a match (see also King, 1998, on 'lads' and 'consumer' fans). They are argued to be contributing to a cultural transformation which involves, as one of its processes, the redefining of masculine values at football.

Many of these 'outsider' fans (although at Anfield perhaps fewer than at other clubs) are also 'new fans', another reason for locals why they should be abused and not be taken too seriously. All these features contribute to their exclusion from 'lad' status (though not that many 'out-of-towners' want to be a 'lad'). They are immediately identifiable and their motivation for supporting Liverpool is, for their doubters, questionable. This isn't to say that all 'out-of-towners' are resented. But many are unmistakably *different* and they do not have, or exhibit, the same local masculine identities or codes of their dominant 'scouse' equivalents. Several female 'out-of-town' fans we interviewed claim to share the same *multiple* feelings of exclusion as local female fans. **Julie,** for example, a season-ticket holder who moved from Cumbria to Liverpool in the late 1980s, recalls standing on the Kop and simply not singing. 'My sister and I were afraid of people hearing our accents. As women we were welcome, but we didn't want people to know that we were from out of town.' 'Out of town' men feel alienated at times because they are 'not allowed' to become part of the 'scouse' Liverpool-supporting community. They feel they are *tolerated* by the locals rather than welcomed as one of the community, and they are certainly made to feel different. One female fan, **Jackie**, actually pointed out that for 'out-of-town' men:

> It's like being a women; you are present, and kind of accepted, but without being one of the lads. Deep down, most 'scousers' believe they are the true fans and that we are hangers-on and aren't really committed. Some think we shouldn't even be allowed tickets until the 'scousers' have been allocated theirs.

In short, 'out-of-towners' can also be held responsible for aspects of the 'feminization', or rather the 'demasculinization' or 'detraditionalization', of football. Women and 'out-of-towners' are still very much the 'other' at football, on occasions.

Mind yer Language

One of the myths of modern-day football, perpetrated in club marketing departments and elsewhere, is the idea that women as a group are more sensitive to swearing in public places than are men. Consequently, so this homogenizing argument goes, men at football must curb their language when women are present. For most women at football this is a rather irritating debate. That women can be so essentialized on this issue and so misunderstood for so long is baffling. True, there are well-documented differences in speech styles between men and women (see for example Johnson and Meinhof, 1997), but it is extremely simplistic to suggest that all women object to swearing. Have men really never heard women swear? Do they think we grow up in a city like Liverpool without being exposed to swearing? Or do they, perhaps, have a preferred image of how women *should* behave, and amend their views accordingly? When we hear a man say 'Watch your language, there's a lady present', some women – and men – will empathize and think he's well-meaning, if somewhat old-fashioned. To swear and then apologize to women for doing so is, however, a way of excluding women (again marginalizing and alienating). It tells us that men feel they have to behave differently simply because we are present.

To generalize in this way, and to brand all women as 'puritans' who are offended by swearing, is insulting and ignores the truth. It is quite simply a myth, perpetuated by men who make assumptions based on prejudice or essentialist or patronizing views of women. However, it is more likely that where differences do exist between men and women it is in the use and acceptance of extreme sexist language. This is hardly surprising really. In a recent (unpublished) survey of swearing at football matches carried out by a group of undergraduate students in the Department of Languages at the Manchester Metropolitan University, the results demonstrated, overwhelmingly, that male and female supporters shared the same attitudes to language at football and most were actually ambivalent towards swearing at the match. Indeed, some fans (of both sexes) expressed disappointment that some grounds were reportedly clamping down on swearing and punishing offenders. Swearing at football is widely seen by fans as a way of venting frustration and emotions in a non-violent manner; it is therefore not unhealthy to swear.

However, when individuals were asked which words or concepts they found offensive, or which they actually employed themselves, marked differences between the sexes became more apparent. Overwhelmingly, the differences in opinion and experience lay in the use of those terms which referred to parts of women's bodies or which were offensive to women as a sex in some way. Some of these terms could not even be classed as swearing. Females found them highly gendered and offensive, and simply didn't use them. Many men used them 'naturally' and had often not given much thought about their overtly sexist nature. To call a player 'You woman!' or 'You tart!' when he is performing badly is not among the most aggressive of insults, and few stewards would act to eject a fan for using such an expression. Yet a 'gentle' insult based, for example, on 'race' could, and occasionally does, quite rightly, lead to some punitive response.

Attempts to make football more female-friendly have been sporadic and poorly targeted. Research seems to suggest that women who like football but don't go to football matches are put off by high prices and the fact that they still carry the burden of family responsibilities which occupies their time (Williams and Perkins, 1999). One of these issues has been addressed by some clubs who have offered (controversially) significant price discounts for women, and some clubs (not Liverpool FC) now have child-minding facilities, such as crèches. Women do not, we would suggest, tend to be discouraged from attending football by abusive or aggressive language but, like some men, they do feel intimidated by the threat of violence. Neither do women relish being singled out as being different from the rest of fans. Few clubs, then, address all these issues and although significant changes were experienced over the last decade of the twentieth century in particular, football still seems to be lagging behind in terms of equality of opportunity and greater acceptance of females into the sports environment.

Most women fans we talked to are not especially interested in attracting more women to football. We do not lack company. Women who do not like football presumably have no desire to become more involved anyway. Those female fans who are already connected to football are often hooked precisely because of the way the game is (or was, when they first became fans), hence they are not keen to change its nature. As has been noted in pertinent observations by Williams and Woodhouse (1991: 105) female fans themselves rarely see gender identity in football as a bone of contention and prefer to play down or even deny accusations that football appeals to the macho side of men and is unwelcoming or threatening to women. We fear that making football more 'female friendly' as a matter of policy might well contribute to the game losing some of its appeal, at least part of which includes being hugged and slobbered over by sweaty, scruffy men who have lost themselves momentarily and gone berserk as we score. Part of us, as committed female fans, seems to want the status quo to be maintained and for football to remain a mainly male domain, but one into which those 'privileged' few women can peek – and even become a part of – thereby awarding us with a special status denied to other females. **Joy** says:

> It's selfish, but true. Going to football gives us an insight into the male world. It's at least partly the aura of masculinity that makes it special. And we have something in common with 'the lads', without having the oppressive pressures of having to be one of them and being forced to behave in a way in which we'd really rather not.

Ch-ch-ch-ch-changes

We are always being told these days that football is 'fashionable' and more accessible to women than ever before. But have things really changed that much? The football authorities are certainly keen to encourage more women to attend matches, strongly believing that better facilities and a more family-oriented promotion of the game will do the trick. If more people of any age or either sex feel more welcome at football matches, then this is a positive step. But is this approach the most appropriate one? Simply to suggest to women that they should like football more, either because it is fashionable and glamorous or because it appeals more to families, is somewhat patronizing. It is also misguided. Actually, male fans are more likely to attend football with children than are female fans today (Williams, 1997).

Women's football in England is still an extremely poor relation of the men's game, as we have seen, and considerably more investment is needed there. Sexism remains institutionalized in professional football at generally, higher administrative levels and in terms of the wider organization of the sport. Perhaps attention might better be directed there, too, rather than strongly at existing football fan cultures in Liverpool and elsewhere, where 'negotiated' change is already taking place.

References

Brimson, E. and Brimson, D. (1997) *Capital Punishment*, London: Headline.
Brunt (1989) 'Raising one voice', *Marxism Today,* September 1989.
Bullock, B. (1999) *Reflected Glory*, Dudley: Brewin Books.
Carrington, B. (1999) 'Too many St. George's crosses to bear', in M. Perryman (ed.) *The Ingerland Factor: Home truths from Abroad*, London and Edinburgh: Mainstream.
Coddington, A. (1997) *One of the Lads: Women Who Follow Football*, London: HarperCollins.
Crolley, L. (1999) 'Lads will be Lads', in M. Perryman (ed.) *The Ingerland Factor: Home Truths from Abroad*, Edinburgh and London: Mainstream.
Dunning, E., Murphy, P. and Williams, J. (1988) *The Roots of Football Hooliganism*, London: Routledge.
Duncan, M. and Messner, M. (1998) 'The media image of sport and gender' in L. Wenner (ed.) *MediaSport*, London: Routledge.
Edge. A (1999) *Faith of Our Fathers*, Edinburgh and London: Mainstream.
Fishwick, N. (1989) *English Football and Society, 1910–1950*, Manchester: Manchester University Press.
Giulianotti, R. (1994) 'Social identity and public order' in R. Giulianotti, N. Bonney and M. Hepworth (eds) *Football Violence and Social Identity*, London: Routledge.
—— (1999) *Football: a Sociology of the Global Game*, Cambridge: Polity Press.
Greendorfe, S. (1987) 'Gender bias in theoretical perspectives: the case of female socialization into sport', in *Psychology of Women Quarterly*, 11.
Hargreaves, J. (1994) *Sporting Females: Critical Issues in the History and Sociology of Women's Sports*, London: Routledge.
Higginson, D. (1985) 'The influence of socializing agents in the female sport-participation process', *Adolescence*, 20.
Hill, D. (1989) *Out of His Skin: the John Barnes Phenomenon*, London: Faber & Faber.
Johnson, S. and Meinhof, U. (1997) *Language and Masculinity*, Oxford: Blackwell.
Kane, M. and Jefferson Lenskyi, H (1998) 'Media treatment of female athletes', in L. Wenner (ed.) *MediaSport,* London: Routledge.

King, A. (1998) *The End of the Terraces?*, London: Leicester University Press.

Lopez, S. (1997) *Women on the Ball: A Guide to Women's Football*, London: Scarlet Press.

Mason, T. (1980) *Association Football and English Society, 1863–1915*, Brighton: Harvester.

Parkinson, M. (1985) *Liverpool on the Brink*, Hermitage, Berks: Policy Journals.

Rudd, A. (1998) *Astroturf Blonde*, London: Headline.

Sabo, D. and Curry Johnson, S. (1998) 'Prometheus unbound: constructions of masculinity in sports media', in L. Wenner (ed.) *MediaSport*, London: Routledge.

Scraton, S. (1986) 'Images of femininity and the teaching of girls' physical education', in J. Evans (ed.) *Physical Education, Sport and Schooling*, London: Falmer Press.

Stacey, J. and Thorne, B. (1985) 'The missing feminist revolution in sociology', in *Social Problems*, **32**(4).

Taylor, R. and Ward, A. with Williams, J. (1993*) Three Sides of the Mersey: an Oral History of Everton, Liverpool and Tranmere Rovers*, London: Robson.

Waddington, I., Dunning, E., Murphy, P. (1996) 'Surveying the social composition of football crowds', *Leisure Studies*, No. 15.

Watt, T. (1993) *The End: 80 Years of Life on Arsenal's North Bank*, Edinburgh and London: Mainstream.

Williams, J. (1987) 'Young people's images of attending football matches: an analysis of essays by Liverpool schoolchildren', Sir Norman Chester Centre for Football Research, Leicester: University of Leicester.

—— (1997) *FA Premier League National Fan Survey 1996/97*, Sir Norman Chester Centre for Football Research, Leicester: University of Leicester.

Williams, J. and Perkins, S. (1999) 'Ticket prices, merchandising and the new business of football', Report to the Football Task Force, SNCCFR, Leicester.

Williams, J. and Woodhouse, D. (1999) *Offside? the Position of Women and Football in Britain*, Reading: South Street Press.

Williams, J. and Woodhouse, J. (1991) 'Can Play, Will Play? Women and Football in Britain', in J. Williams and S. Wagg (eds) *British Football and Social Change*, Leicester : Leicester University Press.

−10−

Liverpool FC in the Global Football Age
Rick Parry

The Shankly Legacy

In football it is easy to focus on tradition in the wrong way. There is an inclination to remember only what was good (which in Liverpool FC's case was extremely good) and a tradition of success creates a weight of expectation that is difficult to bear. This creates a damaging reluctance to change – in the hope that the magic formula will eventually bring everything right again. The outcome is likely to be losing ground on competitors.

But viewed in the right way, tradition is very important and a great strength. It is essential to identify the values, the principles, the essence of what a club such as Liverpool is all about, because these provide a stable framework in an increasingly unstable football world. This is not to be confused, of course, with doing things the *same* way – but it does mean that you always ensure that what you do fits within the established framework.

To me, the traditions that matter at Anfield started with the arrival of Bill Shankly in 1959; we must be talking, in this context, about the twenty-five years of unparalleled on-the-pitch football success. Distilling what every Liverpool supporter instinctively feels about that period into words is a challenge, but not one to be shirked. So what did Shankly bring to the club. He brought winning football played with a certain style – in what Stephen Hopkins in Chapter Four and others elsewhere have described as 'the Liverpool way'. Nothing can be more important than this. Shankly also forged a special bond with the supporters of the club and the people in the city because he understood them and he treated them with openness, honesty and respect. He had huge enthusiasm for the game, which rubbed off on everyone around him. Players and supporters had self-belief and pride, they had passion. There was no place for losers, no place for anyone prepared to give less than one hundred per cent. No individual was bigger than the Club (see Chapter Three for more on Shankly).

The real secret of Liverpool's success at that time was the ability to spot players who were winners; players who would add something to the team. There were always plenty of good players at other clubs, of course – but Liverpool FC repeatedly identified that something special, that extra dimension that made players winners. Look at the number of games that were won in the last few minutes by Shankly's teams and those at Liverpool which followed. This was all down to character and determination, allied to self-belief. It had little to do with coincidence or with luck.

Off the pitch the club also had a reputation for doing things the right way. Nothing flash, nothing pretentious. Envied by others but always respected, never despised. Always planning ahead, never resting on recent glories. Simply put, what matters for this football club, moving forwards, is to win trophies and stay close to its supporters. Easy to say – a little more difficult to do. But, guiding values should be simple so that they are understood and remembered by everyone.

The Origins of the FA Premier League

In what follows I will say nothing about the Heysel and Hillsborough disasters and their consequences. Of course, they have been a central part of shaping the recent history of Liverpool FC, but that issue is covered at length in Chapter Five. Given a whole book, it might be possible to give a comprehensive account of the recent modernization of the game. Given a single chapter, it is necessary to be highly selective and to focus on those elements that have the most direct bearing on the immediate future of Liverpool Football Club. The 1990s saw enormous changes in the game. They have been well documented by the burgeoning army of commentators, analysts and experts that is a by-product of the growing interest in football. But it may be helpful to give a perspective from someone fortunate enough to have been very close to many of the key events.

The origins of recent changes in football in England can probably be traced back to the fact that tensions within the old Football League had escalated during the latter half of the 1980s. Big clubs were uncomfortable with a complex voting structure on policy which tended to favour the clubs in the lower divisions; they constantly cried that the tail was wagging the dog. There were also complaints that a Football League Management Committee comprising club chairmen carried in-built conflicts of interest. Finally, it was argued that the formula for sharing television and sponsorship income resulted not from any kind of objective analysis of what was 'fair', but instead from a series of high-profile rows and horse-trades which had been going on across the previous five years. At best, it represented no more than an uneasy truce.

But it was the Taylor Report on Hillsborough in 1990 that proved to be the catalyst for change and prompted the then 'Big Five' clubs (Liverpool, Everton, Manchester United, Arsenal and Tottenham Hotspur) to take action. These clubs approached the Football Association in late 1990, to seek its support for the foundation of a new breakaway league. It was estimated that £250 million would be required to transform top football stadia in England into all-seated arenas. At the time this seemed (and was) a huge sum of money, and the top clubs felt there was too little direction from the Football League as to exactly from *which* source the money for stadium redevelopment was to come. At the same time, relations between the FA and the League were at a particularly low ebb; the FA was upset about 'power-sharing' proposals which had been promoted by the League as part of the general debate after Hillsborough about 'leadership' in football. Given these circumstances, the governing body was especially receptive to the approach of these five powerful clubs. Hence the FA Premier League was born.

It transpired, however, that it wasn't just the 'Big Five' clubs that wanted a new beginning; many of the other First Division clubs were unhappy too. They were unhappy with the Football League management structure, but they also had a deep mistrust of the 'Big Five' themselves, and they wanted the opportunity to create a new structure, one which had much more transparency. The constitution of the FA Premier League was, therefore, designed to be simple and fair. All decisions were to be made on a one club/one vote basis (with a two-thirds majority to prevent too many damaging mood swings); there were to be no committees; and there was to be an independent Board comprising a Chairman and a Chief Executive. Perhaps most important of all, a formula for the sharing of TV income, which balanced membership, popularity and performance, was devised. To paraphrase the Chairman of one middle-ranking club in the new league: the new structure didn't produce equal *shares* – but it did provide equal *opportunities* for all clubs.

Television and 'New' Football

This constitution worked and after some hairy moments in the first twelve months, there was a unity and sense of purpose among clubs that was quite rare in football. Perhaps inevitably it was the TV deals that grabbed the major headlines and it is instructive to sketch out, briefly, aspects of the history of football on television.

First of all, it is worth noting that there was no live televised League football in England at all until 1983. Then, ITV and the BBC paid £2.6 million per season between them to share the broadcasting of ten games. During the passage of the Broadcasting Bill in 1995, it was amusing to read the misty-eyed reminiscences of politicians and journalists who talked about the grainy black and white images of the great games of the 1960s that were now 'denied' to the public at large with the advent of satellite television. The truth, of course, is that these images of 'live' football on TV never really existed.

In 1985 the League had had the temerity to demand more money from the TV companies, famously pointing out that the broadcasters needed football more than football needed the broadcasters. As a result of the dispute which followed, there was no football on television at all that season until Christmas, when the League backed down and accepted a short-term TV deal – with *no* fee increase. In 1988 British Satellite Broadcasting (BSB) appeared on the scene, breaking the BBC/ ITV duopoly and usefully establishing the principle that when it comes to dealing with broadcasters, two's a cartel but three's competition. After a bout of 'public' negotiating that did little for the image of football or broadcasters, it was the terrestrial ITV which emerged with a four-year agreement to screen eighteen live matches each season for an annual fee, starting at £11 million. A new word entered the football lexicon at this time – 'exclusivity'; ITV paid a significant premium to keep football *away* from the other broadcasters. But this was at the broadcasters' instigation, and it was not a concept that the League itself had devised.

It was this deal that gave rise to most of the mistrust that then existed between clubs; the perception was that some clubs who had taken part in the negotiations were subsequently favoured by ITV. The facts are that over the four years of the contract the 'Big Five' clubs received 65 per cent of all the TV coverage, and in every season of the deal at least six First Division clubs received no TV coverage at all. In turn, this led to an imbalance in the value of sponsorship and advertising contracts at clubs. If you were on TV all the time, sponsors were not difficult to attract.

Hence, the strongly held views among the majority of clubs that with the advent of the FA Premier League, the clubs themselves should no longer be involved in any TV negotiations and that any new TV deal should be subject to the stipulation that *every* club should be covered 'live' at least once each season. Liverpool FC, incidentally, were at the forefront of the push for independent, transparent negotiation along precisely these lines.

The deal that was struck with BSkyB and the BBC in 1992 was worth £214 million over five years (this compared with ITV's losing bid of £165 million). Taking a long-term view, it was crucial from the FA Premier League's point of view that BSkyB grew in strength, otherwise there was a danger of the old cartel reforming. Thus, an element of satellite coverage of top football was important. But the FA Premier League would happily have seen this satellite deal sit alongside terrestrial coverage. ITV, on the other hand, wanted to secure *exclusive* rights in order to stop BSkyB, a dangerous new competitor, growing. The terrestrial channel made it plain that they would bid on an all-or-nothing basis; there would be no sharing of TV rights for them.

Understanding the FA Premier League's genuine concerns about the potential absence of any terrestrial coverage (essential to promote the game to a wider audience), BSkyB forged a new partnership with the BBC. As a result, BBC's *Match of the Day* made a welcome return to the screens after a four-year break and, for the first time ever, offered a comprehensive round-up showing every goal scored in top matches. Another of the attractions of BSkyB was its real commitment to ensure the sort of fair spread of 'live' TV coverage that was so important to the clubs. In fact, in each of the five years of the contract, every club received at least *three* live televised appearances. In addition, BSkyB readily agreed to broadcast a minimum of twenty hours' support programming every week, something no terrestrial broadcaster could offer. Despite early misgivings on the part of some clubs, an excellent working relationship between the new League and the broadcaster developed.

In 1996, the deal with BSkyB and the BBC was renewed for a further four years, on exactly the same basis as before – except that the total fees from the deal rose to £743 million. This time there was competition from two potential pay-TV consortia, each of which included one of the leading ITV companies. Annual rights' fees had risen by a factor of 70 in a little over 10 years, which is impressive growth by any analysis. The reason? In 1983 there was no competition; in 1992 a pay-TV broadcaster did just enough to outbid an advertising-funded broadcaster which was pushed to its limit. By 1996 there was competition between pay-TV broadcasters. Arguably the League had realized the true value of 'live' football TV rights for the first time. Competition in 1996 was driven, of course, by the eagerly anticipated arrival of *digital* transmission.

The nature of the early TV deals was shaped by limitations on *distribution* – initially, there were only two channels and they couldn't even find time in the schedules for a game every week. The multiplicity of digital channels provides almost limitless capacity – there is no reason, in theory, why every match can't be shown live and, as BSkyB have shown, there is scope for an à la carte service, with viewers selecting their own camera angles and commentary tracks. As technologies converge, links to the Internet provide enormous scope for immediate access to statistics and to archive material, interaction and home shopping.

One estimate has argued that the number of digital homes in Europe will grow from three million in 1998 to 53 million in 2005, figures which suggest that enthusiasm from broadcasters for live sport, and in particular for football, is scarcely going to wane. The challenge for football now is to make the most effective use of this exciting, but potentially bewildering, new landscape. Perhaps ironically, given the furore over the first BSkyB deal in 1992, the FA Premier League took a cautious view in 1996. 'If it ain't broke, don't fix it' was the approach, as the urge to rush headlong into all-embracing pay-per-view deals was firmly resisted. Meanwhile, in Italy, in Spain and in France armchair season tickets and impulse pay-per-view football coverage are already established.

The Bosman Effect

In both 1992 and 1996 the BSkyB/BBC deals took the FA Premier League to the top of the European rankings in terms of TV income. This has an increasing relevance thanks to the landmark 'Bosman' ruling in the European Court of Justice in 1995. For several years, a relatively unknown Belgian footballer of average ability, Jean Marc Bosman, had been challenging the football establishment over what he considered to be unfair restrictions at the end of players' contracts. Failing to get satisfaction from the Belgian FA or UEFA, Bosman resorted to law and won an emphatic victory.

In summary, the Court held that it was illegal for there to be any restrictions on the number of players from other EU member states in a team (thus outlawing UEFA's so-called 'three foreigner' rule) and, further, that clubs could no longer demand any transfer fee when a player moved clubs from one EU member state to another at the end of his contract. Had Bosman been playing in England it is likely the problem would never have arisen. The worst excesses of the retain and transfer system here were abolished in 1963, as a result of the challenge brought to them by George Eastham. But the English system was never placed before the European Court and there was no suggestion that modifications that took on board the better elements of our system might now suffice. Nor was proper consideration given to the argument that transfer fees were actually a 'good' thing because they simply recirculate money *within* the game and benefit the majority of players with smaller clubs.

The inevitable, and immediate, impact of the judgment was to increase the movement of players between EU member states and change, forever, the basis on which clubs recruit players. In an effort to retain a degree of stability in England, the FA Premier League went into immediate dialogue with the Professional Footballers Association (PFA) with a view to modernizing the domestic transfer system, but not abandoning it. With a fair dose of goodwill and common sense on both sides it was agreed that there would still be a limit on the number of *non-EU* players that clubs could field in any match (essentially three). It was also agreed that players would only be free to move from one English club to another at the end of contract without a transfer fee once they had reached the age of 24. This provided protection for clubs that develop young players, while at the same time allowing players their first 'free' move before they reach their peak.

From the point of view of clubs, the big shift is that the reward for investing in the development of the players will be four or five years' first-team service rather than a guaranteed pay day, via a transfer fee. This certainly requires smarter thinking and forward planning, but it is by no means the disaster that many predicted. Those clubs that are genuine developers of, rather than traders in, players will be fine.

The European 'Super League' Debate

The changes in the TV landscape – the battle for supremacy amongst the pay TV moguls leading the digital revolution and the constant speculation over pan-European alliances – and also the impact of the Bosman judgment, led to new proposals for a European Super League in 1998. There had been regular talk of such a development for at least a decade and a variety of half-baked plans emerged from time to time. The difference with this particular scheme, conceived and backed by Italian sports rights agency *Media Partners*, was that it had been properly researched and was well thought-through. Attention to detail was impressive, as were the potential rewards.

In brief, the idea was that thirty-two clubs would take part every season. There would be two leagues of sixteen clubs, followed by a knockout phase. The controversial aspects of the scheme were that it would be co-ordinated by a private body, *Media Partners,* rather than by UEFA, and that sixteen founder clubs were to be selected on the basis of historical status rather than current performance. These founder clubs would have guaranteed membership for at least six seasons, being joined each season by sixteen teams that qualified on merit. It was estimated that founder clubs would each earn upwards of £20 million every season from TV income and sponsorship – more than twice as much as the most successful FA Premier League clubs receive, for example, from the BSkyB and BBC contracts.

Liverpool was invited to join the proposed 'super league', but the Liverpool board felt distinctly uneasy about the concept of permanent membership and about its likely impact on the game as a whole, and on the FA Premier League in particular. The club took the position that the matter should be debated by the League as a whole and not by individual clubs; predictably, when *Media Partners* addressed an FA Premier League meeting, the *overall* reaction was very negative.

Elsewhere in Europe, interest in the new concept was stronger. The Spanish footballing giants – Barcelona, Real Madrid – burdened with massive debt, have a voracious appetite for additional revenue. And it is easy to see the dilemma for a club such as Ajax in Holland. Losing its best young players to Spain and Italy as a result of the Bosman ruling, and with modest domestic TV revenues that give no scope to compete in the European market, how on earth does this club, with its great European traditions, maintain its place among Europe's football elite? As it turned out, UEFA responded to the challenge of this new competitor by introducing their own new format for the Champions League. As a result, support for *Media Partners* waned. More guaranteed games and more TV revenue for the major clubs in 1999/2000 was the outcome, and everyone, for now, was happy.

But at what cost? Clubs reaching the final of the Champions League will have to play at least seventeen games, which is an absurd burden. And it is now a fact that in terms of the distribution of TV and sponsorship income, the gulf between the top three clubs in the FA Premier League and the rest is greater than that between the bottom of the FA Premier League and the top of the Nationwide League. There is an argument now that the worst place to finish in the FA Premier League will not be in the lower reaches, but *fourth* – with Champions League wage levels but *without* the necessary revenue to cover them!

Whether we have seen the end of *Media Partners* and their idea of a European Super League remains to be seen. There are uneasy echoes here in Europe of the situation in England in the late 1980s when breakaway threats were met with a succession of offers to increase the First Division's share of the television cake. This delayed, but did not in the end prevent, change. Irrespective of the format of European competition, the distribution of income suggests that over the next five years the emergence of twelve to sixteen 'super clubs' will de facto take place. In marketing parlance, these will be global 'brands' with effective commercial operations spreading worldwide.

A graphic example of this came with the announcement in autumn 1999 that BSkyB were to buy Manchester United. From day one of their links with the FA Premier League, BSkyB had demonstrated a refreshing determination to boost the strength of the League as a whole. This was reflected in the broad spread of their TV coverage and in a desire at BSkyB to rise above club politics. Against this background, the decision to buy the League's biggest and most successful club seemed extraordinary. An analysis of the number of News Corporation companies holding the rights to FA Premier League matches in overseas territories provides some pointers to the logic; increasing promotion of the Manchester United brand worldwide would in turn boost the popularity of growing TV stations. Of course, speculation also linked the purchase of United to European Super League talks, but there is no evidence of a direct connection. However, for those of us striving to bring success back to Liverpool FC, the news of the BSkyB takeover bid for United certainly served to focus minds. To an extent, the focus shifted when the Monopolies and Mergers Commission, rather unexpectedly it must be said, ruled against the bid. Nevertheless, the lid to Pandora's box had been lifted, if not yet completely removed.

Off to Court

While the Manchester United story hogged the domestic headlines there were further developments in Europe which will have repercussions for us, at Liverpool FC. Again they relate to digital television and the growth of European super powers. In Italy and Spain clubs have started to sell rights individually rather than through their domestic league. Bizarrely, Real Madrid and Barcelona have already sold their rights for the period 2003–2008, reportedly for sums in excess of £50 million per annum. Top Italian clubs are making £30 million per season from TV. On one level, we might fear for the implications for domestic leagues of these sorts of developments. Who will be able to compete with the TV 'super rich'? On another, we might say it's no wonder we lost Steve McManaman and on *that* salary.

Thus far in England we have all resolutely supported the principle of collective selling of TV rights on the basis that it is so obviously good for the game.

Obviously? Well, not so obviously to the Director General of Fair Trading. In 1996, the FA Premier League's rule book and the contracts with BSkyB and the BBC were referred to the Restrictive Practices Court on the basis that they contained restrictions which potentially inhibit competition. Uniquely, in this forum, the onus is on the defendant to prove that, on balance, any such restrictions are necessary and not against the public interest. You are, therefore, guilty until proven innocent.

The attack was on two fronts. First of all, the TV contracts were challenged on the basis that exclusivity is anti-competitive. Bearing in mind that exclusivity only emerged in the 1980s at the behest of ITV and was the factor that broke the cosy cartel of TV companies, there is more than a tinge of irony here. More fundamentally, it was argued that by selling rights collectively the FA Premier League operates as a cartel. And cartels are bad.

This always seemed to be an extraordinary analysis which demonstrated simply that the Office of Fair Trading completely misunderstood the way in which sports operate. Very elementary economic theory suggests that there are two key features of a classic cartel. First of all, the cartel comprises producers of a homogeneous product, such as cement, gas or oil. Secondly, the cartel will restrict competition because the members agree to fix prices or to limit supply. Indeed the OFT argued that the FA Premier League restricted the supply of 'live' matches on BSkyB to sixty matches, simply to force the price up.

It is clear that neither of these features actually applies to the FA Premier League. If a cement makers' cartel is disbanded, the members continue to produce cement. The cartel *itself* does not co-operatively produce a distinctive product. But the FA Premier League *does* produce a product that is quite separate and cannot be readily subdivided – it produces the FA Premier League Championship. Every club contributes in equal measure, and every match has a bearing on the outcome of the Championship. The interest in any given game will depend, in part at least, on the relative position of the two teams and on the effect the result might have on other teams. The story of the Championship unfolds, gloriously, across the whole season.

It is a simple matter of fact that the restriction of the number of 'live' TV games to sixty is driven, purely, by football considerations, but even if that is not accepted (and the OFT didn't accept it) then, surely, economic argument falls at the very first hurdle. Why does a cartel restrict supply? It does so because every demand curve tells us that as output rises, the price drops at the point at which the cost of producing extra units exceeds the price at which they can be sold. In other words, a loss is made on each extra unit produced and so there is no incentive to produce more. But hold on. There are 380 Premier League matches, irrespective of any interest at all from TV companies. The 'cost' to the FA Premier League of producing an extra game for television, for increasing coverage from, say, sixty to sixty-one games, is obviously nil. And yet it is clear, by reference to evidence and the application of common sense, that BSkyB would have paid more money for seventy games than for sixty. So, if the FA Premier League simply wanted to *maximize* TV revenues it would actually make more games available.

Is this argument flawed or over-simplistic? Evidently the Restrictive Practices Court didn't think so. And yet it took three years of effort, the compilation of thousands of documents and in excess of £20 million spent on legal fees to get to this point. If this isn't frustrating enough, the resounding victory won by the FA Premier League and the broadcasters has a hollow core. First of all, this is because this was the last case to be brought under the Restrictive Trade Practices Act. The new Competition Act gives greater power to the Director General and applies a whole new set of tests. And, within weeks of the judgment, the European Commission announced that *it* was going to examine the rules and the contracts all over again. Bearing in mind the Commission's quest for harmonization, and the recent developments in Spain and Italy, this examination must be taken seriously.

Liverpool FC's position is still to support the *collective* selling of TV rights because it is good for the FA Premier League as a whole and for the game in general. It brings a fairness of distribution that cannot be replicated. But while a central package will undoubtedly still be a feature, it is almost certain that there will be increasing *individual* selling of club rights. Archive rights will revert to clubs, leading to regional magazine programmes or, perhaps, club channels. And there will be pressure for games not included in the central package to be sold individually through armchair season tickets, or pay-per-view. The truth is that whatever it is that clubs and supporters want, the competition authorities want to see more 'live' football on television.

New Directions for Liverpool FC

It was against this background of constant change, and mindful of the fact that the *rate* of change is undoubtedly quickening, that the Board at Liverpool decided to take stock in early 1999. Instinctively wary of public flotation, and determined to remain a *football* club at heart, it was nevertheless clear that standing still was no longer an option. The guiding principle that matters most at the club is to win trophies. If there is to be a group of 'super clubs', then Liverpool FC has to be one of them. If this means being as successful *off* the pitch as the others, then let's get on with it. But let's be smart; let's try to find a way of doing it without losing the soul of the club.

If this means being in a position to exploit the new television opportunities effectively then let's do it first. And let's be the best at it. Let's *anticipate* the trends rather than follow them. The first priority has to be to get into the Champions

League, quickly; if we can't get into the top three soon there is a danger we'll be left behind. To bring about a rapid restructuring of the team the club needed capital; it could simply not be done from internal resources. But capital alone was not enough. To support a rapidly rising cost base it was essential to find ways of driving turnover up.

A conscious decision was, therefore, taken to find a 'strategic partner'. This would have to be a partner that would invest capital, but one which would also bring the skills and resources needed to help the club exploit the worldwide commercial opportunities it was now presented with, not least those from television. This would also have to be a partner that would allow those running the football club to concentrate, without interference, on football.

It was expected in the wake of the BSkyB/Manchester United talks that there would be widespread changes in the ownership structure of clubs in England. If Liverpool FC took an early, pro-active approach it should have the pick of the potential suitors, and also the *time* to make a properly considered choice, rather than joining the stampede of 'me-too' deals that would inevitably follow. So it was that in July 1999 Liverpool FC announced that the *Granada* group had acquired a 9.9 per cent stake in the club. *Granada* has all the right credentials – in TV terms it is a strong regional player, it has a key voice on the ITV network and, through it's half-share of On-Digital, it is firmly in the digital race. But its skills go well beyond television and they provide an almost perfect fit for the opportunities now presented to a successful football club.

Crucially, too, *Granada* is a company with its roots, firmly, in the North West of England. Many of its customers are Liverpool supporters and, having covered so many of the success stories in the glory years, it understands the importance of a winning team.

In keeping with our focus on building a winning team, all of *Granada*'s investment went into the club rather than to existing shareholders and, with the exception of £2 million invested in the Academy, the proceeds of the deal were devoted wholly to team-building. This is a partnership that should see us well set to face the challenges and opportunities of the new Millennium.

What are the immediate priorities? We need a bigger stadium; to compete with Europe's best we need at least 55,000 seats. We want to stay at Anfield because it is our home. But, significant expansion will require an imaginative partnership to be forged with the City Council and the local community in Liverpool 4. Successful football clubs are demonstrably good for cities. They generate huge publicity on an international scale – why else would our under-19 team have been an integral part of Liverpool's visit to Shanghai to formalize the twinning agreement between the cities in 1999? And professional football clubs do have a direct economic impact. A recent report by the Football Research Unit at the University of Liverpool concluded that 3,000 full-time and 1,400 part-time jobs on Merseyside are dependent on the presence of the two football clubs and that 750,000 visitors come to the city every year *because* of football.

But beyond this, there is every reason to believe that expansion can be a focus for the *regeneration* of the Anfield area. Successful regeneration brings rebirth rather than rebuilding: which means that people come first. The trend in the USA for the construction of functional, multi-purpose edge-of-town stadia, with vast plains of car parks, is starting to reverse. Baseball teams are moving back to purpose-built retro-look urban stadia.

Why is this? It's because the car parks sit empty for vast periods, rendering areas devoid of life and activity. And it is also because spectators travel *through* the surrounding neighbourhoods rather than *to* them. Take away the car parks, and stadia disgorge large number of people *into* a neighbourhood. They will congregate in pubs, before and after games, and spend money in local shops. Such stadia bring vitality to areas and local businesses benefit, too.

Of course such interaction also brings problems which have to be handled sensitively – litter, noise and on-street parking being the obvious ones. But given the will, there are solutions to these understandable concerns. The club has to be mindful of the needs of its neighbours and it has to work *with* the local community. There are many things that can be done – for example directing employment opportunities to local people, encouraging the use of local suppliers, and actively involving people in sporting and educational initiatives. The club must be prepared to turn its face *outwards*.

The desire to stay at Anfield should also be seen as a clear signal that the need to maintain – and, indeed, strengthen – the bond with the local supporters is recognized. Indeed this bond is crucial. And it is wholly *consistent* with the development of the Liverpool FC brand on an international scale. The brand *is* the successful club that cares about its roots. That is exactly what people around the world want to be a part of. And successful commercial development will centre on finding ways of enabling local people to feel a sense of belonging. From this flows a need for better communication. Which, in part, means providing information more effectively, but it also means being better at listening; it has to be a two-way process.

The future is already upon us. At Liverpool we aim to be ahead of the game. We need to continue to develop the club's new Academy at Kirkby. The investment of over £10 million is a clear statement of the club's recognition that, in the post-Bosman era, the development of young players is more important than ever. In economic terms, wage levels simply reflect supply and demand. If outstanding players are in short supply it makes sense to produce more. And if players are free to leave in their mid-twenties this has to be a continuous process. Perhaps more importantly, the longer young players are with us, the more we have the opportunity to influence their attitudes and approach to the game as well as their technical ability; we can ensure that they understand the Liverpool philosophy. It is no coincidence that given the opportunity to choose the postal address of the Academy we instinctively and immediately went for 'The Liverpool Way'.

Afterword: Hillsborough – Flowers and Wasted Words

Colin Moneypenny

In April 1989 Merseyside mourned massively and magnificently for the victims of the Hillsborough Disaster. At least for a couple of weeks the emotional restraint and the masks of respectability we all wear for 'normal life' were set aside just a little. The shock of sudden and needless death on a sunny afternoon on such a scale and involving so many young people united the community in a way not seen before. Public tears merged with private grief throughout that dreadful funereal period.

If the religious ceremonies at both Liverpool Cathedrals served their formal purpose and the funerals fulfilled some of the private needs of individual bereaved families, it was at Anfield that the wider community was able to focus its grief immediately after the disaster. For a time the 'them and us', which had in some way created the conditions for what had happened, was swept away as Liverpool Football Club opened its doors to the public and the bereaved.

Players who, even by 1989, had in many cases begun to live in very different worlds from those who followed their professional fortunes were made available to meet the bereaved, to visit survivors and to attend the far too many funerals. Yet despite the immense efforts of the footballers and in particular their manager, Kenny Dalglish and his wife Marina, it was clear, not least to them, that they were hardly trained to counsel people in such immense trauma.

How sad that, with the exception of local boys such as Steve McMahon and John Aldridge, for some players and officials, as Alan Hansen admits in his autobiography, it was only death on such a large scale which brought it home to them how much the football club meant to its supporters. The pain of the region was symbolized, visually, to the watching world by the spontaneous laying of flowers at Anfield. Within a week this simple gesture of love and loss had escalated as tributes were sent from all corners of Britain and indeed the world. The inspiring carpet of flowers that covered the 'sacred' turf as a result was kept fresh by the ocean of tears that accompanied them.

In the twentieth-century history of Liverpool FC, the photographs of the Anfield pitch in 1989 bedecked with the united colours of nature will surely be images which radiate in historical resonance at least as much as those of the working docks and boats, the May Blitz, the Beatles at the Cavern, or, indeed, the Toxteth riots of 1981.

Many of the flowers sent to Anfield were accompanied by words of love and often extremely moving verse. There's something about the closeness of death, particularly on a large scale and particularly when the young are involved which can make ordinary people, who normally would shun anything to do with poetry, discover the Wilfred Owen inside them. It's almost as if the intense expression of grief can move beyond even the most technologically advanced mortal communication.

The poetry was just one part of the torrent of words, including articles, letters, memoriums and a million traumatized private conversations which poured out after the disaster in a collective attempt to heal the emotional scars and to try to make some sense of the senseless. The agony of having to write such words however was compounded for many by the knowledge of so many wasted words in the previous few years which should have prevented the tragedy and thus made the 'if onlys' unnecessary.

Liverpool Football Club, through its then Secretary, Peter Robinson, had issued warnings to the relevant football authorities about the intended arrangements prior not only to Hillsborough but also the equally awful disaster at the Heysel Stadium in Brussels four years earlier. The warnings, then, about the blatant stupidity of creating a so-called 'neutral' Z section in the midst of the Liverpool 'end' fell on deaf ears, even though the advice given was simple and sensible and would almost certainly have prevented the thirty-nine deaths which occurred on that evening in 1985.

Not to have played such an important match in a crumbling wreck of a stadium would, of course, have been an even simpler way to have avoided the net effects of the mayhem which was created by some elements of both sets of supporters that evening. My overwhelming memory of Heysel is of meeting some Liverpool fans in the centre of Brussels who vividly described, some seven hours *before* the Disaster, the deathtrap conditions which their cursory examination of the stadium had revealed that morning. The question remains unanswered as to why UEFA had sanctioned the playing of the top game in European football at a ground that building surveyors in England would have refused to license for probably any public event whatsoever.

A Belgian journalist once remarked to me that having visited Merseyside, he thought that Liverpool fans only want to talk about Hillsborough – never Heysel. I told him that, obviously, for many of us the hurt of Hillsborough was closer to home, but there were many examples of the huge distress and soul-searching caused locally by the 1985 tragedy. One example is that the week after Heysel, the Football Supporters Association was formed by two Liverpool fans, distraught like so many of us, by such needless loss of life at football.

Their view was that if a group of ordinary Liverpool fans had got together with a group of ordinary Juventus fans prior to the European Cup Final to make the arrangements for that occasion, then they would have made a much better job of it than the highly paid officials of UEFA. Certainly, some Liverpool fans behaved despicably at Heysel, but it is equally the case that the club and its entire fan base took more of the responsibility and the opprobrium generated worldwide than they were really due. This meant that the wider lessons about crowd safety became lost in the headlong rush into condemnation and hooligan hysteria which was eventually to bequeath a terrible legacy.

Despite the fledgling beginnings of a supporter movement through the FSA and the fanzines, the hysteria about hooliganism, fuelled at every instance by the national press, refused to go away. The stone-age approach to the control of football crowds, and particularly those on the standing terraces – perceived as the home of the wildest of the hooligan 'beasts' – paid scant if any attention to safety. It was a mindset carved not out of imagination or intelligence but from a brutal assessment that all standing football fans should be treated as potential criminals.

It was not surprising that against such a backdrop the words of those who cautioned about the inherent dangers of fencing and the militaristic approach to policing were paid scant attention by those with the decision-making powers. For them, safety was a distant consideration obscured by an absolute obsession with 'security' and specifically the sanctity of the professional football pitch.

And so as the disaster in the Leppings Lane unfolded the futility of words when faced with the power of a manufactured perception became chillingly apparent. 'Get us out of here', was screamed in terror. There was nothing here that was vague, equivocal or ambiguous, no double meanings or irony, no nuances or clever repartee, no spin-doctoring to create a softer image or researched wordplay to sell a product. These were soundbites of pure terror and primal screaming born of the original reason for the development of language, the need to communicate an idea or a feeling simply, honestly and speedily.

The message being sent to those a few feet away in safety was that there are people dying here, please do something about it. For the few vital minutes when it could have made a difference, the message received by policemen who were saturated both with years of hooligan hysteria and orders for the day, reflected exactly that same barren and inelastic way of thinking.

The war of the words has continued pretty much unabated ever since the disaster. From the start, the eulogies for the dead were mixed in equal measure with the anger of the living. Recrimination and apportioning blame will follow any disaster that is not an 'act of God', and even many that are. Getting answers to the human failures is essential for the bereaved and survivors whose wish is always to find out exactly what happened and why. In addition, they cherish the idea that their loss will create a future benefit and so they wish to ensure that 'it doesn't happen again'.

Hillsborough, though, has always had another 'victim-blaming' dimension to it that was likely to make the pain worse than it otherwise would have been. No one blames the victims of a train or air disaster but the bereaved and survivors of Hillsborough have always had to combat the quite scandalous allegations, utterly disproven by Lord Justice Taylor, that a drunken, ticketless, rampaging mob were the true cause of the tragedy.

This web of deceit born out of the marriage of leaden stereotypes about football supporters and people from Liverpool and topped with a double helping of 'Heysel' has been so vicious, wide-reaching and persistent that it is impossible to countenance that it has been anything but orchestrated and deliberate. This disinformation has been a permanent backdrop to a campaign for justice – to unlock the 'what happened, and why' – that has stretched interminably from the generic Inquest verdict to the private prosecutions of the two most senior policemen on duty on the day. It does not take much to heed the often used words of Trevor Hicks, to the effect that Hillsborough has been two disasters – the one on the day and the huge miscarriage of justice that has followed ever since.

As well as inflicting more pain on individuals who are already severely traumatized, the campaign of vilification has ranged from the sinister to the bizarre. Bernard Ingham's obsessive but fact-free blaming of Liverpool fans stems from his visit to Sheffield with the Prime Minister the day after the disaster, but he refuses to say from whom he inherited his second-hand opinion. More laughably, Brian Clough's attempts to defend himself after boosting publicity for his autobiography by treading the same path became a farcical descent into abusive stereotypes about 'scousers' which forever destroyed any residual affection for him on Merseyside.

All in all, the press coverage of Hillsborough nationally has been largely disgraceful and has extended far beyond the *Sun* newspaper which at least lost many sales after their sickening '*The Truth*' story provoked a very successful local boycott on Merseyside. Many, many other newspapers, journalists, columnists and broadcasters unfortunately escaped the fury reserved for the *Sun* as they also deserved to be boycotted for the disgraceful comments they have made both about the disaster and in Liverpool since 1989. Of course, the trash has, from time to time, been punctuated and factually corrected by quality journalists such as Brian Reade and James Lawton, but the whole process generally has been one of lies and myths feeding on each other in gratuitous displays of mutually supporting ignorance.

Notwithstanding the immensely important contribution over many years of Liverpool City Council's Hillsborough Working Party, the local authorities of the region and the supporters of Liverpool FC, citizens generally perhaps should ask themselves if their response over the years to this cover-up has been robust enough. The Mersey Partnership these days rightly talks up the positive aspects of the region, but not enough was done to counter the Hillsborough-led stock of negativity which was constantly thrown the way of people in the city after 15 April 1989. More importantly, there is no doubt that this process has weakened the lessons which should have been learned and did increase the probability – as the later Guatemala stadium disaster so tragically showed – that something eerily similar could, and would, happen again.

More positively, Hillsborough, again perhaps only for a short time, shook away the enmity, sometimes bordering on hatred, which can affect relations between fans of rival clubs. Ninety-nine per cent of English football supporters recognized that this was a tragedy which could have happened to them and so their almost universal kindness in the aftermath was accepted with comradely gratitude.

The fact that players from a number of football clubs, including Everton, Tranmere Rovers and Manchester United, attended funerals was similarly appreciated while the salutes from fans further afield and notably the incredibly poignant rendition of 'You'll Never Walk Alone' in Milan, were moving in the extreme. However, in recognizing how so much grief was expressed by, for example, the symbolic tying together of football scarves, it also has to be said that this was a human tragedy which like Heysel (1985), Bradford (1985), Ibrox (1971) and Bolton (1946) transcended all the meaningless rivalries which give football its only meaning.

The ninety-six people who died were mainly, but far from exclusively, from the Greater Liverpool commuter area. Their link in life, as in death, was a passion for Liverpool Football Club, but they were all warm and complex individuals with many more things away from football which they didn't have in common and many differing reasons for living. For all of their love for Liverpool FC and for all of the thoughtless cliches even now still tossed out by dim-witted journalists and footballers, they surely would not have chosen to die for their club. The specific and communal loss across Merseyside should be seen in these human terms and not in football colours. Paying specific tribute to Evertonians is pointless as some Blues will have suffered more personally than many Reds, while some who were most grievously affected will have had no great love for the sport at all.

When the football restarted again in Liverpool, as it did fittingly with a 'derby' match at Goodison Park, it was in a spirit of intense goodwill and fraternity. Of course it was unlikely that that spirit could be maintained forever. Yet, at a time when it is routine in some circles to argue for the degeneration of the relationship between Reds and Blues on Merseyside it is warming to note that on derby day any commemoration of Hillsborough or associated cries for 'Justice' immediately, if briefly, restore the unity of 1989. Hopefully, without the recourse to quoting our beloved Bill Shankly, I hope that future generations of fans on Merseyside will know that, great game that it is, football in the end isn't really *that* important.

Index

Index

Index

and modernisation, 101
and music, 73, 99
and post-industrial problems, 5
and racism, 50, 105, 139
and religion, 19–20, 40–9
as a seaport, 4–6, 22, 102, 155
and unemployment, 5–6, 30
Liverpool Boys, 20
Liverpool & District FA, 15
Liverpool 8, 138–39
Liverpool FC public relations, 153, 158
Liverpool FC turnover, 169
Liverpool FC Youth Academy, 85, 95, 168,
    169, 188, 225–26
Liverpool Ladies FC, 197
the 'Liverpool way', 77–96, 215, 227
    and its decay, 94, 157
Liversedge, S., 84
Liverworld, 122
Lloyd, L., 83
Luton Town, 137–38

McClure, J., 102
McDermott, T., 85
McGovern, J., 115
McInnes, J., 33
McKenna, J., 18–21, 182
McMahon, S., 95, 229
McManaman, S., 138, 163, 166, 168, 222
McQueen, M. 26
Mackin, J., 140
Main Stand fans, 106
management in football, 148–152, 157–59
Manchester City, 2, 93
Manchester United, 2, 6, 7, 20, 28, 80, 87,
    119–120, 151, 154–55, 167, 168, 169, 176,
    181, 187, 222
Marsh, M., 163
Marshall, C., 140
Mason, T., 15, 21, 23
masculinity and English football, 177, 204
masculinity and sport, 196
match fixing, 28
Match of the Day, 202, 218
maximum wage, 22, 30, 34
Media Partners, 221
medical treatment and Liverpool FC, 158
Melwood training ground, 54, 73, 81, 161,
    163–64

Mercer, J., 63
Mersey Partnership, 232
Mersey sound, 101
Merseyside Development Corporation, 8
AC Milan, 233
modernisation and Liverpool, 164
Molby, J., 81, 83
Monopoly and Mergers Commission, 222
Moores, D., 165
Moores, J., 55
Moores family, 153
Moscow Dynamo, 79
Moran, R., 57, 71–2, 82, 87, 161, 166
Munich song, 120
Murdoch, R., 124, 154
music and football, 3

National Women's League, 197
Neal, P., 78, 80–83, 85, 86, 161
Newcastle United, 20, 29, 31, 155
new football, 135, 198, 217–19
News Corporation, 222
Nicholson, B., 73
Nicol, S., 93, 161
Noeux-Les-Mines, 175
northernness, 2, 21, 34
Norwich City, 137
Nottingham Forest, 90

Oakfield Road bank, 24
Office of Fair Trading, 223
O'Hagan, A., 49–50
Old Firm, 50
Olympique Marseilles, 148–49
OnDigital, 225
out-of-town Liverpool fans, 121, 209–210
Orrell, J., 16
Owen, M., 168, 188

Paisley, B., 6, 11, 31, 55, 71
    his death, 95
    and discipline, 85
    and Europe, 88–92
    and football development, 84–5
    and horseracing, 55, 84, 88
    as a moderniser, 84–5
    and players' injuries, 55, 82, 87–8
    and players, 85–6, 141–42
    and retirement, 159

Index

Visual Interventions

Applied Visual Anthropology

Edited by

Sarah Pink

Berghahn Books
New York • Oxford

First published in 2007 by
Berghahn Books
www.berghahnbooks.com

Library of Congress Cataloging-in-Publication Data
Visual interventions : applied visual anthropology / edited by Sarah Pink.
p. cm. – (Studies in public and applied anthropology ; v. 4)
Includes bibliographical references and index.
ISBN 978-1-84545-332-9 (hbk.) -- ISBN 978-1-84545-678-8 (pbk.)
1. Visual anthropology. 2. Toegepaste antropologie. I. Pink, Sarah. II.
Series.

GN347 .V5735 2007
301'.01--ac22

2005055854

British Library Cataloguing in Publication Data
A catalogue record for this book is available from the British Library

Printed in the United States on acid-free paper

ISBN 978-1-84545-332-9 (hardback)
ISBN 978-1-84545-678-8 (paperback)

CONTENTS

————— ∞∞∞ —————

LIST OF ILLUSTRATIONS

LIST OF TABLES

ACKNOWLEDGEMENTS

This book has developed over several years during which time the support and interest of a range of different people has helped in its progress. I would like to thank Peter Biella and Najwa Adra for their support and encouragement during the development of the guest edited issue of *Visual Anthropology Review* (volume 20(1)) in which previous versions of my introduction and the chapters by Chalfen and Rich, Flores, Stadhams, Jhala, and Lovejoy and Steele were published. Susan Levine's chapter was previously published in the preceding issue of *Visual Anthropology Review* (volume 19(1–2)) edited by Peter Biella. Werner Sperschneider's chapter is a revised and much expanded version of an article by Sperschneider and Kirsten Bagger, originally published in 2003 as 'Ethnographic Fieldwork Under Industrial Constraints: Towards Design-in-Context' in the *International Journal of Human-Computer Interaction* (volume 15(1)). Some chapters of this book (by Lammer, van Dienderen and Yiakoumaki) originated from a conference panel on applied visual anthropology that I convened at the EASA conference in Vienna in 2004. Many thanks to those other participants in our panel whose feedback and comments have helped shape the volume. Finally I am very grateful to Marion Berghahn, Anna Wright and Mark Stanton at Berghahn publishers, our anonymous reader and Megan Biesele and Robert Hitchcock for their comments and support with this project.

PART I

INTRODUCTION

Chapter 1

APPLIED VISUAL ANTHROPOLOGY
Social Intervention and Visual Methodologies[1]

Sarah Pink

Visual Interventions examines the practices and value of an applied visual anthropology. It presents a series of detailed case studies, the authors of each recognize the potential of visual anthropology theoretically, methodologically and ethnographically to participate in projects of social intervention. Together they create a powerful argument for an applied visual anthropology. They bring into the public domain examples from across Europe, the United States, Africa and Asia that demonstrate how anthropologically informed visual practices – which variously involve developing visual representations informed by anthropological theory, the analysis of visual aspects of culture, and the use of visual ethnographic research methods – have been used to create social interventions. Their methods and working practices offer a series of templates or models that, they suggest, could be transferable to other contexts. Nevertheless these case studies are not simply presented as a set of practical exercises. Their authors are also academics with present or past posts in or other links to universities. Their applied work is also relevant to academic anthropology: sometimes an academic brief forms part of an applied project; in other cases the academic strand of a project arises as an ethnographic contribution, theoretical implication or methodological innovation. As such *Visual Interventions* and its contributors seek to bridge the gap between applied and academic visual anthropology: first through their own practice, and second by advancing the book's broader argument that applied visual anthropology can contribute to both applied and visual anthropologies and to social anthropology as a whole.[2] *Visual Interventions* brings applied visual anthropology into a public arena by presenting a series of case studies and templates and inviting debate about its role in today's world and its potential contribution to mainstream academic anthropology.

In recent publications I have begun to draw together historical applications of visual anthropology with newer developments in applied visual anthropology practice (Pink 2004b, 2006). In 2004 I guest edited an issue of *Visual Anthropology Review* (Pink 2004b), of which this book is a much expanded version. In Chapter 5 of my book *The Future of Visual Anthropology* (Pink 2006), I discuss applied visual anthropology in the context of a proposal for a visual anthropology for the twenty-first century which develops new engagements both within and outside academia. There I outline a proposal for an applied visual anthropology that urges visual anthropologists to engage the potential of audio visual media for social intervention that has already been demonstrated in accounts of activist and applied uses of video in other disciplines. My approach to the creation of *Visual Interventions* has been different. In part this has been to avoid repeating the discussions I developed in *The Future of Visual Anthropology*. Although some similar ground is inevitably covered here in order to frame and define applied visual anthropology and its methodologies, my focus in each text is different. In *The Future of Visual Anthropology* I suggest that an applied strand of visual anthropology should form part of the future of the subdiscipline as it develops in the twenty-first century. Interlinking with the other strands the book advocates, I situate applied visual anthropology in relation to: interdisciplinary uses of the visual in social intervention and anthropological approaches to indigenous media; the sensory approach that is increasingly popular across mainstream and visual anthropologies; contemporary uses of hypermedia in representation; and the idea of a public anthropology. Here in *Visual Interventions* I follow up that initial statement about applied visual anthropology with a different approach. Here my intention is to take advantage of some of the possibilities for multi-authorship offered by an edited volume. Thus, in this introduction, while also broaching questions of the definition of applied visual anthropology, I focus on the contextualizing, methodological and ethical issues that arise from the wider range of case studies presented here. My interest in applied visual anthropology has become a research project in itself, which has involved seeking the first-hand accounts of the experiences of applied visual anthropologists. In *The Future of Visual Anthropology* I write about and analyse a limited selection of these accounts (some of which are represented by their own authors here). In this edited volume, in contrast, I treat the constitution of applied visual anthropology as a multi-authored project that foregrounds the written and visual representations of the anthropologists who actually experienced the historical developments and recent projects discussed.

Visual Interventions concurrently proposes a contribution and a challenge to visual anthropology as it developed in the twentieth-century. Early advocates of an applied visual anthropology have criticized the subdiscipline's emphasis on ethnographic film-making. Initially this was through their visual practice as it developed since the mid twentieth-century, and more recently in their written discussions of this context (e.g. J. Collier and Latsch 1983, Chalfen and Rich this volume, M. Collier, this volume, and see Pink 2006: 86–7). Recent literature has taken a similar stance (e.g., Banks and Morphy 1997, Pink 2007, Pink et al. 2004) by insisting visual anthropology return to its earlier brief to include the study of visual aspects of culture and visual ethnographic methods as well as visual representation. *Visual Interventions* continues this critique. In Chapter 3 Richard Chalfen and Michael Rich position their own practice within 'a reinvigorated visual anthropology' that is 'considerably advanced beyond the myopic attention to and production of ethnographic film' (Chalfen and Rich, this volume). Several other of the contributors here are not concerned so much with making films, but with using visual anthropology methodologies to understand other people's experiences. Although they are in fact both accomplished ethnographic film-makers, here Jayasinhji Jhala and Werner Sperschneider both describe uses of video for the production of knowledge in projects that do not have ethnographic documentary making as their ultimate aim. In Chapter 8 Jhala outlines his use of video to collaboratively document earthquake damage, while in Chapter 13 Sperschneider shows how anthropologically informed uses of video in design research can engender collaborative approaches to the production of knowledge and analysis. Other contributors situate their work as a critical response to existing ethnographic film representations of the people they have worked with. For instance in Chapter 9 Matthew Durington discusses the romanticized image of hunter-gatherers living in harmony with and from the natural resources of the Kalahari desert, as represented in classic ethnographic film. Arguing that such films perpetuate an inappropriate stereotype, Durington discusses how his participatory video work with San has attempted to represent their contemporary concerns. As a whole the case studies presented here demonstrate how contemporary applied visual anthropology practice departs from the dominant twentieth-century practice of making 'important films' (Ruby 2000). Indeed other examples of 'film-making' discussed in this volume are of edited videos or simply sets of footage, produced in the contexts of local community and development projects (Martínez Pérez, van. Dienderen, Flores), evaluated to understand local impacts in an HIV/AIDS awareness project (Levine), and to 'educate' clinicians (Lammer; Chalfen and Rich), tourist stakeholders (Stadhams) and product designers (Sperschneider). Often the film product itself is not the most important outcome of such projects. Rather, the collaborative and reflexive processes that interweave to produce the film create social interventions in their own right by generating new levels of self-awareness and identity amongst research participants (see especially Chalfen and Rich; Martínez Pérez; van. Dienderen; Flores). Some contributors also depart from ethnographic documentary making to engage with new media, using digital multimedia to combine video, photography and written texts online and in CD-ROM in contexts related to health (Chalfen and Rich), tourism policy and heritage (Yiakoumaki), community work (Martínez Pérez) and commercial consumer ethnography (Lovejoy and Steele).

Visual Interventions is equally a contribution to applied anthropology. Although existing literature in applied anthropology makes scant mention of visual anthropological methods (e.g. MacDonald 2002; Ervin 2000; van Willigen 2002; Nolan 2003; Gwynne 2003),[3] there is increasing evidence of visual methodologies in applied anthropological work. Each case study presented in this volume is an example of how the visual has successfully participated in an applied anthropology project, to provide routes to and representations of other people's knowledge and experience that would be inaccessible through conventional applied anthropology methods. Because the contributors are explicit about their methodological approaches, the methods used, and the relationship of their work to applied, visual and substantive areas of anthropology the case studies provide accessible examples of how a visual dimension of a project might be developed in practice.

Defining Applied Visual Anthropology

The term 'applied visual anthropology' is beginning to gain prominence in academic publishing. For example, in 2003 an issue of *Visual Anthropology Review* edited by Peter Biella[4] focused on the *STEPS to the Future*, a Southern Africa AIDS education film package[5] (see Levine, this volume), followed by my own 2004 issue of *Visual Anthropology Review* on applied visual anthropology. The term does not refer to a circumscribed and predetermined field of practice. Rather its definition is an ongoing process, in which this book and the projects it reports on are participants. It is also inevitably bound up with both visual and applied subdisciplines and any definition must account for contemporary developments in practice and theory in visual anthropology and the global and local contexts applied anthropology is practiced in. Therefore in this section, to map out the characteristics of applied visual anthropology, I refer to existing practices and their relationships to the relevant subdisciplines.

I have previously suggested a broad definition of applied visual anthropology as 'involving using visual anthropological theory, methodology and practice to achieve applied non-academic ends' and, following Chalfen and Rich (this volume), usually entailing problem solving and engaging in 'cultural brokerage' (Pink 2006). This involves first, representing one group's experiences to another and second, working across academic disciplines and organizational cultures. However, within this exists a wide range of actual visual, research and representation practices, interdisciplinary collaborations, project briefs and substantive research areas. The above definition also does not preclude the potential of a project that has applied ends to simultaneously have theoretical, methodological and substantive ambitions within mainstream academic anthropology. The way these relationships might be articulated are exemplified particularly well by the work of some of the contributors to this book. In Chapter 5, for example, Christina Lammer interweaves different levels of visual and written description and analysis, revealing how her theoretical, experiential, ethnographic and applied engagements feed each other. In Chapter 10 Carlos Flores discusses an applied film project that was inextricable from his academic project to assess 'the uses, possibilities and impacts of audiovisual media among indigenous groups in the country from an anthropological perspective'.

In this section I first examine the various historical and contemporary relationships between applied and academic visual anthropologies and the nature of social intervention in applied visual anthropology. Then to conclude the section I return to the question of definition, to reflect on the status of applied visual anthropology as a field of practice in its own right.

Applied Visual Anthropology and Ethnographic Documentary: Historical Interconnections

Since the late nineteenth century, anthropologists have used visual methods to analyse and represent other cultures for nonacademic ends. The interventions such work supported were initially embedded in the power relations of imperialism. For instance, earlier uses involved using photography as part of the objectifying gaze of the colonial project (see Edwards 1992) and in the 1930s film analysis contributed to 'the study of culture at a distance' projects (see Mead and Métraux (2000[1953]), aiming to understand wartime enemies of the United States (e.g., Bateson 1980). However by the mid twentieth-century the visual was being used, in the United States, to create new forms of social intervention: in the 1950s John Collier Jr. began to develop applied photographic and filmic methods of ethnographic research with Native Americans (J. Collier 1967, 1973; Pink 2006; and M. Collier, this volume[6]); and in the 1960s Richard Chalfen began a long-term collaboration with health professionals using visual anthropology methods and media (Chalfen and Rich, this volume). The Centre for Visual Culture Studies (http://uit.no/vcs/) at the University of Tromsø, Norway, also has a long history of applied visual anthropology research. In common with the projects discussed in this book the work of the centre includes using visual methods and media in 'shared' and participatory methods of knowledge production, and training students in these methods. These projects are both academic and applied, producing both social interventions and academic publications. Examples of this work include Lisbet Holtedahl's past and current visual research and film-making projects in West Africa and northern Norway and a current project developed by Trond Waage with Siren Hope and Reni Wright involving working with 'at risk' Norwegian teenagers. However, until very recently, these and other applied innovations in visual anthropology have largely gone unreported in historical reviews of both visual and applied subdisciplines (e.g. Loizos 1993; Banks and Morphy 1997; Grimshaw 2001; van Willigen 2002).[7]

In *The Future of Visual Anthropology* I discuss in more detail the historical context in which applied visual anthropology has developed through an examination of the twentieth-century applications developed by Margaret Mead, Richard Chalfen and John Collier Jr. with their respective colleagues that I noted above (see Pink 2006: 82–7). In *Visual Interventions* this historical context is brought to the fore through the words and images of anthropologists with first-hand experience of it. First, I invited Malcolm Collier to contribute to the volume by way of a photo-essay that represents the applied visual anthropology of John Collier Jr. (his father and often also research collaborator). John Collier is best known for his text *Visual Anthropology: Photography as a Research Method* (J. Collier 1967; J. and M. Collier 1986). Much of his own work discussed there was developed in applied studies. Thus often the methodologies presented, in what was for some thirty years the most influential text in visual methods in anthropology, were developed through visual anthropology projects that combined theoretical approaches with problem solving and social interventions components. The second contribution to *Visual Interventions* to address the historical context is Richard Chalfen and Michael Rich's chapter about their collaborative applications of visual anthropology in medical research contexts. As Chalfen and Rich outline, this work was not developed independently from the questions and methodologies current in academic visual anthropology. Chalfen's approach was rooted in questions raised in visual anthropology concerning how people see their own worlds, often using 'hand over the camera' methods which Chalfen adapted from Sol Worth's bio-documentary methodology.

As these two chapters reveal, applied and academic visual methodologies developed in relation to each other during the second half of the twentieth-century. In the cases of Collier and Chalfen, both of whom have been critical of the dominance of ethnographic documentary film-making in visual anthropology, the methodologies they were developing demonstrated alternative visual anthropology practices. This however is not to say that ethnographic documentary and applied visual anthropology practices are incompatible or opposed to each other. Another strand to the historical context of a contemporary applied visual anthropology can be discerned by tracing its methodological roots back to the work of those twentieth-century ethnographic film-makers who themselves developed innovative collaborative and participatory practices. Of particular interest here is the work of Jean Rouch and of David and Judith MacDougall, whose ethnographic film practice pushed at the boundaries of visual anthropology by developing collaborations with film subjects, often with a political edge that was critical of the power relations in which their film subjects were implicated.[8]

Jean Rouch's notion of a 'shared anthropology' was directly related to the role that film can play in the collaborative production of ethnographic knowledge. For Rouch, the 'first audience' for his films was the film subjects themselves (2003[1973]: 43). Steven Feld suggests this permitted a form of 'feedback' which 'enhances participation and allows the ethnographer-filmmaker to mediate openly and self-critically on his or her role' (2003: 18–19). Rouch saw this form of 'feedback' as fundamental to a 'shared anthropology' (2003[1973]: 44), creating as Paul Stoller has suggested films in which 'no one voice dominates' (1992: 195). However Rouch clearly saw film as having a role to play not only in the representation of people to themselves, but also as a form of 'public anthropology'. His 'second audience' for films produced through a 'shared anthropology' was a wide general public. He argued that there is no better tool than ethnographic film' for creating 'the regard for cultural differences' that he saw as essential to 'the world of tomorrow' (2000[1973]: 45). Also in the 1970s David MacDougall wrote about the idea of 'participatory cinema' as 'one of collaboration and joint authorship between film-makers and their subjects' (1998[1973]: 136) and later redefined this as '*intertextual* cinema' (original italics) which would have 'a principle of multiple authorship' (1998 [1992]: 138). He initially suggested the possibility of 'filmmakers putting themselves at the disposal of the subjects and, with them, inventing the film' (1998 [1973]: 136) and revised this to propose that the idea of multiple authorship might allow ethnographic film to 'address conflicting views of reality in a world in which observers and observed are less clearly separated and in which reciprocal observation and exchange increasingly matter' (1998 [1992]: 138). The ideas of Rouch and MacDougall have been extremely influential in subsequent ethnographic film-making practice, and this influence is also apparent in the applied visual anthropology methodologies outlined by the contributors to this volume. For instance in Chapter 8 Jhala also notes how MacDougall's film-making method informed his applied visual anthropology practice. In their 1979 film *Lorang's Way* David and Judith MacDougall used a single shot method whereby Lorang walks and talks the filmmaker through the material and social context in which he lives. Jhala adapted this method to enable earthquake victims in India to show him the damage to their homes. Although MacDougall's long term film-making relationship with Lorang (MacDougall 1998: 157) differed from the necessarily shorter periods Jhala spent with each of his video subjects, his work also demonstrates the relevance of collaborative ethnographic documentary making practices when adapted to applied visual anthropology. In Chapter 10 Carlos Flores discusses how he developed a version of Rouch's 'shared anthropology' though a collaborative documentary making project with his Q'eqchi' informants in post-war Guatemala. Through this case study Flores explores the potentials, limitations and complexities of the reality of actually producing a shared anthropology which both supports the creation of self-identities and mutually empowers both anthropologist and subject.

Although not all of the contributors attribute their own practices directly to the influence of Rouch or MacDougall, participatory and collaborative methods provide a guiding principle throughout the chapters of this volume. For example in Chapter 6 Dianne Stadhams discusses how she used participatory methods when working with diverse stakeholders in the Gambian tourism industry to research and produce a programme for Gambian television that represented multiple perspectives on and experiences of tourism. In Chapter 9 Matthew Durington draws from MacDougall's points about a 'participatory cinema' to discuss his own participatory strategy in producing a series of video documentaries aiming to represent the issues faced by San Bushmen. In Chapter 11 Ana Martínez Pérez also discusses a collaborative video-making process in which visual anthropologists, psychologists, social workers and 'excluded' people in southern Spain worked together. Taken together these chapters provide examples of how participatory approaches might be developed in quite different contexts. They also advance Rouch's proposal that ethnographic film has a role to play in the world. Stadhams's work aimed to produce a programme to be shown on Gambian national television as well as to key foreign agencies and other stakeholders in the tourism process. Durington discusses the possible role of the video projects he developed with San people as texts that might represent local voices in wider contexts. Ana Martínez Pérez rather differently outlines a context where the local agencies represented by the social workers and local government were themselves collaborators in the project. However, as she states, the film they produced was not only a product of identity construction for its participants, but also aimed to reach the general public and to communicate a message about social exclusion, in part by encouraging its audience to empathize with the subject positions of those represented in the film. As these case studies demonstrate, the 'shared', participatory and multi-authored approaches to ethnographic documentary that Rouch and MacDougall advocated often play a key role in the production of social interventions.

Applied and Academic Visual Anthropologies

Contemporary visual anthropology includes, but is more than, ethnographic film or video making. Following the anthropology of visual communications approach developed by Sol Worth and Jay Ruby in the 1970s it also involves the anthropology of the visual and the use of visual research methods. Thus engaging in 'the anthropology of visual systems, or more broadly visual cultural forms' (Morphy and Banks 1997: 5) and visual methods of anthropological research and representation, encompassing art, drawing, photography, video, new digital and visual media and multimedia technologies including hypermedia (Pink 2001; Pink et al. 2004). Visual anthropology has often been seen as a challenge to mainstream social and cultural anthropology (MacDougall 1997; Grimshaw 2001), and was in large part rejected by it as a serious academic endeavour during the twentieth-century. More recently, along with the decreasing emphasis on ethnographic film in visual anthropology, mainstream anthropologists have increasingly begun to use visual methods and media in their research (if not to represent their work). New media and digital technologies have in some ways drawn the practices of visual and mainstream anthropologists closer together (see Pink et al. 2004). Visual anthropology is a subdiscipline that is both committed to its established forms and practices and to engaging at its 'boundaries' (Edwards 1997). The former include continued developments in ethnographic film-making (e.g. MacDougall 1998; Henley 2005), visual methodology (Banks 2001; Pink 2007[2001]; Pink et al. 2004) and visual and material culture (e.g., Edwards 2001). The latter explores, for instance, visual anthropology and arts practice (e.g., Grimshaw and Ravetz 2005; Schneider and Wright 2006) and examinations of vision itself (Grasseni 2007). Applied visual anthropology can be seen as another of these 'frontier' (Bowman et al 2007) engagements.[9] It connects not only applied and visual anthropologies but also the substantive areas and other disciplines implicated in each project, creating multiple interlinkages and possibilities for visual anthropological approaches to contribute to wider interdisciplinary work. Particularly good examples of this can be seen in the contributions by Chalfen and Rich, Martínez Pérez, and Sperschneider. In Chapter 3 we see how Chalfen's collaborations with clinicians have produced knowledge that is not only used to inform practical interventions. Rather it has become part of the knowledge that is employed in the training of students at Harvard Medical School. In Chapter 11 Ana Martínez Pérez describes an interdisciplinary collaborative programme of work that incorporated anthropological and social work approaches and perspectives. Here, working together, the visual anthropologists and social workers synthesized their approaches, methodologies and understandings of both key concepts and everyday realities. To sum up, applied visual anthropology concerns combining visual anthropology with and adapting it in relation to the demands of other approaches and practices. In common with other recent innovations in visual anthropology it extends outside conventional visual anthropology practice and outside academia to collaborate with other disciplines within particular substantive areas. Its distinguishing feature is that its interdisciplinary collaborations have a particular type of outcome in mind – they aim to produce social interventions.

What is Social Intervention in Applied Visual Anthropology?

Applied visual anthropology is practiced across private, public and NGO sectors, as well as in serendipitous situations, in contexts that are shaped by global, national, transnational, institutional, local and individual agencies.[10] To accommodate these diverse contexts involves a broad understanding of social intervention. This might range from using visual practice to empower research participants with new levels of self-awareness, promote a specific cause to a target audience, or provide decisionmakers in business or policy contexts with 'evidence' that will inform their work.

As social intervention, applied visual anthropology usually takes the form of a problem-solving practice that involves collaborating with research participants and aims to bring about some form of change. This characteristic sets it apart from academic visual anthropology, which is also usually collaborative, but is more often exploratory rather than problem-solving and does not seek to intervene in or change in any way the lives of the research participants (although this might indeed be an indirect result of academic research). Moreover applied visual anthropology usually involves a distinctive form of what we might tentatively refer to as 'cultural brokerage'.

Since both 'culture' and 'cultural' have themselves become contested terms in social and cultural anthropology it is worth briefly outlining what is meant by the concept here. An applied visual anthropology use of culture certainly departs from the notion of 'whole cultures'. Indeed Chalfen and Rich (this volume) use it to refer to subcultures, as a way of defining and analysing difference, between, for example, 'health cultures'. As Arjun Appadurai has suggested it is often most useful to see culture as 'a heuristic device that we can use to talk about difference' (1996: 13). In the context of applied visual anthropology practice the representation of one 'culture' to another usually means representing the experiences and values of a determined sector of society or group of people to a specified audience (which might be or include those people themselves) or client. It involves creating a platform upon which the specificities of others' experiences can become both obvious and at the same time comprehensible to people who will inevitably use their own difference (also specificity) to make sense of them. The process of bringing identities, practices, moralities, and experiences to the fore is not only concerned with the 'brokerage' of representing, for example, the problems of the disempowered to those who might support them or the 'needs' of consumers to business. It can also involve creative and consciousness generating process whereby individuals and groups express (and as such re-constitute) their identities to themselves (see for example Flores; van. Dienderen; Martínez Pérez, this volume).

The idea of brokerage is also a characteristic of much applied anthropology practice, as noted by Chalfen and Rich (this volume). There is nevertheless a notable contrast between the case studies of the work of the international set of applied visual anthropologists collected in this volume and those of the applied anthropologists working in Britain represented in the *Applications of Anthropology* edited volume (Pink 2005b) that sought to explore the range and nature of contemporary applied anthropology in Britain. Whereas the work of some of the applied anthropologists represented there led them into the roles of strategist, project assessor or expert witness, applied visual anthropology practice, as represented by the contributors to this volume, is not identified with such shifts or roles (see in particular Martínez Pérez, this volume), but remains located in the collaborative practice of visual production and communication.

Defining Applied Visual Anthropology

Above I suggested that the term applied visual anthropology should not refer to a circumscribed and predetermined field of practice, but its definition is ongoing and contingent. Moreover as the discussion above has suggested there are many existing and potential continuities between applied and academic visual anthropology. In that most applied visual anthropology projects would have the potential to contribute to processes of social intervention, to substantive knowledge about a particular area of anthropological concern and methodological developments, as well as to academic theory building, there is also a sense in which as a defining statement the term implies an inaccurate distinction between the academic and the applied. In contrasting the aims and outcomes of processes of applied visual intervention and those of academia I have stressed two points. First that some visual anthropologists who have developed applied interventions do indeed regard their work as a challenge to the status of ethnographic documentary making as the dominant form in visual anthropology. Second that the objectives, institutional contexts and specific audiences of applied and academic work engender different demands and work practices. Despite these points of difference I do not believe applied and academic visual anthropologies should be seen as separate fields of practice. I am certainly not suggesting that applied visual anthropology should be another sub-subdiscipline. As the discussion above and the contributions to this volume demonstrate, historical and contemporary applied visual anthropology projects have engaged in all three of the areas of visual anthropology practice: the analysis of visual aspects of culture; the use of visual methodologies; and the production of visual representations. The first is illustrated best here in the chapters by Levine and Jhala, although an understanding of the visual culture of the people one is working with is important in any visual anthropological research. The second two areas are clearly demonstrated in various ways by all of the contributors to this volume. Moreover as I have emphasized earlier the interchanges of methodologies developed in applied and academic visual anthropology projects have both historically and in contemporary practice allowed each to contribute to the methodological development of the other. In addition to this, the development of an applied visual anthropology might be seen as part of a more general contemporary broadening of visual anthropology into a field that is, as I noted above, producing a range of new engagements at its boundaries.

Widening the context to consider briefly the relationship between applied and academic anthropologies, as I describe elsewhere (Pink 2005a: 6–7), it is interesting to note that the historical circumstances of their development in Britain, the United States, France and Canada (Baba and Hill 1997: 10–11) led to their separation. In Britain, for instance, this was largely inspired by a rejection of the applied by an academic project that sought to establish anthropology as a theoretical rather than problem solving discipline (see Mills 2005; Wright 2005). However, as Baba and Hill (1997: 10–11) have pointed out, this contrasts enormously with Central America, Mexico and Israel where applied anthropology is central to the production of the discipline. As such this more general separation between the academic and the applied is a special characteristic of the national contexts in which visual anthropology has emerged as an academic discipline. Elsewhere I have argued that there is much to gain by bridging this gap between applied and academic anthropology (Pink 2005a). *Visual Interventions* makes the same proposal regarding visual anthropology. As the contributors to this volume demonstrate, visual anthropology research can simultaneously integrate and develop academic and applied agendas: it can be productive of both social interventions and academic contributions. Why then, one might ask, call it applied visual anthropology at all? I propose that the term is still useful because it brings to the fore the potential for a visual anthropology that participates in the production of social interventions and is undertaken in relation to and engages with a range of institutional contexts outside academia.

Methods of Research and Representation

Above I have noted how there are identifiable continuities between the methods used in academic visual anthropology and visual anthropology projects that are designed with applied ends. There are also some fundamental factors which commonly influence methods and practices of visual research and representation in applied visual anthropology. For example, these include: project timescales and deadlines, budgets, the sorts of knowledge that are sought, the interdisciplinary collaborations within which methods are developed, the institutional frames within which knowledge needs to be represented and the target audiences to which it will be represented, issues of data ownership, and the ethical codes of the various groups and disciplines involved in the collaboration. There are many different ways that 'types of' applied visual anthropology project could be categorized according to specific methods. My intention here is however to outline some of the broader commonalities that tend to characterize the methods used in applied visual anthropology.

Methods in applied visual anthropology – and more generally in applied anthropology – can meaningfully be divided into those developed to serve projects that permit long-term fieldwork (e.g., Flores; Yiakoumaki; Lammer; van. Dienderen, this volume) and those produced within shorter-term, and sometimes commissioned, projects (e.g., Pink 2004c, 2006; Lovejoy and Steele; Chalfen and Rich; Martínez Pérez; Sperschneider; Jhala this volume). In many instances of short-term fieldwork, the research is based on previous longer-term involvement with the research subjects or theme by either the anthropologist her or himself or others with whom she or he works (e.g., Durington; Martínez Pérez; Sperschneider; Lovejoy and

Steele; Jhala, this volume; Pink 2004a, 2004c). Methods used in applied anthropology already challenge the tendency to define social anthropology in terms of its long-term fieldwork method. Applied anthropology textbooks describe applied methods including not only participant observation and key informant interviewing but surveys, questionnaires, participatory action research, rapid ethnographic assessment, needs assessment, social impact assessment, focus group research, and social network analysis (see for example, Ervin 2000; Gwynne 2003: 36–42). Applied research in which anthropologists are involved is often by shaped not by anthropological agendas alone but though the contexts created by anthropologists' collaborations with informants, clients, co-researchers from other disciplines and other interested parties. Under these circumstances also applied and academic anthropology research methods are likely to sometimes appear quite different. Elsewhere I outline how this requires that we reject the definition of anthropology by its method in favour of seeing applied anthropology as a theoretically informed way of understanding social realities and of formulating and approaching questions, issues and problems (Pink 2005a: 9–10). Here I make a parallel argument. Likewise to take applied visual anthropology seriously we need to depart from definitions that necessarily associate visual anthropological research with long-term participant observation. For example, Paul Henley describes how both observational cinema (the dominant ethnographic film genre) and participant observation share a 'belief that understanding should be achieved through a gradual process of discovery, that is through engagement within the everyday lives of the subjects rather than by placing them within predetermined matrices, whether a script in the case of the filmmakers or a questionnaire in the case of anthropologists' (Henley 2000: 218). In applied visual anthropology such an exploratory approach to discovering and representing other people's lives is not always viable simply due to timescales. However what is striking about the projects discussed by the contributors to this book is that they reveal how in fact practices of scripting can become collaborative knowledge-producing techniques in themselves. For example in Chapter 11 Ana Martínez Pérez describes a project in which the production of a script was a key part of the collaborative process between the film-makers and film subjects. In Chapter 12 An van. Dienderen highlights very well the difference between a script that has been preconceived by a television production company and one that is co-written collaboratively with the film subjects as part of a community film project. The participatory scripting practices outlined here are of course very different from those that Henley disassociates from observational cinema. However they also perhaps indicate a distinction between an applied visual anthropology and observational cinema methods, whereby the former depends more on the research subjects to provide explanations of their lives and experiences, the latter waits for these to unfold on camera over time. A related issue is that since briefs and timescales are sometimes more clearly defined and usually shorter in applied visual anthropology the time required for such long term visual exploration is often simply not available and researchers need to find other methods through which they might produce knowledge about how people experience their realities. Nevertheless the possibility of using visual methods to achieve this is perhaps not so distant from some practices associated with ethnographic film-making as it would first appear. For instance, the idea that using collaborative and participatory methods in filmic research might produce valuable ethnographic knowledge in a shorter time frame was suggested by Jean Rouch in 1973. Rouch wrote of his use of the 'feedback' process I have noted above: 'By studying this film [*Horendi*, about possession dances in Niger] on a small moviescope viewer with my informants, I was able to gather more information in two weeks than I could get in three months of direct observation and interview' (Rouch 2000[1973]: 44). As shown particularly well by Sperschneider in Chapter 13, and Tracey Lovejoy and Nelle Steele in Chapter 14, interviews, photography and video can facilitate these processes of generating coproduced knowledge in significant ways. The idea of an applied visual anthropology invites us to depart from the insistence on long-term immersion (with or without a camera) as the defining method of social and visual anthropology, to consider how shorter-term collaborative and participatory methods of visual research and representation might also produce knowledge of anthropological value.

A second key theme that emerges from viewing the chapters of this volume as a whole is the point that an applied visual anthropology does not entail simply adding an applied component to existing models of film-making or visual analysis, or adding some visual anthropology methods onto existing ones developed in applied anthropology. Rather, applied visual anthropology methods evolve within projects, out of collaborations with colleagues from other disciplines and with research participants. For example in Chapter 3 Chalfen and Rich describe a method they have developed called 'Video Intervention/Prevention Assessment' which sits 'at the nexus of four subdisciplines of contemporary anthropology, namely visual anthropology, applied anthropology, media anthropology, and medical anthropology' (Chalfen and Rich, this volume). Likewise in Chapter 11 Ana Martínez Pérez describes how participants from different disciplines were able to 'synthesize our approaches into a method which both allowed the social workers to verbalize their work ethic of "being without intruding" and was reminiscent of the old ethnographic philosophy (which is still viable today) of "being there as witnesses of the other's gaze"' (Martínez Pérez, this volume).

The results of applied work need to be represented in easily digested forms that will engage otherwise busy professionals and decision-makers. The use of visual methods and media in research provides a wealth of audiovisual materials that, as the contributors to this volume show, can be used in innovative ways. Possibilities include using methods traditional to visual anthropology, such as producing documentary video (Lammer;

Martínez Pérez; Flores; Durington, this volume), TV programmes (Stadhams, this volume) and photographic exhibitions and essays. These might well be combined with conventional applied anthropology formats such as written reports. As for academic visual anthropology representation, in applied contexts the use of video, photography and written words is also being increasingly combined in multimedia hypermedia formats (Chalfen and Rich; Yiakoumaki; Lovejoy and Steele, this volume; Pink 2004c). Through their discussions of their research processes, the contributors to this volume show how the visual representations that are the outcomes of their work are anthropologically informed. However, in these audiovisual texts, as in ethnographic film (MacDougall 1998; Henley 2000), theory and abstraction is subdued in favour of bringing to the fore (sometimes a multiplicity of) individual experiences and narratives. These might, for instance, aim to help a group of project participants arrive at new understandings of their own self-identities (Chalfen and Rich; Flores; van. Dienderen; Martínez Pérez, this volume), generate empathetic understandings of other people's experiences amongst the audience (Lammer; Martínez Pérez; Lovejoy and Steele; Durington, this volume), offer personal narratives that viewers can identify with (Levine) or demonstrate diversity (Stadhams, this volume; and see Pink 2004c) – often in ways that are set to challenge the viewer's existing understandings.

Together the chapters in this volume as well as other existing work (e.g., Biella 2003; Pink 2006) suggest applied visual anthropology is successful in projects that seek to represent how people experience certain dimensions of their everyday worlds and to create platforms on which people can represent their experiences, views or culture. It facilitates aspects of self-representation and anthropological representation that are embodied and that can be expressed audiovisually. It encourages uses of metaphor and the empathetic communication of knowledge and experience that cannot be expressed using only words (see MacDougall 1997). This, combined with the technological possibilities of using visual and digital media, and the interdisciplinary and collaborative nature of applied work, invites particular working practices. The most striking and continuous theme that runs through the case studies presented in *Visual Interventions* is the emphasis the contributors put on the collaborative dimension of the processes of research, visual production and representation in their work. Indeed the greatest differences seem to be not so much in the methods and media of research and representation used across different sectors. Rather they are in the timescales, budgets and institutional structures that frame these projects, and in the nature of the interventions they seek to make. The contributors to this book offer templates for methods of research and representation for visual interventions based on their own experiences and collaborations. This signifies the beginning of a resource of methods for applied visual anthropology which may be appropriated and re-worked in future projects through different interdisciplinary collaborations.

Ethics in Applied Visual Anthropology

Visual methods, as advocated by most visual anthropologists, are by nature collaborative. As is clear from the case studies presented in this book, such collaboration with research participants is fundamental to applied visual anthropology practice – be it in contexts of product development in industry or disaster and crisis work. Indeed when visual methods are not based on collaboration and involve covert recording they would be considered unethical by most anthropologists (Pink 2001; Banks 2001).

Applied visual anthropology raises ethical issues unaccounted for in existing ethical codes for applied or visual anthropology. Ethical codes for practicing anthropologists published in the United States on the websites of the Society for Applied Anthropology (SfAA) and the National Association for the Practice of Anthropology (NAPA) emphasize the responsibility of practicing anthropologists to the people researched and their communities, their colleagues, sponsors and employers, to students, and to society at large.[11] In practice ethical decisions are actually made by individual researchers in the field; they reference specific ethical codes of conduct but are also always contingent on local circumstances. Indeed to be an anthropologist to some degree requires being an anthropologist of ethics (see Pink 2001: 30–46). In the context of applied research this is definitely the case. One needs to assess not only the ethics of one's own research and one's informants, but the ethical codes of one's collaborators, clients and other interested parties, as these could vary from those guiding the anthropological element of the research. This constitutes an informal anthropological analysis of the plural moralities of the applied research context. Additionally visual anthropological research and representation raises ethical issues that do not figure in written anthropology. Elsewhere I argue that an ethical approach to using images in research necessitates understanding local visual cultures and how visual meanings and notions of visual truth will be inferred by those people implicated in the research as well as its audiences (Pink 2001: 30–46). The same applies to applied visual anthropology. Indeed since in applied work the number of stakeholders in the research usually increases, knowledge of how images will be interpreted and used must crucially inform and be informed by decisions about access to and use of the research materials. Questions of ownership of research materials can become complex but should be negotiated and agreed before they are produced.

Three examples bring the key issues to the fore. First, in my own work with Unilever Research (Pink 2004a, 2006), the research materials were actually to be owned by Unilever, to whom I would have to apply for approval to publish work based on them. My informants agreed to participate in the project on the basis of confidentiality. The work was to be used in the business by the research team. After this, in order to use the data for academic publication, I went through two further layers of consent and approval. I sought written consent from those informants whose materials I wanted to use and I asked Unilever to approve my work prior to publication. Second, Chalfen and Rich (this volume) also describe a project in which their informants were similarly initially offered confidentiality but were later given the option of agreeing to their data being disseminated beyond the research team. When informants are unavoidably identifiable on video or in photographs such strategies allow their decisions to be informed by different knowledge at different stages of the research. They can thus give their consent to participate and for their images to be disseminated accordingly. Third, making documentaries for a public audience raises a new set of ethical issues that Garry Marvin addresses in a discussion of the making of a film about his research on fox-hunting in Britain (Marvin 2005). Because TV production companies might work with different codes and procedures regarding consent from those that guide anthropologists, the anthropologist needs to work between these codes, acting not only as a cultural broker to facilitate the representation of one culture to another on film, but also to advise the film subjects through his or her knowledge of the ethics and practices of the film-making culture. Marvin demonstrates how in this situation an anthropologist might become bound up with a series of contractual and moral responsibilities to both informants and film-makers.

Each type of project provides a new context and another set of rights, responsibilities and ethical concerns. This means not only engaging with the ethics of organizations and the ethical practices of nonacademics but also when applied visual anthropological research involves interdisciplinary collaborations, finding ways to combine ethical principles developed in applied and visual anthropology with those of the collaborating discipline. For example, applied visual medical anthropology research is subject to the ethical codes established for medical research. Thus in Chalfen and Rich's collaborative work 'the VIA protocols for the pilot study of asthma', which involved measures to ensure informed consent and confidentiality that gave the participants some control over how the materials were used, were approved by the Children's Hospital Committee on Clinical Investigation (Rich et al. 2000). This might involve a different formal procedure of consent and ethical clearance than would be usual in academic visual anthropology.

Although applied research of any kind often has as one of its aims the intention to intervene to improve the personal or social conditions of its subjects, not all applied visual anthropology is specifically designed to directly benefit the subjects of the research. In these cases, usually for business research and commercial documentary production, we might quite rightly raise the conventional ethical question of what does the research 'give back' to the informants to ask what benefits they do accrue. In much commercial research (see also Roberts 2005) informants are paid a fee for their time and contribution to the research. Ownership of data is clearly stated and further payments will be made for further research events. For more open-ended participant observation repayment is not so simple, particularly when what was an academic project then later becomes a film-making or commercially rewarding enterprise. Here visual anthropologists whose academic work turns out to have profitable applications will be faced with a new set of ethical questions regarding their responsibilities to the research participants, some of which could well be financial.

Above I have briefly surveyed methods and practices in applied anthropology in public sector and NGO contexts and in industry. There are some interesting similarities in these different domains, particularly in terms of their methodology and the time constraints that influence this. However of course there are also key differences, some of which I have touched on already. First, whereas public sector and NGO projects often have as their aim an improvement of social, economic or personal conditions for a target group, industry seeks to increase profit and markets. In each scenario relationships with informants or participants are negotiated accordingly. This does not mean that encounters with paid informants in commercial projects are necessarily any more businesslike or less engaging for both researcher and informant. Nevertheless the intersubjectivity of the encounter often includes an economic transaction and motive that needs to be accounted for. Second questions of confidentiality and ownership of visual data, while always designed with informants' confidentiality as a primary concern, differ in other ways. Whereas original research undertaken in the public sector or NGO research might be disseminated for the sake of sharing good practice as well as research findings, anthropologists working in applied contexts in industry might be limited as sharing the findings of their original research or their innovative methodologies would involve allowing their competitors access to the knowledge that could offer their company a commercial advantage.

The Book

Above I noted a contemporary context where applied visual anthropology is, in various forms, increasingly used across private, public and NGO sectors. In common these different agencies value audiovisual media as a means of producing and disseminating knowledge that is inaccessible through written or verbal media. As a whole, *Visual Interventions* surveys this field by juxtaposing articles that describe applied visual anthropology projects with different aims and clients, in different geographical regions and using different media. The book is divided into 6 sections. In Section 1, Chapter 2, Malcolm Collier brings part of the 'hidden history' of applied visual anthropology to the fore through a photo-essay based on the work of John Collier Jr. in the 1950s and 1960s. This historical theme is also taken up by Chalfen and Rich in Chapter 3. The following five sections are divided according to areas of application which cover: medicine and health; tourism and heritage; conflict and disaster relief; community film-making and empowerment; and industry.[12] These represent a relevant range of substantive areas of the use of applied anthropology and also cross-cut the institutional contexts it is practiced in by describing anthropologists' collaborations with NGOs, governmental agencies and local community initiatives, their work in clinical settings, for European Union projects, in multinational corporations and as activists themselves.

Existing reports on visual work in applied medical anthropology often concern anthropologically informed documentary making, for instance in HIV and AIDS prevention campaigns in the United States (e.g., Tongue et al. 2000; and see Biella 1988) and in Africa (see Biella 2003). Each of the three chapters in Section 2 expands on this to demonstrate a different type of application. In Chapter 3 Chalfen and Rich discuss an example of applied visual anthropology in a medical context where visual production is undertaken by the informants and the target audience is not the general public but clinicians. The visual texts produced are also correspondingly different from those of academic visual anthropological representations, including multimedia CD-ROMs for training clinicians. In Chapter 4 Christina Lammer discusses her collaboration with interventional radiologists in an Austrian hospital. Here, Lammer holds the video camera herself, but her aim is to empathetically understand patients' sensory embodied experiences of interventional radiology and how this is shaped by the clinical interaction. Her findings are communicated to medical staff to help them reflect on their practice. However the project is also applied in a broader sense through Lammer's collaboration with artists to seek ways of communicating sensory experiences using other visual forms. In Chapter 5 Susan Levine discusses the impact of visual media produced for a target audience as part of the *STEPS to the Future,* [13] HIV/AIDS prevention campaign in Southern Africa. Here Levine practiced an applied form of audience ethnography to evaluate the relationship and relevance of the films to local culture and narratives. The authors of each of the three chapters in this section discuss case studies that use different visual methods and draw from visual anthropology practice in different ways. Their research findings that represent the otherwise inaccessible experience of their projects' participants are used to inform social interventions in the health field.

The two chapters in Section 3 focus on projects that engage with tourism and/or heritage policy and management and the local cultures and subjectivities that these intersect with. In different ways and using different visual and digital media each of the publicly funded projects discussed in this section seeks to make social interventions in tourism development by inserting a focus on local culture, voices and subjectivities into the policy-making process (which of course can involve not only public agencies but also the commercial interests of the tourism industry). In Chapter 6 Dianne Stadhams, who works in a poverty alleviation context, discusses a project funded by the British Government Department for

International Development (DfID). Stadhams, a tourism development specialist, produced a television programme collaboratively with Gambian partners. Drawing from visual anthropological methodologies, this project was designed to represent the multiple perspectives of different stakeholders in Gambian tourism. Screened on Gambian television as well as to NGOs the programme promoted awareness, aiming to intervene to establish a process of negotiation and collaboration in the development of tourism as a strategy for poverty alleviation in the Gambia. This work was both framed by and simultaneously challenged development practice by seeking to achieve poverty elimination goals within DfID's parameters yet using innovative methodologies. In Chapter 7 Vassiliki Yiakoumaki discusses a large European Union funded project on urban heritage based in twelve partner cities in the Mediterranean. The anthropologists involved in this research combine digital visual and other ethnographic methods to produce materials for an online multimedia hypermedia database. Their use of the visual ethnographic materials enables them to both serve the policy agendas and categories that frame this European Union project while simultaneously critiquing the generalizing nature of these frames through the visual ethnographic detail that represents the voices and experiences of local participants. Together these two chapters illustrate how applied visual anthropology can insert unique insights and critiques into policy arenas in two ways. First, by using visual and digital media to bring local people's voices into wider domains, thus empowering local actors within the development process. Second, by juxtaposing the agendas and subjectivities of different stakeholders in tourism development and management. Simultaneously each project offers its own alternative to the association of visual anthropology with observational documentary production by developing visual methods and formats of research and representation that are appropriate to the dissemination needs and possibilities of its intended audiences.

The three chapters in section four reflect on how applied visual anthropology can produce social interventions to support peoples whose lives have been disrupted in some way by military conflict, the consequences of environmental disasters or policy agendas that put their ways of life, homes or identities at risk. In Chapter 8 Jayasinhji Jhala discusses how different governmental, NGO, religious, caste and media agencies appropriated visual anthropology methods in the disaster relief context that developed after an earthquake in India in 2001. Considering this alongside his own work in the same context Jhala shows how video can help create culturally appropriate routes for expressing loss or grief. In doing so he argues that applied visual anthropologists have a role as activists and advocates. In Chapter 9 Matthew Durington discusses his recent participatory video work with San people. Criticizing existing romanticized anthropological representation of San Durington discusses how this project attempts to represent San voices and experiences. In Chapter 10 Carlos Flores discusses a collaborative film-making project he developed in a postconflict context with the Maya-Q'eqchi' in Guatemala, who had experienced a traumatic period of civil war. He defines this as a 'shared' anthropology. Flores work produced a form of social intervention by facilitating the local community's self-representation to itself. As such it became part of the process of post-conflict identity construction, but simultaneously served the anthropologists' academic goals. Flores shows how development objectives shaped by NGOs can also shape how indigenous media is produced. His work with the Maya-Q'eqchi' film-makers was produced with equipment provided by a development project. However Flores encouraged the film-makers to collaborate with him to make observational-style videos that reflected both his training in visual anthropology and their own concerns. He argues that a shared anthropology can (amongst other things) allow people to 'gain greater control over which markers of identity they chose to preserve, modify, or reject' (Flores, this volume) as well as allowing the anthropologist to arrive at new understandings. Together these three chapters demonstrate how applied visual anthropology methods can intervene in contexts of crisis by using video to represent local people's voices and experiences, either within their own communities or to wider agencies and audiences.

In Section 5 the focus on local community-based participatory video projects continues but shifts away from developing countries to socially excluded and marginalized groups within developed nations in Europe. In Chapter 11 Ana Martínez Pérez discusses *The Rhythm of Our Dreams* documentary film project produced in Córdoba, Spain. Developed at an interface with local government, social workers and local socially excluded people the film aimed to intervene by both raising public awareness about the experience of social exclusion and representing the work of the social workers to other professionals. In Chapter 12 An van. Dienderen focuses on *The Return of the Swallows* project, developed by a Dutch community filmmaker in a marginalized area of Amsterdam with excluded people including immigrants and sex workers. Here van. Dienderen, an anthropologist and filmmaker herself, both collaborated in the film-making process and was an ethnographer of the production process. Thus applying anthropology both to film-making itself and to comprehending how and why collaborative community film-making projects work to constitute identities and empower marginalized people. Together these chapters demonstrate the enormous scope for social interventions informed by visual anthropology and based on ethnographic research in developed modern Western urban contexts. By using collaborative and participatory methods the two video projects produced films that brought the usually hidden voices of excluded people into a public domain and at the same time allowed these participants to develop their own identity statements in ways that produced both new levels of self-awareness for them as individuals and new local relationships. The films these projects produced also provide alternative models to observational ethnographic film. *The Rhythm of Our Dreams* is an interview-based documentary that shows its participants as people in context, but relies on their verbalized self-representations rather than their observed behaviours. The film produced by the Swallows project, *The March, The Burden, The Desert, The Boredom, The Anger*, is a scripted feature film that represents the experiences of local people through a fictional narrative. Moreover as both chapters demonstrate the film-making process was equally important as a project in social intervention as the final film product itself.

Finally, the two chapters in section 6 focus on applied visual anthropology in industry. This commercial use of visual methodologies constitutes a different form of social intervention to the community-based and development-orientated projects discussed in the previous two chapters, in that the impetus for intervention comes from above. Research is commissioned by a company to solve 'problems'. It usually forms part of the wider multidisciplinary research agenda of the business and, although it normally intends to improve consumer or user experiences, it also aims to generate profit. However in terms of approach and methodology it is also (perhaps surprisingly) similar to work that aims to empower and benefit the disenfranchised. In Chapter 13 Werner Sperschneider discusses the use of video in design anthropology where visual ethnographers use video to understand cultures of work (in particular how people interact with technologies) and to represent these to designers. In doing so he emphasises how this involves collaborative work between researchers and participants and, like the work discussed in previous chapters, communicates stakeholders' perspectives, in this case to designers, as such constituting a form of social intervention. In Chapter 14 Lovejoy and Steele discuss a case study from their work at Microsoft. Based on visual ethnographic research, about the roles technology plays in people's lives in Brazil they constructed an intranet site through which they represented this research, as it developed, to their Microsoft colleagues. Lovejoy and Steele demonstrate how, based on materials generated through anthropological research, this interactive multimedia hypermedia dissemination method provided their audience with a way into understanding the experiences of people living in another culture. Both Sperschneider and Lovejoy and Steele emphasize the time constraints they encounter as visual anthropologists working in industry. They need to produce research and communicate it to product designers and other colleagues within short timescales dictated by the organizations they work for, rather than as considered appropriate by academic anthropology. This however does not so much compromise their ability to represent other people's experiences but stresses the need for their work to be collaborative and reflexive and outlines the role the anthropologist plays as a type of 'cultural broker' who can present other people's experiences to designers.

The Future of Applied Visual Anthropology?

Above I noted that applied visual anthropology has been infrequently reported in the visual anthropology literature. However the contributors to this volume demonstrate that there is much potential for academic insights and outputs to be generated from research materials that began life in applied visual anthropology projects. Flores (this volume) describes how his project involved combining theoretical and methodological perspectives from revisionist approaches to anthropology based in the 'writing culture' debate of the 1980s, visual anthropology, critiques of development, and applied anthropology. The outcomes of his 'shared anthropology' are both academic analysis and anthropologically-informed documentaries which form part of a process of postconflict reconstruction for the Maya-Q'eqchi'. This relationship between applied work and academic outcomes is not only possible in work that, like Flores's, was not governed by a client's brief and timescale. My own consumer video ethnography experiences have inspired me to develop new methodological and substantive areas in my academic work (Pink 2004a, 2006). Of course academic outcomes from applied visual anthropology projects are not inevitable. They may be constrained by time imperatives (especially for anthropologists who carry out applied work full time), or by the competing publishing priorities of an academic anthropologist. Although not every applied visual anthropology project will be reproduced as an academic text, a platform for communication and exchange between applied and academic visual anthropologists will benefit the theory, substantive knowledge and practice of both. It is in this sense that I propose that applied visual anthropology has transformative potential for the discipline – through the introduction of new forms of visual knowledge and visual representation, the acknowledgement of new substantive fields and the development of methodologies suited to them.

Applied anthropology is no longer 'resisted' by the mainstream in the United States and Britain. Nevertheless a divide between applied and academic anthropology and anthropologists persists and is felt by practitioners in their dealings with some elements of the academy. Likewise, there is still work to be done in putting applied visual anthropology on the agenda of professional associations, representing it in panels in mainstream conferences and film festivals, and making public the social and academic benefits of such work. However the current climate is one that is conducive to this task. Visual anthropological methods and media are now becoming increasingly integrated into mainstream anthropological research and representation and visual anthropology is becoming part of undergraduate and postgraduate studies in an increasing number of universities. Likewise applied anthropology is becoming a greater reality, it is more widely practised and its practitioners are increasingly vociferous in demanding that it is taken seriously by the academy and more active in creating links between applied and academic work. *Visual Interventions* is working towards the creation of an identity and a publication and discussion forum for applied visual anthropology. Collectively its contributors have begun to realise the potential of applied visual anthropology practice to make an important contribution to the future development of academic visual anthropology and applied anthropology.

Notes

1. This introduction is an extensively revised version of my introduction to the guest Edited issue of *Visual Anthropology Review* on Applied Visual Anthropology (Pink 2004b). Some of my ideas and research about applied visual anthropology have also been published in Chapter 5 of my book *The Future of Visual Anthropology* (Pink 2006). Some repetition has been inevitable in order to allow me to introduce, and contextualize, the idea of an applied visual anthropology.
2. By examining these questions *Visual Interventions* directly addresses the aim of the *Studies in Applied Anthropology* series – to work towards 'bridging the gap' between applied and 'pure' anthropology.
3. An exception is Tongue et al.'s (2002) discussion of the production of an AIDS awareness documentary as an instance of applied visual anthropology.
4. Biella has been a leading figure in the promotion and practice of applied visual anthropology.
5. http://www.dayzero.co.za/steps/, accessed 6 July 2004.
6. Note that although the dates given for the texts that describe, discuss and reference these projects have been published more recently the examples of applied visual anthropology were actually undertaken during the earlier period noted.
7. Other work involving applied visual anthropology is reported under other subdisciplinary labels. For example, one strand of the anthropology of indigenous media literature focuses on the anthropologist as co-activist (see Ginsburg et al. 2002: 8) and media producer who feels 'a responsibility to support projects by non-western or postcolonial groups who are resisting the impositions of Western or global capitalist media; and to support media use by subaltern groups … or minorities within nation states' (Ginsburg et al. 2002: 22, Ginsburg 1997).
8. I would like to express my thanks to Berghahn's anonymous reader of the draft of this manuscript for bringing these connections to the work of Jean Rouch and David and Judith MacDougall to my attention.
9. The term 'frontier' is taken from the notion of 'The Frontiers of Visual Anthropology', which was also the title of a one-day EASA Visual Anthropology Network seminar I co-organized with Glenn Bowman, Cristina Grasseni and Felicia Hughes-Freeland (held as an event related to the RAI Film Festival at the University of Oxford, 2005).
10. Other aspects of the application of visual anthropology might be seen in interdisciplinary collaborations such as the application of visual anthropology methods to arts practice (e.g. Silva and Pink 2004, Schneider and Wright, 2006). However this area is not covered in this volume since the focus is primarily on social interventions.
11. See the web pages of the National Association for the Practice of Anthropology at http://www.practicinganthropology.org/ and the Society for Applied Anthropology at http://www.sfaa.net/, both accessed 6 July 2004.
12. This set is of course not exhaustive.
13. http://www.dayzero.co.za/steps/, accessed 6 July 2004.

Bibliography

Appadurai, A. 1996. *Modernity at Large*. University of Minnesota Press.

Baba, M. and C. Hill (eds). 1997. *The Global Practice of Anthropology*, Williamsburg Virginia: Department of Anthropology, College of William and Mary.

Banks, M. 2001. *Visual Methods in Social Research*. London: Sage.

Banks, M. and H. Morphy (eds). 1997. *Rethinking Visual Anthropology*. New Haven and London: Yale University Press.

Bateson, G. 1980. 'An Analysis of the Nazi Film "Hitlerjunge Quex"', *Studies in Visual Communication* 6(3): 20–55.

Biella, P. 1988. 'Filming AIDS in the Barrio: A Study in the Pedagogy of the Oppressed', invited paper, Meeting of the American Anthropological Association, Phoenix, AZ.

—— (ed.). 2003. *Steps for the future/A Kalahari Family*. Special issue of *Visual Anthropology Review* 19 (1–2).

Bowman, G., C. Grasseni, F. Hughes-Freeland and S. Pink (eds). 2007. *The Frontiers of Visual Anthropology*. Guest edited issue of *Visual Anthropology*.

Collier, J. 1967. *Visual Anthropology: Photography as a Research Method*. Albuquerque: University of New Mexico Press

—— 1973. *Alaskan Eskimo Education*. Holt, Rinehart, Winston, New York

Collier, J. and M. Collier. 1986. *Visual Anthropology: Photography as a Research Method*. Albuquerque: University of New Mexico Press.

Collier, J. and M. Laatsch. 1983. *Education for Ethnic Diversity: An Ethnography of Multi-Ethnic Classrooms*. San Francisco, CA: Wenner-Gren Foundation.

Edwards, E. 1992. (ed.). *Anthropology & Photography 1860–1920*. New Haven and London: Yale University Press

Edwards, E. 1997. 'Beyond the boundary', in M. Banks and H. Morphy (eds) *Rethinking Visual Anthropology*. London: New Haven Press.

Edwards, E. 2001. *Raw Histories*, Oxford: Berg.

Ervin, A.M. 2000. *Applied Anthropology: Tools and Perspectives for Contemporary Practice*. Boston: Allyn and Bacon.

Feld, S. 2003. 'Introduction' in S. Feld. (ed.) *Cine-Ethnography Jean Rouch*. Minneapolis and London: University of Minnesota Press.

Ginsburg, F. 1997. '"From Little Things, Big Things Grow": Indigenous Media and Cultural Activism', in R.G. Fox and O. Starn (eds) *Between Resistance and Revolution: Cultural Politics and Social Protest*. London: Rutgers University Press.

—— 2002. 'Screen Memories: Resignifying the Traditional in Indigenous Media'. In F. Ginsburg, L. Abu-Lughod and B. Larkin (eds) *Media Worlds: Anthropology on new terrain*. California: University of California Press.

Ginsburg, F., L. Abu-Lughod and B. Larkin, 2002. 'Introduction'. In F. Ginsburg, L. Abu-Lughod and B. Larkin (eds), *Media Worlds: Anthropology on new terrain*. California: University of California Press.

Grasseni, C. (ed.). (2007). *Skilled Visions. Between Apprenticeship and Standards*, Oxford: Berghahn.

Grimshaw, A. 2001. *The Ethnographer's Eye*. Cambridge: Cambridge University Press.

Grimshaw, A. and A. Ravetz. 2005. (eds.). *Visualizing Anthropology*, Bristol: Intellect.

Gwynne, M.A. 2003. *Applied Anthropology: A Career Orientated Approach*. Boston: Allyn and Bacon.

Henley, P. 2000. 'Ethnographic Film: Technology, Practice and Anthropological Theory' *Visual Anthropology* 13: 207–226.

—— 2005. 'Anthropologists in Television: A Disappearing World?', in S. Pink (ed.), *Applications of Anthropology*. Oxford: Berghahn.

Loizos, P. 1993. *Innovation in Ethnographic Film*. Manchester: Manchester University Press.

MacDonald, J.H. (ed.) 2002. *The Applied Anthropology Reader*. Boston: Allyn and Bacon.

MacDougall, D. 1997. 'The Visual in Anthropology' in M. Banks and H. Morphy (eds), *Rethinking Visual Anthropology*. London: New Haven Press.

———— 1998. *Transcultural Cinema*. Princeton: Princeton University Press.

Marvin, G. 2005. 'Research, Representations and Responsibilities: An Anthropologist in the Contested World of Foxhunting', in S. Pink (ed.), *Applications of Anthropology*. Oxford: Berghahn.

Mead, M. and R. Métraux, (eds). 2000 [1953]. *The Study of Culture at a Distance*. Oxford: Berghahn.

Mills, D. 2005. 'Dinner at Claridges? Anthropology and the 'Captains of Industry' 1947–1955' in S. Pink (ed.), *Applications of Anthropology*. Oxford: Berghahn.

Nolan, R. 2003. *Anthropology in Practice: Building a Career Outside the Academy*. London: Lynne Rienner Publishers.

Pink, S. 2004a. *Home Truths*. Oxford: Berg.

———— 2004b. 'Applied Visual Anthropology: Defining the Field', in S. Pink (ed.), *Applied Visual Anthropology*, guest edited issue of *Visual Anthropology Review* 20(1): 3–16.

———— 2004c. 'In And Out Of The Academy: Video Ethnography of the Home', in S. Pink (ed.), *Applied Visual Anthropology*, guest edited issue of *Visual Anthropology Review* 20(1): 82–88.

———— 2005a. 'Applications of Anthropology: Introduction', in S. Pink (ed.), *Applications of Anthropology*. Oxford: Berghahn.

———— (ed.). 2005b. *Applications of Anthropology*. Oxford: Berghahn.

———— 2006. *The Future of Visual Anthropology: Engaging the Senses*. London: Routledge.

———— 2007 [2001]. *Doing Visual Ethnography: Images, Media and Representation in Research*. London: Sage.

Pink, S., L. Kürti and A.I. Afonso (eds). 2004. *Working Images*. London: Routledge.

Rich, M., S. Lamola, J. Gordon and R. Chalfen. 2000. 'Video Intervention/Prevention Assessment: A Patient-centered Methodology for Understanding the Adolescent Illness Experience' *Journal of Adolescent Health* 27(3): 155–65. Retrieved 7 May 2004 from http://www.viaproject.org/VIAMethod.pdf.

Roberts, S. 2005. 'The Pure and the Impure? Applying Anthropology and Doing Ethnography in a Commercial Setting', in S. Pink (ed.), *Applications of Anthropology*. Oxford: Berghahn.

Rouch, J. 2003[1973]. 'The Camera and Man', in S. Feld (ed.), *Cine-Ethnography Jean Rouch*. London: University of Minnesota Press.

Ruby, J. 2000. *Picturing Culture: Explorations of Film and Anthropology*. Chicago: University of Chicago Press.

Schneider, A and C. Wright. 2005. *Contemporary Art and Anthropology*. Oxford: Berg.

Silva, O. and S. Pink. 2004. 'In the Net: ethnographic photography' in S. Pink, L. Kürti and A. Afonso (eds), *Working Images*. London: Routledge

Stoller, P. 1992. *The Cinematic Griot: The Cinema of Jean Rouch*. Chicago and London: University of Chicago Press.

Tongue, N., J. Wheeler and L. Price. 2002. 'At the edge …: Visual Anthropology and HIV Prevention' in P. Higgins and J. A. Paredes (eds), *Classics of Practicing Anthropology 1978–1998*. Oklahoma: Society for Applied Anthropology.

van Willigen, J. 2002. *Applied Anthropology: An Introduction*. London: Bergin and Garvey.

Wright, S. 2005. 'Machetes into a Jungle? A History of Anthropology in Policy and Practice, 1981–1996' in S. Pink (ed.), *Applications of Anthropology*, Oxford: Berghahn.

Filmography

Lorang's Way. 1979. David MacDougall and Judith MacDougall. Rice University Media Centre (U.S.A.). 70 minutes.

Chapter 2

THE APPLIED VISUAL ANTHROPOLOGY OF JOHN COLLIER
A Photo Essay

———— ⋙ ————

by Malcolm Collier

Origins

John Collier Jr is best known within anthropology and sociology as an early and tenacious advocate of visual anthropology, indeed he may have coined the term as part of the title of his 1967 book on the subject. This publication and an enlarged edition in 1986 have served to introduce many to the methodological possibilities of cameras, photographs, and photo elicitation (Collier 1967, Collier and Collier 1986). What may not be evident in those texts is that most of his own work was of an applied nature, most often with a focus on the cultural vitality of ethnic groups within larger societies. When and where can one say this applied work began? The answer is unclear. He turned to photography during the 1930s in part because he saw it as a medium with practical potential that painting (the only area in which he had any formal training) lacked, so his interests were applied from the start. The development of systematic methods took longer. Work for the Farm Security Administration Historical Section (FSA) under Roy Stryker, introduced him to the concept of systematic photographic recording of social phenomena as well as equally organized handling of images after they were made. Subsequent work with Anibal Buitrón in Ecuador and Alexander Leighton in Nova Scotia (not included in this essay) challenged him to begin developing methods for integrating photography into the social sciences, methods whose sophistication would eventually far surpass those learned in the FSA.

John's FSA images often contained the same subjects, including home interiors, overviews of communities, and social processes found in subsequent, specifically applied work, but the later work became more content driven and less concerned with pictorial impact and photographs became part of extended, coordinated coverages that went far beyond anything made for the FSA .[1]

Figure 2.1, chapter title page: John Collier Jr making cultural inventory in northern New Mexico, 1957. Figure 2.2, opposite: This view of Rodarte, New Mexico in 1957 repeats a view made of the community for the FSA in 1943 and is quite typical of landscapes made by John and many other FSA photographers. Figure 2.3, above: Grandfather Romero, age 99, at home in Truchas, New Mexico, 1943. A strong pictorial image, although also containing much information.

The Cornell Fruitland Project

The first specifically applied anthropology project John worked for was the Cornell Fruitland Project in New Mexico in 1953, an agricultural development project associated with the relocation of Navajo families to irrigated lands on the San Juan River. The photographic work was wide in scope, including records of land use, housing, and agricultural practices, and wage workers, as reflected in this essay. Additional images covered family activities, community events, school scenes, and the activities of the project fieldworkers. By this time, work with Alexander Leighton on an extended research study of community mental health in the Maritimes of Canada had produced methods for explicitly anthropological photography and the work in Fruitland included exploration of the effectiveness of some of these methods, most particularly processes of photo elicitation. (Collier, Sasaki, and Tremblay, 1954)

Figure 2.4: Broad views of cultural geography and land use had been part of the FSA repertoire but now were made more systematically, linked in coordinated series that were used in detailed analysis of land use and in photo elicitation sessions intended to derive more complex social and emotional insight from residents. The view below is part of a linked 180 degree panorama. It might be noted that the scope of images used in this section of the essay is limited by project privacy protocols.

Figures 2.5 and 2.6, above: Agricultural practices, Fruitland, New Mexico, 1953.

Figures 2.7 and 2.8, above: Housing study image, part of a large sample of housing types. Below: Navajo wage workers on a natural gas line, New Mexico, 1953.

The Vicos Project

The Vicos project, sponsored by Cornell University and the University of San Marcos and directed by Dr Allan Homberg and Dr Mario Vasquez, remains one of the most controversial efforts in the history of applied anthropology with a considerable literature and mythology. For John, the project provided an opportunity to apply his now well articulated methods of 'photography for social research' (the term 'visual anthropology' was not coined until about 1965) in the context of a full-scale ethnographic and applied project. The twelve months of work in Vicos during 1954 and 1955 produced close to nine-thousand still images plus hours of 16 mm film and represents his most extensive and intensive effort in visual anthropology. Collier took on brief freelance work elsewhere in Peru during the year to help cover the costs of the Vicos photography. In retrospect these photographs provide a larger social context for the photography in Vicos, which had two primary components, a comprehensive visual ethnography of the community and a record of the operation of the project. The visual ethnography was intended to provide both information for immediate use and also as a baseline record for later comparative evaluation of the impact of the project.[2]

Figure 2.9: Traditional plough and rocky (but productive) soil, part of a detailed coverage of all aspects of agricultural technology and practice, both traditional and new.

Figure 2.10: An oblique view of a section of Vicos, part of an extensive photographic mapping of the whole community intended to record patterns of land tenure, habitation, agriculture, geography, and ecology for the whole community. These 'cultural geographies' can be seen as more systematic versions of the overviews done for the FSA. Figures 2.11 and 12.2, opposite: Labour on hacienda lands above and Vicosinos harvesting for themselves below. This selective essay with a handful of images cannot possibly convey the organized quantity and scope of records made in Vicos.

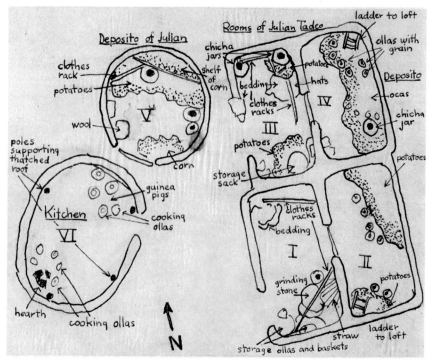

Figures 2.13 and 2.14, opposite: Photograph of family compound with derived diagram below. Figures 2.15, above: Store room with food, clothing, tools. Note identification slate in center.

The photographic ethnography was detailed, as in these examples from coverage of home character, content, and organization. A random sampling of homes was photographed, with records of each compound and every room in it. These were conceived as providing a qualitatively superior understanding of the material status of Vicosinos and as a baseline for later study of change over time. Photographs could be analysed and diagrams derived. While related in broad terms to early records of homes for the FSA, now the process became more systematized and less concerned with the pictorial impact of the photographs.

Figure 2.16, above: Fiesta scene in front of the Vicos church. The vibrancy and creative scope of fiesta activities belied some outsider's perceptions of the Vicosinos as culturally deprived, lacking in creativity and initiative. Figures 2–17 and 2–18, opposite: Family portrait and a meal which, in my memory, was very tasty. John Collier looked for signs of family warmth and processes as important foundations for the future.

John Collier was criticized by some for photographs, both in Vicos and elsewhere, that recorded happiness in the presence of extreme poverty but he felt it important to record the underlying cultural and personal vitality of communities. In Vicos, this included coverages of public events and private lives, ceremony, social relationships, and a host of fine portraits not reflected in this essay.

A record was made of the operations of the applied development project, its staff, and the immediate results of their efforts, including schooling, health care, and development of physical and social infrastructure. Additional photography, not represented here, looked at the relationship of Vicosinos to the surrounding region and to Peruvian society.

Figure 2.19, below and figure 2.20, opposite above: Project staff, including Dr Mario Vasquez on the right, interacting with a community leader. While the immediate goals of the project were better agriculture practices, better nutrition, better health, and other forms of material improvement the primary aims were long term, the political and social empowerment of the community. To that end, Vicosinos were encouraged to argue with project staff, as in the scene to the right, above. Figure 2.21, opposite below: Classroom at the Vicos school, built by community labor with teachers provided by the Peruvian government.

Cross Cultural Schooling

In the late 1960s, John Collier turned his attention to cross-cultural schooling and, in response to the limitations of still photography, started using Super-8 film equipment. The shift to film placed more emphasis on observation and analysis of social interactions and process through time and space. The first major project was a study of schooling in Native communities in Alaska in 1969. This work was explicitly applied and, unlike the work at Vicos, was published, providing important theoretical and practical foundations for new training programmes for Native Alaskan teachers and the development of school programmes more suited to the needs of villages in Alaska during the 1970s and 1980s. While film formed the primary data set for the research, still photographs were made in parallel to the film coverage, both as supplementary sources of information and for use in publications, as in this essay.[3]

Figure 2.22: Teacher aide and students in Tuluksak, Alaska, 1969.

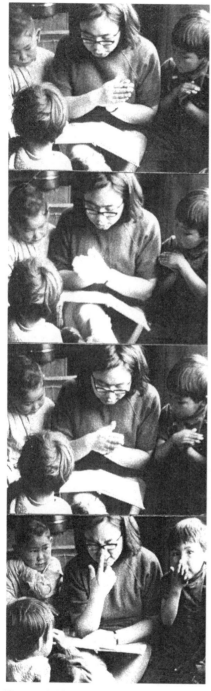

Figures 2.23 and 2.24: Head Start class in Kwethluk, Alaska, 1969. Discontinuous clips on the left, continuous clips on the right. Moving images allowed detailed examination of the social dynamics of schools.

Figure 2.25, above: Still photograph of the Head Start program in Kwethluk, Alaska, 1969. Equipment and materials were minimal but the social processes rich. Figure 2.26, below: Elementary level classroom in government-run school in Tuluksak, Alaska, 1969. Well equipped, with dedicated staff, but not as socially intense as the village-directed Head Start program.

Figure 2.27: Lower grade classroom in the government-run school in Kwethluk, Alaska, 1969. Analysis found considerable contrast between Native-directed situations, like the Head Start programme, characterized by close and extended interactions as compared to the more distant and abbreviated communications found in the well-equipped classrooms of government-operated schools with non-Native teachers from outside Alaska.

Figures 2.28 and 2.29, opposite page: Stills and film were made of homes, daily activities, family life, and community social and religious activity as a basis for comparing Native social circumstance and behavior with those encountered in the formal school settings. These photographs are from various locations in the Lower Koskokwim region of Alaska, 1969.

On completion of the fieldwork in Alaska, the film records were subjected to detailed study and analysis by John and a team of assistants. This analysis, both qualitative and quantitative, focused on the character of communication and relationships in the classrooms as compared to village and family settings. Far more than in previous work, the images were mined for their informational content which, together with a final overview of film and photographs in their totality, formed the basis for writing and publication of findings.

During the 1970s and early 1980s, the investigation of schooling extended to work on the Navajo Nation in Arizona and in a wide range of schools in the San Francisco Bay Area with results that were fed into John's teaching of anthropology and education for credential students at San Francisco State University. This work, not represented visually in this essay, was accomplished almost totally with Super-8 film and was never formally published, although the research was extensively reported in papers at academic conferences.

Conclusion

While in earlier years John Collier Jr's photographs were more classically documentary in character, intended to make statements to viewers for applied purposes, by the 1960s they became explicitly tools for obtaining information and understanding about the circumstances in which they were made. The camera became a more systematically directed tool for data gathering and less of an expressive device. The resulting images were often less individually compelling but the collective informational content became a far more extensive and complete source of information on the circumstances in front of the lens.

Looked at in totality, John Collier Jr's documentary and anthropological photography had a common thread of concern with the cultural vitality of communities. The images, both stills and film, were intended to assist in the recognition of that vitality and in the discovery of means to maintain it in changing circumstances, an applied focus in which the aesthetics of the images, while appreciated, became increasingly secondary.

Notes

1. Given the scope of John Collier's career in photography from 1934 to 1992, this essay provides only a glimpse. The larger collection of images and associated documents is now available to the public at the Maxwell Museum of Anthropology, part of University of New Mexico in Albuquerque, New Mexico, USA.

2. John Collier's work in Vicos was somewhat unofficial and the project made little direct use of the photographs at the time. His work in Vicos, actually a team effort with Mary E.T. Collier, was the most intensive and comprehensive effort of his career. Due to a variety of difficulties, no major publication of this work exist, although they did produce a complete dummy for a photographic book and publish an illustrated article in Scientific American (J. Collier and M.E.T. Collier 1957). There is a considerable body of literature and myth regarding the larger Vicos project: those interested in this subject may start with an article by Paul Doughty (Doughty 1987).

3. Two publications and a number of articles came out of the project (J. Collier 1973; M. Collier 1979). Information on the impact on schooling in Alaska is based on personal communications and a manuscript from Ray Barnhardt of the Center for Cross-Cultural Studies at the University of Alaska, Fairbanks (Barnhardt 1999).

Bibliography

Barnhardt, Ray. 1999. 'John Collier, Jr.: Anthropology, Education and the Quest for Diversity,' available on-line at: http://www.ankn.uaf.edu/Curriculum/Articles/RayBarnhardt/JohnCollier.html

Collier, John 1967. *Visual Anthropology: Photography as a Research Method*. New York: Holt, Rinehart and Winston.

———— 1973. *Alaskan Eskimo Education: a Film Analysis of Cultural Confrontation in the Schools*. New York: Holt, Rinehart and Winston.

Collier, John and Malcolm Collier. 1986. *Visual Anthropology: Photography as a Research Method*. Albuquerque: University of New Mexico Press.

Collier, John Jr. and Mary E.T. Collier. 1957. 'An Experiment in Applied Anthropology,' *Scientific American*, 59: cover and pp 37–49.

Collier, John Jr, Tom Sasaki, and Marc-Adelard Tremblay. 1954 'Navaho Housing in Transition,' *America Indígena*, XIV:3

Collier, Malcolm. 1979. *A Film Study of Classrooms in Western Alaska*. Fairbanks, AK: Center for Cross Cultural studies, University of Alaska.

Doughty, Paul L. 1967. 'Vicos: Success, Rejection, and Rediscovery of a Classic Program.' in *Applied Anthropology in America*, Second edition, Elizabeth M. Eddy and William L. Partridge, editors. New York: Colombia University Press.

PART II

MEDICINE AND HEALTH

Chapter 3

COMBINING THE APPLIED, THE VISUAL AND THE MEDICAL
Patients Teaching Physicians with Visual Narratives

———— ∞∞∞ ————

Richard Chalfen and Michael Rich

Introduction

Health research has always been a fruitful domain for visual methods, manifesting a mutual appreciation of the medical and the visual. In turn, applied anthropology has long-standing interests in health and medical issues (Chambers 1985; van Willigen 2002). The following chapter takes these relationships a few steps further by exploring the interface of visual, applied, media and medical anthropology. This ambitious integration represents a complicated terrain, necessitating a combination of many theoretical, practical and ethical considerations. The visual narratives project combines the production of visual material with an appropriate model of visual analysis coupled with a culturally sensitive mode of intervention and application.

As an orienting perspective, we understand applied visual anthropology to usually include the generation, observation, description, analysis and/or application of visual data to the solution of a human problem. Its objective is to use image representation to identify, define and redesign features of the material, social, biological or symbolic environment by prescribing a solution to a specific problem. The process inevitably requires cultural brokership between identifiable, defined constituencies, with the goal of improving communication and relationships between interacting communities, which sometimes have diverging, even opposing ideologies. The purpose of the applied visual anthropologist is to offer production experience and sociocultural sensitivity to the visual representation of human experience, and exert skills in presenting the audiovisual information to implement social change.

Media within Applied Anthropology

Historically diverse media forms have played significant roles within applied anthropology in both domestic and international contexts. Similarly, medical professionals have used still photography, different film formats, video, and recently CD technology in research, education and practice. Frequently, an audiovisual program is constructed as a didactic document to persuade people to change behavior, to adopt an alternative way of approaching problematic circumstances. With the development of Video Intervention/Prevention Assessment (VIA) (www.cmch.TV/via), we focused on an alternative use for media in applied anthropology. Media can enter a change process at a variety of points and media production is not solely under the control of the research team. VIA asks young people who share a medical diagnosis, such as asthma, obesity, or any chronic disease or condition, to create visual illness narratives, documenting on video their experiences, perceptions, issues, and needs. Typically, applied anthropologists are seen as the teachers; with VIA, members of the patient community teach their clinicians.

Background

The foundations of VIA extend back almost forty years. In 1966, as a recent graduate from the Annenberg School of Communications at the University of Pennsylvania, Richard Chalfen approached the Pennsylvania Hospital (associated with the University of Pennsylvania Medical School) and the Philadelphia Child Guidance Clinic (PCGC, associated with The Children's Hospital of Philadelphia) with a proposal to make 16mm films with local teenagers. Seeking an integration of urban anthropology, and visual anthropology, with methods, results and new questions from the 'Navajo Project' (Worth and Adair 1972) in mind, Chalfen wanted to demonstrate that one did not need to travel two thousand miles and work with a Fourth World culture to record cultural differences in filmic expression. As a complex multicultural society, Philadelphia contained a diversity of ways of seeing the 'same' surroundings in different ways. He wanted to demonstrate that if film-making was introduced in a 'neutral' or hypothetically culture-free manner, the technology would prove to be sensitive enough to record this plurality. Thus he began to research the relationships among sociocultural variables, image expression, and patterns of communication (Chalfen 1981).

Chalfen became a consultant at PCGC to develop the concept of 'socio-documentary film-making' with culturally diverse groups of adolescents. The first project was with a group of African American girls, former gang members (the 'Dedicated Soul Sisters') who had been identified by clinic personnel as 'at risk' for teen pregnancy (Chalfen and Haley 1971). The focal question in this work was to understand better the problematic relationships of subculture, social organization and pictorial expression. However, when the film they created was presented to clinic personnel, the psychologists, psychiatrists and social workers found delight that they could get to know their client populations in new and significant ways, ways they had not seen before. The films were offering them what they felt was an innocently-derived, transparent 'window on life' view of their ethnically diverse constituency. In retrospect, clinic staff had appropriated Chalfen's academically-driven motives to serve their own needs, applying his anthropologically-derived information to the practical matters of a child guidance clinic. In short, without much awareness or acknowledgement, Chalfen was thrown into a model of applied visual anthropology.

Placing VIA and Visual Illness Narratives

Developed by Michael Rich at Children's Hospital Boston, VIA is a research method in which children and adolescents with a chronic medical condition are given the opportunity to create video diaries of their everyday lives with illness. They are asked to 'Teach your clinicians what it means to live with your condition.' The visual illness narratives created by these patients address the experience of illness, health and health care from the patient's perspective. By generating illness narratives in audiovisual forms, VIA seeks a better understanding of what patients know (and clinicians do not know) that may be hindering effective communication and understanding. Arthur Kleinman has written of differing and sometimes divergent 'languages of medicine' operating in different 'health domains.' These medical languages constitute and express 'separate clinical realities, and conflicts between them ... created substantial difficulties in clinical practice' (1980: 144). VIA extends this notion into subculture, and into contrasting epistemes and encompassing belief systems. In this way, VIA gets to the very roots of a health care delivery system.

VIA finds itself at the nexus of four subdisciplines of contemporary anthropology, namely visual anthropology, applied anthropology, media anthropology, and medical anthropology. Our objectives are to understand VIA's motivations, methodology and practice within a framework of applied visual anthropology. Readers are reminded that our culturally sensitive attention to representation firmly positions this project within a reinvigorated visual anthropology, one considerably advanced beyond the myopic attention to and production of ethnographic film. Going one step further, while VIA practice has origins in one important strand of visual anthropology, its primary objectives place it within a framework of applied anthropology. VIA incorporates sociocultural factors and principles of visual studies into its research design, analytic framework and model of application. The intervention-application features of VIA demonstrate the value of its results to date and the potential for a broad range of future applications.

Looking: From Appearance to Seeing

When examining the roots of VIA in visual anthropology, two kinds of 'looking' are called into question. A wide range of documentary projects have focused on important needs to record, illustrate and know how things appear as an indicator of 'how things are.' These projects addressed questions of 'how we/they look' as in how we appear, including issues of body shape, skin color, dress, scarification/tattoos, cosmetics, hair style, gait, gesture and other kinesic issues. This generalized 'how people look' paradigm (Chalfen 1996) predominated visual anthropology until the early 1960s. For example, Robert Flaherty's innovative *Nanook of the North* (1921) is often labelled as 'the first ethnographic film.' The sequential photographs of E.J. Marey (1874) and Eadweard Muybridge (1955) taught researchers much about the mechanics of animal and human locomotion, laying the foundations for modern understanding of functional anatomy.

During the 1960s, another connotation of 'looking' came into play. People began giving more attention to a more literal meaning of looking, one dedicated to problems of perception, interpretation, and questions central to knowing how people 'look at,' know, interpret or otherwise understand their surroundings. Perhaps the best recognized effort which implemented this new way of looking is the 1966 NSF-sponsored *Navajo Film Themselves* project directed by cultural anthropologist John Adair and film communication scholar Sol Worth (Worth and Adair 1972). A small group of Navajo was asked to make individual 16mm black and white films about themselves in their reservation community of Pine Springs, Arizona. This innovative research was driven by interests in cognition, language, and culturally structured connections between verbal and visual communicative codes. In essence, the main objective was to ask the Navajo to show 'us' (acknowledged researchers) how they saw themselves and their surroundings, or even better, how they wanted to show themselves and their lives to outsiders (Chalfen 1997a).

A series of related projects followed, though not as many as initial enthusiasm for *Navajo Film Themselves* might have predicted. The thread of continuity was the researchers' willingness to 'hand over the camera', to reposition the seat of (symbolic) power, encouraging 'subjects' to be 'behind-camera' rather than 'on-camera.' Within anthropology, we have the work of Turner (1990, 1991), Michaels (1985), Asch (1991), Bellman and Jules-Rosette (1977), Balikci and Badger (1995) and additional work with the Navajo in communication studies Light and Henio (1977) among a few others (for full discussion, see Chalfen 1997a, 1997b).

Work in this research orientation began appearing in other contexts, from other disciplines, and in nonfilm media. Examples were found in perceptual psychology (Ziller and Smith 1977, Ziller and Lewis 1981), child psychology (Sutton-Smith et al. 1983, Stokrocki 1994), social work (Small 1981), health education (Wang et al. 1996a, 1996b), photo-therapy (Weiser 1993), video therapy (Skafte 1987, Stoschein 1991), and film communication (Chalfen 1981), among others. Evans et al (1979) developed a research project focused on the results of giving African American sixth-graders 8mm sound cameras and asking them to make films on the topic 'What Alcohol Means to Me.' A modification in protocol was introduced when research efforts did not focus on motivating new imagemaking, but rather studied a corpus of visual material that already existed, such as snapshots and home movies (Chalfen 1987) or videos (Hammond 1988, Jhala 1989). These efforts remained grounded in questions of how people 'look at' and see their physical, social, and symbolic worlds.

Many 'hand the camera over' projects continue to appear in the US – some community-based projects, some as summer activities, some as school-based extracurricular projects, some as esteem-building efforts, and the like (Bigby 1968; Gonzalez 2003; Greenberg 2000; Hall, 2001; Zimmam 1980; Pall 1999). But few are research-based and fewer have any grounding in the sociocultural sensitivity characteristic of anthropological efforts. Almost none are carefully documented in writing. As a rare research effort, Worth's individually-oriented 'bio-documentary' methodology was transformed to the group-oriented 'socio-documentary' when Chalfen began NIMH-sponsored research in Philadelphia in the late 1960s (Chalfen 1981).

Cultural Brokerage

'Applied anthropologists have often described themselves a cultural brokers, maintaining that their activities involve some kind of transfer of knowledge, skill, or service between distinct cultures' (Chambers 1985: 26). Other observers mention cultural brokerage as 'an intervention strategy of research, service and training that links persons of two or more sociocultural systems through an individual' with primary goals of making services more open and responsive to communities (van Willigen 2002: 130). Cultural brokership has intimate connections to the notion of 'cultural competence' which 'consists of the skills, knowledge, and policies that allow a person or organization to provide services effectively in a cross-cultural situation' (van Willigen 2002: 136). Van Willigen suggests that both concepts can be understood as part of the same process, with the former focused on role and the latter on knowledge and practice.

In a broad sense, patients and their physicians represent two subcultures in the medical universe – collections of people, participating in the same illness culture with stated and unstated needs to work together in cooperative ways. But these people do not always understand or even know each other in significant ways. Who or what helps these individual entities to 'get along' or at least allows them to interact in their quests for similar goals? As one answer, Chambers suggests the example of how a nurse 'is often called upon to be a broker among patients, physicians, hospital administrators, and patients' families and friends' (1985: 33): this role 'shares much with the way anthropologists describe the service component of their profession' (1985: 76).

Much clinically applied medical anthropology focuses on cultural brokerage (van Willigen 2002: 43; Gwynne 2003: 253). Within the broader medical context, the most common relationship is between a group of health care providers and individuals or communities that are ethnically distinct (Weidman 1978; Lefley and Bestman 1984). For example, applied anthropologists would usually support the medical staff 'through training, research, or the development of media' (van Willigen 2002: 129). Here we find a need for the production of media, whether written or audiovisual, but we find 'outsiders' producing the media component. VIA upends this construct.

VIA within a Cultural Broker Framework

Weidman (1973) sees five concepts as essential to the understanding of the cultural broker concept: culture, health culture, coculture, culture broker, and culture mediation. What distinguishes VIA in its role of cultural broker lies in its goals of cultural competency, importantly, for both patients and medical personnel. Most relevant here is VIA's conscious awareness of 'health culture,' which Weidman describes as 'all the phenomena associated with the maintenance of well-being and problems of sickness with which people cope in traditional ways within their own social networks … Cognitively, this includes health values and beliefs, guides for health action, and the relevant folk theories of health maintenance, disease, etiology, diagnoses, treatment and care' (van Willigen 2002: 131).

What kind of brokership is facilitated by patient camera-use or subsequent use of audiovisual data? What might visual anthropologists contribute to this mission? In VIA, consumer video technology is used to support the cultural broker role in new and innovative ways (Rich, Lamola, Amory and Schneider 2000). Chambers (1985) identifies five models of cultural broker: representative, facilitator, informant, analyst, and mediator. Two points are critical. The patient-generated illness narratives created through VIA permit cultural brokerage at a distance and, in turn, facilitate the extension of cultural brokerage. In getting the visual illness narratives made, VIA functions as a facilitator. The tapes themselves are representatives. Through the process of logging the content on the videos, VIA is an informant. In interpreting the visual illness narratives, VIA is an analyst. By making recommendations for medical interventions or changes in care based on the findings, VIA serves as a mediator.

One primary objective of VIA's brokerage through imagemaking is to increase the flow of, first, information and second, understanding, between representatives of the illness community and representatives of the medical community. The patient's creation of a visual illness narrative begins this process. VIA participants have said they have never been asked or able to say certain things to their doctors. Participants have revealed how they feel about certain medications in raw, honest ways that would never be directly reported to a clinician. By the same token, they have been able to show in their own visual illness narratives that they had discontinued medications that made them feel bad, even though they could not say such a thing out loud to their clinician. In turn, physicians have admitted that they had never heard or seen their patients' expressions of life circumstances in this depth or freedom. As one physician stated: 'In my twenty-five years of practice, I have never seen what a patient experiences and how an asthma exacerbation develops outside the clinical setting where we can leap in with a variety of acute interventions.' The setting of health care and the knowledge that providers bring to that care not only make that care effective and efficient, it can also obscure the patient's real experiences and needs.

However, these narratives must be understood as more than an information delivery service. Analysis of the videotapes focuses on interpreting the patient-generated data; we must never assume these audiovisual narratives 'can speak for themselves.' The long-term objective has been to develop ways for sharing information about improving a model of discourse – discourse that goes two directions, as a negotiation.

The multifunctional value of the videotapes is another venue of brokerage, a framework in which visual anthropologists should be able to contribute on several fronts. VIA visual illness narratives are a complex collusion of several models of culture, grounded in constellations of understanding about adolescence, media and illness. The visual anthropologist's contribution to interpretation and analysis of the audiovisual data in context goes beyond data generation into culturally sensitive observations of content and meaning. Interpretation of the tapes involves a sensitivity to sociocultural attributes of the patients and to the variants of pictorially mediated expression, many of which focus on how the specifics of culture are attached to audiovisual communication.

Ethical Considerations

With VIA's focus on opening communication between the patient and clinician, unique ethical considerations must be addressed. Unlike other health investigators, VIA researchers collect and analyse recordings of their study participants' images and voices; participants' identities cannot be obscured without significant loss of data. With VIA, there is an unavoidable loss of personal privacy. As with so much applied anthropology, there remains a politics of information. Concern may be raised that VIA might represent a form of surveillance, giving clinicians too much power over the patient. However a critical feature of the VIA method is that the patient–participant collects all of the data.

In the absence of direct information from patients about their issues and needs, medicine typically controls information transfer, framing the questions in medical constructs, and creating management plans based on medical ideals. VIA seeks to increase the patient's power in the clinician-patient dynamic by handing control of the information stream and the setting of the health care agenda to the patient. S/he reveals the important aspects of the illness experience, defines the problems faced, and is able to ask for solutions on personal terms. It is difficult to maintain concern for clinicians having too much power when it is the patients who are taking control of the information and sharing that which they feel is important. The data collected are what the patient deems important for the clinician to know.

Nonetheless, increased attention must be paid to controlling this personal information in the research setting. VIA guidelines stipulate that only the research team has access to the audiovisual data, which cannot go beyond the confines of the research team without the participant's express written permission. The informed consent covers only the data collection and analysis phases of the research, with the assumption that the data are kept secure and confidential. Once a participant's visual illness narrative is complete, s/he is provided with complete copies of the audiovisual data that they have collected and asked for a second consent. Similar to a photographic or recording release, this second stage asks the participant's permission to be able to show or publish some or all of the visual illness narrative as part of the report of the research.

Responses to this second stage informed consent have varied, with complete permission granted by all participants in the VIA–Asthma study to several participants in the VIA-Obesity study requesting that their video not be shown publicly. This double layer of protection for the research participants has led to increased freedom of the participants while videotaping, since they do not have to be fearful that what they show will appear on television or another public forum soon thereafter. They feel secure that they can veto the use of any or all of their visual illness narratives. To date, there have been no complaints from VIA participants or their representatives.

Findings and Applications of Two VIA Studies

As patient-generated documents, the VIA videotapes include a great deal of invaluable ethnographic detail about conditions of everyday life. These tapes reveal information about home conditions, including such topics as interior decoration (including rugs, dust and plant life), dynamics of food consumption (prescriptions and proscriptions), the presence and care of household pets, the bathroom application of hair spray, patient care, interpersonal support, among others. Other revealing scenes provided information about guests smoking in a kitchen, intense dust from a neighboring construction site, the familial sharing of medication as well as incorrect advice of medication use, arguments about exercise, media and food consumption among many others.

Asthma

Since asthma was the first chronic disease studied with VIA, much of the methodology was theorized, implemented, evaluated, and modified on this project. Findings from this study were published in the literature and key modifications of clinical practice followed.

The comprehensive, 'standard of care' medical history missed as much as ninety-five percent of the participants' actual exposure to asthma triggers as visualized by VIA (Rich, Lamola, Amory, Schneider (2000). This finding led to major changes in medical history-taking. Clinical information gathering shifted from an interview that compared a patient's behavior to an abstract medical ideal into a more open-ended, less judgmental discussion of the patient's experiences and needs. This leads naturally to a collaboration between clinician and patient to develop a medical plan that is responsive to the realities of the patient's life.

Analysis of VIA visual narratives found that the patients with moderate to severe asthma had sufficient exposure to asthma education as part of their medical care to have biomedically accurate understandings of their disease, but held explanatory models of disease management that, in some cases, worked against adherence to medical plans and effective self-management of their asthma (Rich, Patashnick, Chalfen 2002). This led to better understanding of a previously confusing lack of correlation between increased asthma education and improved outcomes; increased knowledge did not equal improved health behaviors. Shared ownership of patients' management plans, however, has resulted in improved patient adherence.

Evaluation of asthma patients' illness experiences as related by their visual illness narratives led to an recognition that illness is a social construct, an individual mix of disease status and responses to it by a patient, their family, community, care providers, and belief systems (Rich, Taylor, Chalfen 2000). Thus, patients with equivalent disease by clinical standards can have a wide variety of illness severity, ranging from fully functional to significantly disabled. Clinicians aware of these findings have shifted their medical assessment and decisionmaking from their previous focus on the patient's disease status to an approach to the whole patient's illness. Taking into account the life context in which the patient experiences illness and manages health has led to more sensitive assessments and more effective medical plans.

Most interestingly, VIA itself was evaluated as a therapeutic intervention in the asthma study. Framing the creation of their visual illness narratives, participants completed quantitative asthma-specific quality of life (QOL) measurement instruments. Due to the intermittently symptomatic nature of the disease, we measured QOL twice before VIA to determine whether there was natural fluctuation of their quality of life. It was administered again when VIA participants completed their visual illness narratives, but before either they or the research team had viewed or responded to the information on their tapes. Analysis showed no difference between the two pre–VIA administrations, but a statistically significant improvement in their quality of life after they made their visual illness narratives (Rich et al. 2003). The process of self-examination had resulted in quantifiable improvements in their asthma status, possibly because of the cognitive dissonance between what they observed themselves to be doing and what they knew they should be doing.

Obesity

VIA functioned very differently when used to study obesity, largely because obesity, unlike asthma, is socially stigmatizing and visually obvious. Participants were much more reticent to record behaviors important to understanding their condition, such as eating or physical activity, for which they felt vulnerable to criticism. However, even when they did not document key aspects of their lives with obesity, VIA was again able to function as an intervention. Simply through the increased awareness necessary to avoid showing these aspects of their experience, many of the VIA participants changed those behaviors. Analysis of the VIA–Obesity data continues, but preliminary findings include observations of common behaviors such as self-comforting with food, voracious eating, fidgeting/hyperactive behaviors, and heavy television, video game, and music use. Participants revealed 'unconscious eating' associated with heavy media use, consuming predominantly high salt-, sugar-, and fat-containing foods while completely focused on the screen. This behavior was observed to be associated with oral stimulation rather than hunger satiation, ceasing only when the food item was depleted. Interestingly, many of the participants revealed above average levels of physical activity, although, due to the participant-controlled data collection, it is unclear how frequent these behaviors were and whether they occurred especially for the camcorder. Psychological themes included stigmatization and ostracism by peers, resentment toward attractive celebrities or peers, sexual exploitation because they were perceived as 'desperate,' emotional distress over dietary restrictions, and family conflict over food and weight issues. Participants showed limited insight on their own bodies; some referring to others as 'fat.' They revealed a number of positive features about being obese, ranging from protection against sexual objectification to being appreciated for a sense of humor, from having physical dominance ('I can kill people when I want to'), to making a political statement ('I don't have to conform to your images of what you think a woman should be').

Physicians have been impressed with these tapes for several reasons. Clinicians are used to seeing their patients in relatively sterile unnatural conditions. Instead of working within abstract contexts, the VIA tapes helped medical personnel and students gain access to intimate scenes of personal distress and illness-related anxieties, to personal opinions of illness, treatment plans and related therapies.

Findings to Applications

VIA as research is clearly based in visual anthropology, but it is the use of its findings to intervene on and/or prevent disease that remains the key feature that distinguishes this method as applied visual anthropology. Application of VIA seeks to take advantage of the politics of symbolic forms (Worth 1972); VIA has the potential of upending the political structure of clinician-patient communication by relocating the power base. When patients are given cameras and their clinicians look and listen, patients' perspectives and statements are given authority (Rich and Patashnick 2002). VIA provides patients with opportunities to construct their own narratives to describe and comment on 'back stage' aspects of their illnesses, what their physicians have not seen and do not know. In these ways, patients are contributing new data to their health care problems, broadening the clinical research database. This perspective assumes, of course, that people are listening, hence the necessity for structured analysis and the ability to disseminate research findings to those who can change health care delivery.

Revising Clinical Assessment

One of the first and most obvious applications of these findings is realized when comparing medical information derived through different approaches. VIA research facilitates the acquisition of improved and more complete data about diseases in patients' life contexts. With VIA data, medical personnel gain a different and complementary information source that can be compared with and contrasted to the patient's medical history and QOL scores. Combining methods potentiates medical assessment; qualitative inquiry complements and adds dimension to quantitative measurements. True to human realities, alternative research perspectives do not always agree with one another, suggesting the need to enrich and vary the questions that clinical personnel ask their patients.

The difference in information between patients' visual narratives and medical histories signals a semiotic shift, as when the significant features of a patient's life are too commonplace to be noticed and accounted for in recall interviews. Generally, patients do not necessarily lie or willingly deceive their health care personnel. In actuality, much of our daily lives are taken for granted and not seen as problematic or even dangerous. As a result, important details are 'invisible' to the patient's recall. Because the camera lens and the microphone are indiscriminate in their observation, VIA tends to reveal taken-for-granted aspects of vernacular culture, instances when life is 'too close' to be noticed. VIA methodology has the potential to make the commonplace visible and, in some cases, problematic. Hidden pockets of crucially important lifestyle data are being identified. In short, revisions are being made in what to look for, what to ask about, and what needs to be changed. Researchers gain an opportunity to discover the conditions and circumstances that asthma patients share as members of the same illness subculture. We gain a better sense of what findings can be generalized across participants and, by extension, what changes of medical strategy can be applied to understanding and managing others with the same condition and, more broadly, to a variety of chronic conditions.

Reconceiving Management Plans

VIA reveals hitherto inaccessible information about the life contexts in which patients try to manage their chronic conditions. When they are able to visualize issues such as chaotic households, transportation difficulties, financial shortfalls, language barriers, or other obstacles to optimal care, clinicians have a better chance of addressing unresolved chronic illness management problems. Health care providers get a better handle on problematic medical adherence, why a particular treatment plan may be failing a patient who is living with a particular set of circumstances. Not only does VIA reveal obstacles to effective management, but it also highlights the strengths that a particular patient and family bring to the healing process, the knowledge and experience that can be incorporated into management plans which are sensitive and responsive to patients' everyday lives.

In these ways, VIA results have important roles to play in a revitalized model of medical therapy, where the physical and social context of an illness are broadened and better understood and where the patient brings equal value to the patient–clinician partnership that develops and monitors the patient's health management. This application of VIA brings health education and self-management to the forefront of preventive medical strategies, by giving the clinician needed contextual information with which to collaborate with the better-informed patient in devising more sensitive and, ultimately, more effective medical strategies.

Reenergizing Medical Education and Clinical Training

VIA visual illness narratives are providing new data and visually realized contexts of illness. Health care personnel are gaining information that has never been shared with them before, so it never entered their awareness.

Clinicians have a much better understanding of what might be responsible for a patient's illness when it is observed in life context as compared to what can be evaluated in a clinician's office or emergency room. The visual illness narratives are providing health practitioners with new understandings of the lives and experiences that lie within a specific diagnosis. Through the 'lens' of VIA, clinicians are coming to new understandings of previously perplexing and frustrating problems such as patients not following their treatment plans.

VIA results can be used in educational contexts, to sensitize medical students, residents, and experienced clinicians. 'Visual illness narratives from VIA research projects have been incorporated into Harvard Medical School courses on respiratory pathophysiology, outpatient medical management, and patient–doctor relationships. Patient-created video has proven to be a powerful tool for grounding clinical students in the realities of patient experience and placing medical management in context with their everyday lives' (VIA 2003). Currently, interactive multimedia curricular materials on CD–ROM and DVD are being developed 'so that VIA participants can help educate current and future clinicians to the realities of illness and patients' experiences' (VIA 2003). More broadly, using broadcasting, VIA visual illness narratives can educate and empower other patients, parents, teachers, in fact, all members of the general public, many of whom have some relationship to, but limited awareness of, chronic illness. The 'from the inside out' perspective of these data contributes to a patient-centered medical model and encourages the establishment of a more equal patient–clinician partnership.

Rechanneling Patient Advocacy

Historically, patients, particularly child and adolescent patients, have depended on others to advocate for their needs. Without a voice or a position of power in a society that confers power through a wallet or a vote, advocacy for child patients has been the responsibility of parents, pediatricians, nurses, educators, and social workers. However, information now represents another source of power. By handing control of the information stream to child and adolescent patients, and by looking, listening, and learning from what they show and tell us, VIA gives them the power to advocate for themselves. Patients become empowered to speak and advocate for themselves through audiovisual channels of expression and communication.

There is great potential in the concept of communication competence – feeling that one has a freedom to express oneself and to know with certainty that someone is listening and paying attention to what is being said. Part of the cultural competency of the researcher is to foster the communicative competence of the patient. VIA capitalizes on an adolescent need to be heard and valued – on the sense that 'no one ever listens to me' or 'no one ever pays any attention to me.' 'What is clear is that there is a real potential that can be tapped when young people are given media tools and believe that their expression will be seen and heard' (Rich et al 2006). When this technology and technique allow us to see their worlds, and the issues that they have in navigating them, it helps us be more informed about their needs. Through this direct advocacy, we can look toward the development of improved delivery of health services and more useful and culturally sensitive health care financing.

Control of Image as Related to Improved Management of Treatment

In comparison to the information gained from a doctor's questions, VIA provides a safe, nonjudgmental information conduit to the clinician. This has allowed the emergence of a 'confessional effect', where the VIA participant is able to openly acknowledge issues such as nonadherence that, for fear of disturbing the therapeutic rapport, might never be volunteered in a face-to-face clinical encounter. Participants discontinuing medication due to side effects or their exposure to harmful situations were revealed through VIA to their care providers, even when the same participants were avoiding or obfuscating these issues in their direct dialogues with clinicians. Because they control the acquisition of the information and can reframe what they fear will be seen as their failures, patients are able to acknowledge problems with their medical plans and offer them up for collaborative solutions.

VIA functioned as a therapeutic intervention by facilitating patients' ability to open up about previously uncomfortable truths through self-observation and reflection. 'VIA has also demonstrated a therapeutic effect with asthma patients, possibly because the young people are actively investigating their own illness experience, discovering and reflecting on aspects of their lives that had gone unnoticed but were in contradiction to what they knew they should be doing to care for themselves' (Rich 2003). Working in ways similar to cognitive behavioral therapy, in which a therapist introduces facts that contradict a patient's dysfunctional belief systems, VIA allows the self-introduction of dissonance. The reflexive opportunity provided by the technological mirror of VIA is a model of intra-personal feedback which provokes the patient to reexamine his or her behavior and, hopefully, to self-correct.

A major developmental task of adolescence is the establishment of autonomy, a process that requires finding one's individual identity and taking over control of one's life from parents or other adult authorities, including clinicians. Control is a very significant issue for adolescents and much energy is often expended in resentment toward and rebellion from the control of others. Uniquely suited to the needs and desires of adolescents, VIA offers young patients a medium of communication over which, as a generation raised on television, they feel ownership and in which they can control how they are seen and understood.

The VIA philosophy believes that by working with video, a medium that young people feel comfortable with and by giving them control of the information about their own experiences, feelings, and needs, VIA has created a safe environment in which teens have been able to reveal what has been inaccessible to traditional research methods – realities of their lives and living environment that make adherence to medical plans difficult, perspectives of their families and friends, and their thoughts, fears, and feelings about their condition and its care. Participants who engage with the VIA process discover that they can effectively take charge of the visual medium to tell their stories. As one participant in the asthma study related, 'I was an angry kid. When you gave me a video camera, I thought you were crazy. I could have sold it. But then when I started to shoot, I realized that I could take control of my life story. Then I realized that I could probably take control of my life.' Following the making of their visual illness narratives, many of the VIA participants learned to take charge of their medical management and were able to achieve better control of their asthma. Through VIA, managing a symbolic representation of life may have direct correlates with taking charge of problems in real life. By gaining competence and managing representation and its parent, presentation, these young people were able to develop the confidence to take charge of their lives. Behavioral change, particularly when it involves increased responsibility requires self-efficacy, which is defined as 'the conviction that one can successfully execute the behavior required to produce the outcomes' (Strecher and Rosenstock 1997). That conviction is gained through mastery, mastery that VIA participants achieved in the microcosms of their visual illness narratives. Self-efficacy gained through taking control of their visual illness narratives was then extrapolated to taking control of their lives.

Concluding Thoughts

Beyond the natural application of anthropological information to academics through teaching and publication, most acknowledge that anthropology has historically experienced an uneven relationship with applied realms and domains. Applying anthropological methods or findings has traditionally involved stepping outside the academic setting and, in the minds of some anthropologists, demotion to second class citizenship. This represents a failure of both imagination and interpretation. We have not been imaginative enough to find useful, humanity-promoting applications of the fundamental strengths of visual anthropology. Instead, visual anthropologists have on occasion allowed themselves to be enlisted as foot soldiers of business, consulting on product development and marketing strategies. We have misinterpreted these prosaic activities as the logical and only applications for anthropology, leading 'serious anthropologists' to prize only 'knowledge for knowledge's sake.' Within visual anthropology, the majority of effort has been expended in the direction of applying cultural sensitivities to the production of ethnographic film, and, in turn, promoting a dissemination of the ethnographic information derived into teaching. Visual anthropologists have not sensed the enormous rewards of exploring other avenues and models of both content and application. As disciplines grounded in perspective and not subject matter, anthropology and visual anthropology have a mandate to remain curious and versatile, willing to examine application to a broadly diverse range of interests and activities. Academics can make contributions to the qualitative improvement of the human condition in a variety of ways. Application is neither opposed to nor less than academic pursuit. The difference is only one of emphasis. The model of applied visual anthropology described in this paper offers invaluable opportunities for creativity, personal contact, and feedback, as well as personal and shared reward.

VIA methods and practice are totally appropriate for a time when social scientists want to reduce political friction between observer and observed, with or without cameras: 'Increasingly applied anthropologists work with those studied in a collaborative or participatory mode ... The applied anthropologist shares his or her special skills and knowledge with the community. This serves to transform the community from object to be known to a subject that can control' (van Willigen 2002: 43). At a time when many patients feel that machines are taking the place of doctors and technology is dehumanizing medicine, VIA is demonstrating that visual technology can be used to 'rehumanize' medical care, realigning and energizing relationships between patients and clinicians. VIA reveals ways that a visual model of inquiry can contribute to clinically applied medical anthropology when the objective is to 'introduce into the health care system [visual] anthropological principles and insights that will help biomedical professionals deliver effective and appropriate health care' (Gwynne 2003: 253). Patients controlling the construction of their visual illness narratives and extending those skills to controlling life plans and directions may well be one of the most important keys to improving patient care.

References

Asch, T. with J.I.H. Cabellero and J. Bortolio. 1991. 'The Story We Now Want to Hear is Not Ours to Tell: Relinquishing Control Over Representation: Toward Sharing Visual Communication Skills With the Yanomami', *Visual Anthropology Review* 7(2): 102–106.
Balikci, A. and M. Badger. 1995. 'A Visual Anthropology Seminar for the Native Peoples of Siberian and Alaska', in H.H. Philipsen and B. Markussen (eds), *Advocacy and Indigenous Film-making*, Hojbjerg: Intervention Press, pp. 39–54.

Bellman, B. and B. Jules-Rosette. 1977. *A Paradigm for Looking-Cross Cultural Research with Visual Media.* Norwood: Ablex Publishing Corporation.

Bigby, J. 1968. 'Fade to Black: Seeing Harlem through 8mm Eyes,' *Take One* 1(12): 20–21.

Chalfen, R. 1981. 'A Sociovidistic Approach to Children's Filmmaking: The Philadelphia Project,' *Studies in Visual Communication* 7(1): 1–32.

———— 1987. *Snapshot Versions of Life.* Bowling Green: Popular Press.

———— 1996. 'Photography', in D. Levinson and M. Ember (eds), *The Encyclopedia of Cultural Anthropology.* New York: Henry Holt and Co., pp. 926–931.

———— 1997a. 'Foreword to Revised Edition', in S. Worth, J. Adair and R. Chalfen, *Through Navajo Eyes— An Exploration in Anthropology and Film Communication*, revised 2nd edition. Albuquerque: University of New Mexico Press, pp. ix–xxi.

———— 1997b. 'Afterword to the Revised Edition', in S. Worth, J. Adair and R. Chalfen, *Through Navajo Eyes— An Exploration in Anthropology and Film Communication*, revised 2nd edition. Albuquerque: University of New Mexico Press, pp. 275–341.

Chalfen, R. and J. Haley. 1971. 'Reaction to Socio-Documentary Film Research in a Mental Health Clinic', *American Journal of Orthopsychiatry* 41(1): 91–100.

Chambers, E. 1985. *Applied Anthropology – A Practical Guide.* Englewood Cliffs: Prentice Hall.

Evans, G.B., R.A. Steer and E.W. Fine. 1979. 'Alcohol Value Clarification in Sixth Graders: A Film-making Project', *Journal of Alcohol and Drug Education* 24(2): 1–10.

Gonzalez, D. 2003. 'Young Lives Transformed, Guided by a Camera Lens', *The New York Times*, May 7.

Greenberg, J. 2000. 'Cameras Help Teenagers Look Beyond Bitter Conflicts', *The New York Times*, February 24.

Gwynne, M.A. 2003. *Applied Anthropology—A Career-Oriented Approach.* Boston: Allyn and Bacon.

Hall, K. 2001. 'Their Video Projects Positive Images', *The Boston Globe*, June 10.

Hammond, J. 1988. 'Visualizing Themselves: Tongan Videography in Utah', *Visual Anthropology* 1: 379–400.

Jhala, J. 1989. 'Videography as Indigenous Text and Local Community', *CVA Review* 6: 8–16.

Kleinman, A. 1980. *Patients and Healers in the Context of Culture: An Exploration in the Borderland between Anthropology, Medicine and Psychiatry.* Berkeley: University of California Press.

Lefley, H.P. and E.W. Bestman. 1984. 'Community Mental Health and Minorities: A Multi-Ethnic Approach', in S. Stanley and T. Moore (eds), *The Pluralistic Society: A Community Mental Health Perspective.* News York: Human Sciences Press.

Light, R. and B. Henio. 1977. 'The Role of Media in Ramah Navajo Society', *Audiovisual Instruction* 27(10): 10–12, 45.

Marey, E.J. 1874. *Animal Mechanism: A Treatise on Terrestrial and Aërial Locomotion.* New York: D. Appleton and Co.

Michaels, E. 1985. 'How Video Has Helped a Group of Aborigines in Australia', *Media Development* 1: 16–18.

Muybridge, E. 1955. *The Human Figure in Motion.* New York, Dover Publications.

Pall, E. 1999. 'Video Verite – A 'Media Literacy' Program Helps Teenagers Document their Lives on Camera, and Discover Truths about Themselves along the Way', *Education Life* supplement to *The New York Times*, January 3.

Rich, M. 2003. 'Boy, Mediated: Effects of Entertainment Media on Adolescent Male Health'. in D.S. Rosen and M. Rich (eds), *The Adolescent Male. Special Issue of Adolescent Medicine: State of the Art Reviews* 14(3): 691–716.

Rich, M., S. Taylor and R. Chalfen. 2000. 'Illness as a Social Construct: Understanding What Asthma Means to the Patient to Better Treat the Disease', *The Joint Commission Journal on Quality Improvement* 26(5): 244–253.

Rich, M., S. Lamola, C. Amory and L. Schneider. 2000. 'Asthma in Life Context: Video Intervention/Prevention Assessment (VIA)', *Pediatrics* 105(3): 469–477. [Video illustrations online at www.pediatrics.org]

Rich, M., S. Lamola, J. Gordon and R. Chalfen. 2000. 'Video Intervention/Prevention Assessment: A Patient-centered Methodology for Understanding the Adolescent Illness Experience', *Journal of Adolescent Health* 27(3): 155–165.

Rich, M. and J. Patashnick. 2002. 'Narrative Research with Audiovisual Data: Video Intervention/ Prevention Assessment (VIA) and NVivo', *International Journal of Social Research Methodology* 5(3): 245–261.

Rich, M., J. Patashnick and R. Chalfen. 2002. 'Visual Illness Narratives of Asthma: Explanatory Models and Health-Related Behavior', *American Journal of Health Behavior* 26(6): 442–453.

Rich, M., S. Lamola and E. Woods. 2006. 'Effects of Creating Visual Illness Narratives on Quality of Life with Asthma: A Pilot Intervention Study', *Journal of Adolescent Health* 38(6), 748–752.

Skafte, D. 1987. 'Video in Groups: Implications for a Social Theory of the Self', *International Journal on Group Psychotherapy* 37: 389–402.

Small, E.S. 1981. 'Through Schizophrenic Eyes'. Paper presented at the 35th Annual University Film Association Conference (with Janice Platt).

Stokrocki, M. 1994. 'Through Navajo Children's Eyes: Cultural Influences on Representational Abilities', *Visual Anthropology* 7(1): 47–67.

Stoschein, T.M. 1991. 'Use Your Video Camera to Get to Know Your Students', *Social Studies* 82: 32–33.

Strecher, V.J and I.M. Rosenstock. 1997. *The Health Belief Model*, 2nd ed. San Francisco: Jossey-Bass.

Sutton-Smith, B., M. Griffin and F. Eadie. 1983. 'Filmmaking by Young Filmmakers', *Studies in Visual Communication* 9: 65–75.

Turner, T. 1990. 'Visual Media, Cultural Politics and Anthropological Practice: Some Implications of Recent Uses of Film and Video among the Kayapo of Brazil', *CVA Review* Spring: 8–13.

——— 1991.'The Social Dynamics of Video – Media in an Indigenous Society: The Cultural Meaning and the Personal Politics of Video-making in Kayapo Communities', *Visual Anthropology Review* 7(2): 68–76.

van Willigen, J. 2002. *Applied Anthropology: An Introduction*, 3rd ed. Westport: Bergin & Garvey.

VIA 2003. 'Video Intervention/Prevention Assessment.' Retrieved December 1, 2003 from http://viaproject.org.

Wang, C., Y.Y. Ling and F.M. Ling. 1996a. 'Photovoice as a Tool for Participatory Evaluation: The Community's View of Process and Impact', *The Journal of Contemporary Health* 4: 47–49.

Wang C., M.A. Burris and Y.P. Xiang. 1996b. 'Chinese Village Women as Visual Anthropologists: A Participatory Approach to Reaching Policymakers', *Social Science and Medicine* 42(10): 1391–1400.

Weidman , H.H. 1973. 'Implications of the Culture Broker Concept for the Delivery of Health Care'. Paper delivered at the meetings of the Southern Anthropological Society, Wrightsville Beach, N.C.

Weidman , H.H. 1978. *Mental Health Ecology Report*, Vols 1, 2. Miami: University of Miami School of Medicine.

Weiser, J. 1993. *Photo Therapy Techniques*. San Francisco: Jossey-Bass.

Worth, S. 1972. 'Toward an Anthropological Politics of Symbolic Forms', in D. Hymes (ed.), *Reinventing Anthropology*. New York: Pantheon, pp. 335–365.

Worth, S. and J. Adair. 1972. *Through Navajo Eyes-An Exploration in Film Communication and Anthropology*. Bloomington: Indiana University Press.

Worth, S., J. Adair, and R. Chalfen. 1997. *Through Navajo Eyes—An Exploration in Anthropology and Film Communication*, revised 2nd edition. Albuquerque: University of New Mexico Press.

Ziller, R.C. and D. Lewis. 1981. 'Orientations: Self, Social and Environmental Percepts Through Auto-Photography', *Personality and Social Psychology Bulletin*: 338–343.

Ziller, R.C. and D.E. Smith. 1977. 'A Phenomenological Utilization of Photographs', *Journal of Phenomenological Psychology* 7(2): 172–182.

Zimmam, J. 1980. 'Mental Patients Making Movies', *Tri-Town Transcript*, March 12.

Chapter 4

STEPS FOR THE FUTURE

HIV / AIDS, Media Activism
and Applied Visual Anthropology in Southern Africa

Susan Levine

> I had never heard anyone admit that they have this disease
> (HIV / AIDS), which is strange because it has existed for a long
> time and killed a lot of people, even here in Mohale's Hoek.
>
> Thabo aged twenty, Lesotho

It is 'strange' that people do not talk about a disease that is inscribed into the landscape through burial space shortages, in homes where basic hygiene needs for the ill puts enormous pressure on the 'well', and where billboards are saturated with messages about HIV / AIDS; it is a dangerous silence, so loaded with frustration and impotence that the spoken word cannot, for some, encompass the magnitude of fear that surrounds HIV / AIDS in Southern Africa. Silence, often disguised as disbelief and interpreted as ignorance, is a widely accepted alternative to facing the consequences of disclosure.

Nthombi, a central character from *A Red Ribbon Around My House* (Rankoane 2001), expresses her fear of disclosure when she says 'In our black community (Soweto, South Africa) when you come out and say you are HIV-positive it is the end of you. We don't want you next to us. We don't want to hear your suggestions. To us you are like a living corpse. You know if I knew I was HIV-positive I could keep it to myself until to the grave.'[1]

Figure 4.1 Pinky Tiro and Nthombi Tiro from *A Red Ribbon Around My House*. Photograph courtesy of *Steps for the Future*. © *Steps for the Future* 2006.

In *Ho Ea Rona* (Phakathi 2001), another documentary film from the *Steps for the Future* collection, Moalosi tells three HIV-positive friends 'You know when you do something with your whole heart and then regret it?' He explains that he had been at an HIV/AIDS workshop where he met a lovely woman, but after disclosing his HIV-positive status on stage she said, 'Don't touch me! I'm scared of you!' Before bursting into tears, Moalosi says, 'I shouldn't have disclosed my status publicly.'[2]

The consequences of the complex choices that people face in relation to the HIV/AIDS pandemic are lost on billboard and other dominant media that aim to educate people about the risks of unsafe sex. As Jane Stadler (2003) argues, the documentaries differ significantly from the approach typically taken in media advocacy and public information campaigns.

While the magnitude of the HIV/AIDS pandemic is clearly beyond the scope of visual anthropology to remedy, this paper offers one way forward as it examines communal practices in film viewing that are mobilizing people against the deathly forms of silence that entrench social suffering. By drawing and expanding on methods from visual anthropology, the paper explores the responses of rural and urban audiences in Lesotho, South Africa, and Mozambique. Media activists with mobile cinema units have brought these audiences documentary films from the *Steps for the Future* collection. Their diverse responses offer compelling ethnographic data about the impact of locally-produced documentary film on people who have limited access to film and forums for HIV/AIDS education. The paper highlights new possibilities and directions for emergent practices in applied visual anthropology and HIV/AIDS media activism more generally.

Background to *Steps for the Future*

The *Steps for the Future* initiative was the idea of Ikka Vehkalahti, documentary commissioning editor at YLE Finnish Broadcasting Company, and South African film-maker, Don Edkins. The project is a unique collaboration between international and Southern African film-makers, and is the largest documentary film project to be undertaken in Africa. Vehkalahti and Edkins have produced thirty-six films, ranging in length from four to seventy-four minutes. The project brought together top documentary professionals to work with the *Steps* participants. Their role was to assist the directors without changing the vision of the film-makers.

The films were produced for national and international television and for nonbroadcast distribution in communities across the region. The collection includes different styles of documentary film including music videos, 'vox pop', cinéma vérité, investigative films, and biographical film. They also use a relatively unexplored type of documentary film-making prevalent in Namibia, Zimbabwe, and Mozambique that Jane Stadler (2003) calls 'real enactment': scripts are drawn from life and acted by the characters themselves. Throughout Southern Africa, nongovernmental organisations, local and provincial health authorities, HIV support groups, community centres, church groups and youth organizations have access to the films, a selection of which are available in fifteen local languages. Additionally, *Steps* has produced a facilitator's guide and impact study.

The strength of the films in the *Steps* collection is that they provoke emotional responses from audience members. As Stadler explains, 'Film engages us physically as well as intellectually in acts of perception, attention, imagining, perspective taking; in the experience of empathy and imagination, in resistance or responses to others that are felt bodily' (2003: 88). The films are intentionally nondidactic for the express purpose of transporting people beyond the spectacle of unimaginative condom demonstrations. Film narratives tell stories that resonate with aspects of people's lived experiences. Because of this, facilitated discussions catalyse discussion about sensitive topics related to HIV/AIDS including gender inequality, sexual practices, confidentiality, trust, poverty, political oppression, racism, fear, stigma, rape, grief, death and illness. Transcriptions of such descriptions reveal the intricate process of decoding film messages in a communal setting where meaning is negotiated and contested through discussion and opinion sharing. Most important, perhaps, transcripts made of such discussions make clear that the sessions encourage people to think critically about the punishing metaphors that are commonly associated with people living with HIV/AIDS (Farmer 1992; Sontag 2002; Weiss 1997) as it is apparent that framing HIV/AIDS within a moral web of blame and punishment contributes to people's fears about being tested, disclosure and associating with HIV-positive people.

Research Methodology

In 2002 I was hired as an anthropological consultant to study the impact of the *Steps* project in Lesotho, South Africa, and Mozambique, countries where many of the films were made. As fieldwork required written and spoken proficiency in Xhosa, SeSotho, Portuguese, English, and Afrikaans, I relied on the impressive capacity of students from my medical anthropology, media anthropology and visual anthropology courses at the University of Cape Town (UCT). In turn, the project provided a unique opportunity for my students to bridge medical, visual, and applied anthropology.

The team conducted research in four Western Cape field sites, facilitated by *Steps* educational HIV/AIDS coordinator, Alosha Rayray. Students kept notes of the discussions, including notation of expressions of laughter, whispering, crying, singing, and silence. Prior to the screenings, students assisted audience members in completing a baseline questionnaire. The survey data collected revealed gaps in knowledge about HIV/AIDS transmission and was used to indicate what needed to be communicated during discussion sessions.

Additionally, we identified and interviewed key informants two weeks after each screening. This enabled us to document the 'afterlife' of a film, the reception of a film's messages after screenings.

Results from the Baseline Study

The results of the surveys in Lesotho and South Africa[3] indicate that, while people understand that HIV is transmitted through sex, many are confused about what constitutes safer sex practices. Misunderstandings include the ideas that anal sex is safe sex, using two condoms is safer than one, lubrication on condoms carries HIV, and that insects can spread the virus. While only a few believed that HIV could be transmitted through sweat and urine, there was general confusion about risks associated with kissing. Confusion exists around parent-to-child transmission and transmission from mother-to-child during breast feeding. There remained confusion about the specifics of transmission, which includes direct blood contact due to cracked nipples as well as the risks with the breast milk itself. These and other results from the baseline study indicate the need for careful ethnographic analysis of what people know, what people say they know, and what people do.

Towards an Applied Visual Anthropology

Visual anthropology provides critical debates about what constitutes ethnographic film (Rouch 1974, Ruby 1975), critiques of 'indigenous media' (Ginsburg 1995), and concise methodological applications of visual media for fieldwork (Collier 1986). However, we have perhaps paid less attention to ways that visual media shifts consciousness and behavioural practices, and how these mechanisms can be used to stem the tide of discrimination and stigma that surrounds HIV / AIDS. For example, while there are some excellent studies emerging from the anthropology of media, visual anthropology still has much to offer in terms of understanding the matrix of mechanisms through which people mediate and incorporate audiovisual messages (Abu Lughod 1999). In *The Anthropology of Media*, Kelly Askew (2002) wrestles with the paradigmatic shifts in audience reception theory from the 'hypodermic needle' model to postmodernist interpretive paradigms. She regards these approaches as the furthest ends of a pendulum swing, and argues that we should bring our theoretical gaze to the centre, where we consider the negotiations that take place between the encoding and decoding of messages, and, in particular, the impact of the fields of power and social relations in which the media is embedded. Drawing on this approach, which challenges both the totalitarian nature of the media and audience agency, my understanding is that people are active agents when viewing films, but that the construction of meaning is a dynamic and continuous process that is overdetermined by the particular structural constraints of a given social and political viewing context.

Given that the HIV infection rate in Southern Africa has not decreased despite safer-sex messages saturating the media, it is easy to critique the 'hypodermic needle' model of reception theory. There are over 28.5 million people living with HIV in Sub-Saharan Africa, that is, nine per cent of the population, and the highest number per capita in the world. People are either actively resisting media interventions or are unable to easily engage in safer-sex practices due to myriad structural constraints identified by the respondents in this paper. These constraints include, but are certainly not limited to, patriarchal social relations, sexual violence, poverty, poor health and nutrition, stigma associated with asking for condom use, and trust in relationships.

It is within the context of these constraints that films in the *Steps for the Future* collection form part of a media advocacy campaign that aims to redress the dominant media's shortcomings, while acknowledging the limitations of such an intervention. Where early campaigns relied on fearful images of death by adopting the skull and crossbones as the symbol of the virus, the films in the *Steps* collection tell positive stories about people living with HIV/AIDS. The initiative provides an amazing opportunity for us to re imagine the value of an applied visual anthropology.

Lesotho

16th September 2002
Dear Sesotho Media,
I am very glad to be taught about HIV/AIDS. Indeed I would like to thank brother Thabo for telling us how he feels and got contact with AIDS. I enjoyed all the films especially about the orphans because it tells all students that they should prefer the school as it is the one that takes a person to the happy future. I would like to see our school having some books about the virus, to help some people who want to know or have more knowledge.
Brother Thabo and his friends are proud of telling people about AIDS and I have chosen his words that 'AIDS does not mean death.' That means people can have long life with AIDS. Well I was very happy for your presentation.
Yours sincerely,

Moaki Monki

In Lesotho, the distribution of *Steps* films is organized by Sesotho Media, a public access media centre in the capital city of Maseru. The centre is equipped with a mobile cinema unit that traverses the rugged terrain of the Lesotho highlands. Sesotho Media works in collaboration with Positive Action, a support group for people living with HIV/AIDS that promotes public awareness through poster campaigns, school programmes, and radio shows. Three members of Positive Action – Thabo Rannana, Thabiso Notusi, and Moalosi Thabane – are also the central characters in Dumasani Phakati's film *Ho Ea Rona* (2002), and the main characters in a new documentary by Teboho Edkins called *Ask Me, I'm Positive* (2003), which tracks the road journey of the three activists. This maverick initiative in film advocacy has enabled Thabo, Thabiso and Moalosi to speak beyond the borders of the films in which they appear.

Ho Ea Rona is a cinéma vérité tour de force. It is popular among audiences for addressing the vulnerability of the first four men in Lesotho to have publicly disclosed their HIV-positive status. The most common response from audience members was that 'to see these men in the flesh' made HIV/AIDS real, that, 'Seeing is believing.'

Is Seeing Believing?

'I don't know what AIDS is. I've never seen it nor have I seen or heard anybody say that they have it. I think I would have to see something ... a person would have to show me something to prove that they have that disease ... I don't know what it looks like.'

Mr Mpela, Maseru

Figure 4.2 Thabo Rannana facilitating film screening for school children in Lesotho. Photograph courtesy of *Steps for the Future*. © *Steps for the Future* 2006.

This statement reflects the contradiction between local narratives of disbelief about the existence of HIV/AIDS and actual knowledge about the grave realities of the virus. Ignorance is often blamed for the high rates of HIV infection. Education therefore, is widely regarded as the appropriate intervention to stem the spread of HIV infection, and to ameliorate such imagined ignorance.

At least three troubling features characterize this perspective. First, it is presumptuous, and usually racist, to assume widespread ignorance. Second, education in the form of information about safer-sex practices rarely articulates with local perceptions of HIV/AIDS in this region. Third, many educated, middle-class people find HIV/AIDS information tiresome: they claim they have no need to practice safe sex because it is 'others' who are at risk, the ignorant and poor. A study conducted among UCT students concerning their perceptions and attitudes about HIV/AIDS led us to formulate the concept of *AIDS Information Fatigue Syndrome* (Levine and Ross 2002).

What I want to highlight here, in part to combat the notion that there are 'ignorant' and 'enlightened' citizens who are differentially at risk for HIV, are the overdeterminations and structural constraints that preclude, for the great majority of people in Southern Africa, the possibility of open dialogue about the virus and the ability to practice safer sex. In Lesotho, for example, the inability to speak about HIV/AIDS results from the stigma and discrimination that are often expressed within a discourse of 'disbelief'. I also want to emphasise very strongly that, in the context of communal viewings, locally-produced documentary films are being used effectively to break these codes of disbelief.

It seemed that *Ho Ea Rona* had fulfilled its destiny when audience members at a screening in Lesotho told me that they did not believe HIV/AIDS existed before they saw the film. However, with further discussion the contradiction between the intensity of fear about HIV/AIDS testing and the concurrent narratives of disbelief became increasingly apparent. A key to understanding the contradictory nature of the discourse appears when Thabo says, 'I had never heard anyone admit that they have this disease, which is strange because it has existed for a long time and killed a lot of people, even here in Mohale's Hoek.' Weighed against the probably conservative statistic of 240,000 people living with HIV in a country with 2.1 million people, the narrative of 'disbelief' is a complex linguistic tactic of denial used to deflect knowledge about, and association with, the virus. Therefore, the perlocutionary force of documentary film language creates a critically important space for people to hear others admit that they are HIV-positive. This admission in turn creates the conditions in which socially prescriptive utterances of silence and denial due to stigma can be redressed.

In Mohale's Hoek, Peace Corps workers from the United States assisted Sesotho Media, and in spite of the intense heat inside the community hall, the audience was enthusiastic and participatory. Twenty-year-old Thabo

Mokhele said, '*Ho Ea Rona* impressed me because it was the first time that I had seen someone say "I am HIV-positive", not just in the movie, but actually being there and saying it like that.' The reinforcing of the reality of HIV/AIDS, first through documentary and then through direct contact with the characters, played a major part in Thabo's decision to be tested.

Mpolokeng Peo, an eighteen-year-old woman appreciated *Ho Ea Rona* due to the film shifting her perceptions about men and HIV. She said, '*Ho Ea Rona* impressed me ... because it was boys and usually boys would be shy to disclose their status about this kind of thing. I think a boy would rather go around spreading this thing than actually taking responsibility of doing what these guys are doing.'

The contradiction inherent in Mpolokeng's words is revealing. Here, she acknowledges the courage of the men in *Ho Ea Rona*. In previous remarks, she denied that HIV exists. Yet Mpolokeng could not recognise the mens' courage unless she first understood the social consequences of disclosing, and those consequences are comprehensible only to someone who knows that HIV exists. The association of the virus with pollution and promiscuity indicates that high levels of stigma operate alongside narratives of disbelief. In some instances people who are afflicted with HIV/AIDS are said to suffer from TB or cancer, diseases which carry less metaphorical weight (Sontag 2002, Weiss 1997). In *A Red Ribbon Around My House*, Pinky explains, 'Nobody talks the truth that my sister, my brother, my son, or my daughter died of AIDS. They always have an excuse like it's TB or it's pneumonia'. These linguistic tactics, which are challenged in the films and during facilitated sessions, distance people from the virus.

The Afterlife of Film

I use the concept of a film's 'afterlife' to refer to the social networks through which film messages are communicated during conversations.[4] In order to track these social networks, we first interviewed audience members and later the people with whom they spoke. We found women who had discussed the issues with their children, some children who had spoken with their parents, and, in a few instances, women who had spoken with their husbands. Speaking about HIV/AIDS within the family context is not an unimportant intervention when positioned against the normative silence around sex and HIV/AIDS within families.

In Lesotho as in South Africa we found that strong film characters gave youths the confidence to speak with their parents about HIV/AIDS. 'I didn't tell my mother in detail,' said Thabo, 'but one of the women who had gone to the screening told her and I think she might have told her what the movies were about.' While youths told us how difficult it is to speak with their parents about HIV/AIDS, they also expressed concern for their parents, and hoped that there would be special screenings for them. A teenage boy said:

At home I told my siblings because I think they are old enough to talk about HIV/AIDS. I also told them I saw people who have AIDS. They didn't believe me so I told them to go and ask another girl who stays nearby and when they found out that I wasn't lying they were shocked and they expressed an interest to see these films ... I also told my mother and she was also amazed that I had actually seen HIV-positive people. She was interested to know whether these boys had told their parents and how their parents had reacted, but I told her that even one guy's mother appeared in the movie and she was supportive of her son and this seemed to make her happy.

Thabo Mokhele told a close friend about *Ho Ea Rona* because he wanted his friend to know how serious the virus is:

I told my friend who is usually not interested in HIV/AIDS because he says that this thing doesn't exist. Me and other young people in my village usually organize dramas which we go around showing to people to educate them about HIV/AIDS but he doesn't do this with us. When I told him about what we saw the other day when you came, he showed an interest in seeing the movies ... and I assured him that the mobile movie is going to come back to Mohale's Hoek and he said I should tell him so that he can also come and watch these movies. We talked at length about AIDS and when I asked him what he would do if he got infected he said he would never get such a disease and I told him I wish he could have been there to see those guys who are infected and how they deal with it when they are infected ... he is quite a ladies man, my friend.

Figure 4.3 Teboho Edkins filming *Ask Me I'm Positive* in Lesotho. Photograph courtesy of *Steps for the Future*. © *Steps for the Future* 2006.

Thabo Mokhele said that after he saw *Ho Ea Rona* he felt empowered by having accurate information to share, and that he was keen to become a youth HIV/AIDS activist. Another youth named Mathulo Thulo from Mohale's Hoek said, 'I spoke to the people, including the youth at my village who had not attended the screening because I want all of us to know about this so that we can all work together to fight this thing.'

In Matukeng a 28-year-old woman named Matanki told her friends that she had seen 'people who are not infected actually eating and having a good time together with people who are HIV-positive.' She calls the virus *mokakallane oa setlabocha*, meaning 'a contemporary killer disease'. The chief of Matukeng, Masechaba Letuka, explained that the most common name for HIV/AIDS is *koatsi ea mosolla tlhapi*, meaning 'a disease from abroad'. These names are important in that they challenge the common assumption that rural people conflate symptoms of HIV with those of TB, when in fact, the association is often a way to protect the afflicted from accusations associated with HIV/AIDS-related illness (Farmer 1992).

In Lesotho, as in South Africa and Mozambique, people responded to Pinky, the charismatic character who discloses her status against the wishes of her daughter Nthombi. One young man in Mohale's Hoek said:

> I was impressed by *Red Ribbon* the most because of the way that lady accepted herself even though she is HIV-positive, and especially because her daughter was embarrassed about her mother's status…I learnt that a person should accept him or herself and I hope that if I should ever come out with an HIV-positive test that I will have the courage to do what those guys (who disclose in *Ho Ea Rona*) are doing.

Mpolokeng, a young woman in the audience said:

> If I had tested positive before the screening I think I would have commit suicide because I wouldn't have known how to deal with it, but from the screening I learnt that it doesn't have to be the end of the world. I think that I am now no more afraid to go for a test and if I do and I come out HIV-positive I hope I would have the courage to disclose like the people in those films.

The seeds of widespread HIV awareness and activism are evident from these responses to the films, which is encouraging when we consider the impact of HIV/AIDS activism south of Lesotho, in South Africa.

South Africa

In the biographical film *It's My Life* (Tilley 2001), activist Zackie Achmat declares, 'HIV/AIDS is the new struggle in South Africa.' As founder of the Treatment Action Campaign (TAC), Achmat has rallied national and international support for the struggle to provide affordable anti-retroviral medication, and nevirapine therapy for HIV-positive pregnant women. At the time of filming, Achmat refused to take anti-retroviral drugs. In an emotional scene from the film he says:

> My decision not to take anti-retrovirals is a very difficult decision for me to have made because I can tell you just from last week when I couldn't speak and my mouth was very sore I wanted to say maybe I should take medication...but our politics have become generally empty of moral content … In terms of the majority of people with HIV, they don't have a face, they don't have the political understanding, they are desperate, they are poor, they are alone, and to advocate for their medicines is a very difficult task for all of us, but for me personally with HIV, as someone who can access medication through friends and medical aid … I can't look them in the eye when I take medicine and I know they're going to die because they can't get medicine, and I cannot lead them if that is the case. I want the right to life for myself, but I want to live in a political community in which that right is extended to every person. If such a political community does not exist and the only reason that you die is because you are poor when you're sick, then I do not want to be part of such a community.[5]

Set against what Nicoli Nattrass (2001) calls the 'genocidal' response of South African President Thabo Mbeki to the HIV/AIDS pandemic, Achmat's unflinching support has provided incentive for HIV activists to mobilize countrywide. It is within this political context in South Africa that *Steps* is working.[6]

Zwelethemba Township

Zwelethemba residents are remembered nationally for being among the most active fighters against apartheid (Ross 2003), and many are currently at the forefront of HIV/AIDS campaigns. Some have set up informal 'clinics' that care for the ill, while others lead training workshops in safer sex practices. In 1997, when I conducted fieldwork on child labour in the township, no one spoke about HIV/AIDS. Eight years later, however, as Pinky from *A Red Ribbon* phrases it, the subject is 'on everybody's lips'. In Zwelethemba we found people working in local organisations, educating through workshops and discussion groups. Our *Steps* screening attracted a number of community workers who now use the films in their own outreach programmes. In spite of the general sense of awareness in Zwelethemba, fear of disclosure and gender discrimination continue to dominate group discussions. The films *A Red Ribbon Around My House* (Rankoane 2001) and *Mother to Child* (Lipman 2001)[7] sparked much debate and open discussion about the impact of stigma for people living with HIV/AIDS.

Based on survey findings, only a very small percentage of people are unaware that HIV is transmitted through sex. Such findings contradict the common assertion that people are ignorant about the reality of HIV/AIDS. Respondents said that they received information about HIV/AIDS from television and radio programmes. However, while these survey results indicate that participants know that HIV is transmitted through sex, several people, including HIV/AIDS educators, were confused about what constitutes safer-sex practices. For most audience members, our film screening was the first time they had participated in open discussions about intimate sexual practices.

Activists in Zwelethemba appreciated the detailed nature of our baseline study, and said that they felt more confident and equipped to educate people in the township after the facilitated session.

Nyanga Township

It was late on a Sunday afternoon in May when we arrived in Nyanga Township, near Cape Town, to show *Let's Talk About It* (2001)[8] and *A Red Ribbon* to fifty members of a youth congregation. Sithunyiwe Gece , the director of *Let's Talk About It*, which was filmed in Nyanga, was present. The documentary uses a vox pop style of interviewing, which captures quick responses to questions about condom use, testing and disclosure. The film provoked a useful discussion about condom use. A girl of fourteen said about boys, 'They say they feel nothing. They fear it. When I engage in sexual intercourse I don't use a condom. I'm afraid.' A boy of fifteen responded, 'I want to use a condom, but I think my girlfriend won't.' Another boy raised his hand, 'I want to defend men. If I meet a girl and I say "Let's use a condom", she will say, "Don't you trust me?" Should I tell her that I don't trust her because AIDS/HIV is there?' Among students at UCT, trust is the principal barrier against condom use , and it is evident that trust works negatively in this context (Levine and Ross 2002).

Condom negotiation is a complex process embedded in insecurity, gender roles and expectations, peer and economic pressure, power, and, not least, sexual pleasure. One youth said that he would not use condoms because it constricted his penis in such a way that 'it cannot breathe.' In *A Red Ribbon* the same concern is uttered to Pinky during a workshop with miners, to which she responded that we breathe through our nose, and not our penis. A boy asked if it is safer to use two condoms at once, and another asked if it was necessary to use condoms when you are already HIV-positive. Another asked if men can cure themselves of AIDS by sleeping with young children or virgins. These questions highlight the importance of facilitated sessions for clarifying the misinformation that people have about HIV transmission, and raise serious questions about the nondidactic nature of the films in contexts where facilitation is not an option.

In response to *Let's Talk About It*, youths expressed their fear of being tested. One said, 'If you are HIV-positive, people will treat you differently … From the beginning HIV/AIDS has been presented as a thing of taboo … It's because of fear and ignorance that people show disdain towards HIV-positive people. HIV/AIDS runs parallel to death.'

Children moved from one subject to the next; they focused on their fears about speaking with their parents. A young woman in the congregation explained to Alosha: 'As black people, it's very difficult to sit down and discuss sex with our parents. Our parents are not highly educated. If a child asks, "What will happen if I sleep with a boy?" it's like an insult to our parents. Our parents have a fear that if they talk about it, it will be as if they encourage us to have sex.'

Several of the young girls identified with Nthombi in *A Red Ribbon* and felt that Pinky was selfish in her public disclosure, particularly in church. Interestingly, in Pinky's relationship with her daughter traditional roles are reversed; it is the *daughter's* sense of propriety that creates the conflict. Sitting in church, the youths reflected on Pinky's decision to disclose in church. One youth said, 'The Church should play a major role in the fight against HIV/AIDS. HIV-positive people are church members. Youth should come out and talk about AIDS and the Church should provide support, organize workshops, and talk about it at Sunday school.'

Others in the congregation supported Nthombi. One said, 'If you come out in church, they will see you as a sinner.' Another replied, 'The minister himself should talk about AIDS and sex so that our stubborn parents can hear about it.' A young man interjected that sometimes people hide their status from the church. He said, 'Church members will know about it only after a death. Even their families don't know about it.' A young boy said, 'If we, youth, were trustworthy, if I tell someone about my status it's like burning myself alive for that will spread all over.' Somebody else said, 'People choose whose funerals to attend. If they know that you were HIV-positive, they won't attend your funeral.' For some on that day, the facilitated screening provided a starting point for dialogue and a way forward.

In Conclusion: Mozambique

This concluding section of the paper focuses on a particular outdoor night-screening in Xai Xai, a village approximately three hundred kilometers from the capital city of Maputo. This particular screening demonstrates the success of local cinema to engage audiences, and it also provides a unique opportunity to compare the audience's response to *A Miner's Tale*[9] with the box office hit *Harry Potter and the Chamber of Secrets*, which was screened on the same night. *A Miner's Tale* focuses on the tragic tale of Joaquim, a miner who returns to Mozambique after thirteen years and informs his wife that he is HIV-positive, and that he cannot have more children with her. *Harry Potter* is a story about magical children who can fly on broomsticks among other fantastical things.

The Ufficio di Cooperzione per lo Sviluppo (UTL), an Italian corporation equipped with an impressive mobile cinema unit, is currently screening *Steps* films in rural Mozambique along with international feature films. As seven of the thirty-six *Steps* films were made in Mozambique, it has been a priority to establish routes for nonbroadcast distribution in the country and to assess their impact.

Our night arrival in Xai Xai was stupendous. Flanked by tall palm trees, the crew members of the UTL filmed the audience using digital video cameras that were connected to a very large screen. The audience consisted of approximately eight hundred people, many standing together, holding hands, and dancing. Their delight was apparent as they watched themselves projected high in the sky.

The UTL is currently running an experiment that aims to document the reception of international cinema in rural Mozambique. UTL director of culture and education explained the corporation's desire to introduce rural people to 'other ways of life.' *Harry Potter* is just one of the messengers of 'civilization'. Other ambassadors include *Laurel and Hardy* and *Crocodile Dundee*. Not too surprisingly, follow-up interviews with Xai Xai residents indicate that while they identified with Joaquim from *A Miner's Tale*, they

Figure 4.4 An outdoor screening for a community in Mozambique. Photograph courtesy of *Steps for the Future*. © *Steps for the Future* 2006.

felt confused about the message of *Harry Potter*. Audience members tried to make a connection between the films about HIV and *Harry Potter*. A few people worried that the Italian government was somehow involved in forcing them to consult western doctors. Given the imperialistic nature of the UTL 'experiment', this is not too far-fetched. It could be argued that local interpretations of *Harry Potter* were linked to understandings about the relationship between illness, black magic, and cultural imperialism in the form of national health policies that undermine the centrality of traditional healers. Some media theorists argue for a centrist notion of meaning creation where meaning is a negotiated practice between production and reception; this case suggests that the meaning of a film can be created quite apart from the intention of the film-maker (Askew 2002). Members of the UTL team anticipated that the 'educational' *Steps* films would bore rural audiences, and that what they really wanted were 'entertaining' films. They explained that the international films were a 'reward' for sitting

Figure 4.5 Crew of *A Miner's Tale*. Photograph courtesy of *Steps for the Future*. © *Steps for the Future* 2006.

through the documentaries. Contrary to their expectations, villagers spoke in familiar and enthusiastic terms about *A Miner's Tale*. *Harry Potter* perplexed, but *A Miner's Tale* resonated with their lives.

Joaquim's story brings together local experiences of migrant labour, including the separation and often troublesome reincorporation of family members, HIV/AIDS, questions of transnational polygamy, and the role of traditional healers. In one scene, Joaquim is advised by a traditional healer to sleep with his wife without a condom. The healer says that if his marriage is based on trust he will not infect his wife. Joaquim's wife has waited thirteen years for his return and is desperate to have another child. Joaquim informs the healer that HIV is transmitted through unprotected sex, and that it is 'contagious'.

In Xai Xai, villagers related to Joaquim's predicament. As one woman told us:

> There was a man living here who told his wife that he was not well. The wife spoke to her family and said her husband is not well. The mother and grandmother came to speak with him. Then he left Mozambique to see his wife in South Africa. The wife died of AIDS in South Africa. Then he told his wife here about it. Three weeks later he died. The wife went back to her family's home. She was pregnant and died three weeks later.

'Joaquim', said one young boy, 'taught us how to prevent getting HIV/AIDS'; and a man said, 'We prefer educational movies. We want a message. We prefer it to the beautiful films that don't have a message. I liked *A Miner's Tale* because it taught me something.' 'If I find out that my husband is HIV-positive' said a woman, 'I will not sleep with him unless we use a condom. That is what I learnt from the film.'

The UTL has a copy of our Impact Study, and is working with local anthropologists to further investigate the complexity of the relationship between film messages and audience response to those messages. Through the simple act of speaking to people about their responses to the films, we were able to successfully apply methods from visual anthropology.

This paper can be regarded as an entry point to thinking creatively about the ways that visual anthropology can contribute towards the erasure of stigma, discrimination, and fear that surrounds the HIV/AIDS pandemic. It is my hope that this paper will inspire further research in the area of visual anthropology vis à vis the global HIV/AIDS pandemic and encourage film-makers and visual anthropologists to produce films that tell local stories in local languages about people living with HIV/AIDS.

Notes

1. *A Red Ribbon Around My House* by Portia Rankoane, South Africa 2001, 26 minutes.
    A mother and daughter are in crisis because of their different responses to AIDS. Pinky, flamboyant and loud, lets everybody know she is HIV-positive. Her daughter, Nthombi, strives to be like everyone else. Her mother's courageous and touching refusal to be quiet or passive in the face of AIDS sets them apart. Pinky unapologetically acknowledges the difficulties her openness poses for her daughter. Throughout, her sense of humour and zest for life are apparent. We leave the film with Pinky doing what she does best – living.
2. *Ho Ea Rona (We Are Going Forward)* by Dumisani Phakathi, Sesotho Media Lesotho 2002, 17 minutes.
    Short film about four HIV-positive friends: Thabiso was a national boxer; Thabo is a DJ; Bimbo is an intellectual; and Moalosi an AIDS activist. They meet to reflect on their lives, to cry, but, most importantly, to laugh.
3. Due to the nature of screenings in Mozambique we were unable to conduct a baseline study.
4. On average eighty people attended screenings; on average audience members spoke to ten others. Each screening impacts on about eight hundred people.
5. Zackie Achmat is an AIDS activist. After defeating the multinational drug companies, he takes on the South African government for its confusing policies around HIV/AIDS.
6. In South Africa, film dubbing reflects the most commonly spoken languages: Zulu, Xhosa, SeSotho, Setswana, English, and Afrikaans.
7. *Mother to Child* by Jane Thandi Lipman, Current Affairs Films, South Africa 2001, 44 minutes.
    The prevention of mother-to-child transmission of HIV – the statistics, the people – come vividly to life in this astounding documentary, which follows the lives of two pregnant and HIV-positive women fortunate to be on a drug trial at the Chris Hani Baragwanath Hospital in Soweto. The film charts the lives of Pinkie and Patience as they approach the delivery of their babies. It reveals their expectations, hopes, and inevitable fears concerning not only the health of their babies, but the trauma around the disclosure of their status to their families and partners.
8. *Let's Talk About It* by Sithunyiwe Gece, Day Zero Film and Video, South Africa 2001, 8 minutes.
    The film reflects prevailing attitudes towards HIV/AIDS in the townships of Cape Town. It looks at young people's perceptions of HIV/AIDS and the challenges they face in practicing safer sex.
9. *A Miner's Tale* by Nic Hofmeyr and Gabriel Mondlan, Cool/Uhuru Pictures, Mozambique/South Africa, 40 minutes.
    Joachim is a migrant labourer who is torn between his responsibilities for his junior wife in South Africa and his senior wife and family in Mozambique. When visiting his home village after a long absence, he is torn between his understanding of the responsibilities of his HIV status and what traditional society expects of him. He has to make a choice: he cannot please and protect everybody at the same time.

Bibliography

Abu-Lughod, L. 1999. 'The Interpretation of Culture(s) after Television', in S.B. Ortner (ed.), *The Fate of Culture: Geertz and Beyond*. Berkeley: University of California.

Askew, K. and R.R. Wilk, (eds). 2002. *The Anthropology of Media*. Oxford: Blackwell Publishers.

Collier, J. and M. Collier. 1986. *Visual Anthropology: Photography as a Research Method*. Albuquerque: University of New Mexico Press.

Farmer, P. 1992. *AIDS and Accusation: Haiti and the Geography of Blame.* Berkeley: University of California.

Ginsburg, F. 1995. `Mediating Culture: Indigenous Media, Ethnographic Film and the Production of Identity' in L. Devereaux and R. Hillman (eds), *Fields of Vision: Essays in Film Studies, Visual Anthropology, and Photography.* Berkeley: University of California Press.

Helman, C. 1997. *Culture, Health and Illness. An Introduction for Health Professionals.* Oxford: Butterworth Heinemann.

Levine, S. and F. Ross. 2002. 'Perception of Attitudes to HIV/AIDS among Young Adults in Cape Town', *Social Dynamics* 28 (1): 1–19. Cape Town: Centre for African Studies, University of Cape Town.

Nattrass, N. 2001. 'Ethics, Economics and AIDS Policy in South Africa', *CSSR Working Paper No. 1.* Cape Town: Centre for Social Science Research, University of Cape Town.

Ross, F. 2003. *Bearing Witness: Women and the Truth and Reconciliation Commission in South Africa.* London: Pluto Press.

Rouch, J. 1974. 'The Camera and the Man', *Studies in the Anthropology of Visual Communication* 1 (1): 37–44.

Ruby, J. 1975. 'Is an ethnographic film a filmic ethnography?', *Studies in the Anthropology of Visual Communication* 2 (2): 104–11.

Sontag, S. 2002. *Illness as Metaphor and AIDS and Its Metaphors.* Harmondsworth: Penguin Books.

Stadler, J. 2003. 'Narrative, Understanding and Identification in *Steps for the Future HIV/AIDS Documentaries*', *Visual Anthropology Review* 9 (1 and 2): 86–101.

Weiss, M. 1997. 'Signifying the pandemics: metaphors of AIDS, cancer, and heart disease', *Medical Anthropology Quarterly* 11: 456–476.

Filmography

Harry Potter and the Chamber of Secrets. 2002. C. Columbus. Warner Brothers (Los Angeles). 115 minutes.

Ask Me, I'm Positive. 2004. T. Edkins. Not currently in distribution. Contact Day Zero Film and Video (Cape Town). [http://www.dayzero.co.za/steps/].

Let's Talk About It. 2001. S. Gece. California Newsreel (San Francisco). 8 minutes.

A Miner's Tale. 2001. N. Hofmeyr and G. Mondlan. California Newsreel (San Francisco). 40 minutes.

Mother to Child. 2001. J. Thandi Lipman. California Newsreel (San Francisco). 44 minutes.

Ho Ea Rona. 2002. D. Phakathi. California Newsreel (San Francisco). 17 minutes.

A Red Ribbon Around My House. 2001. P. Rankoane. California Newsreel (San Francisco). 26 minutes.

It's My Life. 2001. B. Tilley. California Newsreel (San Francisco). 74 minutes.

Steps for the Future films are distributed by: California Newsreel, P.O. Box 2284, South Burlington, VT 05407.

Chapter 5

BODYWORK
Social Somatic Interventions in the Operating Theatres of Invasive Radiology

Christina Lammer

Prologue

In this chapter the mutual connectedness of bodies and imaging technologies is discussed in the biomedical context of interventional radiology – a process that renders the blood flow visible, thus enabling diagnosis and therapeutic treatment. During the course of my fieldwork in the radiology department at the Medical University Vienna (MUV), I spoke to fifteen radiologists and fifteen or so medical technical assistants about their professional backgrounds, their work, their daily routines, and their experiences with patients. I was primarily interested in how radiological personnel perceive and define 'contact' as it relates to their interaction with patients. Do they consider that having contact with patients is important? If so, what kind of contact is possible and/or indeed necessary? Is contact established mainly through verbal communication? Or do they see interaction with patients in more multisensual terms? This being the case, what sensual realities are at work in a radiology unit? With regard to the latter, and as I quickly realized whilst conducting research in this particular medical milieu, the task of 'translating' these more tactile sensations into words – both on the part of the researcher and the researched – make the limits of spoken language painfully obvious.

What are the main applied aspects of my research – not only in interventional radiology but also in other biomedical areas and in interdisciplinary clinical teams, where I work with audiovisual media? How can results of my fieldwork activities, which are basically dealing with nonverbal interactions, be communicated back to the clinic personnel in a way that will enable them to be aware of, reflect on, and modify their practices? These questions are particularly challenging within my

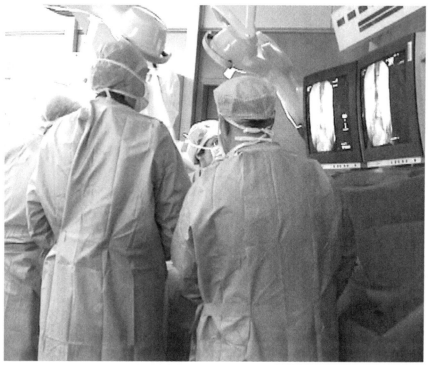

© Christina Lammer 2006

ethnographic interventions in the context of this university hospital. Health professionals (at least at the MUV) have a particular scientific culture. For them statistics and quantitative research methods are central and as such part of their education. Many of them do not quite understand what I am doing and what my (qualitative) scientific approach is about. Before I – in the role of an ethnographer – can talk about scientific aims, objectives and results, I need to explain to them what ethnographic research is, why the use of audiovisual media and other tools and fieldwork devices is important for the investigation of questions about embodiment of knowledge, nonverbal interaction in a surgical theatre, perception of medical images and embodied experiences of being a patient. Only once these 'cultural barriers' are overcome (I discuss my communication strategies with clinical staff and patients in more detail below) are further exchange of information and the mediation of results in multimedia workshops with physicians, technical assistants and nurses possible. Through this I aim to provide 'sensory routes to both researching and representing other people's experiences' (Pink, 2005). Chalfen and Rich (this volume) note, 'The purpose of the applied visual anthropologist is to offer production experience and socio-cultural sensitivity to the visual representation of human experience, and exert skills in presenting the audiovisual information to implement social change'. This goes hand in hand with sharpening my own awareness as an ethnographer of what clinicians and patients need to strengthen their work together as equal partners.

Thus I suggest a process-oriented ethnographic approach, working with my own body, sensitivities and experiences in different biomedical contexts, exploring sensitive depths of people at the hospital with whom I not only closely work together but share research interests. Bodywork in this sense is always reciprocal: creating distance and proximity in a particular sociocultural space, navigating through everyday necessities and routines, dealing with existential dramas of life and death.

Word Flows

In this paper, as in my fieldwork, I adopt a multisensual approach, drawing on visual material that I myself produced whilst in the field (Howes 2003; Seremetakis 1994; Buck-Morss 1994; Stoller 2004; Taussig 1992; Marks 2000; MacDougall 1998). This consists of video footage taken with a digital camera whilst doing 'participant observation' in the operating theatres of invasive radiology. The resulting experimental video piece, *Making Contact,* allows me to 'unfold' the human body, revealing – alongside the network of arteries and veins digitally captured in fluoroscopy images – the body's somewhat more elusive assemblage of sentient layers and emotional depths. Key to this dual act of revealing is that in the production of ethnographic data – be it whilst speaking, writing, videotaping, or conducting any other research activity – I incorporate my own bodily sensations. This integration of the subjective and the personal, and my attempt to externalize what I am feeling, sets up an interesting dialogue between the introspective processes of bodywork and the ongoing drama of the operating theatre. Though this kind of physical and sensual workout that takes place, in part, in front of an editing monitor, and that transforms the digital video camera into a kind of prosthesis, might seem unusual for a fieldworker, I maintain that any information that my body cannot remember and make sense of is of little value given the phenomenological approach to embodiment that I see as central to my work.

In my collaboration with physicians the video footage is used as a mirror. This can cause both emotional reactions and painful effects on the part of clinical personnel. Seeing oneself in a mirror is often an uncomfortable experience. We had workshops and seminars at the interventional radiology department, where people would start to defend themselves. It was too hard for them to watch video pictures of themselves working with patients in one of the operating theatres. Screening research material back to my project partners and informants at the hospital involves a clear distinction between levels of content. It differentiates between how we react when we see ourselves on a video screen, perceiving images of the 'own person', and analyzing the same pictures from a more distanced perspective, focusing on structures such as nonverbal interactions with patients, clothing rituals and their sociocultural meanings, embodiment of knowledge in a surgical theatre, skin as an organ of contact as well as modes of communication. Using audiovisual devices at a hospital and discussing ethnographic footage with health professionals, who want to improve their own practices, requires introducing them to the meanings and functions of mirror images within this highly crafted and experimental applied ethnographic approach.

During my first stage of fieldwork in the radiology department, I quickly realized that time and space meant something quite different in this particular medical context. As I mirrored those involved in the routines of diagnosis and treatment at the hospital, my own movements mimetically took on their bodily rhythms, and my sense of timing fell into synch with their time frequencies. I constantly felt under pressure: perhaps because my own tasks as a fieldworker required a different form of time management from that of my informants; perhaps because I had lost my sense of orientation the moment I began research at the hospital. I could hardly find my way from the core of the radiology unit – a small kitchen where personnel make coffee and take their lunch breaks – to the examination rooms, which are located a mere twenty steps away, or the computer tomography (CT) centre. In addition to affecting the way I physically moved through time and space, the fast-paced environment and my general sense of disorientation within it made me feel as if words and sentences sped up during interviews.

Radiology patients are perceived as 'passengers.' Though they spend a relatively short period of time in the diagnostic department, radiologists tend to agree that personal contact with patients is necessary: 'The contact with patients is important for the diagnosis. Looking at him, talking with him … one gets an impression of how the patient is … Where does it hurt? Where is he swollen? For the anamnesis[1] one has to question the patient, how the complaints look like.' However, as this experienced radiologist goes on to suggest, such contact is hard to achieve:

> Radiology is a special discipline because patients spend only limited time with us. We are not their treating doctors … They are passengers in our area. One develops hardly any contact. … That's dependent on the diagnostic method. I mean for a thorax X-ray we don't have any contact. Assistants would perform the procedures. The patient is already away when I see the pictures. Whereas with ultrasound physicians work directly on the patient. CT scans is another application where one has hardly contact with patients. Fluoroscopy imaging has to be conducted by oneself, which means that one also has contact with the patient during the examination. Mammography is a further crucial area. It's always dependant on the particular method.[2]

In other words, the patients' impressions and experiences are not fully taken into account in radiology because of the limited period of time they spend with radiological personnel. In this way, they are reduced to mere informants with regard to their diagnosis, as opposed to active participants in the process. Conversations with the examining doctor tend to be dry and to the point, with the result that somatic feelings of illness and non-well-being – anything that goes beyond the strict medical 'facts' – are hardly mentioned. A clear-cut discourse based on what a patient's complaint 'looks like' structures the relationship between patients and physicians, and this is particularly true in the realm of radiological diagnosis. This obvious hierarchy of the senses, with its privileging of the visual, can be attributed to the fact that radio-diagnostic techniques are image based. Thus, verbal and personal contact with patients plays a minor role in a radiology department, even though communicating with the patient is understood to be an important aspect of diagnosis according to most of the radiologists I interviewed. This is particularly true when it comes to an anamnesis, where an analysis of the images alone does not provide all the information required to fulfill the various procedures. However, the following quotation hints at just what kinds of procedures are being referred to by radiologists when they suggest this need for more personal contact:

> I meant personal contact. That one with the patient ... I ask the patient what complaints he has before and during I make an ultrasound or X-rays of the stomach. 'Where does it hurt?' Then one very often gets the stupidest answers. They would say, 'I have a gastritis.' I would respond that, 'I don't want to know whether you have a gastritis but rather which complaints you have.' The contact with patients can be difficult and misleading but it is very important for the funding procedures. ... When one recognizes something, then he says that he had a fracture there, things become clearer.[3]

Clearly, this radiologist sees patients harshly. Furthermore, his cynical take on the patient's actual input *through* 'personal contact' does little to challenge the already objectified status assigned to patients by the medical establishment. Reinforcing the hierarchical relationship that exists between doctors and their clientele, the aforementioned radiologist – who is one of the most experienced in the department – is mocking of the vocabulary the patient uses to describe his/her complaint. When the patient says, 'I have a gastritis', s/he affirms her right to partake, like her physician, in biomedical notions and definitions of disease. If this represents a passage of transformation of perception and identity for the patient, his/her efforts are not particularly welcome, and nor do they help to narrow the gap between patient and physician. Rather, the patient's attempt to make him/herself understood is seen as a foreign intrusion into the language of medical expertise – the borrowed words and expressions shifting the patient from the personal emotional context of somatic inner experiences (of either well-being or illness) to that of disease and clinical (authoritarian) judgment. If, for the purposes of the radiologist's reports, such statements are useless, they also, somewhat ironically, serve to bolster his status as 'the expert.' This, as Arthur Kleinman (1988: 135) suggests, is because 'physical complaints are authorized.' As he goes on to explain in his book, *The Illness Narratives*, 'The diagnosis is, in fact, a systematic distortion of the interview: only facts that relate to the disease and its treatment are sought, allowed to emerge, and heard.'

One of the radiologists vividly explains how the development and technological advance of diagnostic tools has led to a transformation of social relationships between clinical personnel and patients:

> I try to talk a lot with patients. Speaking with them before their CT and MR scans – not in a situation like today. When I am alone here, then I certainly do this. Then I see every single patient face-to-face and not only in the tube. That's important for everyone. What is left otherwise? Actually a fully dehumanized and empty proceeding. One also comes to know a lot from the patient. They are so important. Yes? It's all about patients, not about myself or the techniques or the particular medical procedure.[4]

During the course of my interviews, a growing and somewhat uncomfortable sense of self-awareness among radiologists became perceptible to me, though just how this manifested itself is difficult to put into words. In an attempt to convey this feeling, I offer here a short anecdote that touches on my own experience of doing participant observation at the CT centre. I then go on to explain how this experience informed subsequent stages of my research process.

Touching Images

> After spending a few days in the CT funding room, as well as observing fluoroscopy imaging of the act of swallowing, and seeing numerous images of tumors in the bowel and other parts of the intestine, these pictures of disease carry on a disturbing afterlife in my dreams. I vividly imagine myself as a cancer patient. My body even produces painful symptoms. A few weeks later I end up seeing a surgeon, who performs a colonoscopy. An endoscope is introduced into my rectum, and a tube travels up my colon. Fortunately, this uncomfortable procedure does not reveal any sign of a malign growth or inflamed tissue. However, in a flash the imaginative power linked to radiological and biomedical procedures become somatically obvious to me. Later, when I recount this moment of revelation to a young radiologist in training in a self-deprecating manner – playing up the element of embarrassment over my own hypochondria – he is not surprised. In fact, he confesses to having had similar experiences when he first began analyzing CT scans.

In her seminal text, *The Body in Pain*, Elaine Scarry (1985: 164–165) suggests 'that "pain" and "imagining" constitute extreme conditions of, on the one hand, intentionality as a state and, on the other, intentionality as self-objectification; and that between these two boundary conditions all the other more familiar, binary acts-and-objects are located. That is, pain and imagining are the "framing events" within whose boundaries all other perceptual, somatic, and emotional events occur; thus, between the two extremes can be mapped the whole terrain of the human psyche.' In the case of my own research, a new awareness that my imagination and anxieties were playing a crucial role during fieldwork and beyond propelled me to rethink my methodological approach and engage with theoretical concepts in such a way as to incorporate these painful experiences by systematically channeling, analysing and multisensually documenting them.

I started doing participant observation in the angiography and interventional radiology operating theatres, using a digital video camera to focus primarily on nonverbal and sensual interactions during diagnostic procedures. In other words, I used (and still use) the camera as prosthesis – as a physical extension of myself. For instance, the zoom technique enabled me to 'dissect reality' analytically, whereas my own body faced operating procedures from a relatively distanced standpoint on what Susan Buck-Morss (1994: 56) has described as an 'anaesthetizing screen.' The camera allows one to take a distanced position from the operating field, protecting oneself from scenes which are emotionally tough to watch. Thus I could document and record what I thought was important in particular situations during the intervention, without harming myself. In fact, Buck-Morss's notion of cinematic bodies and viewers that are 'anaesthetized' because 'both are absent from the scene' is useful to my own thinking around this project.

Thus, within the context of fieldwork where surgical as well as radiological modes of embodiment are observed, bodies and viewers are both present. You could say that my use of a video camera as prosthesis methodologically mirrors diagnostic and therapeutic techniques of the body, as applied in the operating theatre (Mauss 1992: 455–477). Like my camera, X-ray devices produce moving images of staged bodies, and then project these images on screens. In this particular biomedical field of practice, physicians are dealing with two distinct bodies: the flesh-and-blood body, and a body of images. In interventional radiology, the surgeon and the cameraman (director) are one and the same person. Individuals undergoing an operation face the 'prosthetic organ' (Buck-Morss, 1994) of the screen given that most get only a local anesthetic, and can hence watch their inner 'body landscapes' on monitors. The screen as a mirror matters in manifold ways. As such mirrors are used as 'prosthetic' as well as 'anesthetic organs'.

Producing an awareness of how to utilize moving radiology images on monitors for more 'human' work with patients is only one valuable aspect of my collaborative applied ethnography in the context of interventional radiology. What follows is a description and analysis of scenes from the experimental ethnographic video, *Making Contact*. The narrative is divided into five sections: 'Staged Bodies', 'Embodied Knowledge and its Voices', 'Clothing Rituals', 'Eyes-on', and 'Hands-on'. But first, some remarks with regard to the montage itself. The technique I developed for arranging footage was based on a cut-and-paste model: colourful ink print-offs of screenshots were pasted into sections of the black and white video, thus disrupting the usual structural patterns associated with both still and moving images. My aim was to create an experimental approximation of Walter Benjamin's (1963: 31–32) argument that the cameraman and his (sic) filmic apparatus penetrate reality in the same way that the surgeon does.

In terms of the text accompanying these images, the fact that verbal exchanges between people in the operating theatre took place in German meant that I had to translate their conversations into English.[5] Selected excerpts were inserted into handwritten balloons, similar to those used in comic strips. Why this borrowing from the comic strip format? Comics are a playful medium that, in their combination of the visual with text-based narratives, manage to transcend the usual artistic boundaries dividing drawing, painting, photography, film and video. The generation of text is deeply integrated into the imaginative body – the balloons offering the viewer/reader a useful tool with which to navigate narrative storylines. In consciously avoiding computer-based text, I was also aware that I didn't want to create any associations between my work and those medical soaps on TV.

Making Contact

In the operating theatre, the head of the interventional radiology department describes his practice of diagnosis and treatment:

> These are no particular gifts. Most important is to keep one's senses open for anything which could go wrong. Teaching in this field is relatively difficult. In conventional radiology one can show young [colleagues] a system allowing one to analyse an image. ... In interventional radiology I perceive the picture in toto. Similarly I have to observe how the patient behaves. Does he become very quiet? Is breathing difficult for him? Does he start slightly coughing? That's more difficult and complex. I cannot only concentrate on the X-ray, but furthermore keep my eyes, ears and antennas open to the patient. ... Everything is done directly on the patient and the procedures are invasive and most of them include therapeutic aims. Patients have high expectations, are anxious and often very nervous. One has to tell younger colleagues how they should inform patients and what to say. They need to learn to see the patient as an acting person and not only as a material body proper, which they will examine and treat on the following day ... This can cause a problematic exchange. If it is only a standard examination, for which one

does not need full concentration, then talking with the patient is fine. But if it is a more complicated examination, then I have to explain this to the patient: 'I am sorry, but I need full concentration by now, so that I don't make a mistake.' During the intervention most of the patients – they have a lot of expectations and fears – are very quiet anyway. After the examination, they are often astounded, how harmless all this was. Then they start talking and questioning.[6]

The interventional radiologist speaks about the complex interrelatedness of bodies, machines and images in his daily routines. Helpful here is Arthur W. Frank's (1995: 50) notion of the 'communicative body', and his suggestion that, 'The body itself *is* the message; humans commune through their bodies ... Human communication with the world, and the communion this communication rests on, begins in the body.' As minimally invasive operating techniques, diagnosing and treating the blood flow with the help of video fluoroscopy images offers an exciting insight into how such a 'communion' works, emphasizing as it does the mutual connectedness of bodies, material components and machinery in the biomedical context. It also provokes the following five questions: How are bodies staged in the operating theatre? With which voices can bodies speak during this kind of treatment? Which clothing rituals are at work and how can one make sense of the ideological, biopolitical and sociocultural shaping of corporeality in the clinical institution? How is the division of labour between eyes-on and hands-on procedures organized? And how can the video material be mirrored back to the hospital staff?

In attempting to provide some answers to these questions, *Making Contact* (2004) joins a growing corpus of work that applies a multisensual bodily approach to the field of visual anthropology. Its contribution is that it engages all of the senses to tell a story: incorporating touch, taste and smell into a surreal, sterile yet fleshly audiovisual imagination. True, such an undertaking is unavoidably bounded by the audiovisual medium and form. The challenge, thus, is to use this experiment in ethnographic video production to test out and even transcend apparent limitations. 'You ought to tell us how to speak with patients,' commented an interventional radiologist after he and a few of his colleagues saw some of my early footage in one of the department's monthly seminars. You could say that *Making Contact* is my attempt to do just that. However the applied approach I suggest is not simply about telling physicians how to speak with their patients. Video replay can help clinical personnel to improve performance (Wall 2005: 11): 'During a recent six-week experiment called "ACTION!", six radiology residents at McGill University Hospital Center in Montreal were videotaped while discussing cases at teaching rounds. The residents' performances were reviewed and critiqued by an academic radiology "coach", Jeffrey Chankowsky, MD, and then the residents were taped a second time to see if they improved. At the end of the six weeks, the residents' communication skills ranked higher as did their case based knowledge.'

Staged Bodies

Arthur W. Frank (1995: 118) has observed how illness narratives are often framed as 'quest stories', and thus recounted in the form of a journey. I contend that such a framing aptly applies to people undergoing diagnosis and treatment in interventional radiology: the road, in this case, being one that leads them through a number of different stages. Although my focus here is on the part of the journey that finds patients in the operating theatre, one cannot isolate *communicative bodies* in this particular clinical setting from the social and emotional worlds they habitually live in. The storylines I develop in *Making Contact* start in the 'Abliegezone' – a room where patients, confined to hospital beds, are prepared just prior to being wheeled in for their operations.

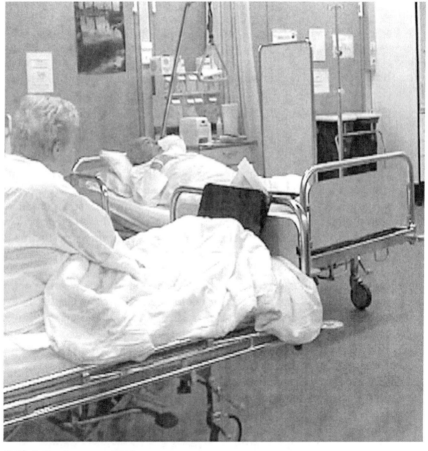

© Christina Lammer 2006.

The word Abliegezone is significant in itself. 'Abliegen' means to 'lie at a distance,' and though there is no exact translation for the word in its entirety, the objectified status of the (sick) person who 'lies at a distance' is implied. After watching the *Making Contact* video, medical technical assistants in the department discussed how they would react if they had to wait for the procedures to begin at the Abliegezone. Their reactions were empathetic and they realized how patients who have to wait in this area feel.

After this period of anxious waiting for the procedure to begin, a male nurse transports the patient to the operating room and gets the patient prepared. People are washed, shaved, positioned on a bed, covered with surgical cloth, and hooked up to sensors and other devices that control bodily functions like breathing and heart rate.

> *Nurse:* Now comes a curtain. You already know this from last time.
> *Patient:* I had this already twice.

The body itself gives hardly anything away. Its shape is artfully concealed. One cannot even localize the person's head or toes beneath the sterile cloth landscape. Only a small square of exposed skin signifies the operating field.

> *Patient:* Through the artery in the liver – the first time one gets a painkiller. Afterwards doctors always want [you to do] without [a painkiller]. But I don't want this. Then they gave me twenty drops.

Through pain and imagining, 'framing events' are created within those boundaries that stage and fix bodies. A 'good story' should be the result of diagnostic and therapeutic operations.

> *Radiologist:* Now you will feel warm again. We will take a control picture. If it does not look beautiful we need to introduce another stent prosthesis.

The patient is dissociated from his or her body during the intervention. Quite literally, s/he *has* a body – a body that is completely in the hands of clinical personnel and technological devices. As Arthur Kleinman (1988: 26) has emphasized, 'Each of us *is* his or her body and *has* (experiences) a body. In this formulation the ... person is the body and also recognizes that he or she has a ... body that is distinct from self and that the person observes as if it were someone else.'

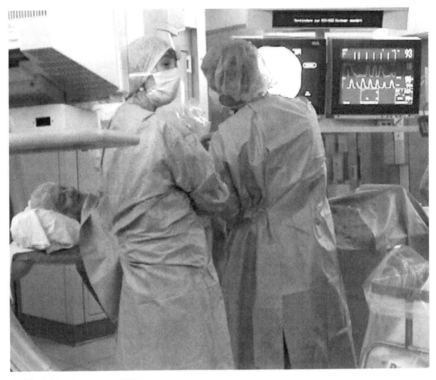

© Christina Lammer 2006.

The body's 'initiation' is performed through the puncturing of an artery. For this the patient gets local anesthesia accompanied by the radiologist's words: 'You will feel a little stitch now.' Henceforth, the exchange between radiologist and patient is reduced to technical explanations, questions and responses pertaining to what is being done. The vocabulary used by the radiologist could just as well be from the field of engineering.

Radiologist: This is quite a plug you have here. Really, it's tough.
Patient: What are we doing now?
Radiologist: Now we are dilating. Immediately you will feel a pressure.
Patient: Yes.
Radiologist: We leave the balloon blown up. Let's see whether it [the blood vessel] remains open. If not, we will put in a stent.

    ...

Radiologist: What sluice is this?
Assistant: A six.
Radiologist: Fits with the stent.

    ...

Radiologist: You will feel warm now [of the contrast, which is introduced in the blood vessel]. We are making a control angiography. Don't move.

Patients undergoing the operation now 'lie at a distance' on the surgery table – their fleshy interiors transformed into abstract X-ray landscapes that appear on a screen before them. Bodies are staged as 'damaged commodities' that, with the help of minimal-invasive devices and embodied techniques, can be fixed.

Embodied Knowledge and Its Voices

In *Transcultural Cinema*, David MacDougall (1988: 53) suggests that, 'We make contact with others not by interpreting the meaning of their conduct, but by imitating what Merleau-Ponty calls a much more generalized postural schema ... This means that in viewing a film a viewer is usually responding not only to the content of images (the postures of the subjects, for example) but also to the postural schema of the film itself, embodying the filmmaker.' Following MacDougall, I argue that what he refers to as the 'phenomenon of physical communion' (ibid.: 52) applies as much to the biomedical practice of (interventional) radiology, as it does to the practice of film-making. Bodies are mutually interpenetrated, leaving deep though invisible somatic traces; filling perception with multisensual flesh.

It is this idea of mutual interpenetration that I want to address now, drawing on Laura Marks's (2000) notions of tactility in her book *The Skin of the Film* to lend texture to my 'thick' descriptions of those surreal landscapes that emerge from the examination/treatment of arteries and veins through various imaging devices and material components, such as metre-long wires, tiny balloons, and catheters. In this particular field of practice, embodiment of knowledge takes place 'under the skin.' The noise of the X-ray machinery almost drowns out the exchange between radiologist and assistant.

Patient:	Until I noticed that there was something wrong I never had complaints during menstruation.
Radiologist:	Mm, did this still hurt?
	...
Radiologist:	Did you feel any improvement since last time [since the last intervention]?
Patient:	It improved ... although because of my diabetes – and the wounds, the wounds are very painful.
Radiologist:	I understand. It's mainly on the right side?
Patient:	[screaming]
Radiologist:	This is a small stitch only – the punctuation.

In the realm of interventional radiology, tactile abilities should be taken seriously. The sense of touch as 'learned' and the whole concept of 'embodied memory' are crucial to this biomedical field of practice. As Laura Marks (2000: 146) explains: 'The interestedness of perception depends upon the memory of what counts as useful information: for example what counts as useful in a given culture will inform whether one perceives an object visually, tactilely, olfactorily, or (usually) in some combination of these and other modalities.' Through learning by doing, young physicians in training simultaneously explore blood vessels with their eyes and their hands, coordinating their somatic repertoire of perception with the tactile qualities of anatomical and pathological bodily exploration. At the start they imitate their teachers. It is through this mimetic process that a sense of embodiment emerges.

> *Radiologist:*   One has to feel tactile resistance. If moving the catheter forward is becoming more difficult, this is an alarming sign. Can I see anything significant on the picture? There is as well something wrong, if the patient is in pain.

During these operations, the bodies of the physicians, assistants and patients are wired up so as to resemble marionettes. The communing body performs a 'secret' choreography in which 'one has to feel tactile resistance' in the arteries and veins as one moves catheters forward, pulls wires out of the body, and inserts stent grafts to keep the blood vessels open. The body, as Marks (2000: 190) suggests, becomes a 'terrain through which we travel.' As she explains: 'Medical technologies such as X-rays, ultrasound, CT scans, and colonoscopy render our viscera visible. They

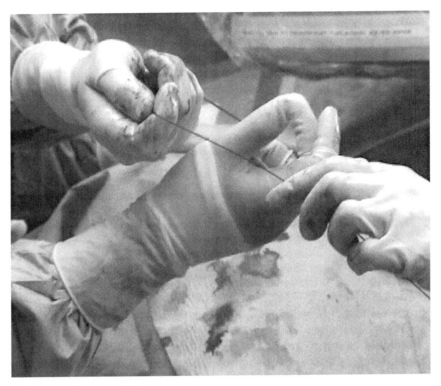

© Christina Lammer 2006.

offer not an embodied visuality, but a visuality that makes our bodies objects to us.' Marks, here, is making reference to the artist Mona Hatoum and her video installation, *Corps étranger* (1996). In this piece, viewers literally travel through Hatoum's body via an endoscopic device attached to an invasive camera eye. According to Marks (ibid.: 190), 'Hatoum can "afford" to treat her body as an object; the effect of this work would be quite different if it were performed with any body but her own.' In my own case, the moving images perceived in the operating theatres of interventional radiology are X-rays of the blood flow. As a layperson, these images haunt me. Devoid of flesh and sinew, the blood vessels look transparent, even ghostly. That said, the patients themselves seem all too aware that what they are seeing on the monitor mirrors the interior of their own body. As regards the overall impact that these images have on patients, it is hard to generalize. Many of the people with whom I have worked have told me, prior to the intervention, that they are not interested in the pictures. However, once they are in the actual situation, they often change their minds. One of the patients – a television journalist – with whom I had intensive contact during one stage of my field research, sent me an email about his experiences:

> Not flesh, not blood, not twitching tissue, angiography images are 'clean' like the pictures of a bomber, which releases a precision bomb. I'm not irritated at all by this. I can look at the pictures during the intervention without feeling tension or nausea. The 'filter' that [means] colour and details are invisible creates calmness and distance. That's what one needs as a patient in this situation. Realizing how the physician manages to penetrate a tough plug in the vessel, setting the balloon, one shares his success. Seeing that the contrast fluid marks the unhindered passage through the former problem zone one experiences incredible relief. In a few minutes only one gets liberated of complaints, which one had for months and made one anxious and depressive. In this moment one experiences an enormous gratefulness.

Interestingly enough, the popular name for the disease that the above patient was being treated for is 'shop window illness' ('Schaufensterkrankheit' in German) – a condition of the leg that makes standing up for long periods of time, and walking great distances, incredibly painful. Window-shopping, obviously, is an activity to be avoided if you suffer from Schaufensterkrankheit.

Unmaking Contact

> Cloth as a metaphor for society, thread for social relations, express[es] more than connectedness ... The softness and ultimate fragility of these materials capture the vulnerability of humans, whose every relationship is transient, subject to the degenerative processes of illness, death, and decay. (Weiner and Schneider 1989: 2)

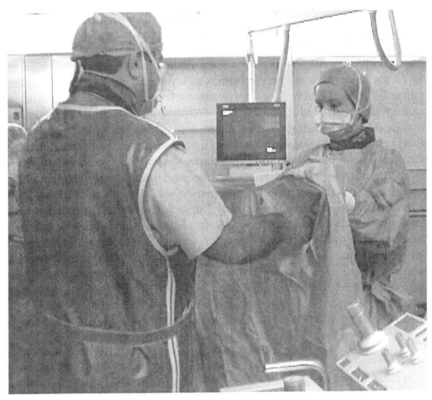

© Christina Lammer 2006.

Clothing Rituals

Cloth has a particular meaning in surgery in general, and interventional radiology specifically. In the section that follows I argue that clothing rituals give the communing body and its staging in the operating theatre its unique sociocultural character. The more a medical practitioner is wrapped in sterile cloth – which is donned with the help of others in a ritualized mode – the more one gets in touch with the patient's body, and the closer one gets to the operating field. Proximity and distance are structured through cleaning rituals involving the body – especially the washing of hands – and through the donning of hygienic clothing. The more cloth one wears, and the more the procedures of pulling on sterile garments are ritualized, the higher up one is in the hierarchical chain of surgical labor.

Sterile clothing rituals are performed like a dance. The patient is already artfully covered with green drapery. Only a small square of skin is exposed – the operating field. According to Drew Leder (1990: 25-27), visceral processes are instances of a 'corporeal disappearance'. For patients undergoing interventional radiology, this corporeal disappearance takes on a different form to that of conventional surgery. Most of those who

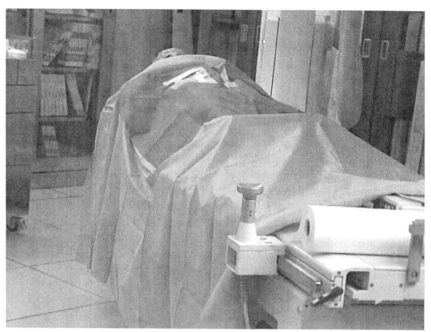

© Christina Lammer 2006.

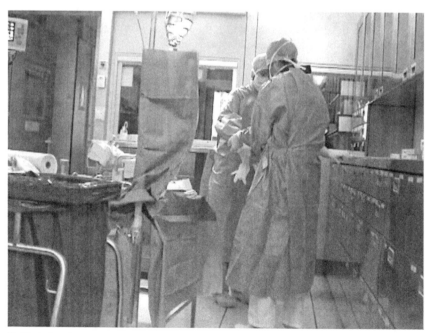

© Christina Lammer 2006.

undergo the former only get a local anesthetic. They consciously experience the whole process: being prepared, hearing the noise of the machinery, seeing the equipment and the material components, waiting for the operator and the medical technical assistant who, after an often considerable delay, finally enter the sterile field. Depending on the nature of the intervention, radiologists either work in conjunction with surgeons or perform the operation on their own. Interventional radiology is one of those fields that transcend disciplinary boundaries.

The more surgical/invasive the procedures are, the more rigidly the body of the operator is enveloped. The cultural development of clothing rituals is embedded in the history of invasiveness within this radiological subdiscipline. Thus, it was not from the beginning that the settings where angiography image-based interventions took place were coded as surgical. Of course, radiological personnel have always had to wear lead aprons in order to protect themselves from diagnostic radiation. However, the sterile field in this area was defined step by step, and still means something quite different from that of conventional surgery. As Katharine Young (1997: 93) elaborates:

> Once I brushed the back of the sleeve of a surgeon's gown with the corner of my notebook and he turned around and snapped, 'Watch out for the sterile field.' The boundaries of the sterile field, palpable and impalpable, are clear to its inhabitants. Along its rim, the field pouches in, as it were, refitting its boundaries around the bodies of the surgical team so that their costumes and accoutrements serve as its finely articulated edges. Surgeons never enter the sterile field in their own bodies. Rather, the boundary of the space is rendered a flexible membrane, which they poke in and which closes around them so that they can manipulate what is inside.

As objects, image devices dominate the creation of the sterile field within most contemporary invasive radiological procedures. Pictures of the body's interior are perceived on monitors and not through surgically cutting into flesh. Tactile epistemology in this particular biomedical field is mediated through digital screenings of the blood flow and other organic inner structures, which are then projected onto TV screens in real time. Thus the sterile field and its boundaries are wired and electronically framed. For this, bodies are washed, prepared, clothed, positioned, staged, moved, touched, perceived, made and unmade in a highly complex choreography.

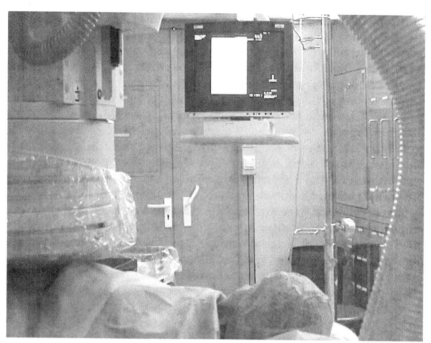

© Christina Lammer 2006.

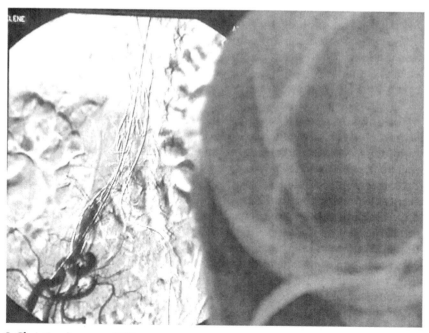

© Christina Lammer 2006.

As it simulates the sterile operating field, the screen has a double function: it works both as 'anesthetic organ', and as 'roadmap'. In this way, it enables radiologists to navigate material components through blood vessels and inner corporeal structures. The wired hands of the operating team seek out their pathways: exploring the carnal terrain beneath the skin; detecting tactile resistances with the help of technologically-rendered moving X-ray landscapes. As such, the sterile field is embedded in continual operations of digitally-mediated simulation. Flesh and blood is simulated on screens in a real time setting, which allows direct manipulation of pathologically defined 'problem zones' inside the patient's body. The epistemological fabric unfolds on video pictures, instead of peeling off skin and tissue.

The radiological gaze explores and palpates the screen as if it were an organ, isolating particular information within complex framing and montage processes. The operator enters after the patient is enveloped and has been properly positioned. One of the medical technical assistants pulls on a sterile surgical gown. S/he will assist the radiologist with the 'hands-on' procedures – passing the catheters, wires and other material components. His or her colleague will take care of the 'eyes-on'[7] operations – the positioning of X-ray tube and monitors, the framing and editing of electronic images during and after the intervention, and bringing over sealed packages of sterile gloves, cloth and other material. In other words, the latter's function is comparable to that of a nurse in conventional surgery.

In order to explain how the 'choreography' that preserves the sterile field in the operating theatre is designed, I offer here a description of some of the video taped scenes from the *Making Contact* footage. Initial cleansing and clothing rituals are highly staged – a prologue to the dance. In an alcove, the radiologist washes his or her hands and forearms with a scrub brush, and enters the operating room, holding hands and fingertips up. S/he wears a heavy lead apron, a surgery cap, and a mask that covers the mouth and nose. Assistants are in attendance. The assistant who is technically 'sterile' opens a folded long-sleeved gown, shaking it out in front of the radiologist 'so that he can walk into it, leaving the opening at the back' (Young 1997: 95). Then the dance begins. At least three performers participate in this complex choreography. The 'non-sterile' assistant comes round and ties the radiologist's gown at the back. In the meantime his colleague takes a pair of gloves from the sterile table, holds the left one by the cuff while the physician inserts a hand. Then, as Young (ibid.: 95) goes on to explain, 'they both take hold of the cuff of the other glove and pull it onto his right hand.' The radiologist wriggles his or her fingers. Finally, s/he hands the 'sterile' assistant one of the ties, turns around, and attaches the gown on the left hand side.

Radiologist:	So, Mr. XY, how are you doing? Good morning.
Patient:	I feel a little bit constricted right now.

Radiologist: Sure, beneath the drapery. No doubt about this – and in addition?

Patient: Not too bad.

...

Scrub nurse: [Helps the surgeon in his sterile gown and gloves, and because the circulating nurse is not in the room she asks me.] Are you able to close this coat? Here?

As to this last directive aimed at myself, my layperson status made me feel nervous about touching the surgeon's sterile gown. Within seconds, I realized the significance behind this seemingly simple request, and was slightly taken aback. In effect, I was being invited to touch the 'sacred boundaries' of the sterile field – a moment of initiation indeed.

'Eyes-on' and 'hands-on':

The scrub nurse included me in the communing body of the operating team. The sense of touch – making and unmaking physical contact – is crucial for the creation of a sterile field and its boundaries. However, the tactile epistemological framework works differently in radiology. In radiological practice 'eyes-on' tactility is embodied with the help of digital X-ray devices, whereas in traditional surgery surgeons are 'hands-on' practitioners, the surgeon's hand literally 'entering the body and cautiously feeling its way around the organs' (Taussig 1993: 31). In fact, and as suggested earlier, interventional radiology combines both modes of embodiment: the 'eyes-on' organ of the screen is wired to 'hands-on' prostheses, which become all the more obvious in the operating theatre.

Radiologist: [to the patient]
Please,
don't breathe, don't move,
don't breathe, don't move.

...

Assistant: Continue breathing.

The radiologist tells the patient what the images are showing, and explains what is about to be done. With his finger he points out sections on the screen. He says:

Radiologist: We take this away, this part there.
Patient: Aha.

Then he continues the 'hands-on' procedure of embolization, filling up blood vessels with tiny liquid plastic pearls. The material is introduced through a catheter. Frequently control angiographies are performed. For this the patient is injected with 'contrast media.' In this way, the blood flow is chemically enhanced and rendered visible on moving fluoroscopy pictures.

Radiologist:	Mr XY, please …
	Don't breathe. Don't move.
	Don't breathe. Don't move.
	…
Assistant:	Are you okay, Mr. XY?
Patient:	Yes, though I can't get enough air.
Radiologist:	Why? Are you in pain?
Patient:	No, you did not say, 'continue breathing'.
	[Personnel break out laughing]
	…
Radiologist:	If I don't say anything then don't breathe just for ten or fifteen seconds – until the noise of the machine leaves off.
Patient:	Ah…

In other words, a 'hands-on' procedure in interventional radiology is a wiring mode. Catheters and sluices are moved in and out of the blood vessels. In fact, it is through wires that the bodies of the patient, radiologist and assistant become intimately connected with one another and with the imaging device. Embodied 'eyes-on' and 'hands-on' procedures are mutually interpenetrated. The eyes of the physician are on the screen, isolating necessary information from the X-ray map of the blood flow, and this enables him or her to navigate material components through the tiniest of vessels. For radiologists, the screen as a prosthesis functions like a window, casting light on the body's innermost crevices. As for the patient-viewer, s/he is bodily dissociated – quietly following the scene on a monitor. The operating field itself is but an opening in the drapery. Through a sluice, which is placed in this opening after the artery has been punctured, thin wires are pushed in and pulled out of the blood vessel. These are the threads, keeping the 'communicative body' and its various parts together. Only a few stitches are required to sew up the wound after the operation is finished. Minimal-invasive interventions leave hardly any visible trace on the body surface.

Radiologist:	So, that's it.
Patient:	Thank you.
Radiologist:	My pleasure.

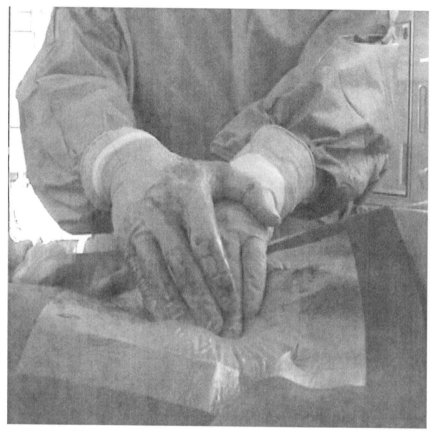

© Christina Lammer 2006.

Epilogue

How do patients see themselves as they watch their own inner bodily workings during these kinds of radiological operations? In the course of my research I tried to get as close as possible to this wired communicative body as it is staged, palpated, profanely illuminated, manipulated, diagnosed, treated, cut open and sewn up. To do this, I drew upon the magic qualities of mimesis through the help of the prosthetic eye of my video camera. Bodies of patients as well as medical personnel are staged through particular acts of framing. The postural schema of imaging technologies produces physical communion between radiologists and patients. Proximity and distance are controlled through cleansing and clothing rituals. The sterile field is created through image devices. I argued that a multisensual approach would encourage empathy and create a deeper sensibility amongst health professionals at a teaching hospital.

Instead of closing here with a conclusion, I will unfold the perspectives of this particular applied bodywork approach, which I have developed for interventional radiology. Since my clinic project is being continued (at least) until the end of 2009 in different biomedical fields, I am already able to report on a follow up project, *CORPOrealities* (www.corporealities.org), which started in October 2004. This work includes case studies in reconstructive and plastic surgery, working with cancer patients, collaborating with interdisciplinary clinic teams and elaborating expressive modes and experimental tools together with two artists, Barbara Graf and Catherine Rollier, and with a curator, Cathrin Pichler, who is not only experienced in the conceptualization of exhibitions and fine art events but has additionally been trained as a medical doctor, psychologist and sociologist. Unfortunately she contributes to the research in a double role, as scientist and patient. Cathrin has multiple sclerosis (MS). She was diagnosed ten years ago, but developed MS more than twenty years ago. Her experiences of living with this disease are extremely influential in our transdisciplinary research collaboration. Our own 'nervous costumes' react more sensitively. We have developed an awareness of how difficult life with such a threatening and painful condition can be.

Another section of *CORPOrealities* involves the use of digital media in a patient record system, *Unified Patient*, which is being developed at the department of Medical Media Services (MMS) at the university hospital and includes research on how this tool is used by clinicians and medical students. The methodological framework goes hand in hand with a problem-oriented approach. Research questions are posed within the different biomedical fields at the hospital. For instance, for the head of the plastic surgery department, Manfred Frey, the socio-cultural background of women who will get reconstructive operations on their breasts is an important issue for planning surgeries. He wants to get a better feeling and understanding of the 'meaning of the breast' for women, and the individual expectations of his patients. Aesthetic problems and suffering are inseparable in reconstructive surgery.

Thus the general aim of an applied visual anthropology approach in the context of biomedicine is the development of communication tools and multimedia applications, which provide mediation between subjective experiences of bodily processes and objective forms of knowledge of the human organism and its inner structures. Notions like empathy and embodiment are investigated to bring apparently unapproachable emotional worlds, which are vividly active at the hospital, to a treatable and manageable surface. For most of the clinicians the development of qualitative standards in their work with patients is at the foreground of their interest in the research.

Patients and clinical staff live with artificially, technically and socioculturally produced artefacts. They embody them in manifold ways. In biomedical practice and beyond the *Unified Patient* becomes part of one's identity. Bodily aspects and tactile qualities are central observational patterns. Within these ethnographic research activities art meets biomedicine through the performance of fieldwork. The results will advance sensitivity to the emotional and imaginary modes of treatment and diagnosis which are involved in biomedical fields of practice.[8]

Notes

1. An 'anamnesis' is a patient's story.
2. The interviewed radiologist is head of the interventional radiology department at the Medical University Vienna (MUV). The interview took place 2004 as part of the field study I conducted at the department. We spoke German. I translated the transcript into English.
3. The interviewed radiologist is head of the surgical unit within the department of radio-diagnostics at the MUV. The interview took place 2002. I translated the German transcript into English.
4. The interviewed radiologist is also staff member of the department of radio diagnostics at the MUV. He is mostly responsible for magnetic resonance imaging (MRI). I translated the transcript into English.
5. Actually the ethnographic video materials are used within the clinical context. Only for screenings of *Making Contact* at international conferences, I needed to translate the documented conversations into English.
6. See footnote 2.
7. These are typologies (made up by myself), which I use to analyze and explain the complexity of sociocultural patterns, relationships and modes of embodiment in interventional radiology.
8. **Acknowledgements:** First I would like to thank Linnet Fawcett for correcting my English. She made this chapter readable and understandable. Further thanks go to all the people who worked together with me during fieldwork at the hospital and beyond:

Patients: J. Bezernek, K. Fehrer, J. Gfrerer, R. Loidl, S. Mozelt, H. Nowitzky, J. Polster, L. Stiefmayer, R. Stoklasek, H.-P. Straka, H. Ullmann, C. Zentner.
Health professionals: A. Bankier, A. Ba-Ssalamah, F. Felberbauer, P. Fitzal, M. Frey, M. Funovics, F. Grabenwöger, G. Heinz-Peer, J. Kettenbach, G. Kretschmer, J. Lammer, G. Lechner, F. Lomoschitz, A. Maier, M. Memarsadeghi, P. Pokieser, T. Rand, M. Schoder, S. Trattnig.
Artists: Barbara Graf, Catherine Rollier.
Curators: Cathrin Pichler, Christa Spatt.

Bibliography

Benjamin, W. 1963. *Das Kunstwerk im Zeitalter seiner technischen Reproduzierbarkeit.* Frankfurt am Main: Suhrkamp.

Buck-Morss, S. 1994. ,The Cinema Screen as Prothesis of Perception', in N.C. Seremetakis (ed.), *The Senses Still. Perception and Memory as Material Culture in Modernity.* Chicago: University of Chicago Press.

Chalfen, R. and M. Rich. 2007. 'Combining the Applied, the Visual and the Medical: Patients Teaching Physicians With Visual Narratives', in S. Pink (ed.) *Visual Interventions.* Oxford: Berghahn.

Frank, A.W. 1995. *The Wounded Storyteller. Body, Illness, and Ethics.* Chicago: University of Chicago Press.

Howes, D. 2003. *Sensual Relations. Engaging the Senses in Culture and Social Theory.* Michigan: University of Michigan Press.

Kleinman, A. 1988. *The Illness Narratives: Suffering, Healing and the Human Condition.* New York: Basic Books.

Leder, D. 1990. *The Absent Body.* Chicago: University of Chicago Press.

MacDougall. 1998. *Transcultural Cinema.* Princeton: Princeton University Press.

Marks, L. 2000. *The Skin of the Film: Intercultural Cinema, Embodiment, and the Senses.* Durham: Duke University Press.

Mauss, M. 1992. ‚Techniques of the Body', in J. Crary and S. Kwinter (eds.), *Incorporations.* New York: ZONE.

Pink, S. 2005. Personal communication (e-mail).

Scarry, E. 1985. *The Body in Pain: The Making and Unmaking of the World.* New York: Oxford University Press.

Seremetakis, N. (ed.) 1994. *The Senses Still: Perception and Memory as Material Culture in Modernity.* Chicago: The University of Chicago Press.

Stoller, P. 2004. *Stranger in the Village of the Sick: A Memoir of Cancer, Sorcery, and Healing.* Boston: Beacon Press.

Taussig, M. 1992. *The Nervous System.* New York: Routledge.

Taussig, M. 1993. *Mimesis and Alterity: A Particular History of the Senses.* New York: Routledge.

Wall, S. 2005. ‚Video Replay Helps Radiology Residents Improve Performance', in *RSNA News,* August 2005: 11–12. Retrieved October 2005 from: http://www.rsna.org/Publications/rsnanews/.

Weiner, A. and Schneider, J. 1989. *Cloth and Human Experience.* Washington: Smithsonian Books.

Young, K. 1997. *Presence in the Flesh: The Body in Medicine.* Cambridge: Harvard University Press.

Filmography

Making Contact. 2004. Christina Lammer. MedArt / somafilm (Vienna, Austria). 20 minutes.

PART III

TOURISM AND HERITAGE

Chapter 6

LOOK TO LEARN
A Role for Visual Ethnography in the Elimination of Poverty

Dianne Stadhams

Figure 6.1 'When I grow up, I want to be a tourist'.[1]

The Challenge

In my work as a tourism development consultant, I see many examples of well-intentioned but poor practice by consultants from the North working with communities in the South. Their reliance on the written word as an effective tool to collect and disseminate information that can improve socio economic conditions in countries with high levels of poverty, illiteracy and an oral culture is flawed.

In this article I suggest that an interdisciplinary approach that combines visual anthropology with the social anthropology of tourism, film and television studies, and pro-poor development economics can produce a more effective communication model that is relevant to the needs and perspectives of communities in the South.

I write from the perspective of a development consultant who has applied methods and approaches from visual anthropology to achieve a metaphorical 'compound eye'.[2] This results in ways of seeing 'the other' that identify the perspective of each 'other' so that cultural values can be distinguished and explained within their context, including that of myself as a research practitioner. From this position of the separation of perspectives, a refocusing to produce a gaze that both separates and assimilates difference, i.e. the compound eye, can be attempted. The second aim of this chapter is therefore to offer a view of how applied visual anthropology might be developed from outside the academy.

First I shall outline the wider context. The 2000 United Nations Millennium Development Goals (DfID 2000) aimed to eliminate world poverty. Policies that identify opportunities for economic growth and strategies to implement these policies have been agreed in support of poverty alleviation goals. Many poor countries view and are encouraged by international aid agencies to see tourism[3] as an opportunity to generate foreign exchange and thereby provide socio economic benefits for local people (Pearce 1981; Krippendorf 1987; Eber 1992; Harrison 1993; Burns and Holden 1995; Badger et al. 1996; Forsyth 1996; Cooper and Wanhill 1997; France 1997; ICRT et al. 2002). However the notion of 'tourism' is a misnomer. It is an umbrella term for a series of inter related commercial activities, which range from primary production, e.g. food for tourist hotels, to manufacturing, e.g. meals for tourist airlines, to service provision, e.g. hospitality staff. Tourism is used to describe a growth sector of the global economy, which represents 10.7 per cent of the total value of world trade and generates 8.2 per cent of total global employment (Miller 2001). Academic research on the impacts and benefits of tourism is fiercely contested. The emphasis has been on economic issues, measurement techniques, management practices and environmental debates (Graefe et al. 1990; Canestrelli and Costa 1991; May 1991; Cater and Goodall 1992; Butler 1993; Hawkins and Middleton 1993; Nelson et al. 1993; Giongo et al. 1994; Lindberg and Enriquez 1994; Prosser 1994; Ritchie and Goeldner 1994; Briassoulis 1995; Buhalis and Fletcher 1995; Croall 1995; Brohman

1996; Roe et al. 1997; Mowforth and Munt 1998; Williams and Shaw 1998; Leask and Yeoman 1999). The trends on tourism impacts and development have been quantified and objectified to form theories which support development models. Whilst this is useful in establishing patterns of behaviour, there is a shortage of well-researched, qualitative opinion from tourism stakeholders in support of models. Anthropologists deploying visual tools, and visual ethnographers, have highlighted the potential that images, moving and still, can make to communicating with and understanding the gaze of the 'other' (Collier and Collier 1986; Crawford and Turton 1992; Hockings 1995; Banks and Morphy 1997; Ruby 2000; Grimshaw 2001; Pink 2001).

Between September 2000 and March 2002, the UK Department for International Development (DfID), funded a pilot project to look at the potential of tourism as a poverty alleviation tool in The Gambia (Goodwin and Stadhams 2000). One output of the pro-poor tourism project was the production of a television programme to raise awareness of the issues amongst a wider audience than tourism stakeholders. The challenge was to create a communication tool that presented the options for tourism as a development route to a population with little positive experience of how official policy links to local practice.

My role was to develop this programme with Gambia television (GRTS), which has only existed since 1995. The programme's primary target audience was Gambians, of whom only twenty-eight per cent are literate (UNDP 2000). Television was seen as a cost-effective vehicle to disseminate accurate information. In The Gambia there are an increasing number of individual televisions in urban households. In rural areas, many villages have access to a communal television. However there was not any research available on audience viewing behaviours.

The Location

The Gambia, situated on the west coast of Africa, is the continent's smallest independent country. Surrounded on three sides by the former French colony, Senegal, it is a country of approximately eleven thousand square kilometres (Tomkinson 2000), which lies within the valley of the River Gambia.

There are five major ethnic groups in The Gambia. They are Mandinka (forty-two per cent, descended from the Mali Empire), Fula (eighteen per cent, migrated from Guinea highlands), Wollof (sixteen per cent, from Senegambia area), Jola (ten per cent, also from Senegambia) and Serrahula (nine per cent, who are descended from traders in Mali and Mauritania). Minority groups, defined by their language and geographical roots, include the Serrerer, Aku and Manjagoes. Five per cent of the population are a mixture of Europeans, Americans, Lebanese, Chinese and refugees from neighbouring countries (Guinea Bissau, Sierra Leone, Senegal). The majority of the population are Muslim (eighty-five per cent) with thirteen per cent Christian and two per cent animist. There is a very tolerant religious atmosphere with a non fundamentalist approach to Islamic practices and worship (Sonko-Godwin 1997; Tomkinson 2000).

The Gambia is ranked as the eleventh poorest nation in the world (UNDP 1998) with an estimated population of 1.3 million, growing at 4.2 per cent, one of the fastest rates in the world. Forty-four of the population is below age fifteen and seventeen per cent are children below age five. Life expectancy is fifty-five years. Only eleven per cent are employed in the formal sector, which includes salaried positions within tourism (e.g., hotel and restaurant staff), civil service (government departments and aid agencies), and some manufacturing and retailing (e.g., Banjul Brewery). Eighty-two per cent of total employment is in the agricultural sector. Sixty-nine per cent of Gambians live below the poverty line.

The economy depends on agriculture, re-export trade and tourism. Agriculture is mainly subsistence with groundnut produce (nuts, oil, cattle cake) contributing ninety per cent of total exports (Concern Universal 2001). There is some forestry and fishing, but no important mineral deposits or natural resources. Tourism represents the largest generator of foreign exchange for the country and accounts for seven per cent of formal sector employment. However, many of these jobs are seasonal and at a menial level (Badger et al. 1996).

Tourism is a recent development in the country and began in 1966 with three hundred package tourists from Sweden. This has grown to nearly sixty thousand during the peak season, November to April. Of the tourist arrivals sixty-six per cent are from the UK, sixteen per cent from Scandinavia and fourteen per cent are from Holland and Germany. The Gambia Government, in its 'Tourism and Infrastructure Project' (1975 – 80), designated a costal strip of land, 750 m wide and 15 km long, west of Banjul along the Atlantic coastline, exclusively for tourism development and offered investment incentive packages to attract development of tourism hotels and facilities. From two hotels in 1965, the country now has twenty-two tourist hotels, an expanding number of small guesthouses, a time share resort, and a few river camps or village accommodations. The majority of tourists arrive on charter flights for cheap 'sun, sea and sand' packages. The Gambia also has acquired a reputation as a sex tourism destination for middle-aged European females in search of young male companions.

However, tourism has not delivered the anticipated development results (McPherson and Radelet 1995). The reasons are complex (Dieke 1998) but can be summarised as a mixture of external economic factors (oil crisis 1979); internal policy and management (inflation, foreign debt, subsequent Structural Adjustment Policy of 1985); perceived political unrest by tourism-generating destinations (general advice from the British Foreign Office Travel Centre 1995); lack of investment in infrastructure, facilities and training; and inadequate resources for destination promotion in a very competitive market. Many Gambians regard tourism as their only hope for survival or potential income source, despite an increasing awareness of its negative impacts. Figures 6.2 and 6.3 illustrate the contrasting attitudes of two project informants.

Figure 6.2 'All benefit'.[4]

Figure 6.3 'Blessing in disguise'.[5]

The Approach

I subscribe to the notion that effective action is rooted in clear thinking. Thus emancipatory action research[6] shaped my approach because it integrated the raising of public awareness by linking policy, i.e., the communication objectives, to practice, i.e., activities with stakeholders.[7] A discussion on the wealth and breadth of academic literature available is outside the scope of this article but Table 6.1 provides a summary of the link between concept and action with key texts listed. The range of academic literature is diverse – from visual anthropology to pro-poor tourism economics to cultural studies.

The key questions framing my research approach were:

- What is my perspective as a researcher and how might this impact on the research approach and data collection methods?
- What am I trying to achieve and how will this shape my role?

Table 6.1 Linking theory to practice.

Key issues in designing the research approach	Proposed resolutions	Theoretical justification and foundation texts
Research aim: • What information is required to produce a public education television programme about tourism for Gambians by GRTS?	• Understand GRTS broadcast culture and technical competencies.	• Plural texts derived from schools of research in social anthropology of tourism, film and television studies, pro-poor development economics and sustainable tourism.
Gaze of researcher: • What do I bring to the project?	• Define positionality.	• Post-modern – John Urry (1990) *The Tourist Gaze*. • Feminist – Ann Kaplan (1997) *Looking for The Other Feminism, Film, and The Imperial Gaze*.
Role of researcher: • How will I approach the project?	• Emancipatory Action. • Reflexivity.	• Participatory – Orton Zuber-Skerritt (1996) *New Directions in Action Research*.
Most appropriate methods to support the gaze and role of the researcher: • Whose work can help?	• Ethnographic • Participant observation.	• Ethnography – Martin Hammersley (1998) *Reading Ethnographic Research*. • Visual Ethnography – Sarah Pink (2001) *Doing Visual Ethnography*; Jay Ruby (2000) *Picturing Culture*; Keyan Tomaselli (1996) *Appropriating Images*.
• Most effective data collection tools to support the gaze and role of the researcher.	• Qualitative interviews with key informants, arranged through a gatekeeper,[8] and recorded on video tape.	• Qualitative interviewing techniques, including video – David Silverman (2000) *Doing Qualitative Research A Practical Handbook*.

The aim of the research was to generate reliable data from which the content and format of a communication tool could be constructed. Thus the data had information potential in its own right but its application to a quantifiable output, i.e., a television programme for broadcast on Gambia national television, was critical. The research data required breadth and depth to meet validity and reliability criteria and the application required a format that reflected this participatory approach. There were two strands of academic literature to be considered – participatory research and the role of multiple voices, each with their versions of 'truth and reality'. In Table 6.1, I have tried to indicate that the nature of the research is both cross disciplinary and inter disciplinary. By this, I mean that the texts are drawn from different approaches to research – for example, anthropology of tourism and film studies. In addition, these approaches describe commonly used terms and practices – such as post modernism and participant observation – with different emphases, nuances, definitions, explanations and textual illustrations, peculiar to that discipline's own academic research traditions. However, although there may be common usage of a term, there is also a fiercely contested exchange of interpretations of some of these terms. Thus the value in the difference between how Urry (1990) defines 'gaze', with his emphasis on cultural construction, and Kaplan's (1997) suggestion that the term is synonymous with a white, gendered, imperial, disinterested-in-engagement way of looking, lies in the intellectual spume, which invites and accommodates interpretations of knowledge constructs.

I also reflected on my own 'gaze' as a white female from a Christian, materially affluent society working in a black, patriarchal, Muslim (non fundamentalist) society. Table 6.2 summarizes my reflection and is presented as a conventional SWOT analysis (McDonald 1986; Westwood 2000) familiar to the commercial world.

Table 6.2 Reflective analysis of my role as facilitator.

Strengths	Weaknesses
• Familiarity with research location and tourism businesses. • Established credentials with Gambian and UK participants from previous work since 1996. • Experienced communicator and commercial tourism practitioner. • Ability as a female to gain access to Gambian women's opinion.	• Not fluent in any local language. • Not resident in the destination. • Disparity of post modern base of the researcher with a modernizing destination in the South.
Opportunities	**Threats**
• Practical action likely to be supported by stakeholders. • Good potential for broad dissemination of research conclusions to substantial audience.	• Suspicion of outsider's role and agenda. • Local scepticism of the value of external European consultants.

The value of Table 6.2 is that it helped me to address the inherent dilemma of power, its negotiation in the research arena and a clarification of how perception is constructed and managed. This process is linked to Foucault's (1973) notions on the power embodied in the 'gaze'. I use the word 'gaze' to imply that:

- Names and values are attached to the subjects and objects perceived.
- The interpretation of the visual and oral matter received is dependent upon the context in which it is perceived and the cultural capital inherited by the persons / group seeing it.
- Context incorporates the power underlying that cultural capital. This power is dynamic (i.e., unstable) and multifaceted with each facet competing and compromising to frame its impact. Thus their economic, religious, ethnic and gendered gaze may shape one person's perception of a given situation. That the individual does not consciously acknowledge these facets does not diminish the power of the impact.

As Ruby (2000: 251) suggests, 'Theories are neither true nor false; they are merely useful.' The outcome of Table 6.2 was that I could reflect on the potential that the opportunities and strengths provided and mitigate the weaknesses and threats through collaborating with a Gambian counterpart, key informants, and using qualitative data collection methods indicated in Table 6.1.

Thus, in moving from theory to practise, my approach was framed by five major questions. They were: What am I doing? Why am I doing it? How will I do it? Who will help me achieve it? How will I be able to tell if I have achieved what I set out to do?

Table 6.3 illustrates an overview of the link between these questions, the research methodology and the practical outputs. This form of presentation can be criticized for its generic approach, which reduces relevant theoretical perspectives and their implications for field practice to a list. This list may be little more than a signpost to useful theoretical information than an integrated approach to thinking and doing. But what is useful in this model of organization is that all activities of the research project are linked to theoretical roots and practical applications. Project personnel, whatever their backgrounds, biases or project functions, can see that action is rooted in thinking and that conceptualizing an approach is linked to practical outputs. My own experience suggests that bridging the gulf between academics and practitioners is a key communication need. If some sort of order is to be given to the structural process of identifying kinds of information, collecting and analysing data, then a log-frame presentation displays a form of sequential progression that permits the positivist, quantifiable approach to be juxtaposed and incorporated within a hermeneutic approach. It seems to give credence to both approaches without denying the essential strengths of both – plural texts can be validated. And, I would argue that the logical framework through its referential structure (in this case study) includes a reflexive dimension. This framework dispels some of the criticisms of qualitative research, particularly those directed at ethnographic traditions, with their emphasis on unstructured interviewing and discovery-based approach. Hammersley (1998: 64) suggests that 'our inability to replicate ethnographic findings does not undermine assessments of their validity, though it may make the task more difficult.'

However, Table 6.3 does not describe the challenges posed to fieldwork!

Table 6.3 An overview of the research methodology and the practical outputs

What am I doing?	Why am I doing it?	How will I do it?	How will I be able to tell if I have achieved what I set out to do?
Goal To develop and broadcast a high rating, informative, entertaining and emancipatory programme on Gambia Television (GRTS)	**Theoretical Foundations** • Applied • Inductive • Interpretative • Qualitative • Postmodernism • Feminist critique	**Application of theory into practice** Broadcast on GRTS	• GRTS would collaborate in the programme development and broadcast • DFID funds to support research and development
Purpose To affect an attitude change amongst all stakeholders in The Gambia towards the potential of tourism to reduce poverty[9]	**Research Approach** • Emancipatory Action • Ethnography • Participant observation	• VHS format, video copies of the broadcast programme available to all organisations representing tourism stakeholders in The Gambia and UK • Written reports describing the research process available to relevant academic and practitioner groups	• Ability to recruit support and participants in The Gambia and UK • Continuing commitment for 20 months from tourism stakeholders to the project
Outputs • To collect and to disseminate knowledge through multiple voices • To identify key issues for tourism stakeholders • To select an appropriate television format for communication • To evaluate the impact of the programme on stakeholders	**Methods** • Semi-structured interviews • Framework analysis • Content analysis • Questionnaire	• Footage of 'talking heads' interviewees in television programme • Discussion of issues in television programme by 'talking heads' • Popular ratings programme – news format • Evaluation report	• Willingness of tourism stakeholders, including tourists, to be video interviewed • Ability of GRTS to provide broadcasting schedules and ratings • Participation by tourism stakeholders to contribute to the television broadcast

Activities	Tools	Programme resume and treatment document	Dependent on DfID funding
• Integrating qualitative and quantitative research into a valid broadcast format with GRTS	• Academic analysis and conclusions		
• Collecting semi-structured video interviews of representatives of tourism stakeholders	• Television production crew with researcher / director	• Content of television programme	
• Discussing in workshops with representatives of tourism stakeholders how to develop a collaborative approach to the television programme and representation of content		• Reports on workshops and conclusions	
• Evaluating and reporting impacts of the television broadcast to all tourism stakeholders		• Audience evaluation survey and analysis of results	
• Disseminating the information through tourism stakeholder organisations in the UK and The Gambia.		• Copies of television programme and written report with extended use of the broadcast by tourism stakeholders	

Implementation

An amusing example of the implementation challenges, which illustrates cultural myths of gender and the power of television, is that I was misperceived as 'Madonna', the pop icon. Figure 6.4 shows me in the field talking to stakeholders about the programme, enlisting their support for interviews and negotiating permission to collect footage in their village. This followed a news item on GRTS for which I had been interviewed about the project. I was therefore surprised by the chief's reaction towards me and to receive feedback from a Gambian colleague that the village believed me to be an international super-celebrity. The 'Chinese whisper' scenario was along the lines of: a white woman on national television (Gambian news enjoys the highest ratings on television), was seen in the company of white men (European consultants and tour operator managers) as well as black men (GRTS staff, Gambia Government officials and local tourism business owners). The erroneous conclusion was this was foreign superstar with an insatiable sexual appetite, i.e., Madonna!

Figure 6.4 'Madonna' gathering stakeholder opinion.

In the field I worked through local trade organisations – ASSET (Association of Small-Scale Enterprises in Tourism), which represented the business interests of entrepreneurs like the fruit sellers and tourist taxis; GHA (Gambia Hotels Association); and GHEHA (Gambia Ground Handlers and Equipment Hirers' Association). Research was conducted between September 2000 and March 2002.

The research was carried out through semi-structured, informal interviews with key informants nominated by gatekeepers in each trade association. Initially I sat through association meetings where the project aim was discussed and in which I answered any questions. From there the group nominated its spokespeople and I spent time with these individuals in a conventional participant observation way. During the same period I attended meetings between stakeholder and association groups where the challenges to collaboration between stakeholders were vociferously debated. In addition I had access to Government officials in The Gambia and to UK tour operator resort staff and their tourist welcome meetings. From attending all these rounds of meetings, I had the opportunity to listen and to learn what stakeholders were saying about their own tourism agendas as well as their perspectives and attitudes on other tourism stakeholders. From the fieldnotes of these meetings, I was able to assemble a framework of common issues and themes around which a script and taped interviews could be collected. Two public meetings attended by representatives of all stakeholder groups were then held where information about each group's perspectives on the strengths of, and obstacles to tourism as a pro-poor strategy could be shared.

From there, data was collected primarily on videotape, analysed using a conversational framework method and disseminated through national television. The conclusions were that a change of action in The Gambia required a change in the gaze of tourism participants. How individuals and groups, with different agendas but sharing a common goal of poverty alleviation, might refocus their social constructs involved both understanding what they could see and collaborating to create new and shared ways of seeing more pertinently. Table 6.4 is a summary of the television programme treatment.

Production

Production was problematic for many reasons. Gathering stakeholder opinion was time- consuming and fraught with local politics around who was selected for interview and how representative their views were of the stakeholders they purported to represent. GRTS production crew had a very low skills base in terms of technical competency. Video recording equipment was not always reliable and crew motivation fluctuated. For example, GRTS production crew are used to working in an environment where the director directs, the cameraman uses the camera, the sound recordist looks to his equipment. The driver is often treated as the 'runner' or general dogsbody, equipment carrier and his cooperation is dependent on his previous relationship with the crew. In this case, I wanted to promote a transfer of skills and cultural knowledge between the Gambian production crew and myself, as well as to reflect the participatory nature of the project approach. It took twelve months of applied effort to achieve a working relationship that can be described as collaborative. However, the professional camaraderie and consultation that developed through the production were rewarding results. Lanzmann's comments are particularly apt, 'I had an obsession … I have made the film and the film has made me –' (Lanzmann 1985, in Bruzzi 2000).

Given the limitations of technology, skills, time and budget I considered the best possible chance of successfully producing a sixty-minute television

Table 6.4 Programme treatment.

Programme Title	Pro-poor tourism in The Gambia.
Programme Type	Current affairs documentary.
Duration	<ul><li>60 minutes maximum for terrestrial broadcast on GRTS.</li><li>Consider re-edit of four 15-minute programmes to build a series for training and education activities by tourism stakeholders in The Gambia and UK.</li></ul>
Resume	Tourism is critical to the economy of The Gambia. Many Gambians view it as one of the few opportunities for employment, where only twelve per cent of the population work in jobs that are not linked to agriculture and fishing. However, the tourism business in the country is perceived to be in crisis with a decline in tourism arrivals and a conflict of interests between tourism stakeholders as they compete for a share of tourist expenditure. The television broadcast has three aims:<ul><li>To provide information on the role of tourism and its stakeholders in The Gambia.</li><li>To highlight the process and results of a pilot project, which seeks to address the issue of whether tourism can contribute to the alleviation of poverty.</li><li>To provoke discussion in The Gambia on tourism as a development tool.</li></ul>
Key issues	<ul><li>What does tourism mean to and for Gambians?</li><li>Who are the stakeholders and how do they see tourism?</li><li>What are the challenges that face tourism stakeholders?</li><li>What can be done?</li><li>Who is involved?</li><li>Who gets the benefits?</li></ul>
Approach	<ul><li>Personal stories.</li><li>Format should reflect the participatory nature of the DfID TCF project.</li><li>Style must be relevant to Gambian viewing audience.</li></ul>
Key characters	<ul><li>Adama Bah: DfID Gambia Project Manager. Articulate, with a good understanding of development issues; experience in working within the formal and informal sectors; access to and trusted by all stakeholders.</li><li>ASSET: Association of Small-Scale Entrepreneurs in Tourism. A number of their executives, Buna Njie (Chair), Geri Mitchell (Vice-chair) and Sheik Tijan Nyang (Secretary) are seasoned tourism participants with strong views and contrasting styles.</li><li>GRTS: Newsreader, Ya Abbis Njie. Positive personal profile with GRTS viewers: clear voice.</li></ul>

Supporting characters	• Informal sector: representatives from two sites in the tourist areas, i.e., Kotu and Senegambia beaches. Representatives include craft vendors, fruit sellers, juice bars, official licensed guides, tourist taxis, bumsters. • Formal sector: representatives from Gambia Hotels Association (GHA), Gambian Ground Handlers and Equipment Hirers Association (GHEHA), Tour Operators. • Official Authorities: British High Commissioner in The Gambia, The Gambia Secretary of State for Tourism and Culture, Association of British Travel Agents, Federation of Tour Operators. • Music: provided by a group Of Gambian musicians working through ECCO, a Norwegian funded cultural exchange non governmental organisation.
Pre-production	September – December 2000.
Production	December 19, 2000; March 9 – 23 2001; May 21 – June 7 2001; November 22 – December 5 2001; January 27 – 31 2002. (26 days in total)
Post-production	July 2001, January – March 2002. (60 days in total)
Broadcast date	March 2002.

programme meant a current affairs type approach with 'talking heads' intercut with supporting location footage. The interview commentaries became the building blocks of information around which the tourism development issues could be grouped. Television is still a relatively new phenomenon in The Gambia and for many people access to a monitor is very recent. Seeing family, colleagues and officials 'live' and discussing topical issues is widely regarded as informative and entertaining. Critical discourse on media representations and programme quality is beyond the knowledge, experience or interest of the majority of the viewing audience. If Gambians were to accept and debate the broadcast information, an authentic visual vehicle, within their own experience, was required.

To link the issues and to create a coherent story, that started with what tourism means to The Gambia through to the impact on Gambians of a foreign-funded but locally-executed pro-poor tourism experiment, part of the script was written after the skeleton edit script was developed. The scripted links were written in the style of the daily GRTS news broadcasts. This was done to guarantee a high level of professional delivery by GRTS presenters with a familiar format and to add gravity and credibility to the programme. It also permitted a reasonable margin for contingencies in case the footage was not usable or technical problems in editing were encountered.

Figure 6.5 Collecting footage with GRTS.

Post-production

The edit became a protracted challenge, as there were significant technical problems with the video footage collected. Although, during each production visit, there had been attempts to encourage the cameraman to set the timing device on the camera, the time codes did not appear on the majority of the taped footage. This made the post-production process much more labour intensive … and expensive. In essence, it meant that logging the footage in the conventional manner, with time codes matched to visual and audio frames, was impossible as there were hundreds of pieces of footage that had the identical time code of 00.00.00.01. The result was that the log had to be done through footage description – for example, 'tourist talking to fruit seller', 'tourist buying banana', rather than 'tourist talking to fruit seller 09.04.32.07 – 09.04.35.10', 'tourist buying banana 09.04.47.01 – 09.06.18.09'. In a correctly time-coded video tape recording, the 09.04.32.07 would indicate that the required footage clip was located on Tape 9 at 4 minutes, 32 seconds, frame 7. As there were 24 tapes of up to 120 minutes each of recording with 24 frames per second, the post-production team were faced with hundreds of thousands of frames of footage that had no equivalent of an ordered filing system. The knock-on effect of this 'organised chaos' meant many, many extra hours were needed in the editing studio identifying the particular clips from the general footage headings.

In addition, the computer was unable to recognise individual footage clips because so many had the same, indistinguishable, time code, i.e., 00.00.00.01. This meant that the conventional editing process could not be followed, i.e., paper edit compiled from 'capturing' those pieces of footage that will be required for the edit; 'storing' them in 'bin lists' or files on the computer, from which the director and editor will source; 'assembling' the footage clips selected from the bin lists at a low resolution of footage to keep costs low and maintain the pace of the edit to fit the budget; doing an on line edit at high resolution and frame accurate to $\frac{1}{25}$ of a second.

The result was that the editor had to work throughout the process with high resolution clips because the computer would not be able to return to the original clips because of the lack of accurate time codes. Given these difficulties and the fact that the editing equipment in The Gambia was proving unreliable with staff uncertain of how they might work with the volume of non time-coded footage in the project time available, it was agreed that the edit would be done in the UK. However, the style of the edit reflected the resources available in The Gambia with GRTS. The finished programme uses only those graphics, techniques and effects which GRTS can manufacture in their own studio. This was agreed to be an acceptable compromise, which could indicate to GRTS staff what was possible within their own establishment.

One further complication was that the footage transcripts were not accurate. The Gambian employed to do the transcriptions experienced difficulty with some of the accents and at other times summarized what interviews meant, rather than what interviewees actually said, in order 'to help me'! This slowed the editing process considerably.

On 25 January, a first six-minute, draft edit of the programme was taken to The Gambia and previewed to an audience of fifty people invited by ASSET. The audience was a mixture of formal and informal sector participants and tourists. Some members of the audience were interviewees on the programme. The audience was then asked for comment and feedback. In general, feedback was very positive on the approach. There was some debate on the use of text on the screen. Some thought it was a very useful tool to introduce and re-enforce issues and aid literacy. Others thought that it would be less successful in rural areas where literacy levels are lower. As a compromise, I suggested that a voice-over accompanied the text, which would cater for all needs. Consequently, the GRTS newsreader script was modified to include voice-overs for text.

GRTS were very supportive of the draft edit and commented on how it appropriately reflected their programming approach. They were critical of many of the foreign-produced programmes broadcast in The Gambia, where sophisticated editing techniques and special effects were deemed inappropriate to a viewing audience that requires clarity and sequential development of programme content. An example of this difference in ways of seeing is the response of the preview audience to a high quality, German-made documentary on tourism shown at the same preview. A beautiful and angled art-house shot of tourists in a canoe was met with squeals of laughter as Gambians told me 'everybody knows that if you sat like that in a canoe you would fall out and drown. Our film is better because it's true.' In the face of all the production challenges such feedback was good for my ego!

The Broadcast and Its Impact

The broadcast of the programme on GRTS was so well received that three days later a live studio debate took place on GRTS. This was to be accompanied by the first viewer telephone vote on the issue of whether tourism really could help to reduce poverty in The Gambia. During a rather fraught hour marred by technical difficulties, it had to be announced that it was impossible to proceed with the telephone vote. Unfortunately, the telephones were not working that evening! The response was overwhelming – deputations of disgruntled viewers, unable to register their opinion, arrived at GRTS studios and my hotel. In response GRTS agreed that a series of one-hour broadcasts on tourism-and poverty-related issues would take place over the following months. They would consist of a short clip from the programme followed by a live studio debate with selected panellists.

It was also agreed that the script for the documentary would permit an easy re-edit of a series of four 15-minute programmes for further use by non governmental and tourism educators in The Gambia. Suggested programmes in the series were:

- What does tourism mean to The Gambia?
- How do tourists and tourism businesses see tourism in The Gambia?
- What is ASSET and how could it help your business?
- How could you use a pro-poor tourism model to increase your income?

Figure 6.6 Ya Abbis Njie, Gambian television programme presenter.[10]

Each programme could be used for information and to stimulate discussion.

Another suggestion was that the script could also be amended to make a shorter version that would be suitable for UK tour operators to use with their destination resort staff as part of a training programme on working responsibly and sensitively in a developing world environment.

Conclusions

For a research-practitioner committed to development in the South, visual ethnography offers enormous potential to collect and disseminate information, which can effect beneficial change. It affords an opportunity for people from the North and the South to meet within a space where there is the possibility for information exchange using methods which present more democratic and egalitarian processes for learning and communication. Researchers need to be open to new ways of seeing conventional anthropological tools. In embracing the multiple visions of human and mechanical lenses, new routes (experimental ethnography) to understanding established destinations (the 'other') could be mapped. I consider that the value of this experimental visual ethnographic approach lies in its attempt to synergise plural meanings from multiple voices across a number of cultures about a social development issue – tourism. In a culture that is visually-and orally-rooted, any chance for a meaningful change in attitude in The Gambia required research that was visually-and orally-based, interpreted and distributed. Visual anthropology demonstrated some very useful lessons which could help those trying to meet those United Nations Millennium Development Goals.

Notes

1. Verbatim statement by Gambian children to me during the project. This stems from their observation that tourists must be wealthy because they sit in the sun and do nothing but eat and drink.
2. I use the term 'compound eye' to describe a way of looking at the world that is experientially positioned and never neutral or objective. It can be likened to the eye of a fly, which has adapted to its environment through a compound eye, which permits each cell in the eye to see a separate image. Simultaneously the fly has multiple images with many pieces of information to support its choices for survival. Humans may not have this physical capacity but I would argue that effective communication and development research may be dependent upon the construction of a metaphorical compound gaze.
3. A comprehensive definition of tourism is beyond the scope of this article. The term is generally used to describe 'going on holiday', i.e., domestic or international travel in pursuit of leisure activities, which include day trips. The World Tourism Organisation (WTO) defines tourism as any form of travel which involves an overnight stay but less than 365 days away from the traveller's home. WTO includes business travel and visits to friends and relations but excludes day trips.

4. 'All seven families [300 people] in Tumani Tenda are represented in the camp ... all benefit ... we believe tourism is the best way to develop the community.' (Sulyman Sonko, Spokesperson for Tumani Tenda Village Camp, which hosts music tours in *Tourism in The Gambia* 2002'.

5. 'Tourism has been a blessing in disguise ... you find children following tourists ... begging. This has polluted our traditions.' (Sheik T'jan Ngang, Secretary of ASSET (Association of Small-Scale Enterprises in Tourism) in *Tourism in The Gambia* 2002'.

6. Emancipatory action research is an approach that reflects the guiding principles extracted from post modern and feminist theories. That is, the approach encourages plural voices; accommodates a variety of texts including written, oral and visual; challenges the validity of conventional approaches to discover 'best approach' strategies for research; is rooted in collaboration between all participants including the researcher; and views theory and practice as independent and interdependent stages of a change process.

7. UK Department for International Development (DfID1995: 17) defines a 'stakeholder' as 'any person, group or institution that has an interest in an aid activity, project or programme. This definition includes both intended beneficiaries and intermediaries, winners and losers, and those involved or excluded from decision-making processes.'

8. The term 'gatekeeper' is used to describe an individual who is a member of a group or organisation into which access needs to be negotiated for research purposes. Although the individual may be extremely useful, e.g., they can speak the languages of the researcher and the researched, there are inherent problems linked to the power and perception of the role. For example the gatekeeper may restrict access to all members of the community or they may be marginalized by parts of the community.

9. The stakeholder list included:
   - The Gambia: Formal sector: Ground Handlers and Equipment Hirers Association, Hoteliers, UK tour operator resort staff, Department for Tourism and Culture. Informal sector: Association of Small Scale Enterprises in Tourism, bumsters, craft market vendors, fruit sellers, juice bar owners, tourist guides, tourist taxi drivers. GRTS viewing public who may benefit directly (employment and repatriation of funds from family working in tourism) and indirectly (socio economic benefits from tourism sector activity trickling down within the country) from tourism.
   - UK: Department for International Development, UK tour operators, Association of British Travel Agents, Association of Independent Travel Operators.

10. Ya Abbis Njie is a well-known and well-liked news presenter in The Gambia who speaks the four languages of broadcasts. There are four regular presenters of the nightly national news bulletin. She was selected as the programme's presenter because women were under-represented in the video interviews (in part due to a lack of confidence as indicated in their camera shyness and their deference to male opinion) and because of the clarity of her English. This was viewed as important to engage UK tourism trade audiences.

Bibliography

Badger, A., P. Barnett, L. Corbyn, J. Keefe (eds). 1996. *Trading Places: Tourism as Trade*. London: Tourism Concern.

Banks, M. and H. Morphy (ed.). 1997. *Rethinking Visual Anthropology*. New Haven: Yale University Press.

Briassoulis, H. 1995. 'The Environmental Internalities of Tourism: Theoretical Analysis and Policy Implications', in H. Coccossis and P. Nijkamp (ed.), *Sustainable Tourism Development*. UK: Ashgate.

Brohman, J. 1996. 'New Directions in Tourism for Third-World Development', in *Annals of Tourism Research* 23(1): 48–70.

Bruzzi, S. 2000. *New Documentary: A Critical Introduction*. New York: Routledge.

Buhalis D. and J. Fletcher. 1995. 'Environmental Impacts on Tourist Destinations: An Economic Analysis', in H. Coccossis and P. Nijkamp (ed.). *Sustainable Tourism Development*. UK: Ashgate.

Burns P. and A. Holden. 1995. *Tourism – A New Perspective*. Harlow: Prentice Hall.

Butler, R.W. 1993. 'Tourism – An Evolutionary Perspective', in J.G. Nelson, R.W. Butler, and G. Wall (eds), *Tourism and Sustainable Development: Monitoring, Planning, Managing*. University of Waterloo, Ontario: Department of Geography.

Canestrelli, E. and P. Costa. 1991. 'Tourist Carrying Capacity: A Fuzzy Approach', in *Annals of Tourism Research* 18: 295–311

Cater, E. and B. Goodall. 1992. 'Must Tourism Destroy Its Resource Base?' in S.R. Bowlby and A.M. Mannion (eds), *Environmental Issues in the 1990s*. Chichester: Wiley.

Collier, J. and M. Collier. 1986. *Visual Anthropology Photography as a Research Method*. Albuquerque: University of New Mexico Press.

Concern Universal. 2001. *Horticultural Production and Marketing in The Gambia: Reality and Recommendations*. The Gambia: Concern Universal.

Cooper, C. and S. Wanhill. 1997. *Tourism Development Environmental and Community Issues*. Chichester: Wiley.

Crawford, P.I. and D. Turton. (eds). 1992. *Film as Ethnography*. Manchester: Manchester University Press.

Croall, J. 1995. *Preserve or Destroy: Tourism and the Environment*. London: Gulbenkian Foundation.

DfID. 1995. *Stakeholder Participation and Analysis*. London: DFID.

DFID. 2000. *Halving World Poverty by 2015, Economic Growth, Equity and Security. Strategies for Achieving the International Development Targets*. London: DFID.

Dieke, P.U.C. 1998. 'Tourism in Sub-Saharan Africa: Development Issues and Possibilities', in A.V. Seaton (ed.), *Tourism: The State of the Art*. Chichester: Wiley.

Eber, S. (ed.). 1992. *Beyond The Green Horizon: Principles for Sustainable Tourism*. Godalming: WWF.

Forsyth, T. 1996. *Sustainable Tourism: Moving from Theory to Practice*. Godalming: WWF.

Foucault, M. 1973. *The Birth of the Clinic: An Archaeology of Medical Perception*, trans. A.M. Sheridan-Smith. New York: Pantheon.

France, L. (ed). 1997. *The Earthscan Reader in Sustainable Tourism*. London: Earthscan.

Giongo, F., J. Bosco-Nizeye and G.N. Wallace. 1994. *A Study of Visitor Management in the World's National Parks and Protected Areas*. Colorado: Ecotourism Society and World Conservation Monitoring Centre.

Goodwin, H. and D. Stadhams. 2000. DfID *Tourism Challenge Fund Application*. London: University of Greenwich School of Earth and Environmental Studies, unpublished manuscript.

Graefe, A.R., F.R. Kuss and J.J. Vaske. 1990. *Visitor Impact Management: The Planning Framework*. Washington: National Parks and Conservation Association.

Grimshaw, A. 2001. *The Ethnographer's Eye: Ways of Seeing in Modern Anthropology*. Cambridge: Cambridge University Press.

Hammersley, M. 1998. *Reading Ethnographic Research*. Harlow: Longman.

Harrison, P. 1993. *Inside the Third World*, 3rd ed. Harmonsworth: Penguin.

Hawkins, R. and V. Middleton. 1993. 'The Environmental Practices and Programmes of Travel and Tourism Companies', in B. J. Richie, and D. Hawkins (eds), *World Travel and Tourism Review: Indicators, Trends and Issues*. Wallingford: Commonwealth Agricultural Bureau International.

Hockings, P. (ed.). 1995. *Principles of Visual Anthropology*. Berlin: Mouton de Gruyter.

ICRT, IIED and ODI. 2002. *The Tourism Industry and Poverty Reduction: A Business Primer*. London: Overseas Development Institute.

Kaplan, A.E. 1997. *Looking for the Other: Feminism, Film and The Imperial Gaze*. New York: Routledge.

Krippendorf, J. 1987. *The Holidaymakers: Understanding the Impact of Leisure Travel*. Oxford: Heinemann.

Leask, A. and I. Yeoman (eds). 1999. *Heritage Visitor Attractions: An Operations Management Perspective*. London: Cassell.

Lindberg, K. and J. Enriquez. 1994. *An Analysis of Ecotourism's Economic Contribution to Conservation and Development in Belize*. Washington: WWF USA and Belize Ministry of Tourism and Environment.

McDonald, M.H.B. 1986. *Marketing Plans*. Oxford: Heinemann.

McPherson, M.F. and S.C. Radelet (eds). 1995. *Economic Recovery in The Gambia: Insights and Adjustments in Sub-Saharan Africa*. Cambridge: Harvard Institute for International Development.

May, V. 1991. 'Tourism, Environment and Development: Values, Sustainability and Stewardship', in *Tourism Management* 12 (2): 112–118

Miller, R. 2001. From a speech, 1 November 2001. Retrieved 18 February 2002 from World Travel and Tourism Council website www.wttc.org/resourcecentre/speeches.asp (This speech is no longer available.)

Mowforth, M. and I. Munt. 1998. *Tourism and Sustainability: New Tourism in the Third World*. London: Routledge.

Nelson, J.G., R.W. Butler and G. Wall (eds). 1993. *Tourism and Sustainable Development: Monitoring, Planning, Managing*. Ontario: University of Waterloo, Department of Geography.

Pearce, D. 1981. *Tourist Development*. Harlow: Longman.

Pink, S. 2001. *Doing Visual Ethnography*. London: Sage Publications.

Prosser, R. 1994. 'Societal Change and the Growth in Alternative Tourism', in E. Cater and G. Lowman (eds), *Ecotourism: A Sustainable Option?* Chichester: Wiley.

Ritchie, B. and C. Goeldner (eds). 1994. *Travel Tourism and Hospitality Research: A Handbook for Managers and Researchers*. Chichester: Wiley.

Roe, D., N. Leader-Williams and B. Dalal-Clayton. 1997. *Take Only Photographs, Leave Only Footprints: The Environmental Impacts of Wildlife Tourism*. London: Wildlife and Development Series No. 10, International Institute for Environment and Development.

Ruby, J. 2000. *Picturing Culture: Explorations of Film and Anthropology*. Chicago: University of Chicago Press.

Silverman, D. 2000. *Doing Qualitative Research: A Practical Handbook*. London: Sage.

Sonko-Godwin, P. 1997. *Social and Political Structures in the Precolonial Periods (Ethnic Groups of The Senegambia Region)*. Banjul: Sunrise Pub.

Tomaselli, K.G. 1996. *Appropriating Images: The Semiotics of Visual Representation*. Højbjerg: Intervention Press.

Tomkinson, M. 2000. *Gambia*. Oxford: Michael Tomkinson Publishing.

UNDP. 1998. *National Human Development Index Report*. New York: United Nations Publishing

UNDP. 2000. *National Human Development Report: The Gambia*. New York: United Nations Publishing.

Urry, J. 1990. *The Tourist Gaze*. London: Sage.

Westwood, J. 2000. *How to Write a Marketing Plan*, 2nd ed. London: The Sunday Times, Kogan Page.

Williams A.M. and G. Shaw. 1998. 'Tourism and the Environment: Sustainability and Economic Restructuring', in C.M. Hall and A.A. Lew (eds), *Sustainable Tourism: A Geographical Perspective*. Harlow: Addison Wesley.

Zuber-Skerritt, O. (ed.). 1996 *New Directions in Action Research*. London: Falmer Press.

Filmography

Shoah. 1985. Claude Lanzmann. Les Films Aleph, Historia Films with French Ministry of Culture (France) 566 minutes.

Tourism In The Gambia. 2002. Dianne Stadhams. International Centre for Communication and Development, Roehampton University (UK). 60 minutes.

Chapter 7

ARCHIVING 'HERITAGE', RECONSTRUCTING THE 'AREA'

Conducting Audiovisual Ethnography in EU-sponsored Research

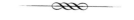

Vassiliki Yiakoumaki

In this chapter I discuss aspects of an ethnographic research project based on the use of audiovisual digital technologies, and realized in the framework of a European Commission Programme on Mediterranean 'urban heritage' in a number of cities across the Mediterranean between 2003 and 2006. As the principal project researcher for one of its thirteen partner-projects, i.e., for the city of Chania, Crete (Greece), I have been responsible for conducting long-term fieldwork based on the exclusive use of digital video and still photography to contribute to a number of audiovisual ethnographic products: a website which now functions as a database of Mediterranean oral histories and urban spaces, as our main collective work, and various audiovisual products which have been developed by each individual research partner.

Here I draw from the three-year empirical work of this project to touch on issues concerning conducting an ethnography that supports an *institutionally* (EU) constructed theoretical framework, which suggests a certain version of Mediterranean cultural unity. As I shall illustrate, what becomes very pertinent in this process is the potential of visual anthropology as an 'applied' discipline, namely, its relevance beyond strictly academic contexts. Therefore I am concerned both with issues relating to the theoretical underpinnings of ethnography, and with questions about the social uses of ethnography, more precisely, audiovisual ethnography. Thus I address questions such as the following: how does an ethnographer come to terms with his/her professional commitment to promote institutionally traditional concepts, such as that of the 'area', which at first sight may seem outdated, or have been long since deconstructed and/or contested by anthropologists? The culture area in question is the Mediterranean, a concept which for many anthropologists suggests a sense of academic parochialism. What role does the visual play in redeploying this term and attaching new meanings to it? Consequently, what can be the sociopolitical significance of such ethnographies, e.g., in terms of the nonacademic character of the projects? Let me note here that the project's declared objective, as is common in many European projects of this kind, has been to contribute to strengthening local actors in Mediterranean cities, in designing 'urban heritage management'.

Therefore my arguments shall follow two directions, one pertaining to the theoretical consequences of articulating a certain discourse, and the other pertaining to the applied nature of this discourse when it comes to civil society. I argue that, while critically approaching EU institutional rhetoric, at the same time one ought to be aware that this rhetoric, i.e., of a Mediterranean urban culture, or cultures, emerges at a specific interface between new agendas – hence pressures – within the EU over the last couple of decades. Therefore traditional area concepts, such as the Mediterranean, are redeployed, hence resignified, in the context of the priorities of these (political, economic, developmental) agendas.

In this process, the visual ethnographer may creatively bypass the issue of subscribing to the idea of a culturally homogeneous area, and offer alternative ways of viewing the urban landscapes in question, which are sensitive to the emerging social realities of each urban setting (e.g., gentrification, immigration, multiculturalist politics). The visual, in other words, may play a crucial role in subverting the potential essentialism of this endeavour.

In the following sections I shall briefly place the current discourse of the Mediterranean in, what I perceive as the broad politico-economic conjuncture from which it emerges, and I shall outline the project in question as a product of this conjuncture. In the main section, by offering examples from individual partner-projects of the programme, I shall discuss and illustrate the potential of visual ethnographies for revisiting traditional concepts such as the Mediterranean, and for viewing the 'area' in ways which can have a social and political impact in the societies under study.

Politico-economic Contexts Pertaining to the (Re-)emergence of the Mediterranean

The current emergence of the Mediterranean in EU institutional discourse and practice is not a reemergence of the concept known to have been popular in anthropology during the 1960s and 1970s. In this earlier stage, the construction of the Mediterranean basin as a 'culture area' was based on the study of Mediterranean societies as structured by the two antithetical codes of 'honour' and 'shame', allegedly prevalent in that world. This approach proposed an alleged persistence of Mediterranean modes of thought, and depicted the Mediterranean world as static, 'simple', and culturally homogeneous.[1]

Although rhetorically it may seem to be reviving the old anthropological paradigm, the EU discourse of the Mediterranean emerging in the 1990s is being articulated in an entirely different context, a context which may be summed up as EU politics at a decisive moment of European integration. This moment has been governed by significant events and processes from the late 1980s until present, such as the dissolution of the Eastern bloc, the European enlargement, and increasing immigration particularly from Southern (i.e., Arab) Mediterranean and African countries towards the European Mediterranean.

The collapse of the so-called Eastern bloc and the subsequent European enlargement, which was realized recently with the integration of a number of new member states from central and Eastern Europe, was a crucial moment by virtue of the fact that it made a new tension perceptible: a tension which can be understood as two opposed forces within the EU, one towards the centre-east, and the other towards the south of Europe.

Specifically, the existing centre of gravity within the EU shifted towards the central-eastern European states, and this shift meant changing European priorities: a new competitive agenda as opposed to the long overdue agenda of a European Mediterranean policy, which had seemed to have been hampered since the 1970s. This development exacerbated already existing tensions between a European North and a European South within the EU, as well as between the Northern Mediterranean and the Southern (non European) Mediterranean.

A Euro-Mediterranean policy should ideally serve needs on both sides of the Mediterranean basin. This would include the economically more vulnerable member states of the European south (Greece, the Mezzogiorno, Spain, and Portugal) and the so-called Third Mediterranean Countries, that is, the Mediterranean nonmembers such as many Arab countries (the prospective Arab 'markets'). Attention to the Arab countries was made even more imperative with the collapse of the Soviet Union and the subsequent emerging presence of the US in the part of the Mediterranean known as the Middle East.

Besides the emergence of the above new state of affairs as a result of the end of the cold war, the lack of political and economic stability amongst the Mediterranean nonmembers became a new challenge. For example, immigration from the Middle East and Arab/African countries towards the European Mediterranean (Spain, Italy, France, etc.) was an alarming event for the EU over the last decades. This situation made more acute the need for a shift of attention towards the Mediterranean, and for a Euro-Mediterranean policy which could tackle the new reality, for example, by means of new economic-developmental initiatives in the Mediterranean region. Therefore a Euro-Mediterranean policy was felt even more urgent by the 1990s, for reasons of European enlargement pressures, maintaining control over Southern Mediterranean (nonmember) markets, and planning a common foreign and security policy in Europe.[2]

It is in this context of European geopolitics that the Mediterranean reentered the EU political agenda in the mid1990s. The shift to the Mediterranean became official with the Barcelona Conference in 1995, which launched the EU's proximity policy towards the Mediterranean region. This policy introduced what has been known since then as the Euro-Mediterranean Partnership, an entity with a majority of Mediterranean partners which are nonmembers.[3] In other words this is a policy for the whole of the Mediterranean, both the European South and the Southern Mediterranean, and it is known as the first of its kind, promoting cooperation between Europe and the Mediterranean. Along with the main core of concerns on the economic and financial fields, of direct relevance to this chapter is the stated concern with so-called 'social, cultural and human questions'. Specifically, as stated in the Barcelona Declaration, the basic axes of the Euro-Mediterranean cooperation are: establishment of 'a common area of peace and stability', establishment of 'economic and financial partnership' and a 'free-trade area' between the EU and its Mediterranean Partners, and establishment of 'partnership in social, cultural, and human affairs ... promoting understanding between cultures and exchanges between civil societies'.[4]

It is for this purpose that Barcelona launched the Euromed Heritage Programme, which is the Commission's regional programme 'aiming at the preservation and development of the Euro-Mediterranean cultural heritage.'[5] Various research projects have been funded under Euromed Heritage, one of them being the *Mediterranean Voices* Programme, discussed in this chapter. Therefore it was at this moment in the mid1990s that the discourse of Euro-Mediterranean cultural unity began to be articulated systematically at the level of EU policy; and it is at the above conjuncture of events that the vision of a Mediterranean community and the stated promotion of a Mediterranean 'cultural heritage' needs to be viewed – in other words, as part of a broader European investment.[6]

The Ethnographer's 'Mediterranean': The Programme as a Visual Project

What seems like an essentialist gaze, then, is not so much essentialist as it is political. The turn towards the Mediterranean is a deployment of the category 'culture' for the purposes of EU politics in this specific historical conjuncture. At the same time it is also a 'gaze' from the point of view of the specific ethnographic endeavour, which is a *visual* rendition of the cultural entity in question.

With this, I can now move from the bureaucratic to the ethnographic. Based on my own empirical work in the project, I shall shed light on the emergence of the Mediterranean from the ethnographer's perspective, that is, on the ways the ethnographers received, and became responsive to, the institutionally provided definition. Specifically I mean how they were able to formulate their public profile as Mediterranean researchers, by negotiating the potential essentialism of the endeavour while remaining faithful to the objectives of the institutional framework.

The programme is called *Mediterranean Voices: Oral History and Cultural Practice in Mediterranean Cities* and it is based on a partnership with a number of different institutions, such as universities (myself representing the University of Crete) and NGOs,[7] conducting research on thirteen Mediterranean cities: Alexandria, Ancona, Beirut, Bethlehem, Chania, Ciutat de Mallorca, Granada, Istanbul, Las Palmas de Gran Canaria, Marseille, Nicosia North, Nicosia South, and Valletta. The map of the Mediterranean which we provide (Figure 7.1) constitutes our own version of the Mediterranean as constructed for the purposes of the research.[8]

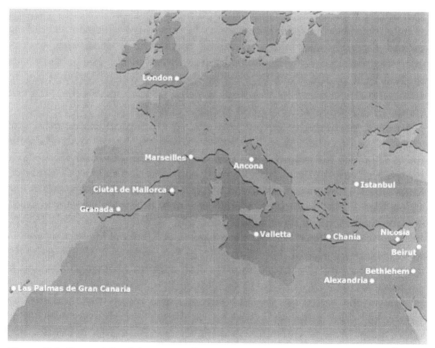

Figure 7.1 Created for this project, the *Mediterranean Voices* map with all the city-partners is but one of many versions in which to perceive the Mediterranean. © London Metropolitan University 2006

Mediterranean Voices is a visual ethnography of the many (urban) nuances of a 'culture area'. According to our official declaration, the aim of the project was 'to promote an awareness of the intangible cultural heritage of Mediterranean urban landscapes' (www.med-voices.org, introduction[9]). In this sense, the declared objective indeed reflects the EU rhetoric on the unity of the culture area.[10] Yet the potential to diverge from an essentialist gaze, as well as to engage in a socially sensitized academic endeavour, was made evident in the declaration: the ethnography was designed to take place by 'collecting and recording the memories and perceptions of neighbourhood residents' (ibid.). This indicated a particular treatment of the concept of 'heritage'. Accordingly, the ethnography did not wish to 'privilege the monumental, or indeed, élite visions of culture and heritage, thus ignoring the presence of popular oral traditions and cultural practices … The Mediterranean Voices project seeks to create a space for the expression of less frequently heard voices which for a variety of reasons are often absent or effaced in monumental aspects of urban cultural heritage' (ibid.). More specifically we expected ourselves, as ethnographers, to 'focus on a variety of neighbourhood-based interactions and experiences which are played out in and through storytelling, personal recollections of historic events, everyday social interactions and cultural practices' (ibid.). The project aimed to shed light on the above by viewing them as 'diverse, yet often fragile, fabric of memories and relationships which help to shape the meaning and character of Mediterranean urban quarters' (ibid.).

In each partner-city project, the above ethnographic material was expected to be collected and recorded exclusively in audiovisual digital form. This way the project generated two categories of visual products: a) the collectively built website, which contains our fieldwork material (interviews, conversations, events, etc.) in the form of image, audio and video files; b) the individual visual products that each partner created, such as documentary films, exhibitions, etc.

Therefore the visual became the means to define local identity, as well as to negotiate the official definition of it. In this process, it also became the mode for the project's involvement in civil society: a principal aim was to promote an awareness of the stated 'intangible cultural heritage' in what is commonly called in the EU bureaucratic idiom the 'stakeholder networks.' The latter is a diverse audience which may consist of educational institutions, policy makers, the media, tourist networks, etc., of which the main target groups are local actors, or networks of local actors, involved in 'urban heritage management' at local level, or becoming empowered to participate in, or contribute to it. For instance, this endeavour may translate into attracting conscientious travellers, in the context of a more sustainable tourist development.

In other words, the visual becomes a 'bottom-up' approach to 'heritage.' This approach, which implies the underlying philosophy of the project, is based on the premise that the actual lived experiences of the inhabitants of the urban quarters under study can point toward a definition of 'heritage', hence of 'heritage management', which is more alert to the local realities of the (Mediterranean) societies in question.

In the following two sections, I shall attempt to illustrate how a visual ethnography can be a site for a constructive and socially engaged encounter between the bureaucratic and the ethnographic. I shall do this by utilizing specific examples from the different partner projects.

An 'Essentialist' Concept as a Tool for an Engaged Anthropology

My task is to reveal the interdependency of processes in a specific power configuration. This means accounting for the emergence of an institutional discourse on culture through a specific geopolitical context, and the ability of this (hegemonic) discourse both to create possibilities for its own constructive debunking through ethnography/anthropology, and to have localized social uses. It is at this point that the visual acquires relevance. My main argument revolves around the idea of the *noncoercive* nature of a bureaucratically established framework for conducting ethnography. The visual, as I illustrate, provides the possibility for such an encounter to be effective, both in terms of the theoretical value of the ethnography and in terms of its applied character.

Specifically, as ethnographers in *Mediterranean Voices*, we found ourselves tackling two interrelated issues: on the one hand, the (re-emergence of the Mediterranean institutionally, and, on the other, the different uses and/or strategic redeployments of the term, from our side. The position of the anthropologists/ethnographers coordinating an EU project which must take for granted a Mediterranean 'cultural unity', can be summed up in the need to make a kind of compromise, which is a challenging task. This position on the one hand consists in a hesitancy to accept what we have very well been trained to call an essentialist term (the 'Mediterranean'), *and* an attempt to de-essentialize it, while on the other, a need to remain faithful to the Commission's objectives and requirements for a politics of urban heritage management.

There seemed to be a necessary and inevitable oscillation, or at times an interplay, between endorsing the 'culture area' and being sceptical about it. This becomes evident in the language of our project declaration as ethnographers:

> The cities and neighbourhoods which form part of the consortium and arenas of activity are not intended to be in any way representative of a Mediterranean urban 'archetype'. However, they do share a number of traits or 'cultures of urbanism' typical of Mediterranean urban quarters and environments, for example, the dense co-presence of an ethnically and socially-mixed population. In addition, these attributes cannot be understood without reference to the trans-Mediterranean ties of trade and mobility which have historically nourished these fluid and cosmopolitan urban social ecologies (www.med-voices.org, introduction).

In the process of this oscillation, ethnographers most often creatively negotiated the officially imposed use of the term Mediterranean. This was both a conscious decision and an unconscious process, which was governed, to a large degree, by the empirical reality of the research. As I illustrate below, this becomes evident in the audiovisual material produced: it is the specific realities of everyday life in each Mediterranean setting (whether it is Chania, or Beirut, or Ancona, or Istanbul) that prompted us to revisit the concept, because of, or rather, in the ways they pertain to, wider social and political realities. The essentialist concept may indeed become a means for producing an ethnography which wishes to be both theoretically grounded and socially sensitive.

With this, I wish neither to reduce the workings of power nor to portray an idealized, hence apolitical, image of fieldwork. As in most collective projects of this kind, there are conflicting perceptions of the 'area' among ethnographers, and there are ethnographers who succumb to an uncritical view of a Mediterranean cultural unity. There are even ethnographic moments in which, for all of us in *Mediterranean Voices*, it became unavoidable to escape a certain degree of folklorism. Yet my intention is less to take stock of such shortcomings, than to speak of the potential of conducting fieldwork legitimized by a particular 'bureaucratic' institutional context and discursive regime. I am not implying anything more than what is common knowledge to us since Foucault, that discourse can be both an effect of power and a site of resistance. Also my intention is to present the visual as a form which, in this research endeavour, acquires an applied aspect. The accessibility of the visual to various types of audiences, such as the 'stakeholder' networks in each city seeking to promote their own, albeit conflicting, perceptions of heritage, helps turn this into a public-sphere issue (local, national, supralocal), with impacts in local power centres and civil society. Therefore I wish less to embark on content analysis of each project's visual material, than to stress the fact of the emergence of visual ethnography/anthropology within an institution such as the EU. Besides the strictly theoretical concerns of *Mediterranean Voices*, it is an endeavour to take anthropology beyond the academy, and have an impact on civil society.

The project focuses on the urban neighbourhood. Neighbourhood and war, neighbourhood and immigration, neighbourhood and multiculturalist politics, neighbourhood and gentrification, neighbourhood and tourism, are some of the cross-cutting themes in the partner-city projects, revealing multiple Mediterranean realities. Through the local inhabitants' personal narrations (histories, memories, recollections) and everyday life events (public and private encounters, performances, e.g., of a song, dance, or a tale), the audiovisual material becomes a registry of another kind of heritage, one which is neglected or understudied in top-down approaches of heritage. In entering the website, this material may become accessible to a variety of social categories of viewers, such as target groups in education, commerce, tourism, and development, or target groups pertaining to civil society (e.g., immigrants and minority groups).

In what follows, I selectively provide examples from the work of some of the partner projects, by highlighting one or two main themes which have emerged in the ethnographic work of each one. By no means do I cover the entire spectrum of cities, or of issues in each city project. Rather, with each visual example, I illustrate how visual methods and/or visual materials are capable of subverting the essentialism of the 'area', by means of focusing on crucial realities shaping local everyday life. The examples come from our collective work on the website, whereby each city-project manages its own page.

Displacement, Gentrification, Immigration, Multiculturalist Politics: On 'Mediterranean' Realities

In the partner projects of Bethlehem, Beirut, North Nicosia (Northern Cyprus), and South Nicosia (Republic of Cyprus), one of the dominant themes emerging in neighbourhood life is the theme of official politics and collective memory in the context of a war (ongoing or bygone). Local narratives constitute an interweaving of recollections, reconciliations, nostalgias, silences, and traumas pertaining to the experience of living in a war, or in the aftermath of a war. In these particular projects, whereby the cities in question are strongly identified with, or reminiscent of, past or present landscapes of conflict and violence, the challenge for the ethnographer is not merely to evade subsuming them under an essentialist Mediterraneanist logic, but also to avoid depicting them as states of handicap, that is, as sensitive areas or war zones. At the same time it is crucial not to lose sight of the aspect of politics.

The projects of Bethlehem and Beirut, in particular, prevent a Mediterraneanist logic primarily through the choice of ethnographers to map vital and pressing existing realities in regard to the recent political history of the areas, thus attempting to keep the projects historically grounded and politically informed. In the Bethlehem project, research mainly pertains to the time period from the post – Ottoman/post – World War II years until the present, a historical period when Israeli-Arab politics critically influenced local life. The researcher cannot avoid viewing local urban life as crucially – and inevitably – influenced by the political events pertaining to the Palestinian issue. One prevalent theme in the ethnographic data is the presence of the border, physical or symbolic. What is made very evident is a sense of a continuous placing of borders disrupting all aspects of everyday life by dividing the physical landscape. The border – in other words the separation, or severance, or segregation – is materialized in forms of various barriers, with all their overt symbolism, whether it is fences, checkpoints, the camps, or the recent Separation Wall (Figure 7.2).

Figure 7.2 'Check Point-1'. © London Metropolitan University 2006. Originator: Centre for Cultural Heritage Preservation (CCHP), Bethlehem.

Figure 7.3 'Clothing-4'. This touches on the theme of urban Palestinians' choice between traditional and European dress, since the first half of the twentieth century. © London Metropolitan University 2006. Originator: Centre for Cultural Heritage Preservation (CCHP), Bethlehem.

At the same time, the city is not merely approached with reference to war. On the contrary, ethnographers shed light on aspects of local life alluding to states of 'normality', such as images of everyday life and social events which are not suggestive of the 'abnormality' of conflict. This may be viewed as a political stance from the researchers' side stating a form of creative resistance to the overwhelming presence of conflict and the irrationality of apartheid-like segregation. To exemplify this, I wish to stress the use of folklore in these ethnographies as a means for the depiction of local urban life, e.g., through a wedding 'custom', a festival, a food, a handicraft, etc. (Figure 7.3). Instead of making easy assumptions about folkloric ethnographies, I suggest, one should rather view such choices as strategic redeployments of folklore from the side of the ethnographer, for the purpose of making politically significant statements. By alluding to the quotidian, folklore may function as an invocation for re-establishing 'normality' despite its possible ideological repercussions of reifying and romanticizing the social subjects in question. In other words, it is useful to see folkloric images in light of the unsettling and overwhelming images of war, because this contrast may render the ordinariness of the quotidian more urgent, hence more powerful. Therefore, folklore may become evocative of the quotidian as a necessary, yet absent, condition.

There is a similar process at work in the case of Nicosia, for instance. Specifically, the military conflict of 1974 in Cyprus resulted in the separation of the island in two different national entities, i.e., the ethnically Turkish Cyprus and the ethnically Greek Cyprus. The separated city of Nicosia, formally divided along the Green Line since then, and hence transformed into two different cities, represents these two collective entities. Here, too, it is important to see folklore in terms of the local historical and political context. In North Nicosia local life is largely depicted through custom, habit, and uses of material culture. This may include food and cuisine (e.g., the culture of bread), clothing and dowry, materials of the domestic environment (utensils, stoves), turkish baths, coffee shops, children's games, shadow-puppet theatre, or museum material. In an urban landscape identified with a history of violent partition, such depictions do not function simply as local colour, capitalizing on the commodification of tradition, but can also function as subversions of a dominant image of Cyprus as a politically turbulent and problematic area. Local life is also depicted through references to the presence of various nonnative (hegemonic) Others on the island (e.g., the British), thus revealing how supralocal the local can be (Figure 7.4). Such references prevent narrow geographical perceptions of Mediterranean locales, and involve a more historically informed perspective, which may mean, in the case of Cyprus, that it is not to be viewed merely as a locus of contention between Greeks and Turks, or Christians and Muslims. This may be particularly useful at local level for understanding the broader contexts producing the ongoing politics of 'difference' in Cyprus.

Figure 7.4 Postbox in North Nicosia: as a sign of the (British) colonial past, it becomes an opportunity to conceptualise the Mediterranean also as supralocal, or supraregional, category. © London Metropolitan University 2006. Originator: Gençlik Merkezi.

The project of South Nicosia also resists being subsumed under a culturally homogeneous Mediterranean. Here the local project stresses the history of the division of the island, the pressing realities of Southern Cyprus's EU accession, the recent 'crossing' (i.e., opening) of the Green Line, the Annan Plan process in 2004[11] and the pertinent referendums. Therefore it integrates Cyprus into a broader geopolitical context of the EU. This has meant touching on the multiple changes in the social landscape, such as the emergence of other Others (e.g., immigrants, foreign students), and the various negotiations between 'European' and 'native', preconflict and postconflict, and 'modern' and 'premodern' realities (Figures 7.5 and 7.6).

Figure 7.5 Quilt maker – South Nicosia. © London Metropolitan University 2006. Originator: *Mediterranean Voices* – South Nicosia.

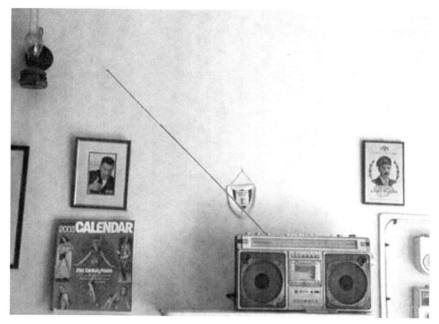

Figure 7.6 Interior space – South Nicosia. © London Metropolitan University 2006. Originator: *Mediterranean Voices* – South Nicosia.

At the same time, because the recent history of this city is equally marked by conflict, the occasional ethnographic focus on local folklore, such as games, cheese making, traditional quilt making, weddings, restaurants and eating habits and the like, may also function here as reminder of the fact that this is no longer a conflict-torn landscape.

In Lebanon, the war is also over; yet the experience of war is only approximately one generation away.[12] The intense focus of the Beirut project on this pressing political reality resists essentialist Mediterranean classifications. In this ethnographic endeavour, the issue of continuities and ruptures in local memory becomes very timely. Specifically in Beirut, life in the urban neighbourhood is in many ways marked by the memory, or lack of memory, of the civil war and the current experience of 'reconstruction'. By recording local narratives in the urban districts of Hamra and Ras Beirut, the partner project aims at mapping Beirut's identity through treatment of the recent civil war in various, official or nonofficial, discourses of local actors. The image of the crane (Figure 7.7), almost omnipresent in Beirut's urban landscape, often in combination with bullet-ridden buildings in the background, functions as a synecdoche for 'reconstruction'. A process which may also signify a reconstruction of history, or, otherwise, an erasure of history, should this become politically necessary . . .

Figure 7.7 Reconstruction in Beirut. © London Metropolitan University 2006. Originator: *Mediterranean Voices* – Beirut

Figure 7.8 'Political Posters – Hizbullah (2)'. Taken in Bashoura, Beirut. © London Metropolitan University 2006. Originator: Centre for Behavioral Research, the American University of Beirut.

The potential registering of local histories into an all-inclusive Mediterranean history is subverted by virtue of the choice of themes by the ethnographer. Rendered into visual material, these themes tie in with urgent political realities, thus 'translating' urban landscape into geopolitical space. Dislocation, conflict resolution, marginalization, and the elusiveness of intimate space emerge as some of the intense realities of urban life in these Mediterranean localities. Their audiovisual rendition is largely a political stance from the side of the ethnographer, which recognizes these histories as histories of power relations. On the other hand, despite having been heavily marked by conflict and violence, these urban landscapes are not perceived as 'states of injury' (Brown 1995), that is, stereotyped as loci of aberration or deviation from a (social/political/historical/ 'human') norm.

Different kinds of experience of displacement and separation are recorded in other city projects, as in the case of Istanbul. This partner project speaks of dislocation experiences of ethnic groups in the local population, in the context of the politics of the nation state. For instance, through fieldwork in the neighbourhoods Arnavutköy, Fatih, Moda, and

Gaziosmanpasa, one of the many foci of this visual ethnography becomes the non-Muslim minorities of Istanbul (e.g., ethnic Greeks and Armenians), forced to leave their city as a result of organized state violence in the 1950s and 1960s. Combined with the opposite movements of mass migration from the countryside (Anatolia) to the city, and from other Balkan countries (e.g., Bulgaria) to Turkey, this process radically changed the landscape of the urban neighbourhood in Istanbul, and redefined self-perceptions of local urban identity. Within this theme, various other issues emerge, such as Turkey's underclasses, and gender roles in contemporary Turkey (Figure 7.9). A similar dislocation experience is recorded in the project of Alexandria, concerned with the memory of the city as a former cosmopolitan multi-ethnic urban centre. Various Alexandrians' life histories, diasporic or not, recount how the different nonnative communities of Alexandria (Greek, Italian, British, French, etc.), which were established since the twentieth century and granted a privileged status in Egyptian society and economy, gradually found themselves having to leave the city, along with many native Arab populations, in the course of the political process of Egypt's nationalization, during the period between World War II and the 1960s.

In both cases, the rupture in local memory caused in the context of nation-state politics often coincides with a romanticization of the past, a past contrasted to the contemporary lived experience of an 'Arab-ized' Alexandria, in one case, and an 'Islamic-ized' Istanbul, in the other. The ethnographic projects view these Mediterranean histories from the perspective of overlapping regional (Eastern or Southern Mediterranean, Balkan, European, etc.) and more global political conjunctures.

Figure 7.9 Istanbul, Fatih district: wedding dresses in shop. © London Metropolitan University 2006. Originator: Gülay Kayacan.

Neighbourhood gentrification in the Mediterranean urban landscape emerges as another prominent theme in the various partner projects. In Granada, gentrification is observed as part of the lived experience in two neighbourhoods. These are Albayzín and Sacromonte, the one known as the old 'Arabic quarter', and the other as 'the gypsy neighbourhood' with its emblematic 'cave-houses' which were the homes of a traditionally underprivileged population in Granada. The Arabic and *gitano* features of the two areas, respectively, bring in new social categories of inhabitants who are attracted by the perceived exoticism of these spaces. In this process, a process of resignification of space, city neighbourhoods are revitalized while becoming spaces of heritage consumption.

Figure 7.10 Sacromonte cave house, renovated (Granada). Heritage consumption, as any type of consumption of tradition, is afforded by emerging social categories compatible with the pursuit of distinctive (Bourdieu 1984) commodities and distinctive ways of life. © London Metropolitan University 2006. Originator: *Mediterranean Voices* – Granada.

The theme of immigration appears prominently in partner projects along the Mediterranean. For instance, in the Marseille project, the city appears marked by the current experiences of immigration, particularly from the Maghreb countries and 'black Africa'. The quarter of Belsunce, chosen for fieldwork, is a historical central quarter symbolic of 'Marseille's cosmopolitanism', yet at the same time experienced today as 'a place of troubling ethnicity' – currently known as *quartier Arab* (www.med-voices.org, Marseille page, introduction). Hence, one scope of the project is to depict the city's process of 'ethnicization' and the ways the local imaginary has overrated the 'Arab' presence in it (Figure 7.11). The figure of the 'black African' becomes a discrete, nonfitting presence in the urban landscape. As such, it subverts a traditionally established image of Marseille as a Mediterranean cosmopolitan harbour-city par excellence, and also becomes suggestive of the (purportedly alarming) increasing emergence of the Islamic Other in Europe.

Figure 7.11 'African' street vendors in Belsunce, Marseille. © London Metropolitan University 2006. Originator: Abdelmajid Arrif.

Multiculturalist politics appears to be a recently emerging issue in Mediterranean locales of the European Union. A study of Mediterranean cities, not as multi-ethnic cities, but as cities endorsing multiculturalist politics, undermines inherited perceptions of the homogeneity and simplicity of Mediterranean societies.

The increasing visibility of what is perceived as a city's 'multicultural heritage' ought to be seen as a product of a politics of multiculturalism and a discourse of 'cultural diversity' in EU institutions over the last couple of decades. On this topic, I draw on the work of the Granada and Chania projects. Among other themes, the Granada project depicts an emerging process of a 'return of Islam', relating itself to the city's Arabic heritage. This is made possible through the presence of Maghrebien immigrants and 'neo-Muslim' Spanish converts, and is materialized through the reopening of mosques, the establishment of spaces for prayer, and the public celebration of religious Muslim feasts (Figure 7.12).

Figure 7.12 'Muslim' dress in Albayzín (Granada). © London Metropolitan University 2006. Originator: *Mediterranean Voices* – Granada.

For the sake of offering a more comprehensive example, I present a more elaborate illustration of emerging multiculturalist landscapes, with the case of the Etz Hayyim Synagogue in the Chania partner project. The Synagogue constitutes a case-study in the *Mediterranean Voices* programme, not merely through the material available on the collective webpage but also through an ethnographic film I produced in the context of my work as researcher in the local project (*Etz Hayyim–Tree of Life* 2005). The audiovisual representation of this case study is concerned with the event of the recent restoration of the Etz Hayyim Synagogue at the city's former Jewish quarter, and the emergence of a new 'community' around it.[13] I explore the unprecedentedness of this presence in the urban landscape of Chania over the last few decades, which has been a city 'without Jews' since the end of World War II. Historically, Chania has been a component of various empires, including the Ottoman. Thus, like the rest of Crete, it is a typical example of a formerly multi-ethnic society. In the postempire era (early twentieth century, in this area), nation-state politics established their own version of collective identity, i.e., the monocultural nation. In Crete, this meant an identity without the traces of ethnic Others, such as Jews, Muslims, and other former Cretans. The almost total extinction of the Jews of Crete in the Holocaust did contribute to the formation of national Greek identity (i.e., Christian and Greek-speaking) in the city of Chania. Since then, the silence on the Jewish past of Chania in the local public sphere, accompanied by the abandonment of the synagogue, went hand in hand with the general state of silence on the Jews at the level of official and public discourse in Greece. The city has had a long Jewish history, yet one not officially displayed, studied, or approached today, and thus unknown.

Both in the database and in the film, I question through interviews and observations how the ethnic Other can be constructed in local memory and the local imaginary in this (Mediterranean? European? Balkan?) society today. I strive to understand how such a project can become viable, and what kind of collectivity/ies it produces. In fact it emerges today as not merely a synagogue but a multi-faith place of prayer and 'multicultural' centre, while a new 'Jewish' collectivity emerges around it, challenging in many ways the definition of 'Jewishness'. This renders its presence politically significant in this Christian and Greek-speaking local society. With my audiovisual fieldwork I aimed at contributing to discussions on issues of tolerance and multiculturalist politics in contemporary European peripheries, particularly in light of European integration and, as such, of new approaches in the official management of ethnic difference.

I view the synagogue film as a project in applied visual anthropology not merely in the sense of the medium, but in terms of its intended impact at a local level in Crete and in the rest of Greece when the film is screened. Not destined only for class or lectures at the University but also for the promotion of stakeholders' interests (to use the bureaucratic jargon), such as those of the synagogue itself, the Jewish communities in Greece and

Figure 7.13 Morning prayers in the Chania synagogue. © London Metropolitan University 2006. Originator: Vassiliki Yiakoumaki.

abroad, or the local tourist industry, this audiovisual ethnographic endeavour becomes a politically sensitive issue, which also involves a number of risks. Although the film enjoys an (unsurprisingly) good reception in Greek academic institutions and in Jewish communities, publicizing the topic can cause a certain awkwardness and, at times, reactionary attitudes in the public sphere at local level. The unprecedented visibility of a silenced issue, and the long established anti-Jewish sentiment in Greece, combined with a more recent pro-Palestinian sentiment, further complicates what might at first seem as a mere renovation project in the historical section of a city.

The tensions in the public sphere, as well as the personal concerns and hesitations of the ethnographer, are part of an ongoing process of writing I am currently carrying out. In this sense, the 'Mediterranean' is very much alive: not as a 'culture area' but as an opportunity to study, and engage in, politically significant and entangled contemporary social realities.

Conclusion

Endeavours such as the *Mediterranean Voices* ethnographic project have what may appear as an inherent contradiction, by virtue of the fact that the bureaucratic/institutional and the intellectual have to come to terms with each other. However, traditional perceptions such as that of the 'culture area', which are institutionally binding, can be resignified or strategically redeployed in the actual process of the work, and in this process, can acquire a practical (in the sense of social and political) significance. It is the actual multiple social realities of each local urban setting as recorded on audio and video, that themselves subvert the idea of Mediterranean cultural homogeneity, at the same time becoming testimonies to a very real and palpable 'Mediterranean'.

By maintaining this as my main argument throughout the chapter, I did not wish to idealize visual ethnography as inherently sensitive to social realities; neither did I wish to depoliticize fieldwork, especially the kind sponsored by EU institutions in the context of European politico-economic agendas. Rather, I aimed at pinpointing the emergence of possibilities for conducting a socially and politically sensitized visual ethnography within the framework of a bureaucratic institution. I have presented aspects of our ethnographic work of mapping the Mediterranean, hoping to have suggested, through some visual examples, the potential of such projects in terms of a) the treatment of 'alarming' concepts, such as that of the 'culture area' and b) potential impacts on civil society.

Overall, I did not intend to offer a simplified model of a top-down versus bottom-up approach, according to which empirical fieldwork presumably subverts the assumed hegemony of the institutional discourse. Rather, I intended to pinpoint the complexity of this relationship, which is determined by the political context in which it emerges every time. In terms of the institutional rhetoric, the concept of the area (the 'Mediterranean', in our case) emerges today in the context of new economic – political realities in EU member states. In terms of the ongoing fieldwork, the area is continually and inevitably both deconstructed and reconstructed in the empirical work, as our work focuses on the everyday realities of the local inhabitants.

I argue that we need to be sceptical about the common anthropological gut-reaction of discarding traditional concepts in contexts where we are institutionally bound to use them, and particularly in contexts where there is an intended impact in local society, i.e., outside the immediate academic context. The use of such concepts, often red banners in contemporary anthropological thought, can be administered without being semantically (thus ideologically) hegemonic. In our case, the audiovisual can be a means for the management of this hegemony. In the *Mediterranean Voices* project, the ethnographer may well achieve the desired Commission's objectives (e.g., support of civil society via cooperation with local actor networks) while at the same time being enabled to leave his/her theoretical and/or political mark on the end result. It is through invoking the Mediterranean, or, rather, by strategically invoking the term that the researcher is enabled to acquire a voice and depict the realities of everyday life in the region. Thus, while, on the one hand, there are institutional constraints in relation to the perception of the area (EU imperatives), on the other hand it is indeed possible for the ethnographer to offer nonessentialist readings of the 'area.' Otherwise put, the institutional does not constitute a constraint for the political engagement of the projects. On the contrary, it has the potential to endow research projects with a timeliness and political significance which may turn out to be important for the process of an engaged anthropology in nonacademic contexts, which is one of our main concerns in this volume.

Notes

All web pages cited were last accessed on 26 June, 2006.

1. For examples of the literature, see, e.g., Peristiany 1965; Davis 1977; Gilmore 1982. For the critique, see, e.g., Herzfeld 1980, 1984; Llobera 1987.
2. For analytical approaches on Euro-Mediterranean policy, one may consult readings such as the relevant Council of Europe series, e.g., Council of Europe 1997; or, e.g., Xenakis and Chryssochoou 2001; Pierros et al 1999; Pollacco 2006.
3. Morocco, Algeria, Tunisia, Egypt, Israel, Jordan, the Palestinian Authority, Lebanon, Syria, Turkey, Cyprus, and Malta (the last two, currently in the process of full EU membership).
4. See the Barcelona Declaration at
   http://ec.europa.eu/comm/external_relations/euromed/bd.htm,
   or http://www.euromedheritage.net/en/euromedheritage/objectives.htm
5. See http://www.euromedheritage.net
6. See, e.g., http://europa.eu.int/comm/europeaid/projects/med/foreword_en.htm, or http://europa.eu.int/comm/external_relations/med_mideast/intro

7. The partner institutions are, respectively: Bibliotheca Alexandrina (Alexandria), University of Bologna, American University of Beirut, Centre for Cultural Heritage Preservation (Bethlehem, Palestinian Authority), University of Crete (Rethimno Campus), University of the Balearic Islands (Palma de Mallorca), University of Granada, Economic and Social History Foundation of Turkey (Istanbul), University of Las Palmas de Gran Canaria, Association d'Anthropologie Méditerranéenne (ADAM) (Aix-en-Provence), Youth Centre Union (Nicosia North, Northern Cyprus), Intercollege (Nicosia South, Republic of Cyprus), and University of Malta. The project is coordinated by a team of anthropologists at London Metropolitan University, the International Institute for Culture Tourism and Development.
8. All visual examples which follow, come from our *Mediterranean Voices* collective work on the website, at www.med-voices.org.
9. Official website of project.
10. The oft repeated desire 'to enhance and conserve the Mediterranean cultural heritage' is a common example within this rhetoric. See, e.g., the Declaration of the Euro-Mediterranean Meeting of Ministers for Culture, in Bologna in 1996, at http://ec.europa.eu/comm/external_relations/euromed/conf/sect/culture.htm
11. The unsuccessful UN proposed plan for resolving the 'Cyprus Problem'.
12. This text was written before the events in Beirut in the summer of 2006, which took place in the context of the new conflict between Lebanon and Israel.
13. The synagogue was proclaimed a World Monument in 1996, and attracted international support for its restoration.

Bibliography

Bourdieu, Pierre 1984. *Distinction: The Social Critique of the Judgment of Taste*, trans. R. Nice. Cambridge: Harvard University Press.

Brown, Wendy 1995. *States of Injury: Power and Freedom in Late Modernity*. Princeton: Princeton University Press.

Council of Europe 1997. *The Challenges Facing European Society with the Approach of the Year 2000. Strategies for the Sustainable Development of European States in the Mediterranean Basin* (Series: European regional planning, vol. 59). Strasbourg: Council of Europe Publishing.

Davis, Jonathan 1977. *People of the Mediterranean: An Essay in Comparative Social Anthropology*. London: Routledge & Kegan Paul.

Gilmore, David D. 1982. 'Anthropology of the Mediterranean Area', in *Annual Review of Anthropology* 11: 175–205.

Herzfeld, Michael 1980. 'Honour and Shame: Problems in the Comparative Analysis of Moral Systems', in *Man* 15 (2): 339–51.

——— 1984. 'The Horns of the Mediterraneanist Dilemma', in *American Ethnologist* 11 (3): 439–54.

Llobera, Josep R. 1987. 'The Anthropology of South Western Europe: The Way Forward', in *Critique of Anthropology* 7 (2): 101–118.

Peristiany, John G. (ed.) 1965. *Honour and Shame: The Values of Mediterranean Society*. London: Weidenfeld and Nicholson.

Pierros, F., J. Meunier, S. Abrams, and C. Williams, 1999. *Bridges and Barriers: The European Union's Mediterranean Policy, 1961–1998*. Aldershot: Ashgate.

Pollacco, Christopher 2006. *The Mediterranean: The European Union's 'Near Abroad'*. Malta: Agenda.

Xenakis, D.K. and D.N. Chryssochoou 2001. *Europe in Change: The Emerging Euro-Mediterranean System*. Manchester: Manchester University Press.

Filmography

Etz Hayyim–Tree of Life: Voices Surrounding a Synagogue. 2005. Vassiliki Yiakoumaki and Chronis Theocharis. University of Crete, Dept. of Sociology (Greece). 71 min.

PART IV

CONFLICT AND DISASTER RELIEF

Chapter 8

EMERGENCY AGENTS

A Birthing of Incipient Applied Visual Anthropology in the
'Media Invisible' Villages of Western India

Jayasinhji Jhala

Introduction

In 2001, Gujarat, India, suffered a terrible earthquake. This chapter examines insights that emerged from the use of visual anthropological field methodology and indigenous video innovation in this crisis. With an indigenous testimonial concept couched in the phrase, *joyun ae janyu*, (to see is to understand), and with visual anthropological methods of investigation, as well as evaluation tools that I call 'the visual ethnography methods and technologies instrument.' I examine the actions of several competing agencies in a belt of 'media invisible' desert villages in Jhalavad in Sauvrastra. These agencies include the central Government of India and its provincial and village authorities, international donor agencies, television organisations, religious charities and caste organisations. The results offer new pragmatic options with which to address the despair of victims and alleviate their suffering.

One aim of the article is to discuss government and donor agencies' uses of audiovisual messages, the appropriation of methods from long-standing visual anthropology practice, and the creation of 'empathy stories' for victims. A second aim of the article is to show how visual anthropology techniques of photographic and video elicitation, observation, interviews, performance, space exploration, public debate and confrontational demonstration were used to manipulate, negotiate and reveal indigenous values. Three case studies will illustrate my argument.

Applied visual anthropology, as it relates to this article, may be defined as the engagement of visual anthropologists in contexts where their actions and products have agency. I also suggest that applied visual anthropology as practice can grow out of unexpected social encounters. My practice of engagement builds on the efforts of important precursors. John Marshall (Durington 2004; Marshall 2002; Kalfam Productions 2001), Jean Rouch (Stoller 1992; Rouch et al. 2003), Ted Carpenter (Carpenter 1974), Vincent

Carelli and Terence Turner (Aufderheide 1992; Turner 1990, 1991, 1992), Eric Michaels (Michaels 1987), Harald Prins (Prins 2002; Prins and Carter 1986), and Richard Chalfen (Chalfen 1981, 1992, 1997; Rich and Chalfen 1999; Chalfen and Rich, this volume) have all contributed to the practice of an applied visual anthropology. Their work and ideas have affected and altered local populations through the three areas pertinent to applied visual anthropology: the technology of visual production, engagement methods, and behavioral adaptation to meet local contingencies.

The Gujarat Earthquake of 2001

The earthquake struck on 26 January 2001, India's Republic Day, when most people were outdoors, working in the fields or attending Republic Day celebrations at parade grounds and on sports fields. Many more could have been hurt had the earthquake occurred at night when people were indoors, or on a day when children were in school. Immediately after the earthquake, regional, national, and international media teams converged on this unfortunate area in search of 'stories.' In addition to television teams, other parties were active in the damage assessment exercise, such as the Indian and Gujarat governments and NGO relief agencies of various types. Their methods of eliciting information established a pattern that I will call the 'television method.' It impacted on local expectations of the ways inquiring individuals behaved and the 'proper' stance that was to be adopted when they interviewed earthquake victims. The privileged victim became the privileging one, granting interviews to a media suppliant, in a reverse empowerment game. The story of the 'Victim Star,' described below, illustrates these expectations.

Figure 8.1 Totally demolished house in Halvad town.
Photo © Jayasinhji Jhala.

Case Study 1: Assessing Damage and the Politics of Method

When the earthquake struck, killing thousands and making many more homeless, the media flocked to areas where access was easiest and where the government was present. This rendered neglected areas invisible. Our work was anchored in these media-invisible areas. In Rann Kantha, where the earthquake damaged most villages and the extent of damage varied from quarter to quarter and from home to home, we had the opportunity to reconstruct the stories of specific traumatic events and document damage to roofs, walls, floors, and courtyards.

Recording victims' stories in the villages of Narali, Jesada, and others always began in a communal setting, where the leading men of the village or caste group congregated, and where the presence of women was minimal.[1] The discussion almost always involved a recounting of the disaster, with different versions offered to particularize stories. These revealed that the nature of damage and injury varied according to the construction of the house. Mud houses with traditional cylindrical tiles and split bamboo rafters were the most vulnerable and most damaged, although fewer people who lived in these constructions were hurt because the roofing elements were relatively light. Stone and mud houses with wooden beams proved most dangerous, as both walls and roofs were potentially lethal to people, animals, and property. The least damaged houses in these villages were those with concrete roofs. Very few collapsed, although none escaped large and small cracks to walls and roof. These modern private homes stood in stark contrast to public buildings built by the government, such as schools, village council meeting rooms, and cooperative milk societies. Almost everywhere, the government-contracted public buildings were destroyed and required rebuilding. Villagers joked about the dishonesty of politicians and government contractors who had been commissioned to build these structures.

Topics of conversation in these village gatherings included inadequate government relief, criticism of nongovernmental organizations (NGOs), partisanship in relief distribution, and ways to request help that could leapfrog the emerging relief and rehabilitation bureaucracy which grew out of the combined efforts of government, international donor agencies, local NGOs, and religious organizations and charities. What was important in these public utterances was that accusations were general and did not attack specific organizations. I heard more pointed criticism when I spoke to people in their own homes or in small groups that shared the same caste or religion. In these contexts, opinions were more vocal and specific. One story, which we heard repeated in several different villages, referred to the powerful Bochasanwasi Shri Akshar Purushottam Swaminarayan Sanstha organization (BAPS). BAPS has a strong following among Hindus of Indian origin in the United States and the United Kingdom and represents the Swaminarayan sect. Its donors often demanded proof of an individual's membership in the sect, including visible markers such as posters of the deified reformer, medallions, and pendant portraits. These demands were not made in the glare of public debate in multicaste situations but in the homes of people claiming to be members of the Swaminarayan community.

Two Methods of Documentation: The Bird's Eye View

Two methods widely used in ethnographic film practice were adopted by the Gujarat government in its attempts to assess the extent of damage, the birds eye view and the 'walk through.' The camera in the Olympian bird's eye view perspective can be set on a moving platform, such as an aeroplane, helicopter, ultralight, parachute, or a land-based radio-operated aircraft. More often in ethnographic film-making it has been positioned on a high platform, tower, treetop or a mountain ledge. From this vantage point the film-maker has explored the spatial canvas by the judicious use of pan, tilt and zoom, creating a narrative of a fixed and fully visible landscape. This distant and probing stance suggests close proximity and mimics telescopic and microscopic investigative endeavors; it reveals important informational detail of the social and cultural domain.

This perspective was made famous by film-maker Robert Gardner in *Dead Birds*, a film on the Dani in Papua New Guinea (Gardner 1964). Gardner used the actual observational tower of the Dani to provide a bird's eye view of the valley, showing, in one long controlled take, the

Figure 8.2 Jibava handing out relief cheque, Jesada village. Photo: Jayasinhji Jhala.

fields, huts, and battlefield clearings. This view enabled the Dani lookout, the filmmaker, and the film's viewer to assess vital topographical information, albeit for different purposes. The Dani lookout who was familiar with the landscape, was interested in movement and movement patterns on the surface. The dearth of movement was as alarming as unusual movement, leading to a response that alerted all members of the community and which, in turn, required people to act in ways that were prescribed for children, women and men. The film-makers, on the other hand, needed a basic understanding of the environment and its theatres of ritual and social and economic activity.

In the earthquake-affected areas, this kind of aerial shot was useful to assess the damage done to a village, its approach bridges, public buildings, and other constructions and to compare the total relative damage of one village with another. In this type of assessment, a village and its hierarchically organized caste subdivisions were united in their attempts to bring attention to the repair needs of roads, railways, bridges, schools, village council buildings, village cooperative buildings, the village bus stop and the embankments of water tanks. The aerial view was divisive, however, when it showed damage spread unequally among homes within a village. As these village communities are organized along caste lines, the view from above shows clearly where each caste community lives. The homes of poorer castes collapsed totally, leaving rubble. Better built areas suffered less visible damage, at least as could be seen from above. Paradoxically, the cheaper destroyed homes cost less and were cheaper to rebuild than the more expensive homes. Some of the latter had cracks and structural damage that could not be seen from a distance but, on closer examination, revealed that they would have to be torn down and rebuilt. Which materials from the debris were reusable led to another complication. Mud, stone, some tiles and some wooden beams and poles that came from the poorer houses could be used again. The earthquake shook the house apart and collapsed it, but all the materials were left on location to be reused. The same could not be said for cement concrete roofs and cement and brick walls. The damaged iron rods and cement concrete could not be used at all. The debris would have to be removed, and new cement and iron supplies brought in at additional cost. Consequently, the camera evidence of the bird's eye view in panoramic survey was contentious in many villages where the unified voice was subverted by squabbling. Opportunistic alliances generated caste tensions that would not be triggered in normal times. The visual evidence was often used to instigate debate and secure advantage for some over others.

The Walk Through: Processing through Landscape to Narrate a Story

In contrast to the panoramic, bird's eye view, the walk through provides a more intimate perspective. A variant of this is an approach that I term, 'processing through landscape to narrate story.' The best example I can recall is from *Lorang's Way*, a film about pastoralists in East Africa by American filmmakers, David and Judith MacDougall (1979). This method utilizes a single shot while moving for the duration of ten minutes, the length of film in the camera. In the shot in question Lorang, the head of a polygamous family, walks through a complex dwelling site made up of a stockade for animals and the dwelling huts of his several wives. The camera follows dutifully behind while Lorang addresses the camera to tell the viewer which wife's area he is in. The camera makes a virtual circle, meandering along paths and allowing for an encounter experience very different from that furnished by a camera floating on high. Furthermore, the camera can go inside structures and behind them, providing a normal three-dimensional experience rather than the flattened two-dimensional experience granted by the bird's eye view. Walking alongside or behind the subject also allows for the maintenance of a human scale and transferable proximity between subject and viewer, whereas the high view can often reduce the person to an organism with whom little direct communication is possible. I hope to illustrate the efficiency of this mode of filming as an alternative way to traverse a landscape and monitor space.

In the earthquake-torn villages of Jhalavad, I documented damage and attempted to identify those who had suffered in order to bring their plight to the attention of potential donors. Our role during this exercise was to intervene and alter, advocate and influence, and select some over others so as to take account of suffering and loss caused by the earthquake. We also wished to alleviate the victimization caused by 'visual neglect' that rendered these victims invisible.

Soon after I first arrived in the Rann Kantha villages of Jesada, Narali, and Sultanpur in early March 2001 (a full month after the earthquake), I discovered a documentation practice established by the state government of Gujarat. Government teams of three – a supervisor with a note pad, a video cameraman, and the supervisor's assistant who carried a measuring tape – made up a unit that documented damage in individual homes. Their procedure was as follows: upon arrival the team would ask to see the head of the household. The video camera would shoot a still of this person standing in front of the house holding a placard with his (or her) name on it. Then the owner would show the inspection team other parts of the house where damage had occurred. The cameraman would shoot short clips of this damage, and sometimes actual measurements were taken of collapsed walls and other structural damage. The team would then move on to the next house and repeat the process.

I adopted a different technique to document the damage. I met with the heads of the households and sat with them in a part of the house they deemed fit for my initial conversation. At this time I described my purpose, and if the person agreed that there was some virtue in my documenting the damage, we would proceed to the next step. This was the walk through taken from *Lorang's Way*. The following pattern emerged: the property owners would stand up saying, 'Let me show you.' They would then walk from point A to point B, talking as they went, describing what happened on the fateful day. At each point of demonstrable damage they would turn around and face the camera while continuing to speak. Once the report was made, we would proceed to the next stop. Finally, we would either return to the site of our initial conversation or to an exit spot from where we would part company.

Victims preferred our method of documentation because it allowed them to recall the story of the disaster, proclaim their presence and gain sympathetic relief from telling their own story. The importance of this psychological benefit and symbolic embrace and recognition should not be discounted in times like these. In addition, and perhaps more to the point, property owners were part of the footage and cinematically attached to the damage they described. This 'storytelling in the frame' mode became popular. I was told that many people soon began to demand such walk throughs with the government teams when their work schedules overlapped with mine.

A few days before I left, however, I was informed that the government teams had now reverted to taking video mug shots of people and video snapshots of damage, as they had done before our arrival. Why did they do this in the face of a victim population that seemed to favor another way to document its loss and seek redress? The official reason given was that our procedure was more time consuming and required more videotape stock. Also, that there was not enough time to look over individual videotapes to decide the category of relief a particular house fell into. The assigned category signalled the extent of the damage and the amount of relief it merited, as well as the attendant priority the victims had to materials for temporary shelter. This may, in fact, have been true, and the reasons given certainly can be defended, but local victims suspected that the walk through left little room for manipulation of the data. With no 'index' in the image (Gell 1998), no person present, one man's actual damage could be ascribed to another. In other words, videotapes of damage could be attached to places, communities, and even villages from which it had not been generated. My way of recording would prevent politicians and administrators who oversaw the government documenting exercise from diverting resources towards favored beneficiaries. Hence while my method avoided separating the victim from the damage the other method reintroduced invisibility, this time with the use of video cameras, rather than by their absence.

Case Study 2: The Victim Star: Adapting Journalistic Practice to Achieve Visibility

'Water? I want Pepsi!' This was the response of a young boy who was trapped with his Rajput mother for three days in a collapsed multistory building in the city of Bhuj, in Kutch, when he was told that the rescuers of a British-led local team had found a way to send a tube down to them through the rubble in which they were still buried. His plucky response caught the imagination of the local press, and the boy became something of a celebrity after he and his mother were finally rescued and returned to the embrace of his father. By the time I met him and his mother in his mother's father's home in Dhrangadhra, the family had endured many video interviews with different members of the press. They were well versed in what they believed the press wanted; they also knew that their story would be more sympathetically received if they catered to journalists' requirements. Consequently, when we arrived at their home, they placed two chairs on a veranda with their backs against the wall and two other chairs facing them, some eight feet away. The two chairs against the wall were intended for the mother and son and the other two for my daughter and me. The already harsh glare of late spring was behind the camera, as it should be, and the two informants had good natural light falling upon them.

In order to contextualize the storytelling performance, I will provide some background on conversational engagements in Surendranagar District. Conversations are always conducted between two seated parties. Talking while sitting is local custom. It does not matter whether one is seated with the pastoralist Bharvad in the desert grassland, in the courtyard of the Bhavaiyas (theatrical performers), in a Rabari camp encircled by camels and sheep, or when talking with women or their maids in the Rajput *zenana*. Not only is being seated a requirement for both parties, I learned that when the informant was seated, the condition itself proclaimed that matters were being addressed seriously. Almost inevitably, the local site chosen by the informant was the spot where he or she habitually sat. In almost every such instance, the informant had a backdrop. A wall, a seated camel or a dung-plastered earth wall made up the background, while the person looked towards the light. In addition to speaking, most informants did something else as well, such as peeling vegetables, cooking tea over a stick and dung fire, knitting, or stitching embroidery (Sandall and Jhala 1980, 1981, 1987; Sandall et al. 2000). These conversations seldom took less than an hour or more than two hours.

Conversations involve ebb and flow and give and take along a continuum that periodically reverses itself. One way to conceive this exchange is to place the inquirer's position at one end of the 'conversation-exchange-narrative' and the informant's position at the other end. The characteristics of any conversation can be presented in a progression that begins with the inquirer as the initiating speaker and the informant as listener, and could end with a reversal of roles, with the informant as speaker and the investigator as listener. The character of these exchange events, or 'social performance dynamos', discussed by Lindsey Powell, may comprise interrogation, interview, conversation, pontification, confession or confidence. In these exchanges power and dominance would flow from inquirer to informant if the sequence were to be held inflexibly. Yet most conversation narratives change in the ebb and flow of the exchange (Powell 2004: 23, 37, 42).[2]

My filming strategy in Jhalavad has evolved to an acceptance of the customary code, and I always try to place people I wish to speak with in 'personal seats of power.' In the film *A Zenana*, about the life of royal women in seclusion, women always occupied such seats of power when I spoke to them (Sandall and Jhala 1980). The head of the household sat in the armchair, and we, the film-makers, sat on the ground; or the maids sat on the ground, and we sat on stools. People we spoke to selected the spots from which they wished to speak to us. The same was true in other films, such as *Tragada Bhavai*, when the theatre troupe leader, Kalu Amra, elected to sit on a raised earth platform beside his mud hut (Sandall and Jhala 1981); *Bharvad Predicament*, in which the farmers' selected the spot near their cotton fields (Sandall and Jhala 1987), and *Close Encounter of No Kind* in which a woman character chose to speak with us in her hut beside the poster of the deified warrior Ram Devji (Sandall et al. 2000). These one-on-one encounters have proved most successful when I have sought insight and a reflective attitude of the informants. It has also been the best environment for individuals to confess, confide, and accuse. In a complex, hierarchical, verbal community, where the spoken word is the main instrument for the making and breaking of reputations, how one speaks and from where one speaks is of great importance. All know this from childhood. Even more important is to know when one should speak.

Bharvad Predicament (Sandall and Jhala 1987) illustrates significant practices that occur when people of one caste enter the social space of another caste. In the film, a delegation of Bharvad leaders go to the higher caste Rajput landowner seeking his help to arbitrate a case in their favour against the local farmers. In this instance, the Rajput man sits on a platform with a cushion and bolster, while the Bharvad leaders sit cross-legged on the dirt floor in a rough arc before him. They present their agenda in humility and deference, using the honorifics required when speaking to a superior. The arbiter appropriately speaks down to them as is the custom. Both act in accordance with caste tradition. By being displaced from their own seats of power, the visiting Bharvad are in a weaker position relative to their hosts.

When the same delegation go to the Kambi headman's house to negotiate a truce with a Kambi delegation of the village, the two parties are on a more even footing, and the exchange is heated. The Kambi outnumber the Bharvad, are in their own place of power, and draw strength from that. The Bharvad, however, do not seem cowed by their small numbers or by being in the opposition camp, and this is probably due to the fact that the arbiter is present, and that the protection and invitation of the superior Rajput landlord guarantees a somewhat level field where discussion and debate can occur.

To return to the story of the 'star victim,' the family had anticipated our need for good indirect light and set up a sitting arrangement where the best natural lighting conditions prevailed. As soon as we sat, a member of the family brought us two cups of sweet tea. Tea drinking is a requirement for anthropologists in this area, for it marks several conditions. Its acceptance signals that the visitors have no caste bias and are happy to take from people of lower castes. It marks the generosity of the homeowners, especially if they are very poor. Tea drinking is used ritually to bind feuding groups, a function that earlier was executed by the ritual consumption of opium to seal a truce (Jhala 1991: 2–67). Finally, tea drinking works to signal visual solidarity. It is drunk several times at night *bhajan* sessions, where a group of people of many castes and religions might gather to sing Hindu devotional songs in a person's home.

The mother began telling the story. She said that she was just about to turn on the television to watch the Republic Day celebrations with her son who had a cold and had therefore stayed home from school, when there was a terrible roar overhead. The building collapsed, and their third floor flat seemed to fall straight down as if it were an elevator. Everything went black, and soon after she heard her son's voice in the dark imploring her to wake up. She felt a heavy weight on her chest that she pushed off with great effort. This permitted her young son to touch her. At this time she realized that her legs were pinned down. Although she was not hurt she could not sit up, as there was little room above her head. She was as if in a rubble coffin. Her son was unharmed and had crawled to her side by pushing away small pieces of debris. She thought a Pakistani military aircraft had dropped a bomb on her building. She never imagined it was an earthquake.

The son said everything was pitch black and silent. For many hours they heard nothing, and then they heard distant sounds. They shouted, but there was no response.

The mother from this point on told her son that his father would rescue them. She repeated this as time went on. Mother and son had nothing to eat or drink. After what seemed some more hours, they heard sounds again. This time the sounds were closer. Mother and son shouted, sometimes together and sometimes separately. Nothing happened. No response. Silence again. After what seemed a short time later they heard a tapping sound. The boy shouted. This time there was tapping in reply. Somebody knew they were there. Now a pattern set in. Every short while there was an exchange of shouting and tapping, and the tapping got closer. Finally, a male voice replied to their shouts and asked, 'Are you hurt?'. The voice then asked how many were trapped, and if they had food and water. Now they could hear heavy things being moved. It was soon after that that a pinprick of light came into their space. Both mother and son were shocked to see that the other looked chalk white. Soon after, the voice told them they were sending down a tube through the cracks for them to have some water, and the boy made his now famous remark, 'Water! I want Pepsi.'

During the narration of this harrowing tale, the mother broke into tears twice and, in one instance, left us and went inside to recover and wash her face. We offered to stop filming, but the family insisted that she cried often even when not being interviewed, and that she would return. When she broke down, the son lovingly stroked his mother's arm. Throughout the conversation, the son seemed more in control, although it was the mother who did most of the talking. His role seemed to be that of stage prompter as he added information that she left out. This sharing of the storytelling task seemed to have evolved for them. While the two roles appeared to be tailored to their personalities, they did not seem rigid, formulaic, or scripted. It was a performance, but it was not feigned. Rather, they seemed to relive their experience through talking about it. The mother's emotional reaction was not a theatrical device meant for the camera but rather a purging of pent up fear of suffocation, starvation, loneliness, death. This purging was beneficial to the couple, for we were told that they were able to sleep better after one of these sessions. Why did they want to tell their story? Why subject oneself to reliving this awful event? Why were we recording this event? Were we exploiting the victims and their plight? Clearly, the mother and son wished to tell their story, and this was in itself beneficial to them. There was no direct gain for them in talking to us, as we were not government representatives. However, we were prominent citizens, and, although there was little we could do about their destroyed home in the town of Bhuj, we could help them locally. The help they asked for and received was admission into a local English-medium school run by my sister-in-law. Yet I do not believe they used the storytelling to secure that objective in a manipulative way. They did not try to manipulate our sympathy for some predetermined goal. Nor were we exploitative or manipulative. Our documentation seemed to serve the family as well as inform other local people about the actual experience of this event. Sharing this common experience became part of the local healing process. It was also an acclamation of their survival.

As visual anthropologists who have worked for a long time in a local environment, we have learned the rules of engagement and refined the techniques of effective enquiry, as well as the most appropriate use and deployment of technology, to help us better understand, study, and know the society we encounter. Our primary purpose is to learn. In this case, however, while learning was important, our purpose as applied visual anthropologists was to help and bring about desired change. We were activists and advocates. Our techniques and insights were shared with our indigenous partners. By this process our methods, strategies and techniques were translated, acquired and, in turn, deployed by indigenous actors, acting entirely independently of us. In fact, once skills are domesticated and internalized, they are used by local people for their own purposes. The example of the Pepsi boy and his family is an illustration of the adaptation of method, understanding, and mindset. So is the case of victims of the house survey who sought to establish an alternate way to document their loss than the method imposed by the government. This point is made to emphasize that applied visual anthropology is not simply the acquisition and use of video or other technology but is also a set of conceptual and methodological approaches. Where you sit, what you ask, how you use technology, all these criteria are important. Even more important is the question of when. Experience in the field teaches us when our engagement is most effective.

Case Study 3: Visualising Shame and the Shame of Visualisation

This section discusses the use of photographs, posters, and banners to allow needy individuals to accept the aid they needed. It involves local definitions of 'giver' (datari) and 'receiver' (mangan), the management of shame, and ways to provide for the needy without demeaning them. In this case, using appropriate visual materials legitimated the status of the givers and changed the character of the aid being given.

As stated earlier, the villages of the Rann Kantha in Jhalavad in Gujarat are complex multicaste societies with a defined hierarchy created over centuries of practice. Relationships of dominance and subordination are actualized and made visible by practices of power. Historically, these have been made visible in the public distribution of the annual grain harvest (Raheja 1988). Specific proportions of the grain harvest were reserved for the village rulers, the landowners, the laborers, and, finally, service castes. Thus, a culture of giving and receiving was based on caste distinctions. Dataris (givers) were ranked in terms of their genealogical proximity to the family and person of the Rajput headman of the village, the Tilayat. From the Tilayat and his family (who were related to the Rajput ruler of the kingdom), power devolved to collateral branches. Together, these made up the ruling caste who were the distributors and givers of grain to all dependents (Jhala 1991: 23–27, 31–43). The earthquake destroyed houses of all villagers, rendering all needy to varying degrees, of aid and assistance. It also created a new set of givers, including the government, international donor agencies, local and national NGOs and religious and relief organisations. I have already described the use of visual markers to allocate aid. Here, I draw attention to the problem caused by visibly depicting need and distress and how this, in turn, made shame visible.

The fear of visible shame prevented the acceptance of aid by some of the needy, and, paradoxically, the adoption of appropriate visual rituals removed this shame, allowing people to accept and live with received aid without feeling the loss of caste and rank status. I concentrate on the dataris because mangans had little difficulty in asking for aid. They have always accepted aid from those they considered their superiors. The *dataris* often refused aid in the early days of the disaster when water, food and shelter were in short supply, even when their need was clear. Their reasons can be summed up in what a widow told me: 'We are givers of grain. In good time and in bad times (datari). From the beginning we give grain. In bad times we give our heads. We never put our hand out. Our hand is always on top, never below. We are not *mangans*.' This widow is describing traditional practice. The subdivisions of the village grain heaped on the threshing grounds is a picture as old as local memory. The giving of heads refers to the historical Rajput defence of villages against marauding outsiders, for which they sometimes gave their lives. The third image is the gesture and position of hands. Recipients put out their hands, palm upwards. Givers, when giving cash, hold the money in their fingers and give in a downward gesture. To be seen as giver or receiver in public proclaims a person's status. Therefore, many Rajput individuals would neither go to the distribution point in the village nor respond to enquiries about their needs. Their standard response was, 'Give to the needy. We can manage.'

If these people would not, or could not, accept aid from outsiders because of caste restrictions, whose gift would they receive? From whom could they accept aid and not lose face? Local organizers found a solution anchored in the visual. Destitute *dataris* could receive aid from the former king, who was both their kinsman and superior. Consequently, supply trucks containing essential items were outfitted with banners saying, *Darbargadh*, or *Dhrangadhra Darbargadh*, implying that they come from the ruler's palace. Darbargadh means palace and Dhrangadhra Darbargadh means the palace of the king of Dhrangadhra, making clear as to where the supplies came from. From these trucks, aid was just as acceptable to *datari* families as it was to the rest of the village population. Distribution of these *Darbari* supplies often occurred at the village temple of the goddess ShaktiMa, principal goddess of the region and clan mother of the local Rajputs. Receiving aid as if it were coming from the Goddess further alleviated the problem, as it promoted the idea that all people could receive from the greatest of *dataris*, ShaktiMa, the great Mother who gives life, food and shelter. The popular poster, showing the Goddess lifting children up, away from a rampaging elephant, was displayed at these distribution events, as was a framed picture of the former Rajput ruler of the area. These visuals served to identify and proclaim the high status of distant but locally relevant *dataris* and rendered the offered aid acceptable.

The key to empowering both receiver and giver of aid lies in the attendant power of the visual in the photograph, the poster and the banner. In adopting these methods of assurance, local organizers borrowed from the long-standing 'photo elicitation' method. Visual anthropologists have for many decades used photographs, posters, and other visual objects as aids and prompts to collect information. Photographs serve to unlock tongues and enable and facilitate discourse. In this instance, the use of visual aids by local organizers was not to gain

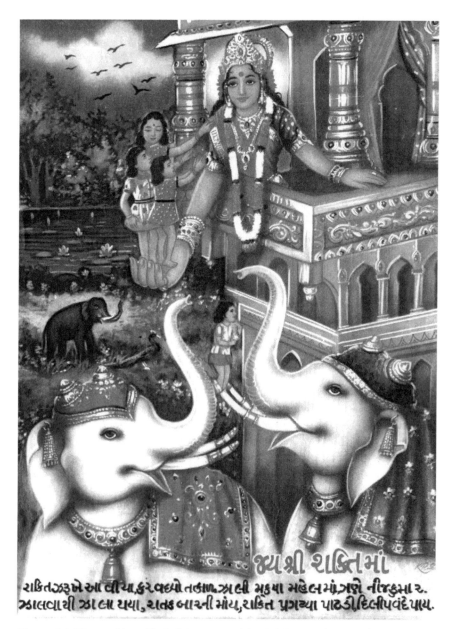

Figure 8.3 The goddess ShaktiMa, giver of food, life and shelter. The display of this poster at distribution centres alleviated the shame of receiving aid for earthquake victims. Courtesy of Jayasinhji Jhala.

Figure 8.4 His Highness Maharaja Raj Mayurdhvajsinhji of Dhrangadhara Uparajpramikh and Rajpramkh of Saurashrtra. This poster was displayed at distribution centres along with the poster of the goddess ShaktiMa. Destitute 'givers' felt comfortable receiving aid from their former king. Courtesy: Jayasinhji Jhala.

insight and information, but to create a new practice in a time of crisis. At this time when the world was turned upside down, a quick acceptance of a new way of acting and thinking was necessary to help victims materially and psychologically.

Conclusion

The case studies I have offered address the uses of visual technology, photo elicitation, videography, poster deployment, behavior modification and media management. Earthquake victims, government and other agencies, and visual anthropologists all contribute to this evidence. This article has underlined the application of traditional anthropological concepts and methods and is witness to their local adaptations by different individuals and institutions. That this engagement responds to a situation of disaster management, calling for maximum collaboration and accommodation, is useful to showcase the possibilities of a vigorous applied visual anthropology. At such times, social structure, political alliances and religious affiliation are revealed more directly than in normal times, when tensions and fissures are often masked. Crisis clarifies what is often lived but denied.

In conclusion, it may be useful to offer a prescription for practice that I have called the 'visual ethnography concepts, methods and technologies instrument.' The following guidelines may assist the novice applied visual anthropologist to work effectively and responsibly:

1. 'Inside resonates – outside provides.' The target population articulates its needs and reveals directions for action. A plan of action based on local ideas may be easier to introduce and implement. Needed resources often come from outside, hence the need to devise appropriate strategies to secure these resources for desirable outcomes.
2. Study the domestication of visual technology and communication by local people and introduce new methods incrementally, so that they can be digested, absorbed and appropriated effectively.
3. Acquire language and behaviour competency. With language and behaviour skills in place, develop humility. Present ideas as suggestions and not as prescriptions. Try to develop reflexivity about personal actions and an alertness to the ways members of the target population treat you in everyday encounters.
4. 'Don't give them fish. Teach them to fish' is a useful mantra. Try to teach local partners the technology and methods of effective practice, so that your ideas are available to locals and add to their repertoire of useful practices.
5. 'Joyun te janeyu' (To see is to know) is a local adage. This phrase refers to the observable world and the activity of the one who visualizes, projects, and anticipates.

These guidelines would allow applied visual anthropologists to assess their place in local society and provide them with an awareness of the concept of personal obsolescence. When the 'visual ethnography concepts, methods and technologies instrument' is adopted, the applied visual anthropologists' teaching task might well be over. When this happens, it is time to begin a withdrawal and leave quietly.

Notes

1. My daughter, Liluye, was camera person, and I conducted the interviews.
2. Spectacle Dynamos: a dynamo is a structure of social relations that produces recurring forms of action. For example, liberal democratic state societies both create and are a response to at least four primary spectacle dynamos: advertising, science, politics, and protest. We are bombarded daily with indexes from these dynamos because these dynamos, or engines, are autocatalytic. They create an interlocking positive feedback loop which sustains them all and makes them grow. Different societies have different dynamos which reflect ongoing processes of power struggle and symbiosis. Earthquake relief created its own dynamo which articulated with ongoing social processes of caste and other social relations (Powell 2004).

Bibliography

Aufderheide, P. 1992. *Video in the Villages. Cross-Cultural Film Guide*. Retrieved 15 January 2004. http://www.library.american.edu/subject/media/aufderheide/villages.html.

Carpenter, T. 1974. *Oh, What a Blow the Phantom Gave Me!* New York: Bantam Books.

Chalfen, R. 1981, 'A Sociovidistic Approach to Children's Filmmaking: The Philadelphia Project' in *Studies in Visual Communication* 7(1):1–32.

Chalfen, R. 1992. 'Picturing Culture Through Indigenous Imagery: A Telling Story,' in Crawford and Turton, (eds), *Film as Ethnography*. Manchester: University of Manchester Press, pp. 222–241.

Chalfen. R. 1997. 'Afterword' in S. Worth, J. Adair and R. Chalfen (eds), *Through Navajo Eyes – An Exploration in Anthropology and Film Communication*, 2nd. Albuquerque: University of New Mexico Press, pp. 275–341.

Chalfen, R. and J. Haley. 1971. 'Reaction to Socio-Documentary Film Research in a Mental Health Clinic,' *American Journal of Orthopsychiatry* 41(1): 91–100.

Durington, M. 2004. 'John Marshall's Kalahari Family,' *American Anthropologist* 106(3): 589–594.

Gell, A. 1998. *Art and Agency: An Anthropological Theory*. Oxford: Oxford University Press.

Jhala, J. 1991. 'Marriage, Hierarchy and Identity in Ideology and Practice: An Anthropological Study of Rajput Society in Western India against a Historical Background, 1090–1990 AD,' Ph.D. dissertation, Cambridge: Harvard University.

Kalfam Productions. 2001. A Kalahari Family. http://www.der.org/kalfam/.

Powell, L. 2004. 'Spectacle and Agency in Japanese Protest,' Ph.D. dissertation. Philadelphia: Temple University.

Raheja, G. 1988. *The Poison in the Gift: Ritual, Prestation, and the Dominant Caste in a North Indian Village*. Chicago: University of Chicago Press.

Rich, M. and R. Chalfen. 1999. 'Showing and Telling Asthma: Children Teaching Physicians with Visual Narratives', *Visual Sociology* 14: 51–71.

Rouch, J., D. Georgakas, U. Gupta, and J. Janda. 2003. 'The Politics of Visual Anthropology' in S. Feld (ed.), *Cine-Ethnography*. Minneapolis: University of Minnesota Press, pp. 210–229.

Stoller, P. 1992. *The Cinematic Griot: The Ethnography of Jean Rouch*. Chicago: University of Chicago Press.

Turner, T. 1990. 'Visual Media, Cultural Politics and Anthropological Practice: Some Implications of Recent Uses of Film and Video among the Kayapo of Brazil.' *CVA Review*, Spring: 8–13.

———, 1991. 'The Social Dynamics of Video-Media in an Indigenous Society: The Cultural Meaning and the Personal Politics of Video-making in Kayapo Communities.' *Visual Anthropology Review* 7(2): 68–76.

Turner, T. 1992. 'Defiant Images: The Kayapo Appropriation of Video,' *Anthropology Today* 8(6): 5–16.

Filmography

Dead Birds. 1964. R. Gardner. 1964. The Film Study Center, Peabody Museum, Harvard University (PR).Cambridge, MA. 83 min.

Lorang's Way. 1979. David MacDougall and Judith MacDougall. Rice University Media Centre (U.S.A.). Documentary Educational Resources. Watertown, MA. 70 min.

Kalahari Family. 2002. John Marshall. Documentary Educational Resources. Watertown, MA.360min.

A Zenana. 1980. Roger Sandall and Jayasinhji. Jhala. Documentary Educational Resources. Watertown, MA. 36 min.

Tragada Bhavai. 1981. Roger Sandall and Jayasinhji. Jhala. Documentary Educational Resources. Watertown, MA. 40 min.

Bharvard Predicament. 1987. Roger Sandall and Jayasinhji. Jhala. Documentary Educational Resources. Watertown, MA. 50 min.

Close Encounter of No Kind. 2000. Roger Sandall, R., Jayasinhji. Jhala and Elizabeth Noznesky. Documentary Educational Resources, Watertown, MA. 60 min.

Chapter 9

THE HUNTERS REDUX
Participatory and Applied Visual Anthropology
with the Botswana San

Matthew Durington

In 1958 ethnographic film-maker and activist John Marshall released *The Hunters*. Described by Marshall himself as 'a romantic film made by an American kid' (1993: 39), the film nevertheless became one of the first pieces of media taken seriously by the field of anthropology (Ruby 2000), becoming a staple in undergraduate courses to visually demonstrate hunter and gatherer culture. Depending upon one's interpretation of the history of ethnographic film, *The Hunters* either instigated or continued a legacy of aberrant and stereotypical readings of indigenous peoples in the genre (Martinez 1992). Despite the decades-long advocacy of countless individuals and other films, and advocacy efforts by John Marshall for the Ju/'hoansi up to his recent death, *The Hunters*, together with feature films like *The Gods Must Be Crazy*, various documentaries and advertising, have all become part of a representational regime throughout Africa and the world that romantically and fictively depicts San[1] as hunters and gatherers still living off of the land in the Kalahari. This is despite the fact that contemporary San are facing the ill effects of modernization, racism and land encroachment initiated historically through colonialism and continued up to the present day. The persistent representation of the 'Bushman' hunter in popular culture as somehow 'closer to nature' or as part of the 'natural fauna' of the Kalahari Desert, depicted in animal skins in a harmonious relationship with nature, stands in direct contrast to the current socio-economic conditions most find themselves in.

The consistent portrayal and exacerbation of the 'Bushman Myth' (Gordon 1992) is also compounded by a history of violence and shifting racial categorizations. At different times, San have been considered vermin and actively exterminated as part of racial national policy, given a variety of different ethnic designations depending on the country in which they find themselves, or they have continued to be shuffled between different homelands with changing land demarcations subject to political cycles and the needs of expanding hunting or nature conservancies and to other encroaching social groups. The anthropological literature on San throughout the Greater Kalahari has not failed to recognize these realities as they have detailed the struggles in which San communities find themselves within the context of various nation-states and time periods (Gordon 1984; Biesele 1992; Hitchcock 2002; Sylvain 2002; Lee 2003). Despite the attention anthropologists and others have devoted to these issues, the predominant representations of San in global popular culture continue to place them in a romantic position that bolsters ill-advised development schemes, racist ideology and continued exploitation. Thus, the ethical representational burden given to anyone attempting to 'represent' San, either textually or visually, requires that one must contextualize these social realities and, as will be argued here, attempt to develop applied strategies to make ethnographic visual documentation work toward social change rather than reinforcing damaging stereotypes. The project described in this chapter, *The Hunters Redux*,[2] addresses current problems being faced by San in one community in Botswana and the overwhelming irony that they are dissuaded from hunting to support themselves and their families. This is despite the fact that they are widely conceived and represented in media, developmental and tourist representations in the same historical fashion as the individuals in John Marshall's original film almost fifty years ago, as the classic 'Bushman' hunter and gatherer.

Reflexive Research Context[3]

During a post-doctorate in South Africa, I accompanied researchers from the University of KwaZulu Natal in the summers of 2003 and 2004 into parts of South Africa and Botswana.[4] The agenda of the initial trip in 2003 was to continue research projects in progress by undergraduate cultural studies students at the university who were attempting to utilize ethnographic methods during fieldwork. My principal role, and meal ticket, was to provide guidance in ethnographic methods and fieldwork practice for these students as a practicing visual anthropologist. I brought along a video camera to possibly work with a couple of students to see if anything developed, but I did not necessarily have the intention of developing an ongoing video project. Once I arrived in the community in Botswana where the research project was taking place this perspective began to change. The fact that I was not focused on conducting fieldwork ironically provided, a sense of liberation and intimacy, as I found myself entering into conversations with local members of the San community in informal settings, albeit through a string of translators code-switching between Setswana, the indigenous language, English, contemporary Afrikaans and a dated dialect of Afrikaans spoken primarily by former San farm labourers. From these mediated and individual conversations I began to hear about the different issues and challenges facing the community and started to discuss the possibility of videotaping testimonial interviews to document these concerns. Within a few days an informal interest sparked by my familiarity with the corpus of anthropological work on San, and the problems I was aware that they were facing broadly, developed into an attempt to formulate and create applied visual anthropology strategies through participatory video projects with members of this particular community.

The community is in a state hunting concession and is a mixed settlement spread over a land space of about two kilometres and made up of about two hundred individuals.[5] The majority are Bakalagadi and Tswana, with the San group making up the minority in the community. It is often assumed that the whole community is 'Basarwa', a term for 'Bushmen' in Botswana that is considered derogatory. It is remote and the environment is sparse, despite tourist literature that would claim otherwise. San individuals in the community are caught between a number of contradictory and competing entities that not only represent the variety of political contexts in which San find themselves in throughout the Kalahari, but also the current socio-political climate in Botswana and the various consequences these various agendas create. As Sylvain has stated, 'One of the most puzzling features of postcolonial life for the San is that, at the very moment they are beginning to travel the world, speak at international conferences, and keep in regular e-mail communication with interested parties overseas, primordialized and essentialized representations of primitive "Bushmen" are being vigorously reasserted in mainstream media and NGO rhetoric' (Sylvain 2005: 354).

The status of San in Botswana and throughout the Kalahari is precarious and being fought for on an international stage. There is constant tension between the Government of Botswana and a number of non-governmental organizations (NGOs) over a variety of issues pertaining to 'Remote Area Dweller' populations in the country. There are also tensions between various NGO groups with competing agendas and perspectives on indigenous populations in Botswana as well. A looming court case addressing a relocation issue in the national court, and the upcoming national elections to be held in October were on the minds of several individuals in the community when I conducted follow-up fieldwork in the summer of 2004. The main subsistence issues still being dealt with by members of the community were similar to the ones in 2003, although better rains had helped the water situation in the previous year.

The main concerns of the participants in the video project and throughout the community were a perceived loss of hunting rights, problems with food deliveries by the state, lack of water despite the presence of boreholes and a loss of a sense of community that is compounded by these problems. Participatory videography initiated in 2003, and continued through 2004 with members of the San community, sought to document these concerns. The intended methodology was to document these issues in a participatory fashion, edit short videos, agree upon content and discuss possible social consequences faced by participants. Once edited, the objective was to return to the community to screen them to individuals who participated and to others, conduct further requested edits on-the-spot, and then to disseminate these videos to different development and government entities in order to make the plight of these communities more visible. Thus, the intention of this ethnographic documentary video work was to reflect an aspect of growing applied strategies within visual anthropology that seek to address human rights issues being faced by individuals under threat.

Exploring a Participatory and Applied Visual Anthropology Practice

As visual anthropology continues to develop into the twenty-first century, a number of questions about the direction of this field, and cultural anthropology at large, are continually centred upon the applied nature of anthropological work. While there is a precedent of applied ethnographic work within traditional anthropology (Willigen 1986; Erwin 2000), the notion of an applied visual anthropology continues to be explored and defined (Levine 2003; Pink 2004). A number of questions unique to the visual medium complicate how one would instigate an applied visual strategy in ethnographic research. This is particularly complex in terms of how to visually document human rights issues among indigenous peoples. For if we are attempting to document and apprehend human rights violations through participant observation and other ethnographic methods, there is no question that the visual medium brings an immediacy and timeliness as a method of representation. In addition, this visual representation is different from the written text in terms of potential impact. Thus, I agree with the notion that 'applied visual anthropology is a practice with a set of methods distinct from those of applied or visual anthropologies' (Pink 2004: 6). Yet, an applied visual anthropology project that is centred on traditional anthropological fieldwork is assisted by revisiting past debates focused on defining what ethnographic media is and the strategies one would employ to ethically document culture. It is the reclaiming of these past strategies and debates within visual anthropology and the questioning of an ethical approach in the creation of ethnographic media that inform the ongoing project.

Visual anthropology is a large analytical terrain whose boundaries are still in negotiation. The field is defined by anthropological media production and studies of the visual world, including various media, dance, art and other forms of symbolic culture. This project is influenced by a conception of visual anthropology and ethnographic media couched in an historical attachment to an anthropology of visual communication that seeks to place film/video as one part of a visual approach to culture (Worth 1981). In recent years, a number of texts have been devoted to contemplating or 'rethinking' what visual anthropology or ethnographic film is, or have looked at the actual scope of the field in recent years, all of which signals an active discipline (Crawford and Turton 1992; Banks and Morphy 1997; Ruby 2000; Pink 2001; Askew and Wilk 2002; Ginsburg et al. 2002). Yet, even with this prolific expansion, visual anthropology suffers from 'the breadth of its agenda and the reluctance to leave any aspect of the study of humans outside its orbit' (Banks and Morphy 1997: 1). Most debates around ethnographic media in the past and at present are focused on representation and strategies in film-making, or on how the content of these projects mediates anthropological knowledge (Barbash and Taylor 1997). Much of these discussions focus on the ethical dilemmas in representing anthropology's traditional subject, a traditionally objectified 'other', and the concomitant power dilemmas that this entails (Ruby 2000). The ethics and criteria for defining ethnographic film, or visual anthropological media representation in general, have been contested since the conception of these two terms, yet they have rarely been discussed explicitly (Asch 1992).

In a seminal commentary entitled 'Beyond Observational Cinema', David MacDougall touches on the unclear origins of ethnographic film when he states, 'ethnographic film-making was a haphazard affair ... it was never employed systematically by anthropologists as a whole' (MacDougall 1998). Despite the continued employment of video and the popularity of visual anthropology and the anthropology of media in the field at large, not much has changed. Visual anthropology is still a haphazard affair. Many consider the inclusion of exotic peoples in remote parts of the world, without any adherence to ethnographic principles in method, substantial enough content for the moniker of ethnographic film. But for those attempting to develop a critical field of intellectual analysis, and perhaps trying to politicize it, there are several factors to be considered when deciding whether a particular film or video can be seen as ethnographic or not. While content could be shared with any type of media attempting to represent individuals in some capacity, the process by which media is created, analysed and *utilized* is what distinguishes the anthropologist's approach to these topics. In terms of producing ethnographic media, a set of ethical criteria is often associated with the way in which a film is shot, or what happens with the material during and after the shooting takes place (Asch 1975; Barbash and Taylor 1997). Perhaps most importantly, it is the method by which a film is made and its revelation of a cultural contact situation that is paramount.

To return once more to MacDougall, I would like to offer two extended quotes that speak to the transition from an observational to a participatory cinema that signalled an ethical shift in film-making style in ethnographic media production in the last two decades. They both represent a cautionary tale regarding the traditional techniques employed in observational cinema and show the potential of a more participatory technique in ethnographic media production that lends itself toward an applied visual practice. As regards observational cinema methods:

The same methodological asceticism that causes film-makers to exclude themselves from the world of their subjects also excludes subjects from the world of the film. Here the implications are ethical as well as practical. By asking nothing of the subjects beyond permission to film them, the film-maker adopts an inherently secretive position. There is no need for further explanation, no need to communicate with the subjects on the basis of the thinking that organizes the work ... in this insularity, the film-maker withholds the very openness that is being asked of the subjects in order to film them. (MacDougall 1998: 133)

Beyond the 'insular world', that the observational film-maker who follows this method emulates, is the promise of a more ethical and open technique in ethnographic media production.

Beyond observational cinema lies the possibility of a *participatory cinema* [author's italics], bearing witness to the 'event' of the film and making strengths of what most films are at pains to conceal. Here the film-maker acknowledges his or her entry upon the world of the subjects and yet asks them to imprint directly upon the film aspects of their own culture. This should not imply a relaxation of purposefulness, nor should it cause film-makers to abandon the perspective that an outsider can bring to another culture. But by revealing their role, film-makers enhance the value of the material as evidence. By entering actively into the world of their subjects, they can provoke a greater flow of information about them. By giving them access to the film, they make possible the corrections, additions, and illuminations that only the subjects' response to the material can elicit. Through such an exchange a film can begin to reflect the ways in which its subjects perceive the world. (MacDougall 1998: 134)

I utilize these two quotes in detail because they reveal the methodological and ethical dilemmas that one must surmount and, I believe, the strategies one must employ in order to initiate an applied participatory project. Also, perhaps not intended by MacDougall, the quotes speak to the political nature of the ethnographic media project and a divide between those who wish to merely represent and those who wish to participate, the latter being able to reveal a cultural contact situation and the film-making process occurring. Thus, the latter attempting to strive for the 'messy' truth of cinema and the complex nature of fieldwork, and, through their dual employment, edge toward a more applied ethnographic cinema in theory. It is a process that has informed collaborative efforts in visual anthropology (Elder 1995) and closely parallels the questioning of reflexivity in the visual project (Ruby 1980). Yet, it is something more than simply a reflexive stance that seeks to reveal the process of the film-making within the content of the film itself. It is a participatory method that engages reflexivity, but makes the reflexive gesture less narcissistic and more subtle, to concentrate on the cultural engagement taking place. It is a method that makes the agreed-upon nature of the participatory process in anthropological fieldwork central to the visual anthropology project.

Banks (1992) follows the initial argument of Jay Ruby (1980) and ponders categories derived from the work of Fabian (1983) to question what criteria are to be considered in defining a film or video as ethnographic in relation to reflexivity. Whereas Ruby followed Fabian's lead of considering the categories of producer, process and product within anthropological analysis to ponder the inclusion of reflexivity in ethnographic film practice, Banks takes this triad and extends it to question the intention, event and reaction toward film as the criteria for defining ethnographic media. As he states, 'Any film can be considered as the outcome of these three phenomena and they are linked ... in a chain to form a process. An intention – to make a film – results in an event – the filming process – which leads to a reaction – the response of the audience to the physical manifestations of the event (the film)' (Banks 1992: 117). Thus, a 'holy triad' of sorts has been developed to consider what type of material could be included in the ethnographic genre. This includes questioning the intention behind a media event, a content analysis of the media event itself, and the contemplation of audience reaction, whether through some type of qualitative or quantitative analysis or by giving voice to some sort of receptive speculation (Crawford and Hafsteinsson 1996). Another step that could be attached to this process would be applied in nature. This would necessitate the screening of material beyond the classroom and academic environment, and the subsequent linkage of this work to larger social processes, such as the exposure of human rights violations. It is this last stage, the dissemination of ethnographic media knowledge to larger entities in an applied fashion, that could define a type of instrumental visual anthropology in the twenty-first century.

The contemporary visual anthropological project entails making visual representations and studying cultures by producing images; examining pre-existing visual representations of culture and exploring the cultural context of media usage in an ethnographic fashion; and collaborating with social actors in the production of visual representations (Pink 2001). Thus, one could make the argument that the participatory method is fully acknowledged within the visual project at this point. Depending on how one interprets the method and outcome of participatory projects, this method has either defined the field of visual anthropology and ethnographic film, from its contested inception with Robert Flaherty that inspired the shared anthropology and revolutionary participatory methods of Jean Rouch, or it has recently come into play through the work of Terence Turner (1990), Vincent Carelli, and Eric Michaels (1986), just to name a few.

The work of these individuals and others, building on historical participatory works like Worth and Adair's Navajo Project (1972), defines participatory ethnographic film with the handing over of the camera to the previously documented subject. Yet one has to make sure not to reduce indigenous-produced media to visual anthropology, or applied visual anthropology for that matter. Indigenous media is often confused with ethnographic film, principally because it is usually instigated by anthropologists and screened for an anthropological audience that shares the same concerns for human rights and justice. The 'handing over of the camera' was the desire of Jean Rouch (1974) and has continued to be the impetus of non-profit organizations, such as Witness and other social projects, that seek to place the tools of representation outside of traditional Western/authoritarian/academic hands (Flores 2004). Whether classified as participatory video, indigenous media or 'faustian contract' (Ginsburg 1991), time has proven that within visual anthropology, participatory video becomes increasingly political as time goes on. This is true whether it is created by an anthropologist or an indigenous film-maker, especially, if the two identities are combined. Also, if one is attempting to work towards handing over the tools of representation, a participatory method grounds the applied nature of this type of project.

The Project

As Richard Lee has warned, one has to continually avoid the twin pitfalls of romanticism and racism when it comes to discussing, representing or conducting development work within San or 'Bushmen' culture (Lee 2003). Unfortunately, the romanticism that Lee warns of continues to inform many of the research, development or representational agendas in the Kalahari (Sylvain 2005). One of the most profound myths associated with this group of people is that they still survive by hunting and gathering or that they have just emerged into the modern world. While attempting to address or document social problems being confronted by individuals in the Kalahari with either development agendas or through video and ethnography, one must negotiate a double-edged sword when it comes to the ethical dilemmas over representation of indigenous or traditional culture. This often entails a confrontation with equal amounts of tranquillity and tragedy, with the representational burden falling on the latter rather than romanticizing over the former. In this sense, one must contextualize the popular imagery associated with San that historically tends to depict them as 'one with nature', part of a 'fauna fantasy' (Marshall 1993) or 'frozen in a past time of hunting and gathering', wearing skins and traditional dress, with real contemporary conditions. As Sylvain states, 'The public face of Bushman identity (as people who still hunt wild animals with poison arrows) and the public face of corporate development ventures (as empowering the San to regain dignity and pride) are clearly at odds with the personal realities of Bushmen who have no say in anything' (Sylvain 2002: 1081).

Many San throughout the Kalahari live in marginal environments, either conglomerating around trade posts or in other settings, where they rely on government subsistence programs.[6] The San throughout the greater Kalahari are suffering from land dispossession, hunger and thirst, alcoholism, domestic violence, discrimination and a rapidly escalating HIV/AIDS infection rate on top of the almost omnipresent tuberculosis that exists in different communities. They are recognized as one of the most disempowered groups in the world and represent the deleterious impacts of modernity couched in active racism and discrimination over time. To quote Sylvain once more, the basic struggle of indigenous San in the Kalahari can be encapsulated in three simple words: land, water and truth (Sylvain 2002). For the community where the project is taking place, hunting is the fourth concern added to this triumvirate.

The people of this community represent a real and semantic dilemma for the Government of Botswana and development agencies working within the country. They live on land that has been designated by the government as part of a hunting concession, so their actual presence complicates images of tourism development and nature conservation based on the natural fauna. Yet, they are often involved in proposed ecotourism for the area and are encouraged to create authentic goods and crafts to sell to tourists as a means of self-empowerment despite the sentiment that profits are unfairly mediated by the entity that controls these transactions. When these individuals show up to sell their goods in second-hand clothes, which show their impoverished condition, it breaks the San myth for tourists, so individuals feel encouraged to wear traditional skins despite the weather conditions (Tomaselli 2001). San are also classified as 'Remote Area Dwellers' and encouraged to work on farms or seek other employment, but all types of employment beside craft making are difficult to come by. Most of the steady work available is to build the roads that signal further encroachment on traditional land. The largest contradiction is in terms of hunting, for it is the 'Bushman' as skilled hunter that is the predominant myth portrayed in a number of ecotourist, NGO and development agendas throughout the Kalahari. Yet, free hunting for subsistence without quotas or licensing is not granted. Thus, one is caught in a semantic and regulatory dilemma that has real life consequences.

As videotaping started in the community in July of 2003, these issues continually arose despite the setting or intended outcome of discussions. Whether it was shooting around a campfire or going to a former hunting ground, the issues of food, hunting and their effect on the community were constantly played out. While the principal goal was to document these concerns, a strategy to undertake an applied visual anthropology was also developed. I offer these steps not to contradict other guides on how to shoot ethnographic media necessarily (Heider 1976; Collier and Collier 1986; Barbash and Taylor 1997) or to offer up the latest in a long series of war stories in ethnographic film production, but to reflect the reality of a haphazard applied project and my ongoing immersion in it, and its complicated political context.

Formulate a Project, Pick the Right Equipment and Go to the Field

Once it was decided that videotaping would take place in 2003, a variety of ethnographic techniques were employed including participant observation, open-ended interviews, collection of life histories and even some kinship and social mapping to get a context for the project. From this rapid assessment fieldwork, initial participants agreed to work on the project. While I initially struggled with the fact that I did not formulate a project or conduct long-term participant observation, I quickly rationalized that the revelation of human rights issues circumvented whether one was in the field for three months or three years.[7] Also, the quick participatory strategy allowed the participants to guide what topics would be breached and what would be shot.

The camera I used facilitated this process as well. Although we all dream of possessing the perfect camera and sound equipment, budgetary constraints and research often contradict this desire. The camera utilized was a small digital video camera with a large omnidirectional microphone. This small set-up allowed a higher sense of intimacy rather than a heightened concern with aesthetics and the isolation this often occurs for a camera operator. In addition, taking a large camera into the Kalahari at this point in the funding cycle was impossible. The camera also possessed a flip-out LCD screen, so participants were able to simultaneously see themselves and guide the action and direction of the shoot. This small technological capacity opened up the realm of participation. As I struggled at times with knowing what to shoot because of the multiple language difficulties, participants would watch what I was framing on the screen and then literally grab my hips and point me toward the conversation that further translation revealed to be of the most importance.

Agree on What to Shoot

There was no scripting of shots or set-ups. Rather, participants would gather prior to that day's activity, usually to have copious amounts of coffee and tea, and talk about which subjects to discuss during the next shoot. These discussions themselves eventually became videotape sessions, as the previous day's activity was often contextualized further. Allowing for distractions that inevitably took place, this plan created productive sessions. On one of the first days of shooting, a collaborative idea was suggested to utilize the vehicles we had in order to return to a hunting-ground to discuss their opinions on the inability to hunt without restrictions. As this particular shoot progressed, the problem with hunting, the concomitant lack of food and the consequences this entailed in terms of hunger and social disintegration became the main topic of discussion.

Discuss Problems in a Participatory Fashion and Shoot It

This particular day was incredibly hot and the glare from the barren pan wreaked havoc with the lens. I was accompanied by a university professor and a doctoral student to help me with sound and videotaping. Although I thought a fluent conversation was taking place, it soon became apparent that the translator could not really understand the dialect being spoken except for a few pieces here and there, mostly due to a lack of teeth by our aging main informant! Making things more difficult, the Afrikaans that became the agreed upon language that particular day was a dated Afrikaans dialect that a contemporary speaker could only understand piecemeal. My limited Afrikaans, practically non-existent Setswana and elementary understanding of the local dialect was problematic and frustrating. In addition, the participants were using bits of English and Setswana at different points in the conversations among themselves. As the footage later revealed, the senior participant knew what needed to be documented anyway and despite the language barrier steered me towards capturing certain images or reiterated certain laments the other individuals were discussing. The footage from that day addressed the topic of hunting and the effect this has had on the community:

> Participant 1: *If one is allowed to hunt then you can cook and eat and raise your children properly. We could get some meat but we are not allowed to. God gave us the meat to eat. Bushmen with dogs and spears do not eat anything. We don't have jobs so we do not have money to buy meat. If we get caught even killing a Gemsbok we go to jail. If you kill something and they find the tracks they follow it right up to your house. They come with a car and take all of the meat. They load it up and take it to (the nearest settlement). They take the money and go on the booze and you go to jail for nothing.*
> Participant 2: *They say that the people will eat all the animals.*
> Participant 1: *They say we will finish off everything but we don't eat like that, (laughter from the rest of the group). If we kill a gemsbok we only kill that one. They eat much more than we do.*
> Participant 3: *Today things are serious.*
> Participant 1: *They say that we must come live with them so that we can become human. I know that they are planning to take us away from here. I don't know where these old people are supposed to go.*

Edit

A topic that is often lacking in discussions of method and the production of ethnographic media is editing. Where does the anthropology occur? Does it occur in intention, in the event, in the reception? Or, does it take place in the crafting and the editing, where meaning is created through the juxtaposition of images, the suspension of real time to create manipulated time, the selection of different quotes and the elimination or addition of context. The preceding quotes are reduced portions of clips, further reduced from the real time context in which they were taped. Yet, they still have the capacity to depict the problems being faced by the community. After leaving the community in the summer of 2003, I spent the next ten months painstakingly translating footage with the assistance of two translators and then editing short clips that pertained to the main topics agreed upon and now revealed in the raw footage. Since the dated dialect of Afrikaans was mostly utilized, I screened these clips to a number of individuals familiar with it and those who had been on the trip to check for clarity and translation. Upon completion of a rough cut and my return to the community in 2004 the footage was approximately 20 minutes in length and addressed a number of issues centred on the irony that 'the hunters' could not hunt to live in the fashion they desired historically.

Return to the Field

One of the complaints often brought up by the individuals I have worked with is that people come, promise something, take stories and are never to be seen or heard from again. This lament is part of the long process that often occurs when San images are used in various documentaries or exercised in marketing campaigns, with the creators of these products never returning any funds or even coming back to share what they have created. This is a major point made by Asch (1992), as well, and I did not want to fall into this stereotype. When I returned in 2004, with a better camera and a laptop editing system, I screened the pieces for the four men who were the main participants, surrounded by about twenty individuals from the community, on a small laptop screen with attached speakers.

As the overall situation had not improved greatly in the previous year this screening was quite emotional, but afterwards we had another session talking about what the individuals had seen and whether or not they felt that they were represented properly. In other words, did the film clips 'tell the truth'? What was of most importance was whether or not the individuals now revealed on videotape, speaking about various parties and other entities, felt that the clips, if shown, could place them in any harm. At this point, two individuals asked if they could see the footage again and we agreed to meet the next day to go over it. With editing software on a small laptop I was able to do on-the-spot edits and eliminate clips that one individual decided were too problematic, although by the end of the trip he returned to tell me that he wanted me to show it anyway. As he stated, 'How much worse could it get if the government sees this? We are dying anyway.'

Shoot Again (and Again)

Building on previous work and continued editing on site, more interviews took place in 2004 that not only addressed the issues brought up in 2003 but also spoke more directly to contemporary political problems being faced. If anything, this speaks to the ongoing efforts that anthropologists must ethically adopt when conducting initial fieldwork, especially if the group of people are under threat. The ethnographic film process never ends, you just decide on an edit out point. This reflects the fact that communities and peoples are not frozen in the past, which is an inherent danger replicated time and time again by the classics of visual anthropology, constantly screened and continually talked about.

Dissemination

Perhaps the most troubling aspect of the completion of what could be considered the first haphazard stage in this project is what to do with the product of our endeavour. While it is incomplete in some respects, it does provide spoken testimonials and visual evidence of human rights issues. Does the video stay within the confines of academia for further speculation and, undoubtedly, critical interrogation? Or, should the focus be placed on attempting to get the video footage in the hands of government officials, NGOs and other development groups that need to be made aware of the local perspective on the situation so they could possibly help in the effort to affect change as soon as possible? What role does the anthropologist have when visual evidence is essentially taken out of his/her hands and screened in various venues for that reason? And, finally, what impact would the dissemination of the video footage have on the continuation of the project and the individuals represented? The participants have stated that they want their voices heard. As the project continues the eventual hope is to replicate past efforts and actually facilitate this desire by turning over the tools of representation to the people of the community themselves. Whether this is feasible or not is dependent upon funding, the availability of resources for sustainability, the political climate in Botswana and the actual existence of the community as time goes on.

Conclusion

Beyond the focus on applied visual strategies in ethnographic fieldwork reflected in this volume, there is an historical precedent of applied sensibilities in the historical, theoretical orientation towards the production of ethnographic media, specifically in the movement from observational to participatory media. The recognition of this precedent is an exercise in reclaiming the implicit applied components of ethnographic media theory and product, perhaps not the intentions of the original creators, but the influence they have had on others as applied visual methods continue to be formulated and developed. Essentially, anthropologists that produce anthropologically intended media have always had the capacity to create applied visual products in both method and theory. For those working with indigenous groups under threat, it is essential. The compression of time and space in the era of globalization (Harvey 1990) creates a smaller void between academic time and real time which necessitates a heightened awareness of the contextual circumstance and immediacy that the visual medium brings. Thus, the opportunity to immediately present applied visual media in public venues, such as the Internet, has compressed the time and space between academic study and presentation, and when this work deals with human rights issues, the demand for an activist sensibility in this type of anthropological work has increased. There have always been divisions between those who merely wish to represent, those who wish to participate, and, frankly, those who would rather just theorize about either practice, while not initiating it themselves. Regardless, an applied sensibility in all three endeavours is paramount for an anthropology of the twenty-first century attempting to deal with human rights issues like those facing San in the Kalahari and elsewhere concerning indigenous people.

The status of San throughout Botswana is precarious, as it is in other nation-states in the Kalahari region. The community where the project took place and the surrounding areas are facing food shortages, a lack of water, health issues and a lack of political representation compounded by multiple representational discourses, outside interests and competing agendas. Reinforcing these socio-economic conditions is the consistent portrayal of the 'Bushman Myth' (Gordon 1992) in media throughout the world. To circumvent this fantasy a representational burden is placed on any researcher or media producer, indigenous or otherwise, that demands a properly contextualized depiction of San groups that reflects current socio-economic realities while avoiding romanticized portrayals. One way to do this is to describe what actually happens on the ground when stereotypes run into reality.

The participatory videography project that I have audaciously titled 'The Hunters Redux' is an attempt to reinforce the fact that the same representational and 'real' problems presented by John Marshall's 1958 film *The Hunters*, and treated in his 2002 film series, *A Kalahari Family*, are ironically still being felt today by San almost fifty years later. This speaks to a larger issue of romanticized indigenous representation in a variety of socio-political circumstances, but it is specifically sharp and contradictory (Tomaselli 2005) considering the legacy of the 'fauna fantasy' (Marhsall 1993) that has marked San throughout the last several decades. An applied sensibility directed towards visual research methodology and the resultant product is a means by which this historical representational weight can begin to be circumvented. As editing and shooting progresses, it is hoped that more awareness can be brought to the struggles of this particular group and larger 'pan-San' identity issues (Sylvain 2005) felt throughout the Kalahari. In this sense, this project is just one more in a series of works by individuals attempting to draw attention to the contradictions that surround indigenous representation and social policies in and outside of anthropology. Focusing on the applied nature of visual work within anthropology provides a means to bring these political issues into immediate relief. Thus, the intention of the resultant ethnographic documentary work from this project is intended to reflect an aspect of growing applied strategies within visual anthropology that seek to address human rights issues being faced by individuals under threat.

Postscript

Conditions for indigenous groups are constantly changing and this community is no exception. Upon returning in 2006 to continue the initial stages of the project many of the same socio-economic problems persisted and many individuals had felt the lure of leaving the community to move to a nearby settlement and to find work elsewhere. Perhaps one of the most significant problems facing the adolescent youth of the community is what to do once schooling has ended, since there is minimal employment. This issue has become a major focus of fieldwork, and a participatory photo elicitation study has been created to provide a means of representation to document this. Video from the *Hunters Redux* project has been screened at a number of venues both domestically in the United States and internationally to bring more attention to the problems faced by the community.

Acknowledgements

This research was partially made possible by a Mellon Postdoctoral Fellowship at the University of KwaZulu-Natal in the Culture, Communication and Media Studies Department from 2003 to 2005. I would also like to thank my informants, research colleagues and others who commented on various versions of this chapter.

Notes

1. Although the proper use of the terms San and Bushmen are contested, I have chosen to use San as the primary term to label the group of people in this work. Whereas San is the primary way that Bushmen are referred to in the West, this term is contested in Southern Africa. In addition, the term Bushmen has become increasingly popular, at least among the individuals I have worked with, to use self-referentially. This popularity is also reflected in many of the NGOs that have developed in Southern Africa in the past decade.
2. I have developed this title, fully aware of its audacity and irony, to bring attention to the absurdity of the fact that many of the same issues dealt with over the last fifty years concerning the representation of San populations are still in debate today.
3. In order to protect the identities of individuals involved in the project and the interest of other research agendas in Botswana, I am not naming the specific community or names of individuals in this publication.

4. Keyan Tomaselli of the University of KwaZulu-Natal has been conducting ongoing research in various parts of the Kalahari concerning issues of identity, tourism and other projects over the past decade. I refer the reader to the website for the program in Culture, Communication and Media Studies (http://www.ukzn.ac.za/ccms/index.asp) for an extensive list of publications by Tomaselli and his students on these topics. I also consider this work to be a component of that ongoing project. See Tomaselli (2005) for an overview of the CCMS project.

5. The number of individuals within the community is variable dependent on students attending school and labourers at work elsewhere.

6. The Botswana government provides periodic subsistence to this community in the form of rations of mealie meal, sugar and tea. Informants in the community have stated that these deliveries do not provide a substantial diet. Therefore, they wish that their diet could be supplemented more frequently with meat gained from free hunting.

7. This is especially pertinent considering the complex political agendas and debates that surround San throughout the Kalahari and in Botswana particularly. As the research project develops, the perspectives of multiple entities are being sought to contextualize the local perspectives granted to us by the participants.

Bibliography

Asch, T. 1992. 'The Ethics of Ethnographic Film-Making', in P.I. Crawford and D. Turton (eds), *Film as Ethnography*. Manchester: Manchester University Press.

Askew, K. and R. Wilk (eds). 2002. *The Anthropology of Media*. Oxford: Blackwell Publishers.

Banks, M. 1992. 'Which Films are the Ethnographic Films?', in P.I. Crawford and D. Turton (eds), *Film as Ethnography*. Manchester: Manchester University Press.

Banks, M. and H. Morphy (eds). 1997. *Rethinking Visual Anthropology*. New Haven: Yale University Press.

Barbash, I. and L. Taylor. 1997. *Cross-cultural Film-making: A Handbook for Making Documentary and Ethnographic Films and Videos*. Berkeley: University of California Press.

Biesele, M. 1992. 'Changing Human Rights for the San in Namibia', *Namibia Brief* 16: 33–38.

Collier, J. and M. Collier. 1986. *Visual Anthropology: Photography as Research Method*. Albuquerque: University of New Mexico Press.

Crawford, P. and S. Hafsteinsson (eds). 1996. *The Construction of the Viewer*. Hojbjerg: Intervention Press.

Crawford, P. and D. Turton (eds). 1992. *Film as Ethnography*. Manchester: Manchester University Press.

Elder, S. 1995. 'Collaborative Film-making: An Open Space for Making Meaning, A Moral Ground for Ethnographic Film', *Visual Anthropology Review*. 11(2): 94–101.

Erwin, A. 2000. *Applied Anthropology: Tools and Perspectives for Contemporary Practice*. Needham Heights: Allyn and Bacon.

Fabian, J. 1983. *Time and the Other: How Anthropology Makes its Object*. New York: Columbia University Press.

Flores, C. 2004. 'Indigenous Video, Development and Shared Anthropology: A Collaborative Experience with Maya-Q'eqchi' Film-makers in Post-war Guatemala', *Visual Anthropology Review* 20(1): 31–44.

Ginsburg, F. 1991. 'Indigenous Media: Faustian Contract or Global Village?', *Cultural Anthropology* 6(1): 92–112.

Ginsburg, F., L. Abu-Lughod and B. Larkin (eds). 2002. *Media Worlds: Anthropology on New Terrain*. Berkeley: University of California Press.

Gordon, R. 1984. *What Future for the Ju/Wasi of Nyae Nyae?* Cambridge: Cultural Survival, Inc.

———. 1992. *The Bushman Myth: The Making of a Namibian Underclass*. Boulder, CO: Westview Press.

Harvey, D. 1990. *The Condition of Postmodernity*. Oxford: Blackwell Publishers.

Heider, K. 1976. *Ethnographic Film*. Austin: University of Texas Press.

Hitchcock, R.K. 2002. 'We Are the First People: Land, Natural Resources and Identity in the Central Kalahari, Botswana', *Journal of Southern African Studies*, 28(4): 797–824.

Lee, R. 2003. *The Dobe Ju/'hoansi*, 3rd ed. Fort Worth: Harcourt Brace College Publications.

Levine, S. 2003. 'Documentary Film and HIV/AIDS: New Directions for Applied Visual Anthropology in Southern Africa', *Visual Anthropology Review*, 19(1/2): 57–72.

MacDougall, D. 1998. *Transcultural Cinema*. Princeton: Princeton University Press.

Marshall, J. 1993. 'Filming and Learning', in J. Ruby (ed.), *The Cinema of John Marshall*. Philadelphia: Harwood Academic Publishers.

Martinez, W. 1992. 'Who Constructs Anthropological Knowledge? Toward a Theory of Ethnographic Film Spectatorship', in P. Crawford and D. Turton (eds), *Film as Ethnography*. Manchester: Manchester University Press.

Michaels, E. 1986. *Aboriginal Invention of Television: Central Australia 1982–1986*. Canberra: Australian Institute for Aboriginal Studies.

Pink, S. 2001. *Doing Visual Ethnography*. London: Sage Publications.

———. 2004. 'Applied Visual Anthropology: Social Intervention, Visual Methodologies and Anthropological Theory', *Visual Anthropology Review* 20(1): 3–16.

Rouch, J. 1974. 'The Camera and Man', in P. Hockings (ed.), *Principles of Visual Anthropology*. The Hague: Mouton.

Ruby, J. 1980. 'Exposing Yourself: Reflexivity, Anthropology and Film', *Semiotica* 30(1/2)(3): 153–179.

———. 2000. *Picturing Culture*. Chicago: University of Chicago Press.

Simpson, J. 2005. 'Bushmen Fight for Homeland', *BBC News Online*. Retrieved 30 August 2005 from http://news.bbc.co.uk/1/hi/world/africa/4480883.stm

Sylvain, R. 2002. 'Land, Water, and Truth: San Identity and Global Indigenism', *American Anthropologist* 104(4): 1074–85.

———. 2005. 'Disorderly Development: Globalization and the Idea of "Culture" in the Kalahari', *American Ethnologist* 32(3): 354–370.

Tomaselli, K. 2001. 'Blue is Hot, Red is Cold: Doing Reverse Cultural Studies in Africa', *Cultural Studies – Critical Methodologies* 1(3): 283–317.

———. 2005. *Where Global Contradictions are the Sharpest: Research Stories from the Kalahari*. Bloemgracht: Rozenberg Publishers.

Turner, T. 1990. 'Visual Media, Cultural Politics and Anthropological Practice: Some Implications of Recent Uses of Film and Video among the Kayapo of Brazil', *Commission on Visual Anthropology Review* Spring: 8–13.

Willigen, J. 1986. *Applied Anthropology: An Introduction*. South Hadley: Bergin and Garvey Publications.

Worth, S. 1981. *Studying Visual Communication*. Philadelphia: University of Pennsylvania Press.

Worth, S. and J. Adair. 1972. *Through Navajo Eyes*. Bloomington: Indiana University Press.

Filmography

The Gods Must Be Crazy. 1980. Jamie Uys. Mimosa Films (Botswana). 109 minutes.

The Hunters. 1958. John Marshall. Documentary Educational Resources (U.S.A.). 73 minutes.

A Kalahari Family. 2002. John Marshall. Documentary Educational Resources (U.S.A.) 360 minutes.

Chapter 10

SHARING ANTHROPOLOGY
Collaborative Video Experiences among Maya Film-makers
in Post-war Guatemala

—— ⊘⊘⊘ ——

Carlos Y. Flores

This paper deals with the role of indigenous video, shared anthropology
and collaborative film-making among Mayan Q'eqchi' communities in Alta
Verapaz, Guatemala. It analyses the subjective and historical conditions
that provided the context for collaborative video production between local
film-makers, communities and visual anthropologist and the implications
these had both for the Q'eqchi' and for my own anthropological practice. I
argue that this community-based video project not only provided
important ethnographic tools, but also new mechanisms for sociocultural
reconstruction and awareness after an intensely traumatic and violent
period of civil war. In this context, the video documents produced provided
a space within a wider practice of shared anthropology where each party
could advance their own goals through hybrid products. Thus, the project
represented an opportunity to explore ways in which anthropology and
ethnographic film-making could be simultaneously of use to the researcher
and also to the communities studied. However, it also highlighted the
contradictions and complexities of collaborative or 'shared' anthropological
practice in the sphere of applied visual anthropology.

Anthropology in a Troubled Home

I went to the Q'eqchi' region of Alta Verapaz, Guatemala, with the aim of
pursuing my Ph.D. research in the second half of the 1990s. This involved
assessing the uses, possibilities and impacts of audiovisual media among
indigenous groups in the country from an anthropological perspective. My
interest, however, was not only academic. During my fieldwork the
country was beginning to emerge from one of the longest and most vicious
armed conflicts in Latin America[1] and the political impact of indigenous
issues at national and international level was steadily increasing. Located in
the so called '*áreas en conflicto*', the Q'eqchi' people of the Alta Verapaz

province, a Mayan group with some 361,000 members, had endured the hardships of the armed conflict and were coming to terms with the violence of the past. In such a context, I believed that the footage obtained through a community video project might eventually provide not only important ethnographic insights about an indigenous group and its recent transformations, but also new mechanisms for cultural reconstruction and social healing after an acute process of social dislocation and militarization.

I had read about other experiences in indigenous media studied by anthropologists in Brazil, Canada, the USA and Australia, and hoped to participate in or to help develop something similar in Guatemala. However, certain features specific to Guatemala distanced it in many respects from other community video practices. Unlike the Brazilian Kayapo or the Australian aborigines, Guatemala's indigenous populations were not minority cultural groups, nor had they secured any measure of territorial autonomy to protect and preserve their distinct identity and way of life. On the contrary, totalling some six million, indigenous people in Guatemala constituted around half of the population and were fully integrated into the national socioeconomic system, albeit in a highly disadvantageous fashion. In fact indigenous people have been essential for the maintenance and reproduction of the country's archaic agro-export model, controlled by a nonindigenous, semi-feudal elite. Another important difference was the armed conflict itself, which had left a deep imprint on the country's indigenous identity and culture.

As a nonindigenous Guatemalan, a *ladino*, I shared a history of conflict with the Mayan people I aimed to work with. Thirteen years previously I had fled Guatemala because of the political violence, going to Mexico where I began my anthropological training, something I was later to continue in the United Kingdom. This research project therefore represented for me an opportunity for reencounter with my country's troubled and unresolved past. In the event, the insight that I gained from studying Q'eqchi' identity and history eventually revealed many issues related to my own identity. The Q'eqchi' narrative about past traumatic events helped me to reconstruct a narrative of myself as Guatemalan in my own country again. This peculiar personal situation made me even more aware of what James Clifford rightly asserts that 'every version of an "other" wherever found, is also the construction of a "self" and the making of ethnographic texts' (Clifford and Marcus 1986: 23). At times, therefore, I was looking at Guatemalan society from the somewhat confusing perspective of a national and a foreigner at the same time.

Undoubtedly, this 'half Guatemalan-ness' coloured my anthropological enterprise since it put me in a peculiar position of both closeness and distance with Guatemalan society in general and the Q'eqchi' people in particular. Despite the fact that I shared cultural and historical roots with them, I was constantly confronted by an elusive and troubling otherness. Yet although the contradictions were many, their historical process was so interwoven with mine that I found it very difficult to try to separate our worlds in the manner of a more traditional Western anthropological practice based on *alterity*. On the contrary, for me fieldwork represented an opportunity for what Michael Jackson has proposed: 'testing and exploring ways in which our experiences conjoin or connect us with others, rather than the ways they set us apart' (Jackson 1989, quoted in Stoller 1992: 214). My desire was to develop an anthropological practice among the Q'eqchi' from a more personal and horizontal perspective framed by shared experiences.

Fortunately I was guided in my methodological pursuits by recent revisionist developments in the discipline. The contemporary concern with understanding the relations established between anthropologists and natives provided new paradigms wherein the univocal voice of the researcher was challenged when the voices of the subjects began to be heard within the academic community. In this process anthropology increased its shift from an 'objective' and positivist approach -aimed basically at 'representing' the cultural 'other'- to a more subjective perspective, where the author's voice began to be regarded as one of a more personal nature. Such approaches, recently advocated by postmodernist currents, supposed the rendering of multiple subjective voices that had value in and of themselves independent of the author's interpretation.[2] These critical movements led to a greater engagement by anthropologists with their subjects, although this happened at different levels and in different ways.

Undoubtedly these theoretical developments provided basic methodological tools to deploy within my own anthropological practice at home, in the sense that they helped me to situate myself as an author within my particular situation as 'native' anthropologist with the people I was working with. They also held out the promise of a more shared and horizontal interaction with the subjects' conceptual universe. Yet they did not answer a fundamental and very practical question which still troubled me: if ethnography had increasingly become a dialogue between multiple voices, why was it that at the end of the day only one of the parties normally benefited from the anthropological practice? In other words, although the production of ethnographic texts and ultimately of knowledge was beginning to be achieved in a more interactive and 'collective' fashion, there was still the problem of ethnographic consumption/appropriation, an area barely touched upon in this revisionist debate. Anthropological theoretical developments, in their textual dimension at least, for all their new and sophisticated methods aimed at 'giving voice to the natives' seemed ultimately to remain largely concerned with issues of 'cultural translation' for the West (see Asad 1986).[3]

I was able to fill some of my methodological gaps by looking to other branches of the discipline concerned with the practical uses of anthropology for the communities involved, notably within the areas of applied and political anthropology. These perspectives provided useful methodological tools to work with subject communities. Their advocates frequently used the knowledge gathered in the field to contribute to development projects and policies. In general, however, such experiences tended to facilitate the promotion of cultural and social change in individuals, communities and societies located principally in the so-called 'Third World', since this kind of interaction was often associated with capitalist 'modernization' and political change. In this respect and independently of the results, such exercises were unattractive since they were often deployed and applied regardless of the natives' opinions. Even when people in the field developed such projects in more participatory manners, it was obviously very difficult for the communities involved to escape the economic and political logic imposed by the national and international donors financing such programmes.

Nevertheless, it was within one such development project in the Q'eqchi' region that I first managed to articulate my anthropological proposal. This provided me with the opportunity to design a research project by combining the methodological insights of postmodernist approaches, particularly their multivocal dimension, with others from applied anthropology. During a short pre-fieldwork period in 1994 I learnt that there was a Maya-Q'eqchi' video team working with the Benedictine Order of the Catholic Church in the city of Cobán. One of the principal ideas behind the Q'eqchi' video project had been to teach members of the communities how to produce video materials in their own language and by themselves, focusing on the areas of health, religion and education. The project was in fact a continuation of the successful experience of Radio Tezulutlán, the local Catholic radio also set up with the help of Father Bernardino, which had been transmitting in Q'eqchi' since the 1970s.[4] Through both forms of electronic media the church was able to bypass the barriers of monolinguism and high illiteracy in the area. In 1994 the Q'eqchi' video project was being sponsored by the US government's Agency for International Development (USAID) and the newly created FONAPAZ (Fondo Nacional para la Paz), the Guatemalan state body set up to channel foreign aid for peace projects. With this information I went to visit them and talked about my academic proposal. After a short discussion the possibility of including me in the video project was accepted. Thus began a collaborative relationship between the local video makers and myself as anthropologist.

Having envisaged this possibility, I systematically gathered information about other indigenous video projects where anthropologists had been involved in their conception and development. Advocates of the 'small media' had written extensively about the ways in which indigenous groups around the globe had been using electronic audiovisual tools during the last two decades 'as new vehicles for internal and external communication, cultural and language maintenance, self-determination, and resistance to outside cultural domination' (Ginsburg 1997: 119).[5] In addition I also consulted data about earlier experiences of collaborative film-making between anthropologists and members of the studied communities. I was particularly impressed by the early efforts of the French ethnographic film-maker Jean Rouch and his ideas of 'shared anthropology', a term coined after he managed to achieve the active involvement of his West African subjects of study in the production of his films.

Setting the Basis for a Collaborative Film-making Experience

In a slow and at times difficult process of integration with the video team, I initially adopted the classical anthropological method of 'participant observation' during their video practices in the city of Cobán and filming in their villages. This basically meant following the video makers and observing them interacting with other members of their communities, developing a rapport with them, asking for explanations where possible, and later registering as much as I could in my field diary. During this process, the video team did not seem bothered by my presence and carried on with their normal activities, although they undoubtedly behaved in a more reserved manner when I was with them.

In this initial period, however, three things attracted my attention because they somehow clashed with my own expectations about indigenous video, stemming from my reading on the subject. The first was that while filming the team paid little attention to what much of the anthropological literature on Mesoamerica referred to as 'essential' Mayan practices, such as ceremonies related to the planting of 'sacred' crops like maize and beans, life-cycle rituals, mythology or references to the important sacred mountain or *Tzuultaq'a*. Instead, they stuck to a strictly developmentalist agenda, recording and screening issues such as hygienic practices, uses of pesticides, construction of latrines, working in cooperatives and so forth. When they did film religious ceremonies, these were normally associated with Catholic, not 'Mayan' festivities. Secondly, despite the fact that many of the Q'eqchi' video makers had been army conscripts and traces of militarism were apparent almost everywhere in their communities, nobody seemed interested in recording events related to the civil war or about the political situation in general. And thirdly, the final video programmes were made in Spanish, a language hardly understood by most members of the communities, the supposed main audience. I later discovered that this outward rather than inwardly oriented behaviour was linked to certain processes of national integration in the post conflict period and the efforts of the still militarized state to develop broader social consensus and legitimacy through the channelling of international funding to projects such as this.

After some weeks among the Q'eqchi' video team, I began to feel uncomfortable that I was the only one without a clear role during the training, filming and editing sessions. The team became aware that I had some experience in TV production and expected me to take a more active involvement in the project. From time to time some of them asked me to contribute by transmitting my knowledge and filming skills. At the beginning I was doubtful about this, fearing that such an external input might somehow spoil or 'contaminate' a particular Q'eqchi' filming narrative. However, I soon realised that such a presumption was nonsense, particularly since this process was happening anyway as the youngsters were permanently exposed to commercial TV and North American and

Mexican feature films, from which they were taking ideas. After some initial hesitation I decided to actively collaborate with them in what could be called a self-consciously interventionist anthropological enterprise. In general, my participation consisted at this point of adding other general video techniques to their already acquired filming skills, such as scripting, lighting, close-ups and details, using more than one camera for the same event, interview techniques, etc.

Feeling more confident among the group and following my visual anthropological instinct, I later proposed experimenting with a reorientation of their topics of interest and filming narratives in order to produce observational documentaries in their own language about what I believed were more 'traditional' or 'ancestral' Mayan customs in their communities. The impact of modernization and civil war had been rapidly eroding such practices and I suggested that keeping a record of some of these would be an important contribution towards the cultural patrimony of future generations. It took a while for the young video makers to accept this proposal, which they finally did after series of internal deliberations and negotiations. However, their parents and the elders of the community selected for filming, Esperanza Chilatz, were enthusiastic about the new project and eager to collaborate almost as soon as they heard about it. Both groups obviously had different perceptions about the possibilities of the project in general. This generational gap was due in many respects to different expectations stemming from age and position within the communities, which had, in turn, been influenced by external factors related to national dynamics and the civil war. Clearly, during the previous fifteen years these events had profoundly affected the nature of internal communal organisation.[6]

We finally agreed on the filming of the rituals associated with the planting of maize, partly because of this activity at the time was a noncontroversial subject in political terms and also because of its key socioeconomic and cultural importance among rural Mayan societies. During the filming process, the elders and their wives enthusiastically helped us in different ways and even suggested that they 're-enact' their cultural practices in front of the camera, something that we politely rejected. However, their previously recorded explanations about the activity made through interviews carried out by the Q'eqchi' video team gave us important clues to follow during the actual filming of the rituals and also structured a good deal of the narrative of the final documentary. Meanwhile, the younger members of the community involved in the video project constantly swapped roles between being video makers and taking part in the maize planting ceremony, blurring the boundaries between recording the ritual and being active participants, or subjects of the filming process. These shifting roles, together with the presence of outsiders among the video crew, stimulated the development of a unique, intimate and revealing window on this annual ritual and on the different roles adopted by the diverse members of the community (see Flores 2000).

Figure 10.1 Filming in the community of Esperanza Chilatz. © Carlos Flores 2006.

Seeking a Shared Narrative

After several months of intermittent filming, we had enough material for the beginning of the editing process. However, I noticed that the interest of members of the video team in the project markedly declined after some days of post production in the cutting room. It was true that the exhausting hours of translating and logging the rushes had tired everybody out by the end of the day, but the filming process had also been a demanding activity which had nevertheless maintained the enthusiasm of the local video makers. After a while, it began to be clear to me that we were working according to different logics and expectations.

As became evident, for the Q'eqchi' video team, to produce a film had more to do with the process than the product in itself.[7] In Mayan communal life, social roles, prestige and power are acquired via individual and collective actions which are perceived by the community as *services*. Although there are several 'invisible' individual services like prayers and offerings (*majehak*), which are culturally understood as beneficial for the rest of the members of the village, in general the most obvious way to project social behaviour is through publicly tangible acts. In this sense, the entire video project in Esperanza Chilatz contained an important dimension of public performance and communal service. The young video makers had already achieved considerable status and leadership in

Esperanza Chilatz through their monopoly on filming skills and their wider general knowledge of developmentalist issues in the fields of education and health. This social position was further underlined by their connections with the powerful external institutions of the military and the Catholic Church and their modernizing agenda. In this context, their ability to mediate with external institutions derived more from their filming skills than from their film products.[8]

However, another factor which might have contributed to their less than enthusiastic behaviour at this stage of the film production was my own presence. During the filming in Esperanza Chilatz my activity was minimal, given my limited understanding of local practices and ability to interact with members of the community due to my lack of fluent Q'eqchi'. In such conditions the video team enjoyed full command of their social space and chose most of the shots and people to be interviewed while I merely provided technical support and some questions to be asked during the interviews. Yet once back in the city, a social space where I felt more comfortable and over which I had in many respects a better command than them, the roles changed and I began to have a more active participation in the process while theirs decreased. Among other things it was taken for granted that I had some additional 'expertise' in video production from my previous experience in TV production and my academic background. It was only later that I realised that my relative assertiveness in the scriptwriting, the editing, and in general about how to produce a more conventional film product might have inhibited the rest of the group, despite my intention to include as many suggestions as possible.

I ultimately had the last word in the editing room and therefore my version and understanding of the ceremony prevailed in the final structure of the audiovisual document. It was an ethnographic visual document characterised by what Clifford has called an 'hierarchical arrangement of discourses' (1986: 17).[9] In any case, the experience ended up being a filming style that borrowed from former practices like Rouch's 'participatory cinema' (Stoller 1992), the Kayapo and the 'Video in the Villages' project in Brazil (Turner 1991), the 'observational' style of the Granada Centre for Visual Anthropology in Manchester, and, of course, the camera and editing expertise of the Q'eqchi' producers themselves (see Flores 1999). Having completed such a product, some of my concerns about the dilemmas stemming from the paternity and destination of the film were eventually addressed. For instance, my experience indicated that the resulting film *Qa Loq Laj Iyaaj* (*Our Sacred Seed*) seemed to be more enjoyable and 'digestible' for a Q'eqchi' or Maya public than for an academic or foreign audience. This was not only because of the subject matter, but also because of the film's particular rhythm and narrative, which were in many senses distinct from the pace of traditional Western filming. Clearly, with such a hybrid exercise it was possible to develop the basics elements of a filming style which proved to be fairly well accepted by the local communities where it was presented and also among other indigenous groups at national and international level.[10]

Figure 10.2 The author with Qawa Zacarías Xol, an elder traditionalist, during the preproduction of *Our Sacred Seed*. © Carlos Flores 2006.

The Production of Rub'el Kurus and the Struggle for Memory

During the distribution of *Our Sacred Seed* through informal channels throughout the Q'eqchi' region, I met Ven de la Cruz, a Filipino priest working in the area of Salawim. I had previously learnt that his mission, the Congregation of The Immaculate Heart of Mary (CICM), had been trying to develop the Catholic Church's work in this former conflict zone after years of missionary absence due to the acute political violence of the previous decade. The priest had seen the film produced in the community of Esperanza Chilatz together with the people his mission was working with. Apparently, the Q'eqchi' audience had enjoyed the film's approach and visual rhythm. He wanted to discuss the possibility of producing another visual document in Q'eqchi' and for Q'eqchi' people using a similar film narrative. I accepted and began to work with him on the main ideas for this new documentary. As would later become evident, this second collaborative film production would have a different focus and objectives compared to the first one, given the different social and political context where it took place.

Months before, the priest's religious community had inaugurated a monument shaped in the form of a fifteen-metre cross on a hill near the village of Sahakok. Inscribed on marble slabs at the foot of the monument were the names of 916 victims of the violence in the area. Most of these people had been killed in the early 1980s by the army's counterinsurgency operations and their bodies dumped in scattered unmarked graves throughout the region. Thousands of the survivors had been also forcibly displaced from their communities and had fled to the mountains before the army captured and in many cases relocated them in semi-militarized villages. For years, the priest told me, people had been terrified and unable to come to terms with the military violence which marked their recent past. Because of this many channels of communication and cultural expression were blocked either by fear or by psychological trauma and confusion. Those violent events constituted an unresolved and conflictive past that permanently haunted people's memory, something that in turn contaminated their sense of self-esteem, identity and community. As Ven de la Cruz explained, his mission wanted a film about this situation in order to help the communities 'to reflect on their recent past of suffering and violence'. 'In learning from their recent past history,' he added, 'they could then go on with their lives'.

When I arrived in Sahakok with Mainor Pacay, one of the Q'eqchi' film-makers I had worked with during the first film production, we immediately received the active support of some leaders of the community for our filming, which in turn facilitated our involvement and work with other villagers who ended up collaborating with us in different ways. Military control and political repression had gradually receded in the area, although local authorities implanted by the army retained important quotas of power and continued to inspire considerable fear among the population. Despite such surveillance networks in many communities, traditional authorities had slowly been occupying the political and symbolic spaces left behind by the army's retreat. One of these spaces was the highly contested field of the recovery of historical memory.[11] Consequently the new film production was inscribed within the local efforts to reconstruct a system of representations severely damaged by war. For the survivors and their allies, such a documentary had the additional potential of being a vehicle of dissemination of such perceptions beyond the community itself. As became evident, the interest in constructing the memorial and, latterly, in producing the film was rooted in efforts to transform those past and fragmented events into formal social discourses. These memory devices contributed to the development of counter-hegemonic accounts reflecting the victims' point of view, ultimately helping to structure meaning within a political discourse about their traumatic past (see Geertz 1993: 19). Therefore, this film process may be understood as one of many therapeutic acts.[12]

After some months, we managed to film and edit the film *Rub'el Kurus* (*Beneath the Cross*), constantly receiving feedback from members of the community – particularly during shooting in the community – and during visits of the elders to the city of Cobán, where we edited the material. As in the first video experience, this was a collaborative practice embedded in

Figure 10.3 In the editing room with Q'eqchi' video maker Mainor Pacay. © Carlos Flores 2006.

a web of social relations where different cultural and historical references met, producing what Marcus and Fisher have called 'a negotiation of meanings' (Marcus and Fisher 1986, quoted in Henley 1998: 51). The distribution of the film throughout different communities in the region also revealed a series of polemical interpretations, which stemmed from the ideological divisions and regime of denial generated by the civil war.[13]

Such polemics notwithstanding, for the relatives of the disappeared of Sahakok the giving of testimony about the violence contributed to the task of reclaiming and legitimizing the physical and social landscape. As people became more able to talk of and rationalize disturbing past events and integrate them in a more organized fashion into their cultural practices and beliefs, those past experiences somehow became more controllable, something which in turn empowered their present actions.[14] Hence the memorial cross – and by extension the film production – became not only a public sphere where the survivors could symbolically reunite with their murdered kin and openly mourn them, but also a space of political denunciation of past atrocities (see Flores 2000).[15]

Conclusion

Collaborative film-making among Q'eqchi' communities within the dynamic context of post-war Guatemala provided varied and rich avenues for exploring the possibilities and limits of shared and applied visual anthropological enterprises. The films *Qa Loq Laj Iyaaj* and *Rub'el Kurus*[16] were produced in a similar cultural milieu during a process of social reconstruction after a period of civil war, militarism and political violence. Within this context, Q'eqchi' people were increasingly asserting their ethnic identity and widening their forms of political expression. Both film projects provided insights and contributed to these processes at the community level, not only by recording a way of life and involving local people in the film production, but also through the different social and cultural responses which these collaborative interactions provoked. In this sense, the experiences were conceived as efforts to make people more self-aware of their specific social, cultural and political behaviour in order for them to gain greater control over which markers of identity they chose to preserve, modify, or reject. Within these processes, my own agenda as an

Figure 10.4 Mourner at Sahakok during the filming of *Rub'el Kurus*. © Werner Goebels 2006.

anthropologist clearly had different ends which were also positively met; through the video interaction I gained access to privileged ethnographic information which enabled me to better understand local events.

From their very inception, neither film was the kind of ethnographic documentary that, once filmed and edited, was intended to be presented to a foreign audience, or solely to the particular community where the events filmed took place. Nor was this an indigenous video enterprise such as the Kayapo experience, where the final material and its narrative were regulated in the last instance by the indigenous producers themselves, together with other members of their ethnic community. Rather, through a more holistic approach involving a co-operative exercise between subjects and anthropologist, it tried to combine different elements of global and local experiences. At a more theoretical level, the practices benefited from different anthropological currents and their revisionist and postmodern variants, particularly in the fields of visual, applied and political anthropology, which have facilitated a more polyphonic construction of the anthropological text. This 'opening' has undoubtedly shifted the ways in which anthropology in general and visual anthropology in particular has been practised, making it possible to conceive of different forms of interaction with subjects in the field and more experimental ways of doing ethnography.

In light of these considerations, however, the quality of being a 'shared' and 'collaborative' venture depends more upon the ability of projects to establish common grounds where those involved can pursue different sets of interests and negotiate, combine and materialize them in a collective fashion. The successes and failures of such joint ventures therefore have to do with their ability to articulate meaningful processes and outcomes for their participants. In the words of Clifford Geertz, rather than projects in search of fixed rules or guidelines, such experiences should be 'interpretative one[s] in search of meaning' (Geertz 1993: 5), and beyond that, I would add, in search of collective action. In short they should be projects which seek to develop an anthropological practice with multiple results and beneficiaries where several projects can be tied together within the same collective process.

Yet collaborative film-making is a complex exercise and not free of risks and contradictions. Different existential and political contexts inevitably mean that each party will have different expectations about the whole project. These mismatches – unavoidable in any cross cultural interaction – derive from the ways in which the identities and needs of the participants have developed. Despite good intentions, the collective construction of a text with multivocal characteristics could easily end up disguising new and sophisticated forms of cultural appropriation where the aims of 'sharing' are only an illusion.[17] In this sense, it is important to be as aware as possible about how and why subjects and subjectivities become objects and are objectivized within the anthropological practice.

Perhaps what is at stake in any anthropological encounter seeking 'shared' processes (and, by extension, 'applied' or 'political' practices) is the way in which the power to act and to propose are established, and the manner in which the outcomes are distributed among the different participants. Nonetheless, within the public sphere where each party operates, collaborative film-making could constitute a constructive relationship wherein each individual is supported and encouraged in the construction of their own sense of selfhood through concrete collective actions. As Paulo Freire (1985) affirmed, research should be an involvement, not an invasion. Ultimately, shared anthropological enterprises should provide spaces for self-discovery and the creative construction of identity: above all they should be processes whereby both anthropologist and subject can be mutually empowered.

Notes

1. With the backing of the international community, the Guatemalan state was negotiating a peace agreement with the guerrilla groups organised in the URNG (Unidad Revolucionaria Nacional Guatemalteca), which eventually put an end to thirty-six years of armed conflict in which, according to the UN, some 200,000 people, mostly indigenous, died.

2. According to Adam Kuper, during these methodological revisions 'the natives had to be given their unedited say. This prescription was justified by a political argument against domination, and in favour of democratic expression' (1986: 542).

3. Abu-Lughod observes that: 'Even attempts to refigure informants as consultants and to "let the other speak" in dialogic or polyvocal texts – decolonizations on the level of the text – leave intact the basic configuration of global power on which anthropology, as linked to other institutions of the world, is based' (Abu-Lughod 1991, quoted in Nordstrom 1997: 30).

4. The Benedictine branch of the Church, based at the Blue Cloud Abbey in Dakota, had arrived in Alta Verapaz in 1964 following the Pope's guidelines of sending ten per cent of its missionaries to Latin America. Its clergymen already had a long-established record working with North American native groups such as Sioux, Dakotas and Metis (a mixture of Chippawa and French people) with the aim of 'little by little Americaniz[ing] the people to facilitate their integration to a more global society' (Benedictine pamphlet about the origins of the order – nd).

5. See also Turner 1991, 1992; Moore 1994; Worth and Adair 1972; McDougall 1994; Chalfen 1992; and McLellan 1987.

6. In the past, power was normally acquired with age inside the communities, but by associating themselves with powerful institutions – first the Catholic Church and subsequently the army – the youngsters managed to acquire positions of authority within the community. Inadvertently, I understood later, my proposal was somehow threatening their prestigious role as brokers of modernity while at the same time re-empowering the elders' authority, which stemmed a good deal from 'traditional' knowledge.

7. I want to thank Sergio Navarrete for his insightful comments on this point.

8. In this sense an important parallel with the Kayapo community video experience in Brazil was discernible; according to Turner, for the Kayapo 'the act of shooting with a video camera can become an even more important mediator of their relations with the dominant Western culture than the video document itself' (1992: 7).

9.   This in itself raised some methodological and ethical questions in line with the interrogations of David MacDougall (1994: 31), who asked, 'if ethnographies now incorporate other voices, what textual independence do these voices actually have? In an absolute sense, all texts used in this way are subordinated to the text of the author'.

10.   *Qa Loq Laj Iyaaj* won the continental price '*Lanza de Amaru de la Nacionalidad Awua para la categoría Cosmovisión*' during the Third Festival of Film and Video of the First Nations of Abya-Yala, which took place in Ecuador in July 1999.

11.   These efforts against forgetting were normally framed in the moral and political language of human rights. As Richard Wilson noted, 'in community-based initiatives throughout the Mayan highlands naming the victims through recording faithfully their names, the "public secrets" of a community are disclosed in order to initiate a break with the regime of denial' (1998: 186).

12.   Nevertheless, the political and personal repercussions of ethnographic film-making in conflictive situations can be potentially as traumatic as therapeutic. Therefore, it is important to assess the convenience or even justification of the entire exercise with care, since sometimes subjects in the field may not be in a position to make a decision that is in their best interests (see Barbash and Taylor 1997: 54, 57).

13.   Clearly, a coincidence of political goals and sympathies with the subjects will generally provide greater collaboration of members of the communities in a shared project, particularly since internal and external forces might prompt individuals in the field to advance their own social and political goals through the power of representation that anthropologists or film-makers are perceived to have. However, in polarized contexts the interests operating within a given area are invariably much more complex than a first impression might reveal and one should be aware that such a partisan approach will inevitably annul or undermine other subaltern voices operating in the same social sphere (see Le Bot 1996, Nordstrom 1995 and Stoll 1999).

14.   According to Judith Zur, 'Chaos enters the memory as an impression of chaos, without taking on meaning. For traces to remain in memory, the experience must be structured: what is well-remembered is what is found in memory as organized units, and ordered memories hangs on ordered experience' (1998: 169).

15.   *Rub'el Kurus* was later screened at the 6th International Festival of Ethnographic Film which took place in Goldsmiths College, University of London, in September 1999. On this occasion the Royal Anthropological Institute generously invited the Q'eqchi' cameraman and editor of the film, Mainor Pacay, to come to discuss with me the shared project from our different perspectives (see Flores 1999).

16.   Both films can be obtained through the Royal Anthropological Institute or directly from the author.

17.   As David MacDougall rightly states, 'the inclusion of indigenous narrative always raises the question of whether the film is making indigenous statements or merely absorbing a device into its own narrative strategies. Inevitably, a method which purports to disperse some of its authority to its subjects is also capable of using this to reinforce its own' (1994: 29).

Bibliography

Abu-Lughod, L. 1991. 'Writing against Culture', in Richard G. Fox (ed), *Recapturing Anthropology: Working in the Present*. Santa Fe: School of American Research Press.

Asad, T. 1986. 'The Concept of Cultural Translation in British Social Anthropology' in J. Clifford and G. Marcus (eds.), *Writing Culture: The Poetics and Politics of Ethnography*. Berkeley: University of California Press.

Barbash, I. and L. Taylor. 1997. *Cross-Cultural Filmmaking: A Handbook for Making Documentary and Ethnographic Films and Videos*. Berkeley: University of California Press.

Benedictine Order, Alta Verapaz, Guatemala, nd. Untitled pamphlet on origins of the order. Unpublished pamphlet.

Chalfen, R. 1992.'Picturing Culture through Indigenous Imagery: A Telling Story', in I. Crawford and D. Turton (eds.), *Film as Ethnography*. Manchester: Manchester University Press.

Clifford, J. and G. Marcus. 1986. *Writing Culture: The Poetics and Politics of Ethnography*. Berkeley: University of California Press.

Clifford, J. 1986. 'Partial Truths' in J. Clifford and G. Marcus (eds.), *Writing Culture: The Poetics and Politics of Ethnography*. Berkeley: University of California Press.

Flores, C. 1999. 'Shared Anthropology in Guatemala', in *Anthropology Today*, 15(1): 19–20.

——— 2000. *Indigenous Video, Memory and Shared Anthropology in Post-War Guatemala: Collaborative Film-making experiences among the Q'eqchi' of Alta Verapaz*. PhD Dissertation. Manchester: University of Manchester.

Freire, P. 1985. *Pedagogy of the Oppressed*. London: Pelican Books.

Geertz, C. 1993. *The Interpretation of Cultures*. London: Fontana Press (first published 1973, New York: Basic Books).

Ginsburg, F. 1997. 'From Little Things, Big Things Grow: Indigenous Media and Cultural Activism' in R. Fox and O. Starn, Orin (eds.), *Between Resistance and Revolution: Cultural Politics and Social Protest*. Brunswick: Rutgers University Press.

Henley, P. 1998. 'Film-making and Ethnographic Research', in J. Prosser (ed.), *Image-based Research: A Sourcebook for Qualitative Researcher*. London: Falmer Press.

Jackson, M. 1989. *Paths Toward a Clearing*. Bloomington: Indiana University Press.

Kuper, A. 1986. 'Culture, Identity and the Project of a Cosmopolitan Anthropology', *Man* 29 (3): 537–554.

Le Bot, Y. 1996. *La Guerra en Tierras Mayas: Comunidad, Violencia y Modernidad en Guatemala (1970–1992)*. Mexico: Fondo de Cultura Económica.

MacDougall, D. 1994. 'Whose Story Is It?', in L. Taylor (ed.), *Visualizing Theory: Selected Essays From V.A.R. 1990–1994*. London: Routledge.

Marcus, G. and M. J. Fischer. 1986. *Anthropology as Cultural Critique: An Experimental Moment in the Human Sciences*. Chicago: University of Chicago Press.

McLellan, I. 1987. 'Video and Narrowcasting: TV for and by Ordinary People', *Media in Education and Development*, 20(4): 144–149.

Moore, R. 1994. 'Marketing Alterity' in *Visualizing Theory: Selected Essays from V.A.R. 1990–1994*. L. Taylor (ed.). London: Routledge.

Nordstrom, C. 1995. 'War on the Front Lines', in C. Nordstrom and A. Robben (eds.), *Fieldwork under Fire: Contemporary Studies of Violence and Survival*. Berkeley: University of California Press.

Stoll, D. 1999. *Rigoberta Menchú: And the Story of all Poor Guatemalans;* Boulder: Westview Press.

Stoller, P. 1992. *The Cinematic Griot: The Ethnography of Jean Rouch*. Chicago: University of Chicago Press.

Turner, T. 1991. 'The Social Dynamics of Video Media in an Indigenous Society: The Cultural Meaning and the Personal Politics of Video-making in Kayapo Communities'. *Visual Anthropology Review*, 7 (2): 68–76.

——— 1992. 'Defiant Images: The Kayapo Appropriation of Video', *Anthropology Today* 8(6): 5–16.

Wilson, R. 1998. 'The Politics of Remembering and Forgetting in Guatemala', in R. Sieder (ed.), *Guatemala after the Peace Accords*. London: Institute of Latin American Studies, University of London.

Worth, S and J. Adair. 1972. *Through Navajo Eyes: An Exploration in Film, Communication and Anthropology*. Bloomington: Indiana University Press.

Zur, J. 1998. *Violent Memories: Mayan War-Widows' Memories of 'La Violencia'*. Boulder: Westview Press.

PART V

COMMUNITY FILM-MAKING
AND EMPOWERMENT

Chapter 11

THE RHYTHM OF OUR DREAMS
A Proposal for an Applied Visual Anthropology*

Ana Martínez Pérez

As we dream we love,
As we love we live,
As we live we die.
I won't say yes or no
But what I will say is that there is no heat without fire.
(Carlos Cano, singer songwriter).

I would like the people who don't believe
in us to see this documentary.
(Manoli, protagonist of *The Rhythm of Our Dreams*).

The Rhythm of Our Dreams as Applied Visual Anthropology

The documentary video *The Rhythm of Our Dreams* (*Al Compás de Los Sueños*) was developed in Córdoba, Spain, in 2002. Above I quote Manoli, one of the film's protagonists. Her words encapsulate how approaches from visual anthropology and social work in marginalized areas were combined in this project: we applied visual anthropology methods to represent the experienced realities of excluded people and their social workers. The project was requested by the local government Department of Youth, Women and Employment and the Association of Social Workers Encuentro en la Calle (Street Encounter), which has worked in the poorest areas in Córdoba for over a decade. It was produced in collaboration with A Buen Común, a multidisciplinary group of social researchers (anthropologists, psychologists and teachers) and film-makers. The project aimed to produce a documentary film that would generate awareness of social exclusion and its causes and show how it is being tackled by Encuentro en la Calle. However this was not simply a film production project. Rather it constituted a joint and collaborative experience of intervention in socially excluded areas and research using audiovisual media, developed by an interdisciplinary group of professionals from the social sciences (anthropology, psychology, education, social work) and audiovisual media.

* Translated by Emma Davey and Sarah Pink.

In this chapter, writing as a social and visual anthropologist and a member of A Buen Común, I explain how we constructed a model for multidisciplinary intervention, which both responded to our differing aims as a group of diverse professionals and remained focused on the main task of making an ethnological documentary. We responded to Encuentro en la Calle's request that we should make the film by developing a methodological device halfway between applied anthropology and visual ethnography. We believe the work plan developed for *The Rhythm of Our Dreams* could be transferred and adequately implemented in other projects with similar objectives. Like all integrated models, by default the interconnectedness of the perspectives that constitute it optimize the tool's versatility.

Approaching Social Intervention

Like many projects in applied anthropology our work involved both interdisciplinary collaboration and working closely with the 'client' (see Pink 2006). In such contexts collaboration also means gaining a clear understanding of the definitions and motivations of the other parties, and this was fundamental to our approach. At the beginning of the project we (the social researchers) met with the social workers and educators from Encuentro en la Calle to discuss common themes in our approaches to social intervention.

Our first point of contact focused on the nature of our fieldwork encounters. We were able to synthesize our approaches into a method which both allowed the social workers to verbalize their work ethic of 'being without intruding' and was reminiscent of the old ethnographic philosophy (which is still viable today) of 'being there as witnesses of the other's gaze'. 'Being without intruding' corresponds with the ethnographic practice of turning fieldwork interactions into a way of life. By establishing a shared approach focused on the commonalities in our existing fieldwork practices we were able to fulfil the objectives that inform social science research and the social workers' proposed intervention.

Second, we shared the social workers' understanding of social exclusion; as referring to people's inability to access economic resources and participate in different areas of city life: employment, housing, education, health, etc. We began with a definition of social exclusion as, on the one hand an element of an incomplete self-identity, and on the other hand a practical inability to access the normal resources the establishment makes available to the general public. We refused to blame the victims of exclusion for their own situation – as those who cannot empathize with the reality of the excluded 'other' often do. With these definitions in mind the documentary opens with images of the symbolic centre of Córdoba, the Patio de los Naranjos of the historic *Mesquita* (Mosque)[1] and the words of the president of the Andaluz Human Rights Association: 'The water reaches all the orange trees equally. If we translate water into social justice it becomes housing, employment, education. When the water is spread out equally no orange tree rots; no person would break down causing social conflict. When the water does not reach the tree the problem is not with the tree itself, which smells, but with the water that never got there'. Audiovisual media, particularly video, were perfect for representing this vision of equality/inequality. Video allowed us to produce and reproduce a series of images that created a polyphonic representation of people who live in areas of exclusion, and of their dreams. This provided us with a basis for developing awareness and reflection among the general public and, because we made it our objective to reveal the reality of social exclusion, for other social workers and researchers the documentary demonstrates a novel form of intervention. While our use of ethnographic methods and audiovisual media were fundamental to the success of the project, the mutual vision, approaches and goals we shared with the social workers, educators and media professionals were equally important in producing a shared context for our interactions. The setting where the events would unfold was also familiar: A Buen Común[2] had already filmed one of our ethnographic documentaries (*Mujeres Invisibles* 2000) in Córdoba and had made two other films in Andalucia (*A Buen Común* 1999; *The Skin of the Mountain*, 2002). Some members of the team are Andalucians and for the rest of us Andalucia is an important point of reference.

The concept of the 'street' used by the social workers represents their daily activities in a way that makes their social intervention very ethnographic. For people in situations of risk or social exclusion the street is where they learn diverse lessons: both good and bad. There is a place for everything on the street. One of the social workers told us: 'When I get home at night, after a day's work, I look at my shoes, if they are dirty and full of mud I know I've done a good job, my job is not sitting behind a desk in an office and filling out forms, my job is on the street' (Q: an educator from Encuentro en la Calle). They are involved with excluded people on an everyday level in a way that has parallels with the way we do ethnography. The metaphor Q used to describe her/his work was so powerful both denotatively and cognitively that it has fed back into my teaching practice – I have successfully used it to inspire students starting their own ethnographic fieldwork.

From a macro-sociological point of view, the social workers' objective is to sensitize a society that constantly turns its back on social exclusion. To understand their brief, both practically and ideologically, it is useful to consider how they understand how their work fits into a wider context. They typify situations of social exclusion with which we live by examining the comparative relationship between notions of First and Third World or developing countries, and those of First and Fourth World[3]. Encuentro en la Calle believes the poverty that is closest to us remains invisible to the general public while in contrast we sometimes represent marginalized people in other latitudes as worthy of receiving help. The following comparative table

Table 11.1 Representation of an ethno-centred vision of the developed world

First World	Third World	Fourth World
Visible	Becoming visible	Invisible
Individualistic	Group (race, country)	Group (family, area)
Responsible for achievements	Not responsible and victim of the economic system	Responsible for their economic and social situation
With opportunities	Worthy to receive help	Given no help or opportunities
Listened to/ and have a say, humans	Listened to/ but have no say, humanized	Not listened to/ have no say, dehumanised

(Table 11.1) illustrates how our ethnocentric vision of the developed world defines the attributes of the people belonging to each of these spheres.

According to the ideology of Encuentro en la Calle, we might rectify the injustices suffered by Fourth World groups through local action that acknowledges this global situation. Like anthropological research, such local action does not intrude on, but respects, the vision of the individuals with whom one is working. The social workers who appear in this documentary believe that integration is a dialectic relationship between two culturally and socioeconomically different communities. The bond between the two groups – the excluded and the street educators – should be established according to principles of equality and not ethnocentricity. Their starting point for any type of social intervention could well head up an applied anthropological manual, it reads as follows: 'We wish to bring together the emotional and the educational, the professionals and the volunteers, we want to be on the street without intruding and intrude in the institutions who, more often than not, want to bring in guidelines which are far from the reality of the problems and the daily life of those areas in exclusion. We are interested in a model of intervention where people are important. A world which in the majority of cases is completely shattered but which, on the other hand, is always worthy of being put back together'.

As such our work with Encuentro en la Calle was based on a series of commonalities that we were able to establish between social science and social work: a nonintrusive 'ethnographic' approach to working with others that respects their ways of being and attempts to live their everyday lives with them; a shared understanding of social inequalities, exclusion and its causes; and a shared vision of using audiovisual media as a means of bringing these issues to a wider public. Establishing and working with shared understandings was also continuous throughout the whole film-making process. This was embedded in the way we made *The Rhythm of Our Dreams* by combining three strands of work. First, the work of the educators from Encuentro en la Calle provided us with the context for the story. Both the educators and the people at risk of, or in a situation of, exclusion were to be the main characters in the documentary. Second, the documentary makers and the audiovisual experts were responsible for developing a film narrative that would appeal to the greatest possible public. Third, the scriptwriters concentrated on creating the hinges that connect the different interests involved in the project. Their role was vital in facilitating the processes through which the different parties came to understand one another's perspectives and negotiated meanings between themselves to produce a film that was not distorted by the interests of any one party. In fact the aims and objectives of *The Rhythm of Our Dreams* were linked more to the intersection of perspectives which occurs during the film-making process, than to the film as product (see van. Dienderen, this volume for a similar approach).

Aims and Objectives

In this section I discuss the proposal Encuentro en la Calle and the Department of Youth, Women and Employment made to us in autumn 2001 and the way this informed the development of our shared project. The objectives of these organizations were two-fold. First they wanted to demonstrate an alternative form of social work practice through participation in marginalized urban areas. Second they wanted to use the documentary to raise awareness and produce empathy amongst the wider population which has no contact with this social reality. Faced with this dual objective we needed a complex device, which responded to both approaches. To develop this we drew from both applied and visual anthropology in way that mirrored the social worker's objectives:

- As applied anthropologists we aimed to promote a form of social intervention which brings resources to people living in marginalized contexts, rather than these groups having to leave their surroundings and search for resources within the depths of the public administration;
- As visual anthropologists we aimed to both divulge a reality totally unknown to the majority of the population and present a form of social intervention to professionals who specialize in areas of exclusion.

Alongside the ethnographic documentary we also proposed to carry out personal development workshops for those who featured in the film. Our proposal was accepted and the project was carried out in 2002. As it was an interdisciplinary project, below I discuss the different perspectives that informed it.

In the context of Spanish municipal politics in a city of more than 300,000 inhabitants, it is significant that issues related to social exclusion are, generally, *excluded* from the agenda. The people that live in the poorer areas of our cities do not usually participate in city life. They are not even involved in the electoral process. They live on the periphery of urban life and are not included in statistics. The organizations that work in areas of social exclusion are sustained by municipal funds and / or by subsidies given by other public bodies, which subcontract different social interventions. In this context two types of social work tend to be practiced. The first is bureaucratic and administrative. Here associations periodically apply for help to cover certain needs, only in part and for a limited amount of time. The second entails complete and intensive intervention in collaboration with the 'beneficiaries'. This is much more costly but very effective in producing profound social transformation. The associations or groups that practice these latter types of intervention are in the minority because it is much more complicated to apply. Not least because they need to transfer their infrastructure to the areas of exclusion; they must leave their offices to work on the street and integrate with the local people they seek to support. The work practices of Encuentro en la Calle provide a good example of this method.

The objectives of *The Rhythm of Our Dreams* were based on the idea that to confront marginalization (or any situation of social conflict) the two parties involved need to arrive at a level of mutual understanding. To make this possible we needed to offer alternative means of communication that would draw together these two understandings of the world. One aim was to make the general public aware of the situation of those who live in exclusion. We were addressing a large public and, above all, a sector of that public who, while ascribing to a politically correct discourse, fails to recognize that the excluded are victims of the contemporary socioeconomic, political and cultural climate. They thus effectively blame the excluded for their own condition. To confront this the documentary presents a series of people from marginalized areas of Córdoba, who have struggled to escape from marginalization. These people work for agencies that support re-integration into society through employment. Their very work centres on the inclusion of those who live, as they once did, at risk of or in a situation of, exclusion. Our second aim was to illustrate how a specific form of social work was undertaken with these people. To achieve this the Encuentro en la Calle educators are also characters in this documentary: who better to tell one's own story but oneself – the excluded – and who better to narrate the process of insertion and integration into normalised society than a direct witness – the social workers.

As applied anthropologists we shared these aims. First, that people and groups living in areas of exclusion in Córdoba should gain easier access to the resources which society has to offer, as such to decrease their needs. Second, that the wealthier middle classes should understand and accept the difference between these two worlds, however slight it may be. The public we wished to reach still ascribes to the idea that we all enter the world with equal potential for development, and this is frequently used to explain or justify social exclusion. We wanted to demonstrate that this is not correct. We also wanted people who have experienced the reality of exclusion to be the main characters in the film because, too often, social interventions neglect the vision of their 'beneficiaries'. At best resources are distributed without accounting for the viewpoint of the community to which they are being directed.

Developing *The Rhythm of Our Dreams* in this way meant rejecting certain existing media narratives. For example the clichés used by television reports (see also Christina Lammer, this volume) would reinforce a negative image of the marginalized people we worked with. Following the media tendency to tell a morbid tale of reality could so easily have become sensationalist. Moreover the reductionism that is essential to journalistic representations would have been offensive to the participants in our film. To avoid this we worked side by side with the protagonists and made only limited use of voice-over.

Simultaneously this project was not simply an evaluation of the work of Encuentro en la Calle. It was not meant to be an analytical device framed by the terminology of institutional analysis. Rather we saw the documentary as a powerful analytical process in itself. *The Rhythm of Our Dreams* set in motion its own dynamic of self-reflection. We set about harnessing this to support the development of the project rather than allowing it to become (consciously or unconsciously) simply a mock evaluation of the educators and social workers' activities. The protagonists of this story were not born working with people in exclusion; each had their own personal path of development and dedicated themselves to the project with very clear ideologies and sense of commitment. There is an important difference between living *from* the exclusion of others and living *for* the struggle of inclusion and we wanted to show how the protagonists of this documentary achieved the latter. We agreed that it would be inappropriate to represent the educators in terms simply of their professional identities, but to show them as individuals. We intended the audience to identify with and recognize themselves in these protagonists, to feel moved and be encouraged to change their perspectives and preconstructed stereotypes. We aimed to highlight the work processes of a group of people who were concerned about bettering the living conditions of the most needy.

Methodological Aspects

Our methodological tool was constructed to respond to the proposal developed by Encuentro en la Calle. It involves a succession of processes of intervention, which create a set of products represented in different media.

Table 11.2 The relationship between tasks (process) and materials (products)

Tasks (Process)	Materials (Products)
Analysis of the demand (interviews and workshops)	Project
Fieldwork (locations and contacts)	Filming plan
Filming	Brute materials
Viewing and drafting	Editing script
Editing	Documentary

The first stage of our work consisted in carrying out a 'needs analysis'. We needed to know what the client wanted to tell, the experiences that they have had through the years with people at risk or in a situation of exclusion. This was not exactly a commission as they contacted us to develop an integral interdisciplinary project of intervention after becoming aware of our previous audiovisual work (*A Buen Común* 1999, *Mujeres Invisibles* 2000, and see also Camas et al 2004, Pink 2004) and a task-training workshop for social intervention, which we carried out in Córdoba. To undertake a proper analysis of their needs and develop transparent work methods with them, we decided to meet those responsible for the idea and organize two coordination workshops from which we would develop the common objectives and strategies discussed at the beginning of this chapter.

The second stage in the organization of the task consisted of 'defining objectives' and locating the most appropriate tools for them. We agreed from the outset that that most appropriate medium to illustrate the way of life of people who live in the marginalized areas of Córdoba was the documentary. We worked together to incorporate audiovisual media into applied anthropology methods: participant observation, in-depth interviews, filmed diaries, and written words. For social work geared towards inclusion, the association's method of intervention involves their alternative scheme of action: of 'being without intruding'. Working on the street, rather than being office-based, they know that 'reality can change on a day-to-day basis, from the most minute detail, from intrahistory. When each individual counts, the street and the area are seen through different eyes' (Encuentro en la Calle 1998). In addition to the objectives noted above, the social workers also wanted the film, by representing their work practices, to present a model for intervention that could be transferred to work in other contexts of social exclusion.

The coordination workshops allowed us to merge our perspectives and develop a collective task. To create a polyphonic (rather than dialogic or monologic) project, the scriptwriters and social workers met over two weekends. Our work plan combined group dynamics and individual contributions, following the principle that while analysis is developed collectively, to attain synthesis, individuality is necessary. The timetable below (Table 11.3) represents our programme of activities for the first coordination workshop in early 2002:

Table 11.3 Programme of activities for the first coordination workshop in early 2002

Friday, 4–5 p.m.	Presentation 'What is *The Rhythm of Our Dreams*?'
Friday, 5–6.30 p.m.	Focus group 'Who are we and what do we feel about the project?'
Friday 6.30–8 p.m.	Individual work 'What and how would you make the documentary?'
Saturday, 10–11 a.m.	Introduction and exhibition of individual work
Saturday, 11–12 a.m.	Presentation of individual work
Saturday, 12–1.30 p.m.	Work in small groups 'As citizens, people in areas of exclusion and educators of Encentro en la Calle how and what do we want the project to be?'
Saturday, 1.30–2 p.m.	Debate about possible operative device

One process led to another and thus we arrived at the fourth stage of 'the development of the script'. The materials generated in these encounters form part of the script. Some of the texts written in the workshops were used as voice-overs, lyrics for certain songs used in the sound track or proposals put to the interviewees who appeared in the film. The coordination of the project, the workshops and the script were carried out with the help of Victoriano Camas. I played the role of participant observer in these workshops, adding a reflexive strand to our practice, I analysed the materials from the coordination workshops and presented this to the group as a 'field diary'. The discussion generated through the reading of these diaries also contributed to the development of the script.

From a formal point of view, the group of social workers from Encuentro en la Calle had accepted the script when we began writing it. Our method of developing a documentary script includes both space for reflecting on the objectives and permits us to generate documents that help organize the successive stages of the project (Camas, Martínez, Muñoz and Ortiz 2004: 131–146). In contrast to fiction film, a socio-anthropological documentary, like a nature film, is unpredictable. Therefore for us the script refers more to the epistemological framework of the project than to a succession of takes and sequences. The script for *The Rhythm of Our Dreams* outlined an production schedule. From this we produced the 'raw materials' that formed the basis for our editing script.

The documentary script represents our analytical and interventional objectives. It is made up of a series of blocks:

1. The introduction outlines the causes of exclusion – why it exists, macro/micro, institutional and personal reasons. Here the educators and other characters appear suggesting a wide range of possible causes.

2. The second part addresses the audience directly through individual characters from marginalized areas: from those who have work and are 'normalized', those who are in the process, to those who have extreme difficulties.

3. The third part proposes possible alternatives to exclusion.

The order of the content represented in these three parts emerged from our objectives to (1) explain the reality of people in a situation of social exclusion, (2) sensitize the population who is unaware of this reality and (3) propose solutions to the spectator. For both an expert audience and those with no experience of the film's themes there would be nothing more negative than ending without providing any solutions to the problems represented in the film. As an alternative the documentary proposes creating efficient work methods rather than a probably nonexistent panacea.

When we arrived at the 'scene' we discovered existing strands of work through which we could integrate different groups into the film project. The children and the young adults from the marginalized areas where we were going to work already participated in a project called 'The Rhythm Workshop'. This group met twice a week to sing, dance and create through flamenco, a deep-rooted art form in these neighbourhoods with a high gypsy population. As part of *The Rhythm of Our Dreams* we decided to incorporate this area of the educators' work with young people by creating a workshop titled 'Let's Put Music to Our Dreams'. We sought to engage with the theme of young people's dreams by using their accounts to compose melodies for the film's soundtrack. One of the members of A Buen Común, Rafael Muñoz, a music teacher in primary education, developed this. The entire workshop was recorded as a visual diary (using a mini DVD digital camera) and a diary written by the participant observer who in this case was also the production assistant, Manuel Ortiz.

The methodology designed for 'Let's Put Music to Our Dreams' worked in parallel with the weekly rhythm workshop. Through this a musical research project was developed to examine dreams through a music therapy approach, normally used for group sessions, to locate a meeting point where educators and children could learn and create together. Having the whole process recorded digitally in both sound and vision by the participating observer, along with the written field diary, provided us with an audiovisual record of the teaching-learning process. When the project was finished the children who dreamt of becoming artists had a taste of what that might feel like. Their concert was recorded onto CD and three of the girls from the project managed to launch themselves commercially, when they formed a group called *Las Chuches* and sold their CD nationwide.

Thus although producing the documentary was our main objective, the existing infrastructure and effort of the participants enabled us to broaden our work to include other media and forms of expression. We also compiled a book based on the written material generated throughout the process, not for general circulation, but as a working document for internal use within Encuentro en la Calle. The documentary's soundtrack was produced from the sessions carried out with young adults in the rhythm workshop. By combining these three products in the same digital medium we finally created a CD-ROM whereby people could read the book, see the documentary and/or listen to the music. In the first stage of preproduction the CD of flamenco music was recorded, in the production stage we made the film and in postproduction we edited both film and the CD-ROM, using all the materials that had been generated. The timetable, which was made in the first of the coordination workshops, was as follows (Table 11.4):

Table 11.4 The timetable for *The Rhythm of Our Dreams*

Task	Jan	Feb	Mar	Apr	May	Jun	Jul	Sep	Oct	Nov
Music CD	Let's Put Music to Our Dreams				Concert					
Coordination workshops	Project	Diary		Script	Diary					
Documentary				Filming plan	Filming	Draft		Editing script	Editing	
CD-ROM						Compilation of written texts				Design

Contributions to *The Rhythm of Our Dreams*

The Rhythm of Our Dreams was a shared experience of applied visual anthropology carried out with and from the specific demand of the social actors who were the film's protagonists and those of us who represented their story. This approach, that combines social intervention, applied media and social research was supported by our production of a methodological tool. Our collaboration was based on a model of integration. On the one hand this entailed the coordination and flamenco workshops, which generated the materials from which the project was produced. On the other hand the audiovisual materials allowed us to represent these work practices to other social workers and raise consciousness amongst the general public.

Our starting metaphor and origin – the 'dream world' – emerged from the coordination workshops. But, why dreams? Why use what is dreamt to reflect what is lived? Dreaming is an essential element of the human condition both in the sense of night dreaming (see Edgar 2004) and as a form of projecting our fantasies and desires, which is our concern here. It is part of the imaginative and creative practice of being an individual and forms part of our agency to instigate processes of change. Once we have defined our desire we dream of the future in the form of a path we intend to follow. However inequalities lie in that some find the obstacles encountered in their chosen path easier to surmount than others. The idea of dreams offers a simple and graphic way of illustrating the distance that both separates and unites us. The contents of dreams reveal the distances between us because while some of us dare to imagine a better future and struggle to achieve it, others dare not even mention desires that are, for them, unattainable: living under a roof with their loved ones, having a dignified job, escaping from a neighbourhood that stigmatizes them and, the most sublime of all, freeing themselves. Viewing inequalities in terms of dreams illuminates two key points. First we gain a sense of how individual creativity becomes a route through which inequalities might be confronted. However, second, by looking at individual's dreams as comparative data we ourselves are confronted with the contrast between the dreams of those who have access to basic resources and those who do not.

The general (dis)position of the social workers towards the project was known and shared by all. What remained was for us (the social researchers) to gain our own sense of ownership of our task. We began by defining our own dreams in the coordination workshops. This allowed us to get closer to what we really wanted from the project. We took time to ask ourselves, individually as people, and not as professionals, to imagine the documentary we each dreamt of. Each of us, as individuals, described our own vision of the film, bringing out the nuances that would inform its making. The texts we contributed to the first coordination workshop reflected the group's general feelings about the project and are closely related to the script and the film. One of these texts was chosen as the only-voice over in *The Rhythm of Our Dreams*:

> To me the rhythm of dreams is about growing and fulfilling dreams. There is a marvellous freedom in dreams which has nothing to do with social classes, prestige, race or First and Fourth Worlds … The rhythm sounds to me like flamenco, like the girls and boys of the rhythm workshops singing and dancing their emotions. Women's dreams, a faint song which escapes unwittingly from a conversation one afternoon in a bar somewhere … I don't know how many types of dreams there are. I have 'dreams dreams': images that appear whilst I am sleeping, I see them in colour, even though some say that we dream in black and white. Others are 'living dreams': longings, desires that surprise me when my mind wanders, fantasies … I have nightmares, dreams about a deep sadness, which appear when I am having a bad time, in difficult situations or when I am tense, whether I am asleep or awake. It is best not to take notice of these dreams at the time. … They come with tiredness or when I can't deal with myself or with anyone else. Bad dreams: personal insecurity, fear of failure, letting down the people I love, allowing people to look over their shoulders at me. I live life feeling excessively guilty and responsible. I feel frightened about the permanently provisional nature of my job … I know that the provisional nature of my job is important in being coherent with our objectives, but I can't avoid having complexes due to the path I have chosen to take in such a class-conscious profession. The temptation to seek protection and fall into line crosses my

mind, but neither the fears nor the temptations are so powerful ... A black fear comes over me when I think that in putting myself in the other person's shoes I won't want to be in them. I dream of a world without contempt, where the person in front of you is what is important. I dream of a world where is no prejudice, where relationships aren't built up around economic, power or sexual favours ... A world for and belonging to everyone ... I dream with the hope that allows us to dream but not to sleep, a world where no one has to grovel, be thankful or ask permission. I dream of a world where Encuentro en la Calle is not an association but a right, where the starting point is the same for everyone. I dream of people who don't look the other way and whose faces don't contort when they laugh ... Having, accumulating, obtaining, working to be and have more. ... Rise, step on others, climb, what for? ... This is a dream with a misleading melody: to be in tune with it would empty us of what is truly important: being me... This is my dream: To be me and live a dignified life ... for me and for everyone else ...

I dream of not losing my dreams ...

To ensure that our work was truly choral and polyphonic the majority of the proposals presented to the group had to be reflected somehow in the final product. Our primordial task as documentary makers was to imagine, or to 'think in images'; to transfer the ideas that we wanted to convey into audiovisual sequences. To talk about exclusion we needed to know how to communicate it visually. This included identifying the images that are commonly associated with exclusion, including those that we would not want to use. What is exclusion and why does it exist? We had the opportunity to think about images without limiting ourselves. Imagination has no limits but the technicians or the budget would soon clip our wings. Which were my images of exclusion? A beggar with a stump at the door of a shopping centre, a shack, prison bars ... Life becomes a lottery where destiny and necessity determine who is excluded, who are plain and simple citizens, and who will become educators. These three perspectives were represented in the group of scriptwriters and integrated in to the film. The images and causes of exclusion are related to a cityworld of concentric circles of the type presented by the Chicago School in the early twentieth century (e.g. Park and Burgess 1925), but adapted to the Spanish city.[4] Here the centre is the power of the banks, political parties, commerce, multinationals – the major players. Moving outwards the middle classes inhabit an intermediate space in an environment characterized by green zones. The territory of exclusion begins where this border ends, it is a territory where the poor struggle, in an environment where police cars patrol streets that often lead to either prison or the cemetery. The privileged centre has the right to live, those in the second circle must work hard to have a decent life, for those in exclusion all that is left is death!

The vision of the educators-social workers presents the dialectic between 'making a living from exclusion' and the more desirable 'working for inclusion'. Plenty of images could represent the former: a woman sitting behind an office desk attends another who is standing; it is raining and the social worker has only one umbrella with which she covers herself. The social worker and client never look each other in the eye; access to the social workers is through doors, obstacles, paperwork and conditions, institutionalized blackmail. However, some social workers do not accept the option of death for the excluded, they seek solutions. This was the approach to social work that we wanted our film to convey by representing a shared sensory world. When the social worker and client sit at a dinner table and share the warmth of a heater and a coffee their relationship shifts: 'We rally together: For social problems we demand social answers!, No to exclusion!, because we live in the same space. We go to the police station and the law courts, the hospital and the schools, to look for employment and to play football, we go to the talks in prison and share moments of discussion next to the fire, we do all these things together'.

The excluded themselves comment on the different faces of exclusion in ways that, like dreams, evoke the visual, aural, tactile and olfactory experience: a truck full of scrap, black hands, wrinkled eyes; the police seizing crates of fruit, the helplessness they feel as the merchandise is confiscated; a car passing by full of 'moon oranges' (stolen in the light of the moon); the letters to the courts; coming off drugs and the experience of this transformation; the mother chasing up her son, the lawyer, the courts; those who live out of a rucksack, searching for temporary work wherever they can ... They speak of fresh running water, the channels that distribute it to the city. As it travels to the excluded neighbourhoods it becomes dirtier and cloudier, it remains there, dirty and stagnant. Now there are no ornamental fountains, no park, now there is nothing. People get up in the morning, unmotivated, they open their windows, look at their reality and retract back into themselves. If they do decide to go into the world they don't understand the bureaucratic language, they don't feel prepared to face the contempt. Women selling rosemary near the mosque. The wastelands of poorer areas, the constant worsening of conditions day after day, always the same. The woman who faints as she leaves the social services where they have taken her children away from her. The way a drug addict walks in fits and starts when looking for his next shot. The child who is expelled from school for bad behaviour and jumps over the fence in the afternoon to play in the grounds of 'his school'. The idea of the right to a dignified life, a job, housing, does not exist, it all comes down to depending on individuals, and not the establishment, to cover their needs. Understandably they don't feel part of the society that marginalized them. When justifying exclusion the excluded begin and end with themselves, not the social system, not anyone else: This is how they see me! Because I am a gypsy and I live in this area ... As they represent it, being 'excluded' is not simply a category one fits in to but a sensory embodied experience with its own rhythm.

Our film aims to reach the general public. When we talk about the causes of exclusion we emphasise that the excluded are not in that position because they want to be, nobody would. We aim to help to break this stereotype. By presenting images of excluded neighbourhoods that were not too shocking we hoped that rather than making our audience feel guilty, we could show them how vulnerable we all are, by urging them to empathize with the film's protagonists we suggest to them how it might feel to live that reality and how easy it would be to slip into that outer circle of exclusion. We hope that through this we can begin to believe more in the people who dream with another rhythm.

Appendix

Table 11.5 *The Rhythm of Our Dreams* filming plan (in Spanish)

DIA	HORA	EQUIPO/LUGAR	TEMA	ENTREVISTA	OBSERVACIONES
1-Mañana	10–14	A: CÓRDOBA	A: RECURSOS. Zona turística.		P. /Q.
		B: CÓRDOBA	B: RECURSOS. Centro ciudad.		M. / Y.
DÍA	**HORA**	**EQUIPO/LUGAR**	**TEMA**	**ENTREVISTA**	**OBSERVACIONES**
1-Tarde	16–20	A: CASA R. Y M.	A: ENTREVISTAS (de 16 a 19 h) Educadores y recursos de M. y R. C. en su casa y por el barrio (de 19 a 20h)	A: Q., P., J..	R. /M
		B: Casa R.-M. CÓRDOBA, BARRIOS	B: Entrevistas (de 16 a 18h) y RECURSOS. Barrios obreros y alrededores (de 18 a 20h).	B: L., T.	J, M, / F,
DÍA	**HORA**	**EQUIPO/LUGAR**	**TEMA**	**ENTREVISTA**	**OBSERVACIONES**
2-Mañana	8–14	A: PALMERAS	A: Seguimiento F., L. y J. Colegio, Guardería (de 8 a 12h). Seguimiento A. (de Palmeras al centro de la ciudad)(de 12 a 14h)		L, / J, / F, / M.M.
		B: TORREMOLINOS	B: Seguimiento Q. y P., Y., J. M. y T. en Surge. RECURSOS de Torremolinos.		Q./ P. / M.J.

DÍA	HORA	EQUIPO/LUGAR	TEMA	ENTREVISTA	OBSERVACIONES
2-T a r d e	16–20	A: LOCAL MORERAS	A: GENTE DE LOS BARRIOS (de 16 a 20h)	A: M., J., F., P. (F. y M. de acompañantes)	Mª LUZ / R. M.
		B: PALMERAS	B: ACTIVIDADES: FÚTBOL, MUJERES. Recursos Palmeras. Escenas de pelota y casa. (de 16 a 20h)		L. / M. J.

DÍA	HORA	EQUIPO/LUGAR	TEMA	ENTREVISTA	OBSERVACIONES
3-M a ñ a n a	8–14	A: CÓRDOBA, FIGUEROA Y CASA JUVENTUD.	A: Seguimiento M. y F. (de 8 a 10h), J. y P. (de 12 a 14h). RECURSOS CÓRDOBA (de 10 a 12h.)		JOSE MANUEL /TOÑI
		B: PATIO CERRO	B: ENTREVISTAS (de 8 a 14h)	B: A., E., M., J. (M. L. y N. acompañan)	MªJESUS / PICHUQUI

Table 11.6 *The Rhythm of Our Dreams* filming plan (in Spanish)

DÍA	EQUIPO	RECURSOS
1-M	A	Córdoba, Judería, Mezquita, Corredera, Potro, Puente Romano, Hoteles, Alcázares, Palacio Congresos, Agua-fuentes, gente pidiendo limosna, vendiendo flores, romero, semáforos… La idea es grabar imágenes de la zona turística, de la limpieza, de las fuentes bellas, del patio de los Naranjos y sus acequias que distribuyen el agua para TODOS los árboles. Hay que sacar imágenes de turistas de espaldas.
1-M	B	Córdoba, Bulevar, Corte Inglés, Paseo Renfe, Cruz Conde, Tendillas, Concepción, Cajasur, rótulos, carteles, agua-fuentes, Colón, Patos, P. Victoria, República Argentina. La idea es grabar el centro económico, comercial y financiero, sus fuentes bellas y ornamentales. Todo está limpio y hay luz en el centro. Grabar las grandes avenidas que salen desde el centro hacia los barrios de clase media y obreros (es un viaje del centro a la periferia)
1-T	A	Después de las entrevistas, la idea es salir al barrio de Palmeras para grabar recursos de R. C. y Miguel, pero además, grabar recursos del barrio a la anochecida, para terminar el viaje centro-periferia (Centro por la mañana; barrios obreros por la tarde, barrios marginales al oscurecer)
1-T	B	Antes de salir, se puede grabar a R. en la escena de la pelota. Después, salir a Córdoba: Fuensanta, Ciudad Jardín, Parque Cruz Conde, Sector Sur (abajo), Avda. Barcelona, P. Alpargate, Alrededores de Palmeras, Torremolinos y Moreras. La idea es seguir con el viaje del centro a la periferia. Estos barrios son el segundo cinturón después del centro. La luz es menos brillante, es de atardecida, los barrios están bien equipados, sus fuentes son funcionales, para beber, y no tanto ornamentales.
2-M	A	Seguimiento F. y L., J. Encuentros con gente, Local. Palmeras: puertas, casas, rejas, descampados, carreteras, calles, patios, colegio, guardería, casa hermano M., vistas, candelas, campo fútbol, fuentes secas, agua estancada, alcantarillas, personajes con niños. El seguimiento a A. desde Palmeras hasta el centro, se sube al bus 8, se baja en el centro y llega a las oficinas del INEM, del Ayto, en un peregrinaje para pedir trabajo.
2-M	B	Seguimiento Q., Paseando, encontrando gente. En la oficina se graba sobre todo a T. y a J. M. trabajando en el ordenador, recibiendo a gente y ayudando, informando, etc. Después salimos a la C/ Torremolinos: gente, pared picadero, local, vistas desde terrazas, candelas, fuentes secas, agua estancada. Campillo de fútbol. Muros, paredes, descampados, puertas, ventanas…
3-M	A	Seguimiento M. y F., J. y P.. Residencia Figueroa, Casa Juventud, Recursos de Córdoba, calles de los barrios en el camino de uno a otro sitio, gente trabajando, yendo y viniendo.
3-T	A	Seguimiento José M. Cárcel antigua y macrocárcel. Hay que grabar recursos con J. M. y otros recursos de la cárcel sin personajes. Grabar puertas, celdas, candados, barrotes…

DÍA	EQUIPO	RECURSOS
3-T	B	Moreras: patios, descampados, límite Pryca, local, local Mariana, pirámides, alrededores local de Encuentro y DD.HH., fuentes secas, agua estancada, grabar personajes por el barrio: E., M., F. Seguimiento a M., paseando por los patios de Moreras, encontrándose con mujeres y niños. Grabar recursos de M, llegando a DDHH, por los alrededores.
4-T	A	Agua: EMACSA, centro ciudad, atardecer, candelas, gente barrios. Habría que grabar recursos de Juanono, Rafa C., Miguel por las candelas y a la atardecida
4-T	B	Polígono y cerro, atardecer, candelas, gente barrios. Grabar a Q., P., por las candelas
5-M	B	Recursos pendientes. Grabar en el mercadillo del Arenal los puestos de algunas familias de los barrios
6-M		Recursos pendientes
7-M		Recursos pendientes

Notes

1. The Mesquita is one of the most important historical and tourist heritage sites in Spain. The Patio de los Naranjos is literally a patio courtyard outside the Mesquita with orange trees.
2. This is an ideology which came about in Bujalance, Córdoba whereby the olive pickers worked as a group; women, men old and young, each person did their part of the job within the bounds of the group and when the work was finished the money was divided equally between the workers without regard for sex or age. We have taken this ideology and used it as our own in our documentary work.
3. Here Fourth World refers to marginalized people within the First World.
4. The layout of Spanish cities tends to differ from the models produced by urban sociologists for British and North American cities. Whereas in Park and Burgess' (1925) model the inner zone represents the poorer area inhabited by immigrants and the urban poor, while the upper and middle classes progressively move out to the suburban periphery, in Spanish cities the city centre tends to be inhabited by the wealthy while the outer suburbs represent the poorest areas of social exclusion.

Bibliography

Camas, V., A. Martínez Pérez, R. Muñoz, and M. Ortiz. 2004. 'Revealing the Hidden' in S. Pink, L. Kurti, and A.I. Afonso (eds), *Working Images: Visual Research and Representation in Ethnography*. London: Routledge.

Edgar, I. 2004. *Guide to Imagework*. London: Routledge.

Encuentro en la Calle. 1988. *Modelo de Intervención en Entornos Socio-familiares de Exclusión*. Seville: Government of Andalucia.

Park, Robert E. and Ernest W. Burgess. 1925. *The City*. Chicago: University of Chicago Press.

Pink S. 2004. 'Conversing Anthropologically' in S. Pink, L. Kürti, and A.I. Afonso (eds), *Working Images: Visual Research and Representation in Ethnography*. London: Routledge.

—— 2006. *The Future of Visual Anthropology: Engaging the Senses*. London: Routledge.

Filmography

A Buen Común. 1999. A Buen Común.
Mujeres Invisibles. 2000. A Buen Común.
The Skin of the Mountain. 2002. A Buen Común.
The Rhythm Of Our Dreams. 2002. A Buen Común.

Documentary Film Credits for *The Rhythm of Our Dreams*

Script and Coordination: Ana Martínez Pérez and Victoriano Camas Baena
Production: Manuel Cerezo Lasne and Ricardo Rivera Pena
Camera operators: Lorenzo María Hormigos and Jesús M. Tirado
Sound technician: Ángel López Alonso
Sound assistants: Raúl Montoto De la Fuente
Salvador López Ajero
Production assistants: Rafael Muñoz Sotelo, Manuel Ortiz Mateos and Ángela García Miranda
Editing: Manuel Cerezo Lasne
Original Idea: Rafa Corpas Reina and Miguel Santiago Losada

Chapter 12

PERFORMING URBAN COLLECTIVITY

Ethnography of the Production Process of a Community-based Film Project in Brussels

An van. Dienderen

This chapter offers an analysis of the process through which a community-based film project was developed. It is a study of a visual social intervention that emphasizes process as the subject of its analysis. I argue that researching processes rather than the final 'text' is of crucial importance in dealing with the way (cultural) identity and visual representation are intertwined (van. Dienderen 2003; 2004). To achieve this goal, I analyse the mediated interactions between the 'author', the 'viewer' and the 'other' in their plural and variable agencies during the preparatory phases of a community project in Brussels. Through this ethnography of a visual arts project I apply visual anthropology to further understanding the kinds of social interventions applied visual arts community projects can produce.

The community art project was titled *The Return of the Swallows* led by artist Els Dietvorst. This work can be regarded as an 'off the map place of dominant media cartographies' (Ginsburg, Abu-Lughod and Larkin 2002: 8). Dietvorst collaborated with a collective she named the Swallows located in a marginalized area of Brussels.[1] Mostly populated by immigrants of different cultural backgrounds, the area can be characterized as a transit zone. Although she had never worked with a video camera before, Dietvorst felt drawn to this medium because of its social and collective qualities, and proposed to make a film with the people of the area. The ultimate goal was to produce a fiction feature film based on the lives of the inhabitants. Abstract notions such as utopia and collectivity, and more pragmatic concerns, such as encouraging communication in the area by inviting the inhabitants to express themselves in a joint experience, were of primary interest. They created a broad area of presentations over the course of five years such as street performances, 'jukebox stories',[2] films and glossy magazines covering the activities of the Swallows. Their final performance was a concluding exhibition of their archive in Bozar, the high cultural palace of 'Beaux Arts' in Brussels.

As a film-maker and anthropologist, I have been involved in this project for more than five years, sometimes as an observer, sometimes as an assistant or consultant. It allowed me to fully submerge myself in the project, to collaborate but also to inspire confidence in the Swallows. The aim of my participatory collaboration was to produce an ethnography of the project. By considering the subject of this ethnography a performative event, while at the same time applying performative methods, I emphasize the turn Fabian proposes from 'an informative to a performative anthropology' (Fabian 1990: 18), 'the kind where the ethnographer does not call the tune but plays along' (ibid.: 19). Being part of this project and at the same time reflecting on it, forced me to develop complex interpersonal roles, affirming the reflexive correspondence (performative) anthropology invites.

This ethnography offers a way of understanding how community arts projects can create social interventions, demonstrating the complexities of imagining or performing collectivity. The project of the Swallows is different from other community-based projects because of its focus on negotiating different values and codes, rather than on a pre-scripted film product. This approach is difficult to analyse solely from artistic end results. I therefore stress the importance of not simply analysing the end product but of attending ethnographically to the processes, relationships and identities that are integral to its production. In doing so, it is my aim to suggest an investigative tool for the examination of the rich potential of audiovisual media in the construction of the self and the formation of socialities. This tool allows me to assess the ideological and social forces at work in film production in a particular context.

The Process of Production as a Site of Critique

Some years ago I worked for the Flemish Broadcasting Corporation as a documentary film-maker. An independent production company that offers programs to different television channels engaged me. Because of my anthropological background, my employers wanted me to work for a documentary series that was sold to Canvas, the so-called quality channel. The story line I was asked to create needed to deal with a family of Turkish descent who were looking for a house. Before I started my research, my series editor, to my utmost surprise, handed me a detailed script in which not only the specific scenes were described but the quotes of the main 'characters' were already written. In this script, stereotypically, the family lives in a scrappy house with lots of relatives, the women are veiled and they all encounter many racist situations. 'Make it happen', my series editor said, clearly affirming that I needed to model my interaction with this yet unknown family in such a way that I made them fit the script. 'Of course, otherwise we couldn't have sold the format', he answered when I asked him whether he was serious. The story quickly ended: I encountered a very interesting family with whom I made a documentary, without connecting to the script, so obviously this experience resulted in my dismissal.

From the perspective of the 'viewer', it seems that crucial information about the production process is obscured. As images are not critically contextualized the way written texts are – there are no footnotes, or bibliographical references – the audience seem to depend on the status of the channel to evaluate the truthfulness of the images they see. In this case that is precisely what is shocking. Next, from the perspective of the Turkish family, this script seems absurd, as they were unwelcome guests in their own script. Finally, from the point of view of the 'author', this story questions the process of production as a site where authors, producers and editors are tangled up in a web of values, responsibilities and audience ratings.

This experience inspired me to scrutinize the production processes of (documentary) film practices through a critical understanding of the image and its impact in our society. My research follows a key strand in anthropological thought, which questions the transparency of the transmission of information claimed by ethnographic methodology and writing. The anthropologist Clifford Geertz has a powerful voice in this debate. He states in his book *Works and Lives* that the construction of texts ostensibly scientific out of experiences broadly biographical, which is after all what ethnographers do, is thoroughly obscured (Geertz 1988: 10). His main goal is to strip off the pretensions of textual discourses which mystify their construction so as to assess critically their authorship and discourse. Written ethnographies are grounded on pseudo-claims such as text-positivism, ethnographic ventriloquism, dispersed authorship and so on (ibid.: 104–145). These pretensions are even harder to challenge in documentary film production. Indeed, as visual media are able actually to present recognizable and even mimetic traces in the audiovisual counterpart, positivist assumptions appear much harder to combat. The idea persists that images represent without any censorship or manipulation whatsoever. This can be explained by their indexical qualities, which Bill Nichols defines as 'signs that bear a physical trace of what they refer to, such as a fingerprint, an X-ray, or a photograph' (Nichols 1994: ix).

In contrast to Geertz's approach, in my exploration of documentary film production it is thus not sufficient to analyse the end result (a film, a documentary), as is classic in cultural and film studies. A final film product would not inform me for instance about the scripting of the producer that I experienced when working for Flemish television. The indexicality of the image and the resulting positivistic assumptions hamper a critical analysis. Rather, I investigate how the audiovisual system is employed by the principal agents who are implicated. I therefore propose to understand the process of production as the mediated and variable relationship between 'author' and 'other' in which the 'viewer' is prefigured. It creates a complex set of interactions, during production, reception and consumption. It involves many stages of and negotiations on the creation and appreciation of visual presentation. This analysis therefore offers a study of a visual social intervention that emphasises process rather than the final 'text' as the subject of its investigation.

The 'author', the 'other' and the 'viewer' are plural positions, related to one another through several aspects of the medium, such as recording, editing and screening. As such, I propose to view these positions as inherently mediated: they cannot be understood without referring to the medium. Furthermore, not only is the 'viewer' prefigured throughout the entire production process but it is also necessary to question how the 'viewer' is perceived as having a critical position within this process (Dornfeld 1998, 2002; Mandel 2002).

> An ethnographic approach to cultural production offers the possibility of rethinking and bridging the theoretical dichotomy between production and consumption, between producers' intentional meanings and audience members' interpreted meanings, and between production studies and reception studies. In doing so, it transcends disabling debates in media studies, moving beyond the binaries of media power versus resistance, ideology versus agency, and production versus reception. (Dornfeld 1998: 12)

Moreover, as Winston and Volckaert both argue, not only is the audiovisual configuration a socially elaborated construal, which is itself ideologically embedded, but it also has certain specific parameters which cannot be ignored as they constitute the very operational forces of this configuration (Volckaert 1995; Winston 1996). I therefore explore the hypothesis that the audiovisual configuration with its social, ideological, operational and technological features determines the interactions between the main agents during (documentary) film production. By examining this hypothesis I want to question the way narratives reconstruct the experience of the real, to investigate the manipulation of the contexts, to trace selection and intrusion and to analyse the technological, social and ideological forces at work.

Fieldwork in a Swallows' Nest

Performing Multivocality

I hope to demonstrate the relevance of investigating film production processes by presenting some examples of my fieldwork in what I like to refer to as 'my tribe of film-makers'. Because of the specific audiovisual choices, be it the elaboration of the medium, the process, the authorship or the narrative, these cases can be referred to as 'alternative', 'experimental' or 'independent' cinema. Without locking these cases into a genre, I understand them as 'off the map' places, a term formulated by Ginsburg, Abu-Lughod and Larkin in reference to the research on indigenous media to point out differences in the cartography of dominant media (Ginsburg, Abu-Lughod and Larkin 2002: 8). In this article I elaborate on the process of a community-based film project in Brussels. Artists Els Dietvorst and Orla Barry in collaboration with a hybrid tribe, which they named the Swallows, directed this project. The film is called: *The March, The Burden, The Desert, The Boredom, The Anger* and had its premiere on May 2004 at the Brussels KunstenFESTIVALdesArts.

To explore my fieldwork I adopt Fabian's reorientation 'from informative to performative ethnography':

> 'Performance' seemed to be a more adequate description both of the ways people realize their culture and of the method by which an ethnographer produces knowledge about that culture. In search for a catching phrase I proposed to move 'from informative to performative ethnography'. This has epistemological significance inasmuch as I recommend an approach that is appropriate to both the nature of cultural knowledge and the nature of knowledge of cultural knowledge. (Fabian 1990: 18)

Fabian claims that a performative approach is not only the subject of ethnographic research – it is 'appropriate to the nature of cultural knowledge' – but it is also descriptive of the ethnographic method - 'appropriate to the nature of knowledge of cultural knowledge'- by which ethnographers continuously engage with the communicative, corporeal, sensory and performative dimensions that define the activity of ethnographic field research (ibid.: 86). Fabian states that various forms of cultural knowledge cannot be represented in discursive statements:

> What has not been given sufficient consideration is that about large areas and important aspects of culture no one, not even the native, has information that can simply be called up and expressed in discursive statements. This sort of knowledge can be represented – made present – only through action, enactment, or performance. ... The ethnographer's role, then, is no longer that of a questioner; he or she is but a provider of occasions, a catalyst in the weakest sense, and a producer (in analogy to theatrical producer) in the strongest. (Ibid.: 6)

Asad also claims that translating another culture is not always best done through the representational discourse of ethnography (Asad 1986: 159). MacDougall highlights that many aspects of social experience are not finally translatable (MacDougall 1998: 266). On the contrary, an interaction, an encounter can simply not be represented by textual discourses without transforming it. Rather, they are productions of the original and not mere interpretations: transformed instances of the original, not authoritative textual representations of it, as Asad underscores (Asad 1986: 159).

I hence view this chapter as a production of my encounter with the Swallows, without any interpretive or even representational pretensions. It is a transformed instance of the original performance and I therefore present it as a performative production – 'the kind where the ethnographer does not call the tune but plays along' (Fabian 1990: 19). I attach three important qualifications to this type of production. The first one is that the subject of my research can be described as the Swallows' performances and their mediated interactions during the preparatory phases of the film. I regard these social interventions as performances. I hence use the word 'performance' in Fabian's first meaning, namely as the way people realize their culture. My research deals with processes, which occurred before the end result was presented. I suggest an ethnographic approach towards film processes that deals with the mediated interactions between the main agents. In doing so I present an alternative to an exclusively text-based interpretation of film. I hence deliberately shift the attention from analyses focusing exclusively on the end result of (documentary) film productions towards an examination of the context of interaction in which this result is submerged.

The second qualification deals with the interactive nature of the methodology of this research. I have been involved in the making of the Swallows' film for several months, sometimes as an observer, sometimes as an assistant. This enabled me to fully submerge myself in the project and to collaborate with the Swallows. This methodology could be regarded as an applied visual anthropological perspective. It values Pink's definition of ethnographic research which aims 'to produce a loyal and reflexive account of other people experiences, an account based on collaboration and recognizes the intersubjectivity of the research

Figure 12.1 Playback night. © Orla Barry 2006.

encounter' (Pink, 2004: 10). Of particular significance in this performative fieldwork is that it involves studying people whose projects have such reflexive correspondence with the practice of ethnography (Dornfeld 1998: 20-21) and applied visual anthropology. Indeed, Pink describes applied visual anthropology as follows:

> [It] entails designing visual productions that are informed by anthropological theory, have ethnographic integrity, are appropriate to the context one is working in, and can communicate with specific target audiences. Here however by ethnographic integrity I do not mean that they are necessarily based on long-term fieldwork, but an understanding of both the researcher's and local people's subjectivities, developed though a reflexive process of collaboration and research. ... In these projects applying visual anthropology involves promoting self awareness by representing individuals and groups to others and to themselves. (Pink, 2004: 8)

Els Dietvorst adopts a practice, which has several similarities with this type of survey, involving concepts such as collaboration, feedback and interaction, aiming at giving a voice to minorities in a collective and integral way. Given my experience as a film-maker, and my 'double' identity in these projects, I faced complex interpersonal roles, forcing me to sustain a reflexive attitude throughout the fieldwork. Ginsburg, Abu-Lughod and Larkin point out that this type of correspondence should be understood by the position of media in society: 'Anthropologists now recognize that we are implicated in the representational practices of those

Figure 12.2 'DLNVDN'. © Orla Barry 2006.

we study; and we are engaged or complicit, as the case may be, in complex ways, with all those communities for whom media are important' (Ginsburg, Abu-Lughod and Larkin 2002: 23).

The third qualification deals with the formal presentation of this fieldwork. This 'produced' fieldwork was deprived of its oral and physical qualities as it transferred to a text. The citations are thus weaved and intertwined with the pictures, as in a multi-vocal conversation, to try to recreate a performative production instead of an authorial representation. This discourse suggests a discussion, a happening where my voice is clearly contextualized as the one who has selected the citations and is situated between others. As Fabian contends, 'Translation is a process; the texts we call "translations" are but documents of that process. They, too, are produced through contingent events – in fact, they may in turn be regarded as rehearsals and performances – and are therefore never definitive' (Fabian 1990: 99).

I interviewed eleven people from the cast and the crew in French or Flemish. The interviews took place immediately after the main shoot in Brussels in June 2003 and before the film had been completed. Because matters such as balance of power, hierarchy and financing were discussed during the interviews, and because of some of the participants' frail position within society, all interviewees remain anonymous. The participants have been divided into three groups: the Swallows/actors, the film crew members and Els Dietvorst. This has allowed me to contextualize the quotes and, at the same time, remain sufficiently vague in order not to reveal the person behind the answer. After a first draft I invited the participants to correct where necessary, thus using their feedback to enhance the understanding of this collective experience.

The interviews consist of open, semi-structured conversations and deal with three broad strands of questions. The first strand looks into the relation between the 'author' and the collective: how does the author handle the parameters of the medium and how are they employed and negotiated with participants? Who introduces what, when and where? What is the barrier between author and participant? I focus on the interviewees' expectations and input at the various stages of the process and the differences between preparations and shooting. I consequently monitor the participants' input in their own representation. Next, I look into the social and ideological forces at work during this type of film production. How are these forces tangled up with the goals of the Swallows? Lastly and briefly, I investigate how this project has impacted on the lives of the Swallows, their self-esteem and community relations. In sum, I investigate how this project 'can lead to innovations that give it the potential to be the basis of theoretical, methodological and substantive contributions to academic visual anthropology' (Pink 2004).

The Breeding of the Swallows

Sculptor Els Dietvorst was invited by a contemporary art gallery in the Anneessens area of Brussels to exhibit her artwork. Although warned by the gallery curators about the area's high crime rate, instead of remaining inside the gallery, she started to explore the area on foot. The area is located near the Southern railway station in the heart of Brussels. Yet whereas other areas in the centre were revived recently through several urban activities by which local government officials invited the inhabitants to designate the most acute problems and helped to solve them (1994–1998), the Anneessens area remained isolated (Demeyer and Van Pee 2003: 164). Main arteries, such as the ring road and two new housing projects, physically lock in the area and so prevent integration with other parts of Brussels. Rubbish dumps, vandalism and neglected public spaces all help to create an atmosphere of carelessness, negligence and sloppiness. Mostly populated by immigrants from different ethnic backgrounds, the area can be characterized as a transit area: its different communities are very separate entities, without any common goal or interest whatsoever.

As Els Dietvorst crossed this area, she experienced various interesting encounters which encouraged her to work with the people of this neighbourhood instead of imposing her works of art on them. Although she had never worked with a video camera before, she felt drawn to this medium because of its social aspects and proposed making a film with the people of the area. According to Dietvorst, it was this type of collective experience that the area lacked. Her ultimate goal was to produce a fiction feature film based on the lives of the inhabitants.

Els Dietvorst's fascination with the area is born out of a deep concern for others. In her words: 'I always want to defend people who are oppressed or deprived of their basic rights.' Her note of intent is reminiscent of George Marcus's notion of 'the activist imaginary'. He describes how subaltern groups turn to film, video and other media not only to 'pursue traditional goals of broad-based social change through a politics of identity and representation' but also out of a utopian desire for 'emancipatory projects... raising fresh issues about citizenship and the shape of public spheres within the frame and terms of traditional discourse on polity and civil society' (Marcus 1996: 6). Dietvorst stipulates that she wanted to encourage communication by inviting the inhabitants to express themselves in a joint experience:

> My dream was to create something collective, not something individual. Call me an old-fashioned Marxist, but I do not believe in a society solely steered by individuals. When it comes to that, I'm a utopian. I believe in collective values, even if we all remain individuals. It's animal nature. Why? I think it's a way of bridging our own culture with others. I'm interested in other people because I think that perhaps I can improve myself by learning what others do. I'm not interested in my own culture, or purely in myself. I'd get terribly bored if I had to draw from my own life. Looking for and finding other

things opens up new perspectives. But to use the words of Lévi-Strauss, there's always a chief. I think a collective needs a chief. I gave the people involved in the project a lot of freedom, which I did deliberately. I wanted to know what the limit was and how far I could go.

Els Dietvorst organized a casting in a container that she planted in Anneessens Square, located in the centre of the area. Although, again, many people warned her about criminal acts, two hundred people presented themselves. Dietvorst invited them to improvise, inspired by texts of Arthur Rimbaud, as he lived in the Anneessens area and wrote on exile and migration. In the container, alone with a video camera, Dietvorst recorded these performances. Rimbaud seemed a stimulating source for them: people sang his texts, recounted emotional slave narratives, some even performed somersaults and other acts of physical prowess.

An:	Let's go back to the moment where you were doing an audition in front of Els. You walked through the door of the container. What happened?
Actor/Swallow:	Well, I'd been given a sheet of paper with several extracts written by Arthur Rimbaud. I read them several times and selected one I particularly liked, a text about slavery. The history of slavery is a subject that has always touched me. When I was standing in front of Els, she said to me: 'Ok, we're listening. You can do whatever you like with the text, you can sing, dance … Do whatever you please'. So I started reading out loud, in my own way and all of a sudden, I don't know whether I actually sang, but I do remember I became one with the text. As soon as I read out a phrase, I saw the image described in the text in my head. That's how I did the audition and that's why Els selected me.

This successful casting was the start of a four-year project funded by several organizations, mainly governmental, and helped by different community groups based in the Anneessens area. With this support, Dietvorst managed to engender a hybrid group she named the Swallows, consisting of people without passports, sex workers, migrants from Moroccan, Iranian and Italian descent, a computer designer and even a Belgian policewoman.

An:	How do you personally feel about the image of the swallow?
Actor/Swallow:	I do feel like a swallow, as a matter of fact. Proof of it is that I can say what I want to say, I can make a film and talk about Togo, about everything that, in terms of politics, goes wrong there. It would be impossible for me to do that in Togo. Over there, I would feel like a sheep or a dog on a leash or a chicken in a coop, whereas here, I feel like a swallow, I can fly to wherever I want and say what I think without having to worry about it.

An: Does this add something to your identity? Have you perhaps taken on a new identity?

Actor/Swallow: I believe I have, for thanks to the Swallows I've been able to meet other people and share my experiences and this has helped me to talk about my problems and the other way round. We've all poured everything out and mixed it all together in order to reduce it to one single issue.

An: What do you mean?

Actor/Swallow: We've all come from countries with different problems. We created 'the Swallows', and shared our experiences in order to create one single problem, namely that of the immigrant living in an environment that is not his.

An: Did your personal background as an immigrant have anything to do with your decision to stay in the group?

Actor/Swallow: It didn't. During the casting I had no idea what the film was going to be about. I didn't know what they were going to shoot, what it was all about. I don't think Els was one hundred percent sure either. I was attracted by the word 'film', like a moth to a flame.

People came and went, Dietvorst insisted on creating an open atmosphere where people felt at ease without having any obligations other than collaborating with the others on an art project.

An: How did you select the participants?

Els Dietvorst: Diplomas are of no importance. In principle M could say: 'I am the king of Belgium'. As long as he's a good actor, he can be the king of Belgium. I'm not going to say to anyone: 'This is not realistic' or 'You're telling a lie'. I don't care. If he invests in the group and wants to be Pinocchio, he can be Pinocchio.

An: Being inspired and feeling passionate about the part was important for you during the auditions?

Els Dietvorst: There were different levels. Some people stayed in the group, like L and G, because of their tremendously positive impact on the group. In the group they had a healing influence. They stayed, although they didn't get the biggest parts. The audition was an open, organic process. Every character that has stayed within the group has his own story.

Els Dietvorst, who rejects strict boundaries between art, community projects and anthropology, deliberately opted for the experimental, even freewheeling, character of the project. She did not focus exclusively on the film during these four years, but remained open to suggestions from the Swallows, who were very creative and inspired by their new nest. There were street performances, jukebox stories based on the lives of the inhabitants and recounted in a local pub, glossy magazines covered the activities of the Swallows in full-colour pictures and rave reviews. The Swallows were invited to experiment, to defy easy categorization or definition, but this sense of experimentation was not always effortless.

Actor/Swallow:	We felt as if we weren't taken seriously, as if we were puppets and had to follow the group, unable to do our own thing, really. At a certain moment we felt like guineapigs. We completely lost the feeling of playing in a movie.
An:	Guineapigs for what kind of experiments?
Actor/Swallow:	The social aspect, the contact with the others, with the area, while we had come to do a film.
Actor/Swallow:	I believe the media strongly romanticize our social performances.
An:	And where's the romance?
Actor/Swallow:	Oh, in that everything is possible.
An:	The fact that, even in a destitute neighborhood, these events are possible?
Actor/Swallow:	That's romanticizing, it doesn't work that way. Although the neighbourhood had promised they'd be quiet, they kept on intruding. However, what happens in between, is not going to be shown.
An:	What do you mean?
Actor/Swallow:	The thefts, for example, how they broke into D's car, the fact that they shouted at us, that the takes were interrupted by blokes wanting to show off and other such things.

It is relevant to contextualize this project in the recent wave of Belgian socio-artistic practices, promoted by the new line of subvention by the Flemish Ministry of Culture, for its potential for promoting cultural participation and cultural competence, and enhancing emancipation by marginalized communities or persons. Principles such as accessibility, a context of encouragement and respect, and a profound exchange of experience between participants are developed to enhance cultural emancipation.

But what was unique about the Swallows is that typical socio-artistic aspects were not the foci of the project. Obviously, whenever a Swallow needed social or legal assistance regarding passport issues, or housing problems (and these occured frequently), Dietvorst helped by assigning them to informed social workers. Although these social aims may have been attained, they were not the 'root principles or cultural intuitions' behind the project.[3] On the contrary, abstract notions such as 'positive energy', 'collective' and 'utopia' inspired Dietvorst and her Swallows to create a challenging process. It is this long, enduring, flexible and vigorous process which stands out from other similar projects: not focused on a pre-scripted product or result, this process enabled the Swallows to search individually and collectively for shared moments, happenings, performances which lead intuitively to this yet unknown art work, preferably a feature film. Dietvorst set the perfect example with her continuous enthusiasm and positive charisma, enabling many to overcome their fears and anxieties about their future by believing in this collective project. By means of negotiating and experimenting the Swallows expanded the notion of author to a more cooperative inspiration.

Collaborative Preparations of the Film

The writing of the script is one of the many interesting examples in this search for a collective and collaborative authorship. Els Dietvorst and Orla Barry invited the Swallows to write their own piece of the script. Interestingly, few wanted to take up autobiographical aspects while writing the script. Many switched identities with roles in society that seemed more appealing to them, for instance the male sex worker choose to be a policeman, the Belgian policewoman choose to be a sex worker. Some chose to fictionalize political traumas they experienced in their home land, while others wrote utopian fantasies about their future life. These performative acts might refer to what Conrad, quoting Schechner, proposes when he promotes performance as a paradigm of liminality: 'Fundamental to all performance is the characteristic of "restored behaviour" or "twice-behaved behaviour" that is "symbolic and reflexive: not empty but loaded behaviour multivocally broadcasting significance . . . [in which] the self can act in/as another" allowing the individual to become someone other than themselves. The play frame opens a liminal space where the "not me" encounters the "not not me"' (Conrad 2004 citing Schechner 1985: 52).

Figure 12.3 '*The March*, a Break'. © Norma Prendergast 2006.

Although a selection had to be made, during long sessions of discussions and feedback the Swallows debated on the different contributions. The collective created a collaborative script, although it is clear that Dietvorst and her co-writer Orla Barry defined the overall type of the film, as they were convinced that it would be pointless to create an experimental film not viewable by some Swallows. They therefore used the idea of 'a real film, based on real lives', to communicate about the project.

An:	You said *The March, The Burden, The Desert, The Boredom, The Anger* had to be a real film. What do you mean by that?
Els Dietvorst:	When the Swallows say that a real film is a feature film, like in a cinema theatre, it should be a film with a story line, characters, something about life, love and death.
An:	So that was their idea, what's yours?
Els Dietvorst:	As an artist, you can go many ways. I understand their idea of a real film. I think that everybody has to admit that when you're watching a film and you start crying, that's a real film. The feelings might be cliché, but we recognize them as part of our own lives.
An:	And that's what you were aiming for?
Els Dietvorst:	It's based on their lives and there are story lines in every life. If I were to make an experimental film based on their lives, I'd find myself a bit abusive. But that's not what it's about. It's about trying to make a film together with this collective, which showed a part of their lives and emotions. I was trying to be the director and steer things in the right direction. But at the end of the day it's not my film. I directed and coached, I introduced visual ideas. But if someone had told me four years ago: 'This is the film you're going to make, this is your film', I would have told them: 'Not entirely ... although everything about it interests me, it's based round a collective'.

An important point that is raised by this concept of 'a real film based on real lives' is the position of the 'viewer' during the shoot. Els Dietvorst projected a personalized 'viewer' – in the form of the 'Swallows'. According to Dietvorst, the first viewer needed to be the Swallows and the people for whom they were preparing this film. As such the film needed to be stretched from an art project to a community project, relating to the Swallows' anticipations and expectations, rather than to art-house audiences.

What is important to note is that Els Dietvorst not only managed to convince the Swallows of their self-identity, that they had something important to share with an audience, but she also handled this in a professional way. According to Pinxten, it is a specific kind of professionalism that differentiates a socio-artistic project from a hobby or occupational therapy (Pinxten 2003: 73). It entails a commitment to learn the specific cultural and sociopolitical codes or competences of not only the artists involved but also of the other participants.

Els Dietvorst:	We started the script by asking people what kind of part they wanted to play. For many Swallows, the part consisted of something they dreamt of being in real life. It's some sort of escape from society, or something society refuses to consider. Like D (actor/Swallow), for example. He chose to be a manager in the film who decides to give everything up and leave and hitch hike. It's a romantic idea of freedom.
An:	Did it not create problems?
Els Dietvorst:	At the beginning, the script contained twenty-one characters with equal parts. We invited some people to read the script and no-one was able to follow it. They didn't even understand what the end was or the beginning.
An:	Did you do that in order to give everyone a part?
Els Dietvorst:	Yes, but having twenty-one characters didn't work. In the end, even we lost track of what everybody was doing. We had to drop some scenes in the end.
An:	For the sake of logic?
Els Dietvorst:	When you develop twenty-one characters and give them two minutes each, you don't get any depth. You never get beyond superficially portraying characters without contents.
An:	By consequence, is a so-called 'democratic way of writing' less productive?
Els Dietvorst:	I think it's possible to do it, providing you have ten hours of film and a lot more means and a lot more money. We were limited by time and the length of the film, the time spent filming. We had to scale down, for the sake of clarity. But we discussed this with everybody, and after that it was OK.
An:	You reconnected the script to the people?
Els Dietvorst:	I did. We have been honest when dealing with the actors. Not all twenty of them were able to devote themselves to the project full-time. Some were only available on Saturdays. People with less time were given smaller parts.

Thus, not only in its relation to the collaborative method with the 'other' and hence the subject of the film but also in terms of specifying the 'viewer', the challenge of this type of project is to experiment with what the fragile limit might be in the relation between a collective and a 'chief', in Dietvorst's words, to invest in the collective not necessarily by finding a consensus. It is a search for the limits of negotiation, the sharing of codes and to invest these in a choice, a decision.

Crew member:	When talking to the actors, it became clear they had objections. Or Els had failed to involve them in certain issues. They give a part of the history of their life, something that happened to them personally, something rather fragile. They simply gave it for her film. I thought

> this was a delicate issue throughout the film. How far can you go in using other people's stories to tell your own? One could say, from an outsider's point of view, that Els created an alibi to use these people for her film.

The script presented a collage of different slices of lives touching upon local, national and transnational issues in which locality, nationality and transnationality were differently defined as subjected to the background of the Swallows in this diaspora community. As such, the script did not pretend to reveal the 'category' of the immigrants of the Anneessens area, nor did it represent them, or put up a mirror trying to mimic this community. On the contrary, the script presented a flexible and playful collage of the (utopian) lives of the Swallows, in which fact and fiction were blurred and in which concepts such as authenticity or reality were ignored, yielding a rich example of the concept of identity dynamics.

Professionalism Revised: The Filming Phase

Figure 12.4 '*The March*, … Shoot'. © Norma Prendergast 2006.

The transformation of a script into the actual film shoot is of crucial importance. Driven by Dietvorst's description of 'a real film' motivated by the viewer (as the Swallows), the production unit organized the shoot as a classical fiction-film set. This meant a rather strict definition of functions: a professional cameraman and his assistants, a sound engineer and his assistant, a script supervisor, a make-up artist, several production assistants etc. Yet they were only subsidized with a very limited budget and needed to film in a limited period of time, four weeks in total. The hierarchy of such an organization contrasted sharply with the dynamic and negotiable production process of the Swallows. Furthermore, although Dietvorst invited the crew on rehearsals and tried to make them sensitive to the overall social background of the project, it remained very difficult for a first-time director to entirely direct this 'machine', as a crew member labelled it.

Crew member: A film set deals with a group of people and you've got to get everybody organized. This way of working is characteristic of fiction-film making. Everyone has their job. But I think that when you make a documentary, people's roles are more interchangeable than with other kinds of film (the sound technician could easily be the camera man, for example). During *'The March'* everything had been neatly laid down and people worked within a specific frame. I believe that to be typical of a fiction-film. You can feel it's more rigid, all the activity, the hustle and bustle of a fiction-film.

The crew thus brought another type of professionalism with them, which created a definitive rupture with the previous performances. This rupture brought changes to the project not only because outsiders infiltrated this rather intimate nest of the Swallows, but more importantly because codes and values such as the parameters of cinema (focus, frame, color, light, composition, and depth among others: Volckaert 1995) were in the hands of professionals, rendering impossible the negotiation on codes, and ultimately distancing Dietvorst from her Swallows.

Els Dietvorst: In fact, no-one dared to overstep the mark during the shooting. In the end everyone stuck to the part they'd learnt. The pressure was terrible. During the rehearsals I never had to ask them to improvise. Things happened because they were meant to be. So I thought I could say to them: 'Now you do this, and you do that, etc.' But this was impossible with all these cameras. No matter what I asked them to do, they'd have been lost for words, unable to do anything because of the stress.

This rupture had different sorts of impact on the Swallows, the neighbourhood and on the project as such. Whereas Dietvorst often felt frustrated, some Swallows felt inspired by the crew and were even discovered as new casting talents. Some people of the neighbourhood were proud of the crew while others saw them as intruders.

Actor/Swallow:	It's true that sometimes I would feel intimidated, impressed by the small audience that had gathered around me, especially when my emotions got the upper hand and I started crying. It's like ... I compare it to ... I'm sorry to make this comparison, but I compare it to having sex ... that's to say, you get started, you get into it, you go for it and suddenly you're so excited because you've arrived at the top, at the point of no return, and then you ejaculate, you explode. During this explosion (as I am playing my part), I hardly recognize myself, I really feel like on the day these things happened, when I genuinely shed my tears. Afterwards I'm a little embarrassed, just like after ejaculating, when you feel a little relaxed, but also a little embarrassed towards your partner.
An:	Was it a way of digesting things?
Actor/Swallow:	I believe it was, I'm sure it was therapy for me, precisely helping me to digest what had happened to me. Just by talking about it, I freed myself. At last I felt relieved from this feeling locked inside me for such a long time.
An:	Did this feeling of relief come about after the shooting or after the rehearsals?
Actor/Swallow:	During the rehearsal I sometimes came close to the feeling, but it was nothing like during the shooting. During the shooting, I got into a trance, which took me back to the place where things happened, which brought about this relief. It wasn't the same thing at all.

Ginsburg suggests that indigenous media present a kind of Faustian contract with the technologies of modernity, enabling some degree of agency to control representation under less than ideal conditions (Ginsburg 1991: 96). The Swallows' culture is not based on a common tradition, language or relationship between generations. They created a community, a tribe, during four years, based on a sharing of codes and values and thus living in diversity. Yet the audiovisual medium threatened this community in a different way: although the script was created collectively, since they created a 'real film' they inscribed their process in this dominant and hence constraining mode of production. For the viewer in the person of the Swallow, the film needed to be projected in a commercial cinema venue, a place referring to dominant film production. The experience of most of the Swallows with film was dominant film production, more precisely the commercial blockbusters. For them to engage in a film project had reference to this type of film-making, which had different social, economic and ideological connotations to the type of project Els Dietvorst had in mind. In the project of the Swallows it was the very form of Western narratives that undermined their intentions. This form can be evaluated by the organization of the crew, which was more rigid than any the Swallows were used to. This was partly due to the number of people on the set and the need to organize them efficiently but

Figure 12.5 'Lara'. © Thomas Sennesael 2006.

Figure 12.6 'Kito and Kokou'. © Thomas Sennesael 2006.

also due to a type of film-making that has become common in Western cinema. Raoul Ruiz uses the concept of a Central Conflict Theory to understand this Western type of cinema (Ruiz 1995: 14). According to him, this theory has turned into a predatory theory, a system of ideas that devours and enslaves any other idea that might restrain its activity. Pink states the ethical codes and understandings of TV companies, and by extension Western film production, differ from those that guide applied visual anthropologists. She therefore urges that 'the anthropologist needs to work between these codes, acting not only as a cultural broker to facilitate the representation of one culture to another on film, but also to protect the local culture through his or her knowledge of the ethics and practices of the filmmaking culture' (Pink, this volume). Yet whenever Dietvorst or the Swallows felt uncertain over a specific choice or decision, due to a lack of experience or under too much pressure, it seemed necessary to rely upon the experience of the professional crew-members, instead of finding resources in their own flexible and dynamic methods that preceded the shoot. Instead of questioning how the relation between Dietvorst and her Swallows could be imagined, questions such as costume continuity and clarity prevailed because of this type of professional dependence on the script and on the type of organization of the set.

The Swallows' Nest Inside Out

In general, the inhabitants of the Anneesens' area appreciated the attention to their neighbourhood, which attracted press people, resulting in several newspapers articles and spots on television. The area had suddenly appeared on the map of Brussels. This social intervention, the film-shoot performance, had a major impact on the area in its stimulation of social cohesion by this collective experience during the shoot and by the expectations it raised about the 'real film' scheduled in one of the large commercial film theatres of Brussels owned by UGC. It had produced various creative moments which stimulated communication in the area. The film shoot thus replaced the image of the destitute transit area with that of a dynamic and vibrant neighbourhood that gave rise to numerous arts events, resulting in such a large-scale feature film production about the community. The shoot, which implicated the entire neighbourhood, enlarged the flexible nest of the Swallows as insiders.

Although the Swallows sometimes complained about money issues, or about the importance of their part in the film, in general their self-esteem had been empowered by the event. Some found jobs because the experience had given them more self-confidence; other continued in an artistic direction by producing their own films; others were stimulated by the social aspects of the process and engaged in emancipatory projects while still others felt depressed because of the ending of the project. Undeniably, this project had empowered each of the Swallows due to the inspiring root intuitions: utopia, enthusiasm and collectivity. They felt privileged to have been part of this undertaking.

I will not analyse the remainder of the performances of the Swallows but I will limit myself by briefly presenting the final activities. These activities demonstrate the impressive transformation of the Swallows' nest. The Swallows organized a final part of the shoot in Morocco as many Swallows were born there, or had relatives there. The film was edited during a long period with several moments of feedback. The film was titled *The March, The Burden, The Desert, The Boredom, The Anger* and was shown at the UGC in Brussels, in the 'golden room', the largest and most impressive theatre of this venue for dominant Hollywood cinema. The theatre was packed: all Swallows were so proud of this project that they had invited all their friends, family relatives, neighbours etc. After this presentation the Swallows decided to end their collective experience with an exhibition where all their events, performances, and films were accessible. They were stunned to hear that BOZAR in Brussels wanted to give them a platform. For a month they were able to present their archive in this high cultural palace of fine arts.

Enlarged by these performances and transformed by the passages through these very differentiated sociocultural areas, ranging from community centres, a high cultural palace to a dominant cinema venue, the Swallows' nest flipped inside out and dissolved, making room for empowered individuals and leaving several traces throughout Brussels.

Figure 12.7 'Birdi'. Els Dietvorst 2000.

Epilogue: A Performative Analysis of Collaborative and Plural Authorship

I have taken a visual anthropology approach to analysing the Swallows project so as to offer a way of understanding how community and arts projects can create social interventions. That is, not by simply analysing the end product - the final 'text' - but by attending ethnographically to the processes, relationships and identities that are integral to its production. I emphasize the necessity of exploring the interactions during the production process in a loyal and reflexive way, based on collaboration and recognizing the intersubjectivity of the research encounter (Pink 2004). In doing so I underscore the performative turn in anthropological thinking influenced by Fabian, when he claims that a performative approach is not only the subject of ethnographic research but it is also descriptive of the ethnographic method (Fabian 1990).

Cultural intuitions such as 'positive energy', 'collective' and 'utopia' inspired Els and her Swallows to create a challenging process. These notions shape the way in which the parameters of cinema are understood or used within the interactions between the main agents. By means of negotiating and experimenting, the Swallows expanded the notion of author to a more cooperative inspiration. The process presented a search for the fragile limits of negotiation, the sharing of codes and an attempt to invest these in a decision in which the 'other' and the 'viewer' were invited and personalized. The project thus stimulated social aims such as encouraging communication, social cohesion in the community and individual growth. Yet it had been situated within the context of a film project, with its specific social and ideological forces. The challenge of this project was to assess the ideological and social forces at work in film production and to invest these in a particular community context. These forces created anticipations, interactions influenced by a dominant mode of production, as the project was designed to create 'a real film based on real lives'. Ginsburg therefore refers to Faust when relating community projects with the technologies of modernity (Ginsburg 1991: 96).

In sum, with this analysis of the production process of a community-based film project in Brussels, I hope to have demonstrated the value of an analysis of the interactions between the 'author' and the 'other' in which the 'viewer' is prefigured during (documentary) film production. Rather than coining (documentary) film production with concepts such as 'reality', 'authenticity', 'fiction' and 'faithful representation', I thus suggest that the mediated interactions during the production process determine the 'flow between fact and fiction' (Trinh 1990: 89). The case of the Swallows offers a unique perspective on authorship and its relationship to the 'other' and the 'viewer', which could not be apprehended by simply analysing the final film. Qualitative methods mostly derived from performative and visual anthropology offer possibilities in investigating the mediated interactions between the different agents. This analysis therefore explores the relations between the production of knowledge, the different contexts in which these processes occur and the position the researcher has in these processes (Alvesson and Sköldberg 2001). As such, I hope to offer an alternative to a strictly interpretative, text-based analysis and representational discourse. As Fabian (1990: 259), notes: '... The theoretical benefit that is to be derived from making performance a guiding idea is a conception of relationships between texts and interpretation, which is neither static nor hierarchical but processual. The burden of such an approach is to show the essential openness of that process.'

Notes

1. More information on this project: http://www.fireflyfilms.be/
2. 'Juke-box stories' are stories based on the lives of people who regularly visited the bar 'Rouge et Noir' in the Anneessens area. Writer Anna Luyten gathered these stories and performed her interpretation in the bar, next to a jukebox.
3. 'Root intuitions' or 'cultural intuitions' are concepts suggested by Pinxten to facilitate ethnographic comparisons (Pinxten 1997: 87).

   What appears at first sight to be varied, chaotic, unconnected or utterly disparate in a culture can, upon closer examination, be recognized to be unified or closely linked because of a common root principle. A somewhat similar argument holds for the synonymous term of cultural intuitions; they express the non-discursive or immediate notions, which are underlying the level of rational discourse.

Bibliography

Asad, T. 1986. 'The Concept of Cultural Translation in British Social Anthropology' in J. Clifford and G.E. Marcus (eds), *Writing Culture*. Berkeley: University of California Press.

Alvesson, M. and K. Sköldberg. 2001. *Reflexive Methodology: New Vistas for Qualitative Research*. London: Sage.

Conrad, D. (2004). 'Exploring Risky Youth Experiences: Popular Theatre as a Participatory, Performative Research Method', *International Journal of Qualitative Methods* 3(1) Article 2. Retrieved [May 2004] from http://www.ualberta.ca/~iiqm/backissues/3_1/html/conrad.html

Demeyer, B. and K. Van Pee 2003. *De sociaal-artistieke praktijk in België. Een kwalitatief onderzoek naar methodiekontwikkeling. (Socio-artistic Practices in Belgium. Qualitative Research of Methodologies)*. Kunst en Democratie – Katholieke Universiteit Leuven.

Dornfeld, B. 1998. *Producing Public Television, Producing Public Culture*. Princeton: Princeton University Press.

——— 2002. 'Putting American Public Television Documentary in Its Places' in F. Ginsberg, L. Abu-Lughod and B. Larkin (eds), *Media Worlds. Anthropology on New Terrain*. Berkeley: University of California Press, pp. 247–63.

Fabian, J. 1990. *Power and Performance. Ethnographic Explorations through Proverbial Wisdom and Theater in Saba, Zaire*. Wisconsin: University of Wisconsin Press.

Geertz, C. 1988. *Works and Lives. The Anthropologist as Author*. Stanford: Stanford University Press.

Ginsburg, F. 1991. 'Indigenous Media: Faustian Contract or Global Village?', *Cultural Anthropology* 6(1), pp. 92–112.

Ginsburg F., L. Abu-Lughod and B. Larkin (eds), 2002. *Media Worlds. Anthropology on New Terrain*. Berkeley: University of California Press.

MacDougall, D. 1998. *Transcultural Cinema*. Edited and Foreword by Lucien Taylor. Princeton: Princeton University Press.

Mandel, R. 2002. 'A Marshall Plan of the Mind: The Political Economy of a Kazakh Soap Opera', in F. Ginsburg, L. Abu-Lughod and B. Larkin (eds), *Media Worlds. Anthropology on New Terrain*. Berkeley: University of California Press, pp. 211–28.

Marcus, G. 1996. 'Introduction' in G. Marcus (ed.), *Connected: Engagements with Media*. Chicago: University of Chicago Press, pp. 1–18.

Nichols, B. 1994. *Blurred Boundaries. Questions in Meaning in Contemporary Culture*. Bloomington: Indiana University Press.

Pink, S. 2004. 'Applied Visual Anthropology: Defining the Field' in S. Pink (ed) *Applied Visual Anthropology* a guest edited issue of *Visual Anthropology Review*, 20(1): 3–16.

Pinxten, R. 1997. *When the Day Breaks. Essays in Anthropology and Philosophy*. Frankfurt-am-Main: Peter Lang.

——— 2003. *De artistieke samenleving. De invloed van kunst op de democratie (The artistic society. Influence of the arts on democracy)*. Antwerp: Houtekiet.

Ruiz, R. 1995. *Poetics of Cinema*. New York: Distributed Art Publishers.

Schechner, R. 1985. *Between Theater and Anthropology*. Philadelphia: University of Pennsylvania Press.

Trinh, T. Minh-ha. 1990. 'Documentary Is/Not a Name', *October* 52, Spring: 76–100.

van. Dienderen, A. 2003. '"Flow between Fact and Fiction": Analysis of Identity Dynamics in Visual Representation', in C. Longman, Pinxten, R. and G. Verstraete (eds), *Culture and Politics: Identity and Conflict in a Multicultural World*. Oxford: Berghahn Books, pp. 117–132.

———, 2004. 'Collectivity on Screen: Balancing between Taxidermy and Negotiation', *Social Justice: Anthropology, Peace and Human Rights*. 4(3-4): 196–227.

Volckaert, D. 1995. *Opkomst en ondergang van Cinema: een Pre-Cinematografische zoektocht naar een kerndefinitie. (Rise and Fall of Cinema, a Pre-Cinematographic Research to a Definition)*, Master's thesis. Brussels: St-Lukas School of Arts 1995.

Winston, B. 1996. *Technologies of Seeing: Photography, Cinematography and Television*. London: British Film Institute.

PART VI

INDUSTRY

Chapter 13

VIDEO ETHNOGRAPHY UNDER INDUSTRIAL CONSTRAINTS
Observational Techniques and Video Analysis

———— ❧ ————

Werner Sperschneider

Introduction

This paper reports on how video is used in design studies to understand particular cultures of work. Ethnographers in the emerging field of design anthropology make extensive use of video to study how people interact with computers and other information technology devices. Many practitioners in design studies find that using video is an effective way to collect and analyse observational visual data to inform product development and design, and to use these findings to communicate with stakeholders. Video helps to invoke an understanding of how people really perform their duties at work, how information technologies in mechatronic products are used and how they interact successfully with machinery. In contrast to many standard laboratory tests and cognitive studies, video of real people in real settings performing real duties brings users (or informants) into the designer's realm for the analysis and evaluation of design solutions. Thus product development becomes a collaborative task of designers and users. Video enables co-design, not in a conventional lab on the designer's premises, but in the collaboratorium.[1]

Human-Computer-Interaction (HCI) is a well-established subfield in computer science. With the emergence of a participatory design approach in the late 1980s, more and more trained ethnographers are hired by big companies to elicit user perspectives for the design of information systems. Being well aware of their proactive stand, ethnographers in design regard their practice as social intervention: the way a tool is designed determines how humans apply it. Ultimately, design is about social intervention.

First, I discuss how video serves to observe users' activities, their embodied skills and knowledge, in regard to mechatronic (mechanical and electronic) devices. This chapter presents five techniques for video-based ethnographic field studies for user-centred design under industrial constraints where video ethnography is being scrutinized as a vigorous research technique. It examines the original meaning of fieldwork in ethnography and discusses how ethnographically inspired fieldwork can enrich research and data gathering. But, in an industrial setting, time and resources for prolonged engagement with informants are limited. Is there a 'quick and dirty' version of 'going native'? Or is this just another approach of 'hit-and-run' ethnography'?

Second, I discuss the 'video card game', which is a powerful tool to evaluate large amounts of qualitative video data. This is a collaborative evaluation tool where users such as informants participate along with designers and other stakeholders, such electronic engineers and marketing managers.

Video has equal potential as a design tool as the pen has as a standard tool for engineers and architects. This chapter shows how using video, in ways that are based on methods developed in visual anthropology, is more than just a mere observational and representational tool, but communicates stakeholders' perspectives to represent design potentials and enable design solutions.

Context

Since 1999 I have been involved in doing ethnographically-inspired user studies for the design of innovative industrial products at Danfoss A/S, a major Danish industrial manufacturer for refrigeration, heating and motion controls. Being a trained visual anthropologist I have learned to combine ethnographic and visual research methods for the benefit of surveying (rather than doing research in the academic sense of the term) the use of industrial products and of their users' environments.

I would like to reflect on the array of ethnographic and visual techniques employed in my daily work and show how video observations effectively inform evaluations for design. The video card game is a structured and systematic analysis method developed in the Danfoss User-Centred Design Department (Buur and Søndergaard 2000). This method has survived a number of variations in many projects. Thus I believe it could be beneficial as well for those visual anthropologists who go about in more conventional anthropological research settings. The visual research techniques and the video card game analysis could well enter the array of methods in visual studies. The word 'user' could be replaced with 'informant'. And the notion 'design' could be replaced with 'ethnographic film', 'empirical data', etc. I would therefore like to make the video observation techniques and the respective analysis method accessible for interested visual researchers.

Fieldwork as Research

The last two decades have seen a strong interest in employing qualitative methods in design for researching users and use in design. Since about 1980 a number of collaborations have arisen between ethnographers, anthropologists, ethnomethodologists and qualitative sociologists on the one hand, and designers, engineers and computer scientists on the other. Especially in Britain and Scandinavia, and increasingly in the U.S., fully-fledged partnerships have grown (Suchman 1995). The nature of these partnerships differs, but they all have in common the goal of analysing the contingencies of information-based work practice as situated in particular times and places, and using that analysis to inform user-centred design.

Ethnographic research has become important in the design of all kinds of new information systems. The participatory design community in particular found its major inspiration in the ethnography genre, where ethnography is conceived as 'a way of seeing' (Wolcott 1995). One of the research techniques that became most popular is the fieldwork method, often employed as ethnographic field study. But what is ethnographic fieldwork?

Even if the term suggests one standard technique, there are many ways of doing it. In fact, fieldwork as research is a way of doing something (Wolcott 1995) that unites many approaches. Fieldwork is a matter of techniques rather than a rigid step-by-step 'how to' prescription. The approaches to fieldwork are alternatives. They should be regarded as choices among strategies rather than selections of proper techniques to be adapted for any particular setting. The essence of qualitative research is that it is designed in the doing. As Wolcott puts it: 'They are intended to allow researchers to follow a suitable course of inquiry rather than to dictate in advance what that course should be' (Wolcott 1995).

Fieldwork in Ethnography

In ethnography and social anthropology, fieldwork is mainly associated with the technique of participant observation. Interviewing is either a complement of participant observation or a major facet of it. The participant observer operates simultaneously both as an insider and as an outsider. Differing from an ordinary participant, who engages in activities appropriate to a social situation, the fieldworker goes beyond ordinary engagement in order to observe the activities, people and physical aspects of a given situation (Spradley 1980). Participant observation in ethnography is best described as a way to 'hang around, talk to folks, and try to get sense of what is going on' (Wolcott 1999). Pragmatic as it is, this advice still generally holds true, although much has since been achieved in methodological sophistication and refinement.

Nowadays participant observation and interview techniques are paired as the 'dynamic duo' of field research. Researchers who need to exert control over what they study design their own research strategy – both before going to and while in the field. Observations are (pre-)informed by a dawning understanding as our understanding is informed by new observations. Thus alteration of the research strategy, even while out in the field, is recommended in the literature (Spradley 1980; Wolcott 1995).

Today's recipe for good ethnographic field research is as follows: 'You want to go there with your mind as open as possible. You want to be surprised and you want to let yourself be surprised, and you want to put yourself where you can be as surprised as possible, and then you wonder what it is like, how does it hang together, what is the picture, and that should be your stimulus to intellectual work analysis.' (Barth, in Sperschneider 2000).

So much for the overall attitude and the doings of a genuine ethnographic fieldworker who works in social contexts. But what about short-term research visits? What if you have to work under time constraints, if your design project does not allow you to hang around, talk to folks, and try to make sense of what is going on? And what about when your goal is not to study social interaction, as in the case of ethnography, but to study change, as in the case of design?

Fieldwork in Participatory Design

When it comes to time constraints, ethnography seems to be the very antithesis of design. The ethnographer goes out into the field – for months, for years, in some cases for a lifetime. Lifelong companionship with field informants is not uncommon among ethnographic fieldworkers. Starting as observing participant, or privileged observer, the ethnographer at the end of their field study might have become a genuine participant. The ethnographer returns to 'their' people – for gathering additional empirical material, for proving a redesigned hypothesis or simply for reasons of solidarity and social engagement. The luckiest ethnographic fieldworker even might become initiated in the culture they study.

In a similar way, the designer might feel attracted to a 'super-user'; for example, a particular company or a supermarket. 'It's always good to know people; and it's always good if they know what one is after', one might argue.

When it comes to formal principles, ethnography again seems to be antithetical to design. Design is experimental. The designer seeks to create a future practice. Ethnographically untrained HCI specialists, who behave as ethnographers at their best – just in a much shorter time – often perform fieldwork in participatory design.

From a user centred design point of view design is a creative, exploratory activity where the designers try to conceptualize, formalize and express (verbally, visually) their ideas of future work practice for example, with new technology. In a participatory design setting the designer (as observer) seeks to understand the user's tacit knowledge in using and interacting with technology.

The ethnographer (as participant observer) would rather talk of studying cultural rules in use and interaction with machinery and tools. More than just a matter of nuance in terminology, the difference lies in the focus of attention (tacit knowledge about technology versus cultural rules in using machinery).

Field research in design does not assume a level of involvement comparable to ethnographic fieldwork in a social setting for studying social interaction. Data gathering requires a minimum length of time and a particular consideration of the social and cultural context. If one knows which data are to be gathered, then once that is done, one soon leaves for home to refine ones inquiry. But in one aspect design and ethnography projects are alike: when employing qualitative methods both refer to an ongoing process rather than to a 'fait accompli' (Wolcott 1995).

Fieldwork and Theory

What remains to be covered in terms of the similarities and differences between these two disciplines is the question of how observations in the field are theorized: the question about which, when and how theory makes an entry into the research process. Different theoretical schools suggest different entry points for theory.

What has been said about design holds true also for ethnography: critical tongues (of course unpublished) always spread rumours of a discipline's poor of theory. Teachers in both disciplines help by advising students to reserve a closing chapter of a dissertation 'where a self-conscious but genuine search for theoretical implications and links begins rather than ends' (Wolcott 1995). Experienced ethnographic fieldworkers, like Fredrik Barth, advise us to think of theories in multiple rather than monothetical form. According to Barth (1994), theories ought to be 'explored and played with.' Fieldwork ought to be 'a stimulus to your intellectual work analysis'; 'you must build your argument on what is there in (the field) and not on what you have brought along (from theorizing at home)' (Sperschneider 2000).

Herein meet problems of methodology and theorizing, of design and ethnography. The fieldworker in design could well follow the ethnographic fieldworker's advice: 'One step at a time, and then you anticipate of what is to result as end product' (Wolcott 1995).

Fieldwork Techniques for User Involvement

The following five video-based research techniques drawn from our own work practice demonstrate some examples of different approaches for an ethnographically-inspired strategy for participant observation research. The order demonstrates our overall desire to intensify user engagement and user centeredness in the design process, as well as telling of our sympathy with the ethnographic ideal of 'going native'.

Experimenting further with this approach by intensifying involvement with users one even might go so far as to hand out video cameras to the users and ask for a record of what they see in their field. The boundaries between users and designers become blurred.

The examples using this approach point to one of the main crucial aspects for the goal of a real participatory design approach: field studies under industrial constraints need to be considered under the overall time constraint.

Whether or not the ethnographer's ideal is to 'go native', it could also be a desirable goal for the designer. When we move beyond the usability lab towards the co-design lab, we need to reconsider some of the basics of our participatory design approach. We need to look again to what we referred to when we drew inspiration from the ethnography genre for formulating a design-in-context approach.

Situated Interview: Tell Me What You Do

The researcher interviews a user on location using qualitative interview techniques. You might have brought along a questionnaire, but you do not force its structure. Some questions formulated in advance will work in the situation you encounter; most will need reformulation to adjust to what is there. Being there in context means that the user can refer to important things at hand.

Simulated Use: Show Me How You Should Do It

This case draws greatly on the basics of the ethnographic fieldwork approach: 'tell me what you think you see'. Unlike an ethnographer's participatory observation approach, you just observe simulated use, not life as it unfolds. The case has been made up, maybe in a laboratory or maybe on location at the workshop. However its defining characteristic is simulation.

Acting Out: Show Me Your Normal Procedure

Users often follow regular procedures in parts of their jobs. When asked, they will often be happy to guide you around to show you explicitly what their working procedures are. While the user acts out their work at particular places, you observe staged work routines. Acting out is about specific life situations as seen by users.

Shadowing: Let Me Walk with You

The designer follows the users in their daily routine. This does not work with a pre -formulated questionnaire, but you might proceed with a working

Figure 13.1 Interview with a French chemical plant operator on the use of valves. (1 h visit). © Werner Sperschneider 2006.

Figure 13.2. Danish heating installers mount a pump on our premises. (1-day workshop). © Werner Sperschneider 2006.

Figure 13.3 Japanese refrigeration mechanic demonstrates his daily round. (1 h visit). © Werner Sperschneider 2006.

Figure 13.4 We follow Danish water treatment plant operators. (1 day visit). © Werner Sperschneider 2006.

hypothesis. You might even provoke the user with a mock-up in a situation you have anticipated before, but you will not limit yourself in learning.

Apprenticeship: Teach Me How

The designer steps into the user's role. You are interested in learning about work routines by doing it yourself. As the user teaches you as their apprentice, you can draw on an insider's perspective. Having observed and tried the work yourself, you can reformulate questions you have brought along. You might even do this in collaboration with the user, who will in a way become a co-designer.

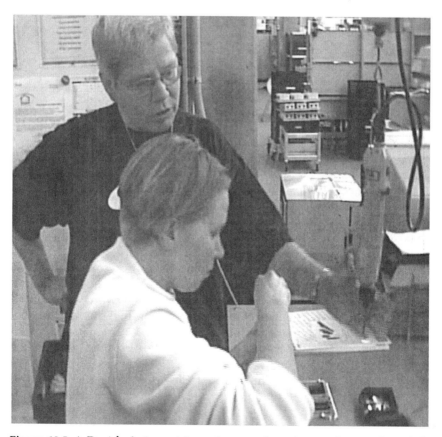

Figure 13.5 A Danish designer tries out a manufacturing work procedure. (1 h visit). © Werner Sperschneider 2006.

Ethnographic Video Observations as Reflection-in-action

Video observations of use, recordings of dialogue among users and interviews with users are various approaches of reflecting on practice. Reflection takes place 'in the middle' of it. This is what Schön calls reflection-in-action (Schön 1983, 1987). Often reflection-in-action is stimulated by surprise. Schön defines reflection-in-action as 'hing[ing] on the experience of surprise. When intuitive, spontaneous performance yields nothing more than the results expected for it, then we tend not to think about it. But when intuitive performance leads to surprises, pleasing and promising or unwanted, we may respond by reflection-in-action' (Schön 1983: 56).

Naturally, reflection-in-action is an intervention in observational practice. Thus the quality of information collected needs to be considered under this constraint. What you get is not what you see – but it points to characteristics, and patterns, of use – practice. From surprises during reflection-in-action observation and interviewing we learn about the relation between work and technology. For design it is necessary to try to understand work practices in specific settings. This understanding can provide a platform for involving users further in the design process. Ethnographic user studies are one of several methods to get hold of use – practice, and to understand what users regard as important and relevant in the activities they carry out.

Design-in-context with Video

Video is used as a catalyst for communication and discussion. The discussion generating process is the most important part of using video (Buur and Søndergaard 2000). It promotes discussions between design team members (Suchman and Trigg 1991; Mackay, Ratzer and Janecek 2000; Buur, Binder and Brandt 2000).

Working with user-centred design in an industrial company challenges the usability expert to do ethnographic fieldwork considering time constraints and tight project budgets. Nevertheless, in the User-Centred Design group at Danfoss we have experimented with variations of fieldwork strategies, trying to compensate for some of the aforementioned problems with using ethnographic fieldwork techniques in industry.

With two case studies we will describe how we have used ethnographic inspiration to move design activities into the field in design projects. We have used the term 'design-in-context' to describe design sessions staged in the user's own work environment and based on scenarios developed by the user.

Improvised Video Scenarios on Location

The first example is from a development project at Danfoss where the User-centred Design group was involved in designing a new flow meter concept with a portable service tool for process operators at a waste water plant.

The design-in-context session involved two designers and two users and it lasted two hours. We had prepared five simple foam mock-ups, emphasizing different features of the flow meter concept we found interesting from a design point of view. We showed the mock-ups to the users at the plant, asked them to select their favourite mock-up and explain why they selected this 'tool'. After they had explained why they favoured certain tools, we asked if they could explore how the ideas would work in their work environment. As we walked out into the plant, we talked about where they would place the tools. The users showed us how a portable tool could be placed on a shelf inside the building while not in use, and how it should fit in their pocket when they worked outdoors.

From this moment on the roles of the designers and the users changed from those in a usual participatory design workshop because now the

Figure 13.6 Waste water plant operators pick a favourite design mock-up. ©Werner Sperschneider 2006.

Figure 13.7. In the plant, the operators improvise a work scenario with the mock-up. ©Werner Sperschneider 2006.

users took control and set the stage for us designers. The users guided us around in their work context and showed us where they would use the tool, how they preferred to interact with it and what the interface of the tool should show in different work situations.

In a setting like this we do not direct the users to follow a scenario we describe. The users themselves create the scenarios as they guide us in their work context using simple foam mock-ups as design props. Despite their very primitive and simple looks, the foam mock-ups play a very important role as 'something to think with' while the users explore and follow new ideas as they design new concepts for future tools and new use situations. For a more detailed description of a similar case at Danfoss see (Buur, Binder and Brandt 2000).

Co-design Game and Movie Making

The second example is a user workshop that took place in a vision project at Danfoss, with the aim of exploring water components for the future (Pedersen and Buur 2000). In the vision project the User-Centred Design group focused on what the user's work environment and its instrumentation would look like in a future waste water plant. What kind of requests would the users come up with for products to accomplish the future water cleaning processes? (Bødker and Buur 2000).

The design event was a day-long user workshop in which thirty process operators, developers, marketing people, designers and usability experts participated. They were divided into three teams and started with a design game in a meeting room at the company. The aim of the first design game session was to build a state of the art waste water plant, with its different water components represented by foam pieces on a map of a plant printed on a game board. In the next session the teams built the instrumentation of a future wastewater plant, using the same game pieces but with an empty game board instead of the plant layout. The third session took place at a nearby waste water plant. The three teams produced an on-site video showing a future scenario with the ideas from the design game. Each team was given a video camera, foam props, tape and markers to design the components used in their future scenario. To get them started we suggested that they imagine a situation where a process operator shows an apprentice their future procedures. As the teams tried to establish the future plant layout from the game board, they started to discuss and explore the solutions in further detail in order to somehow visualize their design ideas and discussions for the video. At the end of the day the teams presented their ideas (the movie and future plant layout) to the other participants. This user workshop, and especially the third session with the on-site video, encouraged the participants to collaborate in a co-design event. Although the participants had different professional backgrounds and languages, during the day they developed a common design language throughout the design game and the design solutions. This helped all participants to understand today's practices and to envision and explore new work practices in a real-use context. The co-design event narrowed the gap between the different professionals and their competences, such as designers and process operators. It worked because everybody was engaged in producing a video expressing their design ideas about future components and work practices. Thus the roles of the observer and the user blurred during the co-design event, where everybody designed and tried to understand work practice in a real use context.

Video Card Game: Method for Analysis and Evaluation of Design Potentials

The video card game (Buur and Søndergaard 2000) is a collaborative analysis method, but given the form of a game. Its name refers to the 'Happy Families' children's game. In this game players collect families of four cards by asking each other in turn for cards. The goal is it to get rid of the bad cards, and to collect a family of four cards that will be assembled in a stack. The player with most stacks wins.

The metaphor of gaming supports the video card method in a playful way. Humans like to play. The video card game is mostly played with stakeholders of a product innovation team. But is has been employed successfully with users as well, with stakeholders collaborating with users in the analysis of video for the evaluation of design potentials and challenges.

The preparatory step is to turn video segments from field observations into paper prints. Thus video becomes transformed and given physicality. Video turns into tangible arguments to support a design team's work (Buur and Søndergaard 2000). The video cards can be referred to as objects and will be handled physically by participants, the 'game players'.

This technique is similar to what an anthropologist does when writing each piece of information on a separate card. Grouping and regrouping the cards in several rounds structure observations, and the anthropologist achieves an understanding of field observation through a bottom-up process.

Making Video Cards and Playing the Video Card Game

Video sequences of a maximum 2 minutes in length are selected subjectively and unconsciously. The selection of video segments basically relies on what the field ethnographer finds potentially significant. After this a key frame of each video segment is used to create cards for the game. Just the sheer number of video cards guarantees a certain degree of objectivity. Typically some 75 to 135 cards are created for between six and nine players (approximately 12-15 cards per player).

The short length of the video clips is important. If the goal is to get participants to focus on particular interesting aspects of the video, then it is important not to overwhelm them with a long video clip containing various ideas or topics. It is also worth noting that the video does not necessarily need to only contain surprising events that trigger reframing in the participants' minds.

For design purposes it is important to collect video segments that display action rather than dialogue. Conversations are of minor interest. Basically we want to see what people do rather than listening what they say they believe they are doing. This of course is also of interest, but on a secondary order level. For design of industrial products we need to see how users handle and deal with products. Video is about action, not interpretation.

A stack of randomly selected video cards (12 to 15) gets distributed among the players. Each player watches the video sequences linked to their cards, describes the action, and notes comments on each card, an activity which lasts at least 30 minutes. In the next round each player groups the cards according to any imaginable topic or headline. No restrictions are made to how the players group their cards as long as it makes subjective sense to them.

One by one each player then chooses a favourite 'family' of cards, describes their favourite 'family' to the assembly and invites other players to contribute with cards to their family. Any player might contribute with what seems to fit in. The receiving player, the 'family' owner, negotiates which cards fit the category under discussion. This serves to help participants understand what the video sequences basically are about; and it gives all participants a relatively good overview of what is on the table.

Recordings can be reviewed several times to find evidence for interpretations or to find other explanations for the interaction of humans with technology. This continues until all agree on the interpretation, or they have found questions that ought to be pursued. In fact the video card game method opens up, what Bødker and Buur call a design 'collaboratorium' (Bødker and Buur 2002) where users and designers again meet for collaborative work.

None of the players will have seen all the video sequences. Therefore all are free to show their sequence to others and to explain why they believe them to be relevant for the 'family' under negotiation. Often the category and phrasing of each 'family' changes in the process. The new extended 'family' of cards is glued onto a separate sheet of paper, with a heading denoting the theme and its characteristics. In this way each player becomes responsible for a design topic, thus making sure that any idea is based on actual user input.

Video Card Game Step by Step

The video card game is a day-long event requiring commitment and engagement of all players for some six to seven hours.

Step 1: Dealing the cards
(30 minutes)
Cards are distributed randomly between the different players, rules are explained, and a simple training exercise in video analysis is run on what is observation and what is interpretation.

Figure 13.8. A video card (with number and title). ©Werner Sperschneider 2006.

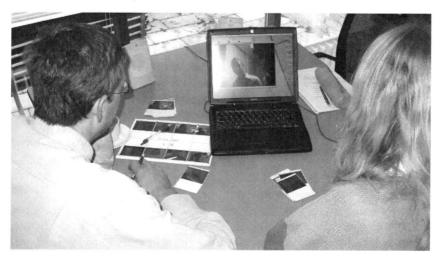

Figure 13. 9 Players read their cards (watch video), making annotations for observation and interpretation. ©Werner Sperschneider 2006.

Step 2: Reading your cards (1 hour)
Players (individually or in pairs) watch video sequences of the cards. Players annotate cards by writing individual comments (observation/ information) to each video sequence directly onto the paper print that represents the sequence. Video cards now have properties of their own; players 'own' cards; they control the interpretation of the observations. Handwritten annotations transform cards from 'public' into 'personal' property. At this stage players are encouraged not to discuss their comments further, and instead to rely on spontaneous subjective experience of the contents.

Step 3: Arranging your hand (30 minutes)
When brought together again, the players are asked to group their cards in 'families' openly in front of them on the table. Hereafter the players describe and explain the ideas behind each 'family'. During their presentation, developers will recognize which clips are relevant to their design activity. Nuances in the problems at hand will become apparent. There are no restrictions to how the players group their cards as long as it makes sense in terms of the design focus.

Step 4: Collecting card families (1 hour)
Each player is then asked to choose a favorite 'family' of cards. One after another the players describe the 'family' they have chosen and invite the other players to contribute with cards that seem to fit into the theme that the 'family' of cards represents.

Figure 13.10 Players in pairs (product specialist/designer) arrange their hand. ©Werner Sperschneider 2006.

Figure 13.11 Players discuss card 'families'. ©Werner Sperschneider 2006.

These new collections of cards are glued onto a separate A 3-sized poster with a heading denoting the theme. The selection of favourite themes ('trick') makes the individual design team member responsible for relating the design to actual user input.

Step 5: Discussing the card 'families' (3 hours)

This is the main activity of the video card game. Following a brief discussion of priorities (where should we start?) the players spend time discussing one 'family' after another, trying to understand what the video clips said and what this 'family' would mean to the design. Since none of the players have seen all clips, they each show their clips to one another and explain why they thought them to be relevant. Tricks glued on A3-size paper are assembled and hung up to discuss further challenges. We find that developers come to use the video again and again throughout such a discussion. It is important to make sure that prototypes and relevant hardware are readily available on the table to point at and think with.

Figure 13.12 Discussion of design potentials and challenges making further annotations (eventually adding sketches). ©Werner Sperschneider 2006.

Reflection

The video card game has been used with ever greater success in a number of design projects. Participants are excited, feel encouraged and play the design game with a great deal of enjoyment that has lead to valuable results.

The video material used for video card games draws from user feedback of different kinds:

- Shadowing technique – user observation and interviews
- Situated interviews – users explain practice in their own context
- User workshops – discussion of design ideas in a meeting room
- Usability evaluations – triggering user feedback with prototypes

Video material that shows actual practice, non-verbal or at least less-verbal video, is referred to much more often than video where verbal explanations are given. Seeing practice is more relevant than user's own interpretation of it. The video card game is less appropriate for non-tangible design tasks. Then the game is likely to turn into a simple card-sorting exercise.

Discussion

I have illustrated the general principles of ethnographic fieldwork for design. I have shown how ethnography has influenced the User-Centred Design approach of the participatory design tradition. With inspiration from ethnographic fieldwork methods, user involvement in industrial practice becomes a 'thick' description. The array of engagement with users in the field ranges from pure observation to involving users in 'design-in-context' sessions and collaborative analysis in the video card game.

'Design-in-context' is collaborative: users participate in workshops in the designer's domain and designers engage with users out in the field. Designers do like the modern ethnographer: the ethnographer invites the informant into their world – for various purposes, such as film editing, transcription, translation and accurate field note analysis and they engage with them in their universe. What develops is a real design collaboratorium (Bødker and Buur 2002) where the emphasis is on contextualization and collaborative analysis.

The lack of a universal fieldwork recipe draws attention to process facilitation. Doing fieldwork is not a question of one particular technique; one must adapt methods to what is there. Any new design project requires rethinking the most applicable and appropriate field research strategy. Applying video techniques for information gathering and for explorations that trigger unanticipated results, thus leading to changes in the design, seems to be a promising way to provoke innovative product ideas.

Even though industrial time constraints seem antithetical to 'real' ethnographic fieldwork, I have experienced, and shown, that much can be achieved in just a few hours. Video is more than just a mere observational and representational tool; it helps to uncover design potentials, and thus to sort out design solutions.

As a way of handling and interpreting field data, the video card game session takes on a quality very different from the traditional ethnographic way of writing-up notes and analysing data. Moreover the evaluation becomes collaborative. Participants/players come up with hypotheses about user practice or improved usability for a product. Participating users offer correctives to designer's interpretations of use practice and interaction principles. In contrast to field note memos and reports, the collaborative interpretation in a 'game' gains a new quality: design solutions are directly linked to the 'real' world and communities of practice (Wenger 1998).

The video card game allows designers and users (or informants) to reflect collaboratively on practice. Thus video is both reflective material and design material at the same time (Buur, Binder and Brandt 2000). The video card game approach takes the collaborative interpretive praxis of participants, and their partial and situated perspectives, into account, thus allowing multiple voices to be expressed in the final 'text', a report, a prototype, etc. The 'text' is as polyphonic, as fragmentary, multiple voiced, evocative and dialogic as other ethnography. Thus the video card game for collaborative user-centred design might also be of interest for many other visual researchers.

Notes

1. The collaboratorium is a laboratory-like space in the users' domain, e.g. a workplace, where designers and users collaborate to survey design experiments (see Bødker and Buur 2002).

Bibliography

Barth, F. 1994. 'A Personal View of Present Tasks and Priorities in Cultural Anthropology', in: R. Borofsky (ed.) *Assessing Cultural Anthropology*. New York: McGraw-Hill, pp. 349–361.
Bødker S., and J. Buur. 2002. 'The Design Collaboratorium: A Place for Usability Design', *ACM Transactions on Computer-Human Interaction*, 9 (2): 152–169.
Buur, J. and A. Søndergaard. 2000. 'Video Card Game: An Augmented Environment for User-Centred Design Discussions', DARE Conference. 2000: ACM – Elsinore.
Buur, J., T. Binder, and E. Brandt. 2000. Taking Video Beyond 'Hard Data' in User-Centred Design, Design. Participatory Design Conference, New York.
Kyng, M. 1994. 'Scandinavian Design: Users in Product Development', *ACM Proceedings Computer-Human-Interaction '94*, 'Human Factors in Computing Systems', pp. 3–9.
Mackay, W., A.V. Ratzer, and P. Janecek. 2000. 'Video Artifacts for Design: Bridging the Gap Between Abstraction and Detail', *DIS 2000*. Brooklyn, New York.

Pedersen, J. and J. Buur. 2000. 'Games and Movies: Towards an Innovative Engagement with Users', CoDesigning Conference, UK.

Schön, D. 1983. *The Reflective Practitioner: How Professionals Think in Action.* New York: Basic Books.

Schön, D. 1987. *Educating the Reflective Practitioner: Toward a New Design for Teaching and Learning in the Professions.* San Francisco: Jossey-Bass.

Spradley, J.P. 1980. *Participant Observation.* New York: Holt, Rinehart and Winston.

Suchman, L. 1995. 'Making Work Visible', *Communications of the ACM* 38 (September 1995), 56–64.

Suchman, L. and R.H. Trigg. 1991. 'Understanding Practice: Video as a Medium for Reflection and Design', J. Greenbaum and M. Kyng (eds), *Design at Work.* Hillsdale, NJ: Lawrence Erlbaum Associates, pp. 65–89.

Wenger, A. 1998. *Communities of Practice: Learning, Meaning and Identity.* Cambridge: Cambridge University Press.

Wolcott, H.F. 1995. *The Art of Fieldwork.* Walnut Creek, CA: AltaMira Press.

Wolcott, H.F. 1999. *Ethnography: A Way of Seeing.* Walnut Creek, CA: AltaMira Press.

Filmography

Filmportrait Fredrik Barth: From Fieldwork to Theory. Werner Sperschneider 2000. Institute for Scientific Film, Video, 60 min. Göttingen.

Chapter 14

ENGAGING OUR AUDIENCE THROUGH PHOTO STORIES

Tracey Lovejoy and Nelle Steele

'Visual anthropology is not going to appear
miraculously some day in the future. It is being
created now, even if we do not always recognize it.'
– David MacDougall (1997)

Introduction

In trying to shape product development at Microsoft[1] – a fast moving international technology corporation headquartered in Redmond, WA, USA – we continually attempt to engage our target audiences[2] in new and distinctive ways. To this end, we recently utilized a new method of data delivery that, though not without its potential pitfalls, is promising both for what it could mean for developing design ideas together with our product team colleagues and for putting the visual at the foreground of doing anthropology in an applied setting.

As ethnographers for Microsoft we conduct studies with many populations in an attempt to more deeply understand people's relationship, or lack thereof, with technology. Our primary goal is to make people's lives and behaviours come to life for our colleagues so these become the cornerstone of product development, with a secondary goal of challenging our colleagues' assumptions while encouraging reflexive critique. In 2003 we launched an international program where we did exploratory field studies designed to bring awareness and actionable knowledge of people in various global markets to the Windows client division as a way of complementing and enriching the statistical measures that had long been used. For the study discussed in this article we spent four weeks in Brazil with four families and four university students in Sao Paulo and Brasilia.[3] Methods included participants creating and talking us through a collage of technology,[4] a full day of observation with each family member, in-context interviews, a semi-structured interview and a follow up diary study.[5] We documented our participants' days with handwritten notes, digital photos and some video.[6]

In an effort to engage our target audience during the course of our work, to offer them opportunities to see and to the extent possible, experience, what it is like in the field, we used a computer application, Microsoft Plus! Photo Story (hereafter referred to as Photo Story), to meld digital photographs from the field with our spoken narratives. The result was a visual and oral excursion into our experiences and impressions of Brazil as well as the lives of our participants.

In doing ethnography in a product design setting, we are intensely focused not only on our data collection and analysis methods, or the forms of production of knowledge, but also on the consumption of that knowledge by our product team colleagues. This consumption of knowledge is not a singular event; it unfolds over time as a dialogue among us, our product team colleagues and participants, and this is where the key transformations happen that will have an impact on the product. Through Microsoft Plus! Photo Story, a new mode of visual communication in our milieu, we brought our colleagues as close to the field as possible, short of actually taking them along with us. Through narrative and images, we reflexively shared our experiences of this new, foreign culture and the daily experiences of our participants, with all of our 'viewers'. In doing so, we collapsed the spatio-temporal distance between ourselves, our colleagues and our participants while allowing for some differing interpretations about what these experiences meant. Photo Story forced us to cede some (though not all) of our authoritative control in interpretation, which ultimately opened the way for us to develop a novel approach of making sense of the data together with our colleagues.

Visual Anthropology in the Corporate Setting

As anthropology begins to be more accepted as a legitimate and important form of corporate research, questions have been raised about the validity of corporate ethnography, both in time and scope. But as Jordan explained, 'in many ways, what we do is no different from what anthropologists and other ethnographically trained practitioners have always done: establish relationships in the study site; "hang out" to become as much as possible a part of the scene; attempt to understand what is going on from the inside out and from the bottom up; and feed back that understanding to the people we work with. But we are also becoming increasingly aware of the fact that our work has changed in significant ways from what we used to do' (Jordan 1997: 12). In particular, while the time lines of the corporate world are much shorter than those we enjoyed while in the academic sector, the principles of our research remain unchanged.

Of course a crucial element that sometimes divides academic and applied anthropology is the end goal. Within our corporation the goal of ethnographic research is to influence product design by introducing a holistic and rich understanding of users' behaviours and needs to the development process. To meet this goal, ethnographic research project time lines need to coincide with the high-paced cycles of corporate product development. Often this means we must narrow the scope of our research design to be conducive to a shorter period of study. Correspondingly, we need to be able to quickly filter and communicate what we learn, as well as translate it into actionable recommendations to a nonacademic audience. These conditions do not lessen the legitimacy of the findings, they simply present challenges to the ethnographer that many academic anthropologists may not have to face.[7]

In many instances, the use of images and narration has proven to be a powerful tool in confronting these challenges because we are able to more quickly and effectively immerse our viewers into participants' daily lives than we can through the use of lengthy papers and reports (which take a long time to author and few ever read fully). In fact, it was often the use of visuals that actually grabbed viewers' interest and made them willing to engage at all. This has caused many more people to tune in and therefore increased the number of people that are exposed to the lives and needs of the users for whom they design. Traditional forms of corporate research, such as surveys and focus groups, have often been unable to achieve this.

Visual anthropology is not new to the corporate setting. In fact, it has been making contributions to corporate anthropology for several years. Video has long been used as a data collection method and as a data analysis method in the form of collaborative watching of video, sometimes with participants (Suchman and Trigg 1991; Jordan and Henderson 1995; Brun-Cottan and Wall 1995; Nardi et al. 1996; Ruhleder and Jordan 1997; Buur, Binder and Brandt 2000; Buur, Binder and Øritsland 2000).

In addition to data analysis, video has been used in the product design process, by both ethnographers and usability engineers, to help bring participants closer to designers and developers, share findings and as a general method of data consumption by those that the research is intended to influence (MacDougall 1997; Buur, Binder and Brandt, 2000). In Wasson's account of the history of corporate ethnography she mentions the appeal of video in the design process: 'Designers also found ethnographic videotape of naturally occurring consumer practices strongly appealing; the profession is visually oriented to begin with and this medium appeared to provide a transparent window onto a whole new dimension of "the user"' (Wasson 2000: 378). Additionally, in two recent papers Johnston argues strongly for the use of video to influence decision makers: 'if we are to see our research implemented and more extensive research employed, then video should take centre stage. Video transforms how our findings are viewed and implemented. While video cannot and should not eliminate the written report, it should have a greater role in the tool kit of the practitioner working in the corporate environment.' (Johnston 2002: 40; Johnston 2003).

It is probable, however, that much of the contribution that visual anthropology makes in corporations has gone and may continue to go unrecognized due to the confidential nature of corporate anthropology: 'Due to both client confidentiality principles and the reticence of design firms for whom research methods constitute a competitive edge, it is impossible to know precisely what contributions ethnography has so far made in the field of design' (Wasson 2000: 383).[8]

As Photo Story is a new technology it is not surprising there is no prior documentation around its use as a tool for visual anthropology, especially the new ability to feed near real time ethnographic data back to those we wish to influence. Several of its aspects make it a very compelling data delivery technique for corporate settings: it is much faster and easier to upload digital photographs to a computer while in the field than video; each story condenses to such a small size that it is possible to send via email, even using dial up; it becomes easily possible to share fieldwork while it happens therefore, allowing your audience to feel closer to the research; many corporations today are supporting intranets, thereby providing a means of distribution and consumption. In the end visual anthropology has already and continues to make a very important contribution to corporate research by making results more interesting and more accessible to a wider audience, thereby extending the reach and importance of corporate anthropology as a discipline. Photo Story, or other tools like it, allow for an evolution of visual anthropology in the corporation.

Setting the Stage

Thursday, June 19th, 7pm. We are highlighting handwritten notes and looking through digital photographs from a full day in the field following a participant in Sao Paulo, Brazil. After scribbling an outline of themes from the data, as well as important moments during the day to constitute 'a day in the life', about twenty photos that best illustrate our participant's day are chosen, pulled into Photo Story, put in chronological order and then narrated to explain the significance of each picture. The entire Photo Story file is saved into a single file, zipped, attached to an email and sent from the hotel room in Sao Paulo to a colleague at the Microsoft headquarters. The following morning the colleague posts the Photo Story file on a website. When our target consumers of data are notified through an email distribution list that a new Photo Story file has been added to the site, they click a link, go to the website and the Photo Story file automatically starts playing. Images of our experiences and our participants' lives in Brazil glide effortlessly across the screen as our voices explain the significance of what our colleagues are seeing. Employees all over the globe are instantly transported, through storytelling and photos, into a 'day in the life' of a Brazilian university student, from her two jobs, onto the metro, inside a mall, on a bus to her university, through her classes and into her friend's car that drops her at a train station that will take her home at night.

As illustrated in the vignette above, after each day in the field we moved our photos from our digital cameras to our laptops and then went through our handwritten notes and photographs to pull together a short, narrated 'slide show' (sometimes adding music or quotes from participants pulled from video) that was posted by a colleague on an intranet site other Microsoft employees could visit. For those who wanted more detail, each Photo Story file had an accompanying text blog, or web log, which added depth and richness to the images and voice annotation they saw and heard. While no single participant can be held up as a representation of all Brazilians, we were able to incorporate information from the literature and statistical data reviews conducted before our study to help present a broader perspective of life within Brazil. In total we created twenty-one Photo Stories over the course of thirty days. We did not have extensive experience with this technology before we went into the field; we loaded the software application on our laptops and briefly reviewed the major feature areas before we departed for Brazil.

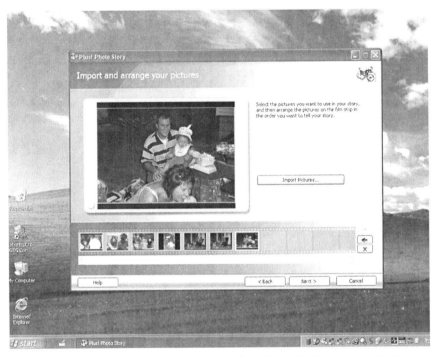

Figure 14.1 Screenshot of a Microsoft Plus! Photo Story file being created: 'Import and arrange your pictures' screen. Here, photos are imported, then arranged and voice-annotated however the creator sees fit (author's personal photos).

Figure 14.2 Screenshot of a Microsoft Plus! Photo Story file under development: 'Advanced Options' screen for panning and zooming photos. You can control how the images actually glide across the screen when the Microsoft Plus! Photo Story file is playing. We never used this manual control, but instead just let the software choose the algorithm it wanted to move the photos for us (author's personal photos).

Windows XP; Microsoft Plus! Photo Story, ©2004 Microsoft Corporation All Rights Reserved.

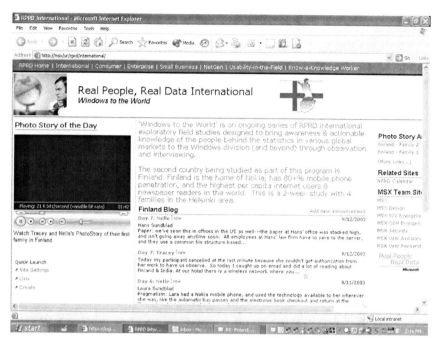

Figure 14.3 Screenshot of a mocked up webpage, originally accessible to Microsoft employees only, that looks nearly identical to the one we use for our international work (pseudonyms used to protect the privacy of participants). Our Photo Story file is in the upper left corner; it begins playing automatically the first time viewers click a link to access our site. Our textual blogs accompanying each Photo Story file are in the centre of the webpage. An example of a typical voice annotation that plays automatically when an initial photo like this one appears in a Photo Story file: 'Hi everyone! Here's how I spent the days with the other half of the family Tracey showed you yesterday. This is Renata, the mother of the kids you've already seen. She is the Executive Assistant to the Director of (a worldwide nongovernmental organisation) in Brazil and the office is about ten minutes from their house.'

Windows XP; Microsoft Plus! Photo Story; Microsoft SharePoint Microsoft Internet Explorer. ©2004 Microsoft Corporation. All rights reserved.

Anthropology and Product Design

In understanding how expressive photographic works fit into the visual anthropological domain, Elizabeth Edwards' (1997) definition of the 'Boundary' focuses on how anthropology as a discipline perceives the boundary between itself and all that it excludes. She argues for inclusion of different forms of the visual, and in particular photographs, by saying that innovation often does not come from inside the Boundary, but from without: 'in this context photography as a medium is not about photography *per se* but about its potential to question, arouse curiosity, tell in different voices, or see through different eyes from beyond the

Boundary' (Edwards 1997: 54). Clifford also writes his concerns of the boundary: 'As every anthropologist knows, boundaries are dangerous spaces: the consideration of the paradigm depends on exclusion or relegation to status of "art" or "impression" these elements of the changing discipline that call the credentials of the discipline itself into question' (Clifford 1988: 135).

In doing ethnography for corporate product development, and in using Photo Stories to deliver data and influence our audience, we problematize, push and reconfigure the Boundary for our particular purposes in our unique space and environment. How? In our Brazil project, we delivered data on the fly, using iteratively analysed text, images and voice, to influence product development in a corporate environment. Our ultimate goal in all our work is to influence product design by getting our product team colleagues to internalize our data and recommendations from cultures and places other than their own. If they can do this, they can then extrapolate to make informed design decisions that will best support people's behaviours and goals in the real world.

We continually fight the seductive path of least resistance in all our ethnographic projects, 'throwing it over the wall', and our work in Brazil was no exception. Writing textual reports based on our analysed data and then handing them off to a colleague in the hope that they will interpret our words in the way we want them to, and then designing their feature to best support people's natural behaviours, is easy for us in the short term, but difficult for us and for our customers in the long term, for two reasons. First, the data has a greater likelihood of being badly misinterpreted if it is presented only in textual form, with no accompanying explanation, either verbal or visual, from us. Second, the data has less of a chance of being internalized by that product team colleague and ultimately enacted in a final product if it is presented in textual form and merely 'handed off' without longer term engagement.

In analysing qualitative data and sharing it with our colleagues, we strive to make meaning together so that what is right for the user gets built. As Jordan writes

> Our emphasis is moving from chasing 'valid and reliable data' to an emphasis on 'making meaning' together with our partners in the organisations in which we work. This means building shared views from which action can be taken, views to which we contribute by making visible the invisible and talking about the unspeakable. From our fieldwork, we attempt to feed the shared view, strengthen the connectedness, stimulate conversations in the company rather than providing authoritative data or advice. (Jordan 1997: 3)

One of the best ways to initiate this process of making meaning together is to get our colleagues who do not get to come into the field as frequently as we do, if ever, a chance to 'meet' our participants and get a more intimate look at their lives through storytelling. We attempt to make our product development colleagues feel like they are there with us in the field; we want them to feel that 'You are there … because I was there' (Clifford 1988: 22). While it may be argued that there are ethical issues in trying to bring colleagues as close to the field as possible because it is still an illusion created by us, any kind of medium, be it text, photos, video, attempts to do this. It is a simulacrum of the culture and this is what anthropology has produced from the beginning. By synthesizing our data, stringing together images and voice narratives and then facilitating the easy consumption of this data, we create an open dialogue with our product team colleagues about what it all means. 'Story telling allows for the construction and communication of interpretation of data to design teams, clients, colleagues and even customers…. [Storytelling's] greatest value is in aligning a group of people around new, but shared understanding. When stories are shared, through telling, a common understanding or even worldview can result' (Roberts 2003: 10).

Photo Story File Creation

Photo Story had only recently been released by Microsoft when we decided to use it for our Brazil ethnography. Because it was new to us and our product team colleagues, our story-creation process evolved as we became more comfortable with the product. Our first Photo Stories were just impressions; we reflexively shared our sense of cultural dislocation and made explicit our own very fresh, raw observations of difference, of cultural 'otherness'. In selecting photos for our later Photo Stories, a sifting and winnowing process occurred: we selected those photos we felt best represented themes that emerged from the participant's day; photos that showed major activity or transition points throughout our participant's day; photos that exemplified both what was similar to American daily life, as well as photos that best exemplified cultural 'otherness', or experiences that were radically different in our eyes from American experiences; and, finally, photos that showed behaviours we surmised were idiosyncratic to that individual.[9] In creating our verbal narrations, we reflexively highlighted our own feelings of cultural dislocation and provided commentary on our participant's activities over the course of the day. We did not agree on this strategy in advance; instead, it emerged as we went through the iterative process of quick data analysis in the field, responding to our viewers' comments and questions, talking with each other about the Photo Stories we were creating, the comments we were receiving and story-creation itself.

As we completed Photo Stories for each participant after each day in the field, themes began to emerge both within and between participants. In the final stages of our research in Brazil, our Photo Stories were still focused on those individual participant's experiences, but through our voice narrations and textual blogs, we not only commented on that participant, but also reinforced dominant themes that had emerged between participants by referencing past Photo Stories, as well as pulling in population level statistics to begin to triangulate data to build a greater picture of life in Brazil.

The Response

The reaction to our Photo Stories was both overwhelming and surprising. For the first three weeks of June 2003, we received over 7,000 hits on our website, which is very high for a user research intranet site at Microsoft. In addition we received dozens of emails from co-workers with comments, corrections to something we had said or written, or questions and requests for additional data.[10]

Our first Photo Stories were images with no accompanying verbal narrative (we actually did not realize we could add verbal annotations until a colleague pointed this out to us). We had textual interpretation in the form of blogs that accompanied the Photo Stories, but we had no control over whether or not our viewers read these (however, previous experience had taught us that people often do not take the time to read text if visual presentations are available). Because there was a good chance consumers of the Photo Stories did not read the accompanying text, and because we did not provide narration, there was much more potential for our colleagues to make interpretations that were not in line with the ethnographic data we collected. 'To the anthropologist who knew the cultural context, the visual image spoke volumes, but that power was also a source of danger. An uncaptioned photograph was full of undirected potential' (MacDougall 1997: 289). We reconsidered this strategy when we received an email from one viewer, a product planner from a different product team whose opinion we valued, alerting us to the fact that we could add voice-over annotations and encouraging us to do so. Adding the audio annotations allowed us to feel more confident that we would be making meaning together.

> **From:** Dave Manningsmith
> **Sent:** Sunday, June 15, 2003 12:46 PM
> **To:** Tracey Lovejoy; Nelle Steele
> **Subject:** RE: Brazilian Blog: http://msx/ur/rprd/international/
>
> The blogs are great. When will you add audio to your photo stories?
> I hope all of your audience enjoys your lessons as much as I do.
> Thanks,
>
> ~Dave

> **From:** Tracey Lovejoy
> **Sent:** Sunday, June 15, 2003 9:55 PM
> **To:** Dave Manningsmith; Nelle Steele
> **Subject:** RE: Brazilian Blog: http://msx/ur/rprd/international/
> Hey Dave, per your email I added voice annotations to the photo stories I made tonight! Thanks!

Tracey Lovejoy
Ethnographer
Real People, Real Data
Check out our daily blogs of our research in Brazil at: http://msx/ur/rprd/international/
From: Dave Manningsmith
Sent: Monday, June 16, 2003 9:42 AM
To: Tracey Lovejoy; Nelle Steele
Subject: RE: Brazilian Blog: http://msx/ur/rprd/international/

Dude, the voice annotations rock! That's what I'm talking about.
This serves two purposes: this is a much richer way to record and share
your experiences; this is a great demonstration of how cool and useful
Plus! Photo Story is.
Thanks again,

~Dave

With our colleague's guidance, we transformed mute images into sensory
experiences that provided a path for the viewer to begin to form their own
interpretations and questions about life in Brazil. This example shows that
creating Photo Stories was really an iterative, collaborative process, where
we ceded some control over data transformation, which in turn more
deeply engaged our audience. Because our viewers knew we were
'listening' to them and responding to their requests quickly (note the time
stamps in the emails above), we potentially created even more
engagement with our work.

The product development cycle at Microsoft can move very rapidly, so
the more quickly and compellingly we can tell the story of our data, the
more likely the data is to have an impact on product development. We
sought to actively integrate co-workers into our research and make them
feel as if they were in on the work by delivering the data in near real time.
We wanted our viewers to get as close to 'being there' as possible without
having to expend as much energy as we did. To this end, another product
team colleague sent us the following comment after viewing our Photo
Stories over the course of our first two weeks in Brazil:

From: Edie Adams
Sent: Wednesday, June 25, 2003 9:32 AM
To: Tracey Lovejoy
Cc: Nelle Steele
Subject: RE: Brazilian Blog: http://msx/ur/rprd/international/

I am loving your stories – especially when you narrate to the pictures and I
can listen and do other work at the same time

Sounds like a great trip.
I have research going on in China right now (discussion groups just
concluded 2 hours ago) so it is great to make comparisons between what
we learn from China PC users and what you report from Brazil.

Edie Adams
Microsoft Corporation

306 | TRACEY LOVEJOY AND NELLE STEELE

Most surprising to us was how emotional some of the responses to our Photo Stories were, particularly from Brazilian Microsoft employees living in Redmond, WA. The nostalgia many of them experienced as they watched was intense; in face to face interactions with them when we returned to Redmond, they told us how our Photo Stories reminded them of things they missed the most about home, for example the food and the social closeness. As MacDougall writes, 'if we consider the visual as offering pathways to the other senses and to social experience more generally, then what may be required of the viewer will often combine psychological or kinaesthetic responses with interpretive ones' (MacDougall 1997: 288). Many Brazilian employees in Redmond began 'tuning in' almost daily for the next instalment.

From: Fabio Motta
Sent: Wednesday, June 18, 2003 8:36 PM
To: Tracey Lovejoy
Cc: Nelle Steele
Subject: from Redmond

Hi Tracey,

I am Brazilian and work here in Redmond. I have been watching your blog. It is very cool and it is the new 'novela' [soap opera] for some Brazilian employees here in Redmond. I found very interesting your observation about the lack of use of mobility due to lack of security and that the student uses the computer as a toy, not for studying.

I have some suggestions/observations:

- Last February, the ex-CEO of (the Latin American branch of an American multinational corporation) gave a lecture over here in Redmond and one of his observations about Microsoft is that is not perceived as 'Brazilian'. The idea is that Brazilians have a strong sense of community and that products that people consume need to be part of that. He mentioned that Brazilians would see his company as Brazilian and integrated into the local culture.

- I have some curiosity about the background of the people who work maintaining the computer infrastructure of the school and the government office. Are they software engineers? Or is what they learn what they read at PC World and/or by studying on their own? (removed text)

- When I am in Brazil, something that calls my attention is small monitors.

There are 140 Brazilians working in the main campus. If you have any questions feel free to e-mail us.

Very nice work,

Fabio Motta

Clearly, Fabio and others were following our visual and oral narratives serially. Another Brazilian Microsoft employee living in Redmond following our Photo Stories realized he had never heard feedback on his own country before he started following our blogs.

From: Rodrigo Santos
Sent: Friday, June 20, 2003 8:31 PM
To: Tracey Lovejoy; Nelle Steele
Subject: Feedback from your blogs

Hello ladies,

I was reading your blogs and having a blast. I've never had the opportunity to read what a foreign person would think about Brazil.

I was reluctant to write to you because I don't want to skew your perception. But I think I should clarify at least a couple of points, some are fun, some are not.

First the boring stuff. Getting late to something is not acceptable but, as you both noticed, Brazilians care a lot about visitors and will cut you some slack. Did anyone working with you get late before you did? I'd be surprised, crazy traffic or not. This changes from region to region and the more south you go, the less polite it is. (removed text)

Rodrigo's concern about skewing our perceptions showed that he was sensitized in some way to research principles, but giving us feedback on our data very quickly was new territory for all concerned. Both he and we were actively negotiating this new landscape of near real time data delivery and collaborative meaning building together.

Why It Worked

As evidenced by the responses above, co-workers found our Photo Stories compelling for a variety of reasons depending on the context from which they came. This reflects Mermin's thoughts on how narrative shapes understanding: 'Context – understood in the broadest sense to include everything from the details of a particular viewer's life to the socio-historical setting of the screening – is essential to the interpretation of the narrative' (Mermin 1997: 45). Depending upon the life experiences of our viewers, and their socio-historical placement, they responded differently.

For Dave, who had no experience of Brazil, the photos were mute representations of life that did not mean much until we added our interpretations. Edie, who also had no Brazil experience, trusted us enough to listen to our narrative as 'the' interpretation she needed to internalize: we did the work of interpreting, and this freed her up to do other things as she watched our Photo Stories. For Fabio, born and raised in Brazil and now living in Redmond, this daily visceral connection to his homeland was a vivid reminder of all that he missed there and an opportunity for him to share his cultural expertise about his country with us. For Rodrigo, also born and raised in Brazil and living in Redmond, our Photo Stories created a moment of reflexivity for him; he had never before heard an outsider's comments about his home country and he enjoyed engaging in dialogue about them, sharing his own ideas and feelings along the way.

To fully understand the impact of using Photo Story on our co-workers, we must also examine both the technology itself and the environment in which it was used. Precisely because Photo Story occupies an in-between space – it is not just photographs, it is not just narrative, it is not video; rather, it is a mélange of all these representations – it is open to a potentially wider range of interpretation and engagement than any of these other media would be on their own. Some of the viewers who responded to our Photo Stories called it 'video' in their comments; was this because they were unsure what medium Photo Stories were? Or because no matter what medium it was, our stories elicited the same responses from them that video would? Additionally, viewers could pick whichever media suited them best: they could watch and listen to the Photo Story file, they could just listen to it, they could just read blog text from that day, or do any combination thereof. Viewers may have responded more enthusiastically than they typically would to ethnographic data because they were not compelled to consume the data in a singular fashion, nor were they compelled to consume it in a linear way.

Microsoft Plus! Photo Story is particularly suited for the milieu in which we work: enthusiasm for new technology, PC use, high-speed internet access, website accessibility and team collaboration is ubiquitous. Another constant is the dearth of time most Microsoft employees feel they have to get their work done. Because our Photo Stories were an on demand data source, they could go to them and consume them whenever they chose. They were not forced to consume the data at a particular time, in a particular place or in one particular way.

Additionally, Brazil was a unique, exotic and exciting subject for many employees. We have surmised that the U.S.-based observation we have done would not have been as popular because the stories may have been seen as more banal and similar to our viewers' daily experiences.

Finally, we answered every single email that we received from our viewers which further entrenched in them a feeling of 'being there', heightening their sense of engagement with the work and our sense of engagement with a community that cared about the data, our participants and Brazil.

What Were the Issues?

Although we might have engaged our product team colleagues with the novelty of new visual and oral forms of data, the downside of all this flexibility is that we had less perceived control over the final interpretations our viewers made. What meaning were they ultimately drawing from all this? What impact did sharing visual data iteratively over time, instead of only sharing a neat and tidy textual analysis at the end of our work, have on product development? Were our viewers watching all our Photo Stories over time and reading all our blogs, or picking and choosing? Did they attend our final presentation that pulled together all the themes and made concrete design recommendations when we were back in Redmond? Many of these questions have only been partially answered thus far.

In her article 'Being Where? Experiencing Narratives of Ethnographic Film', Elizabeth Mermin cites Barthes when discussing how meaning gets created not only by the makers of ethnographic film, but also by viewers of that film: 'Narrative involves several levels of retelling, all of which offer opportunities for unpredictable interpretations and the emergence of new meanings. Trying to limit or control such a network of meanings is endlessly frustrating work' (Mermin 1997: 40). As we progressed through our month in Brazil, we found our proprietary grip on meaning loosening as we interacted more with our viewers. It was refreshing to form an open community with interested colleagues where we continually helped them internalize the data more deeply, steering them clear of dangerous misinterpretations, while remaining open to their way of seeing the world we presented to them.

Photo Story in the Context of Anthropological Hypermedia and Digital Ethnography

We are not the first ethnographers to use electronic tools and constructs to try to be effective in making sense of our data and sharing it with others. Previous work in anthropological hypermedia and digital ethnography has highlighted some of the issues we struggled with in our attempts to engage our target audience at Microsoft, to push the research forward in new directions using visual media and to understand what impact visual media has on our ultimate goal of making product impact.

In 'Mama Kone's *Possession: Scenes from an Interactive Ethnography*', Peter Biella (1997) uses interactive data presentation techniques to tell the story of the spirit possession of Mama Kone and the role he played in the tableau. One of the most powerful parts of his Maasai Interactive project is that he iteratively analysed his data, finding new understandings over a series of years of interacting with the data by himself and with others. We not only get to see how Biella interprets his translator's and Mama Kone's speech and actions after reviewing them a number of times, but we also get to see how Biella himself matures as an anthropologist and a human being. In looking back over interpretations he made years earlier, he writes 'In 1994, I tried to explain my frustrations in this interview by blaming Jonas' anxiety…. The problem is not Jonas' anxiety…. The problem is that I am in a big hurry, I cannot bear being ignorant, and my anxiousness blocks anybody who tries to teach me.' (Biella 1997: 76). Here, Biella challenges the primacy of authoritative control by making clear that he is fallible and that he can also learn from his mistakes, which in a sense makes him even more credible. As he amasses years of experience and reflection, we can see his understanding of his interaction with Mama Kone changing and growing over time.

In a corporate environment like Microsoft's, we would do well to recognize the value of Biella's self-criticism. Even though we might like to, we cannot emulate Biella's approach exactly because of our fast product cycle setting. Working with colleagues who are also trained in anthropology and ethnography is crucial because they can quickly provide feedback on emerging themes, perceptions and research design that we may not be able to iteratively review.

Mason and Dicks' (2001) work on hypermedia ethnography and Story Space highlights another key issue: how do we make sure our viewers walk away with a clear message for product development when our Photo Stories are multilinear journeys and when we do not know which Photo Stories they have seen? In actuality, our product team colleagues have always had to engage with multilinear messages from a variety of sources. Continual engagement with our product team colleagues over time, in a variety of forms, is one remedy for this problem.

Pink (2004) also employs the visual and textual together in her *Women's Worlds* project to try to create deep synthesis of these modes of interaction to provide a rich and nuanced view of her participants' lives, while at the same time referencing anthropological theory and her own interpretations of the data. With our Photo Stories, textual reports, multimedia presentations and face to face meetings at Microsoft, we attempt to do the same.

Biella's hypermedia project, Mason and Dicks' use of Story Space and Pink's *Women's Worlds* project are robust examples of pairing visual data with textual, iterative interpretation. In whatever setting ethnography is used, what we must remain cognizant of is fetishization of the tool; in other words, we must be careful not to focus solely on the technology or tool because the tools and technology will always change. Banks alludes to this in his article on interactive media when he states: 'Ethnographic film is produced, used and enthused over largely for the qualities of the medium itself (it is no surprise that until Wilton Martinez' work, no anthropologist had stopped to consider whether the use of ethnographic film in the classroom was actually effective). This preoccupation with the medium – "Gell's enchantment of technology" – has led to the major use of ethnographic film being in classroom teaching, not in research (Banks 1994). Biella respectfully criticizes Banks in his article on codifications of ethnography by pointing out that Banks says the discussion after screening an ethnographic film is the 'locus of ethnographicness' (Banks 1994). Biella then writes, 'although Banks is correct that it is an error to reduce ethnography to any one medium or quality, he commits the same error by reifying the undeniable achievements of flesh-and-blood, classroom interactions. ... Intentionality, active historical consciousness, shapes definitions by reflecting on interaction of many kinds, those that involve other people and those that involve texts' (Biella 1994).

As Biella points out, it is important not to reduce ethnography to any one medium or quality. From our perspective the most important question is, to what end is the medium employed? What are the ultimate goals of the ethnographic endeavour? The answer to this question should dictate the theory, research methods and tools, visual or not, used to achieve the goals. We must also be flexible in our attitude toward tools. If we find a new tool that can better support our ethnographic goals in data collection, analysis and impact than one we are currently using, we have to be able to shift directions midstream. Technology for technology's sake will only please technologists. What we should consistently strive for is analytical depth and then translating this depth in an engaging way for those who will build the product. In the final analysis, 'making ongoing meaning together' with our product team colleagues through a variety of modes of interaction like Photo Story, face to face meetings, textual reports and large scale multimedia presentations is typically our path to highest effectiveness in product development at Microsoft.

Conclusion

For some, anthropology's boundary maintenance will continue to be critical to the survival of the discipline. As questions of positioning and validity rage on, we will continue to do ethnographic work to make impacts on product design. As MacDougall writes, 'Instead of campaigning for the creation of a mature visual anthropology, with its anthropological principles all in place, we would be wise to look at the principles that emerge when fieldworkers actually try to rethink anthropology through the use of a visual medium' (MacDougall 1997: 293).

Ultimately, the conviction that our product team colleagues believe what we want them to, even when we exercise more perceived authoritative control over the final products of our research through publishing a final textual report versus sharing data in visual form over time, is flawed. Our colleagues make their own assumptions about data all the time; thus, engaging them in this novel way and making explicit the fact that they do make assumptions all the time, allowed us to continually reflect on their assumptions and share our interpretations of them so that we could build shared understandings over time, together.

Notes

1. Microsoft, Windows, Windows XP, Microsoft Plus! Photo Story, Microsoft SharePoint, are either registered trademarks or trademarks of Microsoft Corporation in the United States and/or other countries.

2. Our target audiences are product team colleagues who come from various disciplines and occupy various job roles, such as program manager, developer, tester, designer, user researcher, user assistance expert, product planners and others.

3. We found families with children to be an advantageous way to study behaviour (especially technology behaviour) because it allowed us to see a multitude of age groups in multiple settings, such as work, school, out with friends, shopping, home with the family, etc. It also allowed us to glean a holistic view of participants and how they related to and interacted with each segment of their lives, which in turn proved to be integral to understanding how technology can best fit into each individual's life. Additionally, we thought it important to understand how parents and children perceived technology and if there were cultural consumption patterns around these beliefs. Families were recruited based on several factors, such as number and age of children and size of organization in which parents worked. Additionally, it was required that families have at least one PC with a working internet connection at home. Although families were not recruited on the basis of on socio-economic factors, statistically it is only families in the higher socio-economic levels that own a PC with a working internet connection, and this was reflected in the families we worked with, all falling in the two highest socio-economic classes (denoted by 'SEC (socio-economic class) A' and 'SEC B' in Brazil) . University students varied by age, gender and area of study. They were not required to have a PC at home, but were required to use a PC. Students ranged from SEC A – B. Participants were offered a monetary gratuity for their participation. During the study participants also stated that they enjoyed being part of the study; more specifically, that someone from Microsoft was taking an interest in them personally and that they felt proud to be contributing to a study that would help products become better suited to their needs.

4. Participants were sent a set of pictures taken from Brazilian magazines and asked to create a collage with the intentionally broad instruction to 'show us technology in your life'. They were given the flexibility to use any means they chose: use the pictures provided, use their own images, draw, write, etc. Before observational work we wanted to meet the families involved and build rapport. The collages were reviewed during this meeting. Participants talked us through their collages, explaining what the images represented and why they had chosen them, while we probed into various areas. The collages helped us to get a baseline notion of how each participant defined, understood and described their interactions with technology.

5. The families would choose a morning arrival time, then we would observe morning rituals, travel to work and school (permission always collected prior to data collection), observe while at work and school, observe after work and school activities and travel home with each participant. In-context interviews were done when appropriate and unobtrusive. Most semi-structured interviews happened at the end of each day of observation. We always travelled with Brazilian qualitative researchers who also served as translators. All participants were given a digital camera and paper diary and asked to take photographs of 'technology in their life' as well as to write about why each photo was taken. This was done for one week to give us the opportunity to compare our observations with the participants' perceptions of what technology is and how they felt they interacted with it.

6. Voluntary signed consent was given by each family member that they were willing to participate in the study and that they were aware that photos and video may be taken. Additionally, participants guided us as to when they felt comfortable and/or uncomfortable with our presence or with us taking photos or video. Video was sometimes felt to bring too much attention to our presence and was therefore minimized in schools, work places and public venues such as public transportation.

7. Other factors we must consider in trying to influence product design are, firstly, our team composition: Are there new members on our team? Are they new to Microsoft, new to our product team in particular, or new to product development in general? Do they know what ethnography is? Have they worked with ethnographers before? Secondly, our relationships with our colleagues: Are we viewed as credible? Do team members trust us? Do they know the quality of our work? Do they enjoy working with us? Are they consistently engaged in what we do? And thirdly, the point we are at in the product cycle: Are we at the beginning of a product cycle, when scenarios are being defined? Are we part way into the product cycle, when the software architecture is being defined? Are we farther along in the cycle, when product specifications are being fleshed out? Are we close to the end of a cycle, when secondary, 'beta' products are ready for review? All these factors dictate the choices we make around mode of interaction with team members (textual, visual or face to face), to make product impact.

8. It is important to point out that the same is true for all of the research we do for Microsoft. Therefore we are not able to discuss much of our actual research to maintain participant confidentiality which may cause our participants to appear to be 'mute' or altogether missing from this article. However, one major point of the article is that when we do share information with our colleagues, our Brazilian participants are the centerpiece.

9. It is important to note that while we did show photos that elucidated 'the exotic' or 'otherness' we also had many photos and tales that can be equated to 'sameness'. We fully represented participants' 'day in the life' which included elements that may appear to be 'exotic' and many that may appear to be banal or the same. However, because one of the goals of our study was to understand how product development should be different for different cultures, pointing out 'differences' was a very important component of our data results.

10. Permission was granted from all people whose emails we share in this article. Some of the email text has been edited for the sake of brevity.

Bibliography

Banks, M. 1994. 'Interactive Multimedia and Anthropology: A Sceptical View', Retrieved 4 February 2007 from http://www.bodley.ox.ac.uk/isca/marcus.banks.01.html.

Biella, P 1994. 'Codifications of Ethnography: Linear and Nonlinear', Retrieved 7 May 2004 from http://www.usc.edu/dept/elab/welcome/codifications.html.

———. 1997. 'Mama Kone's Possession: A Scene from an Interactive Ethnography', *Visual Anthropology Review* 12:2.

Brun-Cottan, F. and P. Wall 1995. 'Using Video to Re-present the User', *Communications of the ACM (Association for Computing Machinery)* 38(5): 61–71.

Buur, J.T. Binder and E. Brandt 2000. 'Taking Video Beyond 'Hard Data' in User Centred Design', Retrieved 4 February 2007 from http://www.sdu.dk/Nat/MCI/m/Research/Publications/UCD/VIDEOBEYONDHARDDATA.PDF.

Buur, J.T. Binder and T.A. Øritsland 2000. 'Reflecting on Design Practice: Exploring Video of Designers in Action', *Designing Interactive Systems Conference, ACM (Association for Computing Machinery), New York, 2000*, Retrieved 4 February 2007 from http://www.sdu.dk/Nat/MCI/m/Research/Publications/UCD/VIDEO%20REFLECTION%20SESSION.PDF.

Buur, J. and A. Soendergaard 2000. 'Video Card Game: An Augmented Environment for User Centred Design Discussions'. *Proceedings of DARE 2000, ACM (Association for Computing Machinery)*, Elsinore, Denmark, pp. 63–70.

Clifford, J. 1988. *The Predicament of Culture*. Cambridge, MA: Harvard University Press.

Edwards, E. 1997. 'Beyond the Boundary: A Consideration of the Expressive in Photography and Anthropology', in M. Banks and H. Morphy (eds), *Rethinking Visual Anthropology*. New Haven and London: Yale University Press.

Johnston, G.L. 2002. 'Video, Ethnography, and the Corporate Environment: Adapting Methods of Data Collection and Presentation (Or Convincing the Corporate Monster Not to Eat You), *Practicing Anthropology* 24(4): 40–42.

———. 2003. 'Industrial Soap Operas, Fables, and Morality Tales: Ethnographic Video and Design Implementation', *American Anthropological Association Conference, Chicago, 23 November 2003*.

Jordan, B. 1997. 'Transforming Ethnography – Reinventing Research', *Cultural Anthropology Methods Journal* 9(3): 12–17.

Jordan, B. and A. Henderson 1995. 'Interaction Analysis: Foundations and Practice, *Journal of the Learning Sciences* 4(1): 39–103, Palo Alto.

MacDougall, D. 1997. 'The Visual in Anthropology', in M. Banks and H. Morphy (eds), *Rethinking Visual Anthropology*. New Haven and London: Yale University Press.

Mason, B. and B. Dicks 2001. 'Going Beyond the Code: The Production of Hypermedia Ethnography', *Social Science Computer Review* 9(4): 445–457.

Mermin, E. 1997. 'Being Where? Experiencing Narratives of Ethnographic Film', *Visual Anthropology Review* 13(1): 40–51.

Nardi, B. et al. 1997. 'Video-As-Data: Technical and Social Aspects of a Collaborative Multimedia Application', in K. Finn et al (eds), Video-mediated Communication. Mahwah, NJ: Lawrence Erlbaum.

Pink, S. 2004. 'Conversing Anthropologically: Hypermedia as Anthropological Text', in S. Pink, L. Kurti and A. Afonso (eds), *Working Images*. London: Routledge.

Roberts, M. 2003. 'Border Crossing: The Role of Design Research in International Product Development'. Retrieved 4 February 2007 from www.id.iit.edu/papers/Roberts-Border_Crossing_2001.pdf.

Ruhleder, K. and B. Jordan 1997. 'Capturing Complex, Distributed Activities: Video-Based Interaction Analysis as a Component of Workplace Ethnography', in A.S. Lee, J. Liebenau and J. DeGross, *Information Systems and Qualitative Research*. London: Chapman and Hall, pp. 246–275.

Suchman, L. and R. Trigg 1991. 'Understanding Practice: Video as Medium for Reflection and Design', in J. Greenbaum and M. Kyng (eds) *Design at Work: Approaches to Collaborative Design*, Hillsdale, NJ: Lawrence Erlbaum.

Wasson, C. 2000. 'Ethnography in the Field of Design', *Human Organization* 59(4): 377–388.

NOTES ON CONTRIBUTORS

Richard Chalfen is Emeritus Professor of Anthropology at Temple University in Philadelphia and Tokyo. He is also Senior Scientist, Centre on Media and Health at Children's Hospital in Boston where he continues long-term studies of visual illness narratives. He is author of *Snapshot Versions of Life* (1987), *Turning Leaves* (1991) and co-author of *Through Navajo Eyes* (1997).

Malcolm Collier is an Emeritus faculty member in the College of Ethnic Studies at the San Francisco State University. While holding an MA in Anthropology his primary training in visual anthropology has been in field settings in the United States, Latin America and the Arctic. He has worked extensively in the fields of visual anthropology, anthropology and education, applied anthropology and ethnic studies. He is co-author of the publication, *Visual Anthropology: Photography as a Research Method*, and has served as president of the Society for Visual Anthropology in the American Anthropological Association.

Matthew Durington is an Assistant Professor of Anthropology at Towson University and a graduate of the Anthropology of Visual Communication Ph.D. program at Temple University. He is also a recent recipient of a Mellon Postdoctoral Fellowship and studied at the University of KwaZulu Natal in Durban, South Africa. His areas of specialization include visual anthropology, urban anthropology, suburban development and gated communities in the United States and South Africa, and indigenous land rights in Southern Africa. He is currently completing a manuscript related to doctoral research on a heroin moral panic in the suburban United States.

Carlos Y. Flores completed his Ph.D. in 2000 at the Granada Centre for Visual Anthropology, University of Manchester, under the supervision of Professor Paul Henley. His doctoral work was on shared anthropology and collaborative film-making among Maya-Q'eqchi' communities in post-war Guatemala. Since 1995 he has been involved in community video programmes among Mayan communities and organizations in Guatemala and Chiapas, Mexico. He has taught on the Visual Anthropology programme at Goldsmiths College, University of London, and currently works at the Department of Anthropology of the Universidad Autónoma del Estado de Morelos, Mexico.

Jayasinhji Jhala is an Associate Professor of Anthropology at Temple University, where he serves as the Director of the Visual Anthropology Programme and the Anthropology Media Lab. He has been involved in interpreting culture on film and video for the past twenty years. He has produced, directed, filmed, and edited over fifteen ethnographic films that illustrate the cultures of India and the United States while speaking to various issues in Visual Anthropology and published numerous written texts.

Christina Lammer has a Ph.D. from the University of Vienna, Department of Sociology. She lives and works as a freelance sociologist and lecturer in Vienna. With her recent collaborative research activities – *CorpoRealities* – on empathy and somatic perception in the biomedical context of a teaching hospital she is affiliated at Medical University Vienna (MUV). Christina Lammer is the author of *Die Puppe: Eine Anatomie des Blicks* (1999), *doKU: Kunst und Wirklichkeit inszenieren im Dokumentarfilm*, (2002) and *Günter Brus Kleine Narbenlehre* (2007). She is co-editor of *Puppe.Monster.Tod.* (1999), and editor of *Schneewittchen: Ein Eiskristallbuch* (1999) and *Verköperungen/ Embodiment* (2007). She is currently writing a book about breast cancer and the reconstruction of body image in patients of plastic surgery.

Susan Levine is a Senior Lecturer in the Department of Social Anthropology at the University of Cape Town in South Africa. Her primary research interests include the use of visual media to challenge the widespread stigma, discrimination, and confusion related to HIV / AIDS in Southern Africa. Dr Levine received a Masters Degree in Visual Anthropology from Temple University in the United States in 1997, during which time she produced a visual ethnography of the Toyi Toyi dance in South Africa, and in 2000 completed a Ph.D., also at Temple University, on the impact of new child labour legislation for children who rely on wage labour in South Africa's wine industry.

Tracey Lovejoy works full-time at Microsoft® Corporation as an ethnographer in the Mobile Communications Product Group. She observes people across various demographics, and then integrates the behaviours, practices, needs and issues that emerge during fieldwork into the design and implementation of Microsoft products. Tracey did her Master's work and ethnographic training at the University of Chicago. Although visual anthropology was not her academic field of study, she relies on photographs and video in her applied work.

Ana Martinez Perez is Lecturer in Sociology at Universidad Rey Juan Carlos de Madrid. She has a Ph.D. in social anthropology from the Universidad Complutense Madrid. She is a founder member of the Taller de Antropologia Visual (Visual Anthropology Workshop) in Madrid and of the A Buen Común documentary filmmaking unit with whom she has produced a series of ethnographic video documentaries in applied anthropology projects. She has worked on numerous projects in applied and visual anthropology in Spain and is editor of *Taller de las Cuatro Estaciones* (2002) and co-editor of *Antropologia de los sentidos: la vista* (1996).

Sarah Pink is Professor of Social Sciences, Loughborough University (UK). She is series editor of Berghahn's *Studies in Applied Anthropology* series. Her work falls mainly in the areas of visual anthropology, applied anthropology, gender and the senses. Her academic and applied research is mainly in Spain and Britain and her publications include *Doing Visual Ethnography* (Sage 2007 [2001]), *Home Truths* (Berg 2004), *Applications of Anthropology* (ed) (Berghahn 2005), and *The Future of Visual Anthropology: Engaging the Senses* (Routledge 2005). She is currently doing research about the senses and the urban focusing on the Cittàslow (Slow City) movement in Britain.

Michael Rich is Director of the Center on Media and Child Health at Children's Hospital Boston, an Assistant Professor of Pediatrics at Harvard Medical School, and an Assistant Professor of Society, Human Development, and Health at Harvard School of Public Health. He developed the Video Intervention/Prevention Assessment (VIA) research method and has been principle investigator of VIA research on asthma, obesity, and other chronic and disabling medical conditions.

Werner Sperschneider is a practicing visual anthropologist (Ph.D.) He has worked both as an R&D senior consultant in industry (Danfoss A/S) and in academia (Mads Clausen Institute for Product Innovation, University of Southern Denmark). He currently works as an anthropologist in product profiling for Coloplast (Denmark).

Dianne Stadhams is Director of the International Centre of Communications and Development at Roehampton University (UK). She has a Ph.D. in visual ethnography and twenty years of private sector consultancy experience in marketing and management in Australia, Africa, Europe, North America and South East Asia. Recent projects have included working with Gambia state television to produce its first documentary and a series of programmes on responsible travel for European tourists visiting destinations in the South.

Nelle Steele works full-time at Microsoft® Corporation as an ethnographer in the Windows® Client division. She observes people across various demographics, and then integrates the behaviours, practices, needs and issues that emerge during fieldwork into the design and implementation of Microsoft products. Nelle has Master's degrees in Cultural Anthropology and Industrial Relations from the University of Wisconsin-Madison and is currently on leave from her doctoral program in Cultural Anthropology there. Although visual anthropology was not her academic field of study, she relies on photographs and video in her applied work.

An van. Dienderen obtained a Master in Documentary Film Production at the Art School in Brussels, a Ph.D. in Comparative Cultural Sciences at the Ghent University and has been a visiting scholar at the University of California Berkeley. She has made several documentaries, including *Visitors of the Night* (1998), about the matriarchal Mosuo in Yunnan (GNT Channel Prize for Language Renewal – Rio De Janeiro 1999). With Didier Volckaert she directed *Tu ne verras pas Verapaz* (2002). The film elaborates on the history of the (Belgian) colonization in Guatemala (Belgian Prize for Best Documentary 2002 and 2003). She is currently Assistant Professor of Comparative Cultural Sciences at Ghent University.

Vassiliki Yiakoumaki holds a Ph.D. in Cultural Anthropology from the New School for Social Research, New York. She is lecturer in the Department of History, Archaeology and Social Anthropology, University of Thessaly, Greece. Her research interests involve constructions of European identity in the context of the European integration process, constructions of national heritage, heritage management, and material culture and consumption. She has conducted research for an EU-sponsored project on 'Mediterranean' 'urban heritage'. She is currently working on the Jews of Greece and issues of Jewish identity in the context of multiculturalist politics.

INDEX